Office 2003 XML

Other XML resources from O'Reilly

Office 2003 XML

Evan Lenz, Mary McRae, and Simon St.Laurent

O'REILLY®

Beijing · Cambridge · Farnham · Köln · Paris · Sebastopol · Taipei · Tokyo

Office 2003 XML

by Evan Lenz, Mary McRae, and Simon St.Laurent

Published by O'Reilly Media, Inc., 1005 Gravenstein Highway North, Sebastopol, CA 95472.

O'Reilly books may be purchased for educational, business, or sales promotional use. Online editions are also available for most titles (*safari.oreilly.com*). For more information, contact our corporate/institutional sales department: (800) 998-9938 or *corporate@oreilly.com*.

Editor:	Simon St.Laurent
Production Editor:	Philip Dangler
Cover Designer:	Emma Colby
Interior Designer:	David Futato

Printing History:

June 2004:	First Edition.

 This book uses RepKover,™ a durable and flexible lay-flat binding.

ISBN: 0-596-00538-5

[M]

Table of Contents

Preface

For many users, the appearance of Office 2003 has meant a slightly updated version of a familiar tool, another episode in the continuous development of a popular and widely-used piece of software. For some users, however, the appearance of Office 2003 is a herald of tumultuous change. This version of Office liberates the information stored in millions of documents created using Microsoft's Office software over the past 15 years and makes it readily available to a wide variety of software. At the same time, Office 2003 has substantially improved its abilities for working with data that comes from external sources, making it much easier to use Office for the examination and analysis of information that came from other sources.

XML, the Extensible Markup Language, lies at the heart of this new openness. XML has taken much of the world by storm since its publication in 1998 as a World Wide Web Consortium (W3C) Recommendation. XML provides a standard text-based format for storing labeled structured content. An enormous variety of tools for processing, creating, and storing XML has appeared over the last few years, and XML has become a lingua franca that lets different kinds of computers and different kinds of software communicate with each other—all while preserving a substantial level of human accessibility.

This book explores the intersection between Office 2003 and XML in depth, examining how the various products in the Office suite can both produce and consume XML. While this book generally focuses on Office 2003 itself, some supporting technologies will be important pieces of the integration puzzle. Extensible Stylesheet Language Transformations (XSLT) and W3C XML Schema (which Microsoft abbreviates XSD, for XML Schema Descriptions) are two critical pieces for teaching various parts of Office about the structures of XML documents, while SOAP (an acronym that no longer means anything) and HTTP will be important supporting technologies for communications between Office and other programs.

Who Should Read This Book

This book is written for developers who want to be able to combine Office with other sources of information and information processing. For example, you may be a systems integrator trying connect Office to other workflow processing, you may be a power-user who wants to analyze XML data sets in Excel or Access, or you may be an archivist who needs to extract crucial information from existing Office documents. There are many more possibilities out there, of course.

This book is written for developers who already have an understanding of how to use the various programs in the Microsoft Office suite. Some basic instruction in XML, XSLT, and schema-related technologies is provided in the appendixes, but for the most part this book assumes that you come with an understanding of XML and related technologies.

Who Should Not Read This Book

If all of your work is completely contained within the Office suite itself, you probably don't need this book unless you have a particularly tricky problem integrating information among the programs. If, for instance, you just create Word documents using templates, you may even be able to create XML documents using those templates without reading this book. Similarly, developers who create self-contained spreadsheets and databases will most likely not need to learn about these technologies.

If you have never used Microsoft Office or XML before, you may want to consider exploring those technologies in greater depth before reading this book.

Organization of This Book

This book starts in Chapter 1 with an overview of the XML features included in the various Office 2003 components. While most of the components have XML features, they all interact with XML quite differently, and comparing the stories of each of the products makes sense before leaping into the component-specific details.

The rest of the book explores the individual applications in the Microsoft Office Suite, as all of them take different approaches to working with XML. As learning Microsoft Word's internal XML format, WordprocessingML, is a crucial first step for developing any XML applications around it, Chapter 2 examines how Word represents its documents in XML. Chapter 3 explores the use of XSLT to convert WordML to other forms of XML, and then Chapter 4 returns to Word to combine WordML, XSLT, XML Schema, and the Word user interface to create environments where users can create custom XML documents. Chapter 5 takes a look at Smart Documents, a much more labor-intensive but very powerful combination of Word's features with external code.

Excel offers a slightly different set of features for analyzing and processing XML and for saving spreadsheets as XML. Chapter 6 explores how Excel lets users load and work with XML data in a variety of vocabularies, and Chapter 7 takes a close look at creating and consuming SpreadsheetML.

The XML capabilities of Microsoft Access have been enhanced for Office 2003, and those features are described in Chapter 8. Chapter 9 takes a look at a different set of XML features in Office, those specific to Web Services, and examines how to use them in Excel, Access, and Word.

Chapter 10 takes a close look at InfoPath, an application Microsoft has added to the Enterprise version of the Office suite specifically to let users interact with XML and Web Services through a forms-based interface.

The last section of the book is a collection of appendixes, introducing various XML technologies that may be useful in working with Office. They aren't intended to substitute for a thorough understanding, but hopefully they will be enough to get you started.

Supporting Books

Even if you feel you are ready for this book, you may want to explore some of the XML technologies in greater depth than is possible here. The following lists offer some good places to start.

Appendix A, *The XML You Need for Office*, provides a brief orientation to XML, but other books that go into far more depth are readily available. For a solid grounding in XML, consider these books:

- Erik Ray, *Learning XML* (O'Reilly)
- Elliotte Rusty Harold & W. Scott Means, *XML in a Nutshell* (O'Reilly)
- Elizabeth Castro, *XML for the World Wide Web: Visual QuickStart Guide* (Peachpit Press)

Appendix B, *The XSLT You Need for Office*, provides a brief orientation to XSLT, but many projects may require a more sophisticated understanding of XSLT. For more information on XSLT, try these books:

- Michael Fitzgerald, *Learning XSLT* (O'Reilly)
- Doug Tidwell, *XSLT* (O'Reilly)
- Sal Mangano, *XSLT Cookbook* (O'Reilly)
- Michael Kay, *XSLT Programmer's Reference* (Wrox)
- Jeni Tennsion, *XSLT & XPath: On the Edge* (John Wiley & Sons)
- John E. Simpson, *XPath and XPointer* (O'Reilly)

Appendix C, *The XSD You Need for Office*, explores W3C XML Schema briefly, but this topic is definitely worthy of a much larger book. Some good options include:

- Eric van der Vlist, *XML Schema* (O'Reilly)
- Priscilla Walmsley, *Definitive XML Schema* (Prentice-Hall)

Appendix D, *Using DTDs and RELAX NG Schemas with Office* briefly describes how to use RELAX NG, a simpler alternative to W3C XML Schema, to create W3C XML Schema files. For a more thorough explanation of RELAX NG, see:

- Eric van der Vlist, *RELAX NG* (O'Reilly)

You may also want to complement your XML knowledge with more information on the rapidly growing world of Web Services. For a lot more detail, see:

- Ethan Cerami, *Web Services Essentials* (O'Reilly)
- James Snell, Doug Tidwell, and Pavel Kulchenko, *Programming Web Services with SOAP* (O'Reilly)
- Eric Newcomer, *Understanding Web Services: SOAP, WSDL, and UDDI* (Addison Wesley)
- Alex Ferrara and Matthew MacDonald, *Programming .NET Web Services* (O'Reilly)

O'Reilly also offers a collection of programming books on XML that may prove useful. They include:

- Niel M. Bornstein, *.NET & XML* (O'Reilly)
- Brett McLaughlin, *Java & XML* (O'Reilly)
- Erik T. Ray and Jason McIntosh, *Perl & XML* (O'Reilly)
- Christopher Jones and Fred L. Drake, Jr., *Python & XML* (O'Reilly)

There are also many online resources for XML. Two particularly good places to start looking are *XML.com* and *xmlhack.com*. *XML.com* is part of the O'Reilly Network, and covers the latest news in XML on a weekly basis. For smaller stories and a less formal approach, try *xmlhack.com*. Both have a variety of links to other XML resources and mailing lists.

There is an enormous number of books on Microsoft Office and its component applications. My best advice in this field is to visit a bookstore and examine a few books to see which best fits your learning style and your interests. (The same is true of the XML books, but the list above provides a starting point.) Also, if you'd like to know more about how Office's competitor OpenOffice.org handles XML processing, see J. David Eisenberg's excellent *OpenOffice.org XML Essentials* at *http://books.evc-cit.info/*.

Conventions Used in This Book

The following font conventions are used in this book:

Italic is used for:

- Pathnames, filenames, program names, and stylesheet names
- Internet addresses, such as domain names and URLs
- New items where they are defined

`Constant Width` is used for:

- Command lines and options that should be typed verbatim
- Names and keywords in programs, including method names, variable names, and class names
- XML element tags

`Constant-Width Bold` is used for emphasis in program code lines.

`Constant-Width Italic` is used to indicate replaceable arguments within program code.

Using Code Examples

This book is here to help you get your job done. In general, you may use the code in this book in your programs and documentation. You do not need to contact us for permission unless you're reproducing a significant portion of the code. For example, writing a program that uses several chunks of code from this book does not require permission. Selling or distributing a CD-ROM of examples from O'Reilly books *does* require permission. Answering a question by citing this book and quoting example code does not require permission. Incorporating a significant amount of example code from this book into your product's documentation *does* require permission.

We appreciate, but do not require, attribution. An attribution usually includes the title, author, publisher, and ISBN. For example: "*Office 2003 XML*, by Evan Lenz, Mary McRae, and Simon St.Laurent. Copyright 2004 O'Reilly Media, Inc., 0-596-00538-5."

If you feel your use of code examples falls outside fair use or the permission given above, feel free to contact us at *permissions@oreilly.com*.

How to Contact Us

We have tested and verified the information in this book to the best of our ability, but you may find that features have changed (or even that we have made a few mistakes!). Please let us know about any errors you find, as well as your suggestions for future editions, by writing to:

O'Reilly Media, Inc.
1005 Gravenstein Highway North
Sebastopol, CA 95472
1-800-998-9938 (in the U.S. or Canada)
1-707-829-0515 (international/local)
1-707-829-0104 (fax)

You can also send us messages electronically. To be put on the mailing list or request a catalog, send email to:

info@oreilly.com

To ask technical questions or comment on the book, send email to:

bookquestions@oreilly.com

We have a web site for the book, where we'll list examples, errata, and any plans for future editions. You can access this page at:

http://www.orelly.com/catalog/officexml

For more information abut this book and others, see the O'Reilly web site:

http://www.oreilly.com

Acknowledgments

From Evan Lenz

This project has been a wonderful challenge and personal learning experience. Thank you, Simon, for inviting me to help write this book. You've been a joy to work with, both as my editor and as my co-author. Thanks also to Mary McRae for joining us on short notice, bringing to light some important areas we were too scared to touch. I would also like to thank technical reviewers Jeni Tennison and Jeff Maggard for their helpful insights. Jeni's comments in particular were prompt, thorough, and (as always) spot-on.

There are a number of other people who, directly or indirectly, made it possible for me to help write this book. Special thanks go to: James Cooper at Seattle University School of Law, for so generously allowing me time to work on this book; writers like Michael Kay and Merold Westphal, who showed me that it's possible to be clear without compromising rigor; my dad, Herbert A. Lenz, who always encouraged me to write; my grandfather, Herbert J. Lenz, who lived his life as an example of what it means to give and love sacrificially; my beautiful wife, Lisa, and precious children, Samuel and Morgan, for being patient and tolerant of Daddy's extra working hours; and, finally, to my Lord, who is leading me on a journey—a journey on which this project has been an important step.

From Mary McRae

Learning the intricacies of a newly-developed application during beta testing is never easy, and would not have been possible without the help of several individuals at Microsoft, including Jean Paoli, Joe Andreshak, Brian Jones, Martin Sawicki, and Achint Srivastava. My co-workers, Dave Giusto, Rico McCahon, and Jeff Pouliot, were not only supportive, but also instrumental in helping to resolve technical challenges. Special thanks go to co-authors Simon St.Laurent and Evan Lenz for inviting me to be a part of this project, and most importantly to my family, Steve and Heather, for their love and support, and for keeping the coffee flowing.

From Simon St.Laurent

I'd like to thank my wife, Tracey Cranston, for putting up with me over the course of writing this book. Without her kindness, as usual, I'm sure I would have disappeared in a puff of flame and smoke sometime around the middle of the last chapter. I'm delighted to have had Evan Lenz and Mary McRae as co-authors, and would like to thank Jeni Tennison, Jeff Maggard, and Jeff Webb for their technical insights over the course of reviewing this book. Edd Dumbill contributed a large portion of Appendix A and was kind enough to only gently chide me for pursuing and writing this book.

CHAPTER 1

Microsoft Office and XML

Most people who use Microsoft Office see the individual applications as tools for getting their work done, not as general-purpose interfaces to information. Sure, people regularly exchange Word, Excel, and PowerPoint files over email, and there are lots of times when you need to reuse files you created earlier, but for the most part information created in Microsoft Office stays in Microsoft Office, coming or going from elsewhere largely by cut-and-paste or by often imperfect file conversions.

With the latest Windows-based version of Office, Microsoft has taken a risky step, opening up Office quite drastically. Developers, even those who aren't using Microsoft Office—or even Microsoft Windows—will be able to easily process the information inside of Word and Excel files. Instead of just creating Word documents, users will be able to create data files that can be shared with other processes and systems. Excel users will be able to analyze data from a much wider variety of sources, and Access users will be able to exchange information with other databases and programs much more easily than before. Users of the Enterprise Edition of Office will also have a new forms-based interface, InfoPath, for working with other programs.

All of these things are possible because Microsoft has chosen to integrate XML deeply into the core of Microsoft Office.

Why XML?

Extensible Markup Language (XML) defines a text-based format containing labels and structures. XML looks a lot like HTML, the primary language used by web browsers, but XML lets users and developers create their own formats rather than limiting them to a single vocabulary. The XML 1.0 specification appeared in 1998, and a wide variety of applications have added XML functionality or been built around XML since then, from databases to stock tickers to editors to web browsers to inventory systems. While XML still requires readers and writers of documents to have some shared understandings about the documents they create and interpret, it provides a basic format that is easily processed in a wide variety of different environments—it's even frequently human-readable.

 If you've never worked with XML and need to know the technical details of how to read and create XML documents, you should read Appendix A of this book. This chapter provides a high-level view of what XML makes possible and why it makes sense for Office, not a detailed explanation of what XML is.

Microsoft has been involved with XML for a long time. A Microsoft employee, Jean Paoli (later a product manager for Microsoft Office), was one of the editors of the XML 1.0 specification at the World Wide Web Consortium (W3C). Microsoft has been involved with nearly every XML specification at the W3C since, and has participated in a wide variety of XML-related projects at other organizations as well. Microsoft began work on XML tools before the specification was complete, building the MSXML toolkit into Internet Explorer and then expanding into .NET and Web Services development. More and more Microsoft software has XML at its core, and this latest version of Office joins a large group of Microsoft applications using XML.

XML has been a crucial part of Microsoft's drive to put its programs in more and more environments. XML makes it possible for Microsoft programs to communicate with programs from IBM, Sun, Oracle, and others, and greatly simplifies the task of integrating new tools with custom code. Developers can build applications around XML, and don't have to worry about the internal details of components with which they share XML. Equally important, developers using XML don't have to worry about being locked into a format that's proprietary to a single vendor, because XML is open by design. The rules for what is and what is not a legitimate XML document are very clear, and while it's possible to create XML that is difficult to read, a combination of strict grammatical rules and widely-shared best practices encourages developers to create formats that are easy to work worth. XML also includes features that support internationalization and localization, making it much easier to consistently represent information across language boundaries as well as program boundaries.

By adding XML to the Microsoft Office mix, Microsoft both makes it much easier to integrate Office with Microsoft programs that already understand XML (like SQL Server, SharePoint Server, and the toolkits in Visual Studio) and for developers to create their own combinations of Microsoft Office and other software. This allows Microsoft to connect to a much wider variety of software without making users worry about whether they'll be able to use that information elsewhere. XML also lets users go much further in building custom applications around Microsoft Office.

XML itself is only one piece of a larger XML puzzle. Extensible Stylesheet Language Transformations (XSLT) is an XML-based language for transforming one XML document into another, using templates. XSLT is at the heart of much of the Office XML work, a key ingredient for moving from the XML you have to the XML Office needs and vice-versa. Another specification, W3C XML Schema, provides descriptions of document structures which the various Office applications can use as a foundation for their processing. Microsoft refers to this as XML Schema Definition language, or just XSD, but the W3C itself didn't provide an acronym. Some sources refer to it as WXS (for W3C XML Schema), others as XSD, some as XSDL, and some just as XML Schema. Because Microsoft generally refers to it as XSD, this book will do the same.

One aspect of XML development in particular deserves special mention, because Microsoft has integrated it into Office alongside the more generic XML editing and analysis functions. Web Services, built on the SOAP, WSDL, and UDDI specifications, provide a set of tools for communicating with other programs using XML. You can still read and write files from your local computer, a file server, or a web server, but Web Services expose additional functionality of programs located anywhere on the network.

Different Faces of XML

Each of the Office applications that works with XML is targeted to a particular set of XML uses. While many people think of XML as a general-purpose format that can store any kind of information, there are some serious divisions in the way XML is used and in the practices surrounding that use. While some of these sound like the usual programming divides, where Visual Basic, C#, Perl, and Java programmers all look at the same information slightly differently, some of them are more like the divisions between people who primarily use Word to create documents and people who primarily use Access to create and present databases.

The most commonly discussed division in the XML world is the divide between documents and data. XML's predecessor, Standard Generalized Markup Language (SGML) was used primarily for document management. While having structures in documents was a key feature for organizations with huge numbers of documents like various departments of defense, the U.S. Internal Revenue Service, airplane manufacturers, and publishers, the structures were generally seen as labels applied to documents, not as structures defining the contents of the documents. Documents have to be accessible to humans as well as computers, and document structures need to be able to keep up with the many intricate structures humans create to solve particular problems.

Developers who focus on data structures typically see XML as a tool for creating labeled containers for information. While there may be some variations in that data and perhaps even some intricate data structures, the contents are generally expected to conform to the structures, not the other way around. Programmers who want to exchange data typically start by defining structures, and build code around those structures. Many program structures, especially efficient program structures, are very brittle and don't take kindly to changes because of different contexts or people adding extra layers of labels and structures.

While these two camps are often seen as separate and mutually suspicious, they can and do mix. Many documents contain some strongly structured information, like tables or lists, and sometimes data needs an escape hatch for possibilities that can't all be predicted in advance. Databases have long had fields that can support information in "rich" formats, from simple text with bold and italic to complex multimedia. XML is not a cure-all that can make all of these different views on information play nicely together, but it does offer enormous inherent flexibility for representing different kinds and styles of information. (Sadly, no XML features appear in Macintosh versions of Office.)

Different XML Faces of Office

Microsoft Office has always bundled a set of tools specialized for working with information of particular kinds. The new XML functionality continues that tradition, with each application in the bundle using XML in ways that fit its particular task. Microsoft has also added a new application, InfoPath, to the Enterprise Edition of Microsoft Office, filling a common business need for flexible forms-based interfaces to structured information.

Word: Editing Documents

Word began as a program that let people express their thoughts on paper, and most users tend to think of it as a conveniently editable typewriter. Although Word has added more features over time, like mail merge capabilities and web page editing, it is still squarely focused on documents. While it's possible to use Word as a calculator or a database, its primary strength has always been the creation of documents.

Microsoft has taken Word's traditional document-orientation and extended it into the world of document-oriented XML. Word already deals with structured documents through features like styles, footnotes, forms, and comments, and is quite capable of supporting complex layers of variable structure. When asked what they want in an XML document editor, many people cite their experience using Word—and Microsoft has pretty much given that to them.

Word embraces XML on two levels. Without much effort, users can save any Word document as XML, using a vocabulary that reflects Word's native understanding of the document. Styles, formatting, comments, revision marks, metadata, and everything else that normally goes into a .doc file are preserved. Better still, all this information (except for embedded objects, stored as Base64-encoded strings) is readily accessible, and developers can use any XML tools or even a text editor to explore and process it. Word can open these files as if they were .doc files as well, making it possible for other applications to create XML documents explicitly for consumption by Microsoft Word.

Word takes these features to the next level by allowing developers to create their own XML vocabularies and edit those documents using Word, as shown in Figure 1-1. This takes more effort as well as an understanding of XML, XSLT, and XSD, but that understanding is only necessary to create the templates, not to use them. Once the templates are created, users can simply edit XML within the ordinary confines of Word. They can even tell Word to show them the same information with a different set of presentation choices, making it easy to reuse information or edit documents in a form convenient for editing, while presenting it more formally later.

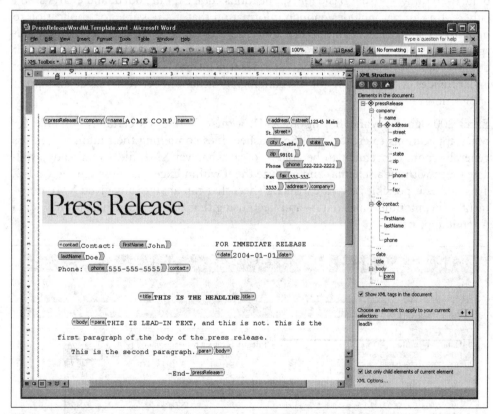

Figure 1-1. Editing an XML document in Microsoft Word 2003

Although Word is a newcomer to XML, Microsoft has driven XML foundations deep into the program. Simply exposing Word information as XML is a sizable step, but Word has aimed higher with its approach to letting users edit the XML of their choice in Word rather than the XML of Microsoft's choice. This should make it much easier to use Word as an interface to a much wider variety of XML-based systems, from Web Services to content management and workflow.

Excel: Analyzing Information

The spreadsheet was a wild new concept when VisiCalc first appeared back in 1981, and spreadsheets are still a fascinating hybrid of data storage and data processing. Excel has grown over the years from a basic calculating tool to a powerful set of features for analyzing and presenting largely numerical data. While many Excel spreadsheets quietly process data on their creators' computers, others have evolved into programs by themselves, providing an interface to problem-solving tools that people beyond their creators can use.

Excel has had its own XML format since Excel XP. While this format doesn't include quite everything—Visual Basic for Applications code isn't included, and charts aren't either—this format includes enough information that it's possible for application to mine Excel spreadsheets and extract their information. A common complaint about spreadsheets (especially among database purists) is that information goes in but doesn't come out. Microsoft's XML Spreadsheet format is relatively easy to interpret and provides a foundation for exchanging information between Excel and other applications.

Excel 2003 goes beyond having an XML format. While it's certainly possible for other applications to create XML Spreadsheet files containing their information, it's generally more convenient to be able to open whatever XML files are already available (even without a schema) and analyze them within Excel, as shown in Figure 1-2. This makes it possible to create a spreadsheet that can analyze any given XML document—say, monthly sales data—and keep using that same spreadsheet on new data when it appears.

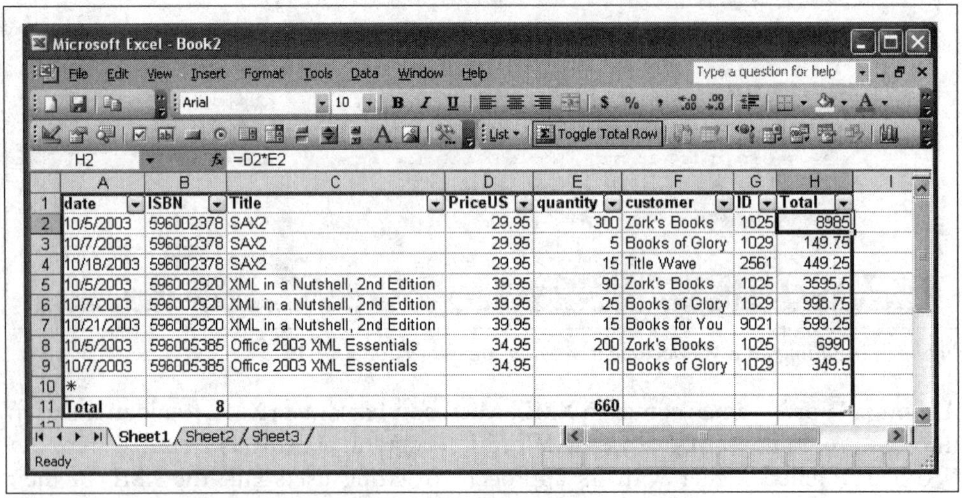

date	ISBN	Title	PriceUS	quantity	customer	ID	Total	
10/5/2003	596002378	SAX2	29.95	300	Zork's Books	1025	8985	
10/7/2003	596002378	SAX2	29.95	5	Books of Glory	1029	149.75	
10/18/2003	596002378	SAX2	29.95	15	Title Wave	2561	449.25	
10/5/2003	596002920	XML in a Nutshell, 2nd Edition	39.95	90	Zork's Books	1025	3595.5	
10/7/2003	596002920	XML in a Nutshell, 2nd Edition	39.95	25	Books of Glory	1029	998.75	
10/21/2003	596002920	XML in a Nutshell, 2nd Edition	39.95	15	Books for You	9021	599.25	
10/5/2003	596005385	Office 2003 XML Essentials	34.95	200	Zork's Books	1025	6990	
10/7/2003	596005385	Office 2003 XML Essentials	34.95	10	Books of Glory	1029	349.5	
*								
Total	8			660				

Figure 1-2. Working with XML data mapped into Microsoft Excel 2003.

The mapping features included in Excel make it much easier to create reusable spreadsheets, and simplify the task of creating Excel-based applications for analyzing data. They also make it much easier to separate the raw data from the Excel spreadsheet, letting the spreadsheet stay up to date even when the data it first analyzed isn't. To some extent this is like connecting Excel to a database, but it's a good deal more flexible. If your document structures are simple enough, you can also use Excel as a simple XML editor.

Access: Sharing Data

Access remains a relational database for the desktop, providing convenient local storage of structured information as well as an interface for information on both local and remote databases. Of all the products in the Office suite, Access is the strictest in demanding that information conform to predefined rules, using those structures as a foundation for all the other work it performs.

Like Excel, Access has had some XML support in earlier versions, supporting an XML vocabulary for importing and exporting information. Access 2003 substantially upgrades that XML support, however. New features include support for XML data that is stored across multiple tables, integrated XSLT transformations when importing or exporting information, and greater standards-compliance for both XSLT and XSD. You can see Access' XML export functionality in Figure 1-3. These features are also now more accessible from applications built using Access.

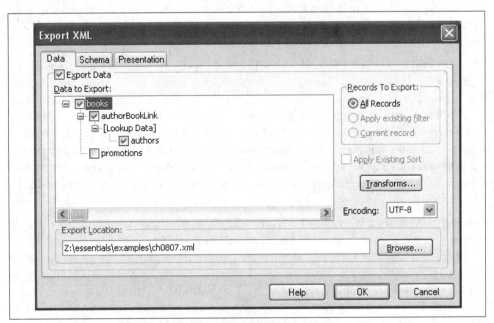

Figure 1-3. Exporting XML in Microsoft Access 2003

Because Access is built on a relational database foundation, it doesn't really make sense to drive XML into its core. It's possible to recreate tables in XML, but that loses the random access and indexing features that make relational databases so good at quickly processing structured information. Storing XML documents inside of relational databases is also possible, but again, the costs are high. Communicating with the outside world using XML seems to provide the best balance between connecting Access to other programs and letting Access do what it does best.

InfoPath: Editing Structured Information

InfoPath is a new addition to Microsoft Office, and only comes in the Enterprise Edition of Office, though it is also available for purchase as a standalone product. Unlike the other Office applications, which are largely self-sufficient, InfoPath is designed to connect users to other services and other users, and was built for the explicit purpose of working with XML. InfoPath provides both an environment for creating forms-based interfaces to structured information (stored in XML, naturally) and a framework for connecting that information to web, web service, and email applications. InfoPath can serve as a frontend to Microsoft's SharePoint Server, but it can also connect to other applications that can process XML.

InfoPath fills a gap between the document-oriented vision of Word and the data-oriented approaches of Excel and Access. A lot of information is too loosely structured to fit easily in a spreadsheet grid or a database table, but not nearly as open-ended as Word makes possible. At the same time, InfoPath provides a more capable set of tools than traditional browser-based HTML forms have provided, and has tied that information more tightly to workflow processes.

InfoPath builds on the same core of XML specifications as the other members of the Office suite: XML, XSLT, and XSD. InfoPath provides a set of tools for creating forms based on the possibilities defined in an XSD schema, letting you drag and drop components and customize them to meet your form-creation needs. An example of form-creation is shown in Figure 1-4. The same information can be presented in multiple views, making it possible, for example, for a customer to fill out a form with the information they know, and have other steps in the process add more information. There's no need for retyping or for mysterious "Office Use Only" sections on forms in this model.

InfoPath also takes advantage of XML to add some features that reflect how people typically work. Forms that collect a lot of information can take a while to fill out, and people frequently start and stop to rest, collect information, or switch to other tasks completely. Because InfoPath stores its information as XML, it's easy to stop the process, save the results, and come back to them later. This also makes it possible, for instance, to send a partially filled-out form to someone else and ask for help. Even if that other person doesn't have InfoPath, they may be able to open the file or apply an XSLT transformation to view the information inside of it.

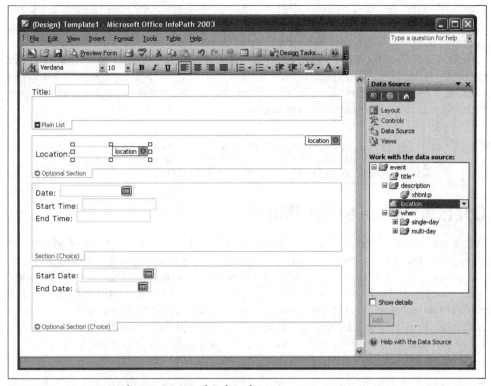

Figure 1-4. Designing a form in Microsoft InfoPath

Other Members of the Office Family

While the XML features in Word, Excel, Access, and InfoPath are especially interesting (and receive the bulk of coverage in this book), most of the other members of Microsoft's Office family of products have an XML story of some sort.

Two members of the Microsoft Office family, PowerPoint and Outlook, are notable for not having an XML story. PowerPoint's developers have continued work on its HTML features, but XML support has been left for later versions. Some developers use their own XML and XSLT to create HTML presentations, but this isn't exactly common practice. Outlook is in a similar position, with new features but none of them XML-related. Future editions of this book may get to explore PowerPoint and Outlook XML, but for now there is no such thing.

Microsoft FrontPage, traditionally a GUI editor for web pages, is growing into a slightly more general tool for creating XSLT stylesheets that can then be easily used to create templates. The XSLT tools in FrontPage remain oriented toward web development and not to general XSLT work, but they may prove very useful for developers who want to create XML documents in Word and present them differently on the Web without users having to lift a finger.

Microsoft Visio has had its own XML format since Visio 2002, but the latest release adds support for Scalable Vector Graphics (SVG), a W3C standard for describing graphics in XML. Visio can import SVG documents and work with them much like regular Visio documents, adding its own markup where it needs to go beyond the capabilities of SVG but preserving the original SVG. Developers who need to exchange diagrams or put them on the Web for readers who don't themselves have Visio should find these features very useful.

 For an example of working with Visio's XML format, see Recipe 11.1 of Sal Mangano's *XSLT Cookbook* (O'Reilly). For more on SVG generally, see J. David Eisenberg's *SVG Essentials* (O'Reilly).

Opening Office to the World

While the *.doc* and *.xls* file formats have served as de facto standard file formats for years, and developers have created a variety of tools for getting information into and out of these formats, writing code that could produce or consume them has never been much fun. Technologies like mail merges and ODBC connections have made it possible to connect the Office applications to other tools, but this is the first time that Microsoft has taken large steps to make Office data accessible through means other than the Office products themselves, and simultaneously has made the applications much more agnostic about where their information comes from.

By freeing users from their applications' traditional perspectives on information sources, Microsoft has created a whole new range of possibilities for using its applications as interactive browsers. Users who have been frustrated by the limited interaction capabilities of web browsers can now access their data, and edit it, in familiar applications supporting many different styles of information manipulation. For the most part, the applications continue to prefer working with local documents and can read documents from the Web, but they have taken a big step toward integration with Web- and XML-based infrastructure.

While the details of each application make a big difference in how the integration works, details which will be covered in later chapters, it's worth examining some potential use cases for the new technology before proceeding into those details.

Generating Word and Excel Documents from Databases

While much of the information that is currently managed by Microsoft Office users is created in Office and manipulated primarily through Office, there is plenty of other information out there. There are also a lot of reasons why organizations may want to keep even their document-like information in more conveniently managed and reused database management systems. While Office has long had pieces for connecting to these systems to extract information, dumping a relational database table into a Word or Excel file has required non-trivial programming. The new XML capabilities open up new possibilities for this kind of work.

The key to this project lies in Microsoft's creation of application-specific XML formats for Word and Excel. Word's WordprocessingML and Excel's SpreadsheetML are formats that these applications can open and interact with just as if they were *.doc* or *.xls* files. (Some restrictions apply, especially for Excel, but enough is available to make this technique useful.)

Developers can create XML documents from databases much the same way that they have created HTML documents from databases for the past decade. Technologies like ASP, PHP, CGI, and all of their siblings are still up to the task. Alternatively, if a database can provide an XML representation of information in response to a query, the server could use XSLT to transform that representation, as shown in Figure 1-5. To create documents for Word, the developer would generate WordprocessingML, while creating documents for Excel would involve generating SpreadsheetML.

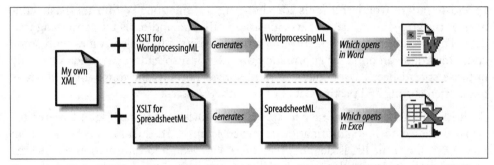

Figure 1-5. Using XSLT to generate WordprocessingML or SpreadsheetML from a custom XML vocabulary

Users of Office 2003 can then open these documents directly, as if they were ordinary Word or Excel files. This works even if the documents are stored on the Web, thanks to Word and Excel's long-time support for opening Web documents. If they need to exchange the information with people using older versions of Office, they can just use Save As… and the *.doc* or *.xls* format for backward-compatibility. Nothing is lost in the transition from XML to the traditional binary formats.

Separating Content from Presentation in Word

Most users treat Word as a tool for creating content that looks the way they want it to look. The gold standard for Word results has generally been the document's appearance on a piece of paper, not the elegance of how that appearance was achieved. While the focus on presentation works well for a lot of applications, it breaks down when developers are trying to use Word's familiar interface to create information that needs to be reused in other ways.

This book, for instance, was written in Word and the *.doc* files converted to FrameMaker using custom tools—tools that only focus on a subset of Word's capabilities, its styles. Users who take advantage of Word's other style features create problems for this converter, and the usual result is that some of the author's intentions are lost in translation.

Word's support for custom XML schemas offers a huge first step toward resolving this problem. Developers can create templates that emphasize structured content rather than presentation, while still using an interface that looks familiar. These templates can even offer users a choice of how to present the content, letting them work on the structures using a view that makes them comfortable. For small projects, this can be a quick and effective way to build forms. For larger, more complicated projects, a more sophisticated set of programming skills is necessary to make this work.

Separating Content from Analysis in Excel

Spreadsheets are wonderful tools for analyzing information. Within the basic confines of the grid system, developers can store both data and tools for processing that data. This paradigm has worked well for twenty years, but it also comes with some costs. Incredible amounts of information are stored in spreadsheets, much of it only in those spreadsheets. Users often use old spreadsheets as the foundations for new ones, often cutting and pasting data in from other sources.

With Excel 2003, it's pretty easy to create a spreadsheet that includes a list area (or areas) designed to hold information retrieved from XML documents, as shown in Figure 1-6. Once the list is defined, the spreadsheet can add information to the area or replace the content with new data. The list can be extended easily to include formulas as well, if desired, and the rest of the spreadsheet can reference the list.

Thanks to these lists, users can keep a standard spreadsheet that they use to analyze information that appears on a regular basis. When new data arrives in XML format—say, a quarterly sales report—those users can just tell Excel to import the new data, and their spreadsheets will reflect the new data. The spreadsheets become small applications themselves, complete with their own XML-based data formats. It's hard to imagine an easier way to write programs that analyze business data.

Creating and Editing XML in Excel

Excel's forte is analysis, but it also provides an easily understood user interface for working with simple structured data. If you need to work with data that fits easily on a grid, Excel offers a convenient tool for working with that data. You can create a list, type data directly into it, and save it as XML without ever seeing a tag. The XML itself can have a slightly more complex structure than the simple grid, though that structure isn't presented to the person working in Excel at all. It's easy to use Excel as a quick interface for creating or editing simple XML documents.

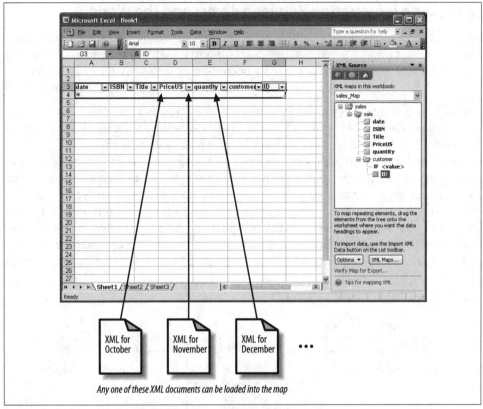

Figure 1-6. Using lists representing XML maps to create reusable Excel spreadsheets that can be applied to different XML data sets

Annotating Word Documents with Additional Information

While Microsoft has described Word's support for custom XML as a feature that makes Word into an XML editor of sorts, the custom markup support has a side effect that gives Word new functionality, whether or not users ever save their files as XML. For many documents, presentation style is a good analog for structure, but there are times when you need to be able to annotate documents in a finer-grained or more complex way than Word's existing styles and comments interfaces provide.

By associating an XML Schema with a Word document, developers can create templates that look like ordinary Word documents but have a hidden layer of additional information, which only surfaces when the document is saved as XML or viewed with XML tags visible. It's more typical for documents to have a single structure, made visible through the traditional WYSIWYG interface, but if you need the document to have two sets of structure, this is definitely an option.

Exchanging Information Between Access and the World

Microsoft Access has traditionally been a desktop application, sharing information among a small group of people. Access now supports XML import and export to and from its tables, meaning that it's rapidly becoming easier to use an Access database as a local host for information that may well come from or go to other systems.

Instead of treating Access databases as islands (or Access as a mere interface to more sophisticated database systems) this new openness makes it easier to treat Access databases as the outer nodes in a hub-spoke system, as shown in Figure 1-7. By picking up information from XML documents and storing it in the database, Access can act as a convenient local container that provides a lot of analytical and interface tools. Access might make an excellent temporary store for users analyzing complex data on disconnected laptops, or as a point of contact for users in remote offices who periodically send and receive updated information. Access can also function as an intermediary between XML and more complex, possibly legacy database systems that don't necessarily support XML but do support import and export to and from Access.

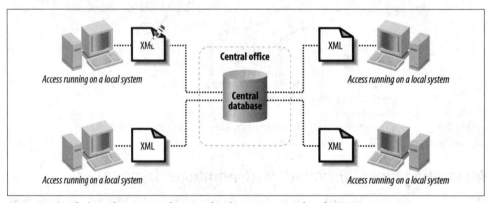

Figure 1-7. A hub-spoke system of Access databases connected with XML

Interacting with Web Services Using InfoPath

Web Services have remained stubbornly buried behind layers of code. Although it's always been possible to write user interfaces for them, it required a lot of interface-building programming. Expanding Web Services (and XML) communications to include people as well as computers hasn't been particularly easy. InfoPath takes direct aim at this project, drastically simplifying the task of designing and deploying interfaces to these services.

Microsoft has made a lot of complete functionality for managing projects using these tools available through the combination of SharePoint Server and InfoPath, but Info-Path can provide a friendly frontend interface to whatever services you'd like. If you need to collect information from users, give them a testing interface to explore a Web Service, or present information to users that they can use or change, InfoPath offers easy access to a wide variety of information types.

Interacting with Web Services Using Excel, Access, or Word

Excel can also be used as an interface to SOAP-based Web Services, not just XML. Doing so requires installing a toolkit and writing some Visual Basic for Applications code, but once you've done that, your Excel spreadsheet can serve as an interface to whatever Web Service you choose. Excel XP supported similar functionality, so this isn't an major change, but it's an important ingredient of the overall Office story.

The same toolkit used to integrate Web Services with Excel can be used with Access and Word. An Access database might use an external web service to support complex calculations or as a source of regularly changing data, while Word users might find Web Services a convenient source of information for documents that need auto-completion of regularly changing or even calculated boilerplate text.

CHAPTER 2

The WordprocessingML Vocabulary

Microsoft Office Word 2003 marks the introduction of XML as a native format for Word documents. Any Word document can now be opened in Word and saved as XML, thereby freeing documents from the tyranny of Word's proprietary *.doc* format. This new format, called WordprocessingML, opens up a multitude of possibilities for generating and processing Word documents. (Read Chapter 3 first if you want some immediate gratification regarding use cases for WordprocessingML.) This chapter includes a basic introduction to WordprocessingML, along with some general technical observations and guidelines for learning more. It is meant to complement, rather than replace, a detailed investigation of the WordprocessingML schema.

An authoritative and thorough source for learning is the Microsoft-supplied XSD schema for WordprocessingML. The "Microsoft Office 2003 XML Reference Schemas" package has been released under a royalty-free license and includes each of the WordprocessingML schema documents, as well as accompanying documentation. It can be found by starting at *http://www.microsoft.com/office/xml/*.

Introduction to WordprocessingML

WordprocessingML is Microsoft's XML format for Word documents. It's what you get when you select Save As... and choose "XML Document." WordprocessingML is a lossless format, which means that it contains all the information that Word needs to re-open a document, just as if it had been saved in the traditional *.doc* format—all text, formatting, styles, document metadata, images, macros, revision history, Smart Tags, etc. (The one exception is that WordprocessingML does not embed TrueType fonts, which is only a disadvantage if the users opening the document do not have the needed font installed on their system.) Indicative of Word's tremendous size and legacy, the WordprocessingML schema file approaches 7,000 lines in length. Fortunately, a little bit of knowledge about WordprocessingML can go a long way.

It was only recently that Microsoft began calling Word's XML format "WordprocessingML," whereas previously it was called, simply, "WordML" (as still reflected in the schema's namespace URI). Why they decided to adopt this new name isn't entirely clear...though it certainly is *wordier*.

To gain an advanced understanding of WordprocessingML, you'll need to first understand the fundamentals of Word itself. While this chapter briefly touches on Word's global architecture and design, books such as the following can provide a more solid foundation:

Word Pocket Guide, by Walter Glenn (O'Reilly)
Word 2000 in a Nutshell, by Walter Glenn (O'Reilly)

In this chapter, we'll examine several increasingly detailed examples of WordprocessingML. First, we'll take a look at the definitive "Hello, World" example for WordprocessingML. Next, after learning some tips for working with WordprocessingML, we'll take a tour through an example WordprocessingML document as output by Word. Then, we'll systematically cover Word's primary formatting constructs: runs, paragraphs, tables, lists, sections, etc. Finally, we'll take another look at one of Word's most important features: the style. Understanding how styles work—how they interact with direct formatting and how they relate to document templates—is essential to an overall understanding of WordprocessingML and Word in general.

A Simple Example

Example 2-1 shows a WordprocessingML document that one might create by hand in a plain text editor. This example represents the simplest non-empty WordprocessingML document possible.

Example 2-1. A simple WordprocessingML document created by hand

```
<?xml version="1.0"?>
<?mso-application progid="Word.Document"?>
<w:wordDocument
  xmlns:w="http://schemas.microsoft.com/office/word/2003/wordml">
  <w:body>
    <w:p>
      <w:r>
        <w:t>Hello, World!</w:t>
      </w:r>
    </w:p>
  </w:body>
</w:wordDocument>
```

The first thing to note about this example is the mso-application processing instruction (PI). This is a generic PI used by various applications within the Microsoft Office

System. Its purpose is to associate the given *.xml* file with a particular application in the Office suite. In this case, the file is associated with Microsoft Word. This has a double effect: not only is the Word application launched when a user double-clicks the file, but Windows Explorer renders the file using a special Word XML icon. This behavior is enabled through an Explorer shell that is automatically installed with Office 2003. All XML documents saved by Word will include this PI. We'll see more uses of the `mso-application` PI in Chapter 7 and Chapter 10.

As mentioned above, Example 2-1 shows the simplest non-empty Wordprocess-ingML document possible. The `w:body` element is the only required child element of the `w:wordDocument` root element. It technically can be empty, but that would make for a pretty boring first example. The `w:p` element stands for "paragraph," `w:r` stands for "run," and `w:t` stands for "text." The namespace prefix `w` maps to the primary Word-processingML namespace: `http://schemas.microsoft.com/office/word/2003/wordml`.

> Beware the default namespace! Word, in its longstanding attempt to be everything to everybody, does something funny when you try to open a WordprocessingML document that uses a default namespace, rather than the `w` (or some other) prefix, for elements in the Wordpro-cessingML namespace. It sees the naked (un-prefixed) body element and thinks "This must be HTML!" The easiest way to avoid this problem is to always use an XML declaration (e.g., `<?xml version="1.0"?>`) at the beginning of an XML document that will be opened by Word. Word will consistently recognize the document as XML if the XML declaration is present.

With few exceptions, all text in a given document is contained within a `w:t` element that's contained within a `w:r` element that's contained within a `w:p` element. A final thing to note is that, except for the `w:wordDocument` element, none of the elements in Example 2-1 (`w:body`, `w:p`, `w:r`, and `w:t`) can have attributes. As we'll see, properties are instead assigned (to paragraphs and runs) using child elements. Figure 2-1 shows the result of opening our example document in Word. We see "Hello, World!" in the default font and font size, in the default view. Word supplies these defaults, because they are not explicitly specified in our WordprocessingML document.

Tips for Learning WordprocessingML

Learning WordprocessingML—particularly how Word behaves when it encounters various markup constructs—is an iterative process. You go back and forth between the text editor and the Word application, closing the document in Word so you can make changes to it elsewhere, and then re-opening it to see what effects those changes have. You make hypotheses and you test them. Anything you can do to speed up the iterations of this process will help. Below are several pieces of advice to consider as you begin this educational journey.

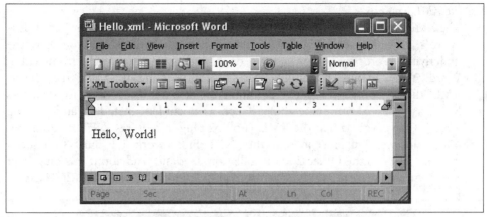

Figure 2-1. Our hand-edited WordprocessingML file, opened in Word

Experiment

Since Microsoft has released fairly limited documentation of Wordprocessing-ML so far, it is often best to learn through experimentation. Create a document in Word that uses various formatting features you are interested in. Save the document as XML. Then, investigate the WordprocessingML for the document, making note of how various document structures are represented as XML. Internet Explorer can be a good tool for viewing WordprocessingML documents. (See the sidebar "Using Internet Explorer to Inspect WordprocessingML Documents.")

Don't try to learn everything

This tip offsets the first one. It is sometimes possible to get hung up on particular theoretical questions or problems when experimenting with Wordprocessing-ML. But if you want to remain productive, you should be prepared to suspend understanding at various turns in your investigation. The beauty of WordprocessingML is that you can accomplish quite a lot without understanding everything in the markup. For example, to create a stylesheet that generates WordprocessingML documents, you would only need to prepare the document in Word itself, save it as XML, and then copy and paste the bulk of it into your stylesheet, zeroing in on only the elements that contain dynamic content.

Use the Reveal Formatting task pane

Word's Reveal Formatting task pane (press Shift-F1) provides a very helpful intermediate view of formatting properties between the WordprocessingML itself and how the document actually looks. Moreover, if you check the "Distinguish style source" checkbox (at the bottom of the task pane), it will identify the source of specific formatting properties, distinguishing between those that are defined in a style and those that are applied as direct formatting. This chapter includes some example screen shots that use the Reveal Formatting task pane.

Use the XML Toolbox

The XML Toolbox was quietly released by Microsoft as a plug-in for Word. It is Word's equivalent of View Source, and it is a godsend. It lets you view the underlying WordprocessingML for a document or selection right from within Word. You can also manually insert WordprocessingML, using the "Insert XML" dialog, shown in Figure 2-2. Ultimately, it is not a substitute for saving as XML, as it leaves out some things (such as document metadata and spelling errors). One caveat is that the XML Toolbox plug-in requires .NET Programmability support. This means that the .NET Framework 1.1 must have been installed prior to the Office 2003 installation. Get and read about this plug-in at *http://msdn.microsoft.com/library/en-us/dnofftalk/html/odc_office01012004.asp*

Figure 2-2. The "Insert XML" dialog, available only with the XML Toolbox plug-in for Word

WordprocessingML's Style of Markup

If you have any XML or HTML markup background, then WordprocessingML's style of markup may surprise you. WordprocessingML was *not* designed from a clean slate for the purpose of creating documents in XML markup. Instead, it is an unveiling of the internal structures that have been present in Microsoft Word for years. Though certain features have been added to make WordprocessingML usable outside the context of Word, by and large it represents a serialization of Word's internal data structures: various kinds of objects associated with myriad property values. Indeed, the object-oriented term "properties" permeates the WordprocessingML schema. If you want to make a run of text bold, you set the bold property. If you want to indent a particular paragraph, you set its indentation property. And so on.

No Mixed Content

Mixed content describes the presence of text content and elements inside the same parent element. It is standard fare in the world of markup, especially when using

Using Internet Explorer to Inspect WordprocessingML Documents

Internet Explorer's default tree-view stylesheet for XML documents provides a handy, readable way to investigate the structure of WordprocessingML documents. However, if you try opening a WordprocessingML document in IE (e.g., by right-clicking the file and selecting Open With → Internet Explorer), IE turns around and launches Word, because it too is now trained to recognize and honor the `mso-application` processing instruction. There are two techniques for getting around this.

The first technique is to simply remove the `mso-application` PI before opening the WordprocessingML document in IE:

1. Save the Word document as XML and then close it.
2. Open the newly saved WordprocessingML document in Notepad.
3. Delete or comment out the `mso-application` PI and re-save.

IE will now display the document using its pretty XML tree view, and will continue to do so even if the document is subsequently updated by Word to include the `mso-application` PI. Once you've initially opened it in IE, you can refresh IE to see how changes to the document from within Word affect the underlying WordprocessingML.

The second technique involves making a temporary global system change, obviating the need to comment out the `mso-application` PI for each and every document you want to inspect.

1. Open the Registry Editor by selecting Start → Run and typing `regedit`.
2. Find the sub-key named *HKEY_LOCAL_MACHINE\SOFTWARE\Microsoft\Office\11.0\Common\Filter\text/xml*.
3. Right-click the Word.Document string value entry, and select Rename.
4. Change the name to something like Word.DocumentDISABLED.

This will make it easy to restore the setting later, by simply renaming it again and removing the "DISABLED" part. With the WordprocessingML filter effectively disabled, IE will now open WordprocessingML documents using its default XML tree-view stylesheet just like any other XML document. Windows Explorer, however, will still continue to associate WordprocessingML documents with Word, which is probably what you will always want.

document-oriented markup. For example, in HTML, to make a sentence bold and only partially italicized, you would use code such as the following:

```
<b>This sentence has <i>mixed</i> formatting.</b>
```

WordprocessingML, however, never uses mixed content. All of the text in a WordprocessingML document resides in `w:t` elements, and `w:t` elements can only contain text (and no elements). The above sentence is represented much differently in

WordprocessingML. The hierarchy is flattened into a sequence of runs having different formatting properties:

```
<w:r>
  <w:rPr>
    <w:b/>
  </w:rPr>
  <w:t>This sentence has </w:t>
</w:r>
<w:r>
  <w:rPr>
    <w:b/>
    <w:i/>
  </w:rPr>
  <w:t>mixed</w:t>
</w:r>
<w:r>
  <w:rPr>
    <w:b/>
  </w:rPr>
  <w:t> formatting.</w:t>
</w:r>
```

As you can see, all of the text occurs by itself (no mixed content), within w:t elements.

Properties Are Set Using Empty Sub-Elements

The above snippet illustrates another general principle in WordprocessingML's style of markup: properties are assigned using empty sub-elements (e.g., w:b and w:i in the above example). For runs, the w:rPr element contains a set of empty elements, each of which sets a particular property on the run. Similarly, for paragraphs (w:p elements), the w:pPr element contains the paragraph formatting properties. For tables, table rows, and table cells, there are the w:tblPr, w:trPr, and w:tcPr elements, respectively. In each case, the *Pr element must come first, so that the general structure of paragraphs, runs, tables, table rows, and table cells looks like this:

```
Object
    Properties
    Content
```

The properties are defined first, and the content follows. If you have any experience with RTF (Rich Text Format), then this pattern may look familiar. Before the advent of WordprocessingML, RTF was the most open format in which Word was willing to save documents. A look at the same sentence after saving it as RTF is demonstrative:

```
{\b\insrsid3691043 This sentence has }
{\b\i\insrsid3691043 mixed}
{\b\insrsid3691043  formatting.}
```

The parallels should be fairly easy to draw, without understanding every detail. There are three runs (delineated by curly braces). The first run has bold turned on by virtue of the \b command. The second run has both bold and italic turned on by virtue of the \b and \i commands. And the third run goes back to using just bold and no italic. From this perspective, WordprocessingML may look more like an XML format for RTF—an estimation that is not too far off the mark.

 To learn more about RTF, consider the *RTF Pocket Guide* (O'Reilly), by Sean M. Burke.

No Hierarchical Document Structures

Nested markup describes the use of element nesting to arbitrary depths. In addition to formatting text, nested markup is useful for structuring documents. For example, a Docbook document may have sections and sub-sections nested to an arbitrary depth, like this:

```
<article>
  <section>
    <title>Section 1</title>
    <para>This is the first section.</para>
    <section>
      <title>Section 1A</title>
      <para>This is a sub-section.</para>
    </section>
  </section>
</article>
```

The above document is represented much differently in WordprocessingML. The hierarchy is flattened into a sequence of four paragraphs having different properties. Below is the w:body element, excerpted from such a document:

```
<w:body>
  <w:p>
    <w:pPr>
      <w:pStyle w:val="Heading1"/>
    </w:pPr>
    <w:r>
      <w:t>Section 1</w:t>
    </w:r>
  </w:p>
  <w:p>
    <w:r>
      <w:t>This is the first section.</w:t>
    </w:r>
  </w:p>
  <w:p>
    <w:pPr>
      <w:pStyle w:val="Heading2"/>
    </w:pPr>
    <w:r>
      <w:t>Section 1A</w:t>
    </w:r>
  </w:p>
```

```
  <w:p>
    <w:r>
      <w:t>This is a sub-section.</w:t>
    </w:r>
  </w:p>
</w:body>
```

In Word, the paragraph is the basic block-oriented element, and paragraphs may not contain other paragraphs. Word does, however, provide a workaround for hierarchical documents, through use of the wx:sub-section element. In fact, if you were to open the above document and then save it from within Word, the result would include wx:sub-section elements that reflect the hierarchy intended by the heading paragraphs. We'll look at how this works in detail later, in "Outline Levels and Sub-Sections."

All Attributes Are Namespace-Qualified

One more peculiarity worth noting about WordprocessingML markup is its use of namespace-qualified attributes. In most XML vocabularies, attributes are not in a namespace. They are generally thought to "belong" to the element to which they are attached. As long as the element is in a namespace, then no naming ambiguities should arise. Namespace qualification, however, can be useful for "global attributes" that can be attached to different elements. Such attributes do not belong to any particular element. The xml:space attribute is a good example of a global attribute. XSLT also has some global attributes, such as the xsl:exclude-result-prefixes attribute, which can occur on any literal result element (in any namespace). These are considered good use cases for qualifying attributes with a namespace.

WordprocessingML, however, does not follow this convention. While there are some "global attributes" in WordprocessingML (such as the w:type attribute, which appears on the aml:annotation element, which we'll see), WordprocessingML does not restrict its use of namespace qualification to those cases. Instead, it universally qualifies all attributes across the board. For this reason, the key thing to remember when working with attributes in WordprocessingML is that they *always* must have a namespace prefix (because there's no such thing as a default namespace for attributes in XML).

A Simple Example Revisited

Example 2-2 shows how our "Hello, World" example looks after opening it in Word, selecting Save As…, and saving the file with a new name, *HelloSaved.xml*. For the sake of readability, we've added line breaks and indentation, neither of which affects the meaning of the file. The highlighted lines in this example correspond to the lines that were present in our original hand-edited WordprocessingML document in Example 2-1. Everything else is new.

Example 2-2. The same Word document, after Word saves it as XML

```xml
<?xml version="1.0" encoding="UTF-8" standalone="yes"?>
<?mso-application progid="Word.Document"?>
<w:wordDocument
  xmlns:w="http://schemas.microsoft.com/office/word/2003/wordml"
  xmlns:v="urn:schemas-microsoft-com:vml"
  xmlns:w10="urn:schemas-microsoft-com:office:word"
  xmlns:sl="http://schemas.microsoft.com/schemaLibrary/2003/core"
  xmlns:aml="http://schemas.microsoft.com/aml/2001/core"
  xmlns:wx="http://schemas.microsoft.com/office/word/2003/auxHint"
  xmlns:o="urn:schemas-microsoft-com:office:office"
  xmlns:dt="uuid:C2F41010-65B3-11d1-A29F-00AA00C14882"
  w:macrosPresent="no" w:embeddedObjPresent="no" w:ocxPresent="no"
  xml:space="preserve">
  <o:DocumentProperties>
    <o:Title>Hello, World</o:Title>
    <o:Author>Evan Lenz</o:Author>
    <o:LastAuthor>Evan Lenz</o:LastAuthor>
    <o:Revision>4</o:Revision>
    <o:TotalTime>15</o:TotalTime>
    <o:Created>2003-12-06T22:45:00Z</o:Created>
    <o:LastSaved>2003-12-18T07:59:00Z</o:LastSaved>
    <o:Pages>1</o:Pages>
    <o:Words>2</o:Words>
    <o:Characters>12</o:Characters>
    <o:Lines>1</o:Lines>
    <o:Paragraphs>1</o:Paragraphs>
    <o:CharactersWithSpaces>13</o:CharactersWithSpaces>
    <o:Version>11.5604</o:Version>
  </o:DocumentProperties>
  <w:fonts>
    <w:defaultFonts w:ascii="Times New Roman" w:fareast="Times New Roman"
                    w:h-ansi="Times New Roman" w:cs="Times New Roman"/>
  </w:fonts>
  <w:styles>
    <w:versionOfBuiltInStylenames w:val="4"/>
    <w:latentStyles w:defLockedState="off" w:latentStyleCount="156"/>
    <w:style w:type="paragraph" w:default="on" w:styleId="Normal">
      <w:name w:val="Normal"/>
      <w:rsid w:val="00B15979"/>
      <w:rPr>
        <wx:font wx:val="Times New Roman"/>
        <w:sz w:val="24"/>
        <w:sz-cs w:val="24"/>
        <w:lang w:val="EN-US" w:fareast="EN-US" w:bidi="AR-SA"/>
      </w:rPr>
    </w:style>
    <w:style w:type="character" w:default="on"
             w:styleId="DefaultParagraphFont">
      <w:name w:val="Default Paragraph Font"/>
      <w:semiHidden/>
    </w:style>
    <w:style w:type="table" w:default="on" w:styleId="TableNormal">
      <w:name w:val="Normal Table"/>
```

Example 2-2. The same Word document, after Word saves it as XML (continued)

```
          <wx:uiName wx:val="Table Normal"/>
          <w:semiHidden/>
          <w:rPr>
            <wx:font wx:val="Times New Roman"/>
          </w:rPr>
          <w:tblPr>
            <w:tblInd w:w="0" w:type="dxa"/>
            <w:tblCellMar>
              <w:top w:w="0" w:type="dxa"/>
              <w:left w:w="108" w:type="dxa"/>
              <w:bottom w:w="0" w:type="dxa"/>
              <w:right w:w="108" w:type="dxa"/>
            </w:tblCellMar>
          </w:tblPr>
        </w:style>
        <w:style w:type="list" w:default="on" w:styleId="NoList">
          <w:name w:val="No List"/>
          <w:semiHidden/>
        </w:style>
      </w:styles>
      <w:docPr>
        <w:view w:val="web"/>
        <w:zoom w:percent="100"/>
        <w:proofState w:spelling="clean" w:grammar="clean"/>
        <w:attachedTemplate w:val=""/>
        <w:defaultTabStop w:val="720"/>
        <w:characterSpacingControl w:val="DontCompress"/>
        <w:validateAgainstSchema/>
        <w:saveInvalidXML w:val="off"/>
        <w:ignoreMixedContent w:val="off"/>
        <w:alwaysShowPlaceholderText w:val="off"/>
        <w:compat/>
      </w:docPr>
      <w:body>
        <wx:sect>
          <w:p>
            <w:r>
              <w:t>Hello, World!</w:t>
            </w:r>
          </w:p>
          <w:sectPr>
            <w:pgSz w:w="12240" w:h="15840"/>
            <w:pgMar w:top="1440" w:right="1800" w:bottom="1440" w:left="1800"
                     w:header="720" w:footer="720" w:gutter="0"/>
            <w:cols w:space="720"/>
            <w:docGrid w:line-pitch="360"/>
          </w:sectPr>
        </wx:sect>
      </w:body>
    </w:wordDocument>
```

The first thing that may come to mind when looking at this example is "Why does the XML contain so much more information when all I did was save it?" Or perhaps you've begun to panic.

Don't. While all of this XML is certainly daunting at first glance, we'll see that for the most part its meaning is straightforward. Take comfort in the fact that, while Word may create markup that's quite verbose, it can handle markup that minimally conforms to its schema without complaining at all. This liberality in what Word accepts makes it much easier to write applications that generate WordprocessingML.

Let's take a tour through this document, examining each top-level element in turn. Getting an overall, top-down view of what goes into a WordprocessingML document will help bring context to the more nitty-gritty, bottom-up examination of the vocabulary that will follow later in this chapter.

The w:wordDocument Element

The root element of Example 2-2, w:wordDocument, has a large number of attributes:

```
<w:wordDocument
  xmlns:w="http://schemas.microsoft.com/office/word/2003/wordml"
  xmlns:v="urn:schemas-microsoft-com:vml"
  xmlns:w10="urn:schemas-microsoft-com:office:word"
  xmlns:sl="http://schemas.microsoft.com/schemaLibrary/2003/core"
  xmlns:aml="http://schemas.microsoft.com/aml/2001/core"
  xmlns:wx="http://schemas.microsoft.com/office/word/2003/auxHint"
  xmlns:o="urn:schemas-microsoft-com:office:office"
  xmlns:dt="uuid:C2F41010-65B3-11d1-A29F-00AA00C14882"
  w:macrosPresent="no" w:embeddedObjPresent="no"
  w:ocxPresent="no" xml:space="preserve">
```

Actually, most of these are technically namespace declarations. They are present on every WordprocessingML document that Word outputs, regardless of whether all the namespaces are actually used in the document. In WordprocessingML, you can safely leave out all the namespace declarations except the ones you actually use, which will minimally include the primary WordprocessingML namespace (normally mapped to the w prefix). Below is a list of the namespaces declared in this document, along with a brief description of the purpose of each.

http://schemas.microsoft.com/office/word/2003/wordml
> Mapped to the w prefix. All of the core WordprocessingML elements and attributes are in this namespace.

urn:schemas-microsoft-com:vml
> Mapped to the v prefix. Elements in this namespace represent embedded Vector Markup Language (VML) images.

urn:schemas-microsoft-com:office:word
> Mapped to the w10 prefix. This namespace is used for legacy elements from Word Ten. It is used in HTML output.

`http://schemas.microsoft.com/schemaLibrary/2003/core`

> Mapped to the `sl` prefix. The `sl:schema` and `sl:schemaLibrary` elements are used with Word's custom XML schema functionality, and are introduced in Chapter 4.

`http://schemas.microsoft.com/aml/2001/core`

> Mapped to the `aml` prefix. The Annotation Markup Language (AML) elements are used to describe tracked changes, comments, and bookmarks.

`http://schemas.microsoft.com/office/word/2003/auxHint`

> Mapped to the `wx` prefix. Elements in this namespace provide "auxiliary hints" for processing WordprocessingML documents outside of Word. They represent derivative information that is useful to us but that is of no internal use to Word. See "Auxiliary Hints in WordprocessingML," later in this chapter.

`urn:schemas-microsoft-com:office:office`

> Mapped to the `o` namespace. This is the namespace for "shared" document properties and custom document properties. They are shared in that they also apply to other Office applications, such as Excel.

`uuid:C2F41010-65B3-11d1-A29F-00AA00C14882`

> Mapped to the `dt` prefix. This is the XML Data Reduced (XDR) namespace, which, in WordprocessingML, qualifies the `dt` (data type) attributes of a document's custom document property elements.

While some confusing legacy is evident in this list, the overall distinction between namespaces is helpful, particularly between the `wx` and `w` namespaces, as we'll see.

The `xml:space` attribute is set to `preserve`, in order that whitespace characters (and even any instances of the empty `w:tab` element) are interpreted correctly. As a matter of best practice, you should include `xml:space="preserve"` on the root element of any WordprocessingML document you create.

The remaining three attributes of the `w:wordDocument` element are all optional and default to the value no.

```
w:macrosPresent="no" w:embeddedObjPresent="no" w:ocxPresent="no"
```

These are consistency checks for when certain kinds of base64-encoded binary objects are embedded in the document. Specifically, `w:macrosPresent` must be set to yes when the `w:docSuppData` element is present (containing toolbar customizations, VBA macros, etc.); `w:embeddedObjPresent` must be set to yes when the `w:docOleData` element is present (containing OLE objects from other applications, such as Excel); and `w:ocxPresent` must be set to yes when a `w:ocx` element is present somewhere in the body of the document (representing a control from Word's Control Toolbox). Unless your document contains any such objects, you can safely leave out these attributes.

The child elements of `w:wordDocument`, as included in this example, represent only a portion of the root element's complete content model. Below is a list of all possible child elements in the order they are supposed to occur, according to the Wordprocessing ML schema. Word tends to be lenient about WordprocessingML documents that contain these elements in a different order, which suggests it does not validate documents against the published schema when they are loaded. However, to be on the safe side, you should ensure that these elements are in the correct order in WordprocessingML documents that you create. As mentioned before, w:body is the only required child element of w:wordDocument. Only the highlighted elements in this list are actually present in Example 2-2.

```
w:ignoreSubtree
w:ignoreElements
o:SmartTagType
o:DocumentProperties
o:CustomDocumentProperties
sl:schemaLibrary
w:fonts
w:frameset
w:lists
w:styles
w:divs
w:docOleData
w:docSuppData
w:shapeDefaults
w:bgPict
w:docPr
w:body
```

Apart from the highlighted elements, the w:lists element is the only one in the above list that will receive further coverage in this chapter.

The o:DocumentProperties Element

The o:DocumentProperties element in Example 2-2, shown again below, is in the general Office namespace (mapped to the o prefix), because it includes properties, such as metadata and statistics, that are common to both Word and Excel:

```xml
<o:DocumentProperties>
  <o:Title>Hello, World</o:Title>
  <o:Author>Evan Lenz</o:Author>
  <o:LastAuthor>Evan Lenz</o:LastAuthor>
  <o:Revision>4</o:Revision>
  <o:TotalTime>15</o:TotalTime>
  <o:Created>2003-12-06T22:45:00Z</o:Created>
  <o:LastSaved>2003-12-18T07:59:00Z</o:LastSaved>
  <o:Pages>1</o:Pages>
  <o:Words>2</o:Words>
  <o:Characters>12</o:Characters>
```

```
    <o:Lines>1</o:Lines>
    <o:Paragraphs>1</o:Paragraphs>
    <o:CharactersWithSpaces>13</o:CharactersWithSpaces>
    <o:Version>11.5604</o:Version>
</o:DocumentProperties>
```

These elements are also serialized as such when Word saves a document as HTML. They correspond primarily to the properties you see when you open the document Properties dialog (by selecting File → Properties). Figure 2-3 shows the Statistics tab of the file Properties dialog.

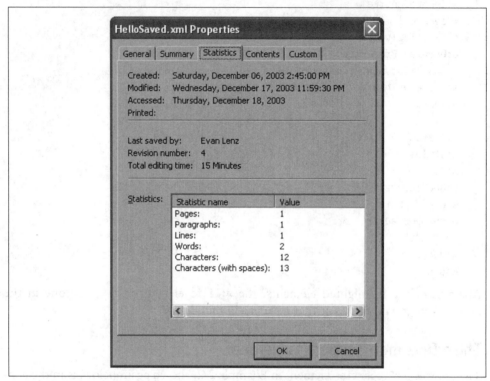

Figure 2-3. The Statistics tab of the Properties dialog, corresponding to values inside the o: DocumentProperties element

There are 12 more valid child elements of o:DocumentProperties not shown here, making a total of 26. A number of these can be added to a document from within Word, at user option. For example, there is an element corresponding to each of the fields in the Summary tab of the file Properties dialog, shown in Figure 2-4.

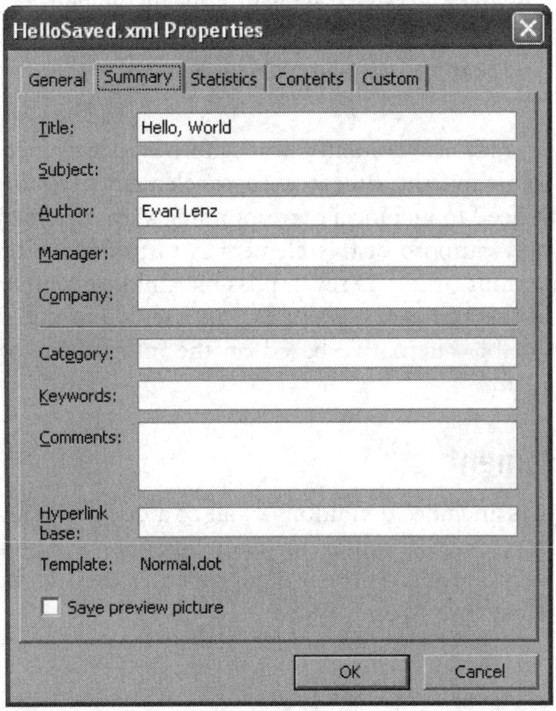

Figure 2-4. Other document properties can be populated at user option

The w:fonts Element

The w:defaultFonts element inside the w:fonts element specifies the *default font* for a document.

```
<w:fonts>
  <w:defaultFonts w:ascii="Times New Roman" w:fareast="Times New Roman"
                  w:h-ansi="Times New Roman" w:cs="Times New Roman"/>
</w:fonts>
```

A document's default font is applied to all of the document's paragraph styles that do not explicitly specify a font. Normally, when you create a new blank document in Word, the default font setting as specified in the *Normal.dot* document template is copied into the document. But our hand-coded WordprocessingML document (Example 2-1) isn't "normal" in this sense. It was created outside of Word and contains no default font definition at all. Word gracefully handles this scenario when it loads the document by automatically inserting a default font, as shown in Example 2-2. Times New Roman is thus the "default default" font. In fact, Times New Roman is also the default font assigned to the *Normal.dot* template when Word is first installed, or when it is forced to create a new *Normal.dot* template because someone deleted the *Normal.dot* file.

The attributes on the w:defaultFonts element indicate which font should be used for each character encoding range among ASCII, high ANSI, complex scripts, and East Asian characters. In Example 2-2, Times New Roman is the default font for all of these ranges.

The w:fonts element may also contain zero or more w:font elements (zero in the case of Example 2-2) following the w:defaultFonts element. The w:font elements are optional; you don't need to include a corresponding w:font element just to use a particular font. The only purpose of this element is to provide Word with descriptive information about a font (using its seven possible child elements) that could be useful in the event that the font is not available on a user's machine. In that case, Word can choose a reasonable alternative based on the information about the font provided in the document.

The w:styles Element

The w:styles element includes definitions of all of a document's styles. Before looking at the WordprocessingML syntax for defining styles, let's establish some basic terminology. A *style* is a group of formatting properties that can be applied as a unit. There are four possible *style types* in Word:

```
paragraph
character
table
list
```

These style types apply respectively to paragraphs, runs, tables, and lists. Every paragraph, run, table, and list in a Word document is necessarily associated with a style of the corresponding type. If a paragraph, run, table, or list in a WordprocessingML document doesn't explicitly specify an associated style (as is the case in Example 2-2), then it takes on the document's *default style* of the appropriate style type. Thus, styles are always involved, regardless of whether you specifically make use of them.

Normally, when you create a new blank document in Word, all of the styles defined in the *Normal.dot* document template are copied into the document. These include, at minimum, a default style definition for each style type. However, our hand-coded WordprocessingML document does not include the w:styles element. Just as Word automatically creates the w:fonts element when absent, Word automatically inserts four w:style elements, corresponding respectively to the four style types (paragraph, character, table, and list):

```
Normal
Default Paragraph Font
Normal Table
No List
```

These four Word-defined styles are what we see inside the w:styles element in Example 2-2. Effectively, they are implicitly present in any WordprocessingML document that does not explicitly define them. (However, to explicitly refer to them from within the body of the document, they must also be explicitly present in the document's w:styles element.) These "default default" styles are also the same four style definitions that are automatically copied into the *Normal.dot* template when Word is first installed, or when it is forced to create a new *Normal.dot* template.

Now let's take a look at the content of the w:styles element, extracted from Example 2-2. Preceding the style definitions themselves are two elements:

```
<w:versionOfBuiltInStylenames w:val="4"/>
<w:latentStyles w:defLockedState="off" w:latentStyleCount="156"/>
```

The w:versionOfBuiltInStylenames and w:latentStyles elements are used to refer to particular built-in styles when document formatting protection is turned on. Since document protection is an important ingredient in building custom XML solutions in Word, these elements will be covered in Chapter 4. For now, all you need to know is that there are no formatting restrictions on this document. In fact, this document would be interpreted no differently if we were to remove these two (optional) elements.

Next, there are four w:style elements, one for each of the "default default" styles listed above:

```
<w:style w:type="paragraph" w:default="on" w:styleId="Normal">
  <w:name w:val="Normal"/>
  <w:rPr>
    <wx:font wx:val="Times New Roman"/>
    <w:sz w:val="24"/>
    <w:sz-cs w:val="24"/>
    <w:lang w:val="EN-US" w:fareast="EN-US" w:bidi="AR-SA"/>
  </w:rPr>
</w:style>
<w:style w:type="character" w:default="on"
         w:styleId="DefaultParagraphFont">
  <w:name w:val="Default Paragraph Font"/>
  <w:semiHidden/>
</w:style>
<w:style w:type="table" w:default="on" w:styleId="TableNormal">
  <w:name w:val="Normal Table"/>
  <wx:uiName wx:val="Table Normal"/>
  <w:semiHidden/>
  <w:rPr>
    <wx:font wx:val="Times New Roman"/>
  </w:rPr>
  <w:tblPr>
    <w:tblInd w:w="0" w:type="dxa"/>
    <w:tblCellMar>
      <w:top w:w="0" w:type="dxa"/>
      <w:left w:w="108" w:type="dxa"/>
      <w:bottom w:w="0" w:type="dxa"/>
```

```
          <w:right w:w="108" w:type="dxa"/>
        </w:tblCellMar>
      </w:tblPr>
    </w:style>
    <w:style w:type="list" w:default="on" w:styleId="NoList">
      <w:name w:val="No List"/>
      <w:semiHidden/>
    </w:style>
```

For now, we'll only look at the lines that are highlighted. The w:type attribute of each w:style element indicates the style type (paragraph, character, table, or list). The presence of w:default="on" denotes that this style is the default style for its style type. This attribute's default value is off.

Each style has two different names, as indicated by the w:styleId attribute and the w:name element. The w:styleId attribute is for intra-document references only; it must be unique within the file. Styles can be referred to either from within the document's body (to associate a paragraph with a certain paragraph style, for example) or from within another style definition (to derive the style from another style, for example). The w:styleId attribute is unused apart from these internal associations. In fact, Word doesn't preserve its value when it opens the document. When a document is subsequently saved as XML, Word auto-generates a value for the w:styleId attribute, usually deriving it from the style's primary name.

The *primary name* of a style is denoted by the w:val attribute of the w:name element. The primary name of a style is what the user sees in the Style drop-down menu in the Word UI. Also, for styles that came from a template, the primary name uniquely identifies the style in the attached template and is the basis by which styles are updated when the "Automatically update document styles" document option is turned on. This name, like the w:styleId attribute, must be unique within the file. Otherwise, Word will try to fix things up, probably not in the way that you intended.

For certain built-in styles, the style name displayed in the Word UI differs from the primary name of the style. For example, the "Normal Table" style appears as "Table Normal" in the UI. This (dubious) privilege is restricted to Word's built-in style names; there is no way in WordprocessingML to define a custom style whose UI name differs from its primary name. Word, however, does throw us a bone when it saves such styles as XML. The wx:uiName element clues us in to the distinction:

```
<wx:uiName wx:val="Table Normal"/>
```

This element is strictly informational. If you were to remove it or change the wx:val attribute's value, Word would behave no differently when opening the file. Elements and attributes in the namespace designated by the wx prefix are for our benefit only and are of no internal use to Word.

The w:docPr Element

Have you ever wondered whether a particular option in the Word UI represents a property of the document you are editing as opposed to a property of the application's state? The answer to your question may lie inside the w:docPr element, which, like one of its siblings mentioned earlier, stands for "document properties." However, unlike the information inside the o:DocumentProperties element, these document properties are unique to Word and describe particular aspects of a document's state, options, and default settings, rather than metadata or statistics that are common to multiple Office applications.

The Tools → Options… dialog in the Word UI, with its many tabs, is rather notorious for being unclear about what exactly the user is modifying, whether global application options or document options. By investigating the contents of the w:docPr element, you can begin to identify which of these options are document-specific and which of them aren't.

The *Pr naming convention that w:docPr follows is common in WordprocessingML. As we'll see, a number of other elements follow this convention, such as w:pPr (paragraph properties), w:rPr (run properties), w:tblPr (table properties), w:trPr (table row properties), w:tcPr (table cell properties), and w:listPr (list properties). In fact, the baseline content model of these elements is also similar: a sequence of mostly empty elements, each standing for a particular property and each having zero or more attributes to set the values of that property. The most commonly used attribute is w:val. You may have noticed by now that WordprocessingML favors putting not only elements but also attributes in its namespace, which means you should get used to typing those w prefixes. (The attributeFormDefault value is set to qualified in each of the WordprocessingML schema documents.)

The w:docPr element has 84 optional child elements. They are declared in the WordprocessingML schema as an ordered sequence (as opposed to a repeating choice group), which suggests that they *must* occur in the declared order. In reality, Word does not enforce this order, though it does appear to follow it in the WordprocessingML documents it creates.

Now, let's look at the w:docPr element as output by Word in Example 2-2:

```
<w:docPr>
  <w:view w:val="web"/>
  <w:zoom w:percent="100"/>
  <w:proofState w:spelling="clean" w:grammar="clean"/>
  <w:attachedTemplate w:val=""/>
  <w:defaultTabStop w:val="720"/>
  <w:characterSpacingControl w:val="DontCompress"/>
  <w:validateAgainstSchema/>
  <w:saveInvalidXML w:val="off"/>
  <w:ignoreMixedContent w:val="off"/>
  <w:alwaysShowPlaceholderText w:val="off"/>
  <w:compat/>
</w:docPr>
```

The 11 child elements shown here provide a fairly representative sampling of these options.

The `w:view` element determines what view to use when opening the document. The default view for a WordprocessingML document that does not specify a view is `web`, which is also Word's default view for opening XML documents in general. That explains why we see the value `web` in this example:

```
<w:view w:val="web"/>
```

This value is the result of Word re-saving a WordprocessingML document that we constructed by hand, without specifying a view. The five possible values of `view` are `print`, `outline`, `normal`, `web`, and `master-pages` (similar to `outline` but applies only to documents that refer to sub-documents).

The `w:zoom` element denotes the zoom percentage that should be set when opening the document:

```
<w:zoom w:percent="100"/>
```

If you change the zoom percentage from within Word and re-save (provided that you also make a substantive change to the document's content to ensure that the file is actually updated), Word will save the document, recording the zoom level that you last used. Alternatively, you could directly edit the zoom property in the WordprocessingML, causing Word to display the document at some other zoom percentage the next time someone opens the file.

The `w:proofState` element records the state of the grammar and spelling checkers (`clean` or `dirty`) at the time Word saved the document:

```
<w:proofState w:spelling="clean" w:grammar="clean"/>
```

Since actual spelling and grammar errors are recorded in the body of the document, this state check reflects not whether there *are* errors in the document, but whether Word had a chance to finish checking for errors before the user saved the document. Thus, its primary purpose is as an optimization hint for Word when it opens the document. Its absence, however, could conceivably be a useful warning for applications that otherwise rely on Word having completed its proofing.

The `w:attachedTemplate` property is one of the two elements representing Templates and Add-Ins options (along with the `w:linkStyles` element):

```
<w:attachedTemplate w:val=""/>
```

Its value in this example is empty, which means simply that the default *Normal.dot* template is attached. Should you attach a different template (through the Tools → Templates and Add-Ins... dialog) and re-save, then this value would be populated with the specific file location of a template. Alternatively, you could manually edit the XML attribute value so that the next time Word opens the document, the new template will already be attached by virtue of your manual change. Note, however, that unless the `w:linkStyles` element is also present inside the `w:docPr` element (as explained later), the fact that a template is merely attached has no immediate effect on the document. The w:attachedTemplate element defines a loose association whose potential is only realized when the w:linkStyles element is also present.

The w:validateAgainstSchema, w:saveInvalidXML, w:ignoreMixedContent, and w:alwaysShowPlaceHolderText properties (among several others not included in this example) are specific to Word's custom XML schema functionality (only available in Office 2003 Professional or standalone Word 2003), which is discussed in Chapter 4.

The w:defaultTabStop element sets the interval between default tab stops in the document:

```
<w:defaultTabStop w:val="720"/>
```

While the Word UI exposes this value in inches (when you select Format → Tabs...), the underlying value is stored in *twips*, or 20ths of a point, or 1,440ths of an inch. (Completing this equation, there are 72 points in an inch.) Since the value of the w:val attribute is 720 twips, the default tab stops for paragraphs in this document occur every half inch. Thus, when Word opens the document, it displays the short vertical lines beneath the ruler, spaced every half inch, as shown in Figure 2-5.

Figure 2-5. Default tab stops every half inch, or 720 twips

Once again, Word supplies this value as an application default, because our original hand-edited document (Example 2-1) did not specify a default tab stop interval. As we'll see, individual paragraphs can define their own custom tab stops too. For those paragraphs, the default tab stops only take effect to the right of the last custom stop.

The w:characterSpacingControl element is one of several Asian Typography options.

```
<w:characterSpacingControl w:val="DontCompress"/>
```

There are three possible self-describing values (DontCompress, CompressPunctuation, or CompressPunctuationAndJapaneseKana) that can be used to sets the compression option for East Asian characters. The default value that Word outputs, as evident in our example, is DontCompress. Of course, this doesn't have any real effect on our document, since it does not contain Asian characters.

Finally, the w:compat element is among the few w:docPr children that may themselves contain child elements (w:mailMerge, w:hdrShapeDefaults, w:footnotePr, w:endnotePr, and w:docVars being the only others). It has 51 possible child elements, corresponding to the compatibility options for a document that are set in the Compatibility tab of the Tools → Options... dialog, as shown in Figure 2-6.

The w:compat element is empty in Example 2-2, because our document does not set any particular compatibility options.

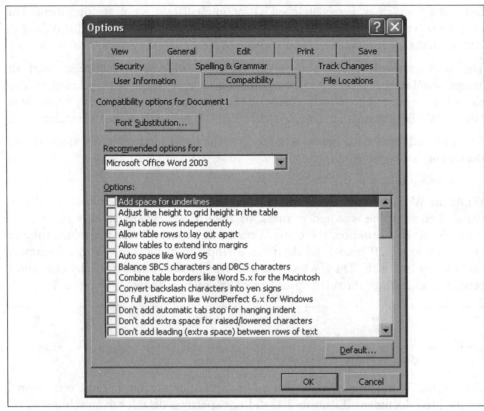

Figure 2-6. Compatibility options, corresponding to the child elements of w:compat

Before moving on, it would be good to point out one more common Wordprocessing-ML convention. Among w:docPr's 84 possible child elements, 49 are declared using the same type in the WordprocessingML schema: the onOffProperty. The declaration for the onOffProperty type in the WordprocessingML schema is as follows:

```
<xsd:complexType name="onOffProperty">
  <xsd:attribute name="val" type="onOffType" default="on"/>
</xsd:complexType>
```

The onOffType type referred to here allows for two possible values: on or off. As you can see, the attribute declaration for w:val specifies a default value of on. This means that for the elements inside the w:docPr element that are defined with this type, the presence of w:val="on" is always implied (and thus redundant), unless overridden by the value off. However, this has no bearing at all on Word's behavior when the property element itself is absent. Default behavior in those cases varies depending on the property, and the WordprocessingML schema itself does not generally cast any light on that question, although annotations therein do sometimes help. Experimentation is probably the best way to determine Word's default behavior when particular property elements are absent.

The wx:sect Element

Finally, we get to the content of our document, residing inside the w:body element. Our hand-coded original (Example 2-1) directly contained a w:p (paragraph) element inside the body. After saving, we now see that the paragraph element has been inserted into an intervening wx:sect element. As mentioned earlier, the namespace mapped to the wx prefix signals a piece of information that may be *useful to us* in processing the XML as output by Word, but that is *ignored by Word* when opening a WordprocessingML file. The wx elements and attributes are of no use to Word internally. In this case, we could remove the wx:sect element's start and end tags, leaving only its contents for Word to read, and Word would behave no differently the next time it opens the file.

That's all well and good, you might be thinking, but what is the wx:sect element *for*? As you might guess, it stands for "section." As is true with many Word documents, our "Hello World!" example document contains only one section, so it's not particularly useful in this case. To learn what sections are and how they are defined using w:sectPr elements, see "Sections" later in this chapter. And to learn how the wx:sect element is a useful aid to external processing, see "Section Containers" later in this chapter.

The w:body Element

It may seem strange to talk about the w:body element after the wx:sect element, when until now we've been traversing our original example in document order. As already noted, however, the wx:sect element is a completely optional intervening element between w:body and its content. So, while in Example 2-2 it is the wx:sect element that contains a w:p element, that content model really belongs to w:body. Using a DTD-like syntax, we can express w:body's entire content model (much more simply than its XSD definition), like this:

```
(w:p|w:tbl|w:cfChunk|w:proofErr|w:permStart|w:permEnd)*, w:sectPr?
```

In other words, w:body may contain any number of w:p, w:tbl, w:cfChunk, w:proofErr, w:permStart, and w:permEnd elements, in any order, followed by an optional w:sectPr element. The w:p element represents a paragraph, the w:tbl element represents a table, and the w:cfChunk element represents a "context-free" chunk of inline default fonts, styles, list definitions, paragraphs, and tables.[*] We'll describe the purpose of the w:proofErr, w:permEnd, and w:permStart elements later, in the section entitled "Proofing, Protection, and Annotation Markings."

---

[*] At least, that is how the WordprocessingML schema advertises it. A plethora of experiments yields few answers as to how this element is actually supposed to be used or how it is supposed to behave. Word tends to fix things up, merging such inline definitions with the document's global definitions. This is one area where more documentation from Microsoft is certainly needed.

The w:sectPr element, included in Example 2-2, defines the section properties for the last (and first, in this case) section of the document. See "Sections," later in the chapter, for more information on how w:sectPr elements are interpreted.

The first part of the w:body element's content model (that is, not including the optional w:sectPr element) is worth repeating:

```
(w:p | w:tbl | w:cfChunk | w:proofErr | w:permStart | w:permEnd)*
```

That's because it also functions as the content model for six other elements in WordprocessingML, namely w:hdr, w:ftr, w:footnote, w:endnote, w:tc, and w:txbxContent. (The only exception is that w:tc may also contain an optional preceding w:tcPr element.) The first two of these elements stand for "header" and "footer," respectively; they occur in the property definitions for a particular section, i.e., inside the w:sectPr element. Footnotes and endnotes may occur inside any "run," or w:r, element. The w:tc element represents a table cell; thus, tables may contain tables. Finally, the w:txbxContent element represents a text box that is embedded inside a VML (Vector Markup Language) image embedded somewhere inside a document's content.

This content model is actually more open than implied above. The WordprocessingML schema also allows any element from any *other* namespace to occur here. This enables annotations from the AML (Annotation Markup Language) namespace, as well as tags from a custom XML schema to be embedded inside WordprocessingML. (See Chapter 4.)

Document Structure and Formatting

Now that you've been inundated with information about lots of document-level constructs, let's move into the actual content of a Word document and how it is represented in WordprocessingML. All Word documents contain three levels of hierarchy: one or more *sections* containing zero or more *paragraphs* containing zero or more *characters*. A *run* is a grouping of contiguous characters that have the same properties. Tables can occur where paragraphs can, and list items are just a special kind of paragraph. You cannot have nested structures in WordprocessingML—sections within sections, or paragraphs within paragraphs. The one exception to this rule is that tables may contain tables.

Runs

A "run" is the basic leaf container for a document's content and is represented by the w:r element. As we've seen, the w:r element may contain w:t elements, which contain text. Including the w:t element, there are 24 valid child elements of the w:r element, representing things like text, images, deleted text, hyphens, breaks, tabs, footnotes, endnotes, footnote and endnote references, page numbers, field text, etc. We'll look at just a few of these.

The w:r element may occur in five separate element contexts: w:p, w:fldSimple, w:hlink, w:rt, and w:rubyBase. The first one, the paragraph, is the most common. The w:fldSimple element represents a Word field, the w:hlink element represents a hyperlink in Word, and the w:rt ("ruby text") and w:rubyBase elements are used together for laying out Asian ruby text.

The run is not an essential part of a Word document in the same way that paragraphs and sections are. Rather, it is WordprocessingML's way of grouping multiple characters (or other objects) that have the same property settings. To illustrate this point, consider the following WordprocessingML paragraph:

```
<w:p>
  <w:r><w:t>H</w:t></w:r>
  <w:r><w:t>e</w:t></w:r>
  <w:r><w:t>l</w:t></w:r>
  <w:r><w:t>l</w:t></w:r>
  <w:r><w:t>o</w:t></w:r>
  <w:r><w:t> </w:t></w:r>
  <w:r><w:t>w</w:t></w:r>
  <w:r><w:t>o</w:t></w:r>
  <w:r><w:t>r</w:t></w:r>
  <w:r><w:t>l</w:t></w:r>
  <w:r><w:t>d</w:t></w:r>
</w:p>
```

The above paragraph is exactly equivalent to the paragraph below:

```
<w:p>
  <w:r>
    <w:t>Hello world</w:t>
  </w:r>
</w:p>
```

When Word saves a document as XML, it merges consecutive runs that have the same property settings. It also merges consecutive w:t elements into a single w:t element. In the above paragraph's case, all of the run properties are assigned through the document's default paragraph and character styles, because no explicit, local property settings are applied (through the w:rPr element).

Text and whitespace handling

The w:t element, which stands for "text," has no attributes and may only contain text. Being one of the few string-valued elements in Word, it is also one of the few contexts in which whitespace is significant. The handling of whitespace within the w:t element can be summarized in three basic rules:

1. Each space character (#x20) is preserved as a space and shows up as a space in Word.

2. Each line-feed character (#xA) and character reference to a carriage-return (#xD) is converted into a space.

3. Each tab character (#x9) is replaced by a w:tab element (broken out into a separate run).

The one exception is that when xml:space="default" is present, tab characters are instead converted to spaces (and w:tab elements ignored altogether).

Tabs and breaks

The run inside the following WordprocessingML paragraph contains text as well as a text-wrapping break and a tab, represented by the w:br and w:tab elements.

```
<?xml version="1.0"?>
<?mso-application progid="Word.Document"?>
<w:wordDocument
    xmlns:w="http://schemas.microsoft.com/office/word/2003/wordml"
    xml:space="preserve">

  <w:body>
    <w:p>
      <w:r>
        <w:t>This is the first line.</w:t>
        <w:br/>
        <w:t>This is a tab:</w:t>
        <w:tab/>
        <w:t>And this is some more text.</w:t>
      </w:r>
    </w:p>
  </w:body>

</w:wordDocument>
```

The first thing to note here is that the presence of xml:space="preserve" is necessary for the w:tab element to be interpreted correctly. Otherwise, the tab is stripped out when the document is loaded (even though it technically doesn't constitute whitespace as far as XML is concerned). Again, for this reason, xml:space="preserve" should be included on the root element of any WordprocessingML document you create.

The w:br element, like its HTML counterpart, inserts a break within the text flow. It is short for <w:br w:type="text-wrapping"/>. The w:type attribute may have two other values: column and page, representing column and page breaks. Figure 2-7 shows the result of opening this document in Word, with formatting marks turned on.

The bent arrow at the end of the first line indicates that this is a text-wrapping break (represented in WordprocessingML by the w:br element) rather than the end of the paragraph. (Word users can insert text-wrapping breaks by pressing Shift-Enter). The right-pointing arrow on the second line denotes the presence of a tab. The w:tab element inserts a tab into the text flow, according to the tab settings for the current paragraph. In this case, since the tab stops for this paragraph are not specified either

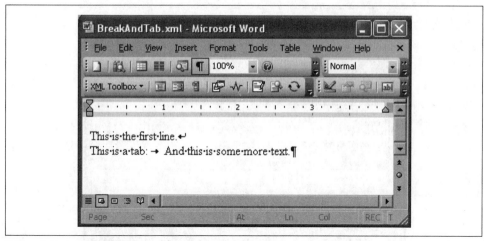

Figure 2-7. A text-wrapping break and a tab inside a single paragraph

locally or in the Normal paragraph style, the tab stops default to the application default: every half inch (as specified by the document's `w:defaultTabStop` element).

Run properties

Among all the valid child elements of `w:r`, the `w:rPr` element is special. It stands for "run properties." All of the other children of `w:r` may occur in any order, but the `w:rPr` element, when present, must come first. Its child elements collectively set properties on the run, controlling primarily how text inside the run is to be displayed. There are 42 possible child elements of the `w:rPr` element, all of which are empty elements. Their various attribute values specify formatting properties such as font, font size, font color, bold, italic, underline, strikethrough, character spacing, text effects, etc. They correspond to the properties you see in Word's Font dialog box, accessed by selecting Format → Font…, as shown in Figure 2-8.

When font settings are applied using a local `w:rPr` element, such settings are called "local settings," "manual formatting," or "direct formatting," as distinct from font settings applied through a selection's associated paragraph and character styles. *Individual font properties applied through direct formatting always override the corresponding properties defined in the associated paragraph or character styles.*

Example 2-3 shows the use of some of these formatting elements, each of which is highlighted.

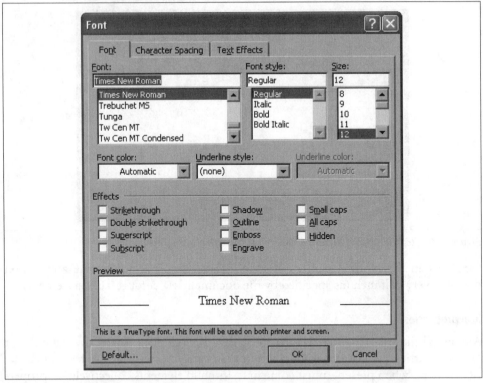

Figure 2-8. Word's font settings which correspond to run properties

Example 2-3. Applying various font properties

```xml
<?xml version="1.0"?>
<?mso-application progid="Word.Document"?>
<w:wordDocument
  xmlns:w="http://schemas.microsoft.com/office/word/2003/wordml"
  xml:space="preserve">
  <w:body>
    <w:p>
      <w:r>
        <w:rPr>
          <w:i w:val="on"/> <!-- turns italics on -->
          <w:b/>            <!-- turns bold on -->
        </w:rPr>
        <w:t>This run is bold and italic. </w:t>
        <w:br/>
      </w:r>
      <w:r>
        <w:rPr>
          <w:u w:val="single"/> <!-- single underline -->
          <w:rFonts w:ascii="Arial"/>
        </w:rPr>
        <w:t>This is Arial and underlined.</w:t>
        <w:br/>
```

Example 2-3. Applying various font properties (continued)

```
      </w:r>
      <w:r>
        <w:rPr>
          <w:sz w:val="56"/>    <!-- 28-point font size -->
        </w:rPr>
        <w:t>This is big.</w:t>
      </w:r>
    </w:p>
  </w:body>
</w:wordDocument>
```

This example contains a single paragraph that contains three runs, each of which contains text. The first two runs also contain trailing text-wrapping breaks (w:br elements), effectively separating the text of each run onto its own line. Each run has different run properties specified in the w:rPr element. These properties, since they are applied as direct formatting, override the corresponding settings in the Normal style (the "default default" paragraph style, as we saw earlier).

The first run introduces the w:b and w:i elements:

```
      <w:rPr>
        <w:i w:val="on"/> <!-- turns italics on -->
        <w:b/>            <!-- turns bold on -->
      </w:rPr>
```

The w:b and w:i elements stand for "bold" and "italic," respectively. They are among 19 of w:rPr's 42 possible child elements that, like many of w:docPr's children, are declared with the onOffProperty type in the WordprocessingML schema. This means that the default value of the w:val attribute is on. Thus, w:val="on" on the w:i element above is technically redundant. As might be guessed, by turning these properties on, all of the text within the run will be formatted in bold weight and italic style.

 The presence of the w:val attribute is necessary to turn *off* a particular property, overriding its setting in the style. For example, if you want to turn off bold for a particular portion of text that's associated as a whole with a style in which the bold property is turned on, then you would include <w:b w:val="off"/> inside the w:rPr element.

The second run in Example 2-3 introduces the w:u and w:rFonts elements:

```
      <w:rPr>
        <w:u w:val="single"/> <!-- single underline -->
        <w:rFonts w:ascii="Arial"/>
      </w:rPr>
```

The w:u element is similar to w:b and w:i, in that it is empty and has a w:val attribute. The difference is that, instead of having only the values on and off, you have a choice between 18 different values, including single (as in this example) and none. These values correspond to the choices in the "Underline style" drop-down menu in Word's Font dialog.

This run also specifies the Arial font, overriding the default Times New Roman font of the Normal style. This is done using the w:rFonts element, which has the same declared type in the WordprocessingML schema as the global w:defaultFonts element we saw earlier. Specifically, it allows the same attributes for specifying the fonts of different character sets: w:ascii, w:h-ansi, w:cs, and w:fareast. In this case, only the w:ascii attribute is supplied, which means that the other character sets still assume the default font.

The third and final run in our single-paragraph document sets the font size using the w:sz element:

```
<w:rPr>
  <w:sz w:val="56"/>   <!-- 28-point font size -->
</w:rPr>
```

The value of the w:val attribute in this case is measured in half-points, or 10 twips, or 144ths of an inch. Thus, while its value is 56 in the XML, the actual font size (in full points) is 28.

Finally, we see the result of opening this document in Word in Figure 2-9.

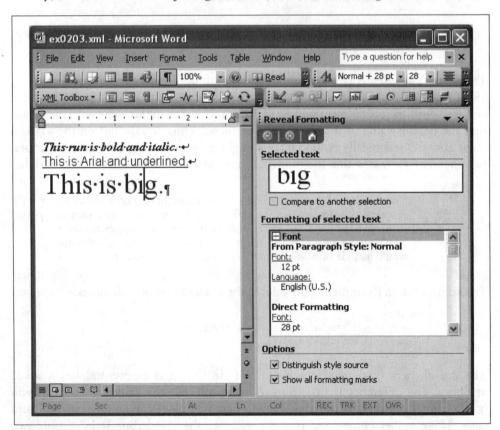

Figure 2-9. Direct formatting using local w:rPr elements

Figure 2-9 also shows how direct formatting is represented in the Word UI. In this case, the cursor is inside the third run, containing the text "This is big." There are two things worth noting about how this direct formatting is represented:

- The style drop-down box, as shown at the top right of the window, says "Normal + 28 pt." This is how all direct formatting is represented here (style name + individual property settings).

- The Reveal Formatting task pane, because "Distinguish style source" is checked, distinguishes between the font size as set in the Normal style (12 pt) and the overriding font size as applied through Direct Formatting (28 pt).

Associating a run with a character style

In addition to specifying direct formatting, a run can explicitly associate itself with one of its document's character styles. This is done using the w:rStyle element. Below are three runs excerpted from a document in which the "Hyperlink" character style is defined. All three runs are associated with the "Hyperlink" style, but the middle run also applies some direct formatting (italics):

```
<w:r>
  <w:rPr>
    <w:rStyle w:val="Hyperlink"/>
  </w:rPr>
  <w:t>This just </w:t>
</w:r>
<w:r>
  <w:rPr>
    <w:rStyle w:val="Hyperlink"/>
    <w:i/>
  </w:rPr>
  <w:t>looks</w:t>
</w:r>
<w:r>
  <w:rPr>
    <w:rStyle w:val="Hyperlink"/>
  </w:rPr>
  <w:t> like a hyperlink.</w:t>
</w:r>
```

Figure 2-10 shows the result of opening this document in Word, assuming it has defined the "Hyperlink" style in its w:styles element (rendering the font blue and underlined).

Once again, the Reveal Formatting task pane shows the distinction between the properties applied through direct formatting ("Italic") and the properties defined in a style ("Font color: Blue" and "Underline"). It also reveals the character style for this run: "Hyperlink."

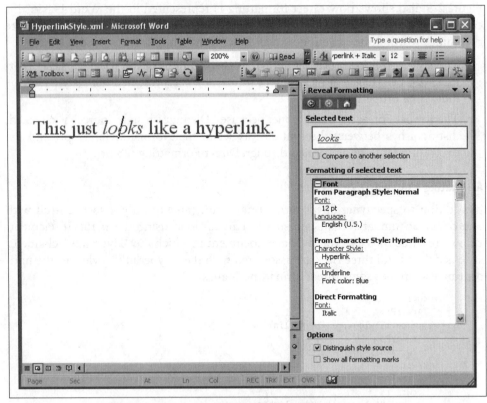

Figure 2-10. A run of text associated with the "Hyperlink" style

Paragraphs

Paragraphs are the basic block-oriented element in Word. All text content within a document is contained within paragraphs, whether it's inside the main body of the document, a table cell, a header, a footer, a footnote, an endnote, or a textbox embedded in an image. Normally, a new paragraph is created whenever a user hits the Enter key while editing.

In WordprocessingML, a paragraph is represented by the w:p element. The area inside the w:p element could be called a "run-level" context, because it is a context in which runs (w:r elements) may appear. Similarly, the area inside the w:body element is a "block-level" context, because it is a context in which paragraphs and tables may appear. The traditional distinction between a block and an *inline* element (or run) is that blocks are laid out on separate lines, whereas inline elements (runs) are laid out continuously, without any hard line breaks.

The content model of the w:p element is simple enough that it's worth showing here (using a DTD-like notation):

```
w:pPr?,
(w:r|w:proofErr|w:permStart|w:permEnd|w:fldSimple|w:hlink|w:subDoc)*
```

This follows the same pattern as w:r's content model: an optional properties element followed by any of a number of element choices in any order. (We didn't show w:r's entire content model because it has so many element choices.)

Three of the elements in w:p's content model, as we've seen, may also occur as children of w:body. The w:proofErr, w:permStart, and w:permEnd elements are thus both block-level and run-level elements. They are explained later in "Proofing, Protection, and Annotation Markings."

The w:fldSimple element represents a Word field, and the w:hlink element represents a hyperlink in Word. You may recall that these elements are also run-level contexts, i.e., they themselves may contain runs. The w:subDoc element represents a link to a sub-document of the current document.

As is the case with the w:body element, w:p's content model is actually more open than implied above. The WordprocessingML schema also allows any element from any *other* namespace to occur here. This enables annotations from the AML (Annotation Markup Language) namespace, as well as tags from a custom XML schema to be embedded inside WordprocessingML. As we'll see in Chapter 4, Word renders custom XML tags differently depending on whether they occur at the block level (inside w:body) or run level (inside w:p).

Paragraph properties

Among all the valid child elements of w:p, the w:pPr element is special. It stands for "paragraph properties." All of the other children of w:p may occur in any order, but the w:pPr element, when present, must come first. Its child elements collectively set properties on the paragraph, controlling how the paragraph will be displayed. There are 34 possible child elements of the w:pPr element, many but not all of which are empty elements. Their various attribute values and child elements specify paragraph properties such as alignment, indentation, spacing, tab stops, widow/orphan control, paragraph borders, etc. Most of these properties correspond to the properties you see in Word's Paragraph dialog box, accessed by selecting Format → Paragraph..., as shown in Figure 2-11.

When paragraph settings are applied using a local w:pPr element, such settings are called "local settings," "manual formatting," or "direct formatting," as distinct from settings applied through a paragraph's associated paragraph style. *Individual paragraph properties applied through direct formatting always override the corresponding properties defined in the associated paragraph style.* If this sounds familiar, it should. It's the same basic rule as for font settings. Local w:rPr and w:pPr elements always

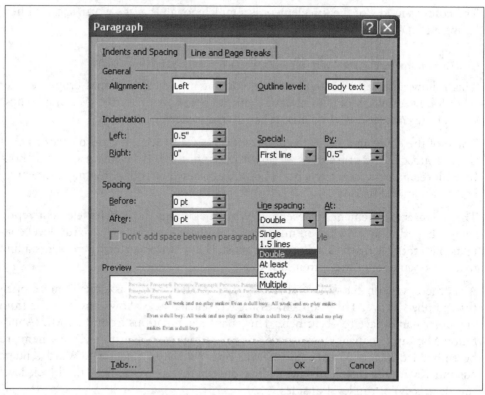

Figure 2-11. Word's Paragraph dialog, corresponding to properties inside the w:pPr element

override settings applied through (explicit or default) style association. Also, the properties within the `w:rPr` and `w:pPr` elements are completely disjoint from each other, so there is no possibility of conflict between these two elements.

Example 2-4 shows the use of some of these paragraph formatting elements, each of which is highlighted.

Example 2-4. Applying various paragraph properties

```
<?xml version="1.0"?>
<?mso-application progid="Word.Document"?>
<w:wordDocument
  xmlns:w="http://schemas.microsoft.com/office/word/2003/wordml"
  xml:space="preserve">
<w:body>
  <w:p>
    <w:pPr>
      <w:jc w:val="center" />
    </w:pPr>
    <w:r>
      <w:t>All work and no play makes Evan a dull boy.</w:t>
    </w:r>
```

Example 2-4. Applying various paragraph properties (continued)

```
    </w:p>
    <w:p />
    <w:p>
      <w:pPr>
        <w:spacing w:line="480" w:line-rule="auto" />
        <w:ind w:left="720" w:first-line="720" />
      </w:pPr>
      <w:r>
        <w:t>All work and no play makes Evan a dull boy. All work and no play makes Evan a
            dull boy. All work and no play makes Evan a dull boy. All work and no play
            makes Evan a dull boy.</w:t>
      </w:r>
    </w:p>
    <w:p>
      <w:pPr>
        <w:ind w:left="2880" w:right="2880" />
      </w:pPr>
      <w:r>
        <w:t>All work and no play makes Evan a dull boy.</w:t>
      </w:r>
    </w:p>
  </w:body>
</w:wordDocument>
```

The result of opening this document in Word is shown in Figure 2-12. Also, the Format → Paragraph... dialog shown earlier in Figure 2-11 reflects the paragraph settings of the third paragraph of this example (note that the second paragraph is empty).

Example 2-4 contains four paragraphs. The second paragraph is empty and does not apply any direct formatting. The other three each specify paragraph properties that override the corresponding settings in the Normal style (the "default default" paragraph style).

The first paragraph is centered. The w:jc element represents the paragraph justification settings:

```
<w:jc w:val="center" />
```

Its w:val attribute value may be left, center, right, both, or one of several other options specific to East Asian text. The first four values correspond to the "Left," "Centered," "Right,", and "Justified" options in the Alignment drop-down menu in the Format → Paragraph... dialog.

The second non-empty paragraph is double-spaced, indented on the left, and has a first-line indent. The double-spacing effect is achieved through the w:spacing element:

```
<w:spacing w:line="480" w:line-rule="auto" />
```

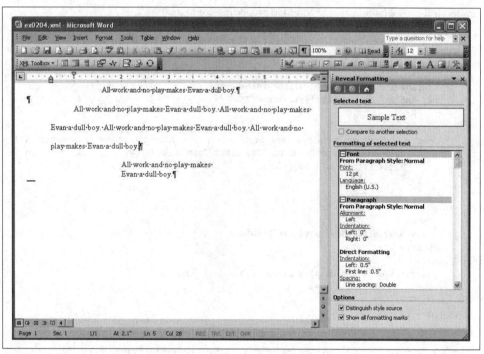

Figure 2-12. Applying paragraph properties as direct formatting

Unlike the w:jc element, which has specific keywords corresponding to each of the UI options, the w:spacing element specifies its values numerically—in twips. The w: line attribute's value of 480 (equivalent to 24 points), in conjunction with the w: line-rule attribute's value of auto, represent the overall setting of "Double" in the Line Spacing drop-down menu in the Format → Paragraph… dialog, as shown earlier in Figure 2-11. When the w:line-rule attribute's value is auto, then the w:line attribute's value is interpreted in a pre-defined way, regardless of the current paragraph's font size. A value of 480 means "Double," 360 means "1.5 line," and 240 means "Single." The actual line spacing distance is automatically adjusted according to the current font size, but the w:line attribute's value stays the same. The other possible values of w:line-rule are exact and at-least. These correspond to the "Exactly" and "At least" options in the Line Spacing drop-down menu and affect how the w:line value is interpreted. For example, a value of exact would fix the line spacing distance to the specified value in the w:line attribute, regardless of the current font size. The w:spacing element also has other attributes (not present in this example) that are used to determine the spacing before and after the paragraph itself.

The indentation of the third paragraph (following the empty second paragraph) is specified using the w:ind element:

```
<w:ind w:left="720" w:first-line="720" />
```

The w:left attribute specifies the left indentation distance as 720 positive twips, or half an inch to the right of the page margin. (Negative indent values move the text into the page margin.) The w:first-line attribute specifies a first-line indent of another half inch. The effect of these settings on Word's ruler is shown in Figure 2-13.

Figure 2-13. A half-inch left indent and a half-inch first-line indent

The w:ind element may also have a w:hanging attribute which specifies a hanging indent. Its presence is mutually exclusive with the w:first-line attribute, because the same paragraph cannot have both first-line and hanging indents. If our example used a hanging indent rather than a first-line indent, then the WordprocessingML would look like this:

```
<w:ind w:left="720" w:hanging="720" />
```

And the ruler would look like Figure 2-14.

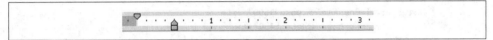

Figure 2-14. A half-inch left indent and a half-inch hanging indent

Interestingly enough, you can also supply negative values for the w:first-line and w:hanging attributes. Since a hanging indent is essentially the opposite of a first-line indent, Word interprets a negative value as if you had supplied a positive value of the other type of indent. In fact, when it subsequently saves the document as WordprocessingML, it replaces one attribute with the other attribute (w:hanging with w:first-line or vice versa) and its negative value with its opposite (positive) value. For example, if you open a document that has this:

```
<w:ind w:hanging="-720" />
```

then Word will normalize it to this instead:

```
<w:ind w:first-line="720" />
```

The two are equivalent.

The last paragraph in Example 2-4 has both right and left indents:

```
<w:ind w:left="2880" w:right="2880" />
```

The positive value (in twips) of 2880 in each of the w:left and w:right attributes means that the paragraph will be indented two inches from the margin on each side.

The w:left, w:right, w:first-line, and w:hanging attributes all measure distance in twips. You can alternatively measure distance in character spaces, by using the w:ind element's other four optional attributes instead: `w:left-chars`, `w:right-chars`, `w:first-line-chars`, and `w:hanging-chars`.

Defining tab stops

Paragraphs can specify custom tab stops, overriding the document's default tab stop interval. This is done using the `w:tabs` child element of a paragraph's `w:pPr` element. Example 2-5 shows a paragraph with custom tab stops as well as some tabs inside the paragraph that make use of those stops.

Example 2-5. Defining custom tab stops

```
<?xml version="1.0"?>
<?mso-application progid="Word.Document"?>
<w:wordDocument
  xmlns:w="http://schemas.microsoft.com/office/word/2003/wordml"
  xml:space="preserve">
  <w:body>
    <w:p>
      <w:pPr>
        <w:tabs>
          <w:tab w:val="left" w:pos="720" />
          <w:tab w:val="center" w:pos="3600" />
          <w:tab w:val="right" w:pos="6480" />
        </w:tabs>
      </w:pPr>
      <w:r>
        <w:tab/>
        <w:t>Left-aligned tab</w:t>
        <w:tab/>
        <w:t>Centered tab</w:t>
        <w:tab/>
        <w:t>Right-aligned tab</w:t>
      </w:r>
    </w:p>
  </w:body>
</w:wordDocument>
```

Each `w:tab` element within the `w:tabs` element defines a different tab stop. Both the `w:val` and `w:pos` attributes are required. The `w:val` attribute indicates the type of tab stop, controlling the alignment of text around it. Its value must be one of `left`, `center`, `right`, `decimal`, `bar`, `list`, or `clear`. (The value `clear` enables tab stops defined in an associated paragraph style to be explicitly cleared.) The `w:pos` attribute specifies the position of the tab stop on the ruler, as the number of twips to the right of the left page margin. The `w:tab` element may also have an optional `w:leader` attribute, which sets the style of the empty space in front of the tab. These properties correspond to the settings found in Word's Format → Tabs... dialog, shown in Figure 2-15, which here is populated with the same tab stops as defined in Example 2-5.

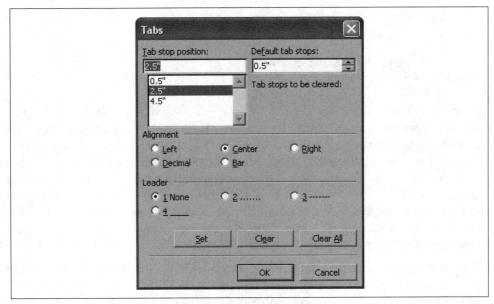

Figure 2-15. Tab stop definitions, corresponding to Example 2-5

Finally, the result of opening this file in Word is shown in Figure 2-16, with formatting marks turned on.

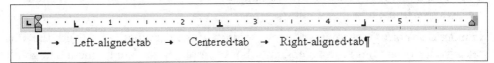

Figure 2-16. Three kinds of custom tab stops

The custom tab stops can be seen on the ruler, and the tabs themselves are signified by arrows in the document content. The document's default tab stops (every half inch) are signified by small vertical lines below the ruler and do not resume until after the last custom tab, beginning at the 5-inch mark.

Paragraph mark properties

You may be surprised to learn that the w:rPr element ("run properties") may also occur as a child of the w:pPr element. Actually, it shows up quite often when editing documents in Word. For example, if you turn bold on, type a short paragraph, and hit Enter, then the resulting paragraph in WordprocessingML will look like this:

```
<w:p>
  <w:pPr>
    <w:rPr>
      <w:b/>
    </w:rPr>
  </w:pPr>
```

```
<w:r>
  <w:rPr>
    <w:b/>
  </w:rPr>
  <w:t>This text is bold.</w:t>
</w:r>
</w:p>
```

This may look redundant, but it isn't. By now, you should be familiar with the purpose of the second w:rPr element above. It sets the properties (in this case, bold) on the run in which it is contained. However, the first w:rPr element (inside the w:pPr element) functions differently than you might expect. Rather than setting properties of the runs inside the paragraph, it represents properties of the paragraph's *paragraph mark*. If we removed the first w:rPr element altogether, it would have no actual effect on the formatting of our document. In fact, we wouldn't even see a difference in the Word UI—unless paragraph marks are turned on. In that case, we might notice whether or not the paragraph mark itself is displayed in bold weight.

The run properties, or font settings, of a paragraph mark, though they do not directly affect the paragraph's formatting, do have an effect on Word's *behavior* when subsequently editing the document. For that reason, you can think of the paragraph mark properties as containing information about your document's editing state rather than its actual formatting. For example, one practical effect of setting bold on a paragraph mark is that if the user selects the paragraph mark (by double-clicking it) and drags and drops it to create a new paragraph, bold will be turned on by default for runs entered in the new paragraph.

In practice, Word synchronizes the font settings of the paragraph mark with the font settings of the last run in the paragraph. For example, if you are typing a paragraph and you hit Enter when italics are turned on, then the paragraph mark of the paragraph you just created will also have italics turned on, as will the paragraph mark of the following paragraph, at least initially. If, on the other hand, you turn italics off right before you hit the Enter key, then the last part of your paragraph will still be italicized, but the paragraph mark won't be, and neither will the following paragraph's paragraph mark.

One final example may help elucidate the function of paragraph mark properties. Consider the WordprocessingML document in Example 2-6. It is devoid of any text content, but it does have one empty paragraph whose paragraph mark has italics turned on.

Example 2-6. An empty paragraph with italics turned on

```
<?xml version="1.0"?>
<?mso-application progid="Word.Document"?>
<w:wordDocument
  xmlns:w="http://schemas.microsoft.com/office/word/2003/wordml"
  xml:space="preserve">
  <w:body>
```

Example 2-6. An empty paragraph with italics turned on (continued)

```
  <w:p>
    <w:pPr>
      <w:rPr>
        <w:i/>
      </w:rPr>
    </w:pPr>
  </w:p>
</w:body>
</w:wordDocument>
```

If we open this document in Word, we'll see nothing but a blank document with a flashing cursor—an *italicized* flashing cursor. This, again, reflects the document's editing state, rather than its formatting. Any time you create a new paragraph while editing, Word tries to remember the formatting properties you had in effect on the last paragraph—even when you create an empty paragraph, save the document, close it, and open it again later, which is what Example 2-6 demonstrates.

It's good to clear up the potential confusion surrounding w:pPr's seemingly redundant w:rPr child. Now that you're cognizant of what instances of this element do *not* represent, you can safely exclude them from WordprocessingML documents that you create. Their absence will have negligible impact on the user's editing experience. Don't worry—Word will still work its magic.

Associating a paragraph with a paragraph style

In addition to specifying direct formatting, a paragraph can explicitly associate itself with one of its document's paragraph styles. This is done using the w:pStyle element. Below is a paragraph excerpted from a document in which the "Heading1" paragraph style is defined:

```
<w:p>
  <w:pPr>
    <w:pStyle w:val="Heading1" />
  </w:pPr>
  <w:r>
    <w:t>This is a heading</w:t>
  </w:r>
</w:p>
```

This paragraph will be formatted according to the explicitly associated paragraph style, provided that the containing document has a style definition that looks something like this:

```
<w:style w:type="paragraph" w:styleId="Heading1">
<w:name w:val="Heading 1"/>
<!-- other style options -->
<w:pPr>
  <!-- paragraph property settings -->
</w:pPr>
```

```
<w:rPr>
  <!-- font property settings -->
</w:rPr>
</w:style>
```

Tables

Tables may occur anywhere that paragraphs may occur (and vice versa), which most commonly is directly inside the w:body element (or inside an intervening wx:sect element when the WordprocessingML is output by Word). The other contexts in which paragraphs and tables may occur are the w:hdr, w:ftr, w:footnote, w:endnote, w:tc, w:txbxContent, and w:cfChunk elements, which we already introduced briefly.

The basic structure of the w:tbl element looks like this:

```
<w:tbl>
    <w:tblPr>...</w:tblPr>
    <w:tblGrid>
      <w:gridCol w:val="..."/>
      <w:gridCol w:val="..."/>
      ...
    </w:tblGrid>
    <w:tr>
      <w:tc>...</w:tc>
      <w:tc>...</w:tc>
      ...
    </w:tr>
    <w:tr>...</w:tr>
    ...
</w:tbl>
```

The content model for the w:tbl element, using a DTD-like syntax, is:

```
aml:annotation*, w:tblPr, w:tblGrid,
(w:tr | w:proofErr | w:permStart | w:permEnd)+
```

In other words, the w:tbl element may contain zero or more aml:annotation elements, followed by a w:tblPr element and a w:tblGrid element, followed by one or more w:tr, w:proofErr, w:permStart, or w:permEnd elements, in any order. The w:tblPr element contains table-wide properties. The w:tblGrid element contains w:gridCol elements that define the widths of columns in the table.

Table rows are represented by the w:tr element. The content model of the w:tr element, using the same notation, is:

```
w:tblPrEx?, w:trPr?, (w:tc | w:proofErr | w:permStart | w:permEnd)+
```

The w:tblPrEx element contains exceptions to the table-wide properties for this row only. The w:trPr element contains table row properties for this row.

Table cells are represented by the w:tc element. The content model of the w:tc element, using the same notation, is:

```
w:tcPr?,(w:p | w:tbl | w:cfChunk | w:proofErr | w:permStart | w:permEnd)*
```

Thus, after optionally specifying the table cell properties (with the w:tcPr element), we are once again inside a block-level context. At this point, paragraphs may contain the text for the table cell, or another table can be nested inside this one.

We've repeatedly seen the trio of w:proofErr, w:permStart, and w:permEnd—now at row-level, cell-level, block-level, and run-level contexts. See "Proofing, Protection, and Annotation Markings," later in this chapter, to find out what exactly these elements are for and how they function.

Example 2-7 shows a simple table that references one of its document's table styles and additionally utilizes several table formatting features.

Example 2-7. A sample table with a style and merged cells

```xml
<?xml version="1.0"?>
<?mso-application progid="Word.Document"?>
<w:wordDocument
  xmlns:w="http://schemas.microsoft.com/office/word/2003/wordml"
  xml:space="preserve">
  <w:styles>
    <w:style w:type="table" w:styleId="MyTableStyle">
      <w:name w:val="My Table Style" />
      <w:tblPr>
        <w:tblBorders>
          <w:top w:val="single"/>
          <w:left w:val="single"/>
          <w:bottom w:val="single"/>
          <w:right w:val="single"/>
          <w:insideH w:val="single"/>
          <w:insideV w:val="single"/>
        </w:tblBorders>
        <w:tblCellMar>
          <w:left w:w="108" w:type="dxa" />
          <w:right w:w="108" w:type="dxa" />
        </w:tblCellMar>
      </w:tblPr>
    </w:style>
  </w:styles>
  <w:body>
    <w:tbl>
      <w:tblPr>
        <w:tblStyle w:val="MyTableStyle" />
      </w:tblPr>
      <w:tr>
        <w:tc>
          <w:p>
            <w:r>
              <w:t>First row, first column</w:t>
            </w:r>
          </w:p>
        </w:tc>
        <w:tc>
          <w:tcPr>
```

Example 2-7. A sample table with a style and merged cells (continued)

```
        <w:vmerge w:val="restart" />
        </w:tcPr>
        <w:p>
          <w:r>
            <w:t>First row, second column (merged with second row, second
            column)</w:t>
          </w:r>
        </w:p>
      </w:tc>
    </w:tr>
    <w:tr>
      <w:tc>
        <w:p>
          <w:r>
            <w:t>Second row, first column</w:t>
          </w:r>
        </w:p>
      </w:tc>
      <w:tc>
        <w:tcPr>
          <w:vmerge />
        </w:tcPr>
        <w:p/>
      </w:tc>
    </w:tr>
  </w:tbl>
 </w:body>
</w:wordDocument>
```

The result of opening this WordprocessingML document in Word is shown in Figure 2-17.

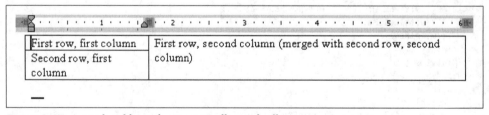

Figure 2-17. A simple table, with automatically sized cells

There are a few things to note about this table:

- The table is associated with "MyTableStyle," which is defined within the document.

- The "MyTableStyle" style adds borders and cell-spacing to the table.

- Word opens the document without complaint, even though it doesn't have a w: tblGrid element; Word automatically sizes the cells to contain the content.

- The w:vmerge element is a table cell property that is used to vertically merge one table cell with another table cell below it—similar to its horizontal equivalent, the w:hmerge element.

- The w:tbl element as generated by Word tends to be much more verbose than this example, explicitly specifying many individual property settings.

There is a lot that this example doesn't cover. To give you an idea just how much more there is to tables, the w:tblPr element has 17 possible child elements (many of which contain their own children), the w:trPr element has 12 possible child elements, and the w:tcPr element has 13 possible child elements. That's not to mention the w:tblPrEx (exceptions for a specific row), w:tblStylePr (for table-style conditional override properties), and w:tblpPr (for specifying the position of a table) elements. If you're writing WordprocessingML for tables, the main things you'll need to configure are the properties of the table, rows, and cells. These work in the same way as the paragraph properties that we've looked at in detail earlier, so we won't go into them here. A quick look at the properties dialogs for tables should give you an idea of what's involved.

Lists

Lists are a rather strange beast in WordprocessingML. Though tables can get pretty hairy, they at least are generally structured the way you would expect: tables containing rows containing cells. Lists, on the other hand, have no such explicit structure in WordprocessingML. Instead, a list consists of a sequence of paragraphs that function as list items. They do not have a common container, nor, unfortunately, does Word provide an auxiliary hint for list containers when outputting WordprocessingML. The member paragraphs of a list are linked to one of its document's "list definitions." These are responsible for maintaining the identity of a single list. When numbering restarts, for example, a new list definition is automatically created. These list definitions, in turn, are linked to one of the document's "base list definitions", which, if there is no subsequent list style link to traverse, define the actual formatting properties of the list. If the phrase "spectacularly convoluted" comes to mind, just wait until you see an example of this.

What makes a paragraph a list item

A paragraph participates as a member of a list under one of these separate circumstances:

- It has a w:listPr element inside its w:pPr element, which refers to a specific list definition (via the w:ilfo element).

- It is associated with a paragraph style that includes list formatting.

Let's take a look at how the first mechanism works. The following paragraph is a member of a list:

```
<w:p>
  <w:pPr>
    <w:listPr>
      <w:ilvl w:val="0"/>
      <w:ilfo w:val="1"/>
    </w:listPr>
  </w:pPr>
  <w:r>
    <w:t>This is item one.</w:t>
  </w:r>
</w:p>
```

The w:ilfo element (whose name may stand for something like "item list format," though Microsoft has not documented what it actually means) refers to one of the document's list definitions, identified by the number 1. The w:ilvl element specifies at what level of nesting this list item occurs. It is incremented each time a list is nested within another list. Since there are nine possible levels of list indentation in Word (starting at 0), its value can be anywhere from 0 to 8. It basically says, "Once you find the definition for how each level of this list is supposed to look, sign me up for the formatting and indentation that are defined for level 0." Finding the list definition is the trick. But before we figure out how that's done, let's take a look at how WordprocessingML lists compare with HTML lists.

Comparing HTML and WordprocessingML lists

Below is a simple nested list in HTML:

```
<ol>
  <li>
    <p>This is top-level item 1</p>
    <ol>
      <li>This is second-level item 1</li>
      <li>This is second-level item 2</li>
    </ol>
  </li>
  <li>This is top-level item 2</li>
</ol>
```

In WordprocessingML, a list like this is expressed much differently. Instead of using a hierarchical structure to express the list hierarchy, we must represent the list as a flat sequence of four sibling paragraphs, assigning them to the same list but to different levels within the list:

```
<w:p>
  <w:pPr>
    <w:listPr>
      <w:ilvl w:val="0"/>
      <w:ilfo w:val="1"/>
    </w:listPr>
```

```
      </w:pPr>
      <w:r>
        <w:t>This is top-level item 1</w:t>
      </w:r>
    </w:p>
    <w:p>
      <w:pPr>
        <w:listPr>
          <w:ilvl w:val="1"/>
          <w:ilfo w:val="1"/>
        </w:listPr>
      </w:pPr>
      <w:r>
        <w:t>This is second-level item 1</w:t>
      </w:r>
    </w:p>
    <w:p>
      <w:pPr>
        <w:listPr>
          <w:ilvl w:val="1"/>
          <w:ilfo w:val="1"/>
        </w:listPr>
      </w:pPr>
      <w:r>
        <w:t>This is second-level item 2</w:t>
      </w:r>
    </w:p>
    <w:p>
      <w:pPr>
        <w:listPr>
          <w:ilvl w:val="0"/>
          <w:ilfo w:val="1"/>
        </w:listPr>
      </w:pPr>
      <w:r>
        <w:t>This is top-level item 2</w:t>
      </w:r>
    </w:p>
```

For this list to display correctly, the document must contain at least one list definition (a w:list element with w:ilfo="1", as we'll see) and a corresponding base list
definition (w:listDef element), which contains the actual formatting information for
list items. Each paragraph's w:ilvl value represents how far it is nested in the list.
The "top-level" paragraphs are each at level 0, whereas the "second-level" paragraphs are each at level 1. Figure 2-18 shows how Word renders this WordprocessingML list, using one of its built-in list styles.

Finding the list definitions

Now let's take a look at where the "list definitions" and "base list definitions" are actually defined. Unsurprisingly, they are both to be found inside the top-level w:lists

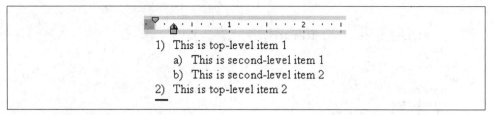

1) This is top-level item 1
   a) This is second-level item 1
   b) This is second-level item 2
2) This is top-level item 2

Figure 2-18. A simple nested list in Word

element, whose basic content model is a sequence of w:listDef elements followed by a sequence of w:list elements:

```
<w:lists>
  <w:listDef ...>
    ...
  </w:listDef>
  <!-- more w:listDef elements -->
  <w:list ...>
    ...
  </w:list>
  <!-- more w:list elements -->
</w:lists>
```

The w:list elements represent what we're calling "list definitions," and the w:listDef elements represent what we're calling "base list definitions."

Consider the first example list paragraph we saw earlier. This will be our starting point for finding the list definitions in the same way that Word does. Here's the paragraph again:

```
<w:p>
  <w:pPr>
    <w:listPr>
      <w:ilvl w:val="0"/>
      <w:ilfo w:val="1"/>
    </w:listPr>
  </w:pPr>
  <w:r>
    <w:t>This is item one.</w:t>
  </w:r>
</w:p>
```

Since our paragraph's w:ilfo element refers to the value 1, we need to find the list definition identified by the number 1. In other words, we need to find a w:list element that looks something like this (whose w:ilfo attribute's value is 1):

```
<w:list w:ilfo="1">
  <w:ilst w:val="5"/>
</w:list>
```

Now that we've found the list definition, the next step is finding the "base list definition." We do that by looking at the value provided by the w:ilst element. In this case, it is referring to a base list definition identified by the number 5. Recalling that the base list definitions are represented by w:listDef elements and that they precede the w:list elements inside the w:lists element, we continue to search further back in our WordprocessingML document. Eventually, we find what we're looking for:

```
<w:listDef w:listDefId="5">
  ...
  <w:lvl w:ilvl="0">...</w:lvl>
  <w:lvl w:ilvl="1">...</w:lvl>
  <w:lvl w:ilvl="2">...</w:lvl>
  <w:lvl w:ilvl="3">...</w:lvl>
  <w:lvl w:ilvl="4">...</w:lvl>
  <w:lvl w:ilvl="5">...</w:lvl>
  <w:lvl w:ilvl="6">...</w:lvl>
  <w:lvl w:ilvl="7">...</w:lvl>
  <w:lvl w:ilvl="8">...</w:lvl>
</w:listDef>
```

The w:listDef element is identified by its w:listDefId attribute and contains one w:lvl element for each level of list nesting for which it defines formatting. While you can create base list definitions that define fewer levels without a problem, Word's built-in list styles define all nine levels of nesting. The content of the w:lvl element includes all kinds of formatting information, such as indentation, tab stops, the number to start on, number format, and bullet images.

Once Word finds the base list definition, with all its formatting information, it then applies the appropriate level's formatting to the paragraph, according to the value of the w:ilvl element that occurs in the paragraph's list properties. Thus, Word applies the level 0 list item formatting to our example paragraph above.

List Styles

An even more complex variation of this approach occurs is when list styles are used. Unlike paragraph, table, and character styles, which can be directly associated with paragraphs, tables, and runs (via the w:pStyle, w:tblStyle, and w:rStyle elements, respectively), list styles are *not* directly associated with paragraphs in WordprocessingML—there is not a corresponding element for direct list style references. For example, when an end user applies the built-in list style "1 / a / i" to a paragraph, the paragraph is effectively associated with a list definition, but it is not *directly* associated with the "1 / a / i" list style that was applied to it. The resulting WordprocessingML paragraph looks essentially no different from the example paragraph we looked at earlier. Here it is again (with the only difference here being that the w:ilfo element happens to refer to a list definition identified by the number 2):

```
<w:p>
  <w:pPr>
    <w:listPr>
      <w:ilvl w:val="0"/>
      <w:ilfo w:val="2"/>
    </w:listPr>
  </w:pPr>
  <w:r>
```

```
      <w:t>This is item one.</w:t>
    </w:r>
  </w:p>
```

This is what the WordprocessingML looks like when an end user applies a list style to a paragraph. Rather than being directly associated with the list style, the paragraph refers to a list definition using the w:ilfo element—no differently than when a list style is not involved. However, the list style association is still retained; it's just that you can't tell that from looking at the paragraph alone. The list style association only becomes evident when we start traversing the graph, and that's where things get complicated. First, the paragraph associates itself with the document's list definition (w:list element), identified by the value 2:

```
<w:list w:ilfo="2">
  <w:ilst w:val="1"/>
</w:list>
```

The list definition, in turn, refers (via the w:ilst element) to a base list definition (w:listDef element) identified by the value 1. So far, so good. Now, here is where a few extra levels of indirection appear. Whereas before we were done at this point (the base list definition contained all the formatting properties for each level of the list), now we're only halfway there. This time, the referenced base list definition doesn't contain any formatting properties (inside w:lvl elements) at all. Instead, it contains yet another reference—the w:listStyleLink element:

```
<w:listDef w:listDefId="1">
  <w:lsid w:val="27DC6005"/>
  <w:plt w:val="Multilevel"/>
  <w:tmpl w:val="0409001D"/>
  <w:listStyleLink w:val="1ai"/>
</w:listDef>
```

This w:listDef element refers, via its w:listStyleLink element, to a list style definition whose w:styleId attribute's value is 1ai. This corresponds to the "1 / a / i" style that the end user applied. Here is the document's list style definition that it refers to:

```
<w:style w:type="list" w:styleId="1ai">
  <w:name w:val="Outline List 1"/>
  <wx:uiName wx:val="1 / a / i"/>
  <w:basedOn w:val="NoList"/>
  <w:rsid w:val="00283CEE"/>
  <w:pPr>
    <w:listPr>
      <w:ilfo w:val="1"/>
    </w:listPr>
  </w:pPr>
</w:style>
```

As you can see, the list style definition, in turn, contains a reference to yet another list definition (identified by the number 1). Dizzy yet?

```
<w:list w:ilfo="1">
  <w:ilst w:val="0"/>
</w:list>
```

This list definition refers to yet another base list definition, identified by the number 0. Finally, we are home free, as this base list definition actually contains the list formatting properties Word needs in order to format each level of the list:

```
<w:listDef w:listDefId="0">
  <w:lsid w:val="1B850634"/>
  <w:plt w:val="Multilevel"/>
  <w:tmpl w:val="0409001D"/>
  <w:styleLink w:val="1ai"/>
  <w:lvl w:ilvl="0">
    <w:start w:val="1"/>
    <w:lvlText w:val="%1)"/>
    <w:lvlJc w:val="left"/>
    <w:pPr>
      <w:tabs>
        <w:tab w:val="list" w:pos="360"/>
      </w:tabs>
      <w:ind w:left="360" w:hanging="360"/>
    </w:pPr>
  </w:lvl>
  <w:lvl w:ilvl="1">
    ...
  </w:lvl>
  <w:lvl w:ilvl="2">
    ...
  </w:lvl>
  <w:lvl w:ilvl="3">
    ...
  </w:lvl>
  <w:lvl w:ilvl="4">
    ...
  </w:lvl>
  ...
  <w:lvl w:ilvl="5">
    ...
  </w:lvl>
  <w:lvl w:ilvl="6">
    ...
  </w:lvl>
  <w:lvl w:ilvl="7">
    ...
  </w:lvl>
  <w:lvl w:ilvl="8">
    ...
  </w:lvl>
</w:listDef>
```

In summary, w:ilfo refers to w:list, which refers to w:listDef, which refers to w:style, which refers to another w:list, which refers to another w:listDef. Home, sweet home. Oh yeah, and the last w:listDef refers back to the same w:style through an element called w:styleLink (which you can see in the last code snippet above)—thereby throwing in a little circularity for good measure.

Sections

A *section* in Word is an area or set of areas within a document, characterized by the same page settings, such as margin width, header and footer size, orientation, border, and print settings. These settings are accessible within the Word UI through the File → Page Setup… dialog, shown in Figure 2-19. Figure 2-19 also shows the five different kinds of section breaks you can insert into a document: "Continuous," "New column," "New page," "Even page," and "Odd page."

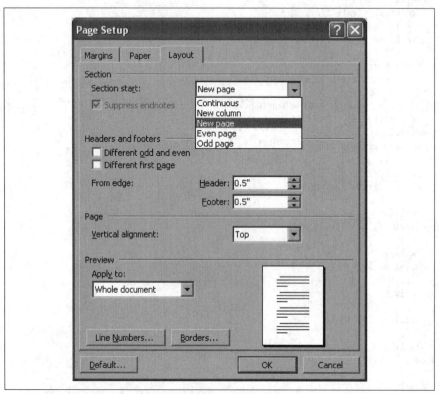

Figure 2-19. The Page Setup dialog for section settings

As mentioned previously, the structure of a Word document consists of one or more sections containing zero or more paragraphs containing zero or more characters. WordprocessingML, however, does not reflect that hierarchy exactly. In fact, there is no section container element in WordprocessingML proper. (As we'll see later in "Section Containers," the wx:sect element helps to fill this void by acting as a surrogate container, thereby aiding external processing.) Rather, sections are represented indirectly through the presence of *section breaks*. A section break is signified in WordprocessingML by the presence of a w:sectPr element inside the w:pPr element of the section's last paragraph. Example 2-8 shows the WordprocessingML for a document that contains two section breaks, and therefore three sections. The w:sectPr elements are highlighted.

Example 2-8. Multiple sections in a document

```xml
<?xml version="1.0"?>
<?mso-application progid="Word.Document"?>
<w:wordDocument
  xmlns:w="http://schemas.microsoft.com/office/word/2003/wordml"
  xml:space="preserve">
  <w:docPr>
    <w:view w:val="normal"/>
  </w:docPr>
  <w:body>
    <w:p>
      <w:pPr>
        <w:sectPr/>
      </w:pPr>
      <w:r>
        <w:t>First section</w:t>
      </w:r>
    </w:p>
    <w:p>
      <w:r>
        <w:t>Second section, first paragraph</w:t>
      </w:r>
    </w:p>
    <w:p>
      <w:pPr>
        <w:sectPr/>
      </w:pPr>
      <w:r>
        <w:t>Second section, second paragraph</w:t>
      </w:r>
    </w:p>
    <w:p>
      <w:r>
        <w:t>Third section, first paragraph</w:t>
      </w:r>
    </w:p>
    <w:p>
      <w:r>
        <w:t>Third section, second paragraph</w:t>
      </w:r>
    </w:p>
    <w:sectPr/>
  </w:body>
</w:wordDocument>
```

The first two w:sectPr elements in this document represent section breaks, because they each occur inside a w:pPr element. One thing to keep in mind about WordprocessingML's way of representing section breaks is that it can be deceiving. Specifically, the w:sectPr elements do not lexically divide the text of the document according to its true section boundaries. For example, though from a first glance it may look as if the paragraph that says "Second section, second paragraph" belongs to the third and final section, that is not the case. It only looks that way because the `w:sectPr` element comes before the text of the paragraph in which it resides. This potential confusion is all the more reason to look forward to "Section Containers," later in this chapter.

The last `w:sectPr` element in Example 2-8 does *not* occur inside the `w:pPr` element. Rather, it is a child of `w:body`, following the last paragraph in the document. This is where Word always expects to see the final `w:sectPr` element of the document. It does not represent a section break; rather, its job is simply to apply properties to the final (and possibly only) section of the document. If it isn't there when Word loads the document, Word will add it. The presence of `w:sectPr` inside a `w:pPr` element always denotes a section break, but the presence of `w:sectPr` as the last child of the `w:body` element does not. It's important to keep this distinction in mind when generating WordprocessingML documents that have multiple sections.

Figure 2-20 shows what we see when Word opens the document in Example 2-8.

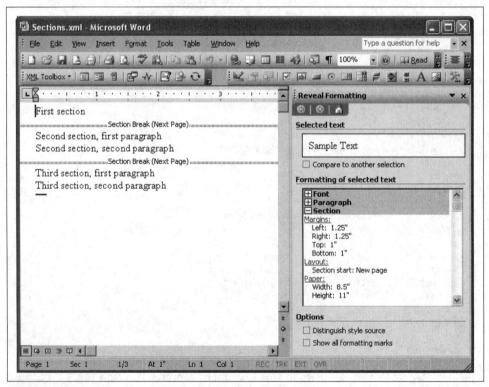

Figure 2-20. Three sections separated by Next Page section breaks

In the "Normal" view (which we see automatically, thanks to Example 2-8's use of the w:view element), all section breaks are visible. The first mystery of the empty w:sectPr section break element is answered: by default it stands for a "Next Page" break. We could have explicitly specified this in our document by using the w:type child element of w:sectPr, like this:

```
<w:sectPr>
  <w:type w:val="next-page"/>
</w:sectPr>
```

Besides next-page, the other possible values (corresponding to the drop-down menu options we saw in Figure 2-19) are next-column, continuous, even-page, and odd-page.

Of course, the insertion of section breaks is not the only responsibility of the w:sectPr element, which stands for "section properties." Its content model, after all, includes 21 possible element children, which collectively represent the settings a user can edit through the File → Page Setup... dialog. The properties specified inside the w:sectPr element apply to the section before the break that it represents (i.e., the section containing the paragraph with which the w:sectPr element is associated).

Normally, when you create a new blank document in Word, all of the page settings defined in the *Normal.dot* document template are copied into the document. These include margins, paper dimensions, vertical alignment, orientation, etc. But our hand-coded WordprocessingML document (Example 2-8) isn't "normal" in this sense. It was created outside of Word and specifies no page settings at all (as the w:sectPr elements are empty). Word gracefully handles this scenario when it loads the document by automatically inserting its application defaults for page settings. These default page settings are the same settings that are automatically copied into the *Normal.dot* template when Word is first installed, or when it is forced to create a new *Normal.dot* template.

We can see Word's application defaults for margins and paper size in the Reveal Formatting task pane in Figure 2-20. The underlying XML representation for these values looks something like this:

```
<w:sectPr>
  <w:pgSz w:w="12240" w:h="15840"/>
  <w:pgMar w:top="1440" w:right="1800" w:bottom="1440" w:left="1800"
          w:header="720" w:footer="720" w:gutter="0"/>
</w:sectPr>
```

All of the attribute values shown here are expressed in twips, or 1,440ths of an inch. The w:pgSz element sets the page size to 8.5" x 11." The w:pgMar element sets the margin widths around the page: one inch on the top and bottom, and 1.25 inches on the right and left. It also sets header and footer areas, each with a height of half an inch.

If you need to override the default page settings for a particular section, you can simply specify your own values, using any of the other child elements of w:sectPr as necessary.

Proofing, Protection, and Annotation Markings

The `w:proofErr`, `w:permStart`, `w:permEnd`, and `aml:annotation` elements have shown up in various places so far without any real explanation. One thing they have in common is that they are all used to mark up ranges of text in a Word document: `w:proofErr` for spelling and grammar errors, `w:permStart` and `w:permEnd` for an editable area within a protected document, and `aml:annotation` for annotating comments, bookmarks, and revisions within a document.

A *range* is a span of text defined by a start character position and an end character position. The distinctive thing about ranges is that they can cross paragraph and section boundaries. From within a VBA application, a commonly used range is the range that corresponds to the user's current selection. Individual sentences and words are also examples of ranges that you can access through the Word object model, but they are not actually stored as part of the information in a Word document. Instead, such ranges are purely derivative and calculated on the fly, as the Word or VBA application demands. However, there are certain kinds of ranges that are necessary to be stored as part of the Word document itself. These include the various kinds of annotations you can make to a document without affecting its actual formatting, and markings that are automatically created, such as proofing marks for grammar and spelling.

There is a problem with representing such ranges of text in XML, because XML only allows you to represent a single tree. The problem of needing to represent multiple, overlapping hierarchies (which is what such annotations amount to) is commonly addressed in XML by inserting markers into the flow for the start and end positions of the range in question. This is exactly what Word does, too.

Figure 2-21 shows a paragraph in Word in which three ranges are overlapping, namely a document protection range, a grammar error range, and a comment annotation range.

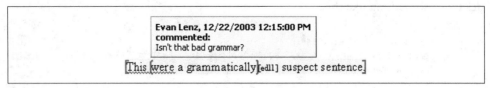

Figure 2-21. Overlapping grammar, protection, and comment markings

The outer brackets surrounding the entire sentence delineate the boundaries of an editing region with particular permissions; the inner parentheses delineate the boundaries of the text about which a comment was made; and the squiggly line under "This were" is a grammar error automatically recognized and flagged as such by Word. Example 2-9 shows the underlying WordprocessingML for this document excerpt, as output by Word. The start and end markers for each range, all of which are empty elements, are highlighted.

Example 2-9. Overlapping protection, proofing, and comment ranges

```
<w:p/>
<w:permStart w:id="0" w:edGrp="everyone"/>
<w:proofErr w:type="gramStart"/>
<w:p>
  <w:r>
    <w:t>This </w:t>
  </w:r>
  <aml:annotation aml:id="0" w:type="Word.Comment.Start"/>
  <w:r>
    <w:t>were</w:t>
  </w:r>
  <w:proofErr w:type="gramEnd"/>
  <w:r>
    <w:t> a grammatically</w:t>
  </w:r>
  <aml:annotation aml:id="0" w:type="Word.Comment.End"/>
  <w:r>
    <w:rPr>
      <w:rStyle w:val="CommentReference"/>
    </w:rPr>
    <aml:annotation aml:id="0" aml:author="Evan Lenz"
                    aml:createdate="2003-12-22T12:15:00Z"
                    w:type="Word.Comment" w:initials="edl">
      <aml:content>
        <w:p>
          <w:pPr>
            <w:pStyle w:val="CommentText"/>
          </w:pPr>
          <w:r>
            <w:rPr>
              <w:rStyle w:val="CommentReference"/>
            </w:rPr>
            <w:annotationRef/>
          </w:r>
          <w:r>
            <w:t>Isn't that bad grammar?</w:t>
          </w:r>
        </w:p>
      </aml:content>
    </aml:annotation>
  </w:r>
  <w:r>
    <w:t> suspect sentence.</w:t>
  </w:r>
  <w:permEnd w:id="0"/>
</w:p>
<w:p/>
```

This example illustrates the use of start and end markers to annotate ranges of text, regardless of whether they overlap each other or other elements, such as paragraphs. This explains, at long last, why these elements crop up in so many places in the

WordprocessingML schema. They need to occur as block-level elements as well as run-level elements. The w:permStart element occurs in this example in a block context, as a sibling of paragraphs, whereas the corresponding w:permEnd element occurs in a run context, before the end of the paragraph. Likewise, the first of the w:proofErr elements occurs as a block-level element, before the beginning of the paragraph, but the second w:proofErr element, which ends the range at the word "were," occurs as a run-level element.

Document protection

Now let's look at how each type of annotation works. The w:permStart and w:permEnd elements work together to identify a range of text that has a particular editing permission enabled. The w:id attribute of each element is used to associate the markers with each other. In this case, we know that they go together, because the w:id attribute value is 0 for both of them:

```
<w:permStart w:id="0" w:edGrp="everyone"/>
    ...
    <w:permEnd w:id="0"/>
```

The value of the w:edGrp attribute denotes a group of people who can edit this region of text. In this case, the value is everyone, which means that there are no restrictions for this particular range. This is useful as a way of overriding a global document protection policy in which the rest of the document is off-limits for making changes. For more information on Word's document protection features, see Chapter 4.

Proof errors

The w:proofErr elements in Example 2-9 are used to identify the start and end points of a grammar error. The type of each marker is denoted by the w:type attribute:

```
<w:proofErr w:type="gramStart"/>
    ...
    <w:proofErr w:type="gramEnd"/>
```

Since grammar, as well as spelling, errors cannot overlap each other, there is no need for an ID attribute to associate start and end markers with each other. Word knows that a grammar error ends at the first gramEnd marker that it finds after the gramStart marker. Spelling errors are represented in the same way, using the values of spellStart and spellEnd for the w:type attribute. Thus, the w:proofError's w:type attribute has four possible values:

```
gramStart
gramEnd
spellStart
spellEnd
```

Comments and other annotations

Example 2-9 also demonstrates how comments are represented in Wordprocessing ML. Every comment is represented using three separate aml:annotation elements. The three are associated with each other by having the same aml:id attribute value (0 in Example 2-9's case). The first two aml:annotation elements are used to denote the start and end of the range that the comment is about:

```
<aml:annotation aml:id="0" w:type="Word.Comment.Start"/>
...
<aml:annotation aml:id="0" w:type="Word.Comment.End"/>
```

The w:type attribute values distinguish the start and end markers from each other: Word.Comment.Start and Word.Comment.End. The third aml:annotation element occurs inside a run (w:r element) that immediately follows the comment end marker:

```
<w:r>
  <w:rPr>
    <w:rStyle w:val="CommentReference"/>
  </w:rPr>
  ...
</w:r>
```

This run is associated with the CommentReference character style, a built-in style that is automatically inserted into the document when you insert a comment. So far, this looks like a normal run that might appear in the flow of document text. The content of the run, however, does not consist of normal document text. Instead, inside the run, we see the third and last aml:annotation element for this comment:

```
<aml:annotation aml:id="0" aml:author="Evan Lenz"
                aml:createdate="2003-12-22T12:15:00Z"
                w:type="Word.Comment" w:initials="edl">
  ...
</aml:annotation>
```

The aml:id attribute's value is 0, which associates this annotation with the previous two. The w:type attribute is Word.Comment, which indicates that this element contains the actual content of the comment. The other three attributes contain metadata about the comment, including who made the comment, their initials, and the date and time they made it.

Inside the aml:annotation element is the aml:content element, which is used to contain the text of the comment:

```
<aml:content>
  <w:p>
    <w:pPr>
      <w:pStyle w:val="CommentText"/>
    </w:pPr>
    <w:r>
      <w:rPr>
        <w:rStyle w:val="CommentReference"/>
      </w:rPr>
```

```
            <w:annotationRef/>
          </w:r>
          <w:r>
            <w:t>Isn't that bad grammar?</w:t>
          </w:r>
        </w:p>
      </aml:content>
```

The comment text is represented using a sequence of Word paragraphs. These paragraphs are "out-of-band" in the sense that they do not occur in the normal flow of document text. After all, they ultimately occur inside a w:r element. A paragraph inside a run isn't normally allowed; it wouldn't make any sense. Only because of the intervening aml:annotation and aml:content elements is the w:p element allowed to occur as a descendant of a w:r element.

In addition to comments, the aml:annotation element is also used to represent bookmarks and revision markings (recorded when "Track Changes" is turned on). In each case, the type of annotation is identified by the value of the w:type attribute, which has these possible values:

```
Word.Insertion
Word.Deletion
Word.Formatting
Word.Bookmark.Start
Word.Bookmark.End
Word.Comment.Start
Word.Comment.End
Word.Insertion.Start
Word.Insertion.End
Word.Deletion.Start
Word.Deletion.End
Word.Comment
Word.Numbering
```

Auxiliary Hints in WordprocessingML

Until now, we've managed to stick to a pretty strict diet of elements and attributes from the WordprocessingML namespace, which has had times more pleasant than others. Now it's time to introduce a set of elements and attributes from another namespace that are designed purely for the purpose of making your life easier. That's right, you guessed it: the wx prefix is your friend (so long as it's mapped to the right namespace: http://schemas.microsoft.com/office/word/2003/auxHint).

There are quite a few contexts in which elements and attributes from the wx namespace appear in WordprocessingML documents saved by Word. We'll be focusing on some of the most significant of these: sections, sub-sections, and list text, as well as formatting hints. These hints save consumers of WordprocessingML documents much grief and processing power that would otherwise be spent on things like traversing the links of a list definition, for example.

Again, elements and attributes in the wx namespace represent information that could be *useful to us* in handling WordprocessingML but that is of *no internal use to Word*. One implication of this distinction is that, while you may write applications that depend on their presence, it hardly ever makes sense to write applications that output elements or attributes in the wx namespace when generating WordprocessingML—except perhaps when doing incremental processing of an existing document such that you want to maintain the auxiliary information that originally came from Word. Even then, you're not really generating it; you're just forwarding it on.

Section Containers

Earlier in the chapter, in "Sections," we introduced WordprocessingML's non-intuitive way of representing a document's sections—how the presence of a w:sectPr element is implicitly interpreted to mean that the current paragraph is the last one in a section. Without a common container in which paragraphs of the same section are grouped together, it's not only counterintuitive but more difficult to process than it would otherwise be. Fortunately, the wx:sect element, which was introduced way back in Example 2-2, is Microsoft's answer to this problem. Whenever Word saves a document as XML, it doesn't just output the content of the w:body element. Instead, it groups the paragraphs and tables inside the body into wx:sect elements, corresponding to sections in the Word document.

To recognize the helpfulness of this feature, all we need to do is have Word open and to re-save the WordprocessingML document from Example 2-8. No longer is it so difficult to figure out where the section boundaries are:

```
<w:body>
  <wx:sect>
    <w:p>
      <w:pPr>
        <w:sectPr>
          <w:pgSz w:w="12240" w:h="15840"/>
          <w:pgMar w:top="1440" w:right="1800" w:bottom="1440"
                   w:left="1800" w:header="720" w:footer="720"
                   w:gutter="0"/>
          <w:cols w:space="720"/>
        </w:sectPr>
      </w:pPr>
      <w:r>
        <w:t>First section</w:t>
      </w:r>
    </w:p>
  </wx:sect>
  <wx:sect>
    <w:p>
```

```
    <w:r>
      <w:t>Second section, first paragraph</w:t>
    </w:r>
  </w:p>
  <w:p>
    <w:pPr>
      <w:sectPr>
        <w:pgSz w:w="12240" w:h="15840"/>
        <w:pgMar w:top="1440" w:right="1800" w:bottom="1440"
                 w:left="1800" w:header="720" w:footer="720"
                 w:gutter="0"/>
        <w:cols w:space="720"/>
      </w:sectPr>
    </w:pPr>
    <w:r>
      <w:t>Second section, second paragraph</w:t>
    </w:r>
  </w:p>
</wx:sect>
<wx:sect>
  <w:p>
    <w:r>
      <w:t>Third section, first paragraph</w:t>
    </w:r>
  </w:p>
  <w:p>
    <w:r>
      <w:t>Third section, second paragraph</w:t>
    </w:r>
  </w:p>
  <w:sectPr>
    <w:pgSz w:w="12240" w:h="15840"/>
      <w:pgMar w:top="1440" w:right="1800" w:bottom="1440"
               w:left="1800" w:header="720" w:footer="720"
               w:gutter="0"/>
    <w:cols w:space="720"/>
    <w:docGrid w:line-pitch="360"/>
  </w:sectPr>
</wx:sect>
</w:body>
```

Note that there are three wx:sect elements, one for each section, and that the paragraphs in each section are clearly grouped together. As mentioned before, we could remove the start and end tags of each wx:sect element, and Word would process the document no differently. Conversely, the meaning of the document as far as Word is concerned is completely unaltered by the addition of the wx:sect element. It only considers the w:sectPr elements to determine where the sections are. The same old rules apply: w:sectPr elements inside w:pPr elements represent section breaks, but the last w:sectPr element (provided it follows the last paragraph inside the w:body element) does not represent a break, but instead simply contains the properties of the last section.

An example using XPath can help demonstrate how the wx:sect element enables easier processing of WordprocessingML documents outside of Word. If we were to write an XPath expression to select all of the paragraphs in, say, the third section, this would be easy (assuming the appropriate namespace bindings):

```
/w:wordDocument/w:body/wx:sect[3]/w:p
```

However, without the aid of the wx:sect element, the task is still possible but not as straightforward and certainly not as intuitive:

```
/w:wordDocument/w:body/w:p[count(preceding::w:sectPr)=2]
```

Clearly, the wx:sect element, though it may have looked cryptic at first sight, is a helpful aid to processing WordprocessingML documents as output by Word.

Outline Levels and Sub-Sections

Word has a special paragraph property that we didn't mention earlier: the outline level. As might be guessed, the outline level property has an effect on the display of a paragraph in Word's "Outline" view. Example paragraph styles for which an outline level is defined include all of Word's built-in Heading styles. In fact, it's no accident that the Outline view supports nine levels and that there are precisely nine Heading styles. Figure 2-22 shows how all of the Heading styles are displayed in Outline view, along with some body text on each rung of the ladder. The body text has no outline level specified, as is the case with most normal paragraphs. All of the Heading paragraphs, however, have the outline level corresponding to their name. Heading 1 has Outline Level 1, Heading 2 has Outline Level 2, etc.

Clearly, the document in Figure 2-22 follows a hierarchical structure (if rather deep). Many people author such hierarchically organized documents in Word. Indeed, the Heading styles in conjunction with Outline view give them incentives for doing so. Unfortunately none of that hierarchical structure made it into WordprocessingML, which remains wedded to the flat-list-of-paragraphs paradigm. Sure, you can make a document *look* like it's hierarchically structured, but underneath the covers it's just a sequence of paragraphs with various formatting properties applied. But all is not lost. Once again, the wx namespace comes to the rescue, in what is arguably the most useful element of all the auxiliary hints: the wx:sub-section element.

Whenever Word saves a WordprocessingML document that has an outline level specified on any of its paragraphs, then at least a one-level depth tree of wx:sub-section elements will be present in the output. Specifically, any time Word comes across a paragraph with an outline level, it establishes a new sub-section context equal in depth of sub-sections to the outline level of the paragraph. For example, if the outline level is 3, then the paragraph will be contained within three nested wx:sub-section elements. This stays in effect for following paragraphs either until it reaches another paragraph with an outline level, or it comes to the end of the section

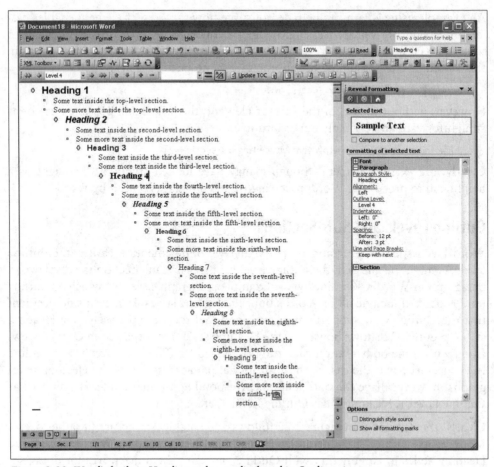

Figure 2-22. Word's built-in Heading styles, as displayed in Outline view

(in which case all of the `wx:sub-section` elements are closed). In the case of the document in Figure 2-22, it would output a structure similar to the following:

```
<wx:sub-section>
  Heading 1
  Body text
  Body text
  <wx:sub-section>
    Heading 2
    Body text
    Body text
    <wx:sub-section>
      Heading 3
      Body text
      Body text
      ...
    </wx:sub-section>
  </wx:sub-section>
</wx:sub-section>
```

You can achieve a similar effect with any custom paragraph style that you develop, simply by adding an outline level to the style definition. While using styles is probably the best way to achieve this effect, the use of styles isn't required. You can also apply the outline level property locally, as direct formatting on your paragraph. Example 2-10 finally demonstrates the syntax for the outline level property, as specified inside a paragraph's w:pPr element. This document contains a series of five paragraphs, two of which specify an outline level using the w:outlineLvl element, whose w:val attribute value must be between 0 and 8 (exposed as 1 through 9 in the Word UI).

Example 2-10. Setting outline levels locally

```
<?xml version="1.0"?>
<?mso-application progid="Word.Document"?>
<w:wordDocument
  xmlns:w="http://schemas.microsoft.com/office/word/2003/wordml"
  xml:space="preserve">
  <w:body>
    <w:p>
      <w:pPr>
        <w:outlineLvl w:val="0"/>
      </w:pPr>
      <w:r><w:t>This is the top-level heading</w:t></w:r>
    </w:p>
    <w:p>
      <w:r><w:t>This is some text inside the top-level sub-
section.</w:t></w:r>
    </w:p>
    <w:p>
      <w:r><w:t>This is some more body text.</w:t></w:r>
    </w:p>
    <w:p>
      <w:pPr>
        <w:outlineLvl w:val="1"/>
      </w:pPr>
      <w:r><w:t>This is a second-level heading</w:t></w:r>
    </w:p>
    <w:p>
      <w:r><w:t>This is some body text under the second-level
heading.</w:t></w:r>
    </w:p>
  </w:body>
</w:wordDocument>
```

First, let's see what this document looks like when opened in Word. Figure 2-23 shows both the Normal view and the Outline view. The outline levels are completely invisible in the Normal view; the paragraphs look no different than any other plain, boring paragraph. Outline view is another story.

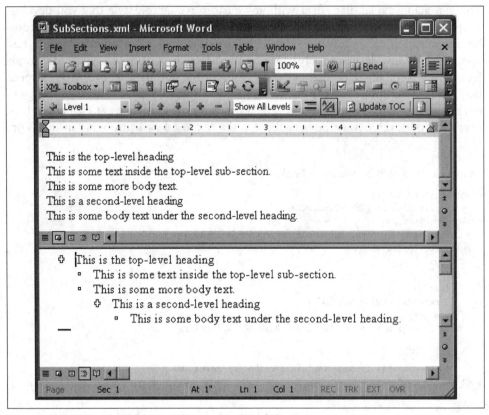

Figure 2-23. Outline levels shown in Normal and Outline views

Finally, we can see the wx:sub-section element in action by resaving the document as XML from within Word. Example 2-11 shows the body content excerpted from the WordprocessingML document as saved by Word.

Example 2-11. A document body with outline levels, when saved as XML in Word

```
<w:body>
  <wx:sect>
    <wx:sub-section>
      <w:p>
        <w:pPr>
          <w:outlineLvl w:val="0"/>
        </w:pPr>
        <w:r>
          <w:t>This is the top-level heading</w:t>
        </w:r>
      </w:p>
      <w:p>
        <w:r>
          <w:t>This is some text inside the top-level sub-section.</w:t>
        </w:r>
```

```
      </w:p>
      <w:p>
        <w:r>
          <w:t>This is some more body text.</w:t>
        </w:r>
      </w:p>
      <wx:sub-section>
        <w:p>
          <w:pPr>
            <w:outlineLvl w:val="1"/>
          </w:pPr>
          <w:r>
            <w:t>This is a second-level heading</w:t>
          </w:r>
        </w:p>
        <w:p>
          <w:r>
            <w:t>This is some body text under the second-level heading.</w:t>
          </w:r>
        </w:p>
        <w:sectPr>
          <w:pgSz w:w="12240" w:h="15840"/>
          <w:pgMar w:top="1440" w:right="1800" w:bottom="1440"
                   w:left="1800" w:header="720" w:footer="720"
                   w:gutter="0"/>
          <w:cols w:space="720"/>
          <w:docGrid w:line-pitch="360"/>
        </w:sectPr>
      </wx:sub-section>
    </wx:sub-section>
  </wx:sect>
</w:body>
```

Example 2-11 demonstrates that Word interprets the outline levels to automatically structure the resulting WordprocessingML into sub-sections, using wx:sub-section elements, which are highlighted. Again, outline levels are most useful when they are associated with particular paragraph styles, rather than assigned directly to individual paragraphs (which, in the Word UI, can only be done in Outline View). Provided that the user applies styles in the order that they are intended, e.g., Heading 1 followed by Heading 2, etc., then the WordprocessingML that Word generates will be structured into sub-sections that reflect the true hierarchical structure of the document, rather than merely a flat sequence of paragraphs.

List Item Formatting Hints

Anything Word wants to provide in the way of making lists easier to process is certainly welcome. As we saw earlier in this chapter, lists in WordprocessingML are rather complicated to process. Generally, you can recognize the presence of a list item by the presence of a w:listPr element inside a paragraph's w:pPr element. While that's a start, if you want to find out anything about how the list item is formatted, including even whether it's a "numbered" or "bulleted" list, you have to traverse a number of intra-document links. How many depends on whether and to what extent paragraph or list styles are involved.

As a matter of fact, Word does rather consistently save us this trouble by outputting the wx:t element inside a paragraph's w:listPr element. The wx:t element has three attributes: wx:val, wx:wTabBefore, and wx:wTabAfter. The wx:val attribute specifies the actual text used for the number or bullet point of this particular list item. The wx:wTabBefore is measured in twips and specifies the width of the tab preceding the line number. This usually corresponds to the indentation of the list item from the page's left margin. The wx:wTabAfter, on the other hand, calculates the distance, in twips, between the end of the text of the line number and the beginning of the editable area. It takes into consideration the font size and length of the line number itself. For example, consider the second list item of the simple list in Figure 2-24.

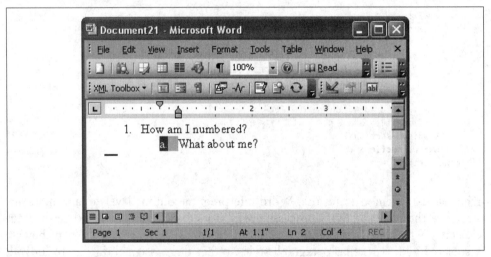

Figure 2-24. A simple list item

The hint as it resultantly appears in this paragraph's w:listPr element (inside its w:pPr element) is as follows:

```
<wx:t wx:val="a." wx:wTabBefore="1080" wx:wTabAfter="195" />
```

The wx:val attribute clearly relates that the line number text is "a." The wx:wTabBefore corresponds to the actual left indent of this paragraph, namely .75 inches, or 1080 twips. And the wx:wTabAfter attribute represents the distance between the "a." text and the contents of the list item—in other words, the gray, highlighted area following "a." in Figure 2-24.

More on Styles

Having come this far in the chapter, you should already know a few key aspects of how styles work in Word and WordprocessingML:

- A style is a grouping of property settings that can be applied as a unit.
- There are four kinds of styles: paragraph, character, table, and list.
- Styles are defined using `w:style` elements inside a WordprocessingML document's `w:styles` element.
- Paragraphs, runs, and tables can be directly associated with a style of the appropriate kind through the `w:pStyle`, `w:rStyle`, and `w:tblStyle` elements, respectively.

You should also know the basic syntax of the `w:style` element, and four aspects in particular:

- The `w:type` attribute, indicating the type of style defined here (`paragraph`, `character`, `table`, or `list`)
- The `w:default` attribute, indicating whether this style is the default style for its type
- The `w:styleId` attribute for intra-document references to this style
- The `w:name` element, indicating the style's primary name as exposed in the Word UI

In this section, we'll look at a few more aspects of how styles are defined, how default styles work (or don't), how to derive styles, and how style conflicts are resolved.

A Document's Styles

All styles that are used within a document must also be defined in the document. This effectively means that you can't leverage Word's built-in styles outside of Word; i.e., you can't simply refer to them by name. When a document uses a built-in Word style, Word makes a *copy of* the built-in style, rather than merely a reference to it. From that point forward, the style is part of the document and begins to exist independently of the built-in style from whence it came. To see a definitive list of the styles that are contained in your document, through the Word UI, select Tools → Templates and Add-Ins... and then click the Organizer... button. The styles listed on the left should correspond one-to-one with the `w:style` definitions in the WordprocessingML serialization of your document.

Default Styles

WordprocessingML's default style mechanism (using the `w:default` attribute) works well for paragraph and table styles. If you have `w:p` and `w:tbl` elements in your document that do not explicitly associate themselves with a style (with `w:pStyle` or `w:tblStyle` elements, respectively), then you can create sweeping formatting changes by simply changing the default style to a different paragraph or table style inside the `w:styles` element. You do this by setting the `w:default` attribute to on:

```
<w:style w:type="paragraph" w:default="on" w:styleId="MyParagraphStyle">
  <w:name w:val="My Paragraph Style"/>
  ...
</w:style>
```

On the other hand, the default style mechanism does *not* work for character styles and lists. If you try to specify a custom default character style, for example, Word will ignore it and will simply set the "Default Paragraph Font" character style as the default. For example, the `w:default` attribute shown here has no effect on Word's behavior:

```
<w:style w:type="character" w:default="on" w:styleId="MyCharacterStyle">
  <w:name w:val="My Character Style"/>
  ...
</w:style>
```

Effectively, this means that runs can only be associated with a character style *explicitly*—through the `w:rStyle` element, like this:

```
<w:r>
  <w:rPr>
    <w:rStyle w:val="MyCharacterStyle"/>
  </w:rPr>
  <w:t>This text is associated with a custom character style.</w:t>
</w:r>
```

Also, while you can freely customize the "Normal" paragraph style properties in your document, Word will discard any changes you attempt to make to the "Default Paragraph Font." Thus, there is no defaulting mechanism for associating runs with a particular character style (other than "Default Paragraph Font," which amounts to "no style"). In some respects, this is disconcerting, as it doesn't seem to match up with what WordprocessingML's syntax implicitly advertises. On the other hand, it reduces the possible combinations, thereby making the overall application of styles somewhat easier to think about.

The `w:default` attribute is essentially "syntax sugar," making it easy to create WordprocessingML documents without having to explicitly associate all of a document's paragraphs with a particular style (using a bunch of `w:pStyle` elements). Since the `w:default` attribute is merely syntax sugar and not part of Word's internal data structures, Word does not preserve your default style choices when it opens your document. Instead, Word always sets `w:default="on"` to the "Normal" style definition when it outputs WordprocessingML, regardless of which paragraph style was the default in the WordprocessingML document it originally opened. This doesn't affect your document's formatting; it just means that the resulting WordprocessingML markup will be a little more verbose if most of your paragraphs don't use the "Normal" style. In that case, your paragraph style will be explicitly referenced via w:pStyle elements, rather than implicitly via the default style association:

```
<w:p>
  <w:pPr>
    <w:pStyle w:val="MyParagraphStyle"/>
  </w:pPr>
  <w:r>
    <w:t>This paragraph is explicitly associated with a para style.</w:t>
  </w:r>
</w:p>
```

Default Font Size for Paragraph Styles

There are two kinds of default font sizes in Word:

- 12 points, the font size of Word's built-in "Normal" style that gets automatically inserted into your document if you don't explicitly define it using a w:style element
- 10 points, the font size of a paragraph style definition (w:style element) that does not explicitly specify a font size using the w:sz element

We have already seen how the first default font size comes about. If you do not explicitly define the "Normal" paragraph style in a document, then Word automatically inserts its built-in "Normal" style, whose font size is 12 points (24 half-points). This scenario is exactly what we saw in Examples 2-1 and 2-2.

However, when you *do* define a paragraph style but do not explicitly specify the font size (using the w:sz element), then the font size of your paragraph style defaults to 10 points (20 half-points). For this reason, if you do define the "Normal" style in your document but without specifying a font size, then you will get a different result than if you didn't define the style at all. Specifically, the font size of your document's text will be 10 points, rather than 12 points. Example 2-12 shows a document that differs from Example 2-1 only in that it contains an empty definition for the "Normal" paragraph style (as identified by the w:name element).

Example 2-12. Defining the "Normal" style without specifying a font size

```
<?xml version="1.0"?>
<?mso-application progid="Word.Document"?>
<w:wordDocument
  xmlns:w="http://schemas.microsoft.com/office/word/2003/wordml">

  <w:styles>
    <w:style w:type="paragraph" w:default="on">
```

```
      <w:name w:val="Normal"/>
    </w:style>
  </w:styles>

  <w:body>
    <w:p>
      <w:r>
        <w:t>Hello, World!</w:t>
      </w:r>
    </w:p>
  </w:body>
</w:wordDocument>
```

When Word opens this document, the text "Hello, World!" is displayed in 10-point, rather than 12-point, Times New Roman. This is because you defined the style in your document, but did not include a w:sz element (inside a w:rPr element):

```
    <w:style w:type="paragraph" w:default="on">
      <w:name w:val="Normal"/>
    </w:style>
```

Word interprets such a paragraph style definition (regardless of whether it's the "Normal" style or some other paragraph style) as having a font size of 10 points. The above definition is equivalent to this one, where the font size of 20 half-points is explicitly specified:

```
    <w:style w:type="paragraph" w:default="on">
      <w:name w:val="Normal"/>
      <w:rPr>
        <w:sz w:val="20"/>
      </w:rPr>
    </w:style>
```

The only case where a paragraph style's font size could be different than 10 points without explicitly specifying a font size is when the style is derived from another paragraph style that has a different font size. As long as both the w:basedOn and w:sz elements are absent, then you can be sure that the paragraph style's font size is 10 points. But if there *is* a w:basedOn element and no w:sz element, then you would have to look at the base style to determine what the font size is.

So, what is the default font size for a WordprocessingML document? The answer is: it depends on what you mean by "default font size." If you're talking about the font size of Word's built-in "Normal" style, the answer is 12 points. If you're talking about the default font size of paragraph style definitions, the answer is 10 points.

Derived Styles

> In MS Word, editing styles is like drilling for oil in the Mariana Trench: by the time you finish the descent through the menus, you're down so deep that you can get the bends trying to remember what you started to do.
>
> —*http://www.linuxjournal.com/article.php?sid=7120*

One of the most powerful aspects of styles is the ability to base one style on another (in WordprocessingML, using the `w:basedOn` element), overriding individual properties as necessary. We'll see a couple examples of derived styles later in "A Pop Quiz," but the basic syntax looks like this:

```
<w:style w:type="paragraph" w:styleId="MyDerivedStyle">
  <w:name w:val="My Derived Style"/>
  <w:basedOn w:val="MyBaseStyle"/>
  <!-- formatting information -->
</w:style>
```

Using style derivation, you can base all of your paragraph styles, for example, on a base "Normal" style. Then, if you want to make a global change to all of your styles, such as font size, you need only make the change in one place—in the base style. This, of course, assumes that none of your derived styles override the base style's font size setting. Unfortunately, the Word UI doesn't give any visual clues as to when a particular property of a derived style is merely inherited from the base style or whether it is hard-wired to the style itself. This can make for some bewildering behavior.

For example, say your document has a base style called "Normal," from which a number of different styles have been derived, all of which merely inherit the font size property from "Normal." Whenever you update the font size of the "Normal" style, all of the derived styles' font sizes will be updated accordingly. So far, so good. But suppose you now want to derive another style, called "Code," that you know upfront should *always* be set to a font size of 9 points, regardless of any changes to the base "Normal" style's font size. This is the tricky part. When you first create the "Code" style and select a font size of 9 points, whether that size will end up being hard-wired to the "Code" style (which is what you want) or whether the "Code" style will merely inherit the font size from "Normal" (not what you want) completely depends on what the font size of "Normal" happens to be at the time you create the style. That's because Word gives you no way of telling it to hard-wire the font size to this style. Instead, it makes an assumption based on the current state of the base style. It assumes, in this case, that if the "Normal" font size is 9 points and you select 9 points when creating the "Code" style, you must want "Code" to always be the same size as "Normal." The only way to get around this is to temporarily change the "Normal" style's font size to something other than 9 points, and then create the new style, changing it back after you're done.

The introduction of WordprocessingML can largely alleviate this problem. By saving as XML, you get a readable (assuming you've pretty-printed), as well as editable, dump of all of your document's style definitions, removing once and for all any doubt about which of a style's properties are inherited and which are hard-wired to the style.

Resolving Conflicts

A given piece of text's formatting information can come from several different places, which raises the question of how conflicts are handled. Even after resolving a document's derived-style inheritance tree, there are still plenty of potential ambiguities, since you still have direct formatting, paragraph styles, and character styles to consider. Understanding how these all interact is fundamental to an understanding of WordprocessingML. In this section, we'll look at how potential conflicts are resolved—first for paragraph properties and then for font properties.

Paragraph property conflicts

A given paragraph can have paragraph properties applied to it in two ways:

- Through the associated paragraph style
- Through direct formatting

There is a simple rule for resolving conflicts between these two ways of applying paragraph properties: *direct formatting always wins*. For example, you can be sure that the following paragraph will be centered, without ever having to look at the MyParagraphStyle definition:

```
<w:p>
  <w:pPr>
    <w:pStyle w:val="MyParagraphStyle"/>
    <w:jc w:val="center"/>
  </w:pPr>
  <w:r>
    <w:t>This text is centered, regardless of what the associated paragraph
style says.</w:t>
  </w:r>
</w:p>
```

The w:jc element in the above snippet is an example of direct paragraph formatting. It is a paragraph property that is applied locally to this specific paragraph, as opposed to being part of a style definition. Any time you see a property setting applied within a local w:pPr element, you can be sure that it will take precedence over any conflicting settings in the associated paragraph style.

Font property conflicts

While paragraph properties can only be applied in two ways, font properties can be applied to a given piece of text in *three* different ways:

- Through the associated paragraph style
- Through the associated character style
- Through direct formatting

For font properties, as with paragraph properties, *direct formatting always wins*. For example, you can be sure that the run of text in the snippet below is italic and not bold without even looking at the MyParagraphStyle or MyCharacterStyle definitions:

```
<w:p>
  <w:pPr>
    <w:pStyle w:val="MyParagraphStyle"/>
  </w:pPr>
  <w:r>
    <w:rPr>
      <w:rStyle w:val="MyCharacterStyle"/>
      <w:i/>
      <w:b w:val="off"/>
    </w:rPr>
    <w:t>This text is italic and not bold, regardless of what the associated
paragraph and character styles say.</w:t>
  </w:r>
</w:p>
```

The w:i and w:b elements in the above snippet are examples of direct font formatting. They are font properties applied locally to this specific run, as opposed to being part of a style definition. Any time you see a property setting applied within a local w:rPr element, you can be sure that it will take precedence over any conflicting settings in the associated paragraph or character styles.

While the rule that "direct formatting always wins" is sufficient to resolve all potential paragraph property conflicts, it does *not* resolve all potential font property conflicts. Resolving font properties is a more complex problem, because—unlike paragraph properties—font properties can be defined in both the character style *and* the paragraph style. What happens when font property settings conflict between a run's associated paragraph and character styles?

To help answer this question, let's consider the different kinds of font properties that can be applied. Word's font properties can be classified into two categories:

- On/off properties
- Everything else (multi-valued properties)

Examples of on/off properties are bold (w:b), italic (w:i), all caps (w:caps), and strikethrough (w:strike). Examples of the other, multi-valued properties include underline (w:u), font (w:rFonts), font size (w:sz), and font color (w:color). For multi-valued properties, the rule is simple: *the character style takes precedence.*

For the on/off properties, the rule isn't about which style has precedence; the paragraph and character styles are considered equally. Instead, the rule is about how their settings are *merged.* Here's the rule: *a given property is turned on only when it is turned on in one style but not the other.*

To help make this more explicit, Table 2-1 shows all four possible combinations for a particular on/off property and the effective result of each.

Table 2-1. How on/off font properties are merged between a paragraph and character style

Paragraph style	Character style	Result
Off	Off	Off
Off	On	On
On	Off	On
On	On	Off

Table 2-1 is essentially a truth table. The first two columns contain the inputs and the third column contains the XOR ("exclusive or") result. If you imagine representing a style's on/off property settings as a binary number (a series of 0s and 1s), then to compute the final result, you would apply an XOR bitmask to the two binary numbers, i.e., to the paragraph and character styles. That is in fact what Word does.

Let's bring this back down to earth with an example. At one time or another, you may have noticed Word's behavior when you applied an italicized character style to text within an italicized paragraph. Rather than keeping the text italic, this action had the opposite effect: the resulting text was *not* italicized. You may have thought that Word was just being clever about interpreting your intentions. After all, if you wanted to emphasize a particular word in a paragraph that is already emphasized as a whole, how else would Word do it? In reality, Word was just following the above rule. Since the italic property was turned on in both the paragraph and the character styles, they effectively cancelled each other out, and the result was not italicized. Example 2-13 illustrates exactly this scenario.

Example 2-13. Turning italics off using a character style

```
<?xml version="1.0"?>
<?mso-application progid="Word.Document"?>
<w:wordDocument
  xmlns:w="http://schemas.microsoft.com/office/word/2003/wordml">

  <w:styles>
    <w:style w:type="paragraph" w:styleId="EmphasizedParagraph">
      <w:name w:val="Emphasized Paragraph"/>
      <w:rPr>
        <w:i/>
```

Example 2-13. Turning italics off using a character style (continued)

```
          <w:b/>
      </w:rPr>
    </w:style>
    <w:style w:type="character" w:styleId="Emphasis">
      <w:name w:val="Emphasis"/>
      <w:rPr>
        <w:i/>
        <w:b w:val="off"/>
      </w:rPr>
    </w:style>
  </w:styles>
  <w:body>
    <w:p>
      <w:pPr>
        <w:pStyle w:val="EmphasizedParagraph"/>
      </w:pPr>
      <w:r>
        <w:t>Most of this paragraph is italicized, but </w:t>
      </w:r>
      <w:r>
        <w:rPr>
          <w:rStyle w:val="Emphasis"/>
        </w:rPr>
        <w:t>this part is not.</w:t>
      </w:r>
    </w:p>
  </w:body>
</w:wordDocument>
```

Figure 2-25 shows what this document looks like when opened in Word. The last part of the paragraph is not italicized. The "Reveal Formatting" task pane shows that the "Emphasis" style contributes the "Not Italic" effect. In any other (non-italicized) paragraph, the "Emphasis" style would have exactly the opposite effect.

The other thing to note about this example is that the entire paragraph is rendered bold, even though the "Emphasis" character style explicitly tries to turn bold off:

```
          <w:b w:val="off"/>
```

This behavior is consistent with the rule that if *either* (but not both) of the paragraph and character styles turns a property on, then that property will effectively be turned on. The only times that explicitly turning a property off will have an overriding effect are either when you are inheriting from another style (using the w:basedOn element) or when you are applying direct formatting (using a local w:rPr element). In those cases, to turn a property off, you explicitly turn it off. In contrast, if you want to use a character style to turn a property off, you have to do the counter-intuitive thing: you turn the property *on*.

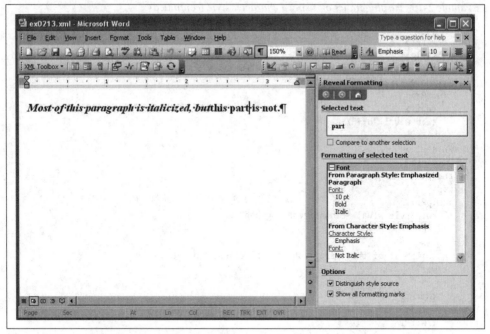

Figure 2-25. How Word renders Example 2-13

 For most on/off font properties, explicitly turning them off in a character style has no effect. However, there are a few exceptions to this rule, including the w:dstrike (double strikethrough), w:noProof (ignore spelling/grammar errors for this run), and w:rtl (right-to-left reading order) elements. Though each of these are on/off properties, they are interpreted more like their multi-valued counterparts, i.e., they have an overriding effect. The character style takes precedence over the paragraph style setting. For example, if a run's paragraph style turns double strikethrough on, but its character style definition includes <w:dstrike w:val="off"/>, then it will be rendered *without* the double strikethrough.

A Pop Quiz

Now it's time for a pop quiz. Considering what you now know about default styles, derived styles, direct formatting, and how paragraph and character styles interact, try to figure out what formatting the runs in Example 2-14 have. There are two runs of text, separated by a soft line break. For each run, ask yourself: Is it bold? Is it italic? Is it both?

Example 2-14. What formatting do I have?

```xml
<?xml version="1.0"?>
<?mso-application progid="Word.Document"?>
<w:wordDocument xmlns:w="http://schemas.microsoft.com/office/word/2003/wordml"
  xml:space="preserve">

  <w:styles>
    <w:style w:styleId="BaseParagraphStyle" w:type="paragraph">
      <w:name w:val="Base Paragraph Style"/>
      <w:rPr>
        <w:b/>
        <w:i/>
      </w:rPr>
    </w:style>
    <w:style w:styleId="DerivedParagraphStyle" w:type="paragraph"
            w:default="on">
      <w:name w:val="Derived Paragraph Style"/>
      <w:basedOn w:val="BaseParagraphStyle"/>
      <w:rPr>
        <w:i w:val="off"/>
      </w:rPr>
    </w:style>
    <w:style w:styleId="BaseCharacterStyle" w:type="character">
      <w:name w:val="Base Character Style"/>
      <w:rPr>
        <w:i/>
      </w:rPr>
    </w:style>
    <w:style w:styleId="DerivedCharacterStyle" w:type="character">
      <w:name w:val="Derived Character Style"/>
      <w:basedOn w:val="BaseCharacterStyle"/>
      <w:rPr>
        <w:b/>
      </w:rPr>
    </w:style>
  </w:styles>

  <w:body>
    <w:p>
      <w:r>
        <w:rPr>
          <w:rStyle w:val="DerivedCharacterStyle"/>
          <w:i w:val="off"/>
        </w:rPr>
        <w:t>What formatting do I have?</w:t>
      </w:r>
      <w:r>
        <w:rPr>
          <w:rStyle w:val="DerivedCharacterStyle"/>
        </w:rPr>
        <w:br/>
        <w:t>And what formatting do I have?</w:t>
      </w:r>
```

Example 2-14. What formatting do I have? (continued)

```
    </w:p>
  </w:body>

</w:wordDocument>
```

Okay, let's figure it out. The first thing we can do is determine what styles are used in the document. The document's one paragraph doesn't explicitly associate itself with a paragraph style; it has no w:pStyle element. Therefore, it adopts whatever the document's default paragraph style is. Looking at the document's style definitions, we see that the "Derived Paragraph Style" definition is the default one:

```
<w:style w:styleId="DerivedParagraphStyle" w:type="paragraph"
        w:default="on">
  <w:name w:val="Derived Paragraph Style"/>
```

Inside the document's paragraph are two runs, both of which are associated with the "Derived Character Style" definition, using the w:rStyle element:

```
<w:rStyle w:val="DerivedCharacterStyle"/>
```

The next thing we need to do is resolve the style derivations to determine exactly what formatting properties are applied by each derived style. The "Base Paragraph Style" turns bold and italic on:

```
<w:b/>
<w:i/>
```

But the "Derived Paragraph Style" turns italic off:

```
<w:i w:val="off"/>
```

Therefore, our document's default paragraph style consists of one font property setting: bold.

The "Base Character Style" turns italic on, and the "Derived Character Style" turns bold on. Nothing is overridden. Therefore, the character style associated with our document's two runs has two font property settings: bold and italic.

Next, we look to the body of the document itself. The first run explicitly turns italic off, so we know that the first run will not be italicized, as direct formatting always has the final word:

```
<w:r>
  <w:rPr>
    <w:rStyle w:val="DerivedCharacterStyle"/>
    <w:i w:val="off"/>
  </w:rPr>
  <w:t>What formatting do I have?</w:t>
</w:r>
```

The next question is whether this run is bold or not. Since, as we've seen, both the fully resolved paragraph style and the fully resolved character style turn bold on, that means bold will effectively be turned *off*. This is in keeping with the rule that a property is on only if one *but not both* styles turns it on. Thus, the first run is rendered in neither bold nor italic type.

The second run is the same as the first, except that italic is not explicitly turned off via direct formatting. In fact, there is no direct formatting:

```
<w:r>
  <w:rPr>
    <w:rStyle w:val="DerivedCharacterStyle"/>
  </w:rPr>
  <w:br/>
  <w:t>And what formatting do I have?</w:t>
</w:r>
```

We've already seen that the paragraph and character styles' bold settings cancel each other out, so the remaining question is whether this run is italicized or not. Since the character style turns italic on but the paragraph style does not, that means that italic will indeed be turned on, because it is turned on in one but not both of the paragraph and character styles. Figure 2-26 shows the result of opening this document in Word (with paragraph marks turned on).

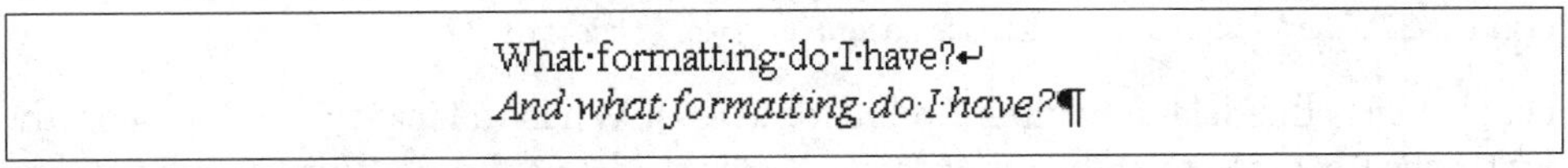

What·formatting·do·I·have?↵
And·what·formatting·do·I·have?¶

Figure 2-26. How Word renders Example 2-14

Dummy Styles

A common advantage of using styles in Word is that they can help to enforce consistency of presentation throughout a document. However, for an XML-oriented user, styles may at first seem to provide yet an additional advantage, especially when they are defined in a template: a way to separate presentation from content in Word. In a limited way they do, because within a document, the style definitions and the content are in distinct places, and changes to a document's style are propagated to all instances of that style throughout the document. However, styles defined externally in a template, rather than remaining separate from a document, are copied into the document when the template is first attached. (This ensures that a document will display uniformly on different machines without requiring all users to have access to the originally attached template.) When a template is attached, all of its styles are copied into the document, and the template's role is essentially over. The document does retain a loose association with the template (as represented by the w:attachedTemplate element), but for all practical purposes the template is no longer needed—*unless* you elect to set the document's "Automatically update document styles" option to true, as shown in Figure 2-27, in the "Templates and Add-ins" dialog box.

WordprocessingML represents this setting through the presence of an empty w: linkStyles element inside the w:docPr element (short for <w:linkStyles w:val="on"/>

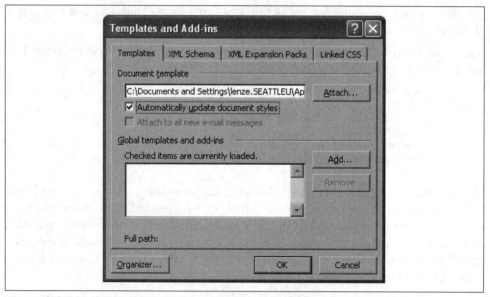

Figure 2-27. The "Automatically update document styles" checkbox

because on is the default attribute value for w:val). When w:linkStyles is present, the w:attachedTemplate reference gains new meaning. The next time Word opens the document, it immediately copies all the style definitions within that template into the document once again, replacing any style definition that has the same name as a style defined in the template. As long as this option is set, Word will continue to update the styles in the document, whenever the document is opened.

There is a practical implication for the XML developer writing XSLT stylesheets to, say, generate Word document reports. Provided that the user who opens the target Word document has access to its attached template, then styles in the template can effectively be referenced without duplicating the entire style definition.

As long as the w:linkStyles option is set, you can rely on Word to supply all the style definitions for you as soon as it opens the document. This greatly simplifies programs (such as XSLT stylesheets) that generate WordprocessingML documents that use styles already defined in a template.

Remember that to use any style within a document, it always must be declared in the top-level w:styles element. You can't just refer to a style from inside the w:body element, even if it's a built-in style. If you try to use a style without declaring it, the style reference will be ignored and discarded. So you must declare the style, giving it an arbitrary internal ID (using the w:styleId attribute) for reference from within the document body. (The w:styleId attribute's value can be any string.) Then, to have Word replace a dummy style definition for you, you must additionally ensure all three of the following:

- The w:linkStyles element is present inside the w:docPr element
- The value of the w:name element's w:val attribute is the same as the name of a style declared in the attached template
- The attached template is available to the user who initially opens the document

Example 2-15 shows a minimal WordprocessingML document created by hand that uses the Code,x style defined in the O'Reilly Word template. Rather than defining the entire style in all its verboseness, along with the ripe potential for error that would entail, this WordprocessingML document simply declares the style, using a dummy definition that includes nothing other than the w:name element, which identifies it as the Code,x style. The only paragraph of the document then is assigned that style using the w:pStyle element inside the w:pPr element. Thanks to the presence of the w:linkStyles element, the complete style definition for Code,x is inserted automatically (along with all of the template's other styles), as soon as Word opens the document.

Example 2-15. Replacing dummy style definitions via w:linkStyles

```
<?xml version="1.0"?>
<?mso-application progid="Word.Document"?>
<w:wordDocument xmlns:w="http://schemas.microsoft.com/office/word/2003/wordml">
  <w:styles>
    <w:style w:styleId="Code">
      <w:name w:val="Code,x"/>
    </w:style>
  </w:styles>

  <w:docPr>
    <w:attachedTemplate w:val="C:\Documents and Settings\lenze.SEATTLEU\Application Data\
Microsoft\Templates\ora.dot"/>
    <w:linkStyles/>
  </w:docPr>

  <w:body>
    <w:p>
      <w:pPr>
        <w:pStyle w:val="Code"/>
      </w:pPr>
      <w:r>
        <w:t>This is a code example.</w:t>
      </w:r>
    </w:p>
  </w:body>
</w:wordDocument>
```

Word will always output complete style definitions in the WordprocessingML it creates. Accordingly, this technique shouldn't be thought of as enabling the separation of presentation and content, but rather as a one-time macro of sorts for getting Word to put all the styles in your document for you. Indeed, this describes the basic role that template attachment plays in the first place.

Linked Styles

The w:link element, when present in a paragraph style definition, represents a link to a character style. Conversely, when present in a character style definition, the w:link element represents a link to a paragraph style. Only paragraph and character styles can be linked to each other. The key characteristic of a paragraph-character style link is that the two styles are exposed in the primary Word UI as a single style, using the name of the paragraph style. Also, changes to the character properties of one style are automatically propagated to the other. Word automatically creates a linked character style when a user applies a paragraph style to only a portion of a paragraph, rather than to a paragraph as a whole. The alternative would be to throw an error, chastising the user for trying to use a paragraph style on anything but a complete paragraph. That being potentially bad business, Word instead gracefully falls back and automatically creates a new character style by copying all of the paragraph style's character properties into the newly created style. Thus a linked character style is born.

Figure 2-28 shows the creation of a linked character style named "Heading 1 Char." Word automatically creates the style, because the user has tried to apply the "Heading 1" style to only a portion of a paragraph (the word "partial"). At the top of the screen, the style is still listed simply as "Heading 1," though the Reveal Formatting task pane and the Style dialog box both reveal the distinction between "Heading 1" and "Heading 1 Char."

The style definitions in the resulting WordprocessingML are shown below, with the w:link elements highlighted:

```
<w:style w:type="paragraph" w:styleId="Heading1">
  <w:name w:val="heading 1"/>
  <wx:uiName wx:val="Heading 1"/>
  <w:basedOn w:val="Normal"/>
  <w:next w:val="Normal"/>
  <w:link w:val="Heading1Char"/>
  <w:rsid w:val="00B33163"/>
  <w:pPr>
    <w:pStyle w:val="Heading1"/>
    <w:keepNext/>
    <w:spacing w:before="240" w:after="60"/>
    <w:outlineLvl w:val="0"/>
  </w:pPr>
  <w:rPr>
    <w:rFonts w:ascii="Arial" w:h-ansi="Arial" w:cs="Arial"/>
    <wx:font wx:val="Arial"/>
    <w:b/>
    <w:b-cs/>
    <w:kern w:val="32"/>
    <w:sz w:val="32"/>
    <w:sz-cs w:val="32"/>
  </w:rPr>
</w:style>
<w:style w:type="character" w:styleId="Heading1Char">
  <w:name w:val="Heading 1 Char"/>
```

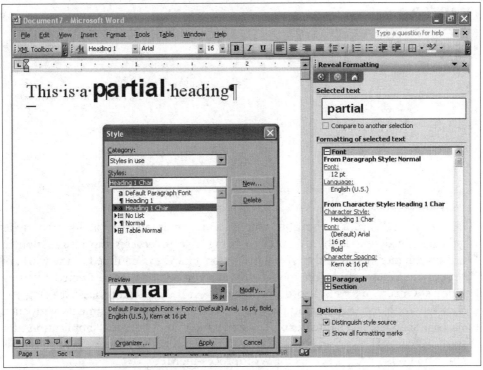

Figure 2-28. An automatically created linked character style, "Heading 1 Char"

```
<w:basedOn w:val="DefaultParagraphFont"/>
<w:link w:val="Heading1"/>
<w:rsid w:val="00B33163"/>
<w:rPr>
  <w:rFonts w:ascii="Arial" w:h-ansi="Arial" w:cs="Arial"/>
  <w:b/>
  <w:b-cs/>
  <w:kern w:val="32"/>
  <w:sz w:val="32"/>
  <w:sz-cs w:val="32"/>
  <w:lang w:val="EN-US" w:fareast="EN-US" w:bidi="AR-SA"/>
</w:rPr>
</w:style>
```

As you can see, all of the run properties from the "Heading 1" style are copied into the new "Heading 1 Char" style. The w:link elements retain the association between the two styles by reference to the w:styleId attribute of the other style. Word maintains the link between the styles and honors it by propagating any character property changes in one style to the other. It's possible to create a "synthetic" WordprocessingML document outside of Word that links two styles that do not share the same character properties. However, as soon as you try to change one of the styles within Word, all of the character properties of each get merged together and are synchronized from that point forward.

CHAPTER 3
Using WordprocessingML

While learning WordprocessingML can be fun and interesting in its own right, what's really exciting is the prospect of being able to *process* the information in Word documents in new and fresh ways. No longer are you confined to the world of VBA and the Microsoft object model. In fact, you're not even restricted to using Windows. Once you save a Word document as XML, you can process it using any tool or environment that supports XML. And creating Word documents with such tools is a snap. This chapter explores some tools and potential applications for WordprocessingML, with an emphasis on XSLT. Essentially, what we present here is a mini-cookbook of XSLT scripts for WordprocessingML.

Endless Possibilities

We have to be careful when talking about use cases for generating and processing Word documents. By defining categories too strictly, we might completely ignore possibilities that others have explored or have yet to explore. The purpose of this chapter is to help open your mind as to what's possible now that the expanse of information found in all the world's Word documents is suddenly capable of being unlocked and exposed as XML. The categories and examples in this chapter are only the tip of the iceberg. Perhaps they will help trigger some of your own ideas and creativity. When reading along, if you think of an example that we failed to cover, then we have succeeded in our goal!

That said, you can break down the scripts in this chapter into three basic categories:

- Input is WordprocessingML
- Output is WordprocessingML
- Both input and output are WordprocessingML

We'll cover examples of each of these under the general activities of *creating*, *extracting*, *modifying*, and *converting*. Creation produces WordprocessingML as output; extraction takes WordprocessingML as input; modification both takes

t as output; and conversion either takes

.s output.

Tools

pter, you'll need an XSLT pro-
dalone editions of Word 2003
load and *onsave* stylesheets, as
1 this chapter assume you will
>le, with a command-line pro-
such utility, *msxsl.exe*, at this
lnxml/html/msxsl.asp.

>ft.org) houses some quite use-
g. I personally use Cygwin (a
p://www.cygwin.com) and the
here are also native Windows
at *http://www.zlatkovic.com/*
>ol in the libxml suite is the
nputs an XML document and
1e breaks and indentation), is
\L and for helping to author
; also instrumental in prepar-

processor, with a command-
e XSLT processors you may
sourceforge.net) and Xalan
are Java-based processors.

:essingML documents using
ed character (LF) rather than
l if your documents contain
>edded images, then you will
:e opening the document in

....., ...rd will not be able to open the document correctly,
even though it is well-formed XML. This is arguably a bug in Word's XML
processing behavior, but it can be explained by the fact that the Base64 specification requires that individual lines end with a CRLF sequence in the
canonical Base64 format. Fortunately, there are easy workarounds. For
example, in a Unix or Cygwin environment, you can run the unix2dos command on your file, converting each instance of the LF character to a CRLF
sequence.

Creating Word Documents

It's very easy to create Word documents from XSLT. We saw the definitive "Hello, World" example for WordprocessingML in Chapter 2. Example 3-1 shows the "Hello, World" example for creating a Word document from XSLT.

Example 3-1. Creating a Word document from XSLT

```
<xsl:stylesheet version="1.0"
  xmlns:xsl="http://www.w3.org/1999/XSL/Transform"
  xmlns:w="http://schemas.microsoft.com/office/word/2003/wordml">

  <xsl:template match="/">
    <xsl:processing-instruction name="mso-application">
      <xsl:text>progid="Word.Document"</xsl:text>
    </xsl:processing-instruction>
    <w:wordDocument>
      <xsl:attribute name="xml:space">preserve</xsl:attribute>
      <w:body>
        <w:p>
          <w:r>
            <w:t>Hello, World!</w:t>
          </w:r>
        </w:p>
      </w:body>
    </w:wordDocument>
  </xsl:template>

</xsl:stylesheet>
```

As you can see, there's little to it, beyond slapping xsl:stylesheet and xsl:template elements around the w:wordDocument element. The only additional provisions you need to make are for generating the mso-application PI and the xml:space="preserve" directive in the result. (Using the xsl:attribute element as opposed to a literal xml:space attribute ensures that whitespace will be preserved in the result but not in the stylesheet.)

Obviously, Example 3-1 isn't terribly interesting in its own right. What *is* interesting is how you can extend it. With XSLT's power and a basic knowledge of WordprocessingML at your disposal, you can create dynamic Word documents quite easily. We'll take a look at one example of doing this: generating data-driven tables in Word.

Generating Data-Driven Tables

Oftentimes, Word documents need to contain tabular data. After all, that's what tables were made for. But it can be quite a pain to manually update tabular data in Word, especially when it's large or frequently changing, such as when generating reports from a database. When that data is exposed as XML—a feature increasingly supported among the latest database products, then it becomes quite easy to generate data-driven Word tables using XSLT. Example 3-2 shows an XML document as output from Microsoft Office Access 2003. This example comes straight out of Chapter 8. We've added some indentation for readability.

Example 3-2. An example XML document generated from a database, books.xml

```
<?xml version="1.0" encoding="UTF-8"?>
<dataroot xmlns:od="urn:schemas-microsoft-com:officedata"
xmlns:xsi="http://www.w3.org/2001/XMLSchema-instance"
xsi:noNamespaceSchemaLocation="books.xsd" generated="2003-03-26T13:49:17">
  <books>
    <ISBN>0596005385</ISBN>
    <Title>Office 2003 XML Essentials</Title>
    <Tagline>Integrating Office with the World</Tagline>
    <Short_x0020_Description>Microsoft has added enormous XML functionality to
Word, Excel, and Access, as well as a new application, Microsoft InfoPath.
This book gets readers started in using those features.
    </Short_x0020_Description>
    <Long_x0020_Description>Microsoft has added enormous XML functionality to
Word, Excel, and Access, as well as a new application, Microsoft InfoPath.
This book gets readers started in using those features.
    </Long_x0020_Description>
    <PriceUS>34.95</PriceUS>
  </books>
  <books>
    <ISBN>0596002920</ISBN>
    <Title>XML in a Nutshell, 2nd Edition</Title>
    <Tagline>A Desktop Quick Reference</Tagline>
    <Short_x0020_Description>This authoritative new edition of XML in a
Nutshell provides developers with a complete guide to the rapidly evolving XML space.</
Short_x0020_Description>
    <Long_x0020_Description>This authoritative new edition of XML in a Nutshell
provides developers with a complete guide to the rapidly evolving XML space.
Serious users of XML will find topics on just about everything they need,
including fundamental syntax rules, details of DTD and XML Schema creation,
XSLT transformations, and APIs used for processing XML documents.  Simply put,
this is the only references of its kind among XML books.
    </Long_x0020_Description>
    <PriceUS>39.95</PriceUS>
  </books>
  <books>
    <ISBN>0596002378</ISBN>
    <Title>SAX2</Title>
    <Tagline>Processing XML Efficiently with Java</Tagline>
    <Short_x0020_Description>This concise book gives you the information you
need to effectively use the Simple API for XML, the dominant API for efficient
XML processing with Java.</Short_x0020_Description>
    <Long_x0020_Description>This concise book gives you the information you
need to effectively use the Simple API for XML, the dominant API for efficient
XML processing with Java.</Long_x0020_Description>
    <PriceUS>29.95</PriceUS>
  </books>
</dataroot>
```

Let's say you want to only display the ISBN, title, tagline, and price of each book. You would start by creating an example four-column table from within Word, formatted however you wish. Figure 3-1 shows one such table.

ISBN	Title	Tagline	Price
0596002920	XML in a Nutshell, 2nd Edition	A Desktop Quick Reference	39.95

Figure 3-1. An example table created from within Word

The table headings in Figure 3-1 are formatted differently than the rest of the cells, using a character style called "CellHeading." The rest of the table cells (containing the data) take on the document's "Normal" paragraph formatting.

Once the table template looks how you want it to look, you would save the document as XML. Then, from a text editor, you would adapt the WordprocessingML into an XSLT stylesheet that generates dynamic tables, using documents like *books.xml* (Example 3-2) as input. Example 3-3 shows just such a stylesheet (*booktable.xsl*). The key parts of the stylesheet that make the resulting table dynamic are highlighted.

Example 3-3. Stylesheet for creating a dynamic books table in Word, booktable.xsl

```
<xsl:stylesheet version="1.0"
  xmlns:xsl="http://www.w3.org/1999/XSL/Transform"
  xmlns:w="http://schemas.microsoft.com/office/word/2003/wordml">

  <xsl:output omit-xml-declaration="no" encoding="UTF-8"/>

  <xsl:template match="/">
    <xsl:processing-instruction name="mso-application">
      <xsl:text>progid="Word.Document"</xsl:text>
    </xsl:processing-instruction>
    <w:wordDocument>
      <xsl:attribute name="xml:space">preserve</xsl:attribute>
      <w:styles>
        <xsl:copy-of select="$styles"/>
      </w:styles>
      <w:body>
        <w:tbl>
          <w:tblPr>
            <w:tblStyle w:val="TableGrid"/>
          </w:tblPr>
          <xsl:copy-of select="$heading-row"/>
          <xsl:apply-templates select="/dataroot/books"/>
        </w:tbl>
      </w:body>
    </w:wordDocument>
  </xsl:template>

  <xsl:template match="books">
```

```
  <w:tr>
    <xsl:apply-templates select="ISBN"/>
    <xsl:apply-templates select="Title"/>
    <xsl:apply-templates select="Tagline"/>
    <xsl:apply-templates select="PriceUS"/>
  </w:tr>
</xsl:template>

<xsl:template match="books/*">
  <w:tc>
    <w:p>
      <w:r>
        <w:t>
          <xsl:value-of select="."/>
        </w:t>
      </w:r>
    </w:p>
  </w:tc>
</xsl:template>

<xsl:variable name="heading-row">
  <w:tr>
    <w:tc>
      <w:tcPr>
        <w:tcW w:w="1216" w:type="dxa"/>
      </w:tcPr>
      <w:p>
        <w:r>
          <w:rPr>
            <w:rStyle w:val="CellHeading"/>
          </w:rPr>
          <w:t>ISBN</w:t>
        </w:r>
      </w:p>
    </w:tc>
    <w:tc>
      <w:tcPr>
        <w:tcW w:w="3032" w:type="dxa"/>
      </w:tcPr>
      <w:p>
        <w:r>
          <w:rPr>
            <w:rStyle w:val="CellHeading"/>
          </w:rPr>
          <w:t>Title</w:t>
        </w:r>
      </w:p>
    </w:tc>
    <w:tc>
      <w:tcPr>
        <w:tcW w:w="3770" w:type="dxa"/>
      </w:tcPr>
```

Example 3-3. Stylesheet for creating a dynamic books table in Word, booktable.xsl (continued)

```
        <w:p>
          <w:r>
            <w:rPr>
              <w:rStyle w:val="CellHeading"/>
            </w:rPr>
            <w:t>Tagline</w:t>
          </w:r>
        </w:p>
      </w:tc>
      <w:tc>
        <w:tcPr>
          <w:tcW w:w="838" w:type="dxa"/>
        </w:tcPr>
        <w:p>
          <w:r>
            <w:rPr>
              <w:rStyle w:val="CellHeading"/>
            </w:rPr>
            <w:t>Price</w:t>
          </w:r>
        </w:p>
      </w:tc>
    </w:tr>
  </xsl:variable>

  <xsl:variable name="styles">
    <!-- list of w:style elements -->
  </xsl:variable>

</xsl:stylesheet>
```

The root template rule in Example 3-3 looks similar to Example 3-1; it creates the mso-application PI, the w:wordDocument root element, and the xml:space attribute:

```
    <xsl:template match="/">
      <xsl:processing-instruction name="mso-application">
        <xsl:text>progid="Word.Document"</xsl:text>
      </xsl:processing-instruction>
      <w:wordDocument>
        <xsl:attribute name="xml:space">preserve</xsl:attribute>
```

Since our result document contains some custom styles, the stylesheet needs to output a w:styles element. To save space and reduce clutter, we've encapsulated all of the w:style definitions into a global variable, $styles, and our stylesheet copies that into the w:styles literal result element:

```
    <w:styles>
      <xsl:copy-of select="$styles"/>
    </w:styles>
```

Next, we create the `w:body` and `w:tbl` elements. The resulting table is associated with the `TableGrid` style, which is defined in the result document's `w:styles` element:

```
<w:body>
  <w:tbl>
    <w:tblPr>
      <w:tblStyle w:val="TableGrid"/>
    </w:tblPr>
```

Then, we create the first table row, which is the heading for our table. Just as we did with the `w:style` elements, we put this row definition in another global variable, `$heading-row`, and copied it:

```
<xsl:copy-of select="$heading-row"/>
```

The heading row dictates the width of each column, which means we don't have to define the column width for each of the remaining rows. Word automatically gives them the same width as the heading row.

Finally, we begin processing each books element in the source document:

```
<xsl:apply-templates select="/dataroot/books"/>
```

Elsewhere in the stylesheet, we define the template rules that create the rows and columns for our dynamic table. The template rule for table rows matches up each books element in the source document with a table row in the result. Then, inside the table row, we process the `ISBN`, `Title`, `Tagline`, and `PriceUS` elements, in that order:

```
<xsl:template match="books">
  <w:tr>
    <xsl:apply-templates select="ISBN"/>
    <xsl:apply-templates select="Title"/>
    <xsl:apply-templates select="Tagline"/>
    <xsl:apply-templates select="PriceUS"/>
  </w:tr>
</xsl:template>
```

The template rule for table cells is quite simple. For each element inside the books element that is processed, it creates a table cell containing a paragraph containing a run containing text. The text is simply the string value of the current element in the source document:

```
<xsl:template match="books/*">
  <w:tc>
    <w:p>
      <w:r>
        <w:t>
          <xsl:value-of select="."/>
        </w:t>
      </w:r>
    </w:p>
  </w:tc>
</xsl:template>
```

Now, let's take a look at what the result looks like. Figure 3-2 shows the result of applying *booktable.xsl* (Example 3-3) to *books.xml* (Example 3-2).

ISBN	Title	Tagline	Price
0596005385	Office 2003 XML Essentials	Integrating Office with the World	34.95
0596002920	XML in a Nutshell, 2nd Edition	A Desktop Quick Reference	39.95
0596002378	SAX2	Processing XML Efficiently with Java	29.95

Figure 3-2. The result of applying booktable.xsl to books.xml

Creating dynamic Word documents is now so easy with Word 2003 that it just might be WordprocessingML's "killer app." But before we jump to any conclusions, let's look at some of the other fun things we can do with WordprocessingML.

 While most constructs in WordprocessingML are straightforward to generate using XSLT, there are certain things, such as VBA macros and embedded images, that cannot be generated using vanilla XSLT. That's because they are encoded in WordprocessingML as Base64 binary, and XSLT has no built-in facilities for processing or generating binary data. However, by utilizing XSLT extension functions, you can get around the limitations of standard XSLT. Oleg Tkachenko has demonstrated in a blog entry how an XSLT stylesheet can generate images in a Word document, using XSLT extensions. For more information, see *http://www.tkachenko.com/blog/archives/000106.html*.

Extracting Information from Word Documents

XSLT can also be used to extract information from existing Word documents. This can be useful for tracking document metadata, aggregating document fragments, listing tracked changes—the sky is the limit. In this section, we'll look at three examples: dumping the text of a document, extracting metadata from a document, and listing a document's comments.

Dumping a Document's Text Content

Sometimes, we are only interested in the textual content of a document and not its formatting. Because of the way that WordprocessingML is structured, dumping all the text content of a document is a very straightforward task. In fact, the empty XSLT stylesheet (shown in Example 3-4) gets us pretty close to what we want to do.

Example 3-4. The empty transformation, empty.xsl

```
<xsl:stylesheet version="1.0"
  xmlns:xsl="http://www.w3.org/1999/XSL/Transform">

</xsl:stylesheet>
```

All text content within a Word document is represented using text nodes in the WordprocessingML document. Since the empty stylesheet does not specify any explicit template rules, only the built-in template rules (defined in the XSLT recommendation) are applied. (See *http://www.w3.org/TR/xslt#built-in-rule*.) The built-in rule for elements is to keep processing (apply templates to children), and the built-in rule for text nodes is to copy them. The resulting behavior of the empty stylesheet is that all the text content of the source document is copied to the result tree without any element markup.

While the empty stylesheet provides a useful and easy way to extract the text content of a Word document, the result is not always easy to read. Figure 3-3 shows an example Word document (*textToDump.xml*) that has two paragraphs containing formatted text.

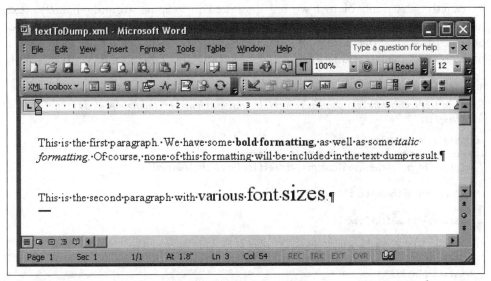

Figure 3-3. A document with two paragraphs and various formatting, textToDump.xml

If we apply the empty stylesheet (*empty.xsl*) to *textToDump.xml*, we will get a result that looks like this:

```
This is the first paragraph  172004-02-22T05:32:00Z2004-02-22T05:40:00Z129196 53
22211.5604This is the first paragraph. We have some bold formatting, as well as
some italic formatting. Of course, none of this formatting will be included in t
he text dump result.This is the second paragraph with various font sizes.
```

While it's true that all the text content of our document is included in this result, there are several problems. For one thing, there is no visible separation between the text in the first and second paragraphs. Also, we see some other gibberish at the beginning of the file; this text comes from the text inside the elements in the o: DocumentProperties element in the source document (o:Title, o:LastSaved, etc.). To get a reasonable text dump, we clearly need a more sophisticated stylesheet than the empty one.

We'll need to handle several other places where non-body text nodes can occur in WordprocessingML:

- If the "Track Changes" feature was turned on when editing the document in Word, then deleted text is represented as text inside w:delText elements.
- Field instruction text is represented as text inside w:instrText elements.
- Embedded objects (VBA, bitmap images, etc.) are represented as Base64-encoded text.
- Headers and footers show up as text nodes deep within the w:sectPr element.

Rather than having to enumerate all of the text that we *don't* want, it's easier to specify exactly what kind of text we *are* interested in keeping around—namely, text inside w:t element descendants of the w:body element. The stylesheet in Example 3-5 does just that. It shows a slightly more sophisticated way to extract the text content of Word documents, taking into consideration the above-mentioned problems with the empty stylesheet.

Example 3-5. Extracting text content grouped by paragraph and excluding non-body text, textDump.xsl

```
<xsl:stylesheet version="1.0"
  xmlns:xsl="http://www.w3.org/1999/XSL/Transform"
  xmlns:w="http://schemas.microsoft.com/office/word/2003/wordml">

  <xsl:output method="text"/>

  <xsl:template match="text()"/>

  <xsl:template match="w:body//w:t/text()">
    <xsl:copy/>
  </xsl:template>

  <xsl:template match="w:p">
    <xsl:apply-templates/>
    <xsl:text>&#xA;&#xA;</xsl:text>
  </xsl:template>

</xsl:stylesheet>
```

First of all, the stylesheet explicitly specifies that the output serialization should be text, which means that no XML markup (e.g., character references) will appear in the result. Rather, it will just be straight text:

```
<xsl:output method="text"/>
```

Unlike the empty stylesheet, the default template rule for text nodes in this stylesheet is to do nothing:

```
<xsl:template match="text()"/>
```

The exception to this rule is that text nodes inside w:t element descendants of the w:body element should be copied:

```
<xsl:template match="w:body//w:t/text()">
  <xsl:copy/>
</xsl:template>
```

Finally, the stylesheet solves the problem of text from multiple paragraphs running together, by explicitly inserting two line breaks after processing the text of each paragraph:

```
<xsl:template match="w:p">
  <xsl:apply-templates/>
  <xsl:text>&#xA;&#xA;</xsl:text>
</xsl:template>
```

If we apply this improved stylesheet (*textDump.xsl*) to the Word document shown in Figure 3-3 (*textToDump.xml*), we'll get a much more reasonable result:

```
This is the first paragraph. We have some bold formatting, as well as some itali
c formatting. Of course, none of this formatting will be included in the text du
mp result.

This is the second paragraph with various font sizes.
```

Now, we only see the actual text content of the document. Also, there is a clear separation between the two paragraphs of the document (two line breaks).

For simple documents, the *textDump.xsl* stylesheet works just fine. However, there are many other formatting features (tables, lists, etc.) that this stylesheet doesn't specifically support. There's a slippery slope between "extraction" and "conversion," but since we're talking about extraction right now, we won't worry about turning this stylesheet into a sophisticated Word-to-text converter. It still gets the job done—it dumps all the text content of the document to the result regardless of what formatting features are used in the source document.

Extracting Metadata

In WordprocessingML, the o:DocumentProperties element stores various pieces of document metadata, such as author, title, and company. An obvious extraction-oriented use case involves pulling that metadata out of the document for isolated processing—or perhaps to load it into a database for continual synchronization with a repository of documents. When extracting data, there are any number of target formats we could choose, such as prettily-formatted HTML, text, or another Word document. For this example, we'll just stick with XML, and, since the o: DocumentProperties element makes up a well-formed document all by itself, we'll just copy it straight on through. Sure, there are much more exciting things we could do, but sometimes all we need is simple extraction. Example 3-6 shows a stylesheet (*extractMetadata.xsl*) for extracting this information.

Example 3-6. A stylesheet for extracting Word document metadata, extractMetadata.xsl

```
<xsl:stylesheet version="1.0"
  xmlns:xsl="http://www.w3.org/1999/XSL/Transform"
  xmlns:w="http://schemas.microsoft.com/office/word/2003/wordml"
  xmlns:o="urn:schemas-microsoft-com:office:office">

  <xsl:output indent="yes"/>

  <xsl:template match="/">
    <xsl:copy-of select="/w:wordDocument/o:DocumentProperties"/>
  </xsl:template>

</xsl:stylesheet>
```

The xsl:output directive in this stylesheet instructs the XSLT processor (by way of indent="yes") to apply some nice whitespace formatting to the result. What "nice" means is completely dependent on the XSLT processor you choose. In the case of the xsltproc tool (see the earlier sidebar "Command-Line Tools"), we apply the command like this:

```
xsltproc extractMetadata.xsl Chapter4.xml
```

And we get the result shown in Example 3-7, which is certainly nice enough.

Example 3-7. The result of applying extractMetadata.xsl to an early draft of Chapter 4

```
<?xml version="1.0"?>
<o:DocumentProperties xmlns:o="urn:schemas-microsoft-com:office:office">
  <o:Title>ORA Word Template</o:Title>
  <o:Author>Evan Lenz</o:Author>
  <o:LastAuthor>Evan Lenz</o:LastAuthor>
  <o:Revision>2</o:Revision>
  <o:TotalTime>1</o:TotalTime>
  <o:LastPrinted>2004-02-10T23:22:00Z</o:LastPrinted>
  <o:Created>2004-02-13T21:39:00Z</o:Created>
  <o:LastSaved>2004-02-13T21:39:00Z</o:LastSaved>
  <o:Pages>1</o:Pages>
  <o:Words>21024</o:Words>
  <o:Characters>119839</o:Characters>
  <o:Company>O'Reilly and Associates, Inc</o:Company>
  <o:Lines>998</o:Lines>
  <o:Paragraphs>281</o:Paragraphs>
  <o:CharactersWithSpaces>140582</o:CharactersWithSpaces>
  <o:Version>11.5604</o:Version>
</o:DocumentProperties>
```

Listing Comments

This book was authored in Word. Our excellent tech reviewers naturally used Word's comment feature to communicate their critique of each chapter. While Word's built-in mechanisms for viewing comments generally sufficed for our purposes, it was sometimes handy to get an alternative summary view of the comments for a particular chapter. With Word 2003, such customized views can be made commonplace. All we had to do was write a simple XSLT stylesheet, save the source document as XML, and apply the stylesheet to the saved WordprocessingML document. Example 3-8 shows a simple XSLT stylesheet (*listComments.xsl*) for extracting comments from a Word document and displaying them in summary form in a new Word document. The relevant code for retrieving the comments is highlighted.

Example 3-8. A stylesheet to list all the comments in a document, listComments.xsl

```
<xsl:stylesheet version="1.0"
  xmlns:xsl="http://www.w3.org/1999/XSL/Transform"
  xmlns:w="http://schemas.microsoft.com/office/word/2003/wordml"
  xmlns:aml="http://schemas.microsoft.com/aml/2001/core">

  <xsl:template match="/">
    <xsl:processing-instruction name="mso-application">
      <xsl:text>progid="Word.Document"</xsl:text>
    </xsl:processing-instruction>
    <w:wordDocument>
      <xsl:attribute name="xml:space">preserve</xsl:attribute>
      <w:body>
        <xsl:apply-templates select="//aml:annotation[@w:type='Word.Comment']"/>
      </w:body>
    </w:wordDocument>
  </xsl:template>

  <xsl:template match="aml:annotation">
    <w:p>
      <w:r>
        <w:t>From <xsl:value-of select="@aml:author"/>:</w:t>
      </w:r>
    </w:p>
    <xsl:copy-of select="aml:content/*"/>
    <w:p/>
  </xsl:template>

</xsl:stylesheet>
```

This stylesheet, since it creates a new Word document as its result, starts off with the standard boilerplate for creating WordprocessingML documents: the mso-application PI, the w:wordDocument root element, and the xml:space attribute:

```
    <xsl:template match="/">
      <xsl:processing-instruction name="mso-application">
        <xsl:text>progid="Word.Document"</xsl:text>
```

```
</xsl:processing-instruction>
<w:wordDocument>
  <xsl:attribute name="xml:space">preserve</xsl:attribute>
```

Then, immediately inside the w:body element, it begins processing each and every aml:annotation element in the document whose w:type attribute is equal to Word. Comment—in short, all of the document's comments:

```
<xsl:apply-templates select="//aml:annotation[@w:type='Word.Comment']"/>
```

The template rule for aml:annotation elements then creates three or more paragraphs in the result for each matched aml:annotation element. The first paragraph lists the author of this comment:

```
<w:p>
  <w:r>
    <w:t>From <xsl:value-of select="@aml:author"/>:</w:t>
  </w:r>
</w:p>
```

The number of middle paragraphs is determined by how many paragraphs are in the comment itself. The comment's paragraphs occur inside the aml:content element. The stylesheet copies all such paragraphs straight through into the result:

```
<xsl:copy-of select="aml:content/*"/>
```

Finally, the stylesheet delineates each comment with an empty paragraph, making the summary view easier to read:

```
<w:p/>
```

Figure 3-4 shows the result of applying this stylesheet (*listComments.xsl*) to an early draft of Chapter 10. As you can see, each comment is identified first by the person who made the comment, and each is separated by a blank paragraph.

Modifying Word Documents

There are plenty of use cases for processing Word documents in which both the input *and* output are Word documents. Since XSLT is a particularly suitable tool for incrementally processing XML, it also works quite nicely for modifying Word documents. An important tool for making incremental modifications to a document is the identity transformation. Example 3-9 shows the canonical identity transformation, exactly as it appears in the XSLT recommendation itself (*http://www.w3.org/TR/xslt#copying*).

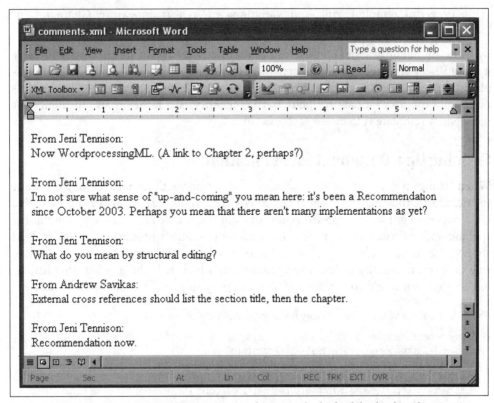

Figure 3-4. The result of applying listComments.xsl to an early draft of this book's Chapter 10

Example 3-9. The identity transformation, identity.xsl

```
<xsl:stylesheet version="1.0"
  xmlns:xsl="http://www.w3.org/1999/XSL/Transform">

  <xsl:template match="@*|node()">
    <xsl:copy>
      <xsl:apply-templates select="@*|node()"/>
    </xsl:copy>
  </xsl:template>

</xsl:stylesheet>
```

What is the identity transformation? Shown in Example 3-9, it's a stylesheet with one template rule that effectively copies the source tree to the result tree unchanged. Here's how it works. The single template rule, with its pattern @*|node( ), matches all elements, attributes, comments, text, and processing instructions in the source tree. Each time the template rule fires, a shallow copy of the node is created (using the xsl:copy element), and templates are applied to all of the node's attributes and children. Thus, the entire source document is recursively copied, one node at a time.

(This powerful template rule and variations of it also appear in Chapter 4, in Example 4-9, *saveDataOnly.xsl*, and Example 4-11, *create-onload-stylesheet.xsl*.)

By using the identity stylesheet as your departure point, you can incrementally alter its default copying behavior by specifying exceptions to the rule, using custom template rules. Since this stylesheet serves as the baseline for each example in this section, we'll use xsl:include to include it (as *identity.xsl*), rather than repeatedly list the identity template rule inside each example.

Cleaning Up a Document for Publication

When Word saves documents, it includes a lot of information that you may not want to include in the final published document that you share with others. Sensitive information might include previous authors, comments, deleted text, revision marks, spelling and grammar error marks, and custom document properties. Example 3-10 shows a stylesheet (*cleanup.xsl*) that removes all such information. Each template rule is accompanied by a descriptive comment, which is highlighted in this listing. Rather than walking through the stylesheet step-by-step, we'll let it speak for itself.

Example 3-10. A stylesheet for cleaning up Word documents, cleanup.xsl

```
<xsl:stylesheet version="1.0"
  xmlns:xsl="http://www.w3.org/1999/XSL/Transform"
  xmlns:w="http://schemas.microsoft.com/office/word/2003/wordml"
  xmlns:o="urn:schemas-microsoft-com:office:office"
  xmlns:aml="http://schemas.microsoft.com/aml/2001/core">

<xsl:include href="identity.xsl"/>

<!-- Normalize document's view and zoom percentage (Normal at 100%) -->
<xsl:template match="w:docPr">
  <xsl:copy>
    <w:view w:val="normal"/>
    <w:zoom w:percent="100"/>
    <xsl:apply-templates select="*[not(self::w:view or self::w:zoom)]"/>
  </xsl:copy>
</xsl:template>

<!-- Remove all but the Author and Title document properties -->
<xsl:template match="o:DocumentProperties">
  <xsl:copy>
    <xsl:copy-of select="o:Author|o:Title"/>
  </xsl:copy>
</xsl:template>

<!-- Remove all custom document properties -->
<xsl:template match="o:CustomDocumentProperties"/>

<!-- Remove all comments and comment references -->
<xsl:template match="aml:annotation[starts-with(@w:type,'Word.Comment')]"/>
```

```
<!-- Remove all spelling and grammar errors -->
<xsl:template match="w:proofErr"/>

<!-- Remove all deletions -->
<xsl:template match="aml:annotation[@w:type='Word.Deletion']"/>

<!-- Remove all formatting changes -->
<xsl:template match="aml:annotation[@w:type='Word.Formatting']"/>

<!-- Remove all insertion marks -->
<xsl:template match="aml:annotation[@w:type='Word.Insertion']">
  <!-- Process content, but do not copy -->
  <xsl:apply-templates select="aml:content/*"/>
</xsl:template>

</xsl:stylesheet>
```

As in all the rest of the examples in this section, we include the *identity.xsl* stylesheet, which establishes the default copying behavior:

```
<xsl:include href="identity.xsl"/>
```

Everything after that is a custom template rule overriding the default behavior for a particular element. A common pattern in this stylesheet is the use of empty xsl: template elements. These are used to *remove* elements from the result document. Since an empty template rule does nothing when fired (overriding the default copying behavior), it effectively strips out the matched node from the resulting document.

This stylesheet by no means provides the definitive cleanup for all the different kinds of documents you might want to publish. More than likely, you'll want to customize it to meet your particular needs. For example, if you don't want to strip out comments, then you would remove the template rule that strips out comments. Similarly, if you want to strip out another kind of information not covered by this stylesheet, then you would add your own template rule for doing that.

Let's take a look at *cleanup.xsl* in action. Figure 3-5 shows a document with lots of cruft—deleted text, tracked insertions (underlined), a tracked formatting change, comments, and some spelling and grammar errors. It was saved in "Web" view with a zoom percentage of 125%.

If we apply *cleanup.xsl* to the WordprocessingML representation of the document shown in Figure 3-5, then we'll get the result shown in Figure 3-6.

Not only have all the comments, proof errors, and tracked changes been removed, but the document's view has also been normalized to the "Normal" view with a zoom percentage of 100%.

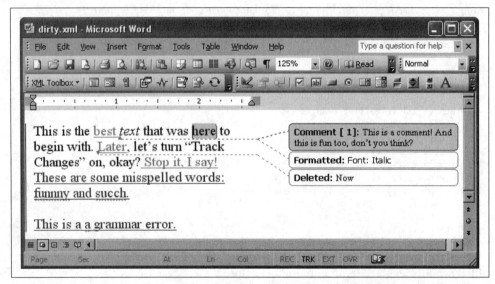

Figure 3-5. A document with comments, tracked changes, and proof errors, dirty.xml

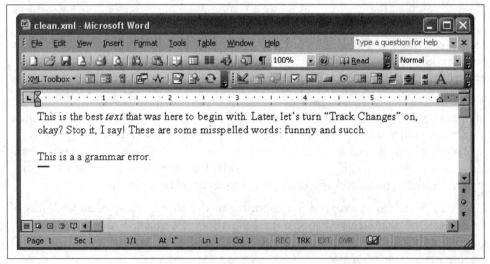

Figure 3-6. clean.xml—the result of applying cleanup.xsl to dirty.xml

 If you publish your documents as WordprocessingML, then you have complete control over what information is contained within them. However, only users that have Word 2003 will be able to view your documents. When publishing .doc files instead, you'll have backward compatibility on your side, but you won't have quite as much control over what metadata is included. For example, whoever last saved the file will be listed under "Last saved by:" (corresponding to the o: LastAuthor element in WordprocessingML).

Removing All Direct (Local) Formatting

A commonly promoted "best practice" in authoring Word documents is to use styles only and no direct formatting. While there is a function in Word that allows you to remove direct formatting (by selecting text and pressing Ctrl-Space), it is sometimes handy to apply such cleanup to an entire document *ex post facto*, using XSLT. Example 3-11 shows a stylesheet that leaves the entire source document intact, except for the paragraph and run properties that have been applied as direct formatting—those are removed.

Example 3-11. A stylesheet for removing direct run and paragraph formatting, removeDirectFormatting.xsl

```
<xsl:stylesheet version="1.0"
  xmlns:xsl="http://www.w3.org/1999/XSL/Transform"
  xmlns:w="http://schemas.microsoft.com/office/word/2003/wordml">

  <xsl:include href="identity.xsl"/>

  <!-- Remove all direct paragraph formatting -->
  <xsl:template match="w:p/w:pPr/*[not(self::w:pStyle)]"/>

  <!-- Remove all direct run formatting -->
  <xsl:template match="w:r/w:rPr/*[not(self::w:rStyle)]"/>

</xsl:stylesheet>
```

Once again, the default behavior for all nodes is to copy them through, because the stylesheet includes the *identity.xsl* stylesheet.

There are two custom template rules in this stylesheet—one for direct paragraph formatting and one for direct run formatting:

```
<xsl:template match="w:p/w:pPr/*[not(self::w:pStyle)]"/>
...
<xsl:template match="w:r/w:rPr/*[not(self::w:rStyle)]"/>
```

Both of these are empty, which means that matched nodes effectively get stripped from the result. All element children of local w:pPr and w:rPr elements get stripped from the document—with one exception in each case. The w:pStyle and w:rStyle elements are preserved. That's because these elements are used not to apply direct formatting but to associate the paragraph or run with a particular style defined in the document. We need to preserve these associations; otherwise, the stylesheet would strip out *all* of the document's formatting, not just direct formatting.

An alternative version of this stylesheet could be customized according to a particular Word template so that, rather than just removing direct formatting, an appropriate style would be used instead. For example, when you come across a run that has italics turned on as direct formatting (using the w:i element), you could convert that to a run that uses the "Emphasis" character style instead (using the w:rStyle element). Such a conversion could go a long way in updating legacy Word documents according to an organization's current authoring standards. Fortunately, with Word 2003's new document protection features (introduced in Chapter 4), such restrictions can now be enforced at authoring time.

Removing Linked "Char" Styles

At the end of Chapter 2, in the section "Linked Styles," we learned about the character styles that Word automatically creates when a user tries to apply a paragraph style to only a portion of a paragraph. Word names the new character style by appending the word "Char" to the end of the existing paragraph style's name. Unfortunately, Word does not provide a way to delete a linked character style without deleting the paragraph style it is linked to. If a user tries to delete the automatically created linked style, Word also deletes the corresponding paragraph style. However, by processing a document's WordprocessingML representation outside of Word, we can overcome that restriction. Example 3-12 shows a stylesheet that strips out linked character styles and references to them, while retaining the paragraph styles they are linked to.

Example 3-12. A stylesheet for removing linked "Char" styles, removeLinkedStyles.xsl

```
<xsl:stylesheet version="1.0"
  xmlns:xsl="http://www.w3.org/1999/XSL/Transform"
  xmlns:w="http://schemas.microsoft.com/office/word/2003/wordml">

  <xsl:include href="identity.xsl"/>

  <!-- Remove all linked character styles -->
  <xsl:template match="w:style[@w:type='character' and w:link]"/>

  <!-- Remove the w:link element from linked paragraph styles -->
  <xsl:template match="w:link"/>

  <!-- Remove w:rStyle elements that refer to linked character styles -->
  <xsl:template match="w:rStyle[@w:val = /w:wordDocument/w:styles/w:style
                     [@w:type='character' and w:link]/@w:styleId]"/>

</xsl:stylesheet>
```

The first custom template rule (overriding the default copying behavior of *identity.xsl*) strips out all linked character styles. A character style definition is easily identified as a w:style element that has a w:type attribute whose value is character and that contains a w:link element:

```
    <xsl:template match="w:style[@w:type='character' and w:link]"/>
```

In addition to stripping out all the linked character styles, we need to strip out otherwise dangling references to them. These occur in two places. First, we strip out the remaining w:link elements (inside linked paragraph style definitions):

```
<xsl:template match="w:link"/>
```

Then, we strip out all of the document's w:rStyle elements that refer to linked character styles:

```
<xsl:template match="w:rStyle[@w:val = /w:wordDocument/w:styles/w:style
                              [@w:type='character' and w:link]/@w:styleId]"/>
```

This pattern is a little more complex, but it is pretty straightforward when you break it down into its respective parts. If we were to translate this pattern into English, it would read something like this:

> "Match all w:rStyle elements whose w:val attribute is equal to the w:styleId attribute of any w:style element that has both a w:link element and a w:type attribute equal to character."

The last part of this translation (beginning with the word "any") could be replaced with simply "any linked character style," thereby reducing the translation to:

> "Match all w:rStyle elements whose w:val attribute is equal to the w:styleId attribute of any linked character style."

Since we know (from Chapter 2) that the w:styleId attribute is precisely what the w:rStyle element refers to in order to associate a run with a particular character style, we can finally reduce the translation to our top-level intent: "Match all references to linked character styles." When a matching w:rStyle element triggers the rule, nothing happens, thereby excluding the linked character style reference from the result.

Adjusting Font Sizes

Word's style inheritance features can help reduce duplicate work when it comes to making global formatting changes to your document. For example, if you want to double the size of all fonts in your document, you may only need to update the "Normal" style, as long as all of your paragraph styles are based on the "Normal" style and do not explicitly override the font size they inherit. However, when that's not the case or when your document also contains direct formatting, such changes have to made in multiple places—a tedious and error-prone process.

Once again, WordprocessingML and XSLT come to the rescue. The stylesheet in Example 3-13 adjusts the font sizes within a document (whether in style definitions or direct formatting) by multiplying them by a factor that you specify (through xsl:param).

Example 3-13. A stylesheet for adjusting the font size of the "Normal" style, adjustFontSize.xsl

```
<xsl:stylesheet version="1.0"
  xmlns:xsl="http://www.w3.org/1999/XSL/Transform"
  xmlns:w="http://schemas.microsoft.com/office/word/2003/wordml">

  <xsl:include href="identity.xsl"/>
```

Example 3-13. A stylesheet for adjusting the font size of the "Normal" style, adjustFontSize.xsl

```
<xsl:param name="factor" select="2"/>

<!-- Adjust all w:sz elements (in style definitions or direct formatting) -->
<xsl:template match="w:sz">
  <w:sz w:val="{floor(@w:val * $factor)}"/>
</xsl:template>

<!-- Account for Word's application default font size (10 points)
     in underived paragraph styles when the w:sz element isn't present  -->
<xsl:template match="w:style[@w:type='paragraph' and
                             not(w:rPr/w:sz) and not(w:basedOn)]">
  <xsl:copy>
    <xsl:apply-templates select="@*|*[not(self::w:rPr)]"/>
    <w:rPr>
      <w:sz w:val="{floor(20 * $factor)}"/>
      <xsl:apply-templates select="w:rPr/*"/>
    </w:rPr>
  </xsl:copy>
</xsl:template>

</xsl:stylesheet>
```

As with the other examples in this section, we include the *identity.xsl* stylesheet module, effecting the default copying behavior of the stylesheet:

```
<xsl:include href="identity.xsl"/>
```

The xsl:param element supplies a default factor of 2, so that the default behavior of the stylesheet (when no external parameters are supplied) is to double the font sizes:

```
<xsl:param name="factor" select="2"/>
```

The first template rule of the stylesheet matches all w:sz elements, whether they occur in a style definition or within a local w:rPr element. The value of the resulting font size is the previous size multiplied by the specified factor. The floor( ) function ensures that the result is an integer:

```
<xsl:template match="w:sz">
  <w:sz w:val="{floor(@w:val * $factor)}"/>
</xsl:template>
```

Our work would be done at this point, if it wasn't for one other scenario we need to handle: paragraph style definitions that do not contain a w:sz element *and* that are not based on (do not derive from) another style. In that case, what is the font size? The answer is: an application default, 10 points (as explained in Chapter 2). To handle that scenario, we use a template rule that matches w:style elements that meet these conditions:

```
<xsl:template match="w:style[@w:type='paragraph' and
                             not(w:rPr/w:sz) and not(w:basedOn)]">
```

We make a shallow copy of the w:style element and then copy all of its attributes and element children, except for the w:rPr element:

```
<xsl:copy>
  <xsl:apply-templates select="@*|*[not(self::w:rPr)]"/>
```

Then, we create the w:sz element, nested inside a new w:rPr element. Its value is the application default (10 points) expressed in hard-coded half-points (20), and multiplied by the specified factor, once again using the floor( ) function to ensure that the result is an integer:

```
<w:rPr>
  <w:sz w:val="{floor(20 * $factor)}"/>
```

Finally, we copy any remaining child elements of the w:rPr element, if present in the source document's style definition:

```
<xsl:apply-templates select="w:rPr/*"/>
```

Now let's take a look at *adjustFontSize.xsl* in action. Figure 3-7 shows an early draft of this book's Chapter 2 (*Chapter2.xml*), using the normal font sizes dictated by the O'Reilly Word template.

Figure 3-8 shows the result of applying *adjustFontSize.xsl* to *Chapter2.xml*, leaving the default factor of 2. As you can see, the font sizes have doubled across the board.

Converting Between WordprocessingML and Other Formats

While it can be very easy to translate simple custom XML formats into WordprocessingML (as we saw with Example 3-1), the reverse is not usually true—at least not when you're interested in preserving all aspects of a document's formatting. The sheer size and complexity of WordprocessingML makes it a very daunting task to write a generic stylesheet for converting WordprocessingML documents into some other format. For that reason, we won't include any actual examples in this section. We can, however, point to some existing work that's being done in this area.

HTML

During the beta program for Office 2003, Microsoft released an XSLT stylesheet for converting WordprocessingML documents to HTML. At just under 4,000 lines long, this stylesheet is an impressive and enlightening look at processing Word documents in XML format. At the time of this writing, Microsoft has not yet released an updated version of the stylesheet. Fortunately, the stylesheet will largely work as-is—provided that you update a few of the top-level namespace declarations. You can find this stylesheet by searching for "wordml" at Microsoft's download center (*http://www.microsoft.com/downloads/search.aspx*). It's quite possible that an updated version of the stylesheet will be available by the time you read this.

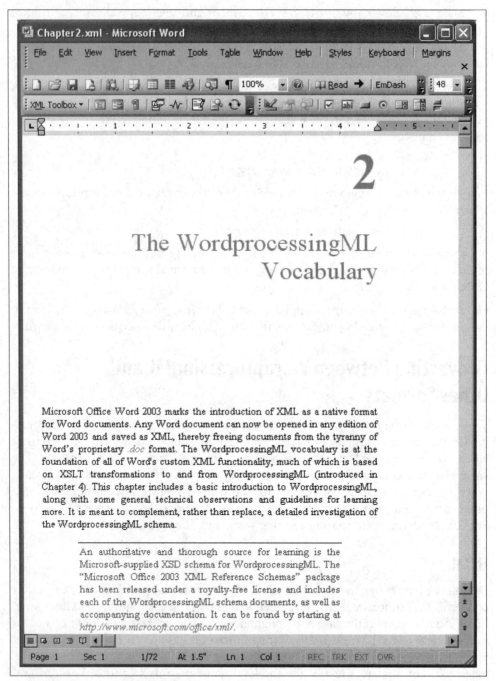

Figure 3-7. A draft of Chapter 2 before font size adjustment

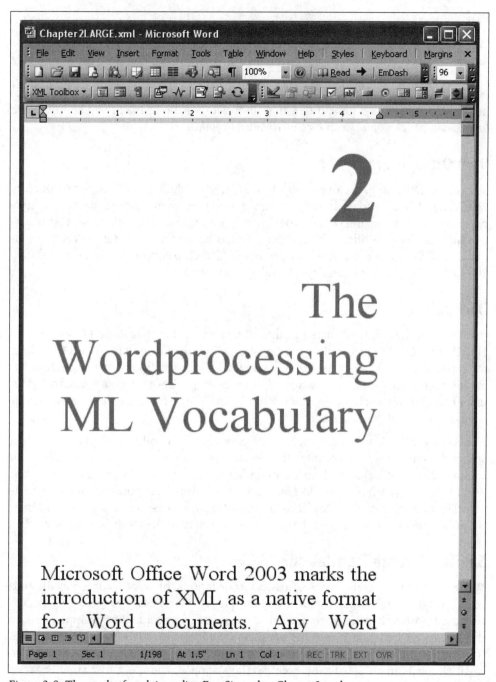

Figure 3-8. The result of applying adjustFontSize.xsl to Chapter2.xml

PDF

Converting Word documents to PDF can, of course, be done using products like Adobe Distiller. However, another possible way to perform this conversion is by way of XSL Formatting Objects (XSL-FO). Antenna House, Inc., maker of a premier XSL-FO processor, has released a (for-pay) XSL stylesheet that does just that. For more information, including some interesting discussion of the problem and solution, see *http://www.antennahouse.com/product/wordmltofo.htm*.

OpenOffice.org

Since OpenOffice.org, the open source alternative to Microsoft Office, saves all of its files using XML format, it only makes sense that there should be translations between WordprocessingML and the OpenOffice.org formats. Of course, this is easier said than done. While nothing significant has been released so far, this is listed on the OpenOffice.org web site as an open issue: "Develop support for Microsoft Office 2003 XML, i.e., WordprocessingML and SpreadsheetML."

Docbook

Just as Norm Walsh has created a suite of stylesheets for transforming Docbook to HTML and XSL-FO, it is only a matter of time before someone releases a stylesheet for converting Docbook to WordprocessingML. Since Docbook provides rich document structure and semantics, while WordprocessingML is only concerned with document formatting, such a conversion would be a "down-translation." Accordingly, it should not, in principle, be difficult.

Converting from WordprocessingML to Docbook, on the other hand, is a much less straightforward task. Certainly the wx:sub-section element (as described in Chapter 2) would be helpful for gleaning hierarchy from the Word document, but overall such a translation would have to be very special-purpose—akin to converting PDF to a meaningful XML format. Usually, such "up-translations" are special-purpose, one-time conversions that must use a variety of heuristics and guesswork.

Special-Purpose Translations

While creating general-purpose, lossless translations of WordprocessingML into other formats is no doubt useful, there are plenty of use cases for creating special-purpose translations specific to particular classes of documents. For example, a set of documents created using the same template could be converted into a custom XML format. This could be done by translating certain parts of the document into custom XML elements in the result, or even by translating paragraph and character styles into custom XML elements. In fact, that's just what part of Chapter 4's primary example does. In the content of press release documents, individual w:p elements are translated to para elements in the result, and certain character styles within the paragraph are translated to custom XML elements in the result.

Creating XML Templates in Word

The standalone and Office 2003 Professional versions of Microsoft Office Word 2003 include additional XML functionality not available in Office 2003 Standard. Specifically, they provide support for custom XML schemas. By providing your own XSD schema, you can create solutions that enable end users to edit custom XML from within Word. While Word's custom XML functionality does not provide as much power as a traditional XML editor, it does give you some helpful building blocks for custom Word-based XML editing applications. Ultimately, if you want to build anything but the simplest XML editing solutions, you will also need to utilize the Document Actions task pane through the use of Smart Document technology, as introduced in Chapter 5.

Clarifying Use Cases

There are two broad use cases for Word's custom XML schema functionality, the first of which is the focus of this chapter:

- Using Word to edit custom XML documents that conform to your schema
- Using custom tags to add richer meaning to Word documents

In many respects, the first use case—using Word as an XML editor—is the most exciting. As XML's role in software engineering grows, one of the most difficult problems continues to be getting end users to create XML documents for all our wonderful back-end systems to process. Word is so familiar and its usage so pervasive that XML editing solutions based on it could take huge steps toward solving this problem. Unfortunately, the extent of Word's built-in custom XML schema functionality leaves a lot to be desired, at least in comparison to other XML editing products on the market. That doesn't mean you won't be able to create fully functional and powerful solutions based on Word, but it does mean you will need to do more actual programming than you might have otherwise expected. Word's base XML schema functionality supports simple business-template use cases (such as memos, purchase orders, and resumes), where the choice of elements used is fixed, there are no optional elements, etc. To handle richer structures such as those found in any document-oriented XML, at least in a user-friendly way, you will need to incorporate Smart Document programming, as described in Chapter 5.

 With the exception of support for mixed content, the InfoPath application provides much of the built-in, schema-driven, and user-friendly structural editing support one might have expected in Word. For more information, see Chapter 10.

The second use case—annotating Word documents with metadata—is essentially another flavor of the business-template scenario. The distinction is that whereas in the first case Word is merely the editor of your underlying data (and in principle could be replaced by any other editor), here you are interested in keeping Word documents around as such, complete with their rich, Word-specific formatting. The XML tags might be used for better document retrieval, or another process might glean the XML data out of the document and into a database, but either way your information is firmly tied to the Word document in which it resides (whether stored as a *.doc* file or as WordprocessingML). Any embedded XML data is supplementary and does not provide the whole story.

This chapter will present the basic components of Word's core XML schema functionality, including related document options and how they are represented in WordprocessingML. We will see how schema attachment, *onload* and *onsave* XSLT stylesheets, placeholder text, and document protection can work together to make a working XML editing solution for Word, according to the first use case mentioned above (using Word as an XML editor).

While this chapter can be seen as a preparation for learning Smart Documents (in Chapter 5), it stands alone in its own right. By the time you are done reading it, you will have traversed a complete XML editing solution in Word—what it is, how it works, and how it was developed. We will push the limits of what can be done with XSLT and Word's base XML functionality to see how far they can take us without venturing into Smart Document programming.

A Working Example

Before we get into the *how* of creating XML editing solutions in Word, let's look at an example of *what* it is we're trying to achieve. This example will reappear throughout the chapter.

Suppose a small Public Relations department wants to create press releases that look good as Word documents but that also can integrate into other systems or that can be published in other formats. Consider also that the people who write such press releases have experience with Word but have no understanding of XML.

By leveraging Word 2003's custom XML schema functionality (in the Office Professional or standalone versions), the IT department can create an XML template[*] for Word that enables end users in the PR department to not only create new press releases in XML but to edit existing ones too. Imagine that they have already defined an XML schema that includes the basic information that a press release needs to represent. Example 4-1 shows just such a schema.

Example 4-1. The press release schema, pressRelease.xsd

```
<xsd:schema xmlns:xsd="http://www.w3.org/2001/XMLSchema"
  xmlns="http://xmlportfolio.com/pressRelease"
  targetNamespace="http://xmlportfolio.com/pressRelease"
  elementFormDefault="qualified">

<xsd:element name="pressRelease" type="prType"/>

<xsd:complexType name="prType">
  <xsd:sequence>
    <xsd:element name="company" type="companyType"/>
    <xsd:element name="contact" type="contactType"/>
    <xsd:element name="date" type="xsd:date"/>
    <xsd:element name="title" type="xsd:string"/>
    <xsd:element name="body" type="bodyType"/>
  </xsd:sequence>
</xsd:complexType>

<xsd:complexType name="companyType">
  <xsd:sequence>
    <xsd:element name="name" type="xsd:string"/>
    <xsd:element name="address" type="addressType"/>
  </xsd:sequence>
</xsd:complexType>

<xsd:complexType name="addressType">
  <xsd:sequence>
    <xsd:element name="street" type="xsd:string"/>
    <xsd:element name="city" type="xsd:string"/>
    <xsd:element name="state" type="xsd:string"/>
    <xsd:element name="zip" type="xsd:integer"/>
    <xsd:element name="phone" type="phoneType"/>
    <xsd:element name="fax" type="phoneType"/>
  </xsd:sequence>
</xsd:complexType>

<xsd:complexType name="contactType">
  <xsd:sequence>
```

---

[*] The word "template" is heavily (and in many ways unavoidably) overloaded in this chapter. It can mean anything from a *.dot* file to an XSLT instruction, from an XML view in Word to an empty XML "skeleton" document. Most often, we use it to mean the general XML editing application, as in "the press release template." Of course, context will be your best guide. Just don't get hung up on thinking it's a technical term; it's not.

Example 4-1. The press release schema, pressRelease.xsd (continued)

```
    <xsd:element name="firstName" type="xsd:string"/>
    <xsd:element name="lastName" type="xsd:string"/>
    <xsd:element name="phone" type="phoneType"/>
  </xsd:sequence>
</xsd:complexType>

<xsd:complexType name="bodyType">
  <xsd:sequence>
    <xsd:element name="para" type="paraType" maxOccurs="unbounded"/>
  </xsd:sequence>
</xsd:complexType>

<xsd:complexType name="paraType" mixed="true">
  <xsd:choice minOccurs="0">
    <xsd:element name="leadIn" type="xsd:string"/>
  </xsd:choice>
</xsd:complexType>

<xsd:simpleType name="phoneType">
  <xsd:restriction base="xsd:string">
    <xsd:pattern value="[0-9]{3}-[0-9]{3}-[0-9]{4}"/>
  </xsd:restriction>
</xsd:simpleType>

</xsd:schema>
```

The XML schema in Example 4-1 declares a title and a body that contains one or more paragraphs. It also contains information about the company making the announcement and the contact person for this press release. Certain fields require their text to conform to a particular format. Specifically, the zip code must be an integer value, the date must conform to the ISO 8601 date format (xsd:date), and each phone number (three in all) must follow a specific format, namely xxx-xxx-xxxx.

Now let's jump to the completed solution. The IT department delivers a single read-only file named *New Press Release.xml* to the PR department. To create a new XML press release, PR department employees simply double-click the file and begin filling out the template. To save their new press release, they select File → Save, as usual. Editing an existing press release is just as easy: double-click the existing press release file, make changes, and save changes. All the while, users need not know that the actual format of the files they are creating and editing is XML, let alone that it conforms to a special schema defined by the IT department.

This sounds simple enough, but what is the editing experience like for the user? How easily can they screw things up? Well, the developers in our imaginary IT department are smart and have figured out a way to use a combination of Word's new XML and document protection features in such a way that users won't be able to screw things up, at least not without some deliberate effort. In fact, they created the solution with several assumptions in mind:

- Users should not have to know anything about XML.
- Users should not be able to inadvertently mess up the template in which they are editing.
- Users should not be required to turn special options on or off.

The last assumption has a catch: while users may not be required to change any settings, they *are* required to leave the default XML and save settings unchanged. As long as they simply edit documents and save them, all should go well. Figure 4-1 shows what the user sees when first opening the *New Press Release.xml* file.

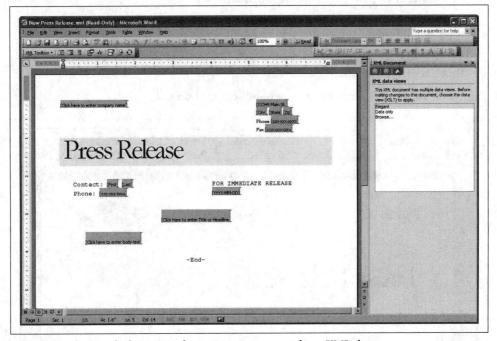

Figure 4-1. The initial editing view for creating new press release XML documents

The gray areas in the "press release" template in Figure 4-1 contain placeholder text, such as "Click here to enter company name." These are familiar constructs in Word templates and are thus familiar to experienced Word users. What is not immediately evident is that these fields correspond to underlying XML elements, a fact which is successfully hidden from the user's view.

The XML Document task pane shown in Figure 4-1 lists one or more "XML data views" that the user can choose from. In this case, the options are "Elegant," "Data only," and "Browse...." Here we only care about the default "Elegant" view, so the user can simply ignore the task pane and begin editing. As soon as they begin editing, the "XML Document" task pane permanently disappears, because it is not possible to choose a different view after changes have been made to the document.

There are several additional things to note about the user's editing experience:

- Invalid values in the document (such as a phone number in the wrong format) are flagged with a pink squiggly underline. The user can see what the problem is by right-clicking it.

- Word will not let the user save the document until all validation errors are resolved.

- Word will not let the user edit any part of the document other than the fields they are supposed to edit. They cannot, for example, inadvertently edit the "Press Release" heading or delete an entire field.

- Word will not let the user apply any direct formatting to the text they enter, e.g., bold or italic.

- Word will not let the user apply any styles to the text they enter, except for those that have been specifically allowed.

Figure 4-2 shows the template after being filled out by a user.

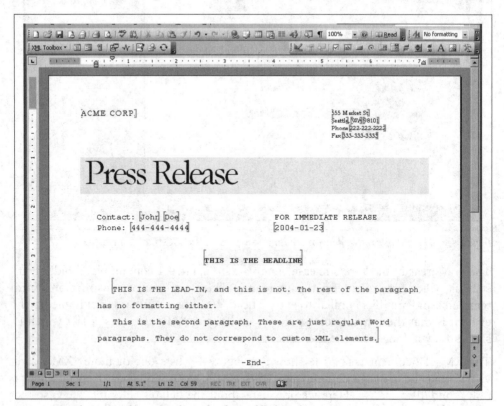

Figure 4-2. The press release template after being filled out by a user

The editable regions shown in Figure 4-2 are bracketed and highlighted yellow; this is the default behavior for when editing restrictions are in force. Also, the squiggly lines are gone, since each value now conforms to its required format.

You can also see in Figure 4-2 that all of the fields in the template are simple text fields—all, that is, except the body of the press release. Here the user can enter multiple paragraphs and can apply some limited formatting. Specifically, there is a character style called "Lead-in Emphasis," which is turned on by default when the user begins typing the body text. This style is used to delineate the lead-in text for the press release. In Figure 4-2, the lead-in text happens to be "This is the lead-in." The only formatting effect that the style has is to make the text all-caps. After the user has finished typing the lead-in text, they can turn the all-caps formatting off by selecting the other special character style they have at their disposal: "No formatting." Figure 4-3 shows the entire style drop-down box that the user sees. Since formatting restrictions are in force, the user only sees the styles they are allowed to apply.

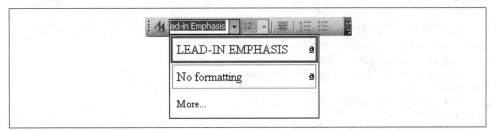

Figure 4-3. The style drop-down box for the press release template

After the user is finished filling out the template and is satisfied with the result, they select File → Save and get the prompt shown in Figure 4-4.

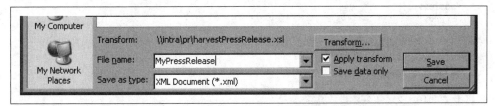

Figure 4-4. Saving the press release XML document

Since the *New Press Release.xml* file is read-only, the user is prompted to select a new file name. Here is where the user must not interfere with the document's default settings. In this case, "Apply transform" must remain checked, and "Save data only" must remain unchecked. After entering a filename (*MyPressRelease.xml* in this case) and clicking "Save," the user is given one final warning before the XML document is saved, shown in Figure 4-5.

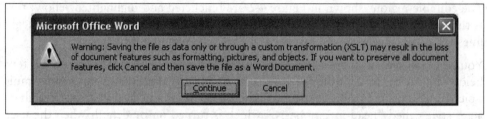

Figure 4-5. Warning the user that WordprocessingML markup may be lost

The purpose of this warning is to alert the user that Word-specific formatting and document features are going to be stripped out of the saved document. Users will have to get used to selecting "Continue," because this is precisely what we want.

Finally, the *MyPressRelease.xml* file is saved with the filename and location that the user chose. The content of this file is shown in Example 4-2 (with indentation added).

Example 4-2. The contents of the press release XML file saved by Word, MyPressRelease.xml

```
<?xml version="1.0" encoding="UTF-8" standalone="no"?>
<?mso-application progid="Word.Document"?>
<pressRelease xmlns="http://xmlportfolio.com/pressRelease">
  <company>
    <name>ACME Corp.</name>
    <address>
      <street>555 Market St.</street>
      <city>Seattle</city>
      <state>WA</state>
      <zip>98101</zip>
      <phone>222-222-2222</phone>
      <fax>333-333-3333</fax>
    </address>
  </company>
  <contact>
    <firstName>John</firstName>
    <lastName>Doe</lastName>
    <phone>444-444-4444</phone>
  </contact>
  <date>2004-01-23</date>
  <title>This is the Headline</title>
  <body>
    <para xml:space="preserve"><leadIn>This is the lead-in,</leadIn> and this is
not. The rest of the paragraph has no formatting either.</para>
    <para xml:space="preserve">This is the second paragraph. These are just regular
Word paragraphs. They do not correspond to custom XML elements.</para>
  </body>
</pressRelease>
```

Note that all of the information that the user entered has been preserved in the final press release XML document. The text in the text-only fields has been preserved verbatim, and the styled paragraphs of the press release body have been converted to our press release schema's custom `para` and `leadIn` elements.

To make subsequent changes to this press release, the user would simply double-click the XML file. Word opens the file and displays the view shown in Figure 4-6. This is very similar to the original template view, the only difference being that all of the fields are already filled out.

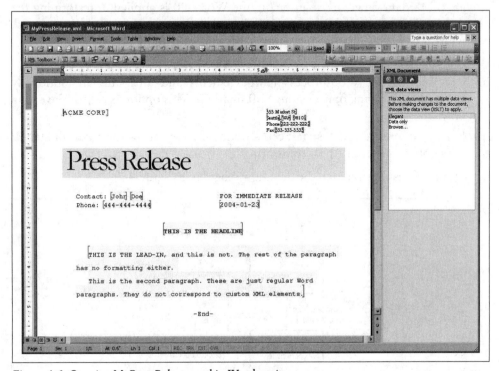

Figure 4-6. Opening MyPressRelease.xml in Word again

When the user is done editing, they simply select File → Save, and the XML file will be updated according to the changes they made.

The rest of this chapter systematically covers the custom XML schema support in Word 2003 (standalone and Office 2003 Professional versions), while continually making reference back to this example. First, we'll detail the components of Word's custom XML schema functionality and how they work. Then, with that knowledge in hand, we'll go step-by-step through the creation of the press release template, in "Steps to Creating the onload Stylesheet." Then, in "Deploying the Template," we'll look at how the application can be deployed in a corporate environment. Finally, we'll conclude by addressing some important limitations of Word's custom XML support.

Word's Processing Model for Editing XML

When Word opens an arbitrary XML document (i.e., an XML document that is not WordprocessingML), that XML document undergoes four primary processes from the time that it is opened to the time that it is saved, in this order:

1. When the document is first opened, an *onload* XSLT stylesheet (variously called an "XML data view" or "solution" in the Word UI) is applied, transforming the raw XML into a WordprocessingML document, usually intermixed, or *merged*, with custom XML tags from the original document.

2. A user edits the document, modifying the underlying merged representation.

3. Upon saving, all WordprocessingML elements and attributes are optionally stripped out, leaving only custom XML markup. This option is called "Save data only."

4. Finally, an *onsave* XSLT stylesheet is optionally applied to the result of step 3. This option is called "Apply transform."

This basic flow is illustrated in the data flow diagram in Figure 4-7.

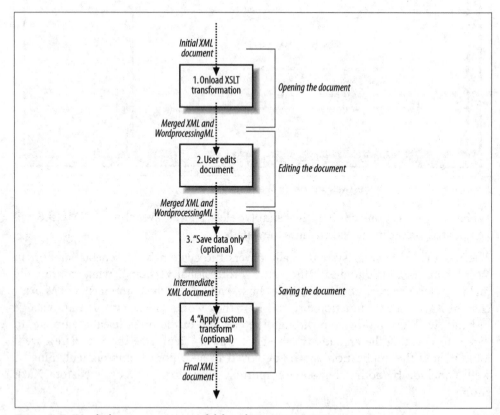

Figure 4-7. Word's basic processing model for editing custom XML

Each arrow in Figure 4-7 represents an XML document in different states of transformation. Each process operates on the result of the previous process. The last two processes, "Save data only" and "Apply custom transform," are both optional. When an option is not elected, you can think of the process as being an identity transform, or a no-op. For example, if "Save data only" is turned off, but "Apply transform" is turned on, then the latter effectively operates on the result of process # 2, "User edits document."

In the next several sections of this chapter, we will detail each of these processes, including how the *onload* XSLT stylesheet is selected, what the merged representation looks like, what editing functionality is available to the user, how the "Save data only" option works and how to set it, and how an *onsave* XSLT transformation is selected. But first let's take a look at the Schema Library, an important ingredient not explicitly evident in this diagram—important because it is consulted both to determine what *onload* XSLT transformation to apply, and to enable on-the-fly schema validation while editing the document.

The Schema Library

The *Schema Library* is a collection of XML schemas and associated files located on the user's machine. Each machine has its own schema library (with each schema library entry having the option of applying to all users or only to the current user). Schema library entries are stored in the Windows Registry. Each schema library entry is identified by a unique target namespace URI, refers to a schema document, and optionally refers to additional supporting files, such as XSLT stylesheets.

The purpose of the schema library is to allow Word (and other applications, such as Excel) to locate schemas and XSLT stylesheets for use in custom XML editing solutions. For example, when Word opens an arbitrary XML document, it checks the schema library to see if there is an appropriate *onload* XSLT stylesheet to apply, based on the namespace of the document's root element. Likewise, once the stylesheet has been applied, it associates the result document with zero or more schemas in the schema library, depending on the namespace declarations present in the result of the *onload* transformation. This association, called "schema attachment," enables on-the-fly schema validation.

Schema library entries can be manually created and modified through the Word UI. Figure 4-8 shows an example of a schema library entry, as shown in the Schema Library dialog, which you can access by selecting Tools → Templates and Add-Ins... → XML Schema → Schema Library....

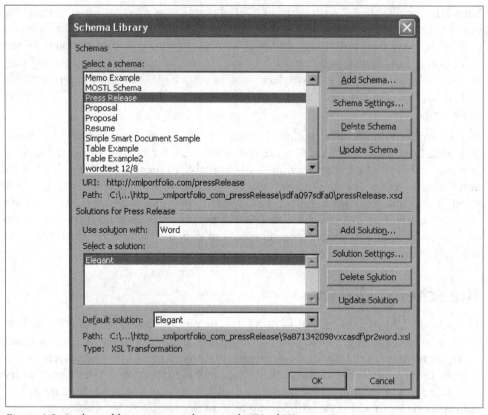

Figure 4-8. A schema library entry as shown in the Word UI

The schema library entry shown in Figure 4-8 is what a user's machine must have in order for our press release example to work correctly. There are several things to note about this entry:

- The friendly name, or alias, for this entry is "Press Release," as shown in the "Select a schema" list.
- The namespace URI is *http://xmlportfolio.com/pressRelease*, which corresponds to the namespace of press release instance documents.
- The schema document is stored as a file named *pressRelease.xsd*.
- There is one "solution" (alias "Elegant") associated with this entry. This refers to an *onload* XSLT stylesheet, which is stored as a file named *pr2word.xsl*. Elsewhere in the Word UI, this is called an "XML data view." Here it is called a "solution."

Although schema library entries can be created manually on each user's machine using the dialog in Figure 4-8, there are also automatic deployment mechanisms that approach the simplicity of the scenario described above (where the IT department simply delivers a *.xml* template file to the PR department). These are discussed briefly later in "Deploying the Template."

Figure 4-9 shows the same schema library entry as represented in the Windows Registry Editor.

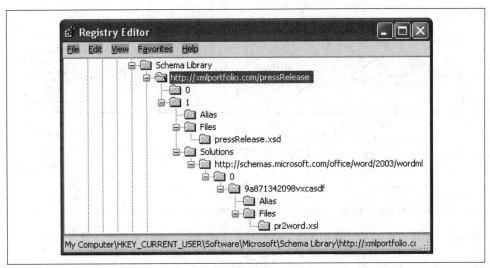

Figure 4-9. A schema library entry as shown in the Windows Registry Editor

Don't worry, you won't be needing to edit your registry directly. We included this just to help demystify how and where the schema library information is stored. Should you want to investigate such entries yourself, the schema library for a specific user is stored under *HKEY_USERS\SID\SOFTWARE\Microsoft\Schema Library*, and the schema library for all users on a machine is stored under *HKEY_LOCAL_MACHINE\SOFTWARE\Microsoft\Schema Library*. As always, be careful you don't make any accidental changes. The Registry Editor is not for the faint of heart.

How the onload XSLT Stylesheet Is Selected

When Word opens an XML file, it first checks to see if the file is a WordprocessingML document, by comparing the namespace URI of the root element with the WordprocessingML namespace (*http://schemas.microsoft.com/office/word/2003/wordml*). If they are not equal, then Word applies an XSLT transformation to the document. Which stylesheet it applies depends on whether there is an entry in the machine's schema library that corresponds to the namespace of the document's root element, and whether that entry has an accompanying XSLT "solution." If Word does not find one, it applies its own default XSLT stylesheet. The flow chart in Figure 4-10 details this logic.

We can relate this back to our press release example very easily. When an employee in our imaginary PR department opens an XML document whose root element's namespace is http://xmlportfolio.com/pressRelease, then Word will apply the

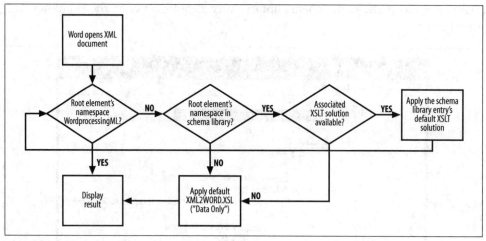

Figure 4-10. How Word decides which XSLT stylesheet to apply, if any

default XSLT stylesheet associated with the "Press Release" solution. This is assuming that the user's machine has the schema and accompanying stylesheets registered in its schema library (as was reflected in the example "Schema Library" dialog in Figure 4-8). So the sequence (with respect to the flow chart in Figure 4-10) goes like this:

1. Word opens a press release XML document.
2. Is the root element's namespace the WordprocessingML namespace? No.
3. Is the root element's namespace in the schema library? Yes.
4. Does that schema library entry have an associated XSLT solution? Yes.
5. Word applies the "Elegant" stylesheet, *pr2word.xsl*, to our press release document.
6. Is the result document's root element in the WordprocessingML namespace? Yes, now it is.
7. Word displays the result.

In Figure 4-6, we saw an example of the result of this sequence—Word displaying the "Elegant" view of a newly opened press release document.

On the other hand, if a user was to open a press release document without ever having installed the Press Release schema in their machine's schema library, then the sequence would be different:

1. Word opens a press release XML document.
2. Is the root element's namespace the WordprocessingML namespace? No.
3. Is the root element's namespace in the schema library? No.
4. Word applies its own default XSLT stylesheet.
5. Word displays the result.

In this case, the user gets a very different view of the XML document, without any custom formatting specific to press releases, and without any document protection features (editing and formatting restrictions) enabled. Figure 4-11 shows an example of Word's generic view for arbitrary XML documents. This view is called "Data only" in the Word UI (not to be confused with the "Save data only" Save option).

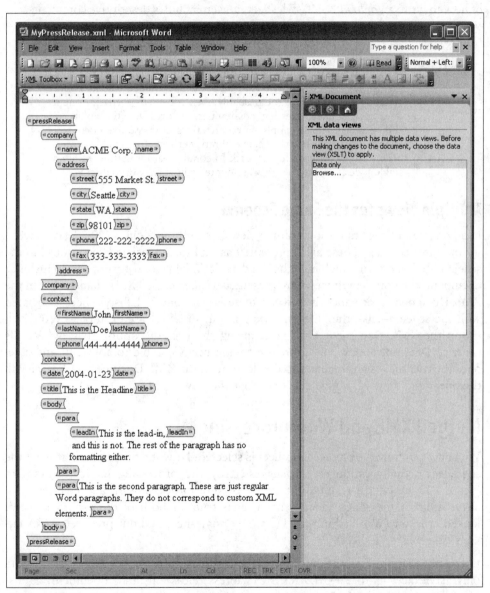

Figure 4-11. The "Data only" view—what Word displays when opening an arbitrary XML document

What we see in Figure 4-11 is the result of applying Word's default *onload* XSLT stylesheet to the press release XML document from Example 4-2. You can find Word's default *onload* stylesheet on your hard disk at *C:\Program Files\Microsoft Office\OFFICE11\XML2WORD.XSL*. This *XML2WORD.XSL* file contains the actual stylesheet that Word executes to display the "Data only" view. It is a good example of how to write an *onload* XSLT stylesheet; it even includes descriptive comments.

> The loop that is present in the flow chart in Figure 4-10 reflects the fact that it is possible to create a switching pipeline of XSLT transformations, where the next stylesheet in the chain is determined based on the namespace of the previous result document's root element. This is certainly not a normal (or probably even intended) scenario, but it does raise some interesting possibilities. It gives you the ability to choose which view to apply based on values in the source document (assuming the necessary schema library entries). It probably always makes the most sense to just stick to conditional formatting within a single stylesheet, but, hey, it was an interesting behavior to discover.

Multiple Views for the Same Schema

It is possible in Word to create multiple views, i.e., multiple *onload* XSLT stylesheets, for the same schema. These are represented as multiple associated "solutions" in the schema library, one of which must be the default. When a user first opens an instance document, the non-default views are presented as alternative "XML data views" in the XML Document task pane. Even when there is only one XSLT stylesheet associated with the schema—like the "Elegant" view in our press release example—Word still shows the XML Document task pane, giving the user the option to view Word's generic "Data only" view, or to browse to another XSLT file to apply. In any case, once the user makes any changes to the document, the XML Document task pane will disappear and they will not be able to change the view again.

Merged XML and WordprocessingML

We have seen how the *onload* stylesheet is selected. Now it's time to look at what the stylesheet actually produces. As suggested by the processing model diagram in Figure 4-7, the typical result is a mixture of WordprocessingML and custom XML elements from the source document. That is true for both of the examples we've looked at so far (Word's built-in "Data only" stylesheet and our press release example's "Elegant" stylesheet).

In the last section, Figure 4-11 showed the result of applying Word's default "Data only" stylesheet (*XML2WORD.XSL*) to a press release instance document, as displayed in the Word UI. The stylesheet generates paragraphs corresponding to the original XML document's element hierarchy, indented to reflect the element nesting. The labeled start and end tags (colored pink), such as pressRelease, company, and name, represent intervening elements not in the WordprocessingML namespace. These custom tags are also included in the WordprocessingML representation; they do not exist separately. They are *merged* together into one document.

Example 4-3 shows an excerpt of the result of this transformation. You can get to the full representation from within Word either by re-saving the document as XML (un-checking the "Save data only" checkbox in the "Save As..." dialog box first) or by viewing the WordprocessingML source using the handy XML Toolbox we introduced in Chapter 2. In this excerpt, indentation has been added for readability, and custom tags from the original source XML document have been highlighted.

Example 4-3. WordprocessingML with merged custom XML elements

```
<w:body>
  <wx:sect>
    <ns2:pressRelease>
      <w:p/>
      <ns2:company>
        <w:p>
          <w:pPr>
            <w:ind w:left="360"/>
          </w:pPr>
        </w:p>
        <ns2:name>
          <w:p>
            <w:pPr>
              <w:ind w:left="720"/>
            </w:pPr>
            <w:r>
              <w:t>ACME Corp.</w:t>
            </w:r>
          </w:p>
        </ns2:name>
        <ns2:address>
          <w:p>
            <w:pPr>
              <w:ind w:left="720"/>
            </w:pPr>
          </w:p>
          <ns2:street>
            <w:p>
              <w:pPr>
                <w:ind w:left="1080"/>
              </w:pPr>
              <w:r>
                <w:t>555 Market St.</w:t>
              </w:r>
            </w:p>
          </ns2:street>
          <ns2:city>
            <w:p>
              <w:pPr>
                <w:ind w:left="1080"/>
```

```
            </w:pPr>
            <w:r>
              <w:t>Seattle</w:t>
            </w:r>
          </w:p>
        </ns2:city>
        <!-- ... -->
        <w:p>
          <w:pPr>
            <w:ind w:left="720"/>
          </w:pPr>
        </w:p>
      </ns2:address>
      <w:p>
        <w:pPr>
          <w:ind w:left="360"/>
        </w:pPr>
      </w:p>
    </ns2:company>
    <!-- ... -->
    <w:p/>
  </ns2:pressRelease>
  <w:sectPr>
    <w:pgSz w:w="12240" w:h="15840"/>
    <w:pgMar w:top="1440" w:right="1800" w:bottom="1440" w:left="1800" w:header="720"
     w:footer="720" w:gutter="0"/>
    <w:cols w:space="720"/>
    <w:docGrid w:line-pitch="360"/>
  </w:sectPr>
  </wx:sect>
</w:body>
```

The indentation of each paragraph in this result is defined using the w:ind element. The value of the w:left attribute in each case is computed (by *XML2WORD.XSL*) based on the paragraph's depth within the merged source document's element hierarchy.

The ns2 namespace prefix on each of the custom XML element names is an auto-generated prefix mapped to the press release namespace, *http://xmlportfolio.com/ pressRelease*, which is declared on the w:wordDocument root element (not shown in this excerpt). Each custom XML element is an intervening element in the hierarchy between w:p elements and the w:body element (ignoring the intervening wx:sect element). Wherever a w:p element may occur, so may a custom XML element. All of the custom XML elements in this example are block-level custom elements, meaning that they occur as siblings and parents of w:p or w:tbl elements (just w:p elements in this example).

Custom XML elements must be present for on-the-fly schema validation to work correctly. Also, by keeping the XML tags around, it is easy to preserve them when the document is saved, simply by stripping out all of the WordprocessingML markup (through the process called "Save data only," which we'll take a closer look at).

Although the result document of an *onload* XSLT transformation must be a WordprocessingML document, strictly speaking it is not required to have any custom XML tags. However, in both of the examples shown so far—Word's built-in "Data only" stylesheet (*XML2WORD.XSL*), and our press release example's "Elegant" stylesheet (*pr2word.xsl*)—the result does include custom XML tags. (The reason you can't see them in the "Elegant" view is that they are hidden by turning off the "Show XML Tags" option; see the next section.)

The only time you might not want to use custom tags is when you are sure you can translate from the plain WordprocessingML format back to your custom XML format when the user saves the document (using an *onsave* XSLT stylesheet), and when you don't need schema validation. By using styles in conjunction with editing and/or formatting restrictions, you may be able to pull this off. Your *onload* and *onsave* XSLT stylesheets would need to translate between your custom XML elements and special editing regions or styles that you have set up for this purpose. In fact, part of our press release example does just this, as we'll see later in the section called "The 'Apply Custom Transform' Document Option." But even in that case, we rely on the use of custom XML tags and on-the-fly validation for other parts of the editing view.

The "Show XML Tags" Option

Another thing to note about the pink tags displayed in Word's "Data only" view is that they can be made invisible. Although the XML Structure task pane (which we'll introduce later) includes a checkbox for turning "Show XML Tags" on and off, there is also a quick keystroke command that will do the trick. Ctrl-Shift-X toggles this option on and off. For example, if you hit Ctrl-Shift-X after opening the document we saw in Figure 4-11, then the tags will disappear, leaving the view shown in Figure 4-12.

The only difference between Figure 4-11 and Figure 4-12 is that the "Show XML tags" option is turned off in Figure 4-12; otherwise, all of the document formatting is identical.

Word's generic "Data only" view and our press-release-specific "Elegant" view both contain custom XML tags. The primary visible difference between them is that "Show XML tags" is turned on in the "Data only" view but turned off in the "Elegant" view. If a particular document does not dictate whether the option should be turned on or off, then Word defaults to the last setting chosen within the Word application. For this reason, both stylesheets explicitly specify the intended setting,

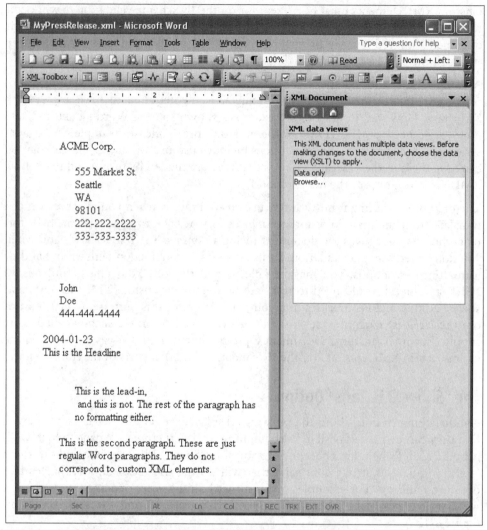

Figure 4-12. The "Data only" view with "Show XML tags" turned off

using the w:showXMLTags literal result element inside the w:docPr element. Here is the relevant excerpt from *XML2WORD.XSL*, Word's default "Data only" stylesheet:

```
        <!-- set Word document properties for raw XML - save as raw XML and
  show XML tags in the document -->
        <w:docPr>
            <w:view w:val="web" />
            <w:removeWordSchemaOnSave w:val="on" />
            <w:showXMLTags w:val="on" />
        </w:docPr>
```

As you can see, the w:showXMLTags option has the explicit value of on. In contrast, the "Elegant" stylesheet for press releases, *pr2word.xsl*, explicitly turns this document option *off*:

```
<w:docPr>
  <!-- ... -->
  <w:showXMLTags w:val="off"/>
</w:docPr>
```

Just to prove that the custom XML elements really are present in the "Elegant" press release view, Figure 4-13 shows what the view would look like if a user turned "Show XML tags" on, for example, by pressing Ctrl-Shift-X.

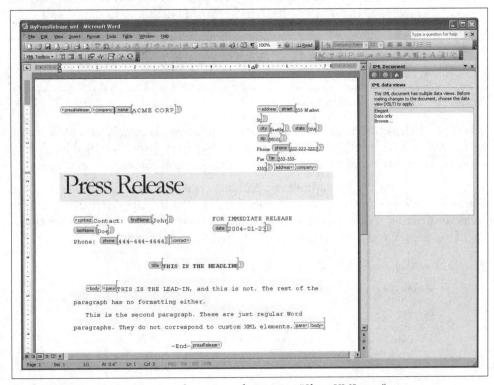

Figure 4-13. The "Elegant" press release view after turning "Show XML tags" on

Block-Level, Run-Level, Row-Level, and Cell-Level Tags

In the merged representation of custom XML and WordprocessingML that we saw in Example 4-3, there were only block-level custom tags, i.e., custom XML elements that occurred as siblings and parents of w:p (or w:tbl) elements. As it happens, custom XML elements may also occur at other places within the WordprocessingML document hierarchy. They may occur as "inline," or run-level, elements (siblings and parents of w:r elements), row-level elements (siblings and parents of w:tr elements), and cell-level elements (siblings and parents of w:tc elements). In each case, they behave slightly differently. In this section, we'll examine block-level and run-level custom tags. See "Table Rows and Repeating Elements" later for a discussion of row-level and cell-level custom tags.

Run-level custom tags are necessary to support multiple elements within the same paragraph. Whenever mixed content is needed, run-level tags are necessary. Word renders run-level tags slightly differently than their block-level, row-level, and cell-level counterparts. Instead of labeling both the start and end tags, Word labels only the start tag and colors both the start and end tags solid pink. Figure 4-14 shows a close up of Word's block-level and run-level tags in an excerpt from our original press release template (with "Show XML tags" turned on).

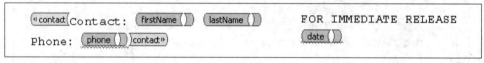

Figure 4-14. Block-level versus run-level tags

The contact element is a block-level tag. It contains two paragraphs and itself is contained within a table cell, which, like the main document body, is a legal block-level context. The firstName, lastName, phone, and date elements are all run-level tags.

Example 4-4 shows the WordprocessingML that corresponds to the visual excerpt in Figure 4-14. We've left out some details for now (particularly having to do with styles and editing restrictions) so that it would be easy to follow the basic structure. All of the custom tags within this excerpt are highlighted.

Example 4-4. Block-level and run-level custom tags in WordprocessingML

```
<w:tbl>
  <!-- ... -->
  <w:tr>
    <w:tc>
      <w:tcPr><!-- ... --></w:tcPr>
      <ns0:contact>
        <w:p>
          <w:r>
            <w:t>Contact: </w:t>
          </w:r>
          <ns0:firstName w:placeholder="[First]">
            <w:r>
              <w:t/>
            </w:r>
          </ns0:firstName>
          <w:r>
            <w:t> </w:t>
          </w:r>
          <ns0:lastName w:placeholder="[Last]"/>
            <w:r>
              <w:t/>
```

```
          </w:r>
        </ns0:lastName>
      </w:p>
      <w:p>
        <w:r>
          <w:t>Phone: </w:t>
        </w:r>
        <ns0:phone w:placeholder="[xxx-xxx-xxxx]"/>
          <w:r>
            <w:t/>
          </w:r>
        </ns0:phone>
      </w:p>
    </ns0:contact>
  </w:tc>
  <w:tc>
    <w:tcPr><!-- ... --></w:tcPr>
    <w:p>
      <w:r>
        <w:t>FOR IMMEDIATE RELEASE</w:t>
      </w:r>
    </w:p>
    <w:p>
      <ns0:date w:placeholder="[YYYY-MM-DD]"/>
        <w:r>
          <w:t/>
        </w:r>
      </ns0:date>
    </w:p>
  </w:tc>
  </w:tr>
</w:tbl>
```

Once again, the namespace prefix (ns0) is an automatically generated prefix mapped to the namespace URI for our press release schema. The ns0:contact element is a block-level element, in that it is a parent of w:p elements and could have w:p (or w:tbl) element siblings. The ns0:firstName, ns0:lastName, ns0:phone, and ns0:date elements are all run-level elements, in that they are contained in run-level contexts—as children of w:p elements and as siblings of w:r elements. They themselves also contain w:r elements. Although all of these elements occur inside a table, none of them happen to occur as row-level or cell-level elements.

Placeholder Text

Another thing that Example 4-4 shows is how placeholders for custom XML elements are represented in WordprocessingML. The placeholder text is a property of the element instance itself, represented by the w:placeholder attribute. Placeholder text is only visible on an element field when the "Show XML tags" option is turned off, when the element is a leaf node (i.e., it contains no other custom XML tags), and when the element is currently empty of any text content. Figure 4-15 shows what the placeholder text looks like for this excerpt, after turning "Show XML tags" back off.

Figure 4-15. Placeholder text

Placeholder text can be applied to any custom XML tag, whether block-level, run-level, row-level, or cell-level.

Table Rows and Repeating Elements

Without the help of Smart Documents, end users normally won't be able to create or delete custom XML elements (let alone attributes) in a reliable and user-friendly way. Instead, they are limited to filling out static templates of fixed XML elements. For the most part, this scenario is what our press release example illustrates. However, you can enable end users to edit a repeating list of XML elements without invoking Smart Document technology by exploiting a special property of row-level custom XML tags.

Here's how it works. Given a table row that has a row-level custom tag applied to it, the user can create new rows in the table, complete with custom tags, simply by hitting the Tab key. This is easiest to explain by example. Consider the WordprocessingML document in Example 4-5. It contains a table with one row and two cells, each of which are contained within custom XML elements. Appropriately named, the myRow element is a row-level tag, and the myCell1 and myCell2 elements are cell-level tags.

Example 4-5. A table with row-level and cell-level custom tags

```
<?xml version="1.0"?>
<?mso-application progid="Word.Document"?>
<w:wordDocument xmlns:w="http://schemas.microsoft.com/office/word/2003/wordml">

  <w:body>
    <myRoot>
      <w:p/>
      <w:tbl>
        <myRow>
          <w:tr>
            <myCell1>
              <w:tc>
                <w:tcPr>
                  <w:tcW w:w="4000" w:type="dxa"/>
                </w:tcPr>
                <w:p/>
```

```
            </w:tc>
          </myCell1>
          <myCell2>
            <w:tc>
              <w:tcPr>
                <w:tcW w:w="4000" w:type="dxa"/>
              </w:tcPr>
              <w:p/>
            </w:tc>
          </myCell2>
        </w:tr>
      </myRow>
    </w:tbl>
    <w:p/>
  </myRoot>
</w:body>

</w:wordDocument>
```

Figure 4-16 shows that the user can easily create new rows in this document just by hitting the Tab key at the end of each row. Each new row is contained within a myRow element, and each row contains myCell1 and myCell2 elements. The final product you deliver to end users, of course, will have "Show XML tags" turned off, and will probably include some meaningful labels, etc.

This behavior also holds true for cell-level custom tags regardless of whether they are contained in a custom row-level tag. For example, if we removed the myRow tags from Example 4-5, the myCell1 and myCell2 elements would still repeat when the user inserts a new row into the table. Even block-level custom tags inside table cells exhibit this behavior—provided that the initial block-level custom tag contains the entire content of the table cell, i.e., it has no sibling w:p or w:tbl elements. Run-level tags in table cells never behave this way; they are never automatically replicated on table row insertion.

When a new row is created, the newly created XML element automatically adopts the same placeholder text that the original had. However, custom XML attributes (which, as we'll see, are represented as literal attributes on custom XML elements) are not replicated.

You can leverage the unique behavior of custom tags and table rows to allow end users to create new instances of a repeating element type declared in your schema. Unfortunately, apart from the visible schema violation flags, the definitions in your schema have no effect on the behavior of the table. If a custom XML tag is wired to a table row or cell in one of the ways described above, then Word will replicate that tag on row insertion, regardless of how the element is declared in the schema.

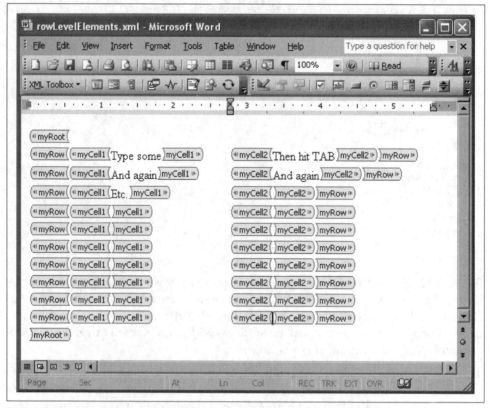

Figure 4-16. Using table rows to create repeating elements

Attaching Schemas to a Document

A given WordprocessingML document can have one or more schemas "attached" to it. The purpose of schema attachment is to enable two things:

- On-the-fly schema validation as the user edits the document
- Schema-driven editing functionality

Schema validation happens automatically as a user edits the document. If a particular element declared in an attached schema is present in the document and does not conform to the type defined in the schema, then Word will flag this as an error. We've seen examples of this in our press release example, for certain simple types such as xsd:date.

Schema-driven editing functionality is exposed through the XML Structure task pane (covered below) and the Document Actions task pane (covered in Chapter 5).

The Word UI allows you to manually attach schemas to the currently open document. Figure 4-17 shows the appropriate dialog, which you can access by selecting Tools → Templates and Add-Ins → XML Schema.

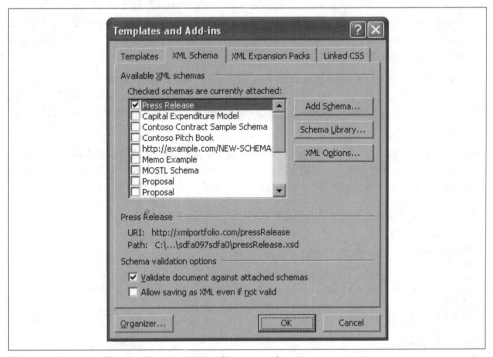

Figure 4-17. Manually attaching an XML schema to a document

The "Available XML schemas" list contains the aliases for all of the schemas in the schema library. In this example, the Press Release checkbox is checked, which means that the press release schema is attached to the current document. Multiple schemas can be attached to the same document, just as elements from multiple namespaces can be used in the same XML document.

The Add Schema... button lets you browse for an XSD schema document file in order to add it to your machine's schema library. By default, it also attaches the schema to the document—automatically checking the corresponding checkbox that newly appears in the "Available XML schemas" list. The Schema Library button opens the Schema Library dialog, which we looked at earlier.

Demystifying Schema Attachment

If all you ever do is manually attach schemas through the Word UI, the process of "schema attachment" may seem a little mysterious. The first thing to do is to stop thinking of it as a *process*. Instead, think of it as a *property* of the underlying Word-processingML document. Secondly, it's important to understand that Word treats namespaces and schemas as virtually synonymous. That a "schema is attached" to a document means nothing more than the fact that a non-WordprocessingML namespace declaration is present somewhere inside the WordprocessingML document. A "non-WordprocessingML namespace declaration" is a declaration for any namespace other than the namespaces reserved for Word that were introduced in Chapter 2. So when Word says that a schema is attached to a document, it really means that a *namespace* is attached.

The fact that a schema is attached to the document is independent of whether a corresponding schema library entry is present on the current user's machine. It doesn't even matter if the document contains an element or attribute that uses the namespace.

Example 4-6 shows a simple WordprocessingML document with a schema attached, i.e., with a namespace declaration that is not among one of Word's reserved namespaces.

Example 4-6. A WordprocessingML document with a "schema attached"

```
<?xml version="1.0"?>
<?mso-application progid="Word.Document"?>
<w:wordDocument
  xmlns:w="http://schemas.microsoft.com/office/word/2003/wordml"
  xmlns:foo="http://xmlportfolio.com/pressRelease">

  <w:body/>

</w:wordDocument>
```

If someone in our imaginary PR department opened this document in Word and selected Tools → Templates and Add-Ins… → XML Schema, they would see something very similar to the dialog box we saw in Figure 4-8 (assuming they already have the Press Release schema in their schema library). Specifically, the Press Release checkbox would be checked. As far as Word is concerned, the mere presence of the namespace declaration (anywhere in the document) means that the schema is attached, regardless even of whether any elements or attributes in the document use the namespace.

What happens if the user doesn't have a corresponding schema library entry? In that case, the schema is no less attached, because we've defined "schema attachment" as the presence of a non-WordprocessingML namespace declaration. However, in this case, the attached schema would be considered "unavailable." Figure 4-18 shows how the Word UI handles this scenario.

As you can see, a checkbox is still checked, meaning that "a schema is attached." The only difference is that, since there is no corresponding schema library entry, this schema is considered to be "Unavailable." And without a corresponding XSD schema document, schema validation and schema-driven editing are not possible.

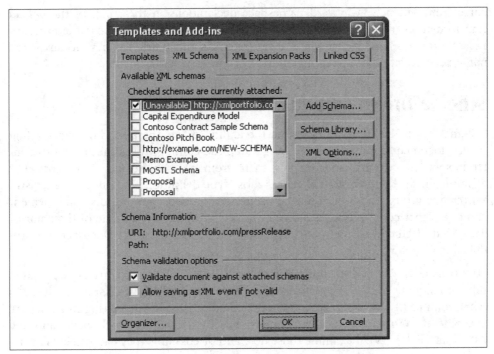

Figure 4-18. An attached, but unavailable, schema

Thus, for schema validation to work correctly, two conditions must hold:

- The schema must be attached (the namespace must be declared in the document)
- The schema must be available (in the machine's schema library).

Now let's relate all of this back to our primary use case—using Word as an XML editor. If you recall the basic processing model, the first thing that happens when Word opens an arbitrary XML document is that an XSLT stylesheet is applied to it, converting it to WordprocessingML. Even though the schema library is consulted to see which XSLT stylesheet to apply (based on the namespace of the document's root element), no schemas have been attached at this point.

Whether a schema is ultimately attached to the document that the user edits is completely determined by whether the result of the *onload* XSLT transformation includes any non-WordprocessingML namespace declarations. Of course, if the result document contains any custom XML elements in your schema's namespace, then the schema will *de facto* be attached (because you can't have an element without declaring its namespace). And since schema validation is usually only useful when custom XML elements are already present, schema attachment is usually an automatic thing you don't have to think about; it just happens. Even so, understanding *how* it works is helpful for debugging and for explaining where unwanted "unavailable" schemas come from—namely, wayward namespace declarations in the result of the *onload* transformation. (The *onload* XSLT stylesheets will therefore often use the exclude-result-prefixes and extension-element-prefixes attributes to prevent unwanted namespace declarations appearing in the WordprocessingML document.)

Schema-Driven Editing

Schema-driven XML editing describes the ability to give the user choices according to the document context they are in, guiding the editing process according to constraints in the schema, and keeping them from creating invalid documents. For example, in the context of an element whose type definition consists of an exclusive xsd:choice group, the user could be prompted to choose among the valid element choices in that context but disallowed from selecting more than one of the choices. This kind of guided editing perfectly describes the aim of Smart Documents, introduced in Chapter 5.

Unfortunately, Word does not provide any sort of robust, schema-driven editing functionality out of the box. (Once again, check out InfoPath in Chapter 10, if that's what you need.) However, there is some limited schema-aware editing functionality available in Word, specifically through the XML Structure task pane and the Attributes dialog. We'll examine those now and discuss how they can still be useful.

The XML Structure Task Pane

The XML Structure task pane is available whenever a document has a schema attached to it. It provides a tree view of the custom XML elements in the merged instance document. Figure 4-19 shows the XML Structure task pane for our press release template.

The tree view shows the local name of each custom XML element in the document. The small yellow "X" icons represent schema validation errors. Since this document is our empty press release template, a number of elements are not yet valid, because they are empty. Specifically, the zip, phone, fax, phone, and date elements are all invalid. You can see the specific validation error by right-clicking the element name. In this case, the user has right-clicked "date," yielding a pop-up message showing the details of the problem.

By clicking on different parts of the tree, you can jump to different parts of the document. Though the main pane isn't shown here, you can determine that the cursor is currently inside the company element, because "company" is highlighted in the XML Structure task pane.

Clicking the "Show XML tags in the document" checkbox is equivalent to pressing Ctrl-Shift-X; it toggles the option on or off.

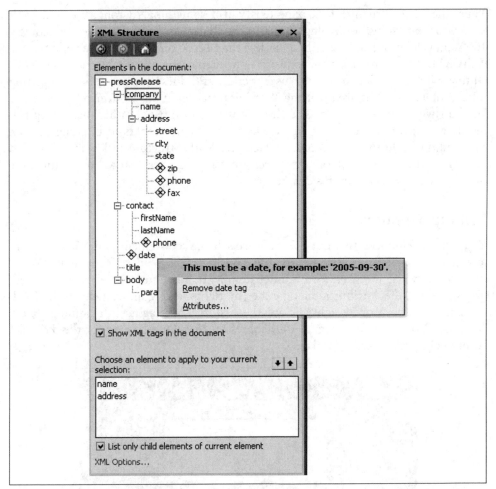

Figure 4-19. The XML Structure task pane

Finally, the list at the bottom of the task pane gives you some choices of elements to insert into the document at the current cursor position or to "apply" to your current selection in the document. If you click one of these names, Word will insert a new instance of that element into the document. If the "List only child elements of current element" checkbox is checked (which it is, by default), the list will contain only the possible children of the current element, according to the schema. If it is unchecked, you'll get a list of all element names declared in the schema. In this case, since the checkbox is checked and the current context is the company element, only the name and address elements are listed. The list does not change according to what elements are already present in the document or what order they're in; it's not that smart. In other words, it won't keep you from making invalid insertions.

Thus, the XML Structure task pane tells you if something's wrong, but it doesn't keep you from doing something wrong in the first place. In that respect, it scores a 100% on validation, and something far less than 100% on schema-driven editing. So, if the XML Structure task pane is just a poor man's version of schema-driven XML editing, what good is it? If it's not user-friendly and doesn't keep users from getting into trouble, why is it a part of the Word application at all? Fortunately, there is a good answer to this question. The XML Structure task pane, rather than being primarily a tool for end users, is an excellent tool for developers in building custom XML editing solutions for Word. In fact, the XML Structure task pane was used heavily in the creation of our press release template. See "Steps to Creating the onload Stylesheet" later in this chapter.

Editing Attributes

You may have noticed that our press release schema (conveniently) does not declare any attributes. There is a reason for this. Without using Smart Documents, Word provides only one way to directly edit custom XML attributes: the Attributes dialog. You can open the Attributes dialog either by right-clicking an element in the XML Structure task pane or by right-clicking the custom XML tag itself (assuming "Show XML tags" is turned on). Figure 4-20 shows the Attributes dialog for the date element in our press release template.

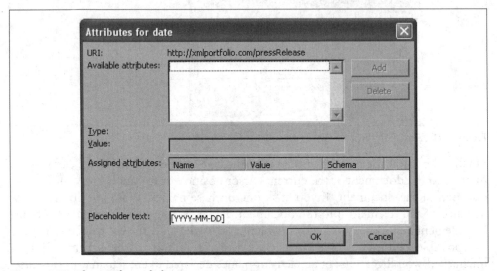

Figure 4-20. The Attributes dialog

Since our schema does not declare any attributes for the date element (or any other element for that matter), the list of "Available attributes" is empty. If there were legal attributes for the date element, then the user could select one from the list, enter its value in the Value text box, and click the Add button. The attribute would then be added to the "Assigned attributes" list, and would be added as a normal XML attribute to the start tag of the date element in the underlying WordprocessingML representation.

The Attributes dialog performs one other function; it lets you specify what the placeholder text for a particular element instance should be. In this case, the placeholder text for the date element is [YYYY-MM-DD]. While this feature may seem out of place in the Attributes dialog, in a certain sense it is appropriately positioned, because the underlying representation of placeholder text (as we saw in Example 4-4) is an attribute, namely the w:placeholder attribute. In any case, this is not something the end user would normally edit. This adds support to the argument that it's unreasonable to force users to edit attributes using the Attributes dialog.

Like the XML Structure task pane, the Attributes dialog may not be terribly useful for end users, but it can be handy for developers in creating custom XML editing solutions, at least insofar as it allows you to insert placeholder text via the Word UI, as you are constructing your template. See "Steps to Creating the onload Stylesheet" later in this chapter.

A workaround for editing attributes

As implied above, the use of Smart Documents could allow users to edit attributes without using the generic Attributes dialog. However, there is also a way to enable users to edit attribute values without resorting to Smart Document programming. It is true that the Attributes dialog is the only way to *directly* edit custom XML attributes in Word, but by using both an *onload* stylesheet and an *onsave* stylesheet, you can enable users to *indirectly* edit attributes without using the Attributes dialog. Here's how it works. First, the *onload* XSLT stylesheet translates the attributes to elements, so that users can edit them as elements. Then, the *onsave* stylesheet translates them back to attributes when the user saves the document. In this approach, the schema in the schema library does not necessarily reflect the actual structure of the XML documents being edited, but rather an intermediate structure that exists only for the purpose of editing within Word. Such restructuring is a typical use case for *onsave* XSLT transformations, which we'll discuss in "The 'Apply Custom Transform' Document Option" later in this chapter.

Schema Validation

When a schema is attached to a document, Word performs on-the-fly schema validation of the document's embedded custom XML, visibly flagging errors as the user edits. However, since the custom XML tags are intertwined with WordprocessingML elements, Word first needs to strip out the Word-specific markup before it can validate the document. This is actually the same process—the "Save data only" process—that optionally occurs in step 3 of our processing model diagram (in Figure 4-7), when a user saves the document. What is not evident in that diagram is the fact that the "Save data only" process is also invoked repeatedly while the user is editing the document (during step 2). The difference here is that, rather than permanently stripping out the WordprocessingML markup, it does so temporarily just for the purpose of validation.

The "Ignore Mixed Content" Document Option

When Word strips out the WordprocessingML markup in order to validate the embedded XML document, by default it leaves all text content (inside w:t elements) intact. Our press release template, however, includes boilerplate text that is not actually part of our data. If this text is included in the remaining XML document, then it will be invalid according to the press release schema. Example 4-7 shows what a press release XML document would look like if all of the text remained intact after stripping out the WordprocessingML markup.

Example 4-7. An invalid press release document, including template boilerplate text

```
<?xml version="1.0" encoding="UTF-8" standalone="no"?>
<?mso-application progid="Word.Document"?>
<pressRelease xmlns="http://xmlportfolio.com/pressRelease"><company><name>ACME
Corp.</name><address><street>555 Market St.</street><city>Seattle</city>,
<state>WA</state>   <zip>98101</zip>Phone <phone>222-222-2222</phone>Fax <fax>333-
333-3333</fax></address></company>Press Release<contact>Contact:
<firstName>John</firstName> <lastName>Doe</lastName>Phone: <phone>444-444-
4444</phone></contact>FOR IMMEDIATE RELEASE<date>2004-01-23</date><title>This is
the Headline</title><body><para>This is the lead-in, and this is not. The rest of
the paragraph has no formatting either.This is the second paragraph. These are just
regular Word paragraphs. They do not correspond to custom XML
elements.</para></body>-End-</pressRelease>
```

The highlighted segments of Example 4-7, such as Phone and FOR IMMEDIATE RELEASE, are pieces of boilerplate text from the press release template. They are not supposed to be part of the data. Thus, merely stripping out the WordprocessingML markup is not sufficient. It is also necessary to strip out the boilerplate text. How is this done? Well, the boilerplate text in this example happens to represent the only mixed content text in the document, and Word happens to provide a document option called "Ignore mixed content." By turning this option on, you can effectively strip out the boilerplate text in this and other similar examples, for the purpose of validation.

The "Ignore mixed content" document option can be viewed as a parameter to the "Save data only" process. It affects both on-the-fly schema validation as well as the document saving process when the "Save data only" document option is turned on. (The precise behavior of this process is approximated using an XSLT stylesheet listed later in this chapter, under "The 'Save Data Only' Document Option".)

In our press release template, the "Ignore mixed content" document option is turned *on*, but the "Save data only" document option is turned *off*. This means that mixed content text is stripped out for the purpose of on-the-fly schema validation, but it is not stripped out when the document is saved. (Instead, our press release template uses a custom *onsave* XSLT stylesheet applied directly to the merged XML and WordprocessingML representation.)

The "Ignore mixed content" document option is represented in WordprocessingML using the w:ignoreMixedContent element. Our press release application's "Elegant" stylesheet, *pr2word.xsl*, turns the option on by generating a w:ignoreMixedContent element in the result document, just like this one:

```
<w:docPr>
  <!-- ... -->
  <w:ignoreMixedContent/>
  <!-- ... -->
</w:docPr>
```

Document Protection

Microsoft Office Word 2003 introduces some powerful new document protection features. While these features are not specifically XML-related, they can help to make custom XML editing solutions in Word more robust. There are two kinds of document protection options: *editing restrictions* and *formatting restrictions*. Our press release template relies heavily on both kinds of restrictions.

Editing Restrictions

Editing restrictions let you protect a document in various ways—for example, by making it read-only or by allowing comments only. You can also make exceptions to the overall document policy for particular regions of the document. Our press release template protects the entire document as read-only but designates particular areas of the document as unrestricted. These areas correspond exactly to the custom XML leaf elements embedded in the WordprocessingML template. By restricting user changes to the text within XML leaf nodes, you can ensure that users won't inadvertently alter the template's boilerplate text, or worse, delete a custom XML element.

The global policy is set using the w:documentProtection element inside the w:docPr element:

```
<w:docPr>
  <!-- ... -->
  <w:documentProtection w:edit="read-only" w:formatting="on"
                        w:enforcement="on"/>
  <!-- ... -->
</w:docPr>
```

This element specifies that the document is read-only, that formatting restrictions are also turned on, and that all such restrictions are currently being enforced. The w:documentProtection element also takes an optional w:unprotectPassword attribute which contains a hex-encoded password key. In that case, users will not be able to remove the document protection without entering the correct password. The *onload* stylesheet for our press release template, *pr2word.xsl*, turns document protection on by generating a w:documentProtection element just like the one shown above.

Individual exceptions to a document's read-only policy are represented in the body of the WordprocessingML document using the w:permStart and w:permEnd elements. Example 4-8 shows an excerpt of our press release template's *onload* stylesheet, *pr2word.xsl*. Both the custom XML elements and the w:permStart and w:permEnd elements are highlighted.

Example 4-8. Document protection boundaries and custom XML elements

```
<w:tbl>
  <w:tblPr>
    <w:tblW w:w="0" w:type="auto"/>
    <w:tblInd w:w="475" w:type="dxa"/>
  </w:tblPr>
  <w:tblGrid>
    <w:gridCol w:w="5303"/>
    <w:gridCol w:w="4590"/>
  </w:tblGrid>
  <w:tr>
    <w:tc>
      <w:tcPr>
        <w:tcW w:w="5303" w:type="dxa"/>
      </w:tcPr>
      <ns1:contact>
        <w:p>
          <w:pPr>
            <w:pStyle w:val="Contact"/>
          </w:pPr>
          <w:r>
            <w:t>Contact: </w:t>
          </w:r>
          <ns1:firstName w:placeholder="[First]">
            <w:permStart w:id="7" w:edGrp="everyone"/>
            <w:r>
              <w:t>
                <xsl:value-of
                select="/ns1:pressRelease/ns1:contact/ns1:firstName"/>
              </w:t>
            </w:r>
            <w:permEnd w:id="7"/>
          </ns1:firstName>
          <w:r>
            <w:t>
              <xsl:text> </xsl:text>
            </w:t>
          </w:r>
          <ns1:lastName w:placeholder="[Last]">
```

```
          <w:permStart w:id="8" w:edGrp="everyone"/>
          <w:r>
            <w:t>
              <xsl:value-of
              select="/ns1:pressRelease/ns1:contact/ns1:lastName"/>
            </w:t>
          </w:r>
          <w:permEnd w:id="8"/>
        </ns1:lastName>
        <w:r>
          <w:t>
            <xsl:text> </xsl:text>
          </w:t>
        </w:r>
      </w:p>
      <w:p>
        <w:pPr>
          <w:pStyle w:val="Contact"/>
        </w:pPr>
        <w:r>
          <w:t>Phone: </w:t>
        </w:r>
        <ns1:phone w:placeholder="[xxx-xxx-xxxx]">
          <w:permStart w:id="9" w:edGrp="everyone"/>
          <w:r>
            <w:t>
              <xsl:value-of
                 select="/ns1:pressRelease/ns1:contact/ns1:phone"/>
            </w:t>
          </w:r>
          <w:permEnd w:id="9"/>
        </ns1:phone>
      </w:p>
    </ns1:contact>
  </w:tc>
  <w:tc>
    <w:tcPr>
      <w:tcW w:w="4590" w:type="dxa"/>
    </w:tcPr>
    <w:p>
      <w:pPr>
        <w:pStyle w:val="Date"/>
      </w:pPr>
      <w:r>
        <w:t>FOR IMMEDIATE RELEASE</w:t>
      </w:r>
    </w:p>
    <w:p>
      <w:pPr>
        <w:pStyle w:val="Date"/>
      </w:pPr>
      <ns1:date w:placeholder="[YYYY-MM-DD]">
```

```
                    <w:permStart w:id="10" w:edGrp="everyone"/>
                    <w:r>
                      <w:t>
                        <xsl:value-of select="/ns1:pressRelease/ns1:date"/>
                      </w:t>
                    </w:r>
                    <w:permEnd w:id="10"/>
                  </ns1:date>
                </w:p>
              </w:tc>
            </w:tr>
          </w:tbl>
```

The w:edGrp attribute of each w:permStart element indicates that "everyone" is allowed to edit the given region. (The value of "everyone" means that there are no restrictions. Other values may be groups defined on the local machine or network.) The w:id attributes on the w:permStart and w:permEnd elements maintain the association between the start and end elements of each range. The editable regions are carefully placed directly inside the custom XML elements, so that users may edit the contents of the XML tags but may not move or delete the XML elements themselves.

The excerpt in Example 4-8 also illustrates how data is pulled from the source document into the merged XML and WordprocessingML editing view—through the use of an xsl:value-of instruction inside each custom XML leaf element.

Formatting Restrictions

Formatting restrictions enable you to restrict formatting to a selection of zero or more styles. This also means that users will not be able to apply direct formatting, such as italic or bold. Unlike editing restrictions, you cannot designate different regions of the document to have different formatting restrictions. The restricted selection of styles is a global setting for the entire document.

Formatting restrictions are enabled when the w:formatting and w:enforcement attributes of the w:documentProtection element both have the value on (as shown above), and when the w:defLockedState attribute of the w:latentStyles element (inside the top-level w:styles element) also has the value on:

```
<w:latentStyles w:defLockedState="on" w:latentStyleCount="156"/>
```

Individual styles defined within the document are either locked or available, depending on the presence of the w:locked element in the style's w:style definition. If w:locked is present (and not explicitly off), it means that the style is locked and cannot be used. If not, then the style is among the limited selection of styles that the user can apply. Note that the document may already contain paragraphs or runs that use locked styles. That is okay; users just won't be able to create *new* runs or paragraphs that use those styles. (Note that the w:defLockedState attribute sets the "default locked state" only for the built-in styles; it does *not* affect styles defined

---

within the document, whose locked state is determined solely based on the presence of the w:locked element.)

In our press release template, there are three styles available for the user to apply: a paragraph style called "Body Text," a character style called "Lead-in Emphasis," and a character style called "No formatting." All of these are used for the body text of the press release. The "Lead-in Emphasis" style is used normally only for the first phrase of the first paragraph, as a traditional all-caps lead-in to the content of the press release. The "No formatting" style is based on the built-in "Default Paragraph Font" style and does not include any additional formatting. Its purpose is to let the user conveniently turn off the "Lead-in Emphasis" style after they are done typing the lead-in text.

You may be wondering, "Why use styles at all when the WordprocessingML markup is just going to get stripped out when the document is saved?" The answer is that our press release template uses an *onsave* XSLT stylesheet to convert a run having the "Lead-in Emphasis" style to an actual leadIn element in the saved XML document. Similarly, the *onload* XSLT stylesheet converts a leadIn element in a newly opened press release XML document to a run having the "Lead-in Emphasis" style. By defining these mappings, our imaginary IT department is able to support a limited form of mixed content editing without having to invoke Smart Document programming.

XML Save Options

When a user tries to save a document as XML, Word presents several options. The "Save As" dialog, shown again in Figure 4-21, includes two checkboxes representing XML save options: the "Apply transform" checkbox and the "Save data only" checkbox. These options correspond to the final two (optional) processes in our processing model diagram (Figure 4-7).

Rather than solely relying on the user to make the right choice, you can specify default save settings for a particular document, obviating the need for user intervention. You can set these through the Word UI (in the Tools → Templates and Add-Ins... → XML Schema → XML Options dialog), or by declaring them in the underlying WordprocessingML representation. In our primary XML editing scenario, the *onload* XSLT transformation that Word applies when opening the document is what determines what the default XML save settings for a document will be.

In our press release template, the *onload* stylesheet turns "Save data only" *off* and "Apply custom transform" *on*. It does this by generating declarations for these settings inside the w:docPr element. Below is the relevant excerpt from the stylesheet:

```
<w:docPr>
  <!-- ... -->
  <w:removeWordSchemaOnSave w:val="off"/>
  <w:useXSLTWhenSaving/>
  <w:saveThroughXSLT w:xslt="\\intra\pr\harvestPressRelease.xsl"/>
</w:docPr>
```

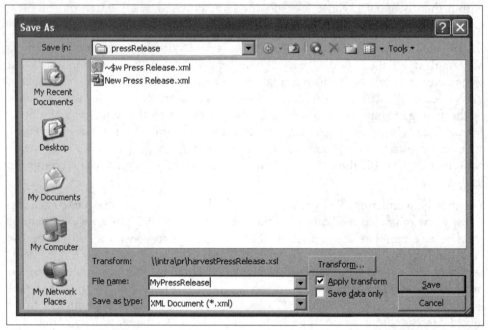

Figure 4-21. XML save options in the "Save As" dialog

The w:removeWordSchemaOnSave element corresponds to the "Save data only" option. Here, it is explicitly turned off. The w:useXSLTWhenSaving element turns the "Apply custom transform" option on. Finally, the w:saveThroughXSLT element specifies the file name of the particular XSLT stylesheet to apply when the w:useXSLTWhenSaving option is turned on.

The "Save Data Only" Document Option

When the "Save data only" option is turned on (via the w:removeWordSchemaOnSave element), Word strips all WordprocessingML markup from the document when the user saves it, leaving only custom XML elements and attributes. This is the same process that Word uses to prepare an embedded XML document for schema validation. In both cases, the "Ignore mixed content" document option parameterizes the behavior of the process, optionally causing it to subsequently strip out remaining mixed content text after it has stripped out the WordprocessingML markup.

Unlike Word's default *onload* rendering process for arbitrary XML documents (which the *XML2WORD.XSL* stylesheet implements), its default *onsave* process ("Save data only") is not implemented in an XSLT stylesheet that you can view—at least not one that's included in the files installed with Office. However, since it is important to understand exactly what this process does, we've included in Example 4-9 an XSLT stylesheet that approximates its behavior. This stylesheet is designed to produce the exact same result as the "Save data only" process, when selected as the transform to apply when saving a document.*

Example 4-9. An approximation of the "Save data only" process, saveDataOnly.xsl

```
<xsl:stylesheet version="1.0"
  xmlns:xsl="http://www.w3.org/1999/XSL/Transform"
  xmlns:msxsl="urn:schemas-microsoft-com:xslt"
  xmlns:w="http://schemas.microsoft.com/office/word/2003/wordml"
  xmlns:sl="http://schemas.microsoft.com/schemaLibrary/2003/core"
  xmlns:aml="http://schemas.microsoft.com/aml/2001/core"
  xmlns:wx="http://schemas.microsoft.com/office/word/2003/auxHint"
  xmlns:w10="urn:schemas-microsoft-com:office:word"
  xmlns:v="urn:schemas-microsoft-com:office:vml"
  xmlns:o="urn:schemas-microsoft-com:office:office"
  xmlns:dt="uuid:C2F41010-65B3-11d1-A29F-00AA00C14882"
  xmlns:st="urn:schemas-microsoft-com:office:smarttags">

  <!-- UTF-8 encoding and standalone declaration -->
  <xsl:output encoding="UTF-8" standalone="no"/>


  <!-- *************************************************************** -->
  <!--                      Global Variables                         -->
  <!-- *************************************************************** -->

  <!-- True if w:ignoreMixedContent is present and @w:val isn't "off" -->
  <xsl:variable name="ignoreMixedContent"
                select="/w:wordDocument/w:docPr/w:ignoreMixedContent
                        [not(@w:val='off')]"/>

  <!-- Result of first pass (before optionally stripping mixed content text) -->
  <xsl:variable name="first-pass-result">
    <xsl:apply-templates select="/*"/>
  </xsl:variable>


  <!-- *************************************************************** -->
  <!--              Template rules in default mode                   -->
  <!-- *************************************************************** -->

  <!-- Start here -->
  <xsl:template match="/">

    <!-- line break after XML declaration -->
    <xsl:text>&#xA;</xsl:text>

    <!-- Re-create any PIs preserved inside o:CustomDocumentProperties -->
```

---

* For this stylesheet to work as intended, the "Apply transform" checkbox must be checked, the *saveDataOnly.xsl* file must be selected as the transform to apply, and the "Save data only" checkbox must be *unchecked*. The reason it must be unchecked is that the *saveDataOnly.xsl* stylesheet is designed to be applied to the document *instead* of the "Save data only" process, rather than in addition to it.

```
    <xsl:call-template name="create-pis">
      <xsl:with-param name="escaped-pis" select="string(
        /w:wordDocument/o:CustomDocumentProperties/o:processingInstructions)"/>
    </xsl:call-template>

    <!-- Apply a second pass to strip mixed content text only if
         $ignoreMixedContent is true -->
    <xsl:choose>
      <xsl:when test="$ignoreMixedContent">
        <xsl:apply-templates select="msxsl:node-set($first-pass-result)/node()"
                             mode="strip-mixed-content"/>
      </xsl:when>
      <xsl:otherwise>
        <xsl:copy-of select="$first-pass-result"/>
      </xsl:otherwise>
    </xsl:choose>
  </xsl:template>

  <!-- Replicate all elements by default
       (filtering out unnecessary namespace nodes) -->
  <xsl:template match="*">
    <xsl:element name="{local-name()}" namespace="{namespace-uri()}">
      <xsl:apply-templates select="@*|node()"/>
    </xsl:element>
  </xsl:template>

  <!-- Copy attributes by default -->
  <xsl:template match="@*">
    <xsl:copy/>
  </xsl:template>

  <!-- Preserve text inside w:t elements (other than headers, footers, etc.) -->
  <xsl:template match="w:t[not(ancestor::w:sectPr)]/text()">
    <xsl:copy/>
  </xsl:template>

  <!-- Strip out all other text (field instructions, doc properties, etc.) -->
  <xsl:template match="text()"/>

  <!-- Process children of, but do not copy, elements in Word's namespaces -->
  <xsl:template match="w:*|sl:*|aml:*|wx:*|w10:*|v:*|o:*|dt:*|st:*">
    <xsl:apply-templates/>
  </xsl:template>

  <!-- Strip out all attributes in Word's namespaces -->
  <xsl:template match="@w:*|@sl:*|@aml:*|@wx:*|@w10:*|@v:*|@o:*|@dt:*|@st:*"/>


  <!-- ************************************************************** -->
  <!--          Template rules in "strip-mixed-content" mode         -->
  <!-- ************************************************************** -->

  <!-- Copy elements, attributes, PIs, and text straight through -->
```

```
<xsl:template match="@*|node( )" mode="strip-mixed-content">
  <xsl:copy>
    <xsl:apply-templates select="@*|node( )" mode="strip-mixed-content"/>
  </xsl:copy>
</xsl:template>

<!-- But strip out mixed content text -->
<xsl:template match="text( )[preceding-sibling::* or following-sibling::*]"
              mode="strip-mixed-content"/>


<!-- *************************************************************** -->
<!--                      Named templates                          -->
<!-- *************************************************************** -->

<!-- For re-creating PIs stored as text in o:CustomDocumentProperties;
     (See XML2WORD.XSL) -->
<xsl:template name="create-pis">
  <xsl:param name="escaped-pis"/>
  <xsl:if test="$escaped-pis">
    <xsl:processing-instruction
        name="{substring-before(
                  substring-after($escaped-pis,'&lt;?'),
                  ' ')}">
      <xsl:value-of select="substring-before(
                              substring-after($escaped-pis,' '),
                              '?>')"/>
    </xsl:processing-instruction>
    <xsl:text>&#xA;</xsl:text>
    <xsl:call-template name="create-pis">
      <xsl:with-param name="escaped-pis"
                  select="substring-after($escaped-pis,'?>')"/>
    </xsl:call-template>
  </xsl:if>
</xsl:template>
```

```
</xsl:stylesheet>
```

The highlighted template rules in Example 4-9 define the essence of what the "Save data only" process does. They strip out elements and attributes in any of the Word-specific namespaces but preserve all elements and attributes in other namespaces. The rest of the stylesheet is concerned with implementing two other features of the "Save data only" process: stripping mixed content and preserving processing instructions.

Stripping mixed content

Also like Word's built-in "Save data only" process, the stylesheet in Example 4-9 alters its behavior according to whether the "Ignore mixed content" document option is turned on or off.

First, the stylesheet defines a global variable named $ignoreMixedContent that is true as long as the w:ignoreMixedContent element is present and is not turned off.

```
<!-- True if w:ignoreMixedContent is present and @w:val isn't "off" -->
<xsl:variable name="ignoreMixedContent"
              select="/w:wordDocument/w:docPr/w:ignoreMixedContent
                     [not(@w:val='off')]"/>
```

Then, after stripping out the Word-specific markup, the stylesheet further processes the document if and only if $ignoreMixedContent is true. This is implemented as a second pass (with the help of the msxsl:node-set( ) extension function):

```
<!-- Apply a second pass to strip mixed content text only if
     $ignoreMixedContent is true -->
<xsl:choose>
  <xsl:when test="$ignoreMixedContent">
    <xsl:apply-templates select="msxsl:node-set($first-pass-result)/node( )"
                         mode="strip-mixed-content"/>
  </xsl:when>
  <xsl:otherwise>
    <xsl:copy-of select="$first-pass-result"/>
  </xsl:otherwise>
</xsl:choose>
```

Finally, the template rules in the strip-mixed-content mode effect an identity transformation with one exception. The operative template rule strips out all mixed content text in the document, i.e., all text nodes that have any element siblings, by doing nothing:

```
<xsl:template match="text( )[preceding-sibling::* or following-sibling::*]"
             mode="strip-mixed-content"/>
```

Thus, the *saveDataOnly.xsl* stylesheet behaves like the "Save data only" process, stripping out mixed content text only if the "Ignore mixed content" document option is turned on.

Preserving processing instructions

When opening an arbitrary XML document that has one or more processing instructions (PIs) outside the root element, Word's default *onload* stylesheet (*XML2WORD.XSL*) preserves those PIs by escaping the PI markup as text and storing the resulting string in a custom document property named o:processingInstructions (in the o: CustomDocumentProperties element). Then, when the user saves the document, the "Save data only" process converts the escaped PI markup back to literal processing instructions in the final XML document saved by Word.

The *saveDataOnly.xsl* stylesheet in Example 4-9 exhibits the same behavior. First, it calls a named template, passing it the string value of the o:processingInstructions element:

```
<!-- Re-create any PIs preserved inside o:CustomDocumentProperties -->
<xsl:call-template name="create-pis">
```

```
    <xsl:with-param name="escaped-pis" select="string(
        /w:wordDocument/o:CustomDocumentProperties/o:processingInstructions)"/>
  </xsl:call-template>
```

Then, the template named `create-pis` does the actual work of converting the value of the `$escaped-pis` parameter to real processing instructions in the result document. It recursively parses the escaped PI markup until no processing instructions are left:

```
<!-- For re-creating PIs stored as text in o:CustomDocumentProperties;
    (See XML2WORD.XSL) -->
<xsl:template name="create-pis">
  <xsl:param name="escaped-pis"/>
  <xsl:if test="$escaped-pis">
    <xsl:processing-instruction
        name="{substring-before(
                substring-after($escaped-pis,'&lt;?'),
                ' ')}">
      <xsl:value-of select="substring-before(
                            substring-after($escaped-pis,' '),
                            '?>')"/>
    </xsl:processing-instruction>
    <xsl:text>&#xA;</xsl:text>
    <xsl:call-template name="create-pis">
      <xsl:with-param name="escaped-pis"
                    select="substring-after($escaped-pis,'?>')"/>
    </xsl:call-template>
  </xsl:if>
</xsl:template>
```

This PI re-creation process only works when the *onload* stylesheet preserves the PIs in exactly the way that the "Save data only" process expects. If you want your own custom *onload* stylesheets to preserve PIs, take a look at the *XML2WORD.XSL* file to see exactly how it's done. Basically, it converts a single PI to a string with these components:

```
'<?' <PITarget> <nbsp> <PIText> '?>'
```

Each subsequent escaped PI is concatenated to the end of the last one. And the final value is stored in the `o:processingInstructions` element.

In our press release template, the *onload* stylesheet preserves PIs from the source document in the same way that the *XML2WORD.XSL* stylesheet does. However, rather than using the "Save data only" process to re-create the PIs, the press release template declares its own custom *onsave* stylesheet, which re-creates them in the same way that the "Save data only" process would have. Of course, when you have control over both the *onload* and *onsave* stylesheets, you can choose whatever mechanism you'd like for preserving PIs. The press release template could have used a different approach, but the approach used by *XML2WORD.XSL* and the "Save data only" process works perfectly fine. Rather than reinventing the wheel, the press release template takes the same approach.

One favorable consequence of preserving processing instructions from the source document is that the `mso-application` PI is preserved in XML documents that Word edits, retaining the file's association with the Word application. This means that users don't have to do anything special to open the file in Word; they just double-click it like any other Word document. Conversely, the `mso-application` PI is only present in the saved document when it was already present in the XML document that Word opened. Word does not automatically output the `mso-application` PI whenever it saves a custom XML document. On the contrary, it is quite possible to open, edit, and save XML documents in Word without leaving any evidence that Word was ever used to edit the file. The point is that you as the developer do have control over what processing instructions appear in the result.

> To *force* the presence of the `mso-application` (or any other) processing instruction in your result document (regardless of whether it was present in the source document), you can simply use the `xsl:processing-instruction` element in your *onsave* stylesheet. Or, if you are using "Save data only" with no *onsave* stylesheet, you can use your *onload* stylesheet to effectively hard-code the PI to the list of escaped PIs in the `o:processingInstructions` custom document property. In this case, the "Save data only" process will regenerate the PI just as if it was preserved from the source document.

The "Apply Custom Transform" Document Option

The "Apply Custom Transform" document option allows you to save an XML document through an *onsave* XSLT stylesheet. As reflected in our original processing model diagram in Figure 4-7, what document the *onsave* stylesheet is applied to depends on whether the "Save data only" option is turned on. If "Save data only" is turned off, then the *onsave* stylesheet is applied directly to the WordprocessingML document. If "Save data only" is turned on, then the *onsave* stylesheet is applied to the result of stripping the Word-specific markup from the merged XML and WordprocessingML view.

Our press release template uses an *onsave* stylesheet called *harvestPressRelease.xsl*. Since the "Save data only" option is turned off, this stylesheet is applied to the entire WordprocessingML document when the user saves it. The purpose of *harvestPressRelease.xsl* is to behave just like the "Save data only" process, with some notable exceptions: it converts `w:p` elements in the body of the press release to `para` elements in the result, and it converts a run with the "Lead-in Emphasis" style to a `leadIn` element in the result.

The *harvestPressRelease.xsl* stylesheet behaves just like the "Save data only" process in the sense that it strips out all Word-specific markup from the result, and, except for the `para` element, it leaves all custom tags intact. It turns out that the *saveDataOnly.xsl* stylesheet introduced in the last section possesses more than academic interest. It not only can be used to understand the precise behavior of the "Save data only" process, i.e., as a learning aid, but it can also be used directly by custom *onsave* stylesheets that want to slightly alter its behavior. Our press release template's *onsave* stylesheet does just that—it imports the *saveDataOnly.xsl* stylesheet, selectively modifying its behavior. Example 4-10 shows *harvestPressRelease.xsl* in its entirety.

Example 4-10. The onsave stylesheet for the harvestPressRelease.xsl template

```
<xsl:stylesheet version="1.0"
  xmlns:xsl="http://www.w3.org/1999/XSL/Transform"
  xmlns:w="http://schemas.microsoft.com/office/word/2003/wordml"
  xmlns:pr="http://xmlportfolio.com/pressRelease"
  xmlns="http://xmlportfolio.com/pressRelease"
  exclude-result-prefixes="w pr">

  <xsl:import href="saveDataOnly.xsl"/>

  <!-- Skip by the single surrogate paragraph -->
  <xsl:template match="pr:para">
    <!-- Apply templates to all non-empty Word paragraphs -->
    <xsl:apply-templates select="w:p[normalize-space(.)]"/>
  </xsl:template>

  <!-- Convert w:p elements inside PR body to para elements -->
  <xsl:template match="pr:para/w:p">
    <para>
      <!-- This element contains mixed content; explicitly preserve space -->
      <xsl:attribute name="xml:space">preserve</xsl:attribute>
      <xsl:apply-templates/>
    </para>
  </xsl:template>

  <!-- Convert "Lead-in Emphasis" runs to leadIn elements -->
  <xsl:template match="w:r[w:rPr/w:rStyle/@w:val =
                          /w:wordDocument/w:styles/w:style
                            [w:name/@w:val='Lead-in Emphasis']/@w:styleId]">

    <!-- Only process this run if the immediately preceding
         run does not have the same style -->
    <xsl:if test="not(preceding-sibling::w:r[1]
                      [w:rPr/w:rStyle/@w:val = current( )/w:rPr/w:rStyle/@w:val]
                    )">
      <leadIn>
        <xsl:call-template name="merge-adjacent-style-runs"/>
      </leadIn>
    </xsl:if>
  </xsl:template>

  <!-- Merge adjacent runs that have the same style -->
  <xsl:template name="merge-adjacent-style-runs" match="w:r" mode="merge-runs">
    <xsl:apply-templates/>

    <!-- Recursively apply to the immediately following run
```

```
            only if it has the same style -->
  <xsl:apply-templates
        select="following-sibling::w:r[1]
                [w:rPr/w:rStyle/@w:val = current( )/w:rPr/w:rStyle/@w:val]"
        mode="merge-runs"/>
</xsl:template>

<!-- Override mixed-content-stripping for text inside pr:para elements -->
<xsl:template match="pr:para/text( )" mode="strip-mixed-content">
  <xsl:copy/>
</xsl:template>

</xsl:stylesheet>
```

As you can see, this stylesheet imports the *saveDataOnly.xsl* stylesheet we looked at earlier:

```
  <xsl:import href="saveDataOnly.xsl"/>
```

Now, let's briefly walk through each template rule in the stylesheet. The first custom rule that will get triggered is also the first one listed in the document. It matches the single pr:para element (where pr maps to the press release namespace) that contains the body text of the press release. Rather than creating a shallow copy of the element, as *saveDataOnly.xsl* would have done by default, it instructs processing to skip by the element altogether and to process its non-empty paragraph (w:p) children instead:

```
  <!-- Skip by the single surrogate paragraph -->
  <xsl:template match="pr:para">
    <!-- Apply templates to all non-empty Word paragraphs -->
    <xsl:apply-templates select="w:p[normalize-space(.)]"/>
  </xsl:template>
```

The next template rule matches the paragraph (w:p) children of pr:para. Each w:p element is effectively replaced by a para element (in the press release namespace). The xml:space="preserve" attribute is programmatically added to the result so that Word (and other potential processes) won't strip out what it deems to be insignificant whitespace from the document when it loads it again. Since the para element contains mixed content, all child text nodes, including whitespace-only text nodes, should be considered significant:

```
  <!-- Convert w:p elements inside PR body to para elements -->
  <xsl:template match="pr:para/w:p">
    <para>
      <!-- This element contains mixed content; explicitly preserve space -->
      <xsl:attribute name="xml:space">preserve</xsl:attribute>
      <xsl:apply-templates/>
    </para>
  </xsl:template>
```

The next template rule gets triggered by runs that have the "Lead-in Emphasis" character style. The purpose of this template rule is to convert such runs into leadIn elements. However, its job is complicated by the fact that Word has a tendency to output adjacent runs that have the same style. Rather that creating a separate `leadIn` element for each of these, this template rule, with help from the recursive template named `merge-adjacent-style-runs`, does just that; it merges adjacent runs in the same style so that only one `leadIn` element is created per contiguous sequence:

```
<!-- Convert "Lead-in Emphasis" runs to leadIn elements -->
<xsl:template match="w:r[w:rPr/w:rStyle/@w:val =
                        /w:wordDocument/w:styles/w:style
                            [w:name/@w:val='Lead-in Emphasis']/@w:styleId]">

    <!-- Only process this run if the immediately preceding
         run does not have the same style -->
    <xsl:if test="not(preceding-sibling::w:r[1]
                        [w:rPr/w:rStyle/@w:val = current( )/w:rPr/w:rStyle/@w:val]
                    )">
        <leadIn>
          <xsl:call-template name="merge-adjacent-style-runs"/>
        </leadIn>
    </xsl:if>
</xsl:template>
```

Finally, *harvestPressRelease.xsl* must override one other aspect of *saveDataOnly.xsl*'s behavior. Rather than strip out all mixed content text (which *saveDataOnly.xsl* does when "Ignore mixed content" is turned on, as it is in the press release template), it must preserve the mixed content text found inside the newly created `pr:para` elements. It does this by overriding the default template rule for text nodes in the strip-mixed-content mode, explicitly copying text nodes that are children of `pr:para` elements:

```
<!-- Override mixed-content-stripping for text inside pr:para elements -->
<xsl:template match="pr:para/text( )" mode="strip-mixed-content">
  <xsl:copy/>
</xsl:template>
```

Thus, the *harvestPressRelease.xsl* stylesheet behaves very similarly to Word's "Save data only" process. In fact, for most of the elements in a press release document, it behaves identically, thanks to the *saveDataOnly.xsl* stylesheet that it imports. However, by incrementally overriding the default behavior of *saveDataOnly.xsl*, it enables limited but effective support for repeating paragraphs and mixed content.

When to Use These Options

Between the "Save data only" and "Apply custom transform" options, there are four possible combinations. When does it make sense to choose one combination over another? Table 4-1 lists some possible use cases for each combination.

Table 4-1. XML save settings and corresponding use cases

"Save data only"	"Apply custom transform"	Example use cases
off	off	Saving the document as WordprocessingML
on	off	Saving custom markup only (most common configuration for Smart Documents)
off	on	Converting Word paragraphs to custom elements; converting styled text to custom elements
on	on	Converting elements back to attributes; re-ordering or otherwise re-structuring the document

When you are using an *onsave* XSLT stylesheet and you need to decide whether or not to turn "Save data only" on, ask yourself these questions: Is all the information I need to create my final, saved XML document present in the XML elements and attributes that are embedded in the Word document being edited? Or do I need to query some aspect of the WordprocessingML markup, because the embedded XML tags do not tell the whole story? The *onsave* stylesheet for our press release template, since it converts Word paragraphs to custom paragraphs, for example, indeed does need to have access to the WordprocessingML markup. Therefore, the press release template takes the third approach shown in this table; it turns "Save data only" *off* and "Apply custom transform" *on*.

Reviewing the XML-Specific Document Options

So far, we've introduced a number of different XML-related document options in various contexts. Now let's take a look at them together, including some new ones. You can configure most of these through the XML Options dialog. Figure 4-22 shows the XML Options dialog with the default XML settings. To open this dialog, select Tools → Templates and Add-Ins → XML Schema → XML Options.

The options in Figure 4-22 correspond to these elements in WordprocessingML:

1. w:removeWordSchemaOnSave—When enabled, Word removes all Word-specific markup from the document when saving.

2. w:useXSLTWhenSaving—When enabled, Word applies an XSLT stylesheet to the document when saving.

3. w:saveThroughXSLT—When the "Apply custom transform" option is on, this element's w:xslt attribute determines what stylesheet will be applied.

4. w:validateAgainstSchema—When enabled, Word validates the document while the user is editing it. This option is turned on by default unless explicitly turned off.

5. w:doNotUnderlineInvalidXML—When enabled, Word does not display validation errors in the document being edited.

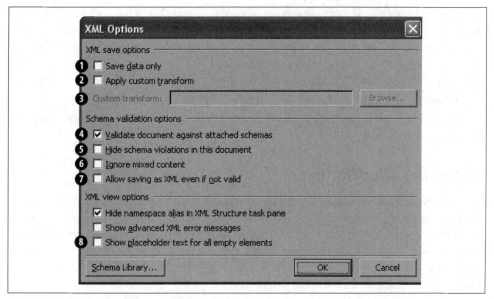

Figure 4-22. The XML Options dialog

6. `w:ignoreMixedContent`—When checked, Word strips out mixed content text for the purpose of validation, as well as for the purpose of saving (when the "Save data only" option is on).

7. `w:saveInvalidXML`—When checked, Word will not disallow the user from saving a document as XML even though the embedded XML document is invalid according to its schema.

8. `w:alwaysShowPlaceholderText`—When checked, Word automatically displays the name of each empty leaf element as placeholder text when "Show XML tags" is turned off, and when the element does not explicitly specify its own placeholder text.

Except for the `w:saveThroughXSLT` element, all of these options are Boolean options. Each of their corresponding elements is defined in the WordprocessingML schema to use the `onOffProperty` type, which means that it is an empty element and that it has a `w:val` attribute whose value can be either `on` or `off`. When the element is present but the attribute is absent, then it defaults to `on`.

The other two checkboxes listed under "XML view options" in Figure 4-22 are not document-specific options and so do not have a WordprocessingML representation.

Steps to Creating the onload Stylesheet

As we mentioned earlier, the XML Structure task pane, though not terribly useful to end users, is an important tool for developers of Word XML templates. By using it to apply XML elements to different parts of a regular Word document, you can create a merged document that contains both WordprocessingML and custom XML elements from your schema. After saving it as XML (WordprocessingML and all), you suddenly have an example of what your *onload* stylesheet needs to generate as a result document. Adapting this document to an XSLT stylesheet is often as simple as slapping `xsl:stylesheet` and `xsl:template` elements around the document and replacing text inside leaf-node custom elements with `xsl:value-of` instructions.

With this end in view, let's take a look at the necessary steps to preparing the press release template within Word.

Start with a Word Document

First, create a regular Word document that contains all of the formatting and boilerplate text you want to include in your template. Our imaginary IT department's press release template began its life as a regular Word document, adapted from a template available on Office Online. After simplifying it a bit to meet their requirements, they were ready to begin. Figure 4-23 shows the pristine Word document before it was introduced to XML.

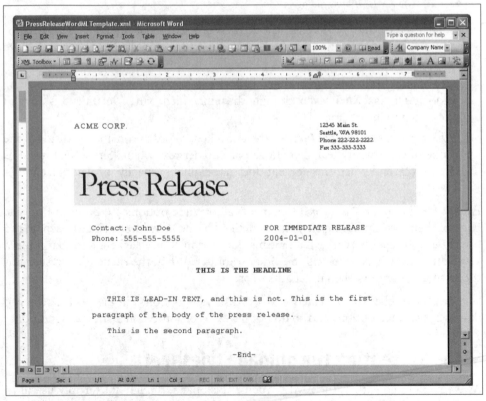

Figure 4-23. PressReleaseWordMLTemplate.xml, a regular Word document with no custom XML

Attach a Schema

Once you have your regular Word document ready, the next thing to do is to attach your schema to it. We saw the schema document for press releases, *pressRelease.xsd*, way back in Example 4-1. Select Tools → Templates and Add-Ins, and click the XML Schema tab to open the dialog shown in Figure 4-24.

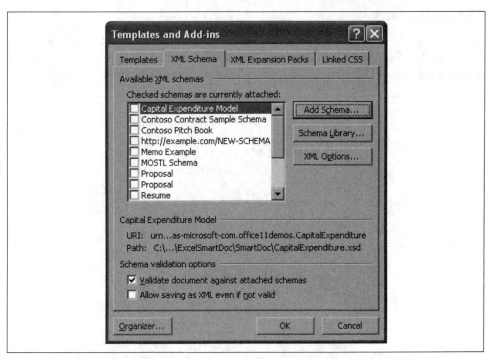

Figure 4-24. The XML Schema dialog

This dialog should look familiar, as we introduced it earlier in "Attaching Schemas to a Document." Click the Add Schema... button and browse to find the file named *pressRelease.xsd*. After you select the schema file, you'll get the Schema Settings dialog, shown in Figure 4-25.

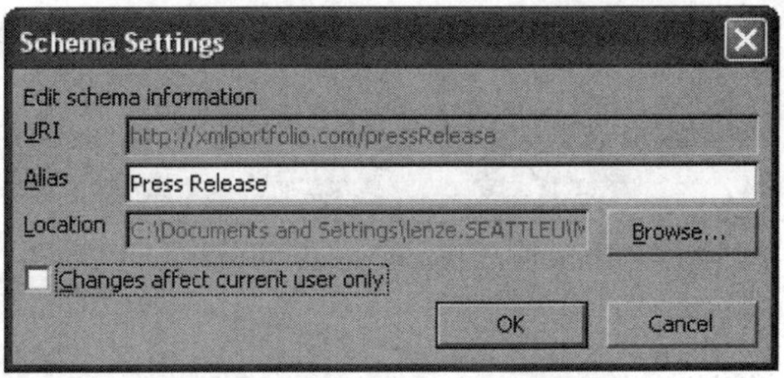

Figure 4-25. The Schema Settings dialog

Enter a friendly name for this schema, such as "Press Release." Uncheck the "Changes affect current user only" checkbox if you want this entry in the schema library to be available to all users on your machine. (Since this schema library entry is initially for development purposes only, on the developer's machine, it probably doesn't matter what you choose.)

Apply XML Tags

After hitting the OK button, you will see that the newly created "Press Release" checkbox has been checked for you in the XML Schema dialog. After clicking OK once more, the XML Structure task pane will appear, as shown in Figure 4-26.

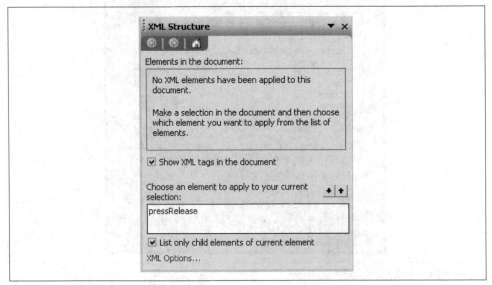

Figure 4-26. The XML Structure task pane immediately after attaching a schema

Click "pressRelease" at the bottom of the task pane to apply your schema's pressRelease element to the entire document. You will see the dialog shown in Figure 4-27.

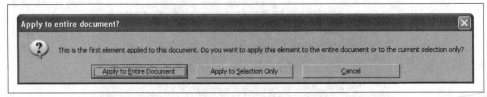

Figure 4-27. "Apply to entire document?" dialog

Select "Apply to Entire Document." The result is shown in Figure 4-28.

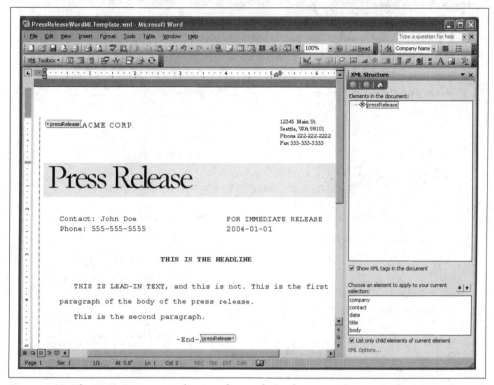

Figure 4-28. The XML Structure task pane after applying the pressRelease root element

At this point, you are ready to begin applying individual elements to their corresponding selections of text in the press release document. To do this, select the text to be contained within the element, and then click the corresponding element name at the bottom of the XML Structure task pane. Since the XML Structure task pane, by default, displays only the elements that are legal in the current context, it works best to apply elements in a top-down order, e.g., company before name and address. Once you have applied all the elements of the document, your document should look something like that in Figure 4-29.

In Figure 4-29, most of the elements have been applied to places where you would expect, e.g., firstName to "John," lastName to "Doe." The one exception is the para element, which has not been applied to each of the two paragraphs in the body of the press release but rather to *all* of the text within the body. Without utilizing Smart Document technology, Word does not provide an easy way for end users to create repeating elements (except with table rows, which aren't used here). Since the para element nevertheless needs to be repeating, we use regular Word paragraphs (w:p elements instead of literal para elements) and convert back and forth between real para elements through the *onload* and *onsave* stylesheets. The only reason we include a lit-

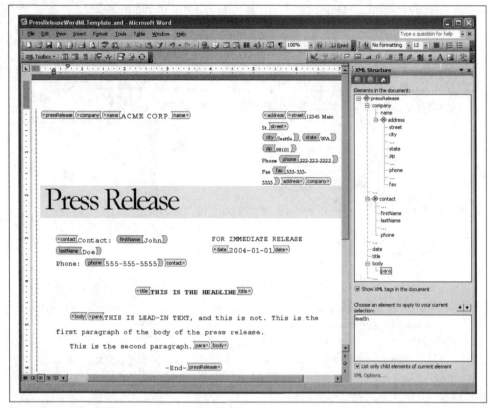

Figure 4-29. The document after applying all XML elements

eral para element in the template is to enable the document to be valid. The schema requires at least one para element to be present. Rather than creating a temporary, special-purpose schema in which para elements are optional, we make the document valid by letting a single, fixed para element contain the Word paragraphs. The *onload* and *onsave* stylesheets translate back and forth between this intermediate representation (one para element containing multiple w:p elements) and the true, desired representation (a sequence of one or more para elements). We'll see both sides of this translation shortly.

Convert Block-Level Leaf Tags to Run-Level Tags

When you apply XML tags to a document through the XML Structure task pane, Word automatically decides at what level of the WordprocessingML hierarchy to insert the tags, based on the current selection. In Figure 4-29, the street element, for example, got inserted as a block-level tag (inside a table cell), while the city and state elements got inserted as run-level tags. This was necessary because city and state were applied to text within the same paragraph. Oftentimes, you do not want to just stick with what Word chooses. While you can't always turn a run-level tag into a block-level tag, you can certainly turn a block-level *leaf* tag (i.e., that contains no more custom elements) into a run-level tag. And, as it turns out, there is a very good reason for doing so.

Block-level tags allow users to insert multiple Word paragraphs (w:p elements) inside them. Unless you have an *onsave* stylesheet that specifically handles this case, the text from the multiple paragraphs will get merged together when the Wordprocessing ML is stripped from the document. This inevitably causes whitespace formatting problems, e.g., the absence of a space between the last sentence of one paragraph and the first sentence of the next. As it happens, our press release template's *onsave* stylesheet *does* expect there to be multiple Word paragraphs (w:p elements) inside the para element (from which it will derive corresponding para elements in the final result). But it does *not* expect multiple paragraphs anywhere else in the template. Thus, it behooves us to change other block-level leaf tags to run-level tags instead. In fact, we can generalize the advice: *whenever possible, use run-level tags for leaf elements when all you want is a single line of text*. In the press release template, there are four such candidates for change: the name, street, date, and title elements.

The easiest way to change a block-level tag into a run-level tag from within the Word UI is to place the cursor just to the right of the end tag and hit the spacebar. Since there can't be text outside the block-level tag yet on the same line, Word automatically converts the block-level tag to a run-level tag. Then, you can just hit Backspace to remove the space character if you want. The tag will continue to be a run-level tag.

Figure 4-30 shows a close-up of the name and street elements in their default block-level state, before any changes are made.

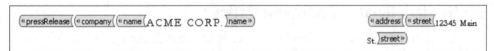

Figure 4-30. The name and street elements as block-level tags

And Figure 4-31 shows the name and street elements after we have changed them to run-level tags using the space/Backspace technique described above.

Figure 4-31. The name and street elements as run-level tags

Provided that we also convert the date and title elements, our new template—supplemented with editing restrictions—will now be more robust. It will prevent users from hitting Enter to create new paragraphs inside fields that are designed to contain only one line of text.

Assign Placeholder Text

Once all of the custom tags are in place, you can assign placeholder text to each custom leaf element by right-clicking the element in the main pane or in the XML Structure task pane and selecting Attributes.... In the Attributes dialog, enter the placeholder text for the element in the "Placeholder text" text box, as shown in Figure 4-32.

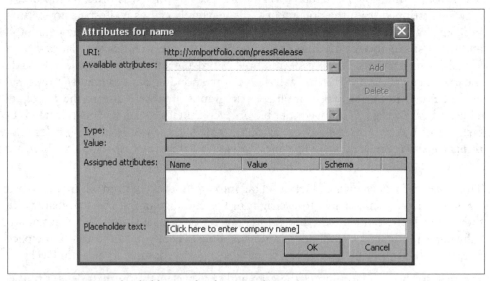

Figure 4-32. Entering placeholder text for the name element

Set the XML-Related Document Options

One thing to note about our template so far is that the document is still flagged as invalid, even though all of the elements in the document have been applied to valid values. The XML Structure task pane alerts us to the problem, shown up close in Figure 4-33.

Right-clicking the address element in the tree shows that the problem is that text is contained directly inside the address element, which the schema disallows. Each mixed content text node is represented in the XML Structure task pane as an ellipsis (...). For the address element, the culprits are the comma (,) between the city and state elements, and the words Phone and Fax. These text nodes are not part of our data; instead, they are part of our template's boilerplate text. To ignore mixed content for purposes of validation, we will need to turn on the "Ignore mixed content" document option.

To view and modify the current document's XML options, click the "XML Options..." link at the bottom of the XML Structure task pane. (This dialog is also accessible through a button on the Tools → Templates and Add-Ins... → XML Schema dialog.)

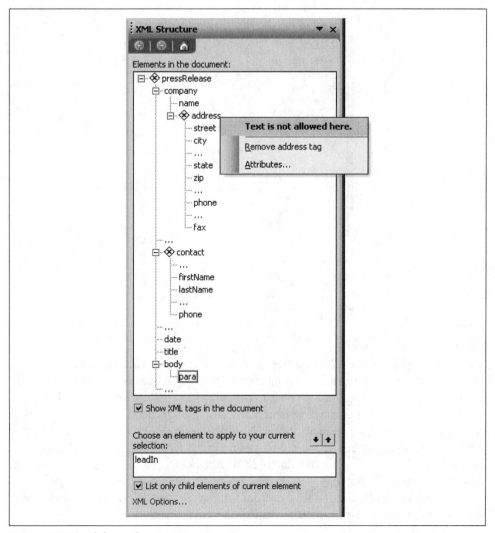

Figure 4-33. Invalid mixed content text

Here is where we can check the "Ignore mixed content" checkbox so that the boiler-plate text in our template gets stripped out for validation purposes. If we check this checkbox and click OK, then the XML Structure task pane no longer complains that our document is invalid, as shown in Figure 4-34.

Note that the ellipses are now gone. Since "Ignore mixed content" is turned on, all mixed content text nodes are ignored for validation purposes and no longer appear in the XML Structure task pane's tree view of the document. For that reason, the validation errors are gone now too.

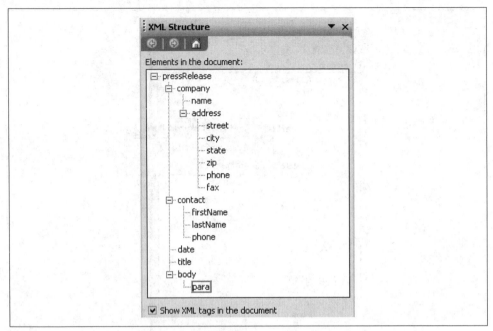

Figure 4-34. The XML Structure task pane with "Ignore mixed content" turned on

For now, we'll leave the XML save options alone. It is true that our ultimate *onload* stylesheet will need to turn the "Apply custom transform" option on, pointing to the *onsave* stylesheet for our press release template, *harvestPressRelease.xsl*. However, we are not there yet. For development purposes, we still need to save the template we are currently preparing in Word as WordprocessingML, so that we can adapt it into an *onload* stylesheet. If we try to prematurely set our ultimately desired save options, we'll be faced with the Catch-22 of not being able to save the underlying WordprocessingML, because we've asked Word to apply our *onsave* stylesheet to it. Instead, the ultimately desired save options will have to be set *manually* inside the w: docPr element in the *onload* stylesheet once we've created it.

Enable Editing Restrictions

Now that you have assigned all of the XML elements in your document, along with placeholder text, it's time to turn on editing restrictions, so that users don't inadvertently delete boilerplate text or custom XML elements. To do this, open the Protect Document task pane, click the box next to "Allow only this type of editing in the document," and leave the default type of restriction in the drop-down box—"No changes (Read only)." Figure 4-35 shows the Protect Document task pane.

At this point, if you start enforcing the protection, no one will be able to edit any part of the document. That's obviously not what you want. To designate a particular area within your document to be editable, you need to select the area and then click

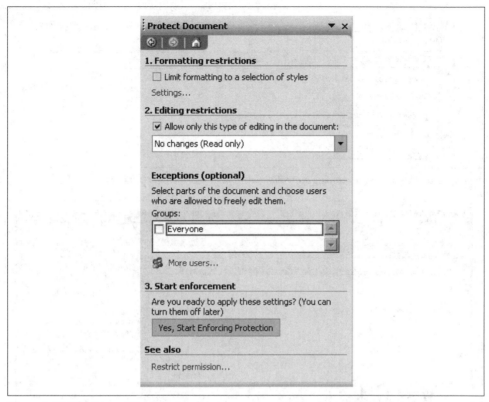

Figure 4-35. The Protect Document task pane

the Everyone checkbox under "Exceptions" to indicate that the designated area can be edited by anyone. With the "Show XML tags" option turned on, you can proceed throughout your document, selecting the text inside each leaf custom XML tag and then clicking "Everyone."

Better yet, you can skip this tedious process by using a feature of the XML Toolbox plug-in (which we introduced in Chapter 2). If you select XML Toolbox → Document Protection → Set All Nodes to EVERYONE Permission, as shown in Figure 4-36, all of the text inside leaf node XML elements will be selected and delineated as editable by "everyone."

The result of applying editing permissions either manually or through the XML Toolbox plug-in is shown in Figure 4-37.

You're almost done setting the editing restrictions. We just have one more recommendation. For the remaining block-level leaf element (para), it helps to avoid certain usability problems if you include para's end tag inside the editable region. Don't worry, the user won't be able to delete the tag. This just ensures that they will be able to hit Enter and create a new paragraph as expected and that all paragraphs they

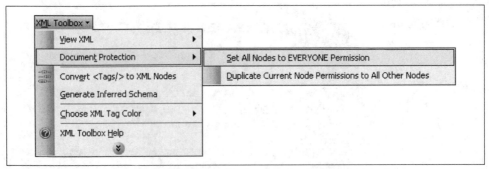

Figure 4-36. Automating document protection with the XML Toolbox plug-in

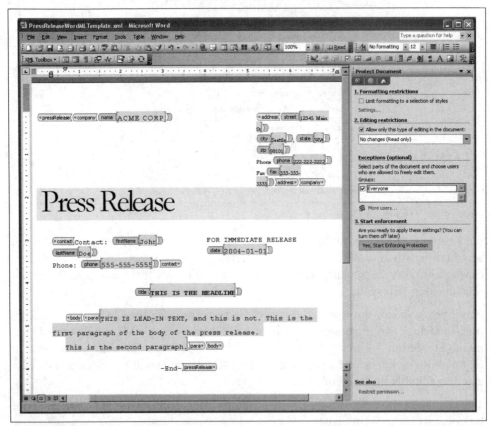

Figure 4-37. Exceptions to the read-only editing restriction

do create stay within the editing region. To do this, highlight the para end tag and click the "Everyone" checkbox in the Protect Document task pane. The result should look like the close-up of the paragraph tags shown in Figure 4-38.

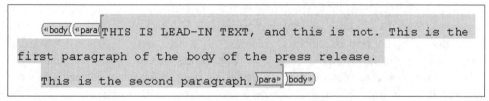

Figure 4-38. Extending the editing region to include the end tag of the para element

Note that the editing region includes the end tag but not the start tag. If you included the start tag too, then the user would be allowed to delete the para element, which is definitely not what you want.

Before we start enforcing protection, we first need to configure our formatting restrictions.

Enable Formatting Restrictions

To enable formatting restrictions, check the box next to "Limit formatting to a selection of styles" in the Protect Document task pane. Then click the "Settings…" link. You will see the dialog shown in Figure 4-39.

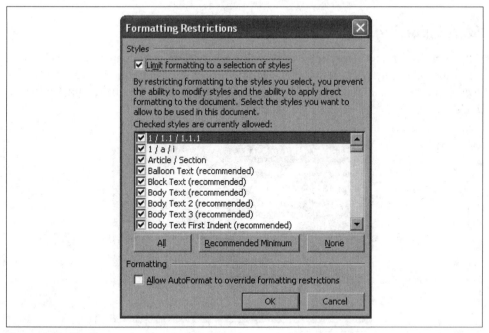

Figure 4-39. The Formatting Restrictions dialog

In the press release template, there are only three styles we want to let users have access to. Start by clicking the "None" button to uncheck all of the styles. Then, scroll down the list and check the boxes next to "Body Text," "Lead-in Emphasis," and "No formatting." Finally, click OK. The dialog box in Figure 4-40 asks you whether you want to remove existing styles in the document that aren't in your allowed list of styles.

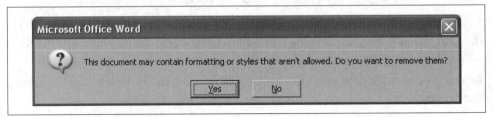

Figure 4-40. Do you want to strip out restricted styles from this document?

At this point, it is important that you click the No button. Otherwise, the other styles in the document that control how the template looks and feels will get stripped out. Thus, there is a distinction between styles that the user is allowed to apply and styles that are already present in the document.

Start Enforcing Protection

After specifying the formatting and editing restrictions, you can put those restrictions into effect by clicking the "Yes, Start Enforcing Protection" button in the Protect Document task pane. You will then be prompted with the dialog shown in Figure 4-41.

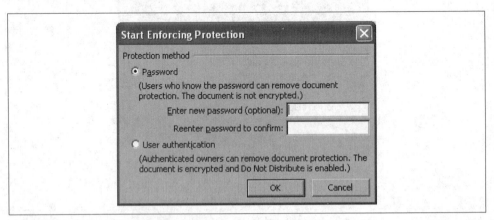

Figure 4-41. Optional password for removing document protection

Here, you can enter an optional password that users need to enter to turn document protection off. If you don't want to specify a password, just click OK.

Convert the Document to an XSLT Stylesheet

We are finally ready to adapt the document's underlying WordprocessingML into an *onload* XSLT stylesheet. As we already mentioned, converting the document to a stylesheet is often as simple as inserting `xsl:value-of` instructions into key places in the document. While this is usually a straightforward task, it can also be somewhat tedious, depending on how many elements are in your template.

A utility for generating onload stylesheets

Unfortunately (and strangely), Word does not provide a mechanism for generating *onload* XSLT stylesheets for you. To address this deficiency, we've developed a fairly simple stylesheet that can be applied as an *onsave* stylesheet to the template you prepared in Word using the XML Structure task pane. The stylesheet is called *create-onload-stylesheet.xsl*, and, as the name suggests, it creates an example *onload* stylesheet. (Yes, that's using XSLT to create XSLT.) Chances are, you will need to manually tweak the resulting stylesheet, but for templates like our press release example, it gets you about 90% of the way there. It does this simply by replacing text inside leaf-node custom elements with `xsl:value-of` instructions.

 Even though the press release template makes use of some heavy XSLT, it is quite possible to build XML templates for Word without doing any XSLT coding at all. If your template doesn't require an *onsave* stylesheet or any custom logic, then the *create-onload-stylesheet.xsl* utility could be all that you need to generate your *onload* stylesheet.

To use this utility, check the "Apply transform" checkbox in the "Save As" dialog once you've finished preparing your template in Word. Then click the Transform... button to browse for the file named *create-onload-stylesheet.xsl*. Lastly, click Save. Just like that, you have transformed your static template prepared in Word to a dynamic template that can be used as an *onload* stylesheet.

Example 4-11 shows the *create-onload-stylesheet.xsl* in its entirety. We'll take a closer look at certain parts of the stylesheet to explain what they do. This stylesheet substantially emulates what you as a developer would otherwise have to do manually to get from the merged XML template prepared in Word to a functioning *onload* stylesheet.

Example 4-11. create-onload-stylesheet.xsl, a utility for creating onload stylesheets

```
<xsl:stylesheet version="1.0"
  xmlns:xsl="http://www.w3.org/1999/XSL/Transform"
  xmlns:out="dummy"
  xmlns:w="http://schemas.microsoft.com/office/word/2003/wordml"
  xmlns:sl="http://schemas.microsoft.com/schemaLibrary/2003/core"
  xmlns:aml="http://schemas.microsoft.com/aml/2001/core"
```

```
  xmlns:wx="http://schemas.microsoft.com/office/word/2003/auxHint"
  xmlns:w10="urn:schemas-microsoft-com:office:word"
  xmlns:v="urn:schemas-microsoft-com:office:vml"
  xmlns:o="urn:schemas-microsoft-com:office:office"
  xmlns:dt="uuid:C2F41010-65B3-11d1-A29F-00AA00C14882"
  xmlns:st="urn:schemas-microsoft-com:office:smarttags"
  exclude-result-prefixes="v st">

  <xsl:output indent="yes" encoding="utf-8"/>

  <!-- Use the "out" prefix for XSLT instructions in the result stylesheet -->
  <xsl:namespace-alias stylesheet-prefix="out" result-prefix="xsl"/>

  <!-- Create stylesheet root element and root template rule -->
  <xsl:template match="/">
    <out:stylesheet version="1.0">
      <out:template match="/">
        <xsl:apply-templates/>
      </out:template>
    </out:stylesheet>
  </xsl:template>

  <!-- By default, copy all elements, attributes, and text straight through
       so they will function as literal result elements, etc. -->
  <xsl:template match="@* | * | text()">
    <xsl:copy>
      <xsl:apply-templates select="@*|node()"/>
    </xsl:copy>
  </xsl:template>

  <!-- Selectively copy attributes and top-level children of w:wordDocument -->
  <xsl:template match="w:wordDocument">
    <xsl:copy>

      <!-- Create xml:space attribute only in the final result
           of the onload transformation -->
      <out:attribute name="xml:space">preserve</out:attribute>

      <!-- Copy the rest of w:wordDocument's attributes -->
      <xsl:apply-templates select="@*[not(name()='xml:space')]"/>

      <!-- Copy any top-level elements that come before o:DocumentProperties -->
      <xsl:apply-templates select="o:DocumentProperties/preceding-sibling::*"/>

      <!-- Preserve only the o:Title property; leave out all private info -->
      <o:DocumentProperties>
        <xsl:copy-of select="o:DocumentProperties/o:Title"/>
      </o:DocumentProperties>

      <!-- Preserve processing instructions inside o:CustomDocumentProperties
           (in the same way that XML2WORD.XSL does) -->
      <o:CustomDocumentProperties>
```

```
    <out:if test="processing-instruction()">
      <o:processingInstructions dt:dt="string">
        <out:for-each select="processing-instruction()">
          <out:text>&lt;?</out:text>
          <out:value-of select="name()"/>
          <out:text> </out:text>
          <out:value-of select="."/>
          <out:text>?></out:text>
        </out:for-each>
      </o:processingInstructions>
      <!-- Copy any other custom document properties -->
      <xsl:apply-templates select="o:CustomDocumentProperties/*"/>
    </out:if>
  </o:CustomDocumentProperties>

  <!-- Process the rest of the top-level children of w:wordDocument -->
  <xsl:apply-templates select="o:DocumentProperties/following-sibling::*
                               [not(self::o:CustomDocumentProperties)]"/>

  </xsl:copy>
</xsl:template>

<!-- Set some XML-specific document options -->
<xsl:template match="w:docPr">
  <xsl:copy>

    <!-- Process all other document options -->
    <xsl:apply-templates select="*[not(self::w:removeWordSchemaOnSave or
                                 self::w:showXMLTags)]"/>

    <!-- Turn "Save data only" back on (as it was likely only off in the
         first place so that this stylesheet could be applied) -->
    <w:removeWordSchemaOnSave/>

    <!-- Force "Show XML tags" to "off", as opposed to application state -->
    <w:showXMLTags w:val="off"/>

    <!-- Insert some commented-out XML document options that you may want
         to manually turn on -->
    <xsl:comment><![CDATA[
      These are some XML save options you may want to set:
        <w:ignoreMixedContent/>
        <w:useXSLTWhenSaving/>
        <w:saveThroughXSLT w:xslt=""/>
        <w:saveInvalidXML/>
    ]]></xsl:comment>
  </xsl:copy>
</xsl:template>

<!-- Remove these settings, because they were probably only set
     to enable this transformation in the first place -->
<xsl:template match="w:useXSLTWhenSaving | w:saveThroughXSLT |
                     w:saveInvalidXML"/>
```

```
<!-- Insert xsl:value-of instructions into custom run-level leaf tags
     (identified by the presence of placeholder text) -->
<xsl:template match="*[@w:placeholder][ancestor::w:p]">
  <xsl:copy>
    <xsl:copy-of select="@*"/>
    <xsl:copy-of select="w:permStart"/>
    <w:r>
      <xsl:copy-of select="(w:r/w:rPr)[1]"/>
      <w:t>
        <out:value-of>
          <xsl:attribute name="select">
            <xsl:call-template name="xpath-expression"/>
          </xsl:attribute>
        </out:value-of>
      </w:t>
    </w:r>
    <xsl:copy-of select="w:permEnd"/>
  </xsl:copy>
</xsl:template>

<!-- Wrap whitespace-only text in w:t elements with xsl:text to ensure
     that it doesn't get stripped when Word loads the onload stylesheet -->
<xsl:template match="w:t[not(normalize-space(.))]">
  <xsl:copy>
    <out:text>
      <xsl:value-of select="."/>
    </out:text>
  </xsl:copy>
</xsl:template>

<!-- Generate XPath expressions for the select attributes of
     xsl:value-of instructions that we create -->
<xsl:template name="xpath-expression">
  <xsl:variable name="ancestor-elements"
    select="ancestor-or-self::*[not(self::w:* or self::sl:* or self::aml:* or
                                    self::wx:* or self::w10:* or self::v:* or
                                    self::o:* or self::dt:* or self::st:*)]"/>
  <xsl:for-each select="$ancestor-elements">
    <xsl:text>/</xsl:text>
    <xsl:value-of select="name()"/>
  </xsl:for-each>
</xsl:template>

</xsl:stylesheet>
```

The highlighted template rule in Example 4-11 is the most important template rule of this stylesheet. Let's step through it to see precisely what it does. Whereas the default behavior of the stylesheet is to copy all elements, attributes, and text straight through, this template rule makes an exception for custom run-level leaf tags. It matches them using this pattern:

```
<xsl:template match="*[@w:placeholder][ancestor::w:p]">
```

This pattern matches elements that have both a `w:placeholder` attribute and an ancestor `w:p` element. The presence of the `w:placeholder` attribute indicates that this is a leaf node (i.e., a custom tag that contains text only), and the presence of an ancestor `w:p` indicates that this must be a run-level tag (as opposed to a block-level, row-level, or cell-level tag). The pattern assumes that you have explicitly specified placeholder text for all of your leaf elements, which is true for the press release template and also a good practice in general.

Instead of just copying the element through as-is, the template rule creates a shallow copy of the element along with its attributes (including the `w:placeholder` attribute):

```
<xsl:copy>
  <xsl:copy-of select="@*"/>
```

Then, it copies the `w:permStart` element if present:

```
<xsl:copy-of select="w:permStart"/>
```

Next, instead of copying all the runs and text straight through, it creates a single `w:r` element, preserving any run properties that you defined when preparing the template in Word:

```
<w:r>
  <xsl:copy-of select="(w:r/w:rPr)[1]"/>
```

Then, it creates a single `w:t` element that, instead of text, contains an `xsl:value-of` instruction:*

```
<w:t>
  <out:value-of>
```

To generate the value of the `select` attribute, a template named `xpath-expression` is invoked, generating an XPath expression that represents the precise path to the current custom element:

```
<xsl:attribute name="select">
  <xsl:call-template name="xpath-expression"/>
</xsl:attribute>
```

Finally, the open elements are closed and the `w:permEnd` element is copied through, if present:

```
      </out:value-of>
    </w:t>
  </w:r>
  <xsl:copy-of select="w:permEnd"/>
  </xsl:copy>
</xsl:template>
```

---

* The out prefix is used (in conjunction with the top-level `xsl:namespace-alias` instruction) to disambiguate between XSLT instructions that are a part of this stylesheet and XSLT instructions that are part of the result stylesheet. The XSLT processor treats `out:value-of` as a literal result element that will effectively output an `xsl:value-of` instruction in the final result.

The reason this is the most important template rule is that it inserts `xsl:value-of` instructions into the resulting stylesheet, thereby making your Word template dynamic. When Word opens a press release XML document, for example, the `xsl:value-of` instructions in the *onload* stylesheet dynamically populate the fields in the press release template with values from the source XML document.

Whether you manually insert `xsl:value-of` instructions into the XML template you prepare in Word or you use a utility like *create-onload-stylesheet.xsl*, your ultimate *onload* stylesheet should contain excerpts that look like this:

```
<ns1:street w:placeholder="12345 Main Street">
  <w:permStart w:id="1" w:edGrp="everyone"/>
  <w:r>
    <w:t>
      <xsl:value-of select="/ns1:pressRelease/ns1:company/ns1:address/ns1:street"/>
    </w:t>
  </w:r>
  <w:permEnd w:id="1"/>
</ns1:street>
```

The above is excerpted from *pr2word.xsl*, the *onload* stylesheet for our press release template. Again, `ns1` is an auto-generated namespace prefix mapped to the namespace for press release documents.

Manually customizing the onload stylesheet

Although the XSLT stylesheet created by *create-onload-stylesheet.xsl* may perfectly suffice for some templates, the press release template needs some further customizations. In particular, it needs to handle the body text of press release documents. As such, a stylesheet created by *create-onload-stylesheet.xsl* will not dynamically populate any block-level elements, since the utility only supports run-level leaf elements. You will need to make some modifications to the resulting stylesheet, because the body text is contained (necessarily) within a block-level element.

After finding the relevant spot in the resulting stylesheet, remove the hard-coded `w:p` elements inside the `ns1:para` element. You want the contents of `ns1:para` to be dynamically populated based on the presence of para elements in the source document being opened, so begin processing those:

```
<ns1:body>
  <ns1:para w:placeholder="[Click here to enter body text]">
    <w:permStart w:id="12" w:edGrp="everyone" w:displacedBySDT="prev"/>
    <!-- ************* MANUAL CUSTOMIZATIONS ************** -->
    <xsl:apply-templates select="/ns1:pressRelease/ns1:body/ns1:para"/>
    <!-- ************************************************** -->
  </ns1:para>
  <w:permEnd w:id="12" w:displacedBySDT="next"/>
</ns1:body>
```

Next, define some template rules that convert para elements in the source document to w:p elements, and leadIn elements to runs having the "Lead-in Emphasis" style. All of the needed custom template rules are shown below:

```
<!-- ************ MANUAL CUSTOMIZATIONS ************** -->
<xsl:template match="ns1:para">
  <w:p>
    <w:pPr>
      <w:pStyle w:val="BodyText"/>
      <xsl:if test="not(node())">
        <w:rPr>
          <w:rStyle w:val="Lead-inEmphasis"/>
        </w:rPr>
      </xsl:if>
    </w:pPr>
    <xsl:apply-templates/>
  </w:p>
</xsl:template>

<xsl:template match="ns1:leadIn">
  <w:r>
    <w:rPr>
      <w:rStyle w:val="Lead-inEmphasis"/>
    </w:rPr>
    <xsl:apply-templates/>
  </w:r>
</xsl:template>

<xsl:template match="ns1:para/text()">
  <w:r>
    <w:t>
      <xsl:copy/>
    </w:t>
  </w:r>
</xsl:template>

<xsl:template match="ns1:leadIn/text()">
  <w:t>
    <xsl:copy/>
  </w:t>
</xsl:template>
<!-- *************************************************** -->
```

These are all very straightforward. There is just one twist. In the template rule for para elements, there is a test to see if the current element is empty:

```
<xsl:if test="not(node())">
  <w:rPr>
    <w:rStyle w:val="Lead-inEmphasis"/>
  </w:rPr>
</xsl:if>
```

If you recall from Chapter 2, the w:rPr element, when inside the w:pPr element, signifies the run properties of the paragraph mark. By assigning the "Lead-in Emphasis" style to the paragraph mark, you dictate the character style that text will be in when the user begins typing. This is exactly the sort of behavior you want for lead-in text when a user is first filling out the template. One way you'll know whether the user is filling out the template for the first time is if the source document contains no data yet, i.e., if it contains a single *empty* para element—hence the test to see if the current element is empty.

There is one more place where you need to make some manual modifications to the *onload* stylesheet. At this point, you have finished defining the mappings between para elements in the source document and styled paragraphs in the WordprocessingML document. However, you still haven't shown Word how to do the reverse— how to translate styled paragraphs back to your custom XML. You do have the *onsave* stylesheet, *harvestPressRelease.xsl*, up and ready to go; you just need to point Word to it. Edit the literal result elements inside w:docPr so that "Save data only" will be turned off, "Apply custom transform" will be turned on, and the *onsave* stylesheet will be correctly referenced. Your changes should look something like this:

```
<!-- ************* MANUAL CUSTOMIZATIONS ************** -->
<w:removeWordSchemaOnSave w:val="off"/>
<w:useXSLTWhenSaving/>
<w:saveThroughXSLT w:xslt="\\intra\pr\harvestPressRelease.xsl"/>
<!-- *************************************************** -->
```

Finally, your final *onload* stylesheet, *pr2word.xsl*, is ready to deploy.

Deploying the Template

There are a number of different ways to deploy XML editing solutions for Word. In this section, we'll look at one possible way to deploy the press release template that works best in a corporate environment. Since deployment is an even bigger topic in the context of Smart Documents, Chapter 5 will cover this topic in greater detail.

So far in this chapter, we have seen the contents (or partial contents, in the case of *pr2word.xsl*) of four of the press release template's source files:

- *pressRelease.xsd* (the press release schema)
- *pr2word.xsl* (the *onload* stylesheet)
- *harvestPressRelease.xsl* (the *onsave* stylesheet)
- *saveDataOnly.xsl* (imported by the *onsave* stylesheet)

There are two more files we need to include (making a total of six): the initial XML template file, *New Press Release.xml*, and a deployment manifest called *manifest.xml*. Together, these files help fulfill the generally twofold aim of deployment:

- Give users a way to create new XML documents (such as a template file to open)
- Populate the schema library on each user's machine so that the solution will be invoked automatically when opening existing XML documents

Now let's look at *New Press Release.xml* and *manifest.xml* in turn to see how they fulfill these goals.

The Initial XML Template File

The *New Press Release.xml* file, which we mentioned at the very beginning of the chapter, is what the IT department delivers to the PR department. This could be deployed, for example, on a web site or on a local network share. Example 4-12 shows the contents of this file.

Example 4-12. The initial XML template, New Press Release.xml

```
<?xml version="1.0"?>
<?mso-application progid="Word.Document"?>
<?mso-solutionextension URI="http://xmlportfolio.com/pressRelease"
                        manifestPath="\\intra\pr\manifest.xml"?>
<pressRelease xmlns="http://xmlportfolio.com/pressRelease">
  <company>
    <name/>
    <address>
      <street/>
      <city/>
      <state/>
      <zip/>
      <phone/>
      <fax/>
    </address>
  </company>
  <contact>
    <firstName/>
    <lastName/>
    <phone/>
  </contact>
  <date/>
  <title/>
  <body>
    <para/>
  </body>
</pressRelease>
```

This document consists of an empty "skeleton" instance of our schema. All of the expected elements are present, but the leaf nodes are empty. They have not been filled out yet. When a user who already has the press release template installed in their schema library opens this document, the *pr2word.xsl* stylesheet is applied to it, producing the press release view we saw originally in Figure 4-1.

The key line that concerns us here is the `mso-solutionextension` PI:

```
<?mso-solutionextension URI="http://xmlportfolio.com/pressRelease"
                        manifestPath="\\intra\pr\manifest.xml"?>
```

This processing instruction doesn't add any value for users who already have the press release template installed on their machine. For users who don't, however, it instructs Word to retrieve the manifest file for this "solution." (The URI pseudo-attribute contains the target namespace URI for the schema.) In this way, Word can automatically install the necessary files into the machine's schema library without manual intervention. It automatically retrieves the manifest file located at \\intra\pr\ manifest.xml after confirming from the user that this is okay.

The Manifest File

The manifest file contains a reference to the schema and *onload* stylesheet files for the press release template. It could also include other files, such as Smart Document code, secondary view stylesheets, etc. Example 4-13 shows the manifest file for the press release template, *manifest.xml*.

Example 4-13. The manifest file for the press release template, manifest.xml

```xml
<?xml version="1.0" encoding="UTF-8" standalone="no"?>
<manifest xmlns="http://schemas.microsoft.com/office/xmlexpansionpacks/2003">
   <version>1.0</version>
   <uri>http://xmlportfolio.com/pressRelease</uri>
   <solution>
     <solutionID>sdfa097sdfa0</solutionID>
     <type>schema</type>
     <alias>Press Release</alias>
     <file>
       <type>schema</type>
       <version>1.0</version>
       <filePath>\\intra\pr\pressRelease.xsd</filePath>
     </file>
   </solution>
   <solution>
     <solutionID>9a871342098vxcasdf</solutionID>
     <type>transform</type>
     <alias>Elegant</alias>
     <documentSpecific>false</documentSpecific>
     <context>http://schemas.microsoft.com/office/word/2003/wordml</context>
     <file>
       <type>primaryTransform</type>
       <version>1.0</version>
       <filePath>\\intra\pr\pr2word.xsl</filePath>
     </file>
   </solution>
</manifest>
```

When Word installs this "XML expansion pack," it retrieves each of the files referenced within the manifest. In this case, it downloads the *pressRelease.xsd* and *pr2word.xsl* files and installs them into the schema library.

Ideally, the manifest would include *all* the files of our template, not just the schema and *onload* stylesheet files. This would allow for a central point of deployment. However, as of this writing, we have not yet figured out a way to reference *onsave* stylesheets installed in the schema library. Recall the relevant line from our *onload* stylesheet, *pr2word.xsl*:

```
<w:saveThroughXSLT w:xslt="\\intra\pr\harvestPressRelease.xsl"/>
```

The w:xslt attribute must point to the file location of an *onsave* stylesheet. According to the WordprocessingML schema, the w:saveThroughXSLT element can also have a w:solutionID attribute, which sounds like precisely what we would use to reference a stylesheet installed in the schema library. Unfortunately, Microsoft has not documented how to go about making that reference, and everything we've tried so far has failed. For that reason, the manifest for the press release template does not install the *onsave* stylesheet. Instead, the stylesheet must remain in a shared location to be accessed directly each time it is used. In this case, that location is *\\intra\pr\harvestPressRelease.xsl*.

Limitations of Word 2003's XML Support

As you've probably already figured out, there are some serious limitations to this first version of Word's custom XML schema support. To conclude the chapter, we'll explicitly address some of these, if for no other reason than to assure you that, no, you're not missing something.

Schemas and Namespaces

In Word 2003's world view, there is a one-to-one correspondence between schemas and namespace URIs. The schema library can contain only one schema for a given namespace URI. In fact, Word uses "schema" as basically synonymous with "namespace URI." Considering the fact that it is the namespace of a given XML document's root element that determines what *onload* "XML data view" stylesheet to apply, this means that there are two important limitations to keep in mind:

- You cannot create two separate editing solutions (using different schemas) that have the same namespace URI
- Any XML document you wish to edit in Word must have a namespace, which rules out, for example, Docbook.

This assumes that you need the *onload* stylesheet to be applied automatically without the user's intervention. If you are willing to force users to manually browse for the XSLT stylesheet to apply, then it is possible to overcome both of these limitations. Depending on your users, it may or may not be feasible to rely on their doing this. Also, if you want on-the-fly schema validation to work, your stylesheet will need to transform the source XML document into an XML document that is in a namespace that uniquely identifies an XML schema in the schema library. In that case, you would also need to provide an *onsave* XSLT stylesheet to change or remove the namespace when the user saves the document. However, these are burdens on the developer that can be overcome with a bit of cleverness. In the end, the real question is whether it's feasible to require users to manually find the appropriate *onload* XSLT stylesheet each time they open a particular type of XML document. If not, then you'll have to stick to using a unique namespace for each document type's root element.

 This problem is somewhat alleviated by the fact that Word, when it opens an arbitrary XML document, also lists any XSLT stylesheets referenced through the xml-stylesheet PI, in its list of "XML Data Views." For instance documents that don't use namespaces, this is the only way to automatically associate the document with an XSLT stylesheet. If you're willing to include an xml-stylesheet PI just for the sake of Word, then this may effectively solve this bootstrapping problem without requiring too much user intervention.

Document Protection Doesn't Go Far Enough

Document protection is an independently introduced feature in Word 2003. It is not tightly integrated with the XML editing features. It is up to the developer to maintain common boundaries between permission areas and custom XML tags.

Formatting restrictions are all or nothing. You can't distinguish between the allowed styles for one field and the allowed styles for another. There is no way to associate particular styles with particular elements except through the use of Smart Documents.

Also, while formatting restrictions prevent the user from applying direct formatting and from using any forbidden styles, it does not prevent the user from inserting tables, images, or other objects.

Document Protection Conflicts with Multiple Views

Editing restrictions unfortunately don't play nicely with XML data views. They are excessively sticky. In other words, once the default *onload* stylesheet has been applied, Word fails to update the document protection settings for the loaded document when it applies another view as elected by the user. In the press release template, for example, the default view has editing restrictions turned on. If the user tries switching to the "Data only" or some other view, Word chokes and is not able to make the transition correctly. Conversely, when the default view does *not* have editing restrictions turned on, they won't be turned on when the user switches to a different view either, regardless of whether the other view defines editing restrictions to be in force. Effectively, you have to choose between using document protection and providing multiple editing views for the same document type. This is most likely buggy behavior exploited by the press release template. Hopefully it will be addressed soon in a future update.

Only One View at a Time

Once the user has begun editing a document after selecting a particular XML data view, they cannot subsequently change the view. This limitation is more a logical consequence of Word's architecture for editing XML than it is a particular deficiency of the product. The reason it is impossible to change the view is that the WordprocessingML document that's a result of the *onload* stylesheet retains no knowledge of the source document from which it was derived. Once the user makes a change to it, there is no way to automatically propagate those changes back to the source document. It could have tried to apply the document's default save settings to reconstruct the document, but this doesn't necessarily make sense for all of the use cases that the custom Word XML functionality is designed to support.

Contrast this with InfoPath's "mapping" approach, which uses XSLT to define a single, round-trip mapping between the source document and editing view, allowing users to switch views while in the middle of editing. See Chapter 10.

CHAPTER 5

Developing Smart Document Solutions

Microsoft Word's built-in capabilities for integrating XML shown in the previous chapter provide a foundation for creating XML documents in Word. The results, however, feel more like an import/export option than a complete application. In many cases, that functionality is perfectly acceptable, but Microsoft also provides a set of options for creating more interactive environments for editing XML documents in Word through the Smart Documents framework.

Smart Documents let you create templates that help users create the information that goes in the document, taking a huge step beyond the material covered in the previous chapter, which showed how to build spaces in the document where users could work. The Smart Document approach lets you integrate all kinds of data sources, from multiple XML documents to web services, and expands Word's XML frontiers substantially.

At the same time, however, Smart Documents come with a price: they require working with managed code, the application object model, and an API that is far from elegant. It takes a fair amount of effort to move from an XML-enabled Word document to Smart Documents, and you'll need to evaluate your projects carefully to determine if the benefits are worth the effort.

What's a Smart Document?

A Smart Document has built-in intelligence that assists the information worker in the process of creating and updating documents and spreadsheets. Smart Documents can query a web service for the latest financial information about a company and automatically insert the returned data into the document. They can access a corporate database and retrieve client information necessary to complete a contract. They can connect to a document repository or portal site and retrieve reusable fragments, such as standard legal notices and disclaimers, or product and service descriptions, and add them to a new or existing document. They can validate that a user has supplied all of the necessary information before saving and forwarding it on to the next step in the workflow. Providing quick and easy access to accurate, up-to-date information and eliminating the need for re-keying or copying from one application to another, Smart Documents can be of tremendous benefit to the end user, especially for editing XML documents.

Word 2003's core XML support provides no method for associating elements in context with Word styles. This is standard functionality in the market-leading XML-for-documents applications and is typically accomplished through some type of stylesheet (DSSSL, FOSI, CSS, or proprietary solutions). As we saw in Chapter 4, an onload XSLT stylesheet can apply styles to an existing XML instance when it is first opened in Microsoft Word. However, once any changes have been made to the document, the XML Document task pane (which is used to select an onload stylesheet) is no longer available. Without a Smart Document solution, not only would the end user have to manually select each of the appropriate elements to be inserted into the document (using the XML Structure task pane or selecting "Apply XML Element" from the pop-up menu), they would also need to manually associate formatting information with each text fragment created.

Unlike traditional XML authoring applications such as Arbortext's Epic Editor or Adobe's FrameMaker, Smart Documents are capable of keeping the markup under the covers; users can peek if they wish, but there is no requirement for them to learn all about XML schemas and the particular vocabulary and grammar associated with their documents.

Smart Document technology is new in Office 2003 and designed to work with Word and Excel. An extension of the Smart Tags API introduced in Office XP, Smart Documents extend the programmability of these desktop tools to support development of *solutions*. A solution is dedicated to a particular task, such as writing a technical manual, a sales proposal, a quarterly SEC filing, or an expense report, and incorporates functionality designed to make the information worker's job easier. Smart Documents require an XML framework, and can include all of the features and functionality of the applications themselves through the use of the Word or Excel Object Models. Smart Documents can also be extended through the use of Web Services, SharePoint Services, and other database connectivity methods to dynamically populate and update content. Smart Documents can also incorporate workflow capabilities, such as checking on save that all required components have been supplied and then forwarding the document to a manager for approval. Microsoft provides support for Smart Document development in several languages: Visual Basic 6.0, Visual C++ 6.0, Visual Basic .NET, and Visual C# .NET.

The Smart Document SDK (*sdocsdk.msi*) can be downloaded from the Microsoft web site. Since the location is subject to change, the best way to locate the file is to go to: *http://www.microsoft.com* and search for *sdocsdk.msi*. The SDK includes documentation, help files, and several sample applications (including source code) developed in each of the four supported languages.

While it has been possible for quite some time to automate certain functions within the Microsoft Office Suite, a Smart Document raises the art to a new level. The Microsoft Office 2003 "System" provides a robust software development environment for building custom applications within no-longer-ordinary desktop tools. Rather than macros residing in individual template or document files, Smart Document code is distributed via a *.dll* that is associated with the document or spreadsheet through a manifest file. The developer is given access to the Task Pane where numerous actions are displayed for the end user along with help content. New protection functionality means that user access can be controlled on a granular level. You can restrict the use of styles, allowing you, rather than the end user, to control the formatting through the Smart Document application. Sections of the document can be protected, ensuring that required content is not accidentally removed. The document appears to have some level of intelligence about what it is and how it works.

Smart Document Solutions

A solution, also referred to as an "expansion pack," consists of several components. At a minimum, an expansion pack contains the following:

- A *.dll*
- A schema
- A manifest file

In addition, it most likely will also include one or more templates and help files, XSLT files, and potentially media files (images, audio or video clips, etc.). Microsoft Word solutions might also include document fragments.

 While Smart Document solutions can be built for either Word or Excel, this chapter focuses on the intricacies of developing solutions for Microsoft Office Word 2003.

Smart Document Components

Each component of a Smart Document plays an integral part in the overall solution. Care must be taken to ensure that each component is synchronized with the others; if an element name has been modified in the schema and is the subject of a Smart Document control, it must also be updated in the programming code and any XSLT files. Since pointers to fragments are to absolute paths, care must be taken to ensure that each file is included in the installation and placed in the appropriate location. The Smart Document components are as follows:

Schemas

Schemas are the foundation of any structured markup implementation. A schema defines a *vocabulary* and *grammar* for a specific purpose, such as the creation of semiconductor datasheets, legal contracts, or user manuals. "Vocabulary" refers to the unique identifiers assigned to each of the components of the information set (i.e., elements), and "grammar" refers to the rules of how the words can be put together to form larger groups. Careful analysis of the information set is required to ensure that the schema to be used will provide the necessary support.

Styles and templates

Templates are, for the most part, empty documents that contain all the necessary information about a particular document type to allow new document instances to be created. In particular, this includes page layouts, styles, header/footer information, and fonts. There are four style categories in Word: paragraph, character, list, and table. Each named style is based on one of these four types and contains numerous settings that define the placement and appearance of any content associated with that specific style. For a Smart Document solution, there is another critical component: a shell XML instance with placeholder text. Boilerplate content may also be included.

XSL transformations

XSL transformations play a vital role in a Word Smart Document solution. As described in Chapter 4, transformations can be called when either opening or saving a document, manipulating the source or resulting data as necessary. Transformations can also be incorporated into the solution itself to apply styles and other formatting characteristics, or otherwise affect the result of an action.

.dll files

The functionality of a Smart Document solution operates through the ISmartDocument interface. The properties and methods of ISmartDocument, in conjunction with the objects, properties, and methods of the Word or Excel Object Model, are the workhorses of the solution.

Manifest file

The manifest file is an XML instance that defines each of the expansion pack components and their locations. It also contains other valuable information about the solution that can be used to automatically trigger updates.

Miscellaneous files

There can be numerous files associated with a Smart Document solution, including image, sound and video files, document fragments, help files, Access database files, other XML files, and just about anything else that may be necessary (or useful) for your particular application.

Creating a Smart Document Solution

The document shown in Figures 5-1 and 5-2 was created using a fairly simple Smart Document solution. The remainder of the chapter will walk through each of the steps involved in building a similar application. While far from robust, it touches on each of the major capabilities incorporated into the Smart Document API and will hopefully set your imagination in motion.

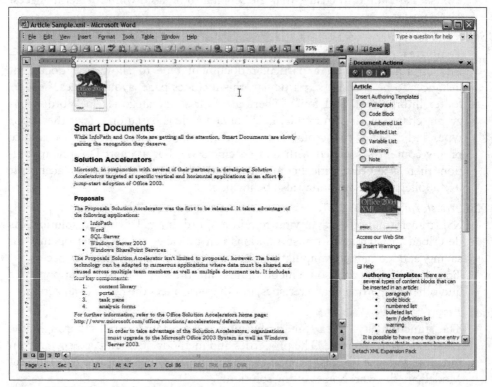

Figure 5-1. Article created with Smart Document solution

Smart Document solutions can be created using Visual Basic 6, Visual Basic .NET, C++ 6, or C# .NET. The examples in this section are all written using VB .NET; however, the Microsoft Office 2003 Smart Document SDK includes examples in all four languages.

A number of articles relating to the creation of Smart Documents can be found on the MSDN web site at *http://msdn.microsoft.com/office*.

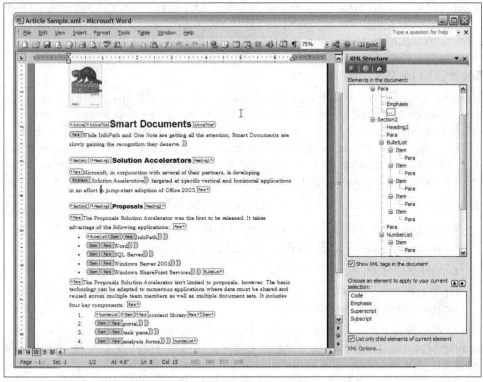

Figure 5-2. Article with XML Tag View on

The following components (schemas, XML instance, templates, and styles) will be used as the basis for the examples in this section. The schema is fairly simplistic and included for demonstration purposes only; the intended usage is for magazine article submissions.

Schemas

As mentioned in Chapter 2, Microsoft Office 2003 supports only W3C XML schemas. If you're working with existing SGML or XML document instances, it's likely that you'll have DTDs rather than schemas associated with these instances. This section provides some insight about migrating or extending existing XML environments to Microsoft Word. While far from an exact science, the following guidelines will help you avoid problem areas. Only through experimentation will you be able to determine what works best for your particular applications.

Existing Word environments

Chances are good that if your users are already using Microsoft Word to author, revise, and maintain their documents, you'll be able to create a schema and build a suitable XML-based Smart Document solution. Documents that incorporate information from external sources can take advantage of database connectivity and web services to automatically populate information and ensure that it is always current.

Existing XML (or SGML) environments

Numerous organizations already take advantage of structured markup for document authoring, editing, and delivery. If you are planning to develop a smart document solution using an existing DTD or schema, give careful consideration to the applicability of such schemas to the goals of the tasks to be designed in Word. If you are working with a schema that is fairly complex, it might be more appropriate to create subsets and build a suite of solutions focused on specific tasks.

Characteristics of a complex schema include, but are not limited to:

- More than a handful of elements allowed at common insertion points
- Numerous elements with similar meaning that can easily be confused
- Elements rarely used
- Deep structures (common to DTDs and schemas that are designed to produce multi-volume information sets)

If your organization has an existing repository of XML documents, an analysis of the markup actually used versus what is allowed by the schema can be a valuable resource. Not only will this aid in the development of any Smart Document solutions, it can also serve to simplify any other tools already in existence that must be supported.

 Refer to Appendix D for information on converting already-existing DTDs to schemas.

Starting from scratch

If your organization doesn't already have DTDs or schemas in place, you will need to either create your own, or find schemas in the public domain suited to the task at hand. It's important to keep the goals of the project in mind while developing schemas; these goals will play an important role in determining the level of granularity to be supported and the specificity of the markup itself, while ensuring that markup will be interchangeable with any other known processes.

Customer-specific DTDs or schemas. The process of performing an analysis on an information set for the purpose of creating schemas can be quick and easy, drawn out and complex, or anywhere in between. It depends on several factors:

- Depth of information set (very complex markup models to support external processes, such as reference works or aircraft documentation versus newspaper articles or consumer-oriented user guides)

- Breadth of information set (multiple information delivery types from a single source, such as user guides, administrative manuals, reference manuals, training materials, and marketing materials versus single-purpose documents such as sales proposals or white papers)
- External information sets (compatibility with other data sets that will become inputs, integrated with, or accept result data from the solution)

Any and all potential users should have some input into the analysis; it is common for different departments to use different names for similar components, or to view data in very different ways from each other. These differences do not need to be reconciled; instead, unique Smart Document solutions can be created that are targeted to the various groups. One common information set with XML at its core; different frontend applications designed to meet the needs of the individual information worker: that's the power of XML!

DTDs or schemas developed by committee. Organizations often use industry-standard or consortia-developed schemas. One mistake to avoid is choosing an existing schema rather than developing your own because it seems like the easier thing to do. Before making this decision, it is important that an analysis is performed of your organization's information set, and that the goals and objectives of your overall project are documented. The results can then be evaluated against the existing schema to determine whether or not the chosen schema is appropriate for your organization. Chances are that once you've done the analysis work, you'll discover that creating the actual schema is a simple task, and your organization won't be dependent an outside group for maintenance and revisions.

When using a particular schema in order to meet governmental or corporate requirements, it is usually possible to create a simplified subset for your particular application. The subset will be valid within the overall schema, yet the developers and end users will not need to deal with some of the inherent complexities of these behemoths. Another alternative is to create a *mapping* from your internal schema to the one required. This will allow your end users to work in an environment that is familiar to them, yet still enable your organization to meet the stated requirements by transforming the resulting information set.

Microsoft Word has always been suited to a certain class of documents, and this hasn't really changed in Office 2003. If you are currently using Word to produce your documents, then chances are that you'll be able to build an XML-enabled smart document solution to accommodate it. If your documents currently require a more sophisticated composition tool, such as Adobe's FrameMaker, or a full-time dedicated XML editor, such as Arbortext's EpicEditor, then Word, even with Smart Documents, most likely will not be able to support your requirements unless you are creating a simplified solution.

The SDArticle schema

The SDArticle schema is by no means comprehensive, but it is enough to show how Smart Documents work. As shown in Example 5-1, it consists of an article root element, followed by a title and introductory paragraphs. From there the article is divided into four levels of sections, which contain a mix of paragraphs, lists, warnings, notes, and code blocks. Inline elements consist of emphasis, subscript, superscript, and code.

Example 5-1. The SDArticle example schema (whitespace added for readability)

```
<xs:schema targetNamespace="http://www.office-xml.com/ns/sdarticle"
   xmlns:xs="http://www.w3.org/2001/XMLSchema"
   xmlns="http://www.office-xml.com/ns/sdarticle"
   elementFormDefault="qualified">

<xs:element name='Article'>
  <xs:complexType>
   <xs:sequence>
    <xs:element ref='ArticleTitle'/>
    <xs:choice maxOccurs='unbounded'>
     <xs:element ref='Para'/>
     <xs:element ref='Section1'/>
    </xs:choice>
   </xs:sequence>
  </xs:complexType>
 </xs:element>

<xs:element name='ArticleTitle'>
  <xs:complexType mixed='true'>
  </xs:complexType>
 </xs:element>

 <xs:element name='BulletList'>
  <xs:complexType>
   <xs:sequence>
    <xs:element ref='Item' maxOccurs='unbounded'/>
   </xs:sequence>
  </xs:complexType>
 </xs:element>

<xs:element name='Code'>
  <xs:complexType mixed='true'>
  </xs:complexType>
 </xs:element>

 <xs:element name='CodeExample'>
  <xs:complexType mixed='true'>
   <xs:choice minOccurs='0' maxOccurs='unbounded'>
    <xs:element ref='Emphasis'/>
    <xs:element ref='Superscript'/>
    <xs:element ref='Subscript'/>
   </xs:choice>
```

```
  </xs:complexType>
</xs:element>

<xs:element name='Definition'>
 <xs:complexType>
  <xs:sequence>
    <xs:element ref='Para' maxOccurs='unbounded'/>
  </xs:sequence>
 </xs:complexType>
</xs:element>

<xs:element name='Emphasis'>
 <xs:complexType mixed='true'>
 <xs:attribute name='CDATA' default='italic'>
  <xs:simpleType>
   <xs:restriction base='xs:string'>
    <xs:enumeration value='bold'/>
    <xs:enumeration value='italic'/>
    <xs:enumeration value='underscore'/>
   </xs:restriction>
  </xs:simpleType>
 </xs:attribute>
 </xs:complexType>
</xs:element>

<xs:element name='Heading1'>
 <xs:complexType mixed='true'>
 </xs:complexType>
</xs:element>

<xs:element name='Heading2'>
 <xs:complexType mixed='true'>
 </xs:complexType>
</xs:element>

<xs:element name='Heading3'>
 <xs:complexType mixed='true'>
 </xs:complexType>
</xs:element>

<xs:element name='Heading4'>
 <xs:complexType mixed='true'>
 </xs:complexType>
</xs:element>

<xs:element name='Item'>
 <xs:complexType>
  <xs:sequence>
    <xs:element ref='Para' maxOccurs='unbounded'/>
  </xs:sequence>
 </xs:complexType>
</xs:element>
```

```
<xs:element name='Note'>
 <xs:complexType>
  <xs:choice maxOccurs='unbounded'>
    <xs:element ref='Para'/>
    <xs:element ref='NumberList'/>
    <xs:element ref='BulletList'/>
  </xs:choice>
 </xs:complexType>
</xs:element>

<xs:element name='NumberList'>
 <xs:complexType>
  <xs:sequence>
    <xs:element ref='Item' maxOccurs='unbounded'/>
  </xs:sequence>
 </xs:complexType>
</xs:element>

<xs:element name='Para'>
 <xs:complexType mixed='true'>
  <xs:choice minOccurs='0' maxOccurs='unbounded'>
   <xs:element ref='Code'/>
   <xs:element ref='Emphasis'/>
   <xs:element ref='Superscript'/>
   <xs:element ref='Subscript'/>
  </xs:choice>
 </xs:complexType>
</xs:element>

<xs:element name='Section1'>
 <xs:complexType>
  <xs:sequence>
    <xs:element ref='Heading1'/>
    <xs:choice minOccurs='0' maxOccurs='unbounded'>
      <xs:element ref='Para'/>
      <xs:element ref='CodeExample'/>
      <xs:element ref='VariableList'/>
      <xs:element ref='NumberList'/>
      <xs:element ref='BulletList'/>
      <xs:element ref='Note'/>
      <xs:element ref='Warning'/>
    </xs:choice>
    <xs:element ref='Section2' minOccurs='0' maxOccurs='unbounded'/>
  </xs:sequence>
 </xs:complexType>
</xs:element>

<xs:element name='Section2'>
 <xs:complexType>
  <xs:sequence>
    <xs:element ref='Heading2'/>
    <xs:choice minOccurs='0' maxOccurs='unbounded'>
```

```
        <xs:element ref='Para'/>
        <xs:element ref='CodeExample'/>
        <xs:element ref='VariableList'/>
        <xs:element ref='NumberList'/>
        <xs:element ref='BulletList'/>
        <xs:element ref='Note'/>
        <xs:element ref='Warning'/>
      </xs:choice>
      <xs:element ref='Section3' minOccurs='0' maxOccurs='unbounded'/>
    </xs:sequence>
  </xs:complexType>
</xs:element>

<xs:element name='Section3'>
  <xs:complexType>
    <xs:sequence>
      <xs:element ref='Heading3'/>
      <xs:choice minOccurs='0' maxOccurs='unbounded'>
        <xs:element ref='Para'/>
        <xs:element ref='CodeExample'/>
        <xs:element ref='VariableList'/>
        <xs:element ref='NumberList'/>
        <xs:element ref='BulletList'/>
        <xs:element ref='Note'/>
        <xs:element ref='Warning'/>
      </xs:choice>
      <xs:element ref='Section4' minOccurs='0' maxOccurs='unbounded'/>
    </xs:sequence>
  </xs:complexType>
</xs:element>

<xs:element name='Section4'>
  <xs:complexType>
    <xs:sequence>
      <xs:element ref='Heading4'/>
      <xs:choice minOccurs='0' maxOccurs='unbounded'>
        <xs:element ref='Para'/>
        <xs:element ref='CodeExample'/>
        <xs:element ref='VariableList'/>
        <xs:element ref='NumberList'/>
        <xs:element ref='BulletList'/>
        <xs:element ref='Note'/>
        <xs:element ref='Warning'/>
      </xs:choice>
    </xs:sequence>
  </xs:complexType>
</xs:element>

<xs:element name='Subscript'>
  <xs:complexType mixed='true'>
  </xs:complexType>
</xs:element>
```

```
<xs:element name='Superscript'>
 <xs:complexType mixed='true'>
 </xs:complexType>
</xs:element>

<xs:element name='Term'>
 <xs:complexType mixed='true'>
 </xs:complexType>
</xs:element>

<xs:element name='VariableEntry'>
 <xs:complexType>
  <xs:sequence>
    <xs:element ref='Term'/>
    <xs:element ref='Definition'/>
  </xs:sequence>
 </xs:complexType>
</xs:element>

<xs:element name='VariableList'>
 <xs:complexType>
  <xs:sequence>
    <xs:element ref='VariableEntry' maxOccurs='unbounded'/>
  </xs:sequence>
 </xs:complexType>
</xs:element>

<xs:element name='Warning'>
 <xs:complexType>
  <xs:choice maxOccurs='unbounded'>
    <xs:element ref='Para'/>
    <xs:element ref='NumberList'/>
    <xs:element ref='BulletList'/>
  </xs:choice>
 </xs:complexType>
</xs:element>
</xs:schema>
```

While having a schema is important, it is also a good idea to create a sample instance for development and testing that incorporates each of the elements (and their possible attribute values) and the context in which they can occur. This helps to ensure that you don't leave anything out, whether in your style setup, your actions pane, or your transformations. Example 5-2 shows just such a sample instance.

Example 5-2. A sample document conforming to the SDArticle schema

```
<?xml version="1.0" encoding="UTF-8"?>
<Article xmlns="http://www.office-xml.com/ns/sdarticle">
 <ArticleTitle>Article Title</ArticleTitle>
 <Para>This is the introductory paragraph.</Para>
 <Section1>
```

```
<Heading1>Heading 1</Heading1>
<Para>This is a paragraph. ... This is a paragraph.
 <Emphasis CDATA="italic">This sentence is in italics.</Emphasis>
 This is a paragraph.<Superscript>1</Superscript>
</Para>
<CodeExample>Code Example Code Example Code Example
 Code Example Code Example Code Example
 Code Example Code Example Code Example</CodeExample>
<VariableList>
 <VariableEntry>
  <Term>Term1</Term>
  <Definition>
   <Para>Definition of term1.</Para>
  </Definition>
 </VariableEntry>
 <VariableEntry>
  <Term>Term2</Term>
  <Definition>
   <Para>Definition of term2.</Para>
  </Definition>
 </VariableEntry>
</VariableList>
<NumberList>
 <Item>
  <Para>Numbered list item 1</Para>
 </Item>
 <Item>
  <Para>Numbered list item 2</Para>
 </Item>
 ...
</NumberList>
<BulletList>
 <Item>
  <Para>Bulleted list item 1</Para>
 </Item>
 <Item>
  <Para>Bulleted list item 2</Para>
 </Item>
 ...
</BulletList>
<Note>
 <Para>This is a note. ... This is a note.</Para>
 <NumberList>
  <Item>
   <Para>Numbered list inside a note - item 1.</Para>
  </Item>
  <Item>
   <Para>Numbered list inside a note - item 2.</Para>
  </Item>
 </NumberList>
</Note>
<Warning>
```

Example 5-2. A sample document conforming to the SDArticle schema (continued)

```
   <Para>This is a warning. ... This is a warning.</Para>
   <BulletList>
    <Item>
     <Para>Bulleted list inside a warning - item 1</Para>
    </Item>
    <Item>
     <Para>Bulleted list inside a warning - item 2</Para>
    </Item>
   </BulletList>
  </Warning>
  <Section2>
   <Heading2>Heading 2</Heading2>
   <Para>This is a paragraph. <Emphasis CDATA="italic">This sentence
   is bold.</Emphasis> This is a paragraph.<Superscript>2</Superscript>
   </Para>
   ...
   <Section3>
    <Heading3>Heading 3</Heading3>
    <Para>This is a paragraph. <Emphasis CDATA="italic">This sentence
    Is underscored.</Emphasis> This is a paragraph.
    <Superscript>3</Superscript>
    </Para>
    ...
    <Section4>
     <Heading4>Heading 4</Heading4>
     <Para>This is a paragraph. <Code>This is inline code.</Code>
     This is a paragraph.<Superscript>4</Superscript>
     </Para>
     ...
    </Section4>
   </Section3>
  </Section2>
 </Section1>
</Article>
```

Figure 5-3 shows Example 5-2 loaded into Word 2003.

Templates

Templates are keepers of styles. It is not uncommon to have several templates, each using the same set of style names, but with different formatting characteristics and page layouts defined in each. This allows the same XML schema, transformations, and Smart Document code to be used to create multiple document types.

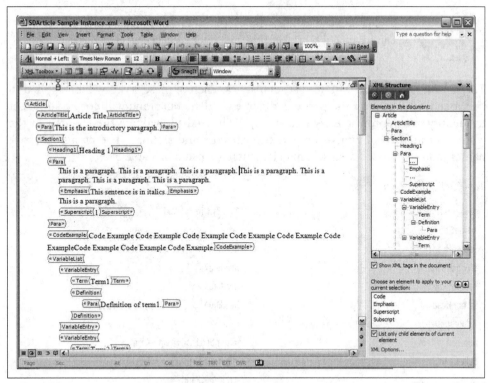

Figure 5-3. Sample instance in Word 2003

Styles

The most common way to associate formatting characteristics with XML elements is through the use of styles. A *style* is merely shorthand for any number of individual traits, such as font, point size, leading, indent, pre-space, post-space, widow/orphan rules, hyphenation rules, and the like. While it is possible to use individual codes (often referred to as *primitives*) to affect the desired visual appearance, it is typically avoided.

When creating a Smart Document solution, a set of styles should be created that conforms to the desired look. You will need to create a separate style for each level of heading, for various types of paragraphs, and for any other unique components that are part of your document set. You should also create character styles to apply inline formatting characteristics such as bold, bold italic, superscripts, and the like. Office 2003 allows styles to be *protected*; by creating named styles for each type of formatting required you can prevent the end user from creating new styles, modifying existing styles, and using the formatting icons on the toolbar, ensuring a consistent appearance for your documents.

For more information on creating styles and templates, refer to Walter Glenn's *Word 2000 in a Nutshell* and *Word Pocket Guide* (O'Reilly).

The sample application will need several styles. Each of these styles will be applied to the document based on the particular element. Elements alone will not be sufficient to identify the appropriate style; instead, we'll need to evaluate the element in the context of its surroundings—its parent, ancestors and siblings. The paragraph style names (and their associated schema elements) are listed in Table 5-1.

Table 5-1. Paragraph styles

Paragraph style name	Element-in-context
ArticleTitle	ArticleTitle
SectionHead1	Heading1
SectionHead2	Heading2
SectionHead3	Heading3
SectionHead4	Heading4
ParagraphDefault	Para
NumberListItem	\<NumberList>\<Item>\<Para>
BulletListItem	\<BulletList>\<Item>\<Para>
Note	\<Note>\<Para>
NoteNumberListItem	\<Note>\<NumberList>\<Item>\<Para>
NoteBulletListItem	\<Note>\<BulletList>\<Item>\<Para>
Warning	\<Warning>\<Para>
WarningNumberListItem	\<Warning>\<NumberList>\<Item>\<Para>
WarningBulletListItem	\<Warning>\<BulletList>\<Item>\<Para>
VariableListEntry	\<VariableEntry>
CodeBlock	\<CodeExample>

Character styles, listed in Table 5-2, are also necessary. Note that several styles are determined by an attribute value rather than by an element's positioning within the overall structure of the document instance.

Table 5-2. Character styles

Character style name	Element-in-context
Italic	\<Emphasis type="italic">
Bold	\<Emphasis type="bold">
Underscore	\<Emphasis type="underscore">

Table 5-2. Character styles (continued)

Character style name	Element-in-context
Superscript	\<Superscript\>
Subscript	\<Subscript\>
InlineCode	\<Code\>

As long as you keep the names of your styles consistent, you will be able to use the same transformations and smart document solution code with multiple styles and templates.

Our sample XML instance in Word 2003, with styles associated as indicated above and with the Styles and Formatting task pane displayed, is shown in Figure 5-4.

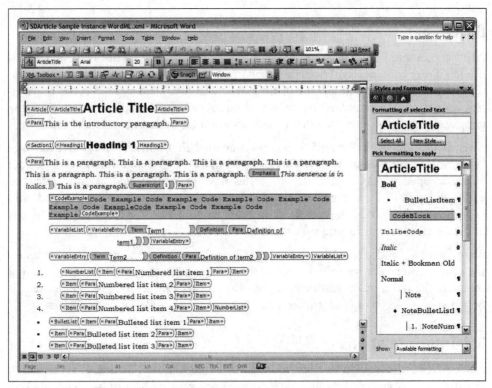

Figure 5-4. Sample XML instance in Word 2003

Shell Instance

Many Word templates contain *placeholder text*; that is, text that describes to the end user the type of content that is to be inserted at a particular location within the document. When creating a template for a Smart Document solution, the template should include a shell XML instance, containing at least the top-level element that will be used for the particular document type as well as any required elements and structure guidelines. When tags are turned off (which is anticipated to be the default mode for most Smart Document applications), the user will see, instead, placeholder text. Not only does this serve as a form of help, it also ensures that the information worker knows exactly where content is allowed within the XML document structure. Once the shell is in place, the Document Actions Task Pane will take over the job of displaying the various options that are allowed at any particular point within the instance.

Boilerplate

Another common feature of a template is boilerplate text. This may be default header/footer content, legal notices, company descriptions, or any other information that is routinely included as part of the particular document type. Storing the content directly in the template means it will be included automatically each time the template is used and also provides a single location for updating.

A template, shown in Figure 5-5, has been created that contains the requisite page layout information along with the styles listed in Tables 5-1 and 5-2. Since styles are linked to specific XML elements, the styles have been *protected*, meaning that no additional styles can be added to the document, the styles cannot be changed, and only those styles listed can be used. A minimal document instance is included as part of the template to get the end user started.

Note the placeholder text (the shaded gray areas) as well as the grayed out areas on the toolbar. Since the styles have been protected, the user does not have the option of selecting the bold, italic, justification, or other formatting icons. Placeholder text is only displayed when tags are turned off, the anticipated mode for most end users.

XSL Transformations

XSLT plays a vital role in any Smart Document solution. As illustrated in Chapter 4, transformations are used to integrate external schemas with WordprocessingML in order to create formatted Word documents. Transformations can also be invoked when saving a document, including the built-in transform that extracts all Word-related markup, leaving only the external schema-related markup in the result instance. A third use for transformations may not be quite as obvious: transformations can be invoked as part of any *action* called from the Document Actions Task Pane. This allows for styles to be applied as markup is inserted in the instance.

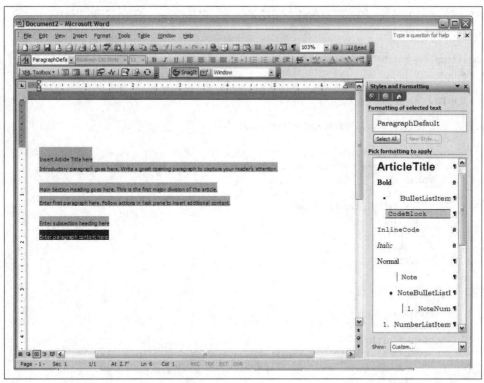

Figure 5-5. Smart document authoring template with protected styles

Only the `InsertXML` method, available on both `Selection` and `Range` objects, supports running transformations within document actions. This can be very handy when inserting blocks of XML markup, associated styles, and placeholder text. For instance:

```
Range.InsertXML("<VariableList></VariableList> ", "path\transform.xsl")
```

will insert the element `VariableList` and then call the named XSLT file. `InsertXML` must return a valid WordprocessingML document; upon matching the root, all the necessary WordprocessingML markup is inserted down to the opening `w:body` element. At that point, the appropriate template is selected (matching the element `VariableList`). Rather than executing the numerous steps involved one by one, the transform, as shown in Example 5-3, performs all steps in a single pass.

Example 5-3. An XSLT transformation for applying style to markup inserted in an instance

```
<xsl:template match="/">

    <w:body>
      <xsl:apply-templates select="*"/>
    </w:body>
  </w:wordDocument>
```

Example 5-3. An XSLT transformation for applying style to markup inserted in an instance

```
</xsl:template>

<xsl:template match="VariableList">
  <w:p/>
  <ns0:VariableList>
    <w:p>
      <w:pPr>
        <w:pStyle w:val="VariableListEntry"/>
      </w:pPr>
      <ns0:VariableEntry>
        <ns0:Term w:placeholder="Enter term here">
          <w:r>
            <w:rPr>
              <w:rStyle w:val="Term"/>
            </w:rPr>
            <w:r>
              <w:t/>
            </w:r>
          </w:r>
        </ns0:Term>
        <w:r>
          <w:tab/>
        </w:r>
        <ns0:Definition>
          <ns0:Para w:placeholder="Enter description or definition of term">
            <w:r>
              <w:t/>
            </w:r>
          </ns0:Para>
        </ns0:Definition>
      </ns0:VariableEntry>
    </w:p>
  </ns0:VariableList>
  <w:p/>
</xsl:template>
```

When creating action transformations, keep your WordprocessingML markup to a minimum; that is, only use what is required to create a valid WordprocessingML document instance. Otherwise you may suffer from performance issues.

See Chapter 4 and Appendix B for more information on using XSLT with Word.

Coding the Smart Document

Now that you have the XML foundation laid, it's time to integrate the data with code for manipulating it.

Required Document Actions

For our Smart Document solution, several actions will be required:

- Apply markup and style to inline components (superscript, subscript, bold, italic, underscore, and code).
- Insert block-level components (paragraphs, code blocks, lists, notes, and warnings).
- Insert additional entries into lists.
- Insert boilerplate warnings.
- Add a graphic.
- Create a hyperlink to a specific location.

Each action will contain a caption, a description, and help information for the end user. Upon selection, the appropriate markup will be inserted and styles applied. Pay careful attention to the Notes and Warnings; Microsoft Word, in this first release of Smart Document functionality, doesn't always behave as expected.

In general, beware of the cursor location. The values returned by your code may not be what you anticipated; this might be due to the current setting of the tag display.

Also, paragraph styles can only be applied to objects that look like a paragraph. If your markup runs in with another style, it will either inherit the current style characteristics or change the entire block to the new style.

Designing the Document Actions Task Pane

You have created, tested, tweaked, and refined your schemas. Your stylesheets are elegant, sophisticated, funky, or whatever other look is suited to the task at hand. The XSL transformations take your existing XML instances and magically convert them into documents any Word user would love. Unfortunately, the end users will never see most of this work. Instead, they will use a very simple interface that masks the complexities buried deep inside the solution. They will use it to add content, to manipulate the markup, and to serve as a guide throughout the document creation and revision cycles.

Remember—it's all about end users. If your solution does not make users' jobs easier, increase their productivity, raise the quality of the final products they produce, and provide other clearly visible benefits, end users will not use it. Or they will not use it properly. The XML that comes out of the backend will be useless—or at least in need of some help. The reason knowledge workers have been anxiously awaiting the time when they could work with their structured content in Microsoft Word is because of Word's familiar interface. The goal of the UI designer is to ensure that the Document Actions task pane meets their expectations.

Achieving this goal may not be easy. The Document Actions task pane is the end user's interface to the Smart Document solution. It would be nice if the Microsoft Word developers had created a method by which you could associate actions with a specific element, or even better yet, an element in context (such as title when its parent element is table versus title when its parent element is chapter), but that isn't how it works. Actions *are* associated with elements, but rather than limit the action to the confines of the element boundaries, the actions instead are inherited by child and descendent elements as well. This means that if your structure contains five levels—<document><section><procedure><step><paragraph>—and the cursor is positioned somewhere within paragraph, any actions associated with the document, section, procedure, step, and paragraph elements will be visible in the task pane.

The Document Actions task pane refreshes each time the location of the insertion point within the document instance changes. Be sure to design the interface with this in mind, eliminating lengthy re-draws whenever possible.

The task pane, shown in Figure 5-6, appears by default on the right-hand side of the application window. It automatically displays any available document actions whenever a Smart Document solution is attached. As it takes up only about 20% of the available real estate, it's important that the content associated with each of the actions is clear and concise, taking maximum advantage of the limited space.

For each Smart Document element defined, the task pane will display one or more controls associated with the element (as long as the element is an ancestor of the current insertion point). There are only a few options available to help format the display. In order to make the task pane as user-friendly as possible, each control group should begin with a caption and possibly some very brief explanatory text indicating how the actual control(s) should be used, followed by the controls themselves, and some help text that provides additional details about their usage.

Good user interface design principles call for consistent usage of display elements. While it is possible to use all 15 control types within a single Smart Document solution, selecting the best control for the task at hand and then using that same control for similar tasks will shorten training time and help ensure proper usage.

The Word Object Model

If you've ever written Word macros or done Visual Basic for Applications (VBA) programming, you've probably encountered the Word Object Model. An interactive map of the model can be found in Microsoft Office Word 2003 Help → Microsoft Word Visual Basic Reference → Microsoft Word Object Model. Unfortunately, all of the sample code contained in the help files is written in VBA rather than VB.NET or

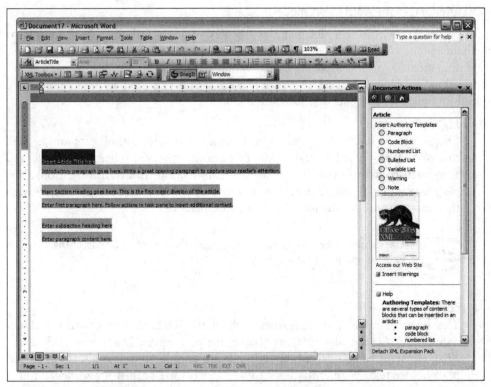

Figure 5-6. Authoring template and Document Actions task pane

any of the other languages used for creating Smart Documents. All is not lost, however; there's a section in the Visual Studio Tools for Office help system that discusses converting code from VBA to VB.NET.

The two most commonly used objects are Range and Selection. The Selection object represents the area currently selected, or the current insertion point. The Range object can be either manually set or created from a Selection object. In most of our code samples, we begin by determining the current cursor location and setting a Range object equivalent to an XML element and its content (XML Node); that is, everything between a start and end element tag, including the tags themselves. We then typically collapse the node so we can insert a new element, assign the appropriate style, and then add placeholder text so the end user will know exactly where to enter the new content.

The Word object model is covered in depth in the Microsoft Word Visual Basic Reference included in the Microsoft Office Word 2003 help files, and in *Writing Word Macros* by Steven Roman (O'Reilly). There are a number of additions to the Word Object Model in Word 2003; a few are detailed below. They are the objects and methods most likely to be referenced in a Smart Document application since they deal specifically with XML.

XML additions to the Word object model

The Word 2003 object model includes five new objects and collections as well as enhancements to the Application, Document, Range, and Selection objects. These are documented in the Microsoft Office Word 2003 help files under "What's New" as well as under their respective group headings. Some of the key pieces that you'll need for Smart Documents development include:

InsertXML

> The InsertXML method applies to both Range and Selection objects and is used to insert either WordprocessingML or customer-specific schema elements and associated content. It can also be used in conjunction with transformations, taking some minimal source data, running through a transform to apply styles, and then inserting the results into the document instance.

 Use caution when using the InsertXML method as it will replace any existing text in the Range or Selection object.

XMLNode(s)

> The XMLNodes collection represents each of the XML elements within a document. The XMLNode object is the workhorse of a Smart Document and allows XML elements to be selected, added, deleted, or validated. It is also used to add placeholder text. Numerous tests can be performed against an XMLNode, and it can be used to access first child, last child, parent, previous sibling, and other objects.

XMLParentNode

> The XMLParentNode property is used, as the name suggests, to return the parent node of the current XML node. It is used in conjunction with ranges and selections:

```
Dim oParagraphNode As Word.XMLNode
oParagraphNode = Selection.XMLParentNode
```

In addition to being able to guide the information worker through the process of creating, revising, and updating documents, most XML-related events can be captured and cause code to be executed:

XMLAfterInsert

> Any time that new XML markup is inserted in the document, the XMLAfterInsert event will be accessible. If the end user is inserting markup through the XML Structure task pane, this event could be used to add appropriate style information or other WordprocessingML markup. It could also be used to populate required child elements, mimicking some of the types of functions that could be programmed into the Document Actions task pane.

XMLBeforeDelete

While the Smart Document solution described in this chapter will handle the creation of an XML instance, making modifications to that document could easily result in an instance that is no longer valid. This is particularly true if the user tries to perform cut and paste operations. By trapping the XMLBeforeDelete event, the developer can ensure that the content to be deleted will not result in breaking the document structure by preventing the deletion of any elements that would result in an invalid instance. Instead, additional actions could be triggered that would guide the author through the editorial process.

XMLValidationError

Any time a validation error occurs within a document instance, the XMLValidationError event will be activated. It returns the XML node that is invalid, and can be used to either remove the offending node or add the necessary components to return the instance to a valid state.

XMLSelectionChange

Each time the parent node of the current cursor position changes, the XMLSelectionChange event is initiated. Both the previous and new nodes can be evaluated, along with the reason:

- Delete—the previous selection was deleted
- Insert—text has been inserted
- Move—the insertion point has been moved

Coding in VB.NET

We're finally ready to begin writing the actual code, a task more tedious than difficult. The ISmartDocument interface is cumbersome, requiring numerous steps to set up the task pane controls. A bit of planning before beginning to actually write the code can be very beneficial. Here's what you're going to need to know:

- the number of XML elements that will have actions associated with them
- the actual name of each of those elements (including namespace)
- The caption to be associated with each of those actions
- The number of individual controls that will be used in each action
- The name to be associated with each control
- The caption to be associated with each control
- The type (C_TYPE) to be associated with each control
- The location of any external document fragments or images
- The actual copy for document fragments that will be coded within the *.dll*

- Help content for each control (either embedded within the *.dll* or external file references)
- The individual choices for any list boxes, combo boxes, and radio groups
- A description of each control's behavior

In order to write code that will integrate all of this, we'll review some of the basic features of the Word object model in conjunction with Visual Basic. Each of these specific tasks is explained in more detail below.

Creating a New Project

Creating a Smart Document project in Visual Studio is a straightforward task. If you are familiar with the Microsoft Office development environment, you might anticipate being able to use Visual Studio Tools for Office to automate the process. Unfortunately, this isn't the case. Visual Studio Tools for Office (VSTO) is basically a set of wizards that facilitate the creation of managed code development projects for Word documents, templates, and Excel spreadsheets. It automatically associates the appropriate Office Primary Interop Assemblies (PIAs) with the project and uses the custom properties dataset to associate the *.dll* with the actual document. Instead, we'll manually create the project and reference the necessary libraries. The steps below walk you through creating a new Visual Basic project.

1. Launch Visual Studio .NET.
2. Create a New Project.
3. Select Visual Basic Projects as the Project Type.
4. Select Class Library as the Template.
5. Specify a name and location for your project. Your screen should now look like Figure 5-7.
6. Verify that the information you provided is accurate, and click OK to generate the project.

The next step is to include the libraries for Word, Smart Tags, and Internet Explorer Controls (the last of which is needed to enable a hypertext link, one of our requisite actions).

1. Right-click on References in the Solution Explorer and select Add Reference.
2. Select the COM tab, and locate Microsoft Smart Tags 2.0 Type Library.
3. Double-click to add the reference.
4. Locate Microsoft Word 11.0 Object Library.
5. Double-click to add the reference.
6. Locate Microsoft Internet Controls.
7. Double-click to add the reference.

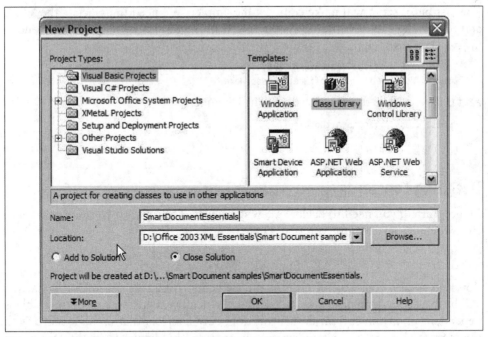

Figure 5-7. Visual Studio .NET 2003 New Project window

Your Solution Explorer pane should look like Figure 5-8.

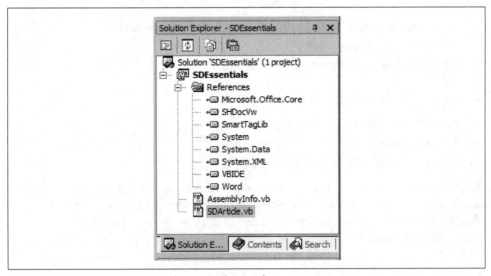

Figure 5-8. Visual Studio .NET Solution Explorer references

The last bit of setup will make coding a bit simpler. We need to associate the Word and Smart Tag Primary Interop Assemblies (PIAs) with our code. Insert the following two `Imports` statements into the code window:

```
Imports Microsoft.Office.Interop.SmartTag
Imports Word = Microsoft.office.Interop.Word
```

And finally, declare the class for the Smart Document:

```
Public Class ArticleSmartDocument

End Class
```

Declaring Constants

To get started, you need to declare a few constants. The first is a constant that references the namespace of the external schema:

```
'Namespace constant
Const cNAMESPACE As String = "http://www.office-xml.com/ns/sdarticle"
```

You also need a constant for each of the elements within the external schema that will have a set of controls associated with it. Remember, which controls are visible is dependent upon the current cursor location. Any controls that are associated with the current element, its parent, or an ancestor will be displayed in the Document Actions task pane. By looking at the ancestry of each of the desired actions, we can determine where best to place the controls. Once again, our requisite actions are as follows:

- Apply markup and style to inline components (superscript, subscript, bold, italic, underscore, and code).
- Insert block-level components (paragraphs, code blocks, lists, notes and warnings).
- Insert additional entries into lists.
- Insert boilerplate warnings.
- Add a graphic.
- Create a hyperlink to a specific location.

The first action involves mixed content. It will insert the selected element at the current cursor location; therefore the action should be displayed only if such elements would be valid. Since the only two elements that allow these elements as children are `Para` and `CodeExample`, an action will need to be created for each of those two elements.

The next action involves inserting block-level structures. These can be inserted at numerous points throughout the document instance; therefore it makes the most sense to place these controls on the `Article` element where they will always be visible.

Similar to inline elements, the Item element is only allowed in one specific context—as child of a list. Similarly, VariableEntry is only allowed in a variable list. Separate controls should be created for each of the three list type elements.

The boilerplate Warning is another block-level structure; it already contains the actual content of the warning itself.

The last two actions do not involve the creation of markup. We'll place those on the root element as well.

Table 5-3 lists the actions we'll incorporate in this document.

Table 5-3. Actions used in the sample document

Desired action	Elements	Parent elements	Control element
Insert superscript, subscript, bold, italic, underscore, and inline code	Emphasis Subscript Superscript	Para	Para
Insert paragraphs, code blocks, lists, notes, and warnings	Para VariableList NumberList BulletList Note Warning	Section1 Section2 Section3 Section4 Note Warning	Article
Insert additional list items	Item VariableEntry	NumberList BulletList VariableList	NumberList BulletList VariableList
Insert boilerplate warnings	Warning	Section1 Section2 Section3 Section4	Article
Insert a logo graphic			Article
Insert a hyperlink reference			Article

To define the constants for the individual elements, the element identifier is preceded by a pound (#) symbol and appended to the namespace:

```
'Element constants
Public Const cARTICLE As String = cNAMESPACE & "#Article"
Public Const cPARAGRAPH As String = cNAMESPACE & "#Para"
Public Const cCODE As String = cNAMESPACE & "#CodeExample"
Public Const cBULLET_LIST As String = cNAMESPACE & "#BulletList"
Public Const cNUMBER_LIST As String = cNAMESPACE & "#NumberList"
Public Const cVARIABLE_ENTRY As String = cNAMESPACE & "#VariableEntry"
```

Make sure that the element identifier is spelled correctly, including proper capitalization.

The last constant defines the number of elements in our schema that will have controls associated with them; this is simply a tally of the constants defined earlier:

```
'Number of types (or element constants)
Const cTYPES As Integer = 6
```

The ISmartDocument interface

In order to access the ISmartDocument interface, it must first be implemented in the class:

```
Implements ISmartDocument
```

All members of the interface must be implemented, whether or not they will actually be used. Omission is considered a syntax error. In Visual Studio .NET 2003, merely entering the above line will automatically add each member to the code window. If you are using Visual Studio .NET 2002, you will need to manually add each member.

Visual Studio .NET 2003 adds each of the requisite interfaces in alphabetical order; Table 5-4 shows them in order of completion.

Table 5-4. Members of the ISmartDocument interface

Member name	Description
SmartDocInitialize	Runs when an expansion pack is attached to a document or a Smart Document is opened
SmartDocXmlTypeCount	Specifies the number of elements that have actions assigned to them
SmartDocXmlTypeName	Name of an element with associated controls
SmartDocXmlTypeCaption	Caption for a group of controls
ControlCount	Specifies the number of controls
ControlID	Unique number for an individual control
ControlNameFromID	Associates a name with an ID
ControlCaptionFromID	Specifies the Smart Document control captions
ControlTypeFromID	Specifies the type of control
PopulateActiveXProps	Specifies the content of the control type with the values provided
PopulateCheckbox	Specifies the content of the control type with the values provided
PopulateDocumentFragment	Specifies the content of the control type with the values provided
PopulateHelpContent	Specifies the content of the control type with the values provided
PopulateImage	Specifies the content of the control type with the values provided
PopulateListOrComboContent	Specifies the content of the control type with the values provided
PopulateOther	Specifies the content of the control type with the values provided
PopulateRadioGroup	Specifies the content of the control type with the values provided
PopulateTextboxContent	Specifies the content of the control type with the values provided
ImageClick	Specifies actions to be performed when clicked by the user

Table 5-4. Members of the ISmartDocument interface (continued)

Member name	Description
InvokeControl	Specifies actions to be performed when clicked by the user
OnCheckboxChange	Specifies actions to be performed when clicked by the user
OnListOrComboSelectChange	Specifies actions to be performed when clicked by the user
OnRadioGroupSelectChange	Specifies actions to be performed when clicked by the user
OnPaneUpdateComplete	Specifies actions to be performed when the task pane has been updated and populated
OnTextboxContentChange	Specifies actions to be performed when the user changes the value of a text box

SmartDoc Initialization and Foundations

The first few members of the ISmartDocument that you'll need to deal with handle initialization and basic setup.

SmartDocInitialize. Any actions that need to be run when a Smart Document is opened or attached, such as initializing variables, should be called here. In our sample application, we do not have any required actions on initialize other than to set a constant to the installation path of the Smart Document components. This will allow future references to file components without having to explicitly identify the absolute path:

```
Public Sub SmartDocInitialize(ByVal ApplicationName As String, _
ByVal Document As Object, ByVal SolutionPath As String, _
ByVal SolutionRegKeyRoot As String) _
Implements Microsoft.Office.Interop.SmartTag.ISmartDocument.SmartDocInitialize
' set strPath to installation path
    strPath = SolutionPath & "\"
End Sub
```

Remember the long list of items to gather before you actually begin to code your Smart Document actions? Here's where they get put to good use as part of the tedious process required to set up the Smart Document task pane and tell the application when each control should be displayed.

SmartDocXMLTypeCount. This is the first property that must be defined. It specifies the number of elements defined in the schema that will have controls associated with them. This value is passed to SmartDocXMLTypeName. Since we created a constant earlier, we can simply return its value:

```
Public ReadOnly Property SmartDocXmlTypeCount() As Integer _
Implements Microsoft.Office.Interop.SmartTag.ISmartDocument.SmartDocXmlTypeCount
    Get
        Return cTYPES
    End Get
End Property
```

SmartDocXMLTypeName. Once the number of control sets has been defined, each one must now be assigned a name, which will be used to reference the control set in the other properties. The names themselves are arbitrary:

```
Public ReadOnly Property SmartDocXmlTypeName(ByVal XMLTypeID As Integer) As String_
Implements Microsoft.Office.Interop.SmartTag.ISmartDocument.SmartDocXmlTypeName
    Get
        Select Case XMLTypeID
            Case 1 'element Article
                Return cARTICLE
            Case 2 'element Para
                Return cPARAGRAPH
            Case 3 'element CodeExample
                Return cCODE_EXAMPLE
            Case 4 'element BulletList
                Return cBULLET_LIST
            Case 5 'element NumberList
                Return cNUMBER_LIST
            Case 6 'element VariableEntry
                Return cVARIABLE_ENTRY
        End Select
    End Get
End Property
```

SmartDocXMLTypeCaption. While the name assigned in `SmartDocXMLTypeName` will be used by the actual code, the caption is what will be displayed in the Document Actions task pane—formatted as a bold heading over the individual controls:

```
Public ReadOnly Property SmartDocXmlTypeCaption(ByVal XMLTypeID As Integer, _
ByVal LocaleID As Integer) As String _
Implements Microsoft.Office.Interop.SmartTag.ISmartDocument.SmartDocXmlTypeCaption
    Get
        Select Case XMLTypeID
            Case 1 'element Article
                Return "Article"
            Case 2 'element Para
                Return "Character Formatting (Paragraph)"
            Case 3 'element CodeExample
                Return "Character Formatting (Code Block)"
            Case 4 'element BulletList
                Return "Bulleted List Items"
            Case 5 'element NumberList
                Return "Numbered List Items"
            Case 6 'element VariableEntry
                Return "Variable List Items"
        End Select
    End Get
End Property
```

A caption must be created for each Case defined earlier. The caption should be something that will be meaningful to your end users.

Without a caption, any associated controls will not appear in the task pane. This can be used to your benefit; while the default behavior is to always display controls that are active based on current cursor location, setting one or more captions to null will prevent them from being displayed.

The next few members of the ISmartDocument interface are about managing GUI components, called controls.

ControlCount. The ControlCount property defines how many individual controls will be used in each of the defined cases. For each of the list elements only one control is needed; the appropriate option will be chosen and the action will be taken immediately. In the inline scenario (for both paragraphs and code blocks) we'll need three: a text box, a choice group, and a submit button. We'll need four for the root element: one for the block templates, one for the hypertext link, one for the logo insertion, and one for the insertion of boilerplate text.

There are two additional controls that can be added to each element set: a separator and help content. While not absolutely necessary, displaying help in the Document Actions task pane will provide the end user with an easily accessible reference:

```
Public ReadOnly Property ControlCount(ByVal XMLTypeName As String) As Integer _
Implements Microsoft.Office.Interop.SmartTag.ISmartDocument.ControlCount
    Get
        Select Case XMLTypeID
            Case cARTICLE
                Return 6
            Case cPARAGRAPH
                Return 5
            Case cCODE_EXAMPLE
                Return 5
            Case cBULLET_LIST
                Return 3
            Case cNUMBER_LIST
                Return 3
            Case cVARIABLE_ENTRY
                Return 3
        End Select
    End Get
End Property
```

ControlID. Unique IDs must be assigned to each control in the task pane. This is important because it is common to have more than one set of controls active at any point in time. Assigning IDs is a two-step process. The first step is to associate a range of IDs with each element. The ControlIndex will always start with 1. Here we just increment each additional control set by 100:

```
Public ReadOnly Property ControlID(ByVal XMLTypeName As String, _
ByVal ControlIndex As Integer) As Integer _
Implements Microsoft.Office.Interop.SmartTag.ISmartDocument.ControlID
```

```
    Get
        Select Case XMLTypeName
            Case cARTICLE
                Return ControlIndex
            Case cPARAGRAPH
                Return ControlIndex + 100
            Case cCODE_EXAMPLE
                Return ControlIndex + 200
            Case cBULLET_LIST
                Return ControlIndex + 300
            Case cNUMBER_LIST
                Return ControlIndex + 400
            Case cVARIABLE_ENTRY
                Return ControlIndex + 500
            Case Else
                Return 0
        End Select
    End Get
End Property
```

ControlNameFromID. The next step is to associate each individual control with a unique ID, based on the values declared above. We don't have to list each and every name/ID pair; this method will take care of it for us:

```
Public ReadOnly Property ControlNameFromID(ByVal ControlID As Integer) As String _
Implements Microsoft.Office.Interop.SmartTag.ISmartDocument.ControlNameFromID
    Get
        Return cNAMESPACE & ControlID.ToString
    End Get
End Property
```

ControlCaptionFromID. Now that each control has a unique ID, individual captions can be defined:

```
Public ReadOnly Property ControlCaptionFromID(ByVal ControlID As Integer, _
ByVal ApplicationName As String, ByVal LocaleID As Integer, _
ByVal Text As String, ByVal Xml As String, ByVal Target As Object) As String _
Implements Microsoft.Office.Interop.SmartTag.ISmartDocument.ControlCaptionFromID
    Get
        Select Case ControlID
                'element Article
            Case 1
                Return "Insert Authoring Templates"
            Case 2
                Return "Insert Logo"
            Case 3
                Return "Access our Web Site"
            Case 4
                Return "Insert Warnings"
            Case 5
                Return "Separator"
            Case 6
                Return "Help"
                    'element Para
```

```
        Case 101
            Return "Enter word or phrase"
        Case 102
            Return "Select formatting style"
        Case 103
            Return "INSERT"
        Case 104
            Return "Separator"
        Case 105
            Return "Help"
                'element CodeExample
        Case 201
            Return "Enter word or phrase"
        Case 202
            Return "Select formatting style"
        Case 203
            Return "INSERT"
        Case 204
            Return "Separator"
        Case 205
            Return "Help"
                'element BulletList
        Case 301
            Return "INSERT"
        Case 302
            Return "Separator"
        Case 303
            Return "Help"
                'element NumberList
        Case 401
            Return "INSERT"
        Case 402
            Return "Separator"
        Case 403
            Return "Help"
                'element VariableEntry
        Case 501
            Return "INSERT"
        Case 502
            Return "Separator"
        Case 503
            Return "Help"
    End Select
  End Get
End Property
```

Captions on individual controls are most often displayed directly above the control, captions for text boxes are displayed to the left, and captions for buttons are displayed on the actual button.

In the case of an ActiveX control, the return value would be set to the GUID (Global Unique Identifier) of the control.

If an element only has a single control associated with it, the control caption can be used to provide additional information that will be helpful to the end user.

ControlTypeFromID. The last step in defining the controls is to identify the specific type of control to be associated with each unique ID. There are 15 control types:

- C_TYPE.C_TYPE_ACTIVEX
- C_TYPE.C_TYPE_BUTTON
- C_TYPE.C_TYPE_CHECKBOX
- C_TYPE.C_TYPE_COMBO
- C_TYPE.C_TYPE_DOCUMENTFRAGMENT
- C_TYPE.C_TYPE_DOCUMENTFRAGMENTURL
- C_TYPE.C_TYPE_HELP
- C_TYPE.C_TYPE_HELPURL
- C_TYPE.C_TYPE_IMAGE
- C_TYPE.C_TYPE_LABEL
- C_TYPE.C_TYPE_LINK
- C_TYPE.C_TYPE_LISTBOX
- C_TYPE.C_TYPE_RADIOGROUP
- C_TYPE.C_TYPE_SEPARATOR
- C_TYPE.C_TYPE_TEXTBOX

This gives the developer a number of choices for designing the look and feel of the Document Actions task pane. While it is possible to use all 15 control types in a single Smart Document solution, it isn't recommended. In particular, check boxes, combo boxes, list boxes, and radio groups can all be applied to similar use cases. Choose one of these four choice types and use it consistently throughout the application.

The ability to add ActiveX controls extends the possibilities available to the developer. There are hundreds of ActiveX controls available from Microsoft and third-party developers, or you can custom-build your own. Using ActiveX controls in Smart Documents can be a bit tricky, as they often do not behave as expected. If you are new to the world of Microsoft application development, you may want to stick with the other control types until you become more familiar with some of the intricacies of ActiveX objects.

```
Public ReadOnly Property ControlTypeFromID(ByVal ControlID As Integer, _
ByVal ApplicationName As String, ByVal LocaleID As Integer) _
As Microsoft.Office.Interop.SmartTag.C_TYPE _
Implements Microsoft.Office.Interop.SmartTag.ISmartDocument.ControlTypeFromID
    Get
        Select Case ControlID
```

```vbnet
'element Article
Case 1
    Return C_TYPE.C_TYPE_RADIOGROUP
Case 2
    Return C_TYPE.C_TYPE_IMAGE
Case 3
    Return C_TYPE.C_TYPE_LINK
Case 4
    Return C_TYPE.C_TYPE_DOCUMENTFRAGMENTURL
Case 5
    Return C_TYPE.C_TYPE_SEPARATOR
Case 6
    Return C_TYPE.C_TYPE_HELPURL

    'element Para
Case 101
    Return C_TYPE.C_TYPE_TEXTBOX
Case 102
    Return C_TYPE.C_TYPE_LISTBOX
Case 103
    Return C_TYPE.C_TYPE_BUTTON
Case 104
    Return C_TYPE.C_TYPE_SEPARATOR
Case 105
    Return C_TYPE.C_TYPE_HELPURL

    'element CodeExample
Case 201
    Return C_TYPE.C_TYPE_TEXTBOX
Case 202
    Return C_TYPE.C_TYPE_COMBO
Case 203
    Return C_TYPE.C_TYPE_BUTTON
Case 204
    Return C_TYPE.C_TYPE_SEPARATOR
Case 205
    Return C_TYPE.C_TYPE_HELPURL

    'element BulletList
Case 301
    Return C_TYPE.C_TYPE_CHECKBOX
Case 302
    Return C_TYPE.C_TYPE_SEPARATOR
Case 303
    Return C_TYPE.C_TYPE_HELP

    'element NumberList
Case 401
    Return C_TYPE.C_TYPE_CHECKBOX
Case 402
    Return C_TYPE.C_TYPE_SEPARATOR
Case 403
    Return C_TYPE.C_TYPE_HELP
```

```
                    'element VariableEntry
            Case 501
                Return C_TYPE.C_TYPE_CHECKBOX
            Case 502
                Return C_TYPE.C_TYPE_SEPARATOR
            Case 503
                Return C_TYPE.C_TYPE_HELP
        End Select
    End Get
End Property
```

Populating controls

Now that each of the individual controls has a unique identifier, a caption, and a type, the contents of the individual controls can be populated. There are multiple methods involved, each one focused on a specific type (or types) of control.

The ISmartDocProperties interface is a common set of key/value pairs that can be used to control the appearance of the Document Actions task pane. They are accessed via the Populate methods.

The only method applicable to ISmartDocProperties is the write method, which is set through the use of key/value pairs:

```
Props.Write("Expanded", "False")
```

Table 5-5 lists the properties you can set with the write method and what they do.

Table 5-5. Writeable ISmartDocProperties keys

Property (key)	Applies to	Description
X	All controls	The left starting position in the task pane
Y	All controls	The starting distance from the top of the task pane or the previous control
H	All controls	The height of the control
W	All controls	The width of the control
Align	All controls	Horizontal justification (left, right, center)
Layout	All controls	Direction of text flow in control (LTR, RTL)
SectionCaptionDirection	All controls	Direction of text flow in caption (LTR, RTL)
FontFace	Text captions	Typeface
FontSize	Text captions	Point size
FontStyle	Text captions	Special formatting (none, italic, underline, strikeout)
FontWeight	Text captions	Weight (normal, bold)
NumberOfLines	Text box, list box, combo box	Number of lines visible without scrolling
IsEditable	Text box, list box, combo box	Whether or not the user can modify the contents (true, false)

Table 5-5. Writeable ISmartDocProperties keys (continued)

Property (key)	Applies to	Description
ControlOnSameLine	Text box, list box, combo box	Whether caption is displayed on same line as control (true, false)
PasswordCharacter	Text box only	Single character to be used to mask password entry
IsMultiline	Text box only	Whether text box allows multiple lines (true, false)
Border	Images only	Whether a border is displayed on image (true, false)
Expanded	Fragments only	Whether fragment should be displayed or collapsed (true, false)
ExpandHelp	Help only	Whether help should be displayed or collapsed (true, false)
ExpandToFill	ActiveX only	Whether ActiveX control should fill the task pane (true, false)
KeepAlive	ActiveX only	Whether control remains active when cursor position changes (true, false)

PopulateActiveXProps. This method allows the developer to set the display parameters for each ActiveX control used in the solution. Custom properties (that is, those other than defined for the ISmartdDocProperties interface, above) can be accessed by using the appropriate key/value combinations as defined in the control:

```
Props.Write(Key:="Special", Value:="200")
```

PopulateCheckbox. A checkbox allows the end user to select an individual control. Three controls have been defined as C_TYPE_CHECKBOX; the checked parameter indicates the initial state for the checkbox. The text that appears next to the checkbox is set in the ControlCaptionFromID method. There are no additional formatting properties associated with the checkboxes.

```
Public Sub PopulateCheckbox(ByVal ControlID As Integer, _
ByVal ApplicationName As String, ByVal LocaleID As Integer, _
ByVal Text As String, ByVal Xml As String, ByVal Target As Object, _
ByVal Props As Microsoft.Office.Interop.SmartTag.ISmartDocProperties, _
ByRef Checked As Boolean) _
Implements Microsoft.Office.Interop.SmartTag.ISmartDocument.PopulateCheckbox
    Select Case ControlID
        Case 301
            Checked = False
        Case 401
            Checked = False
        Case 501
            Checked = False
    End Select
End Sub
```

PopulateDocumentFragment. A document fragment can be expressed directly in the code, or it can be incorporated via a URL reference. In most applications it is preferred to leave such fragments external to the code itself; this will allow for quick and easy modifications to the fragments that would otherwise require the code itself to be modified, recompiled, and distributed.

External document fragments must contain valid WordML document instances; they can be created either by transforming existing XML instances into the necessary merged fragments or created directly in Office 2003 and saved as *.xml*.

In an effort to optimize space in the Document Actions task pane, fragments can be displayed or collapsed. By default, fragments will be displayed. The example code below uses properties of the ISmartDocProperties interface to set the display option to false.

As of this writing, the Smart Document SDK help file incorrectly identifies the key as Expand rather than Expanded.

```
Public Sub PopulateDocumentFragment(ByVal ControlID As Integer, _
ByVal ApplicationName As String, ByVal LocaleID As Integer, _
ByVal Text As String, ByVal Xml As String, ByVal Target As Object, _
ByVal Props As Microsoft.Office.Interop.SmartTag.ISmartDocProperties, _
ByRef DocumentFragment As String) _
Implements _
Microsoft.Office.Interop.SmartTag.ISmartDocument.PopulateDocumentFragment
    Select Case ControlID
        Case 4 'url
            DocumentFragment = strPath & "warning.xml"
            Props.Write("Expanded", "False")
    End Select
End Sub
```

PopulateHelpContent. Help provides online documentation for the knowledge worker. It can be collapsed in order to preserve real estate, but should not be omitted. Formatting is done with XHTML and CSS. Help text can either be coded directly in your program or can be maintained in separate files and referenced via a URL. When using the C_TYPE_HELPURL, the location must be an absolute path.

Similar to document fragments, by default help content is expanded in the Document Actions Task Pane. It can be collapsed by setting the property key ExpandHelp to False.

Not all XHTML and CSS elements are supported. Refer to the Smart Document SDK for specifics.

```
Public Sub PopulateHelpContent(ByVal ControlID As Integer, _
ByVal ApplicationName As String, ByVal LocaleID As Integer, _
ByVal Text As String, ByVal Xml As String, ByVal Target As Object, _
ByVal Props As Microsoft.Office.Interop.SmartTag.ISmartDocProperties, _
ByRef Content As String) _
Implements Microsoft.Office.Interop.SmartTag.ISmartDocument.PopulateHelpContent
    Select Case ControlID
```

```
        Case 6 'url
            Content = strPath & "article.htm"
            Props.Write("ExpandHelp", "False")
        Case 105 'url
            Content = strPath & "para.htm"
            Props.Write("ExpandHelp", "False")
        Case 205 'url
            Content = strPath & "code.htm"
            Props.Write("ExpandHelp", "False")
        Case 303 'inline
            Content = "<html><body><p>Click in the box to add a new" & _
            "item to the list.</p></body></html>"
        Case 403 'inline
            Content = "<html><body><p>Click in the box to add a new" & _
            "item to the list.</p></body></html>"
        Case 503 'inline
            Content = "<html><body><p>Click in the box to add a new" & _
            "item to the list.</p></body></html>"
    End Select
End Sub
```

PopulateImage. Images can be displayed in the task pane and either incorporated into the document instance or used to activate a control. Similar to help and document fragments, the path given must be an absolute path.

```
Public Sub PopulateImage(ByVal ControlID As Integer, _
ByVal ApplicationName As String, ByVal LocaleID As Integer, _
ByVal Text As String, ByVal Xml As String, ByVal Target As Object, _
ByVal Props As Microsoft.Office.Interop.SmartTag.ISmartDocProperties, _
ByRef ImageSrc As String) _
Implements Microsoft.Office.Interop.SmartTag.ISmartDocument.PopulateImage
    Select Case ControlID
        Case 2
            ImageSrc = strPath & "cover.jpg"
    End Select
End Sub
```

PopulateListOrComboContent. For each control defined as either a list box (displayed as a box showing each selection on an individual line) or combo box (displayed as a drop-down list), the number of items must be declared along with the text to be associated with each item. Setting the InitialSelected property to −1 ensures that no action will be selected by default.

```
Public Sub PopulateListOrComboContent(ByVal ControlID As Integer, _
ByVal ApplicationName As String, ByVal LocaleID As Integer, _
ByVal Text As String, ByVal Xml As String, ByVal Target As Object, _
ByVal Props As Microsoft.Office.Interop.SmartTag.ISmartDocProperties, _
ByRef List As System.Array, ByRef Count As Integer, _
ByRef InitialSelected As Integer) _
Implements _
Microsoft.Office.Interop.SmartTag.ISmartDocument.PopulateListOrComboContent
    Select Case ControlID
```

```
        Case 102 'listbox
            Count = 5
            List(1) = "Bold"
            List(2) = "Italic"
            List(3) = "Underscore"
            List(4) = "Superscript"
            List(5) = "Subscript"
            InitialSelected = -1
        Case 202 'combo box
            Count = 5
            List(1) = "Bold"
            List(2) = "Italic"
            List(3) = "Underscore"
            List(4) = "Superscript"
            List(5) = "Subscript"
            InitialSelected = -1
    End Select
End Sub
```

PopulateOther. While the separator and label controls don't really *do* anything, they provide visual clues to the end user. A liberal sprinkling throughout is highly recommended. PopulateOther allows display options to be set for each of the control types that do not have their own Populate method—buttons, labels, links, and separators.

```
Public Sub PopulateOther(ByVal ControlID As Integer, _
ByVal ApplicationName As String, ByVal LocaleID As Integer, _
ByVal Text As String, ByVal Xml As String, ByVal Target As Object, _
ByVal Props As Microsoft.Office.Interop.SmartTag.ISmartDocProperties) _
Implements Microsoft.Office.Interop.SmartTag.ISmartDocument.PopulateOther
    Select Case ControlID
        Case 3 'link
        Case 5 'separator
        Case 104 'separator
        Case 204 'separator
        Case 302 'separator
        Case 402 'separator
        Case 502 'separator
        Case 103 'button
        Case 203 'button
    End Select
End Sub
```

PopulateRadioGroup. Another method for presenting a choice list to the end user is via a radio group. The user selects the specific option by clicking on the appropriate radio button. Again, InitialSelected is set to –1 to ensure that the list will not have any option set by default.

```
Public Sub PopulateRadioGroup(ByVal ControlID As Integer, _
ByVal ApplicationName As String, ByVal LocaleID As Integer, _
ByVal Text As String, ByVal Xml As String, ByVal Target As Object, _
ByVal Props As Microsoft.Office.Interop.SmartTag.ISmartDocProperties, _
ByRef List As System.Array, ByRef Count As Integer, _
```

```
      ByRef InitialSelected As Integer) _
   Implements Microsoft.Office.Interop.SmartTag.ISmartDocument.PopulateRadioGroup
       Select Case ControlID
           Case 1
               Count = 7
               List(1) = "Paragraph"
               List(2) = "Code Block"
               List(3) = "Numbered List"
               List(4) = "Bulleted List"
               List(5) = "Variable List"
               List(6) = "Warning"
               List(7) = "Note"
               InitialSelected = -1
       End Select
   End Sub
```

PopulateTextboxContent. Text boxes allow the end user to enter text that is then returned to the Smart Document application for further processing. In the sample application, text boxes are used to input inline content that is to have special markup associated with it, such as emphasis, superscript, or subscript. PopulateTextboxContent will automatically supply default information in the text box, such as a formatting template for a telephone number or date.

Defining document actions

We have finally reached the point in the process where we begin to actually *do* something, or at least write the code that will allow the end user to cause an event to fire through the Document Actions task pane. Here's where the Word Object Model will be put to use. Once each of the controls has been defined and populated, the actions can be programmed. While it would have been more intuitive to have each method align with its populate counterpart, the developer is left to reconcile the differences. For practical purposes, some methods are often intentionally left blank. Refer to Figure 5-4 for a glimpse at the Document Actions task pane.

Adding a graphic: the ImageClick method. The ImageClick method is used to define the action to be taken when the user selects an image displayed in the task pane. The code below will insert the image into the document itself. Since there are no positioning parameters specified, it will automatically be placed according to the AutoShapeDefaults parameters as defined in the template.

The single line of code that does all of the work uses the Word Object Model to add a picture to the shapes collection of the active document.

```
   Public Sub ImageClick(ByVal ControlID As Integer, _
   ByVal ApplicationName As String, ByVal Target As Object, _
   ByVal Text As String, ByVal Xml As String, ByVal LocaleID As Integer, _
   ByVal XCoordinate As Integer, ByVal YCoordinate As Integer) _
   Implements Microsoft.Office.Interop.SmartTag.ISmartDocument.ImageClick
       Dim strImage As String
```

```
        Select Case ControlID
            Case 2
                strImage = strPath & "cover.jpg"
                Target.Application.ActiveDocument.Shapes.AddPicture(strImage)
        End Select
    End Sub
```

Figure 5-9 shows the result of clicking on the image in the Document Actions task pane. It has been positioned according to the parameters defined for image placement.

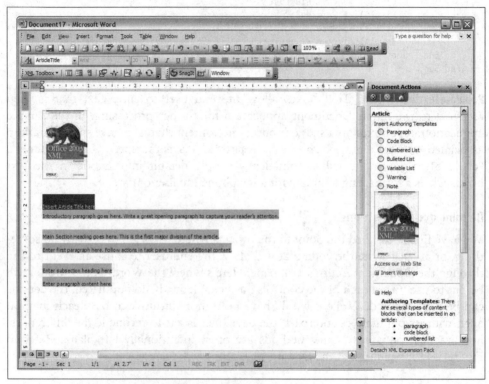

Figure 5-9. Document Template after the image has been inserted

The next item on our list of actions is to apply markup and style to inline components (superscript, subscript, bold, italic, underscore, and code). This requires three separate actions: capturing the contents of the text box, capturing the specific type of formatting selected through either the list or combo box, and inserting the appropriate markup, text, and style information when the user clicks on the Insert button.

OnTextboxContentChange. Whenever a user enters content into the textbox, this method will be activated. We need to capture any content entered into textbox into a variable so we can insert it into the document later. There are two textboxes defined—one used to insert inline elements in paragraphs, and a second used to insert inline elements in code blocks. First, two variables must be defined:

```
Dim varCodeText As String
Dim varParaText As String
```

Now the contents of the text box can be stored for later use by using those variable names. Of course, you could just insert it into the document instance at this point, or use the results to trigger some other action.

```
Public Sub OnTextboxContentChange(ByVal ControlID As Integer, _
ByVal Target As Object, ByVal Value As String) _
Implements Microsoft.Office.Interop.SmartTag.ISmartDocument.OnTextboxContentChange

    Select Case ControlID
        Case 101 'para inlines
            varParaText = Value
        Case 201 'code inlines
            varCodeText = Value
    End Select
End Sub
```

OnListOrComboSelectChange. The next piece in our three-piece control is the results of the choice list presented to the end user. After entering text, the user must choose one of the several possible inline types to be applied to the text. Selecting one of the options will cause this event to fire. We'll need another variable:

```
Dim varSelect As String
```

For each possible choice, we need to set the varSelect variable to a value that we can test on in our final step:

```
Public Sub OnListOrComboSelectChange(ByVal ControlID As Integer, _
ByVal Target As Object, ByVal Selected As Integer, ByVal Value As String) _
Implements _
Microsoft.Office.Interop.SmartTag.ISmartDocument.OnListOrComboSelectChange

    Select Case ControlID
        Case 102 'format options
            If Value = "Bold" Then
                varSelect = "bold"
            ElseIf Value = "Italic" Then
                varSelect = "italic"
            ElseIf Value = "Underscore" Then
                varSelect = "underscore"
            ElseIf Value = "Superscript" Then
                varSelect = "superscript"
            ElseIf Value = "Subscript" Then
                varSelect = "subscript"
            End If

        Case 202 'format options
            If Value = "Bold" Then
                varSelect = "bold"
```

```
            ElseIf Value = "Italic" Then
                varSelect = "italic"
            ElseIf Value = "Underscore" Then
                varSelect = "underscore"
            ElseIf Value = "Superscript" Then
                varSelect = "superscript"
            ElseIf Value = "Subscript" Then
                varSelect = "subscript"
            End If
        End Select
    End Sub
```

InvokeControl. The InvokeControl method applies to buttons, hyperlinks, and document fragments. There are two buttons, one hyperlink, and one fragment that must be defined.

The buttons used in combination with text boxes and choice lists are the third piece to the inlines puzzle. The only action taken in the first two steps was to capture the values into variables. Again, we will need some new variables, this time defined as XML nodes in the Word object model:

```
Dim oBoldNode As Word.XMLNode
Dim oItalicNode As Word.XMLNode
Dim oUnderscoreNode As Word.XMLNode
Dim oSubscriptNode As Word.XMLNode
Dim oSuperscriptNode As Word.XMLNode
```

First, we have to define the current cursor location as a selection. The next step is to test for the value of the variable associated with the choice list. Once a match is found, the Add method is used to insert the appropriate element name. The element node is then defined as a range (which includes both the start and end tags and any content), and the text that was originally entered in the text box is inserted. The last step is to apply the appropriate character style to the content.

 For more information on the new XML objects incorporated into Word 2003, refer to "The Word Object Model" section in this chapter and the Microsoft Word Visual Basic Reference help files.

Note that bold, italic, and underscore all resolve to a single element, emphasis. Rather than having three distinct elements, the role attribute is used instead. It has three possible values defined: bold, italic, and underscore. By selecting the Attributes property of the XMLNode, attribute values can be populated without additional user intervention.

```
Case 103 'para
    Dim oWordRange As Word.Range = CType(Target, Word.Range)
    Dim localRange As Word.Range = CType(Target, Word.Range)
    Dim selection As Word.Selection = _
    localRange.Application.ActiveWindow.Selection
```

```
    If varSelect = "bold" Then
        oBoldNode = selection.XMLNodes.Add("Emphasis", cNAMESPACE)
        oWordRange = oBoldNode.Range
        oBoldNode.Range.Text = varParaText
        oBoldNode.Attributes.Add("role", "")
        oBoldNode.SelectSingleNode("@role", "").NodeValue = "bold"
        oBoldNode.Range.Style = "Bold"

    ElseIf varSelect = "italic" Then
        oItalicNode = selection.XMLNodes.Add("Emphasis", cNAMESPACE)
        oWordRange = oItalicNode.Range
        oItalicNode.Range.Text = varParaText
        oItalicNode.Attributes.Add("role", "")
        oItalicNode.SelectSingleNode("@role", "").NodeValue = "italic"
        oItalicNode.Range.Style = "Italic"

    ElseIf varSelect = "underscore" Then
        oUnderscoreNode = selection.XMLNodes.Add("Emphasis", cNAMESPACE)
        oWordRange = oUnderscoreNode.Range
        oUnderscoreNode.Range.Text = varParaText
        oUnderscoreNode.Attributes.Add("role", "")
        oUnderscoreNode.SelectSingleNode("@role", "").NodeValue = "underscore"
        oUnderscoreNode.Range.Style = "Underscore"

    ElseIf varSelect = "superscript" Then
        oSuperscriptNode = selection.XMLNodes.Add("Superscript", cNAMESPACE)
        oWordRange = oSuperscriptNode.Range
        oSuperscriptNode.Range.Text = varParaText
        oSuperscriptNode.Range.Style = "Superscript"

    ElseIf varSelect = "subscript" Then
        oSubscriptNode = selection.XMLNodes.Add("Subscript", cNAMESPACE)
        oWordRange = oSubscriptNode.Range
        oSubscriptNode.Range.Text = varParaText
        oSubscriptNode.Range.Style = "Subscript"
    End If

Case 203 'code
    Dim oWordRange As Word.Range = CType(Target, Word.Range)
    Dim localRange As Word.Range = CType(Target, Word.Range)
    Dim selection As Word.Selection = _
    localRange.Application.ActiveWindow.Selection

    If varSelect = "bold" Then
        oBoldNode = selection.XMLNodes.Add("Emphasis", cNAMESPACE)
        oWordRange = oBoldNode.Range
        oBoldNode.Range.Text = varCodeText
        oBoldNode.Attributes.Add("role", "")
        oBoldNode.SelectSingleNode("@role", "").NodeValue = "bold"
        oBoldNode.Range.Style = "Bold"

    ElseIf varSelect = "italic" Then
        oItalicNode = selection.XMLNodes.Add("Emphasis", cNAMESPACE)
        oWordRange = oItalicNode.Range
```

```
            oItalicNode.Range.Text = varCodeText
            oItalicNode.Attributes.Add("role", "")
            oItalicNode.SelectSingleNode("@role", "").NodeValue = "italic"
            oItalicNode.Range.Style = "Italic"

        ElseIf varSelect = "underscore" Then
            oUnderscoreNode = selection.XMLNodes.Add("Emphasis", cNAMESPACE)
            oWordRange = oUnderscoreNode.Range
            oUnderscoreNode.Range.Text = varCodeText
            oUnderscoreNode.Attributes.Add("role", "")
            oUnderscoreNode.SelectSingleNode("@role", "").NodeValue = "underscore"
            oUnderscoreNode.Range.Style = "Underscore"

        ElseIf varSelect = "superscript" Then
            oSuperscriptNode = selection.XMLNodes.Add("Superscript", cNAMESPACE)
            oWordRange = oSuperscriptNode.Range
            oSuperscriptNode.Range.Text = varCodeText
            oSuperscriptNode.Range.Style = "Superscript"

        ElseIf varSelect = "subscript" Then
            oSubscriptNode = selection.XMLNodes.Add("Subscript", cNAMESPACE)
            oWordRange = oSubscriptNode.Range
            oSubscriptNode.Range.Text = varCodeText
            oSubscriptNode.Range.Style = "Subscript"
        End If
```

The end result of all of this code is shown in Figure 5-10. Here the user has entered the word "new" in the textbox, and selected the style "Italic" from the list displayed. Figure 5-11 shows the results of clicking the INSERT button. The text has been inserted in the paragraph, the attribute value has been set, and the appropriate style has been applied.

The actions associated with the hyperlink and document fragment are to be executed upon selection. Let's start with the hyperlink. While it looks like a hyperlink in the task pane, it isn't really. At least not yet. We need some code that will do the navigating when the "link" is clicked. The following code implements the Internet Explorer Navigate method to open a browser window and load the O'Reilly home page:

```
Public Sub InvokeControl(ByVal ControlID As Integer, _
ByVal ApplicationName As String, ByVal Target As Object, _
ByVal Text As String, ByVal Xml As String, ByVal LocaleID As Integer) _
Implements Microsoft.Office.Interop.SmartTag.ISmartDocument.InvokeControl

    Dim objNav As SHDocVw.InternetExplorer
    Select Case ControlID
        Case 3
            objNav = New SHDocVw.InternetExplorer
            objNav.Navigate("http://www.oreilly.com")
            objNav.Visible = True

'more to follow here

    End Select
End Sub
```

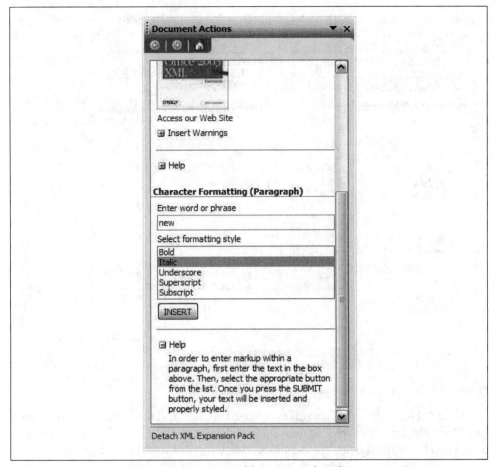

Figure 5-10. Document Actions with content and formatting selected

The last piece of our `InvokeControl` routine is to insert a selected document fragment. Word will display the first page of any document fragment in the task pane. An alternative approach is to specify one file to use in the task pane display, and another for the actual fragment to be inserted. Note in Figure 5-12 that the style associated with the Warning is indented; the task pane also displays this style, making it a bit difficult to read without having to adjust the horizontal positioning of the task pane. An alternate view could be created that does not reference the indented style, making it easier for the end user to read.

OnCheckboxChange. Whenever a user clicks on a checkbox, it will activate the `OnCheckboxChange` method. Our sample application uses a checkbox to indicate when the user would like to insert a new item into an existing list. Since there are three types of lists (`BulletList`, `NumberList`, and `VariableList`) and we want to limit when the control is displayed on the task pane, they have each been defined separately and will display only when the cursor is currently located within one of these three elements.

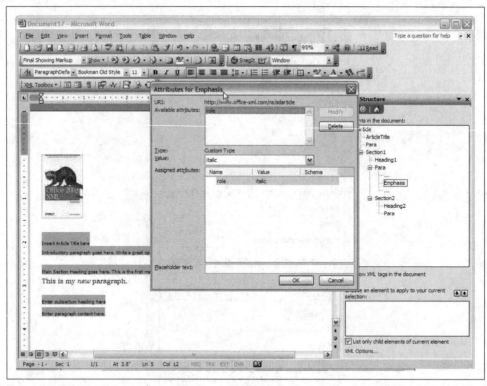

Figure 5-11. Document template with new content added

For both `BulletList` and `NumberList`, we need to add an `Item` element along with a child `Para` element. Variable lists have a `VariableEntry` child, which in turn contains a `Term` and `Definition` pair. The definition element requires at least one `Para`.

There is also paragraph-level formatting that must be applied to ensure that the new content is displayed properly. `BulletListItem`, `NumberListItem`, and `VariableListEntry` are defined in the template for this purpose.

The following routine begins by setting the variable node to the element of the current cursor location. The `XMLParentNode` is a bit deceiving; we're really looking for the name of the current element, but that's the way it works. Once we have the `XMLNode` selected, we then test where we are, move up the tree if required, and finally arrive at the `BulletList` element. The range is then collapsed back to a single cursor location and the `Item` element is added. Before moving on, we insert a paragraph marker. This will move the new list entry onto a new line. We don't have to set the style since it will automatically carry over the style from the previous paragraph. The range is

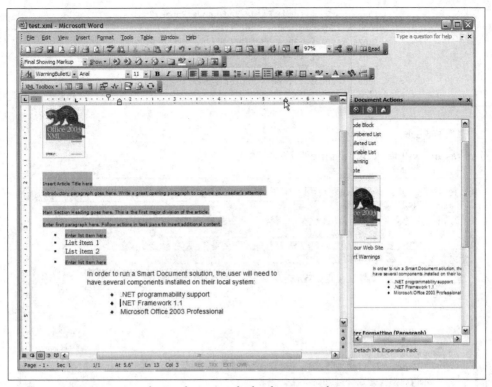

Figure 5-12. Document template with warning boilerplate inserted

again collapsed and the `Para` element is inserted. The last step is to add placeholder text for the end user:

```
Public Sub OnCheckboxChange(ByVal ControlID As Integer, _
ByVal Target As Object, ByVal Checked As Boolean) _
Implements Microsoft.Office.Interop.SmartTag.ISmartDocument.OnCheckboxChange

    Select Case ControlID
        Case 301 'bullet list
            Dim range As Word.Range = CType(Target, Word.Range)
            Dim selection As Word.Selection = _
            range.Application.ActiveWindow.Selection
            Dim node As Word.XMLNode = selection.XMLParentNode

            If node.BaseName = "Para" Then
                node = node.ParentNode
            End If

            If node.BaseName = "Item" Then
                node = node.ParentNode
            End If

            If node.BaseName = "BulletList" Then
```

```
            range.SetRange(node.Range.End, node.Range.End)
            node = range.XMLNodes.Add("Item", cNAMESPACE)
            range.InsertParagraphBefore()
            range.SetRange(node.Range.End, node.Range.End)
            node = range.XMLNodes.Add("Para", cNAMESPACE)
            node.PlaceholderText = "Enter list item here"
        End If

    End Select
End Sub
```

The results will look like Figure 5-13.

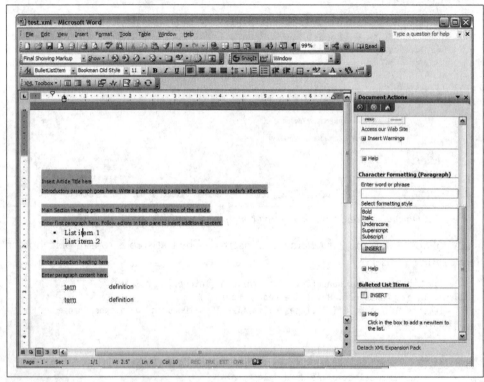

Figure 5-13. Template with bulleted list inserted

The routine for numbered lists is basically the same and is not listed here (but is included in the sample code available for download). The variable list entry, however, has an extra step or two. First, there are more elements in the tree to test and ascend. Next, there are two child elements of `VariableEntry`: Term and Definition. Definition contains a required child Para element. And both Term and Para should have placeholder text added:

```
Select Case ControlID
    Case 501 'variable list
        Dim range As Word.Range = CType(Target, Word.Range)
        Dim selection As Word.Selection = _
```

```
    range.Application.ActiveWindow.Selection
Dim node As Word.XMLNode = selection.XMLParentNode
Dim Nnode As Word.XMLNode = selection.XMLParentNode

If node.BaseName = "Para" Then
    node = node.ParentNode
End If

If node.BaseName = "Definition" Then
    node = node.ParentNode
End If

If node.BaseName = "Term" Then
    node = node.ParentNode
End If

If node.BaseName = "VariableEntry" Then
    node = node.ParentNode
End If

If node.BaseName = "VariableList" Then
    range.SetRange(node.Range.End, node.Range.End)
    node = range.XMLNodes.Add("VariableEntry", cNAMESPACE)
    range.InsertParagraphBefore()
    range.SetRange(node.Range.End, node.Range.End)
    Nnode = range.XMLNodes.Add("Term", cNAMESPACE)
    Nnode.PlaceholderText = "Enter term here"
    range.SetRange(node.Range.End, node.Range.End)
    node = range.XMLNodes.Add("Definition", cNAMESPACE)
    range.SetRange(node.Range.End, node.Range.End)
    node = range.XMLNodes.Add("Para", cNAMESPACE)
    node.PlaceholderText = "Enter definition here"
End If

    End Select
End Sub
```

This code will produce results like those shown in Figure 5-14.

OnRadioGroupSelectChange. Our authoring templates for block-level items are associated with radio buttons. Whenever a user clicks on a radio button, it will become selected and the OnRadioGroupSelectChange method will be activated. As with the list or combo box, the appropriate selection must be identified from the set of options presented to the end user.

The code necessary to accomplish the set of tasks defined in the radio group control is more complex than the previous examples. In order to code for these tasks, a combination of methods will need to be employed, including the possible use of XPath, testing for valid children, and an additional validation pass before committing the results back to the end user. Alternatively, the conditions could be narrowed, resulting in an easier coding implementation. However, that would most likely result in

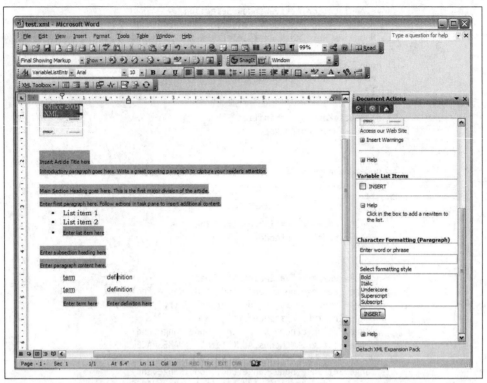

Figure 5-14. Template with an additional variable list entry inserted

severely hampering the Document Actions task pane with numerous controls and excessive refreshes.

The code below uses XPath to locate a particular element and then insert the markup as the last node of that element. It also demonstrates how to apply styles. Note that the lists, and particularly the variable list, have numerous children that also need to be inserted. Another approach would be to insert just the first node, and then apply a transform that would supply the remaining children. This method would give you more control over the exact placement of formatting.

```
Public Sub OnRadioGroupSelectChange(ByVal ControlID As Integer, _
ByVal Target As Object, ByVal Selected As Integer, ByVal Value As String) _
Implements _
Microsoft.Office.Interop.SmartTag.ISmartDocument.OnRadioGroupSelectChange

    Dim range As Word.Range = CType(Target, Word.Range)
    Dim selection As Word.Selection = range.Application.ActiveWindow.Selection
    Dim node As Word.XMLNode = range.Document.SelectSingleNode("//ns:Section1", _
    "xmlns:ns='" & cNAMESPACE & "'")

    Select Case ControlID
        Case 1 'authoring templates
```

```
If Value = "Paragraph" Then
    range.SetRange(node.Range.End, node.Range.End)
    node = range.XMLNodes.Add("Para", cNAMESPACE)
    range.InsertParagraphBefore()
    node.PlaceholderText = "Enter paragraph here"
    node.Range.Style = "ParagraphDefault"

ElseIf Value = "Code Block" Then
    range.SetRange(node.Range.End, node.Range.End)
    node = range.XMLNodes.Add("CodeExample", cNAMESPACE)
    range.InsertParagraphBefore()
    node.PlaceholderText = "Enter code sample here"
    node.Range.Style = "CodeBlock"

ElseIf Value = "Numbered List" Then
    range.SetRange(node.Range.End, node.Range.End)
    node = range.XMLNodes.Add("NumberList", cNAMESPACE)
    range.InsertParagraphBefore()
    range.SetRange(node.Range.End, node.Range.End)
    node = range.XMLNodes.Add("Item", cNAMESPACE)
    range.SetRange(node.Range.End, node.Range.End)
    node = range.XMLNodes.Add("Para", cNAMESPACE)
    node.PlaceholderText = "Enter list item here"
    node.Range.Style = "NumberListItem"

ElseIf Value = "Bulleted List" Then
    range.SetRange(node.Range.End, node.Range.End)
    node = range.XMLNodes.Add("BulletList", cNAMESPACE)
    range.InsertParagraphBefore()
    range.SetRange(node.Range.End, node.Range.End)
    node = range.XMLNodes.Add("Item", cNAMESPACE)
    range.SetRange(node.Range.End, node.Range.End)
    node = range.XMLNodes.Add("Para", cNAMESPACE)
    node.PlaceholderText = "Enter list item here"
    node.Range.Style = "BulletListItem"

ElseIf Value = "Variable List" Then
    Dim Nnode As Word.XMLNode = selection.XMLParentNode
    range.SetRange(node.Range.End, node.Range.End)
    node = range.XMLNodes.Add("VariableList", cNAMESPACE)
    range.InsertParagraphBefore()
    range.SetRange(node.Range.End, node.Range.End)
    node = range.XMLNodes.Add("VariableEntry", cNAMESPACE)
    node.Range.Style = "VariableListEntry"
    range.SetRange(node.Range.End, node.Range.End)
    Nnode = range.XMLNodes.Add("Term", cNAMESPACE)
    Nnode.PlaceholderText = "Enter term here"
    range.SetRange(node.Range.End, node.Range.End)
    node = range.XMLNodes.Add("Definition", cNAMESPACE)
    range.SetRange(node.Range.End, node.Range.End)
    node = range.XMLNodes.Add("Para", cNAMESPACE)
    node.PlaceholderText = "Enter definition here"
```

```
            ElseIf Value = "Warning" Then
                range.SetRange(node.Range.End, node.Range.End)
                node = range.XMLNodes.Add("Warning", cNAMESPACE)
                range.InsertParagraphBefore( )
                range.SetRange(node.Range.End, node.Range.End)
                node = range.XMLNodes.Add("Para", cNAMESPACE)
                node.PlaceholderText = "Enter warning here here"
                node.Range.Style = "Warning"

            ElseIf Value = "Note" Then
                range.SetRange(node.Range.End, node.Range.End)
                node = range.XMLNodes.Add("Note", cNAMESPACE)
                range.InsertParagraphBefore( )
                range.SetRange(node.Range.End, node.Range.End)
                node = range.XMLNodes.Add("Para", cNAMESPACE)
                node.PlaceholderText = "Enter note here"
                node.Range.Style = "Note"

            End If
        End Select
    End Sub
```

The result of this code is shown in Figures 5-15 and 5-16

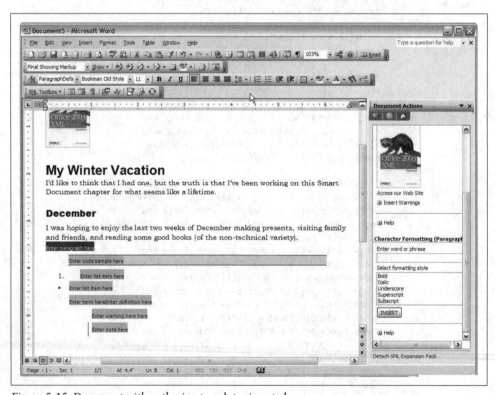

Figure 5-15. Document with authoring templates inserted

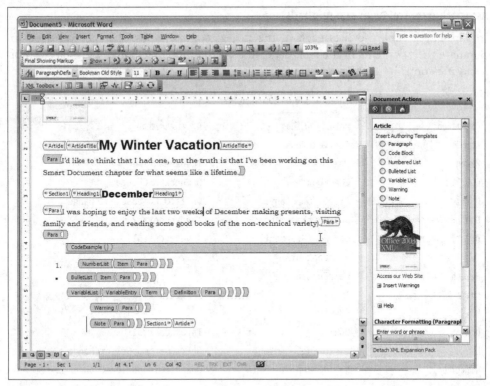

Figure 5-16. Document with authoring templates inserted (tags on)

This fairly simple example works well in our sample since we're beginning with a template and then creating a new document. However, if we were editing an existing document, we would most likely want to place the block-level elements at the next valid location in relation to the cursor position. This requires significantly more coding.

OnPaneUpdateComplete. Our sample did not need to use the OnPaneUpdateComplete method, which is triggered on two separate events: when a document is first opened and the expansion pack loaded, and each time the cursor is placed within a different element. Both of these events cause the task pane to be redrawn; once rendering is complete this method is activated.

 If the code placed in the OnPaneUpdateComplete results in the task pane being reloaded, an infinite loop will result.

Associating control types and methods

In summary, Table 5-6 lists each of the fifteen control types, the method used to populate their contents in the task pane, and the method associated with selection of a specific control.

Table 5-6. Control types available in Smart Documents

Control type	Populate method	Activate method
ActiveX	ActiveXProps	
Button	Other	InvokeControl
Checkbox	Checkbox	OnCheckboxChange
Combo	ListOrComboContent	OnListOrComboSelectChange
DocumentFragment	DocumentFragment	InvokeControl
DocumentFragmentURL	DocumentFragment	InvokeControl
Help	HelpContent	
HelpURL	HelpContent	
Image	Image	ImageClick
Label	Other	
Link	Other	InvokeControl
Listbox	ListOrComboContent	OnListOrComboSelectChange
RadioGroup	RadioGroup	OnRadioGroupSelectChange
Separator	Other	
Text box	TextboxContent	OnTextboxContentChange

Manifest Files

Once the code is complete, all of the components must be prepared and made ready for delivery. The manifest file is an XML instance that identifies each of the components associated with the Smart Document expansion pack. It is the equivalent of a packing list, identifying each of the components necessary to make the Smart Document solution run and where they can be found. It is attached to a Word document or template through the Templates and Add-Ins menu or through a processing instruction incorporated into the document instance itself:

```
<?mso-solutionextension URI="namespace" manifestPath="path">
```

If any components cannot be located, an error message will be returned to the end user. One of the novel uses of the manifest file is to track versions. The most common Smart Document deployment scenario involves placing the files on a server where each end user will access them. Once the update frequency value has been reached, the application will check for a more recent version on the server (as indicated by the version number in the manifest file). While a schema for the manifest file has been published and can be found in the Microsoft Office 2003 Smart Document SDK, it does not appear that it is actually used for validation, as the samples provided in the SDK do not conform to it.

There are several key components to a manifest file, as follows:

manifest

> The manifest element has two different content models, depending whether it is the root element or a child of manifestCollection. When listed as part of a collection, it is nothing other than a pointer to the individual manifest files, containing the URI and path for each. When used as the root element, it contains the version, updateFrequency, uri, manifestURL, and solution elements.

version

> The version element (*major.minor*) contains the release number for the expansion pack and is used to determine whether or not a more recent expansion pack is available (see updateFrequency, below).

updateFrequency

> The update frequency is expressed in minutes. Once this amount of time has elapsed, the user will be prompted to check for an updated expansion pack. The version number of the expansion pack located on the server is then compared with that on the user's system. If the version number on the server is higher, the new expansion pack will be downloaded.

solution

> Each solution element within a manifest file describes either one solution type (smart document, schema, transform, or other) or one targetApplication type (Word or Excel). There can be multiple solution elements within a single manifest. The solutionID element is required and contains the GUID associated with the *.dll*. An alias is also required, and associates a user-friendly name with the solution. The file element is described below.

file

> A file element should be included for each individual file that is associated with the solution. This includes help files, document fragments, images, templates, and any other collections that are part of the overall Smart Document solution.

For a managed solution, a unique Solution ID must be generated. A utility to generate unique identifiers, *guidgen.exe*, shown in action in Figure 5-17, is included with Visual Studio .NET and can be found at *C:\Program Files\Microsoft Visual Studio .NET 2003\ Common7\Tools\guidgen.exe*. When the expansion pack is attached, the *.dll* is entered into the registry with the specified key.

> It should be noted that while the manifest file does have an associated schema, Microsoft Office 2003 will not necessarily generate an error if the instance is not valid. This can be tested by validating any of the *manifest.xml* files distributed with the Smart Document SDK in Microsoft Office Word 2003.

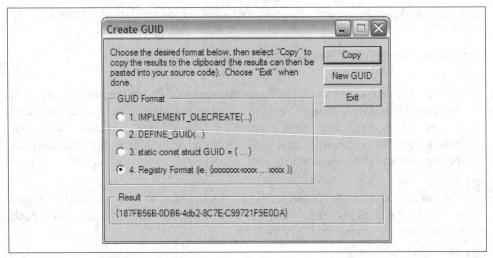

Figure 5-17. Create GUID user interface

Here is a sample *manifest.xml* file:

```xml
<?xml version="1.0" encoding="UTF-8" standalone="no"?>
<manifest xmlns="http://schemas.microsoft.com/office/xmlexpansionpacks/2003">
  <version>1.0</version>
  <updateFrequency>20160</updateFrequency>
  <uri>http://www.office-xml.com/ns/sdarticle</uri>
  <solution>
    <solutionID>{1E15F399-9BFF-4ac9-A68A-737788C1B462}</solutionID>
    <type>smartDocument</type>
    <alias lcid="1033">Essentials Article Solution</alias>
    <documentSpecific>false</documentSpecific>
    <targetApplication>Word.Application.11</targetApplication>
    <file>
      <runFromServer/>
      <type>solutionActionHandler</type>
      <managed/>
      <version>1.0</version>
      <filePath>SDEssentials.dll</filePath>
      <CLSNAME>SDEssentials.ArticleSmartDocument</CLSNAME>
    </file>
    <file>
      <runFromServer/>
      <type>other</type>
      <version>1.0</version>
      <filePath>help/article.htm</filePath>
    </file>
    <file>
      <runFromServer/>
      <type>other</type>
      <version>1.0</version>
      <filePath>help/para.htm</filePath>
    </file>
```

```xml
    <file>
      <runFromServer/>
      <type>other</type>
      <version>1.0</version>
      <filePath>help/code.htm</filePath>
    </file>
    <file>
      <runFromServer/>
       <type>other</type>
      <version>1.0</version>
      <filePath>images/cover.jpg</filePath>
    </file>
  </solution>
  <solution>
    <solutionID>schema</solutionID>
    <type>schema</type>
    <alias lcid="1033">SDArticle</alias>
    <file>
      <type>schema</type>
      <version>1.0</version>
      <filePath>SDArticle.xsd</filePath>
    </file>
  </solution>
</manifest>
```

Other Files

A Smart Document solution is likely to contain numerous files—help files, templates, XSL transformations, document fragments, and media clips, not to mention the actual *.dll*, manifest file, and schema. Each of these files should be listed in the manifest; when the expansion pack is attached to the document or template, the application will check to ensure that it can locate each referenced file.

It is important to note, however, that the references to these files in the *.dll* must be absolute pathnames or URLs. If the Smart Document solution cannot locate a referenced file, it will just ignore it. Building in some error checking to test that the files actually exist in the designated file locations is highly recommended.

One method for resolving the absolute pathname is to set a constant to the installation directory of the Smart Document solution in the `SmartDocInitialize` method. By prepending this constant to the specific directory and filename, the files can be located by the application and the developer does not have to worry about where they were actually installed.

If a specific installation directory is not given in the manifest file, the solution is loaded in the schema folder under the Application Data folder in the user's Documents and Settings folder (*C:\Documents and Settings\<username>\Local Settings\ Application Data\Microsoft\Schemas*).

Subdirectories appear to be flattened when copied to the installation directory; that is, if you created subdirectories for components such as help files, images, and XML fragments, those subdirectories will not be created when the solution is installed on the user's system; instead the files will be aggregated into a single directory. Because of this behavior it is strongly recommended that filenames are unique across the entire solution set.

When building and testing Smart Document solutions, it is a good idea to continually delete temporary files. Common locations for these files are:

C:\Documents and Settings\username\Local Settings\Application Data\Microsoft\Schemas

C:\Documents and Settings\username\Local Settings\Application Data\Assembly

C:\Documents and Settings\username\Local Settings\Temp

Help files

Help files are created using a subset of XHTML. The most important thing to remember when creating help files is that the task pane is only a small percentage of the overall screen size, and there are numerous components to be displayed in this limited space. Keep help text clear and concise. In general, you will create one help file for each control included in the Smart Document solution. Table 5-7 lists the supported elements.

Table 5-7. Supported elements in help file XHTML

Element	Purpose
A	Anchor for hypertext links
B	Bold
BR	Break
CENTER	Centers text in task pane
FONT	Font characteristics
H1–H6	Headings
I	Italic
LI	List item
OL	Ordered (numbered) list
P	Paragraph
SPAN	Inline text block
U	Underline
UL	Unordered (bulleted) list

Here's a listing of the help file that's associated with the authoring templates control:

```
<p><b>Authoring Templates</b>: There are several types of content blocks
that can be inserted in an article:</p>
<ul>
    <li>paragraph</li>
    <li>code block</li>
    <li>numbered list</li>
    <li>bulleted list</li>
    <li>term / definition list</li>
    <li>warning</li>
    <li>note</li>
</ul>
<p>It is possible to have more than one entry for any type; that is,
you may have three authors and two editors. Click on the radio button
next to the desired selection.</p>
<p><b>Logo</b>: Select the appropriate logo from the images below.</p>
<p><b>Website</b>: For additional help, click on the link below.</p>
<p><b>Required Warning</b>: The Warning below, if needed, must be
incorporated into your document without modification. Click on the
content and it will automatically be inserted into your document.</p>
```

Document Fragments

The world of structured document authoring has been using fragments for quite some time, either managed as file entities or as objects in a content management system. Smart Document technology opens this potential to Microsoft Word 2003 users.

Let's say that you work in a law firm. More likely than not, you have a library of document fragments that can be used to create contracts, wills and trusts, and other legal documents. Or maybe you have to search through existing documents to find the right pieces you need, and then cut and paste. You can now access those components directly through the task pane and can build in sufficient intelligence so that only relevant fragments are displayed. Or maybe your sales and marketing group struggles with the process of creating proposals for your products and services. By managing independent descriptions that are targeted to various types of customers (such as government, commercial, or industry-specific) your salespeople will be able to quickly assemble proposals that contain the most up-to-date, accurate information along with any boilerplate required by your legal department. Yet another common usage is in the area of technical documentation. Warnings, cautions, and notes have legal implications and must typically go through an approval process. Once approved, the text cannot be modified. By taking advantage of document fragments, the content can be automatically inserted into the document making sure that no errors occurred during a copy and paste operation, and the content can then be protected to prevent the end user from making any unauthorized changes.

By default, Word will display the first page of any document fragment in the task pane. For lengthy fragments this can be cumbersome. Another option is to create two versions of the fragment—one that is displayed in the task pane and the other containing the complete dataset. Document fragments must be valid WordprocessingML instances. The easiest way to create such fragments is to use Microsoft Office Word 2003 with the Smart Document solution attached as described in the next section. This enables you to take advantage of the templates and styles to apply your schema-specific markup along with the necessary WordprocessingML markup and style information. When saving, save as XML. Fragments can also be created by taking existing XML components and running them through an XSL transform. Here's the listing for our Warning document fragment (with most of the heading information omitted). Note that it contains both WordprocessingML (prefixed by w) and our own schema elements (prefixed by ns0):

```
<?xml version="1.0" encoding="UTF-8" standalone="yes"?>
<?mso-application progid="Word.Document"?>
<w:wordDocument
xmlns:w="http://schemas.microsoft.com/office/word/2003/wordml" xmlns:v="urn:schemas-
microsoft-com:vml"
xmlns:w10="urn:schemas-microsoft-com:office:word" xmlns:sl="http://schemas.microsoft.
com/schemaLibrary/2003/core" xmlns:aml="http://schemas.microsoft.com/aml/2001/core"
xmlns:wx="http://schemas.microsoft.com/office/word/2003/auxHint" xmlns:o="urn:
schemas-microsoft-com:office:office"
xmlns:dt="uuid:C2F41010-65B3-11d1-A29F-00AA00C14882"
xmlns:ns0="http://www.office-xml.com/ns/sdarticle"
w:macrosPresent="no" w:embeddedObjPresent="no"
w:ocxPresent="no" xml:space="preserve">
...
<w:body>
<ns0:Warning>
<ns0:Para>
<w:p><w:pPr><w:pStyle w:val="Warning"/></w:pPr><w:r>
<w:t>In order to run a Smart Document solution, the user will
need to have several components installed on their local system:
</w:t></w:r></w:p></ns0:Para></ns0:Warning>
<w:p/>
</w:body>
</w:wordDocument>
```

Attaching the Smart Document Expansion Pack

Before you can use your Smart Document solution with a Microsoft Word document, you must attach the expansion pack. As a developer, you will first want to run the "Disable XML Expansion Pack Manifest Security" utility included in the Smart Document SDK. This will prevent you from having to re-sign the manifest file each time it is updated. Note, however, that if you disable the security check, you will be reminded each time you attach the expansion pack that security has been disabled. You will then be asked whether or not you wish to re-enable security. Beware—the default response is yes.

Each time you make modifications to your code that you want to test in the user's environment, you will need to rebuild your code, then detach and reattach the manifest file to the Word document or template. This will force the updated code to be loaded into the temporary directories.

 Word 2003 has been known to crash after detaching and then reattaching an expansion pack. Be prepared.

To attach an expansion pack:

1. Open the Word document or template you wish to use with the expansion pack.
2. Select Tools → Templates and Add-Ins... from the menu bar.
3. Select the XML Expansion Packs tab.
4. Click on the Add button.
5. Navigate to the manifest file and select it. The expansion pack should now download.

 If there are problems locating any of the components defined in the expansion pack, an error message will be generated.

6. When the alias you have defined for the Smart Document solution displays in the window, select it. Then click Attach and OK.

 If there are problems with the expansion pack itself, a cryptic error message about your expansion pack being identified as either missing or invalid will be displayed. Unfortunately it's not a very useful error message, and can point to a dozen or more problems.

To delete an expansion pack:

1. Open the Word document or template you wish to use with the expansion pack.
2. Select Tools → Templates and Add-Ins... from the menu bar.
3. Select the XML Expansion Packs tab.
4. Highlight the name of the Expansion Pack and select Delete.
5. You will be prompted about whether or not you want to remove the expansion pack from your system. Click Yes.

Do not use the Remove button; this will remove the expansion pack from that particular document, but will not delete the expansion pack from its install location.

Deploying Your Smart Document Solution

There are a few requirements that must be met before an expansion pack can be installed. Most of these are related to security issues, particularly if your solution is intended to be distributed via the Internet. If you aren't the system administrator, you may need to find the person who is and enlist their services. This is not intended to be a thorough discussion of security and installation; the subject encompasses entire volumes. Refer to the Microsoft Smart Document SDK and MSDN for more detailed information.

Internal Deployment

The easiest way to distribute solutions is to run the "Disable XML Expansion Pack Manifest Security" utility included in the Smart Document SDK. This is easy, but not necessarily secure. It is intended to be used in a development environment only.

The best way to deploy and update a Smart Document solution is from a shared network location, a web server, or another location accessible by all users. If possible, attach the expansion pack to any templates or other documents that are part of the solution. That will eliminate the end user from having to attach the expansion pack manually.

When opening a Smart Document with an attached XML expansion pack that is located on a web server, Office checks to see if the server is located within an intranet zone or is listed as a trusted site. If either of those conditions is true, the expansion pack is retrieved and the standard security check is performed. If, however, neither of those two conditions is true, the expansion pack will not be retrieved.

External Deployment

The optimum approach for external distribution is to create an installer package that will place each of the files in the appropriate location and add the necessary entries to the registry. If it's a managed code solution, client computers must have the Microsoft .NET Framework 1.1 and .NET Programmability Support installed. The optimum installation procedure is as follows:

1. Install Microsoft .NET Framework 1.1 (available for download from Microsoft Windows Update).

2. Install Microsoft Office Professional Edition 2003—complete. This will automatically install the .NET Programmability Support option (the Primary Interop Assemblies or PIAs necessary to make managed code run with Word).

If Office 2003 is already in place, the following procedure will update the environment:

1. Install .NET Framework 1.1.
2. Select "Add or Remove Programs" from the Control Panel.
3. Locate Microsoft Office Professional Edition 2003 (or appropriate) and click Change.
4. Select "Add or remove features" and click Next.
5. Select "Choose advanced customization of applications" and click Next.
6. On the Advanced Customization panel, expand Microsoft Office Word by clicking on the plus sign (+).
7. The first option listed should be ".NET Programmability Support." Click on the down arrow icon to the left of the option name. If not already installed, select "Run from My Computer." and then click Update.

COM Versus Managed Code

In all cases, Office 2003 requires that Smart Document developers sign the XML expansion pack manifest file. Internal certificates can be created with the "Digital Certificate for VBA Projects" included with the Microsoft Office Tools kit. For managed code solutions, there are two additional requirements:

- The Microsoft .NET Framework 1.1 must be installed on the client computer.
- The assembly .dll must have FULLTRUST permissions explicitly granted on the user's machine.

 Refer to the Smart Document SDK and online resources for more information about managing security.

Template Files

If your Smart Document solution contains one or more template (.dot) files, they should be placed in the default template directory as specified in the File Locations tab in the Options menu. This will allow the end user to create new documents by selecting File → New from the menu bar and then selecting the appropriate template. Attaching the expansion pack to the template will ensure that it is automatically enabled.

A Few Last Words on Smart Documents

Now that you've seen the parts involved, it's worth considering which aspects of Smart Documents need your focus.

Range and Selection Objects

The Word object model consists of hundreds of objects, yet no two are more powerful than range and selection. These two objects are used to identify the parts of the document that are to be manipulated by the accompanying code. What is confusing is that, for most cases, either object can be used. The main difference is that a range is not visible to the end user; that is, you can identify a range and manipulate it, and the end user's cursor location will not move. selection, on the other hand, does exactly what you'd expect—literally highlighting the selection on the end user's screen. More often than not, range is preferred over selection for several reasons, not the least of which is performance.

Both the range and selection objects have dozens of properties and methods associated with them—everything from cut, insert, and delete to XMLNodes. For a thorough explanation of range and selection, see *Writing Word Macros* by Steven Roman (O'Reilly).

Inserting Markup

One of the powerful features of Word is its ability to quickly change the "view" of any document on the screen. You can turn individual formatting markers on or off, change the overall look from outline to print layout, view field codes or placeholder text. What may not have been apparent in the past but now becomes clearly evident is what, if any, impact these changes have on the cursor position. When determining what elements are allowed in context, the context referred to is the current cursor location. When programming Smart Documents, you must determine the current view; otherwise your tests may yield undesired results.

Validation

The "Valid elements for insertion" list as displayed in the XML Structure task pane does not pay attention to sequence or occurrence. If the cursor is currently positioned within an element that has children, all of those child elements will be displayed. Word will, however, display an error once an invalid child has been inserted, via both squiggly lines in the document pane and symbols in the XML Structure view. The developer can take advantage of the XMLValidationError method to prevent the user from creating an invalid instance and to provide additional guidance. If the user does not use the XML Structure task pane to insert markup, this problem is avoided.

Inserting Styles

Microsoft Word has four types of styles: character, paragraph, list, and table. When applying styles to content, the surrounding WordprocessingML markup becomes very important. If applying a paragraph-level style to some text (paragraph styles and list styles), that content must be both preceded and followed by a paragraph marker. If the text is not preceded by a paragraph marker, then when the style is applied it will be applied to the entire block; that is, to all content until either a preceding paragraph marker is located or to the top of the document itself. Similarly, if the text following the content to be formatted is not separated by a paragraph marker, it too will take on the particular style characteristics meant to be associated with the content.

Stories or Streams

Word objects such as headers, footers, footnotes, endnotes, comments, and text frames are maintained separately from the main body of a document. They each have their own object model and are accessible programmatically, but if they contain XML markup, your resulting instance when saving the document will most likely result in errors. The best way to handle these separate streams is through direct use of the Word tools; capture them on save by making use of a transform that will convert the WordprocessingML to your specific markup and place the contents in the right location within the XML document instance.

Some Final Thoughts

While far from perfect, Smart Document technology gives the developer tremendous flexibility in creating intelligent document applications that will readily handle time-consuming tasks such as locating information, retrieving it, and inserting it into a document, as well as support for the creation of documents with built-in intelligence thanks to the incorporation of XML markup. For the most part, applications developed as of this writing have proven to be fairly stable, other than the areas specifically pointed out in this chapter.

While the resulting applications are working well, the development process tends to leave substantial amounts of garbage that goes uncollected. Be sure to clean out all temp files regularly (at least daily) to avoid additional problems. The frequent act of attaching/detaching manifest files/expansion packs may be necessary during development and testing is likely to cause Word to crash. Be sure you don't have any other Word documents open while debugging; you may end up losing some of your work.

As mentioned earlier, most sample applications provided in the Smart Document SDK or articles posted to the MSDN web site revolve around "data islands" combined with generic content elements that hold all of the content that is not associated with specific XML markup. For a number of applications, this approach is perfectly reasonable and should be considered.

CHAPTER 6

Working with XML Data in Excel Spreadsheets

Microsoft Office Excel 2003 offers two rather different kinds of XML functionality. Excel (in the Professional and Enterprise editions) allows users to build spreadsheets that load data from XML files, making it easy to analyze information sent from various sources using the same spreadsheet. The data that a spreadsheet analyzes can be separated from the logic used to analyze it very easily this way, making it simpler to create spreadsheets that work more like ordinary applications. Excel 2003 (and XP) also offer the ability to save and open spreadsheets which are themselves saved in Excel's own XML format; these features will be explored in Chapter 7.

The features described in this chapter are available only to users of the Professional or Enterprise editions of Microsoft Office Excel. Sadly, the Standard edition does not include these capabilities. If you have problems finding the XML features in your copy of Excel, check to see which edition you're using. (The Small Business Edition appears to include the Standard, not the Professional, version.)

Separating Data and Logic

When spreadsheets first appeared, they brilliantly blurred the distinction between programming and information. Spreadsheet users could enter their data and work on it without having to do things like "programming." All the information could reside in a single file, readily shared, and copy and paste functionality along with a few basic functions ensured that spreadsheets were easy to learn. An unknown but clearly vast amount of business decision-making has rested on spreadsheets, and an incredible amount of business data is stored in spreadsheets.

This power has come at some cost, however. While spreadsheets are accessible, their mixing of data and logic has created a few problems. While copy and paste works well for simple spreadsheets, it becomes complicated quickly if, for example, users try to combine logic from multiple spreadsheets. Suddenly development style matters. Spreadsheet software, with its smart copy and paste features and support for multiple workbooks, has done a lot to simplify this process, but the work involved in making these pieces communicate is still very real. Mergers and acquisitions, for instance, often face a serious challenge in reconciling the spreadsheets used by decision-makers at the various organizations.

Even on a smaller scale, the combination of data and logic that make spreadsheets so powerful can create some substantial annoyances. I work, for example, with data I need to analyze on a weekly, monthly, quarterly, and annual basis. I use the same basic logic for all of this analysis. The company I work for makes it available in Excel spreadsheets, generated from a database. I end up with an enormous number of largely duplicate spreadsheets over time, as only the data has changed. There's no simple way for me to aggregate the information from multiple spreadsheets, and if I want to make a change to the logic, I have to make that change every time I download new information. That thoroughly discourages me from making logic changes.

 Another cost of spreadsheets is that they act as roach motels: data comes in but it never goes back out to databases, except as spreadsheets. This problem will be addressed in the next chapter.

Excel has addressed these issues to some degree with features like ODBC integration with databases. Instead of storing all the information in spreadsheets directly, the user can specify an area of the spreadsheet to be populated with information from a database query. In places where you trust your users with such access or can provide secure facilities to provide the information, this can be genuinely useful stuff. Users can analyze information using the CPU power on their desktops, customize how they see the data, and manipulate it without ever (hopefully) having to request development of custom processes. They can load new data into their spreadsheets whenever they need to do so, without fear of overwriting the logic they've so painstakingly created.

Unfortunately, that scenario only works for a limited number of cases where users have direct (or nearly direct) access to information. There are many untrusted users, as well as users who travel or are otherwise disconnected. There are lots of users who need access to historical information, and may need to process that information a few times before actually letting it into the final spreadsheet. There are users with intermittent connections, who access their information through things like web servers and file servers.

In these cases, using XML as a base format for data works very nicely. XML files are self-contained, and are easily sent as attachments in email or loaded from a file or web server without any special infrastructure. Instead of users having direct access to a database, they can be given access to copies of the parts of the database that interest them. If users want to tinker with the data—for forecasting, for instance, or just to make themselves feel briefly better about their results—they can tinker without having any impact on the original data source. Users who want to aggregate information from multiple data sources can do so using either Excel's own tools or the wide variety of XML-processing tools available.

Users can also treat Excel as a tool for creating and manipulating XML data, provided that the data structures fit neatly into Excel's expectations of columns and rows. While Excel is in some ways a more limited XML editor than Word, it also provides a much simpler interface, one that is easy for users to set up and use themselves.

Loading XML into an Excel Spreadsheet

There are several different ways to load XML data into Excel. Some are useful mostly for quick exploration and maybe some editing, while others are more appropriate for creating spreadsheets that use XML as a data source that can be easily replaced with new data whenever appropriate. All of these mechanisms share a common approach for showing XML data in the spreadsheet, so it's worth taking a moment to examine how Excel handles XML structures before moving into the mechanics of importing data.

When Excel opens an XML file, it imports data from it. If you make changes to the XML file while Excel is working with the data it has imported from that file, changes to the XML will not be reflected in the Excel spreadsheet.

Tables and Trees

Excel, like all spreadsheets, is built on a grid. Information is organized into rows and columns, and this worksheet grid (as well as relationships among multiple worksheet grids in a workbook) is used to create cross-references between different sections of information. Within the grid, Excel is enormously flexible. Information doesn't have to follow neat table structures—pricing data could, if desired, run diagonally down a spreadsheet. It's easier to work with ranges of information if it stays in a single row or column, though, so most spreadsheets combine table areas that contain raw data and then either tables of results or cells along the fringes of the tables.

XML has no built-in notion of a grid. While it's certainly possible to represent a spreadsheet's rows and columns of cells within a worksheet as XML (and Chapter 7 will explore how Microsoft's chosen to do this), there's no guarantee that any given XML document will neatly fit into the native structures of Excel. There are a few simple but critical conditions that must apply to XML documents for them to be used easily as source data for Excel:

Tree structures that produce rows
> Excel works best on XML documents when they conform to its structural expectations. The root element of the XML document should act as the primary container for a table of information. Each of the child elements of the root element

should represent a row. Each of the child elements (or attributes) of the row elements should represent a cell in the grid. Roughly, this looks like:

```
<table>
  <row>
    <cell-name1>...value...</cell-name1>
    <cell-name2>...value...</cell-name2>
    <cell-name3>...value...</cell-name3>
    <cell-name4>...value...</cell-name4>
  </row>
  <row>
    <cell-name1>...value...</cell-name1>
    <cell-name2>...value...</cell-name2>
    <cell-name3>...value...</cell-name3>
    <cell-name4>...value...</cell-name4>
  </row>
  ....
</table>
```

Excel also works well with cells expressed as attributes:

```
<table>
  <row cell-name1="value" cell-name2="value" cell-name3="value"
    cell-name4="value" />
  <row cell-name1="value" cell-name2="value" cell-name3="value"
    cell-name4="value" />
  ....
</table>
```

Attributes and elements can also be mixed:

```
<table>
  <row cell-name3="value" cell-name4="value">
    <cell-name1>...value...</cell-name1>
    <cell-name2>...value...</cell-name2>
  </row>
  <row cell-name3="value" cell-name4="value">
    <cell-name1>...value...</cell-name1>
    <cell-name2>...value...</cell-name2>
  </row>
  ....
</table>
```

Excel is pretty relaxed about the order in which these appear as well, as it uses the names of elements and attributes rather than their order when creating a map.

 It is possible to extract portions of XML documents that look like these structures, even if the rest of the document looks different, but it does take a few extra steps.

Regular structure

When Excel works with an XML document, it represents the data as rows and columns. It's very difficult for Excel to determine which rows and columns to create if the data of the document isn't consistent. It does make a best effort, but there are limits. The occasional missing piece of information shouldn't cause drastic difficulties, but extra information may not be imported, and consistency makes results much more predictable.

No mixed content

One of XML's best features for working with documents is the ability to mix elements and text together freely. A classic simple use of mixed content is highlighting information in bold or italic:

```
<sentence><b>This is in bold</b> and <i>this is in italic</i>.</sentence>
```

Unfortunately, these structures fit very badly with Excel's view of XML data as cells in a grid. If you need to process XML data that includes mixed content, you should either use Word (which is designed to support it) or pre-process your XML to strip out the extra markup.

Schema for type information (optional)

While Excel doesn't require XML Schema files that describe the XML documents you use, schemas can be a very convenient tool both for describing the information that you'll be including in a spreadsheet to Excel and for sanity-checking the documents users work with in the Excel environment. If there isn't a schema, Excel makes a pretty good best effort to analyze data and guess what schema would be appropriate.

Limited depth

Excel does well with lists of information, but can really only present two levels of lists, representing rows and cells. If a document has many layers of lists, or uses elements containing elements with the same name (recursive markup, commonly used in lists), Excel will not be able to import all of the data.

Effectively, Excel only works well with a small subset of the many possible XML document structures. The Excel subset, however, is an extremely common subset in practice. Enormous amounts of data are available in XML formats that work well with Excel.

Opening XML Documents Directly

The standard Excel dialog box for opening files shows XML files (or files ending in the extension *.xml*) right along with Excel spreadsheets, as shown in Figure 6-1.

Only one of the choices presented here is a traditional Excel spreadsheet, *twoPlusTwo.xls*. The other files are XML files. XML files that Excel knows belong to Microsoft Word (thanks to the mso-application processing instruction), the *ch02-x* series, are marked with the Word icon, while *ch0601.xml*, an Excel SpreadsheetML

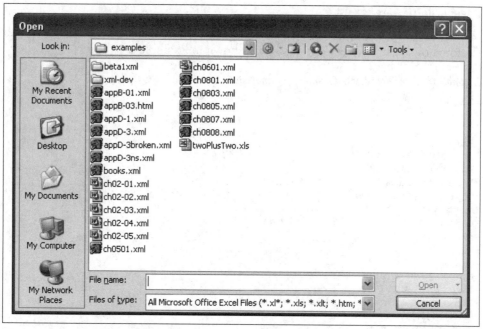

Figure 6-1. XML files appearing in the Excel Open dialog box

file, has the Excel icon. XML files using other vocabularies get a different icon. On my system, they get a Mozilla logo, but they may have a different logo on your system, depending on what XML-processing software you have installed.

Whatever logo appears, however, you can attempt to open any XML file. If the XML contains anything other than Excel's own SpreadsheetML, covered in Chapter 7, you'll see the dialog box shown in Figure 6-2.

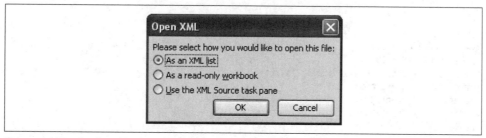

Figure 6-2. Dialog box for choosing how to handle XML document importation

 If the XML document you open contains any elements named html, you won't see the dialog box shown in Figure 6-2. Instead, Excel will attempt to open it as an HTML document. It even seems to do this if the elements that look like HTML are in another namespace.

Opening documents as a list

We'll start with a simple XML document recording (imaginary) sales of books to explore how these different options work, shown in Example 6-1.

Example 6-1. A simple XML document for analysis in Excel

```xml
<?xml version="1.0" encoding="UTF-8"?>
<sales>

<sale>
<date>10/5/2003</date>
<ISBN>0596005385</ISBN>
<Title>Office 2003 XML Essentials</Title>
<PriceUS>34.95</PriceUS>
<quantity>200</quantity>
<customer ID="1025">Zork's Books</customer>
</sale>

<sale>
<date>10/5/2003</date>
<ISBN>0596002920</ISBN>
<Title>XML in a Nutshell, 2nd Edition</Title>
<PriceUS>39.95</PriceUS>
<quantity>90</quantity>
<customer ID="1025">Zork's Books</customer>
</sale>

<sale>
<date>10/5/2003</date>
<ISBN>0596002378</ISBN>
<Title>SAX2</Title>
<PriceUS>29.95</PriceUS>
<quantity>300</quantity>
<customer ID="1025">Zork's Books</customer>
</sale>

<sale>
<date>10/7/2003</date>
<ISBN>0596005385</ISBN>
<Title>Office 2003 XML Essentials</Title>
<PriceUS>34.95</PriceUS>
<quantity>10</quantity>
<customer ID="1029">Books of Glory</customer>
</sale>

<sale>
<date>10/7/2003</date>
<ISBN>0596002920</ISBN>
<Title>XML in a Nutshell, 2nd Edition</Title>
<PriceUS>39.95</PriceUS>
<quantity>25</quantity>
<customer ID="1029">Books of Glory</customer>
</sale>
```

Example 6-1. A simple XML document for analysis in Excel (continued)

```
<sale>
<date>10/7/2003</date>
<ISBN>0596002378</ISBN>
<Title>SAX2</Title>
<PriceUS>29.95</PriceUS>
<quantity>5</quantity>
<customer ID="1029">Books of Glory</customer>
</sale>

<sale>
<date>10/18/2003</date>
<ISBN>0596002378</ISBN>
<Title>SAX2</Title>
<PriceUS>29.95</PriceUS>
<quantity>15</quantity>
<customer ID="2561">Title Wave</customer>
</sale>

<sale>
<date>10/21/2003</date>
<ISBN>0596002920</ISBN>
<Title>XML in a Nutshell, 2nd Edition</Title>
<PriceUS>39.95</PriceUS>
<quantity>15</quantity>
<customer ID="9021">Books for You</customer>
</sale>

</sales>
```

If you open this document from Excel and choose "Open as an XML List," you'll see the dialog box shown in Figure 6-3.

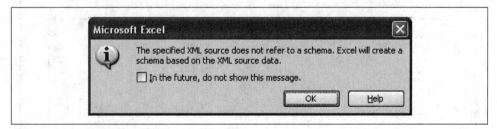

Figure 6-3. Excel's warning that no schema is in use

If you just go ahead and click OK, Excel will look at the document, infer a schema for it, build a list based on that schema, and import the contents of the XML document into that list. You'll be rewarded with the spreadsheet result shown in Figure 6-4.

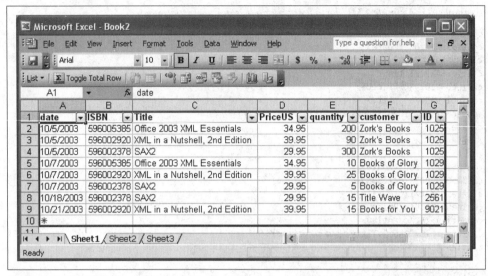

Figure 6-4. The XML document shown in Example 6-1 presented as an XML list in Excel

Excel not only imports the data from the XML document, it uses the element and attribute names as list headers. The drop down tabs to the right of the list headers let you organize the information as you'd like, as shown in Figure 6-5.

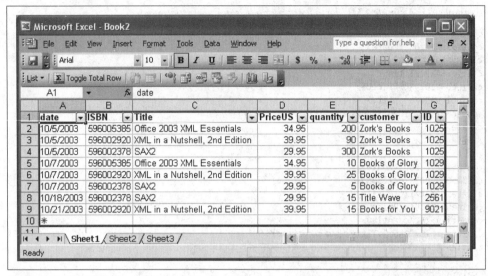

Figure 6-5. Choosing a sort or filter from a drop-down

If you choose "Sort Ascending," for instance, you'd see the list sorted by ISBN, as shown in Figure 6-6.

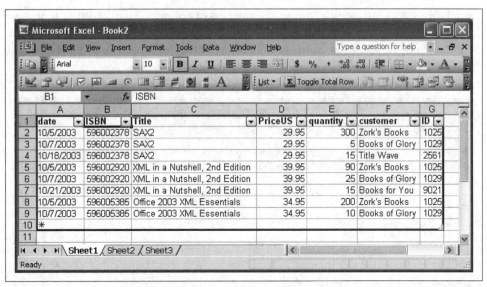

Figure 6-6. Sorting the data from the XML document by ISBN

Excel also offers some basic functionality for totaling and averaging the contents of these lists. Right-clicking on the list—anywhere inside the blue box—brings up a menu. If you choose List → Total Row, you'll see an extra row appear at the bottom of the list, as shown in Figure 6-7.

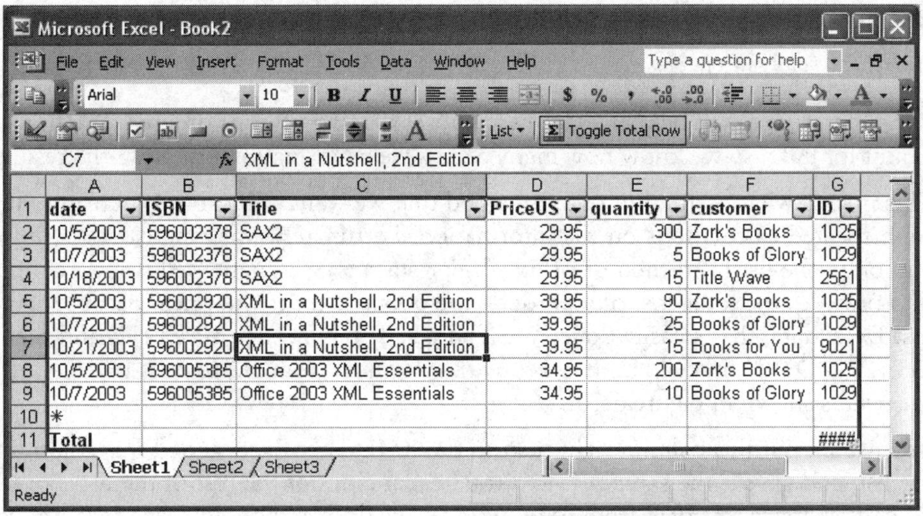

Figure 6-7. A total row added to the spreadsheet

By default, Excel just does a sum of the right-most column. That's common practice for spreadsheets, though in this case it works badly, since the IDs aren't exactly addable. Clicking on the cells in the total row brings up a drop-down tab. Figure 6-8 shows the choices it offers.

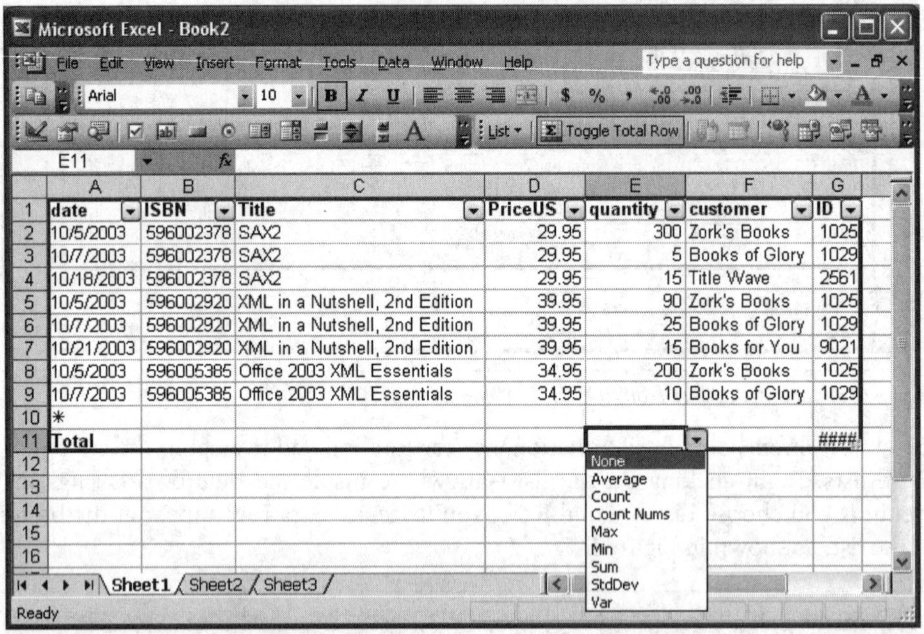

Figure 6-8. Total row options

For quantity, it might be nice to know the total number of units ordered. We'll select Count for ISBN so we know how many orders we have. Figure 6-9 shows the results.

This is somewhat useful, but odds are good that we want to be able to perform more sophisticated calculations on the information. Fortunately, we can access the information in the list from the rest of Excel. For starters, we might well want a column that provides the total cost of an order—the quantity times the price. Because this is just Excel data, that's easily done. We'll add a "Total" header in cell H1, and then a formula, =D2*E2, in cell H2. If we copy that formula from H2 to cells H3–9, we get the results shown in Figure 6-10.

Because we put this column right next to the XML data, Excel added this column to the list, and gave it the same sort and total capabilities of the rest of the list. Formulas can reference this data from other workbooks or from non-adjacent cells, though they won't be built into the list the same way.

While Excel provides no means of referring to data in this list by list name and column, you can safely reference the range and have Excel automatically adjust if a user reloads the XML document or modifies the information.

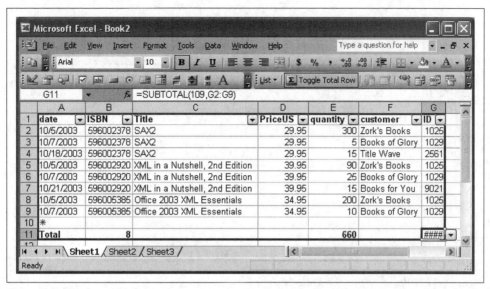

Figure 6-9. Total row results

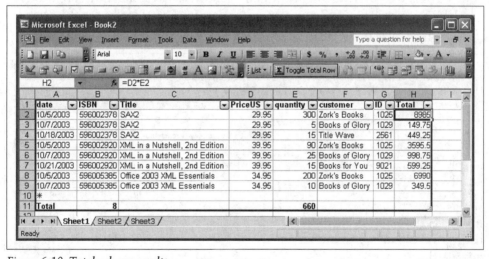

Figure 6-10. Total column results

 This only works on a list that already has data in it. If you base your formulas on an empty list, the ranges won't expand properly. The last row of the list is an entry area, which Excel doesn't count when it adjusts ranges.

To show how to reference data, we'll create some formulas on Sheet2 that reference the range containing the XML data in Sheet1, as shown in Figure 6-11.

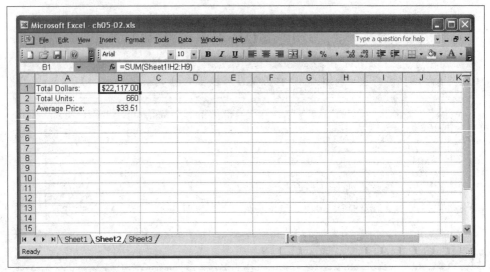

Figure 6-11. Calculations on the XML data

If we go back to Sheet1, and right-click on the XML list area, the XML sub-menu lets you Import... new data. When we import the data in *ch0602.xml*, a slightly extended version of the same information, Excel presents the data as shown in Figure 6-12.

	A	B	C	D	E	F	G	H
1	date	ISBN	Title	PriceUS	quantity	customer	ID	Total
2	10/5/2003	596005385	Office 2003 XML Essentials	34.95	200	Zork's Books	1025	6990
3	10/5/2003	596002920	XML in a Nutshell, 2nd Edition	39.95	90	Zork's Books	1025	3595.5
4	10/5/2003	596002378	SAX2	29.95	300	Zork's Books	1025	8985
5	10/7/2003	596005385	Office 2003 XML Essentials	34.95	10	Books of Glory	1029	349.5
6	10/7/2003	596002920	XML in a Nutshell, 2nd Edition	39.95	25	Books of Glory	1029	998.75
7	10/7/2003	596002378	SAX2	29.95	5	Books of Glory	1029	149.75
8	10/18/2003	596002378	SAX2	29.95	15	Title Wave	2561	449.25
9	10/21/2003	596002920	XML in a Nutshell, 2nd Edition	39.95	15	Books for You	9021	599.25
10	11/01/2003	596002378	SAX2	29.95	65	Spronkmeister	1543	1946.75
11	11/5/2003	596002920	XML in a Nutshell, 2nd Edition	39.95	15	Dryden's Markup Poetry	1783	599.25
12	*							
13	Total	10			740			
14								
15								

Figure 6-12. Adding more XML data

It's the same data, with a few extra sales. If we now return to Sheet2, as shown in Figure 6-13, we can see that the sales figures and the formulas have updated smoothly.

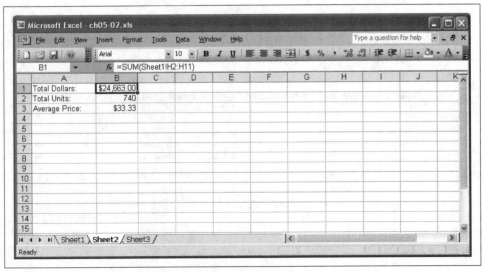

Figure 6-13. Automatically updated calculations on the XML data

Excel only does this updating when new data is imported, not when changes are made to the original file, so you should set user expectations appropriately. This is a very simple example, admittedly, but you can build much more sophisticated spreadsheet applications on these same principles.

 Using sample documents to create a list this way is very convenient, but you should be aware that if you re-use the list on another XML document that contains more structures than appeared in the original document, those extra structures won't get imported.

Opening documents as a read-only workbook

If you're extracting data from XML documents, you may find it useful to open them as read-only workbooks. The presentation of the information is very different, and there's no option for exporting the XML back out of the spreadsheet, but more explicit information about where the information came from is provided in the header rows. If we open *ch0601.xml* and select "Open as a read-only workbook," we see the result shown in Figure 6-14.

Information about where the data came from is provided in the XPath-like headers. The #agg information seems to be aggregated information, though in this case there's only one item per column.

The name "read-only workbook" is slightly misleading. You can make changes to the data, and you can save this file elsewhere. The "read-only" just means that you can't make changes to the original XML document using this approach; if you save the file, it's saved as an Excel workbook. It isn't nearly as flexible as the list approach, but it also lets you extract information from a wider variety of documents. Given its

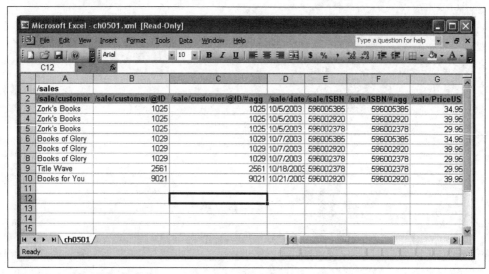

Figure 6-14. Sales data loaded as a read-only workbook

lack of flexibility and Microsoft's lack of documentation for the resulting format, this feature is probably best used only when you want to dump content from a document into Excel and don't mind doing a lot of organization yourself.

Using the XML source task pane

Opening an XML document using the XML Source task pane produces results that are much like the list created by opening the document as an XML list, but it allows you to have more control over what appears in the list and what doesn't. Many XML documents, for example, have header information followed by repeating sections. If opened directly as a list, Excel will produce a lot of columns that repeat the header information, when it really only appeared once. Using the XML Source task pane lets you choose what elements or attributes you want to appear in the Excel grid, and is especially useful when you only want to see or work with a subset of the information used in a document.

To show off the source task pane, we'll open *ch0601.xml* and select "Use the XML Source task pane." If, like *ch0601.xml*, the XML document doesn't contain a reference to an XML Schema, Excel displays the same warning that was shown in Figure 6-3, and then generates a schema based on what it finds in the document, producing the XML task pane contents shown in Figure 6-15.

To put information on to the spreadsheet, click on items in the task pane and drag them over to the grid. If you drag the date over to cell A3, you'll see the result shown in Figure 6-16.

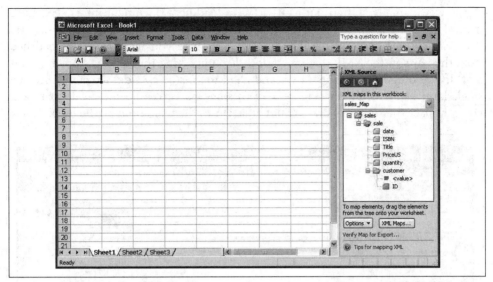

Figure 6-15. Using the XML Source task pane to select XML document parts for display in Excel

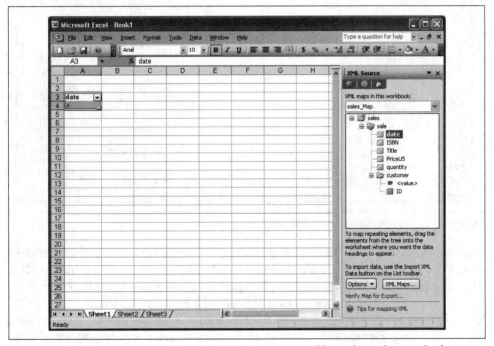

Figure 6-16. Adding a component from the XML Source pane adds a column, but not the data

While we originally started out as if we were loading a document into Excel, Excel instead loaded the structure of the document rather than its contents. Using the XML Source task pane means building the structure you want in the spreadsheet from the parts in the XML document and *then* importing the XML document's content. If you drag more of them over and align them side by side, Excel will create a single large list, as shown in Figure 6-17 (If some parts of a document don't repeat, you can place them in cells that are not adjacent to the main body of the list.).

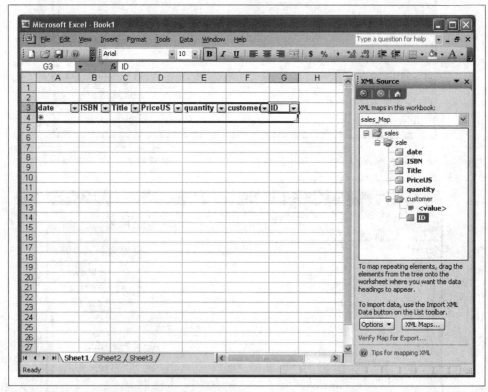

Figure 6-17. A list, created from the task pane

Populating that list takes an extra step. If the List toolbar is visible (and you can find it at View → Toolbars if it isn't already visible), you can click on the Import XML Data button, as the task pane advises, find your XML document, and import it. If the toolbar isn't visible, right-clicking on the list will bring up a menu with an XML entry. Select Import… from that menu, choose your XML document, and Excel will import the data. Figure 6-18 shows what Excel produces if you import *ch0601.xml* into this list.

At this point, you can work with the list the same way you could when the list was loaded directly. One important feature of building the list this way that you don't get when documents are loaded directly is that you can also place non-repeating elements

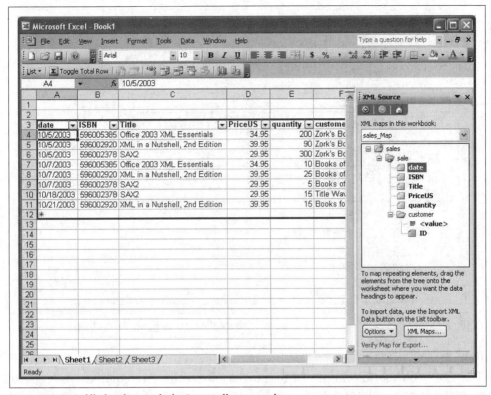

Figure 6-18. A filled-in list, with the List toolbar turned on

on the spreadsheet. Let's suppose the sales element also contained an element named store, identifying which store had these sales. Figure 6-19 shows the store element placed above the rest of the list, displaying the value of store once and only once.

Working with XML Maps

Opening XML documents directly is a great way to get started or to quickly analyze information, but in the long run you'll probably want to build spreadsheets that take a more structured approach. The XML Source pane lets you define XML Maps, describing the relationships between XML document structures and the lists that actually appear in your spreadsheet. These maps are built on XML Schemas, though they may either be schemas you specify or, as the previous examples showed, schemas that Excel derived by example from documents.

Most interactions with XML Maps take place through the task pane's XML Source view, or through schemas or documents which you use as a foundation for the map. Once you've created a map, there isn't much you can do through the Excel interface to change its basic structures, so getting your schema right in the first place is a critical step in creating spreadsheets that work with XML.

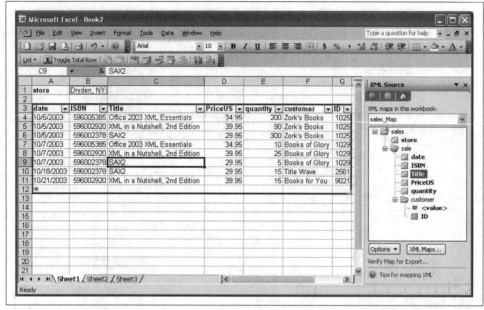

Figure 6-19. A filled-in list, with a single element above the repeating portion of the list

Excel and XML Schema

The XML Schema Recommendation provides a much more comprehensive set of tools for describing information than Excel actually needs. As noted earlier, Excel is good primarily for interacting with certain kinds of document structures, so some document-oriented features of XML Schema (like types that use mixed content) don't work with Excel. Similarly, Excel has had its own set of types for internal consumption for over a decade, and retrofitting Excel with the complete XML Schema datatype system probably would not be wise. Microsoft uses a combination of existing types to support the larger XML Schema system, as shown in Table 6-1.

More information on creating schemas with a variety of tools is covered in Appendixes C and D.

Table 6-1. Mappings between XSD datatypes and Excel datatypes

XSD Datatype	Excel Format	Limitations
time	h:mm:ss	If time zones are used, stored as text.
dateTime	m/d/yyyy h:mm (may vary with local versions of Excel)	No time zones. Excel doesn't understand years below 1900 or above 9999. If either of those violated, stored as text.
date	m/d/yyyy (may vary with local versions of Excel)	No time zones. Excel doesn't understand years below 1900 or above 9999. If either of those violated, stored as text.

Table 6-1. Mappings between XSD datatypes and Excel datatypes (continued)

XSD Datatype	Excel Format	Limitations
gYear	Number, integers only	No time zones. Excel doesn't understand years below 1900 or above 9999. If either of those violated, stored as text.
gDay, gMonth	Number, integers only	If time zones are used, stored as text.
gYearMonth	mmm-yy	No time zones. Excel doesn't understand years below 1900 or above 9999. If either of those violated, stored as text.
gMonthDay	d-mmm	
anyType, anyURI, base64Binary, duration, ENTITIES, ENTITY, hexBinary, ID, IDREF, IDREFS, language, Name, NCName, NMTOKEN, NMTOKENS, normalizedString, NOTATION, QName, string, token	Text	
boolean	Boolean	
decimal, float, double	General	Insignificant zeros will be dropped, and only negative signs will be displayed. All of these forms, despite their XSD differences, are used in calculations using 15 digits of precision.
byte, int, integer, long, negativeInteger, nonNegativeInteger, nonPositiveInteger, positiveInteger, short, unsignedByte, unsignedInt, unsignedLong, unsignedShort.	General	

These differences mean that you should not expect Excel to keep close track of the validation specified by the schema. Excel will behave as it has always behaved, with a set of rules for mapping between Excel and XSD. Formats that are represented as text will be imported or exported as they appear, while formats that have a more complex type may be formatted by Excel in the spreadsheet and according to XSD rules in the XML.

Excel also performs similar simplifications on content models. Excel is not designed as an über–XML-document processor, and it doesn't need the structural type information provided by XML Schema. From Excel's perspective, it needs to know what data goes together as a row and in what columns. Simpler structures are more manageable, and far less likely to break. While there may be times you need to work with XML that arrived with a complex schema, it may be easier in such cases to break the documents into smaller pieces and use simpler schemas if possible.

Creating an XML Map

Although some of the techniques described earlier in "Opening XML Documents Directly" create XML Maps, there are times when you'll want to incorporate data from XML documents in an existing spreadsheet, and those techniques don't work as well for that.

To create an XML Map in an existing spreadsheet, you need to bring up the task pane (View → Task Pane, if it's not already there) and select XML Source from the drop-down menu at the top of the task pane. Unless you've done XML work with this spreadsheet before, you should have an empty task pane, like the one shown in Figure 6-20.

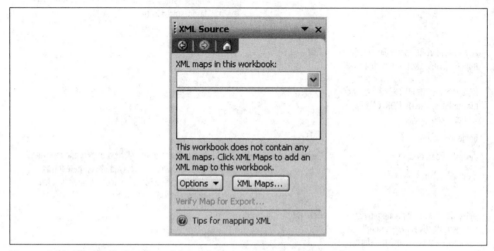

Figure 6-20. The XML Source task pane, before any sources are listed

To create an XML Map, click on the XML Maps... button. The XML Maps dialog box, shown in Figure 6-21, will appear, empty.

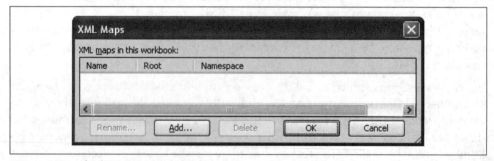

Figure 6-21. A fresh XML Maps dialog box

To add a map, click the Add... button. For an example, we'll use a document structure that both fits the Excel grid approach and tests out how it handles a variety of the XML Schema datatypes listed Table 6-1, using a contract management system as a guide.

For more information about creating the XML Schemas that are the foundations for these maps, see Appendix C. You may want to explore the tools mentioned at the end of that Appendix for inferring schemas from documents in particular.

These are some pretty simple contracts, which are just about payments on birthdays, enough information to get a sense of how Excel treats different datatypes. The schema for the contract description is listed in Example 6-2.

Example 6-2. A simple schema for contracts

```
<?xml version="1.0" encoding="UTF-8"?>
<xs:schema xmlns:xs="http://www.w3.org/2001/XMLSchema" elementFormDefault="qualified"
targetNamespace="http://simonstl.com/ns/example/contract" xmlns:contract="http://simonstl.
com/ns/example/contract">
  <xs:element name="contracts">
    <xs:complexType>
      <xs:sequence>
        <xs:element maxOccurs="unbounded" ref="contract:contract"/>
      </xs:sequence>
    </xs:complexType>
  </xs:element>
  <xs:element name="contract">
    <xs:complexType>
      <xs:sequence>
        <xs:element ref="contract:recipient"/>
        <xs:element ref="contract:signing_date"/>
        <xs:element ref="contract:signing_time"/>
        <xs:element ref="contract:birthyear"/>
        <xs:element ref="contract:birthday"/>
        <xs:element ref="contract:male"/>
        <xs:element ref="contract:payment_amount"/>
        <xs:element ref="contract:years_to_pay"/>
      </xs:sequence>
    </xs:complexType>
  </xs:element>
  <xs:element name="recipient" type="xs:string"/>
  <xs:element name="signing_date" type="xs:date"/>
  <xs:element name="signing_time" type="xs:time"/>
  <xs:element name="birthyear" type="xs:gYear"/>
  <xs:element name="birthday" type="xs:gMonthDay"/>
  <xs:element name="male" type="xs:boolean"/>
  <xs:element name="payment_amount" type="xs:decimal"/>
  <xs:element name="years_to_pay" type="xs:integer"/>
</xs:schema>
```

We'll use this schema to create an XML map by clicking the Add… button and selecting this schema from the browse dialog that appears. When the Multiple Roots dialog box shown in Figure 6-22 appears, select "contracts" from the list and click OK.

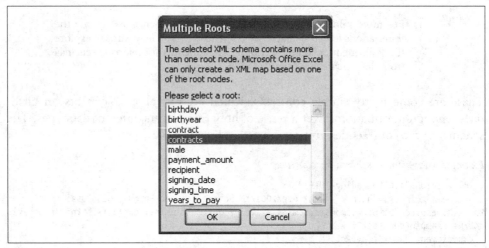

Figure 6-22. Choosing the root element for the map

You'll be rewarded with the result shown in Figure 6-23, a new XML Map that is named contract_map, after the root element, which describes the namespace http://simonstl.com/ns/example/contract.

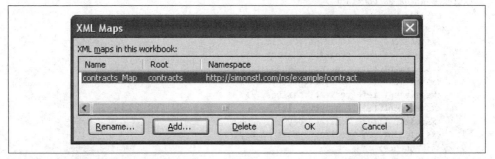

Figure 6-23. The XML Map, ready to go

You may notice that your choices for manipulating this map are very limited. You can rename it or delete it, but you can make no changes. Chapter 7 will explore how you can, if necessary, make changes to XML Maps through SpreadsheetML's XML representation of them.

If you click OK, you'll see XML components ready to be used in the XML Source task pane, as shown in Figure 6-24.

The XML Source pane uses a number of icons to describe the structure of the XML document, much like those used to represent files and folders in the Windows Explorer. These icons are shown in Table 6-2.

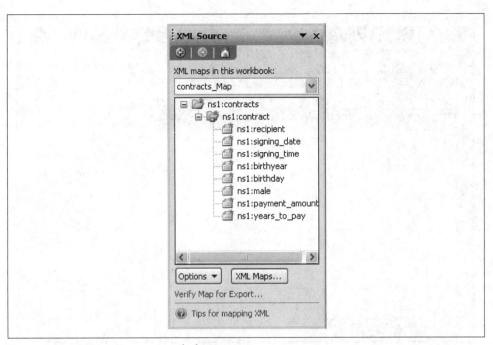

Figure 6-24. XML components, ready for use

Table 6-2. XML Source pane icons

Icon	Description
	Used to represent a container element that may appear one or many times, most typically the root element of the document. (Root elements aren't actually optional, but perhaps Excel does this to support the possibility of an empty map.)
	Used to represent a container element that may only appear once, often an element that contains attributes.
	Used to represent a container element that may appear repeatedly, most typically an element that represents rows.
	Used to represent a data element that must appear once and that contains data rather than other elements.
	Used to represent a data element that may appear once (or not all), which contains data rather than other elements. (The same icon, very slightly darker, is used for attributes.)
	Used to represent a data element that may appear multiple times. These often give Excel trouble as they often break out of the simple grid structure.
≡ <value>	Used to represent the value of an element, typically when the element also has an attribute or attributes. This allows you to put an element's content into the grid separately from the values of any attributes it may have.

If you drag the ns1:contract icon to cell A1, you'll get a list based on this map set up and ready for use, as shown in Figure 6-25.

I tend to clean these up and remove the "ns1" prefixes, as you'll see in later examples. You can also dismiss the XML Source pane, and bring it back up only if you need its "Verify Map for Export…" option.

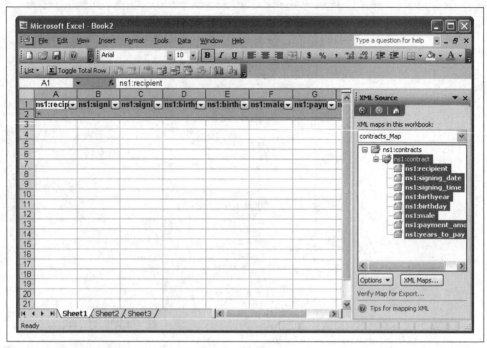

Figure 6-25. A list based on the XML Map, ready for use

If you select a cell in Row 2, and select Format → Cells, you can see how Excel has formatted the data automatically. For example, if you do this to the signing date, you'll see the result in Figure 6-26.

While Excel has used the schema to determine cell formatting, it is not currently using the datatypes in the schema for any kind of data validation. If you import an XML document (or type in data) that doesn't correspond to Excel's expectations, it will format it as text. To make Excel use the schema for validation—which only happens on import and export in any event—you need to right-click on the list, select the XML sub-menu, and then select XML Map Properties. The dialog box shown in Figure 6-27 will appear.

The "Validate data against schema for import and export" is always turned off by default. While that may seem strange in contexts where you want validation to check user data, it also avoids some odd problems. It's possible that users will want to import documents that have problems so that they can repair them. It's also possible that users will be so frustrated by a document that they want to send it to someone else to sort out, without being told they can't save the file.

We'll use two test documents to explore how this works. The first one, shown in Example 6-3, is a deliberately invalid XML document, with all kinds of data that doesn't match the datatypes used by the schema. The second, shown in Example 6-4, is a document that is valid against the schema we've used.

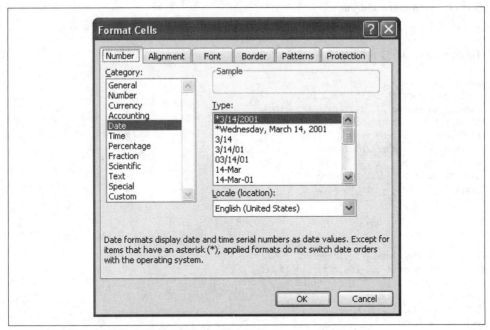

Figure 6-26. Cell formatting applied by Excel to dates

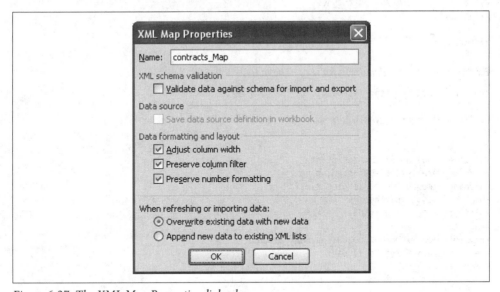

Figure 6-27. The XML Map Properties dialog box

Example 6-3. An invalid document for use in the map

```
<contracts xmlns="http://simonstl.com/ns/example/contract">

<!--This document is NOT VALID.-->

<contract>
<recipient>Jedidiah Smith</recipient>
<signing_date>June 27, 1992</signing_date>
<signing_time>4 PM</signing_time>
<birthyear>62</birthyear>
<birthday>23 November</birthday>
<male>yes</male>
<payment_amount>$27</payment_amount>
<years_to_pay>two</years_to_pay>
</contract>


<contract>
<recipient>Jane Zinger</recipient>
<signing_date>April 22, 2001</signing_date>
<signing_time>6:30 PM</signing_time>
<birthyear>75</birthyear>
<birthday>19 July</birthday>
<male>no</male>
<payment_amount>$42</payment_amount>
<years_to_pay>four</years_to_pay>
</contract>

</contracts>
```

Example 6-4. A valid document for use in the map

```
<contracts xmlns="http://simonstl.com/ns/example/contract">

<!--This document is VALID.-->

<contract>
<recipient>Josiah Smith</recipient>
<signing_date>1999-06-03</signing_date>
<signing_time>09:03:22</signing_time>
<birthyear>1962</birthyear>
<birthday>--06-21</birthday>
<male>true</male>
<payment_amount>0004002.00200</payment_amount>
<years_to_pay>26</years_to_pay>
</contract>

<contract>
<recipient>Jane Zang</recipient>
```

Example 6-4. A valid document for use in the map (continued)

```
<signing_date>1999-04-03</signing_date>
<signing_time>11:04:28</signing_time>
<birthyear>1968</birthyear>
<birthday>--04-23</birthday>
<male>false</male>
<payment_amount>000401.0200</payment_amount>
<years_to_pay>2</years_to_pay>
</contract>

</contracts>
```

If a user attempts to import Example 6-3 into this map, they'll get the list of warnings shown in Figure 6-28.

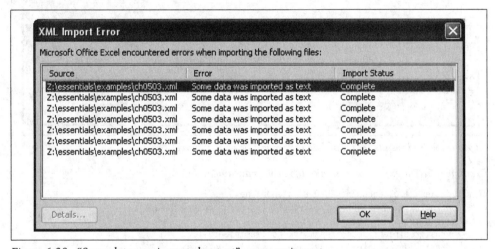

Figure 6-28. "Some data was imported as text" errors on import

While this may dissuade some users, it doesn't sound like a big deal, and all those "Complete"s are pretty reassuring. The map also looks all right in Excel, if you aren't cued in to the formatting. Figure 6-29 shows the import results.

If you export this map, as shown in the next section, Excel goes right ahead with it. If you use the "Verify Map for Export" link on the XML Source task pane, Excel notifies you that "contract_map is exportable." The results of the export, shown in Example 6-5, make it clear that Excel has imported and exported the document, as it's added the ns1 prefix everywhere.

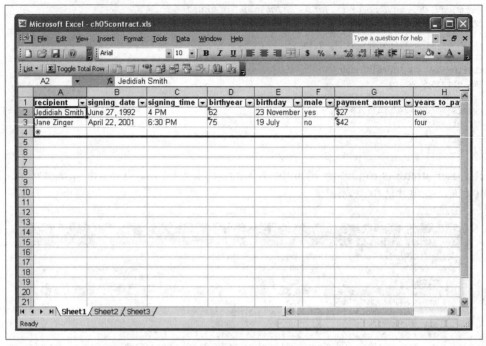

Figure 6-29. Bad results that look like they might be okay in Excel

Example 6-5. The exported version of the broken document

```xml
<?xml version="1.0" encoding="UTF-8" standalone="yes"?>
<ns1:contracts xmlns:ns1="http://simonstl.com/ns/example/contract">
    <ns1:contract>
        <ns1:recipient>Jedidiah Smith</ns1:recipient>
        <ns1:signing_date>June 27, 1992</ns1:signing_date>
        <ns1:signing_time>4 PM</ns1:signing_time>
        <ns1:birthyear>62</ns1:birthyear>
        <ns1:birthday>23 November</ns1:birthday>
        <ns1:male>yes</ns1:male>
        <ns1:payment_amount>$27</ns1:payment_amount>
        <ns1:years_to_pay>two</ns1:years_to_pay>
    </ns1:contract>
    <ns1:contract>
        <ns1:recipient>Jane Zinger</ns1:recipient>
        <ns1:signing_date>April 22, 2001</ns1:signing_date>
        <ns1:signing_time>6:30 PM</ns1:signing_time>
        <ns1:birthyear>75</ns1:birthyear>
        <ns1:birthday>19 July</ns1:birthday>
        <ns1:male>no</ns1:male>
        <ns1:payment_amount>$42</ns1:payment_amount>
        <ns1:years_to_pay>four</ns1:years_to_pay>
    </ns1:contract>
</ns1:contracts>
```

If, however, we turn on "Validate data against schema for import and export," we'll get an extra error message, shown in Figure 6-30.

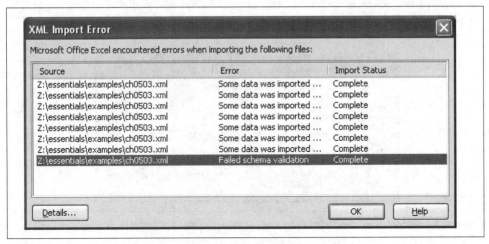

Figure 6-30. An error message produced by failed validation

Close that window, however, and you have the same imported result shown in Figure 6-29. Excel is not very interested in blocking bad data. If you select the schema validation error and click Details... you'll see the information presented in Figure 6-31.

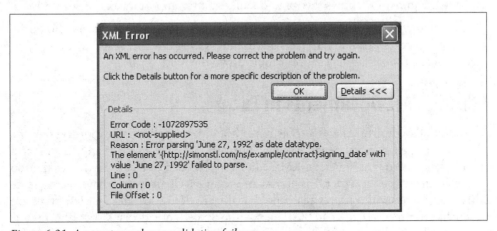

Figure 6-31. A report on schema validation failure

This is somewhat more meaningful, but:

- It only reports on the first of many errors it encountered.
- It presents the element name in a form that's not familiar to many users.
- The line, column, and offset information is inaccurate and useless.

Hopefully, future versions of Excel will provide better support for validation on import that is more helpful to users and more useful for developers. Similarly, exporting this document produces the same result already shown in Example 6-5, but produces a warning message, shown in Figure 6-32.

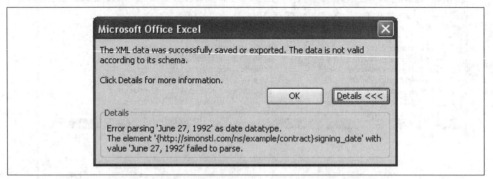

Figure 6-32. The error message from exporting an invalid XML document

Hopefully users will see this and at least know there's a problem, and perhaps being able to export XML will make it easier for them to pass it to someone else who can clean it up before schema-dependent processing takes place.

If, on the other, we import Example 6-4, the valid document, we get no error messages and a spreadsheet whose formatting conforms to the expectations described in Table 6-1. Figure 6-33 shows this valid document after import into our list area.

This document also exports perfectly well. Given good examples, users should be able to produce good results. If users get used to seeing error messages with no obvious ill effects, though, it may cause trouble down the road.

Editing XML Documents in Excel

While Excel's powerful analysis tools make it an ideal application for processing the data found in XML documents, Excel's expectation that data must appear in a grid limits its capabilities as a general XML editor. If you need to create XML files that do fit Excel's interface, however, Excel may prove an excellent way to have users create XML documents without ever realizing that they're doing so. The first few steps are much like those used to load XML data into Excel spreadsheets, but the user is encouraged to add data and save the results. In this case, Excel serves as an editor for a relatively simple class of XML documents.

As an example, we'll use a document format that is designed to represent a portion of a forest, and used to generate a *stand map*. Stand maps are circular maps that represent one-fifth of an acre of land, as shown in Figure 6-34.

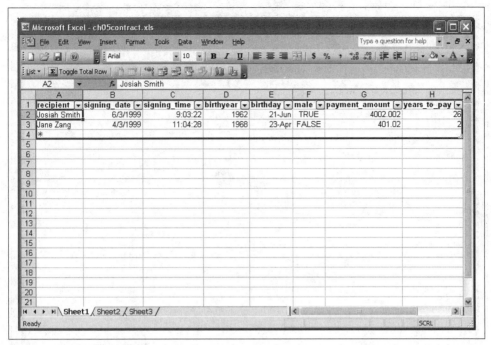

Figure 6-33. A valid XML document, imported

Though you can't see the color in this book, you can get the general idea. Trees are measured from a center point in a forest, using their distance and their compass degree. The species and diameter at breast height (dbh) are also recorded, and there may be additional notes. The data behind the map is generally recorded as a table, often on paper. (The first stand map I made was on a four-foot circle of paper, recorded using markers, templates, a compass, and a ruler.) While stand maps only represent a small section of a forest, they can provide baseline information for comparing the different contents of different forests or sections of forests. For example, the forest shown in Figure 6-34 is largely maple, with some hemlocks and some large tulip poplars just outside the ring. The forest shown in Figure 6-35 is largely black locust, with other species mixed in.

Creating these maps is beyond the capabilities of Excel's charting functions (that's done using XSLT with some trigonometry extensions to generate Scalable Vector Graphics, or SVG), but Excel is very useful in this instance as a tool for collecting data. Laptops have become more and more common in the forest, as they're far more convenient than four-foot circular tables for collecting data.

The XML data format behind these maps is pretty simple. A sample is shown in Example 6-6.

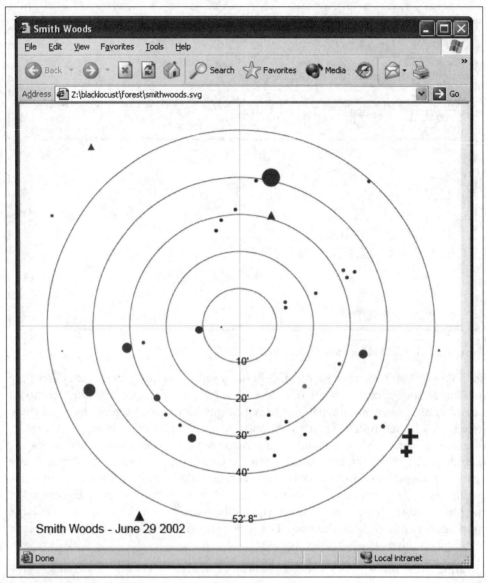

Figure 6-34. A stand map generated from an XML document

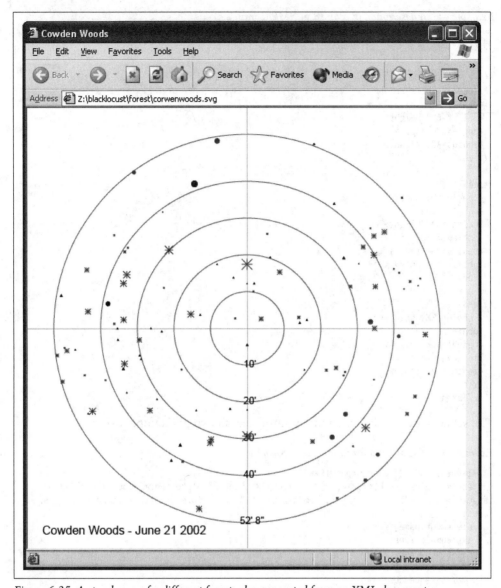

Figure 6-35. A stand map of a different forest, also generated from an XML document

Example 6-6. A description of a forest in XML

```
<forest xmlns="http://simonstl.com/ns/forest/">

<tree>
  <species>STM</species>
  <dbh>6</dbh>
  <height>13</height>
  <angle>6.5</angle>
```

Example 6-6. A description of a forest in XML (continued)

```
  <radius>39</radius>
</tree>

<tree>
  <species>SM</species>
  <dbh>37.5</dbh>
  <height>67</height>
  <angle>12</angle>
  <radius>38.5</radius>
</tree>

<tree>
  <species>H</species>
  <dbh>31</dbh>
  <height>63</height>
  <angle>16</angle>
  <radius>29</radius>
  <note>snag</note>
</tree>

<tree>
  <species>SM</species>
  <dbh>6</dbh>
  <height>30</height>
  <angle>42</angle>
  <radius>52</radius>
</tree>
...</forest>
```

The schema for this data is similarly simple, as shown in Example 6-7.

Example 6-7. The schema for forest map information

```
<?xml version="1.0" encoding="UTF-8"?>
<xs:schema xmlns:xs="http://www.w3.org/2001/XMLSchema" elementFormDefault="qualified"
targetNamespace="http://simonstl.com/ns/forest/" xmlns:forest="http://simonstl.com/ns/
forest/">
  <xs:element name="forest">
    <xs:complexType>
      <xs:sequence>
        <xs:element maxOccurs="unbounded" ref="forest:tree"/>
      </xs:sequence>
    </xs:complexType>
  </xs:element>
  <xs:element name="tree">
    <xs:complexType>
      <xs:sequence>
        <xs:element ref="forest:species"/>
        <xs:element ref="forest:dbh"/>
        <xs:element ref="forest:height"/>
        <xs:element ref="forest:angle"/>
        <xs:element ref="forest:radius"/>
```

Example 6-7. The schema for forest map information (continued)

```
        <xs:element minOccurs="0" ref="forest:note"/>
      </xs:sequence>
    </xs:complexType>
  </xs:element>
  <xs:element name="species" type="xs:NCName"/>
  <xs:element name="dbh" type="xs:decimal"/>
  <xs:element name="height" type="xs:decimal"/>
  <xs:element name="angle" type="xs:decimal"/>
  <xs:element name="radius" type="xs:decimal"/>
  <xs:element name="note" type="xs:string"/>
</xs:schema>
```

Most of the declarations that directly affect users' work are those at the bottom of the schema. The abbreviations for species are non-colonized names (NCNames), while the measurements are decimals and the notes are strings. Using this schema, we'll create a map and put a list into a spreadsheet that users can treat as a recording device for their measurements in the field.

Using the XML Source task pane, add a map to the spreadsheet, using the schema as a base. You'll need to select a root (forest), and then the task pane will be populated with choices for inclusion in the spreadsheet, as shown in Figure 6-36.

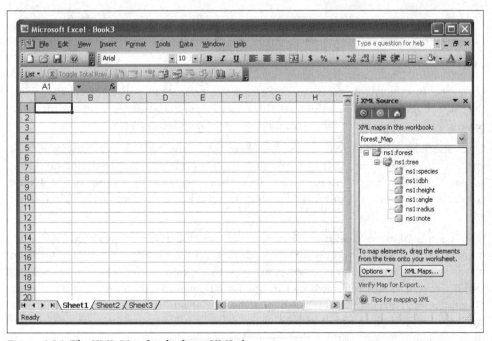

Figure 6-36. The XML Map for the forest XML document

One mildly irritating feature of this map is the ns1 prefix Excel has applied to the element names. Fortunately, this is only an issue when you work with the map directly, as it can be edited out of the list headers with no harm to the data structure. Figure 6-37 shows what our new spreadsheet—with edited headers—looks like.

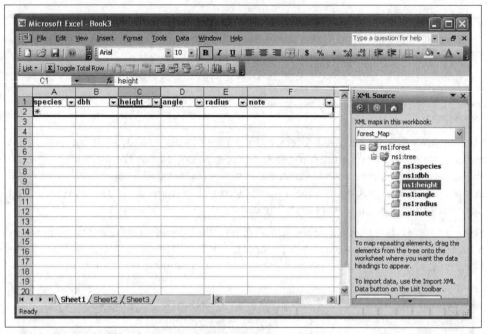

Figure 6-37. A spreadsheet for creating forest map XML

Using this interface is pretty easy. Researchers just enter one row per tree, filling out the required species, dbh, height, angle, and radius, and adding a note if there's a reason. Figure 6-38 shows what this data entry process looks like.

One especially nice feature of this spreadsheet is that the XML Source task pane isn't visible. There's no need for the people working with this interface to understand that they're doing anything at all unusual. The sorting and filtering features of the list are conveniences, but they don't interfere with the data entry. Tabbing from field to field works beautifully.

Also, there's an extra sheet here, the key sheet, which is itself an imported XML document. Because this mapping format is designed to be used around the world, in places that have very different species of trees, the species codes are stored in a separate document that is reference by the XSLT that generates the map. The developers of this spreadsheet have included that information as well. Mostly this is a convenience, to help humans remember codes, but it also opens the possibility that those same humans might use the spreadsheet to modify the codes and their resulting maps. (If you don't want to permit them to save the codes back out as XML, just cut the information and paste it back in outside of a list context.) Figure 6-39 shows the key tab.

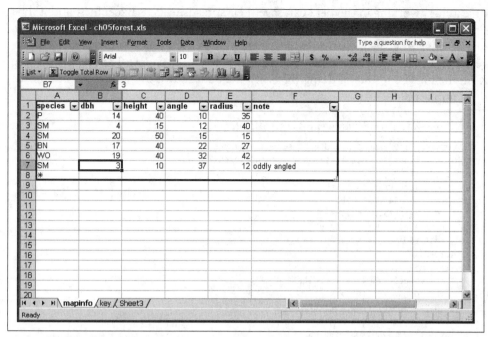

Figure 6-38. Entering new forest information

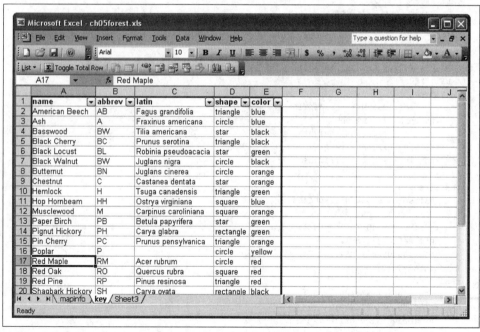

Figure 6-39. Additional key information, also stored as XML

Researchers working in the field can save their spreadsheets as Excel files, and it'll be simple enough to extract the XML information when they return to a place where they're analyzing them. If they want to extract the information in the field, say to generate a map, they can right-click on their data and choose Export… from the XML menu. The results of doing that with the data shown in Figure 6-38 are shown in Example 6-8.

Example 6-8. XML created through Excel's XML interfaces

```xml
<?xml version="1.0" encoding="UTF-8" standalone="yes"?>
<ns1:forest xmlns:ns1="http://simonstl.com/ns/forest/">
    <ns1:tree>
        <ns1:species>P</ns1:species>
        <ns1:dbh>14</ns1:dbh>
        <ns1:height>40</ns1:height>
        <ns1:angle>10</ns1:angle>
        <ns1:radius>35</ns1:radius>
    </ns1:tree>
    <ns1:tree>
        <ns1:species>SM</ns1:species>
        <ns1:dbh>4</ns1:dbh>
        <ns1:height>15</ns1:height>
        <ns1:angle>12</ns1:angle>
        <ns1:radius>40</ns1:radius>
    </ns1:tree>
    <ns1:tree>
        <ns1:species>SM</ns1:species>
        <ns1:dbh>20</ns1:dbh>
        <ns1:height>50</ns1:height>
        <ns1:angle>15</ns1:angle>
        <ns1:radius>15</ns1:radius>
    </ns1:tree>
    <ns1:tree>
        <ns1:species>BN</ns1:species>
        <ns1:dbh>17</ns1:dbh>
        <ns1:height>40</ns1:height>
        <ns1:angle>22</ns1:angle>
        <ns1:radius>27</ns1:radius>
    </ns1:tree>
    <ns1:tree>
        <ns1:species>WO</ns1:species>
        <ns1:dbh>19</ns1:dbh>
        <ns1:height>40</ns1:height>
        <ns1:angle>32</ns1:angle>
        <ns1:radius>42</ns1:radius>
    </ns1:tree>
    <ns1:tree>
        <ns1:species>SM</ns1:species>
        <ns1:dbh>3</ns1:dbh>
        <ns1:height>10</ns1:height>
        <ns1:angle>37</ns1:angle>
        <ns1:radius>12</ns1:radius>
```

Example 6-8. XML created through Excel's XML interfaces (continued)

```
        <ns1:note>oddly angled</ns1:note>
    </ns1:tree>
</ns1:forest>
```

Excel has, unfortunately, applied the ns1 prefix to everything, but the information comes through clearly and can be processed by all the tools built around the format shown originally in Example 6-6.

Your data doesn't have to be this flat for Excel to be capable of editing it. It could, for instance, look like the data in Example 6-9.

Example 6-9. A description of a forest in XML with some gratuitous structure

```
<forest xmlns="http://simonstl.com/ns/forest/">

<tree>
  <details>
    <species>STM</species>
    <dbh>6</dbh>
    <height>13</height>
  </details>
  <location>
    <angle>6.5</angle>
    <radius>39</radius>
  </location>
</tree>

<tree>
  <details>
    <species>SM</species>
    <dbh>37.5</dbh>
    <height>67</height>
  </details>
  <location>
    <angle>12</angle>
    <radius>38.5</radius>
  </location>
</tree>

<tree>
  <details>
    <species>H</species>
    <dbh>31</dbh>
    <height>63</height>
    <note>snag</note>
  </details>
  <location>
    <angle>16</angle>
    <radius>29</radius>
  </location>
</tree>
```

Example 6-9. A description of a forest in XML with some gratuitous structure (continued)

```
<tree>
  <details>
    <species>SM</species>
    <dbh>6</dbh>
    <height>30</height>
  </details>
  <location>
    <angle>42</angle>
    <radius>52</radius>
  </location>
</tree>
...</forest>
```

You could edit it in a spreadsheet that looked just like Figure 6-38. Excel doesn't mind the extra container elements at all, so long as they don't interfere with its expectations for repeating list content.

 If a map only represents part of an XML document, and you export it back to XML, only the parts of the XML document that were shown by the map will be exported. Don't try to use Excel to edit tables in larger documents, for instance!

Loading and Saving XML Documents from VBA

While the GUI provides a convenient way to work with whatever XML you encounter, you may want to create applications that work with XML on a regular basis, and don't want the user of the spreadsheet to have to interact with XML directly. Using Visual Basic for Applications, you can create spreadsheets that load XML and save XML through Excel's maps without the user even needing to know where their data is coming from. The spreadsheet shown in Figures 6-40 and 6-41 will be used to demonstrate how this works.

The worksheet shown in Figure 6-40 contains four buttons, a checkbox linked to cell D2, and two XML maps. The left-hand map expects data like that shown in Example 6-10, while the right-hand map expects data like that shown in cell B4 of Figure 6-41 or like that shown in Example 6-11.

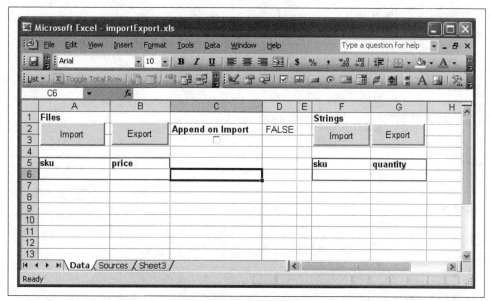

Figure 6-40. XML maps and user interface

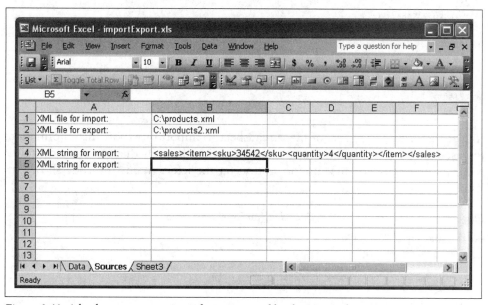

Figure 6-41. A backstage area storing information used by the VBA code

Example 6-10. Simple product information format

```
<products>
   <item>
      <sku>34542</sku>
      <price>29.42</price>
   </item>
   <item>
      <sku>34546</sku>
      <price>19.24</price>
   </item>
   <item>
      <sku>34548</sku>
      <price>99.42</price>
   </item>
</products>
```

Example 6-11. Simple sales information format

```
<sales>
   <item>
      <sku>34542</sku>
      <quantity>10</quantity>
   </item>
   <item>
      <sku>34546</sku>
      <quantity>4</quantity>
   </item>
   <item>
      <sku>34548</sku>
      <quantity>1</quantity>
   </item>
</sales>
```

Rather than expecting users of the spreadsheet to import or export this information themselves using the GUI, this spreadsheet provides buttons that import and export XML information. The first Import button on the left contains the code shown in Example 6-12.

Example 6-12. Importing from an XML file to an Excel XML map

```
Private Sub ImportFile_Click( )
    Dim myMap As XmlMap
    'reference map by name
    Set myMap = ActiveWorkbook.XmlMaps("products_Map")

    Dim source As String
    source = Worksheets(2).Range("B1").Text

    Dim append As Boolean

    append = Range("D2").Value
```

Example 6-12. Importing from an XML file to an Excel XML map (continued)

```
    myMap.AppendOnImport = append
    myMap.AdjustColumnWidth = False

    myMap.Import (source)

End Sub
```

First, this code retrieves the first XML map in the Excel spreadsheet from the workbook's XmlMaps collection. Next, it gets the source file from which it is to import from cell B1 of the worksheet shown in Figure 6-41. It collects the value of cell D2 on the main worksheet so it can tell Excel whether to append new data or replace the existing data in the map with the new data, by setting the AppendOnImport property of the map. To avoid columns changing sizes, the script explicitly sets AdjustColumnWidth to false. Finally, it calls the map object's Import method, giving it the source argument collected at the beginning. (That source can be a URL, not just a file reference.)

If the *products.xml* file listed in Example 6-10 is at the location specified by cell B1 of the Source sheet, you'll see a result like that of Figure 6-42.

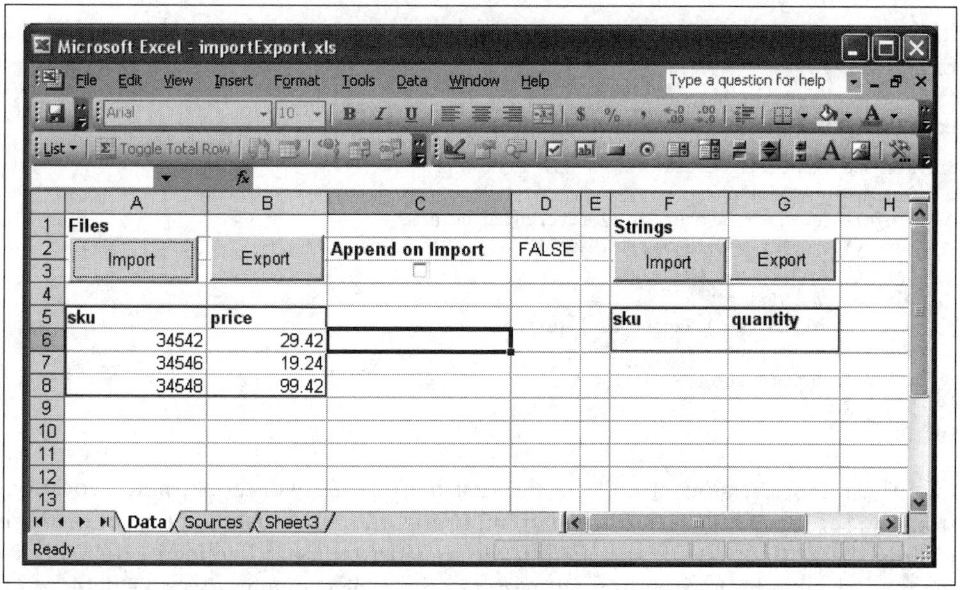

Figure 6-42. Result of the first import from a file

If you check the "Append on Import" checkbox, thereby changing cell D2's contents to true, and then click Import again, it will add the same three values to the map again, as shown in Figure 6-43.

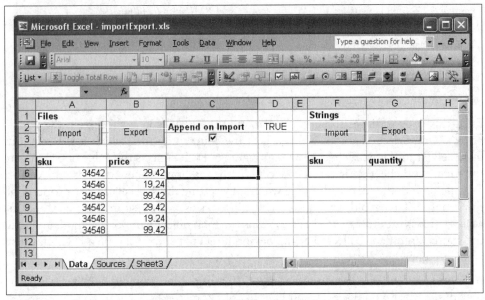

Figure 6-43. Result of the second import from a file, with append

Its companion Export button is simpler, containing the code shown in Example 6-13.

Example 6-13. Exporting from an XML file to an Excel XML map

```
Private Sub ExportFile_Click()
    Dim myMap As XmlMap
    'reference map by number (6-12 referenced by name)
    Set myMap = ActiveWorkbook.XmlMaps(1)

    Dim dest As String
    dest = Worksheets(2).Range("B2").Text

    myMap.Export (dest)

End Sub
```

Like the Import version, it collects the first map in the workbook, and a location from the Sources worksheet. Instead of importing, though, it uses the Export method to drop the XML in the file specified. If the spreadsheet looks like Figure 6-43, clicking the right-hand Export button will produce the code shown in Example 6-14.

Example 6-14. Exporting from an Excel XML map to an XML file

```
<?xml version="1.0" encoding="UTF-8" standalone="yes"?>
<products xmlns:xsi="http://www.w3.org/2001/XMLSchema-instance">
    <item>
```

Example 6-14. Exporting from an Excel XML map to an XML file (continued)

```
        <sku>34542</sku>
        <price>29.42</price>
    </item>
    <item>
        <sku>34546</sku>
        <price>19.24</price>
    </item>
    <item>
        <sku>34548</sku>
        <price>99.42</price>
    </item>
    <item>
        <sku>34542</sku>
        <price>29.42</price>
    </item>
    <item>
        <sku>34546</sku>
        <price>19.24</price>
    </item>
    <item>
        <sku>34548</sku>
        <price>99.42</price>
    </item>
</products>
```

The map and buttons on the right-hand side behave differently. Rather than importing from and exporting to files, they import from and export to strings, using the ImportXML and ExportXML methods instead of Import and Export. You might want to do this if your data came from someplace other than a file, or if you need to do something to the XML before the import or export takes place. The string import method is shown in Example 6-15 and the string export method is shown in Example 6-16.

Example 6-15. Importing from an XML string to an Excel XML map

```
Private Sub ImportString_Click( )
    Dim myMap As XmlMap
    Set myMap = ActiveWorkbook.XmlMaps(2)

    Dim sourceData As String

    sourceData = Worksheets(2).Range("B4").Text

    Dim append As Boolean

    append = Range("D2").Value

    myMap.AppendOnImport = append
    myMap.AdjustColumnWidth = False
```

Example 6-15. Importing from an XML string to an Excel XML map (continued)

```
    myMap.ImportXml (sourceData)

End Sub
```

Example 6-16. Exporting from an Excel XML map to an XML string

```
Private Sub ExportString_Click( )
    Dim myMap As XmlMap
    Set myMap = ActiveWorkbook.XmlMaps(2)

    Dim result As String

    myMap.ExportXml result


    Worksheets(2).Range("B5").Value = result

End Sub
```

If the Sources sheet looks like Figure 6-41, clicking on the right-hand Import button of the Data sheet will produce the result shown in Figure 6-44.

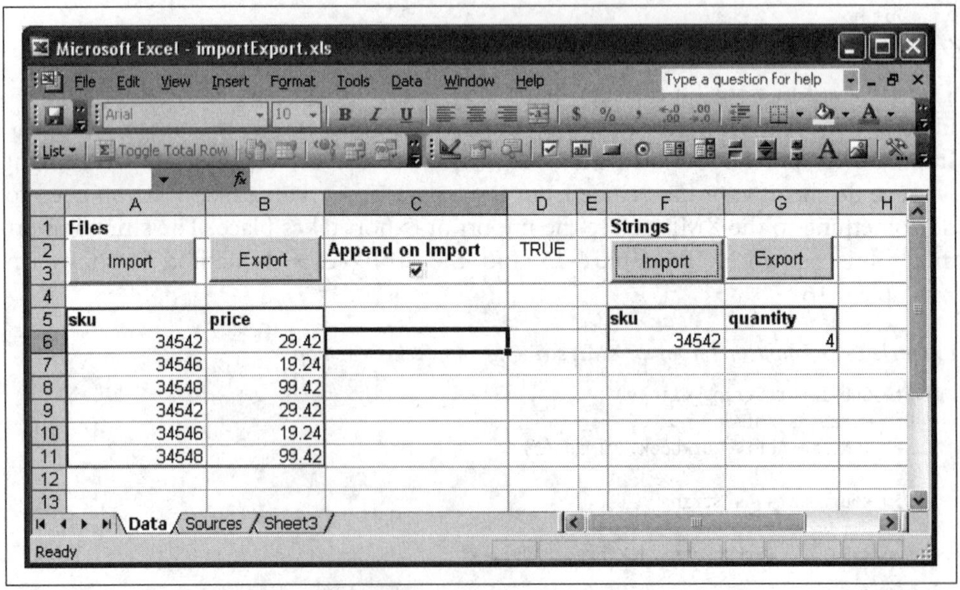

Figure 6-44. Importing from a string on the Sources sheet

If you now click on the right-hand Export button and then go look at the Sources sheet, you'll see the result shown in Figure 6-45.

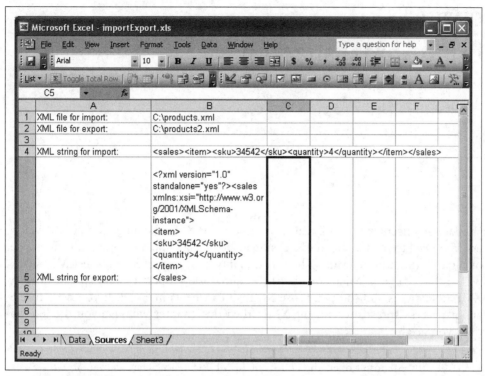

Figure 6-45. The Sources sheet after an export

While these examples are fairly simple, they've demonstrated several ways to get information into and out of Excel. You can extend these examples with more VBA to create applications that update their data automatically, issue queries against web sites and present results, or pass XML information to custom processes for further work.

CHAPTER 7

Using SpreadsheetML

While many users will find Excel's easy import of XML documents useful, developers who need to read or create Excel spreadsheets may find a completely different set of capabilities more relevant. The functionality provided in Spreadsheet ML, which was also available in Microsoft Excel XP, allows developers to save spreadsheets as XML documents and to open those XML spreadsheets in Excel. If you need to create or process spreadsheets using XML, then this chapter will give you the foundations you need.

> Microsoft offers the Office 2003 XML Reference Schemas from *http://microsoft.com/downloads/*. If you want a complete definition of every component in SpreadsheetML, the schema and its documentation are much more detailed than this chapter can be.

Saving and Opening XML Spreadsheets

Excel treats XML spreadsheet files pretty much like regular *.xls* binary files. Microsoft has captured nearly all of the information stored in Excel workbooks in its XML format, with some major exceptions, including embedded Visual Basic for Applications (VBA), charting information, OLE objects, and drawing objects. It works very well for basic data import and export, but not as well for more sophisticated spreadsheets. While you can, for example, use VBA and charting on information stored in the XML maps described in Chapter 6, that functionality will be lost if you save the spreadsheet itself in SpreadsheetML and don't keep a *.xls* copy.

> If you need access to Excel features that SpreadsheetML doesn't support, you might try tools like Spreadsheet::WriteExcel, a Perl module, available through *http://cpan.org*, or POI, a Java library available at *http://jakarta.apache.org/poi/*. These both operate on *.xls* files, not SpreadsheetML, and have their own limitations, but they tend to be different limitations than those of SpreadsheetML.

From the Excel user's perspective, opening a SpreadsheetML XML document is just like opening a spreadsheet—with one minor complication. Excel shows all the XML documents in the current directory as choices to open, when they may not in fact contain SpreadsheetML. Excel looks for the `mso-application` processing instruction at the start of an XML document. If it finds one, it marks the file with a Word, Excel, or other Office logo, as shown in Figure 7-1.

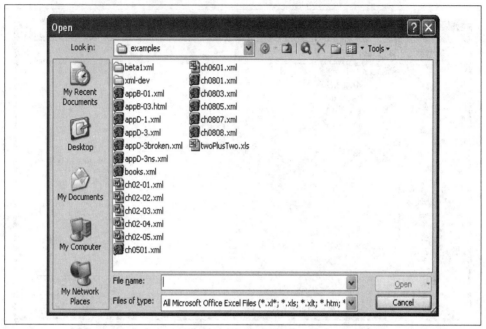

Figure 7-1. The Open dialog box showing SpreadsheetML, WordML, other XML, and regular Excel files

If a user happens to pick an XML file that Excel doesn't understand automatically (even, for instance, a WordML file), they'll be confronted with the dialog box shown in Figure 7-2.

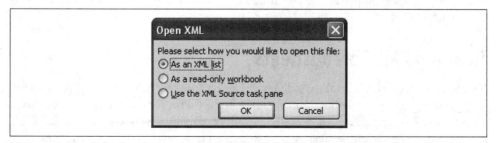

Figure 7-2. The dialog box for opening XML files that don't contain SpreadsheetML

This dialog box is very useful for the functionality described in Chapter 6, but users who open XML files containing SpreadsheetML will never have to deal with it—everything looks just like it does when opening a traditional *.xls* file.

Saving Excel files as SpreadsheetML files is similarly simple. The Save As dialog box, shown in Figure 7-3, offers an "XML Spreadsheet (*.xml)" option right under the usual "Microsoft Excel Workbook (*.xls)" choice.

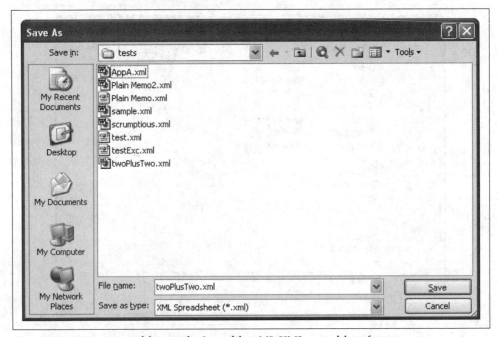

Figure 7-3. Saving a spreadsheet to the SpreadsheetML XML spreadsheet format

If you're especially gung-ho about working with XML spreadsheets, you can set "XML Spreadsheet" to be your default file format in the Transition tab of the dialog box opened by selecting Options… from the Tools menu, as shown in Figure 7-4.

Using any of these approaches, you'll be able to read and write XML Spreadsheets from within XML.

Reading XML Spreadsheets

The SpreadsheetML vocabulary is generally much smaller than the WordML vocabulary, and more approachable. While it also comes with lots of metadata, the structured nature of spreadsheets is easily captured with relatively concise XML. We'll start with a very simple test spreadsheet, adding two numbers, as shown in Figure 7-5.

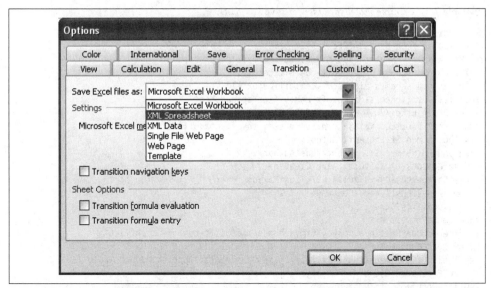

Figure 7-4. Setting the SpreadsheetML XML spreadsheet format to be the default

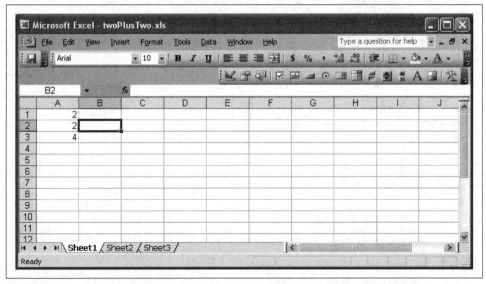

Figure 7-5. A simple spreadsheet for an initial test

This spreadsheet adds 2 and 2, using the SUM function in cell A3 to add the values of cells A1 and A2. If we save the spreadsheet shown in Figure 7-5 as an XML Spreadsheet, Excel generates the XML file shown in Example 7-1.

Example 7-1. A simple Excel spreadsheet saved as XML

```xml
<?xml version="1.0"?>
<?mso-application progid="Excel.Sheet"?>
<Workbook xmlns="urn:schemas-microsoft-com:office:spreadsheet"
 xmlns:o="urn:schemas-microsoft-com:office:office"
 xmlns:x="urn:schemas-microsoft-com:office:excel"
 xmlns:ss="urn:schemas-microsoft-com:office:spreadsheet"
 xmlns:html="http://www.w3.org/TR/REC-html40">
 <DocumentProperties xmlns="urn:schemas-microsoft-com:office:office">
  <Author>Simon St.Laurent</Author>
  <LastAuthor>Simon St.Laurent</LastAuthor>
  <Created>2003-03-19T20:21:31Z</Created>
  <LastSaved>2003-03-19T20:23:08Z</LastSaved>
  <Company>simonstl.com</Company>
  <Version>11.4920</Version>
 </DocumentProperties>
 <OfficeDocumentSettings xmlns="urn:schemas-microsoft-com:office:office">
  <DownloadComponents/>
  <LocationOfComponents HRef="file:///C:\MSOCache\All%20Users\20000409-6000-11D3
     8CFE-0150048383C9\"/>
 </OfficeDocumentSettings>
 <ExcelWorkbook xmlns="urn:schemas-microsoft-com:office:excel">
  <WindowHeight>8955</WindowHeight>
  <WindowWidth>11355</WindowWidth>
  <WindowTopX>360</WindowTopX>
  <WindowTopY>120</WindowTopY>
  <ProtectStructure>False</ProtectStructure>
  <ProtectWindows>False</ProtectWindows>
 </ExcelWorkbook>
 <Styles>
  <Style ss:ID="Default" ss:Name="Normal">
   <Alignment ss:Vertical="Bottom"/>
   <Borders/>
   <Font/>
   <Interior/>
   <NumberFormat/>
   <Protection/>
  </Style>
 </Styles>
 <Worksheet ss:Name="Sheet1">
  <Table ss:ExpandedColumnCount="1" ss:ExpandedRowCount="3" x:FullColumns="1"
   x:FullRows="1">
   <Row>
    <Cell><Data ss:Type="Number">2</Data></Cell>
   </Row>
   <Row>
    <Cell><Data ss:Type="Number">2</Data></Cell>
   </Row>
   <Row>
    <Cell ss:Formula="=SUM(R[-2]C, R[-1]C)"><Data ss:Type="Number">4</Data></Cell>
   </Row>
  </Table>
  <WorksheetOptions xmlns="urn:schemas-microsoft-com:office:excel">
```

Example 7-1. A simple Excel spreadsheet saved as XML (continued)

```
  <Print>
   <ValidPrinterInfo/>
   <HorizontalResolution>600</HorizontalResolution>
   <VerticalResolution>600</VerticalResolution>
  </Print>
  <Selected/>
  <Panes>
   <Pane>
    <Number>3</Number>
    <ActiveRow>1</ActiveRow>
    <ActiveCol>1</ActiveCol>
   </Pane>
  </Panes>
  <ProtectObjects>False</ProtectObjects>
  <ProtectScenarios>False</ProtectScenarios>
 </WorksheetOptions>
</Worksheet>
<Worksheet ss:Name="Sheet2">
 <WorksheetOptions xmlns="urn:schemas-microsoft-com:office:excel">
  <ProtectObjects>False</ProtectObjects>
  <ProtectScenarios>False</ProtectScenarios>
 </WorksheetOptions>
</Worksheet>
<Worksheet ss:Name="Sheet3">
 <WorksheetOptions xmlns="urn:schemas-microsoft-com:office:excel">
  <ProtectObjects>False</ProtectObjects>
  <ProtectScenarios>False</ProtectScenarios>
 </WorksheetOptions>
</Worksheet>
</Workbook>
```

The spreadsheet begins with an XML declaration and a processing instruction identifying this document as an Excel.sheet:

```
<?xml version="1.0"?>
<?mso-application progid="Excel.Sheet"?>
```

After those formalities, the Workbook element appears. The Workbook element is the root element for all SpreadsheetML files, and contains most of the namespace declarations that will be used in the rest of the document:

```
<Workbook xmlns="urn:schemas-microsoft-com:office:spreadsheet"
 xmlns:o="urn:schemas-microsoft-com:office:office"
 xmlns:x="urn:schemas-microsoft-com:office:excel"
 xmlns:ss="urn:schemas-microsoft-com:office:spreadsheet"
 xmlns:html="http://www.w3.org/TR/REC-html40">
```

Unlike Word, which prefixed all of its element and attribute names with w, Excel uses no namespace prefix by default, using xmlns="urn:schemas-microsoft-com:office:spreadsheet" to declare its default namespace, the namespace you'll undoubtedly find most important if you need to get to the data contained in the spreadsheet grid.

Because unprefixed attributes don't have a namespace, Excel also uses the declaration xmlns:ss="urn:schemas-microsoft-com:office:spreadsheet" to associate the ss (for spreadsheet) prefix with the same URI. The elements in the document will be unprefixed, while their attributes will be prefixed with ss, but all of these components will have precisely the same namespace URI, "urn:schemas-microsoft-com:office:spreadsheet".

As we'll see, the declaration for the o prefix doesn't actually get used in this document. The x prefix is used for a few attributes later, and the html prefix is used if there is HTML in the spreadsheet somewhere.

The first child element, DocumentProperties, contains the metadata about the document. While all of these elements use no namespace prefix, the DocumentProperties element redefines the default namespace with its own xmlns attribute. Unprefixed elements in this space have the same namespace URI as the o prefix elsewhere.

```
<DocumentProperties xmlns="urn:schemas-microsoft-com:office:office">
  <Author>Simon St.Laurent</Author>
  <LastAuthor>Simon St.Laurent</LastAuthor>
  <Created>2003-03-19T20:21:31Z</Created>
  <LastSaved>2003-03-19T20:23:08Z</LastSaved>
  <Company>simonstl.com</Company>
  <Version>11.4920</Version>
</DocumentProperties>
```

Most of this information is pretty straightforward. Perhaps the most interesting aspect is that the markup is extremely similar to its counterpart in Word, except for whitespace and the meaningless namespace prefix. Excel stores less information than Word, as Example 7-2 demonstrates, but content managers can rely on these pieces to collect metadata from both Word and Excel files without concern for the surrounding context.

Example 7-2. WordML document properties (whitespace added for readability)

```
<o:DocumentProperties>
  <o:Title>Hello World</o:Title>
  <o:Author>Simon St.Laurent</o:Author>
  <o:LastAuthor>Simon St.Laurent</o:LastAuthor>
  <o:Revision>2</o:Revision>
  <o:TotalTime>0</o:TotalTime>
  <o:Created>2003-03-14T00:21:00Z</o:Created>
  <o:LastSaved>2003-03-14T00:21:00Z</o:LastSaved>
  <o:Pages>1</o:Pages>
  <o:Words>1</o:Words>
  <o:Characters>12</o:Characters>
  <o:Company>O'Reilly &amp; Associates</o:Company>
  <o:Lines>1</o:Lines>
  <o:Paragraphs>1</o:Paragraphs>
  <o:CharactersWithSpaces>12</o:CharactersWithSpaces>
  <o:Version>11.4920</o:Version>
</o:DocumentProperties>
```

Getting back to the Excel markup, the next piece is pretty application-specific and probably not very useful to other applications. Like the DocumentProperties element, it declares its own default namespace rather than using the o prefix defined at the start of the document.

```
<OfficeDocumentSettings xmlns="urn:schemas-microsoft-com:office:office">
  <DownloadComponents/>
  <LocationOfComponents HRef="file:///C:\MSOCache\All%20Users\20000409-6000-11D3
    8CFE-0150048383C9\"/>
</OfficeDocumentSettings>
```

Next we have the ExcelWorkbook element, with information about the window settings and protected status of the workbook:

```
<ExcelWorkbook xmlns="urn:schemas-microsoft-com:office:excel">
  <WindowHeight>8955</WindowHeight>
  <WindowWidth>11355</WindowWidth>
  <WindowTopX>360</WindowTopX>
  <WindowTopY>120</WindowTopY>
  <ProtectStructure>False</ProtectStructure>
  <ProtectWindows>False</ProtectWindows>
</ExcelWorkbook>
```

Again, this element could have used the x prefix defined in the root element, but opts to redeclare the default namespace. After this information about the presentation of the spreadsheet generally, we have information about the styles used in the document, stored in the Styles element:

```
<Styles>
  <Style ss:ID="Default" ss:Name="Normal">
    <Alignment ss:Vertical="Bottom"/>
    <Borders/>
    <Font/>
    <Interior/>
    <NumberFormat/>
    <Protection/>
  </Style>
</Styles>
```

Because this spreadsheet is very very simple, there are just a few defaults here. All of the cells in this stylesheet use the Normal style, with no special formatting. Nevertheless, this empty set of elements gives you some idea of what you can do here.

After these preparations, we reach the Worksheet elements. Each of these elements represents one complete worksheet in Excel. Since Excel created three worksheets by default, there are three Worksheet elements here. Spreadsheets with more or fewer worksheets will have as many Worksheet elements as appropriate. The first of the three Worksheet elements is the one containing our data:

```
<Worksheet ss:Name="Sheet1">
  <Table ss:ExpandedColumnCount="1" ss:ExpandedRowCount="3" x:FullColumns="1"
      x:FullRows="1">
    <Row>
```

```
   <Cell><Data ss:Type="Number">2</Data></Cell>
  </Row>
  <Row>
   <Cell><Data ss:Type="Number">2</Data></Cell>
  </Row>
  <Row>
   <Cell ss:Formula="=SUM(R[-2]C, R[-1]C)"><Data ss:Type="Number">4</Data></Cell>
  </Row>
 </Table>
 <WorksheetOptions xmlns="urn:schemas-microsoft-com:office:excel">
  <Print>
   <ValidPrinterInfo/>
   <HorizontalResolution>600</HorizontalResolution>
   <VerticalResolution>600</VerticalResolution>
  </Print>
  <Selected/>
  <Panes>
   <Pane>
    <Number>3</Number>
    <ActiveRow>1</ActiveRow>
    <ActiveCol>1</ActiveCol>
   </Pane>
  </Panes>
  <ProtectObjects>False</ProtectObjects>
  <ProtectScenarios>False</ProtectScenarios>
 </WorksheetOptions>
</Worksheet>
```

The guts of the worksheet are stored in the Table element, while other information about the worksheet is stored in the WorksheetOptions element. For the most part, if you're trying to extract the contents of spreadsheets or create new spreadsheets from existing information, the Table element will be at the heart of your work. The Table element defines the space it contains:

```
<Table ss:ExpandedColumnCount="1" ss:ExpandedRowCount="3" x:FullColumns="1"
    x:FullRows="1">
```

The ss:ExpandedColumnCount indicates that this spreadsheet has one column, while ss:ExpandedRowCount indicates that this spreadsheet has three rows. Knowing the number of rows and columns gives Excel a chance to prepare for the incoming data. The x:FullColumns and x:FullRows attributes appear to do nothing.

In current versions of SpreadsheetML, multiple Table elements are permitted, but Excel only uses the first of them. According to Microsoft's "Overview of SpreadsheetML," which comes with the Microsoft Office XML Schemas mentioned at the start of this chapter, this will let future versions of Excel "support multiple overlapping ranges by having multiple Table elements."

The contents of the Table element represent the stylesheet as a set of Row elements which themselves contain Cell elements:

```
<Row>
 <Cell><Data ss:Type="Number">2</Data></Cell>
</Row>
<Row>
 <Cell><Data ss:Type="Number">2</Data></Cell>
</Row>
<Row>
 <Cell ss:Formula="=SUM(R[-2]C, R[-1]C)"><Data ss:Type="Number">4</Data></Cell>
</Row>
```

The first two of these Row elements are identical, containing a Cell element whose Data element contains the value 2. The ss:Type attribute identifies this information as a Number—a notable departure from the W3C XML Schema data typing used elsewhere in the Office applications, but consistent with the mapping previously described in Table 6-1. The third row contains a calculated result, the 4 inside of the Data element, as well as the type information and the formula by which that result was calculated. The inclusion of calculated values may make some kinds of import from Excel much easier, and you can always check for the presence of the ss:Formula attribute if you want to exclude calculated values from your processing.

Looking more closely at the ss:Formula attribute, it's fairly clear that using these formulas in other contexts will require reconstructing the table:

```
ss:Formula="=SUM(R[-2]C, R[-1]C)"
```

The formula reflects Excel's internal expectations for working with the information, most notably the expectation that the entire table will be available for navigation using relative references between cells. The Row and Cell elements reflect this same structure, so programs built around this XML have a good chance of interpreting these formulas, but decoding them will take some custom logic (XSLT 1.0 won't easily build and navigate this grid) and an object model for storing all the rows and cells at any given time. Depending on the type of information you need from the spreadsheet, this may not matter. If you're importing it into another spreadsheet-like structure, you may have a lot of work to do. If you just want the data, ignoring the formulas shouldn't be a problem.

The WorksheetOptions element contains other information about the worksheet's presentation and operation:

```
<WorksheetOptions xmlns="urn:schemas-microsoft-com:office:excel">
 <Print>
  <ValidPrinterInfo/>
  <HorizontalResolution>600</HorizontalResolution>
  <VerticalResolution>600</VerticalResolution>
 </Print>
 <Selected/>
 <Panes>
  <Pane>
```

```
            <Number>3</Number>
            <ActiveRow>1</ActiveRow>
            <ActiveCol>1</ActiveCol>
          </Pane>
        </Panes>
        <ProtectObjects>False</ProtectObjects>
        <ProtectScenarios>False</ProtectScenarios>
      </WorksheetOptions>
```

Again, the WorksheetOptions element redefines the default namespace, assigning the same value to no prefix that was assigned to the x prefix at the start of the document. All of this information is considered specific to Excel, not to the spreadsheet generally. While the data here can be useful if you're creating spreadsheet applications, it's not information you'll use for the spreadsheet data itself.

The next two worksheets are empty, so they are represented by relatively minimal placeholders, followed by the closing tag of Workbook:

```
    <Worksheet ss:Name="Sheet2">
      <WorksheetOptions xmlns="urn:schemas-microsoft-com:office:excel">
        <ProtectObjects>False</ProtectObjects>
        <ProtectScenarios>False</ProtectScenarios>
      </WorksheetOptions>
    </Worksheet>
    <Worksheet ss:Name="Sheet3">
      <WorksheetOptions xmlns="urn:schemas-microsoft-com:office:excel">
        <ProtectObjects>False</ProtectObjects>
        <ProtectScenarios>False</ProtectScenarios>
      </WorksheetOptions>
    </Worksheet>
  </Workbook>
```

If all you're concerned with is extracting the data from the spreadsheet, you now have a solid set of basic parts: the Workbook, Worksheet, Row, Cell, and Data elements. For getting information into and out of Excel, that core provides most of the substance you'll need.

Working with More Complex Spreadsheets

While the 2+2=4 example does a nice job of showing the basic structure Excel uses to store spreadsheets in XML, the odds are excellent that you'll need to work with more complicated spreadsheets and formulas. Excel also offers a few structures—notably named cells and ranges—that can make it much easier to work with Excel data, reducing the otherwise constant need to keep track of how an XML cell corresponds to a particular location on the spreadsheet grid.

We'll start with the spreadsheet shown in Figure 7-6, a list of items sold, with IDs, descriptions, prices, named ranges for all of those, and a calculated total for each transaction.

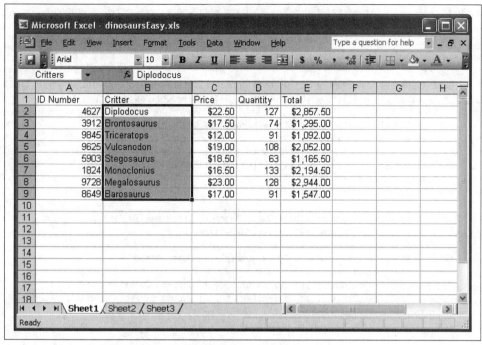

Figure 7-6. A spreadsheet with more data and named ranges

The "Critters" named range includes the contents of the Critter column, and so on. When this spreadsheet is saved as an XML document, the Worksheet element representing Sheet1 looks like Example 7-3.

Example 7-3. The Worksheet portion of the XML representation of Figure 7-6

```
<Worksheet ss:Name="Sheet1">
 <Table ss:ExpandedColumnCount="5" ss:ExpandedRowCount="9" x:FullColumns="1"
    x:FullRows="1">
  <Column ss:AutoFitWidth="0" ss:Width="73.5"/>
  <Column ss:AutoFitWidth="0" ss:Width="96.75"/>
  <Column ss:Index="5" ss:AutoFitWidth="0" ss:Width="56.25"/>
  <Row>
   <Cell><Data ss:Type="String">ID Number</Data></Cell>
   <Cell><Data ss:Type="String">Critter</Data></Cell>
   <Cell><Data ss:Type="String">Price</Data></Cell>
   <Cell><Data ss:Type="String">Quantity</Data></Cell>
   <Cell><Data ss:Type="String">Total</Data></Cell>
  </Row>
  <Row>
   <Cell><Data ss:Type="Number">4627</Data><NamedCell ss:Name="ID"/></Cell>
   <Cell><Data ss:Type="String">Diplodocus</Data><NamedCell ss:Name="Critters"/>
      </Cell>
   <Cell ss:StyleID="s21"><Data ss:Type="Number">22.5</Data><NamedCell
     ss:Name="Price"/></Cell>
   <Cell><Data ss:Type="Number">127</Data><NamedCell ss:Name="Quantity"/></Cell>
```

Example 7-3. The Worksheet portion of the XML representation of Figure 7-6 (continued)

```
   <Cell ss:StyleID="s21" ss:Formula="=RC[-2]*RC[-1]"><Data ss:Type="Number">2857.5</
Data></Cell>
  </Row>
  <Row>
   <Cell><Data ss:Type="Number">3912</Data><NamedCell ss:Name="ID"/></Cell>
   <Cell><Data ss:Type="String">Brontosaurus</Data><NamedCell ss
      Name="Critters"/></Cell>
   <Cell ss:StyleID="s21"><Data ss:Type="Number">17.5</Data><NamedCell
    ss:Name="Price"/></Cell>
   <Cell><Data ss:Type="Number">74</Data><NamedCell ss:Name="Quantity"/></Cell>
   <Cell ss:StyleID="s21" ss:Formula="=RC[-2]*RC[-1]"><Data ss:Type="Number"
      1295</Data></Cell>
  </Row>
  <Row>
   <Cell><Data ss:Type="Number">9845</Data><NamedCell ss:Name="ID"/></Cell>
   <Cell><Data ss:Type="String">Triceratops</Data>
      <NamedCell ss:Name="Critters"/></Cell>
   <Cell ss:StyleID="s21"><Data ss:Type="Number">12</Data><NamedCell
    ss:Name="Price"/></Cell>
   <Cell><Data ss:Type="Number">91</Data><NamedCell ss:Name="Quantity"/></Cell>
   <Cell ss:StyleID="s21" ss:Formula="=RC[-2]*RC[-1]"><Data ss:Type="Number">
      1092</Data></Cell>
  </Row>
  <Row>
   <Cell><Data ss:Type="Number">9625</Data><NamedCell ss:Name="ID"/></Cell>
   <Cell><Data ss:Type="String">Vulcanodon</Data><NamedCell ss:Name="Critters"/>
      </Cell>
   <Cell ss:StyleID="s21"><Data ss:Type="Number">19</Data><NamedCell
    ss:Name="Price"/></Cell>
   <Cell><Data ss:Type="Number">108</Data><NamedCell ss:Name="Quantity"/></Cell>
   <Cell ss:StyleID="s21" ss:Formula="=RC[-2]*RC[-1]"><Data ss:Type="Number">
      2052</Data></Cell>
  </Row>
  <Row>
   <Cell><Data ss:Type="Number">5903</Data><NamedCell ss:Name="ID"/></Cell>
   <Cell><Data ss:Type="String">Stegosaurus</Data>
      <NamedCell ss:Name="Critters"/></Cell>
   <Cell ss:StyleID="s21"><Data ss:Type="Number">18.5</Data><NamedCell
    ss:Name="Price"/></Cell>
   <Cell><Data ss:Type="Number">63</Data><NamedCell ss:Name="Quantity"/></Cell>
   <Cell ss:StyleID="s21" ss:Formula="=RC[-2]*RC[-1]"><Data ss:Type="Number">
      1165.5</Data></Cell>
  </Row>
  <Row>
   <Cell><Data ss:Type="Number">1824</Data><NamedCell ss:Name="ID"/></Cell>
   <Cell><Data ss:Type="String">Monoclonius</Data>
      <NamedCell ss:Name="Critters"/></Cell>
   <Cell ss:StyleID="s21"><Data ss:Type="Number">16.5</Data><NamedCell
    ss:Name="Price"/></Cell>
   <Cell><Data ss:Type="Number">133</Data><NamedCell ss:Name="Quantity"/></Cell>
   <Cell ss:StyleID="s21" ss:Formula="=RC[-2]*RC[-1]"><Data ss:Type="Number">
      2194.5</Data></Cell>
```

Example 7-3. The Worksheet portion of the XML representation of Figure 7-6 (continued)

```
 </Row>
 <Row>
  <Cell><Data ss:Type="Number">9728</Data><NamedCell ss:Name="ID"/></Cell>
  <Cell><Data ss:Type="String">Megalosaurus</Data>
      <NamedCell ss:Name="Critters"/></Cell>
  <Cell ss:StyleID="s21"><Data ss:Type="Number">23</Data><NamedCell
    ss:Name="Price"/></Cell>
  <Cell><Data ss:Type="Number">128</Data><NamedCell ss:Name="Quantity"/></Cell>
  <Cell ss:StyleID="s21" ss:Formula="=RC[-2]*RC[-1]"><Data ss:Type="Number">
      2944</Data></Cell>
 </Row>
 <Row>
  <Cell><Data ss:Type="Number">8649</Data><NamedCell ss:Name="ID"/></Cell>
  <Cell><Data ss:Type="String">Barosaurus</Data><NamedCell ss:Name="Critters"/>
      </Cell>
  <Cell ss:StyleID="s21"><Data ss:Type="Number">17</Data><NamedCell
    ss:Name="Price"/></Cell>
  <Cell><Data ss:Type="Number">91</Data><NamedCell ss:Name="Quantity"/></Cell>
  <Cell ss:StyleID="s21" ss:Formula="=RC[-2]*RC[-1]"><Data ss:Type="Number">
      1547</Data></Cell>
 </Row>
 </Table>
 <WorksheetOptions xmlns="urn:schemas-microsoft-com:office:excel">
  <Print>
   <ValidPrinterInfo/>
   <HorizontalResolution>600</HorizontalResolution>
   <VerticalResolution>600</VerticalResolution>
  </Print>
  <Selected/>
  <Panes>
   <Pane>
    <Number>3</Number>
    <ActiveRow>8</ActiveRow>
    <ActiveCol>4</ActiveCol>
   </Pane>
  </Panes>
  <ProtectObjects>False</ProtectObjects>
  <ProtectScenarios>False</ProtectScenarios>
 </WorksheetOptions>
</Worksheet>
```

It has the same pattern of Row elements containing Cell elements (the Column information is strictly for formatting), and the same surrounding metadata, but it also now contains additional information in many of its Cell elements:

```
<Row>
 <Cell><Data ss:Type="Number">4627</Data><NamedCell ss:Name="ID"/></Cell>
 <Cell><Data ss:Type="String">Diplodocus</Data>
     <NamedCell ss:Name="Critters"/></Cell>
 <Cell ss:StyleID="s21"><Data ss:Type="Number">22.5</Data><NamedCell
   ss:Name="Price"/></Cell>
 <Cell><Data ss:Type="Number">127</Data><NamedCell ss:Name="Quantity"/></Cell>
```

```
    <Cell ss:StyleID="s21" ss:Formula="=RC[-2]*RC[-1]">
        <Data ss:Type="Number">2857.5</Data></Cell>
    </Row>
```

With the addition of the NamedCell element and its ss:Name attribute, we now have a way to select cells from the row by name in addition to position. The XML spreadsheet also contains a summary of the named ranges in a Names element that precedes the Worksheet elements:

```
<Names>
  <NamedRange ss:Name="Critters" ss:RefersTo="=Sheet1!R2C2:R9C2"/>
  <NamedRange ss:Name="ID" ss:RefersTo="=Sheet1!R2C1:R9C1"/>
  <NamedRange ss:Name="Price" ss:RefersTo="=Sheet1!R2C3:R9C3"/>
  <NamedRange ss:Name="Quantity" ss:RefersTo="=Sheet1!R2C4:R9C4"/>
</Names>
```

While the Names element is useful to Excel in loading a document, you may not find processing it (or even creating it) with other applications, notably XSLT and XPath, to be much fun—once again, you need to have the grid available to figure out (or assign) the references. Fortunately, Excel can recreate named ranges from just the NamedCell information, so you don't need to worry about this extra step unless you want to.

Extracting Information from XML Spreadsheets

When the spreadsheet data arrives in a form like Example 7-3, it's easy to extract the data using tools like XSLT. All the cells in the area used contain data, and it's just a simple table. If, for example, we wanted to extract the data in this spreadsheet and produce a much lighter XML document containing just the data, the stylesheet might look like that shown in Example 7-4.

Example 7-4. A simple stylesheet for extracting data from Excel tables

```
<xsl:stylesheet version="1.0"
  xmlns:xsl="http://www.w3.org/1999/XSL/Transform"
  xmlns="http://simonstl.com/ns/dinosaurs/"
  xmlns:ss="urn:schemas-microsoft-com:office:spreadsheet"
 >
<xsl:output method="xml" omit-xml-declaration="yes" indent="yes" encoding="US-
  ASCII"/>
<xsl:template match="/">
  <xsl:apply-templates select="ss:Workbook"/>
</xsl:template>
<xsl:template match="ss:Workbook">
  <dinosaurs>
      <xsl:apply-templates select="ss:Worksheet[@ss:Name = 'Sheet1']"/>
  </dinosaurs>
</xsl:template>
<xsl:template match="ss:Worksheet">
```

Example 7-4. A simple stylesheet for extracting data from Excel tables (continued)

```
    <xsl:apply-templates select="ss:Table" />
</xsl:template>
<xsl:template match="ss:Table">
    <xsl:apply-templates select="ss:Row[position( ) &gt; 1]" />
</xsl:template>
<xsl:template match="ss:Row">
<sale>
    <IDnum><xsl:apply-templates select="ss:Cell[1]" /></IDnum>
    <critter><xsl:apply-templates select="ss:Cell[2]" /></critter>
    <price><xsl:apply-templates select="ss:Cell[3]" /></price>
    <quantity><xsl:apply-templates select="ss:Cell[4]" /></quantity>
    <total><xsl:apply-templates select="ss:Cell[5]" /></total>
</sale>
</xsl:template>
</xsl:stylesheet>
```

Note the namespace declarations in the root xsl:stylesheet element. If you forget any of these, your stylesheet won't behave as expected, even though everything else looks right.

> See Appendix B for more information if you're unfamiliar with XSLT and XSLT processing tools.

Most of the work here is done by the last template, which just matches the rows in Sheet1. The prior templates guide the stylesheet past all the Excel metadata, into Sheet1, and make sure that it skips the first Row element, which contains the column titles. The last template puts the contents of the first Cell element into an element named IDnum, the second Cell element into an element named critter, and so on. The results of running this stylesheet against the XML document in Example 7-2 are shown in Example 7-5.

Example 7-5. Simple XML produced by using XSLT on SpreadsheetML

```
<dinosaurs xmlns="http://simonstl.com/ns/dinosaurs/" xmlns:ss="urn:schemas-microsoft-com:
office:spreadsheet">
<sale>
<IDnum>4627</IDnum>
<critter>Diplodocus</critter>
<price>22.5</price>
<quantity>127</quantity>
<total>2857.5</total>
</sale>
<sale>
<IDnum>3912</IDnum>
<critter>Brontosaurus</critter>
<price>17.5</price>
<quantity>74</quantity>
<total>1295</total>
```

```
    </sale>
    <sale>
    <IDnum>9845</IDnum>
    <critter>Triceratops</critter>
    <price>12</price>
    <quantity>91</quantity>
    <total>1092</total>
    </sale>
    <sale>
    <IDnum>9625</IDnum>
    <critter>Vulcanodon</critter>
    <price>19</price>
    <quantity>108</quantity>
    <total>2052</total>
    </sale>
    <sale>
    <IDnum>5903</IDnum>
    <critter>Stegosaurus</critter>
    <price>18.5</price>
    <quantity>63</quantity>
    <total>1165.5</total>
    </sale>
    <sale>
    <IDnum>1824</IDnum>
    <critter>Monoclonius</critter>
    <price>16.5</price>
    <quantity>133</quantity>
    <total>2194.5</total>
    </sale>
    <sale>
    <IDnum>9728</IDnum>
    <critter>Megalosaurus</critter>
    <price>23</price>
    <quantity>128</quantity>
    <total>2944</total>
    </sale>
    <sale>
    <IDnum>8649</IDnum>
    <critter>Barosaurus</critter>
    <price>17</price>
    <quantity>91</quantity>
    <total>1547</total>
    </sale>
    </dinosaurs>
```

This kind of extraction is easy, but it's fairly unusual that real-world spreadsheets will be this convenient. It's not impossible, of course—I get a spreadsheet whose first sheet is structured like this once a week—but there are many tougher cases. Lots of spreadsheets skip rows and cells, have areas that are used for different kinds of content, and present additional challenges to developers who need to extract information from them. Fortunately, while every spreadsheet is different, there are a few basic patterns that can help you reach into them. Figure 7-7 shows a spreadsheet with much the same data as that in Figure 7-6, but with a few complicating factors.

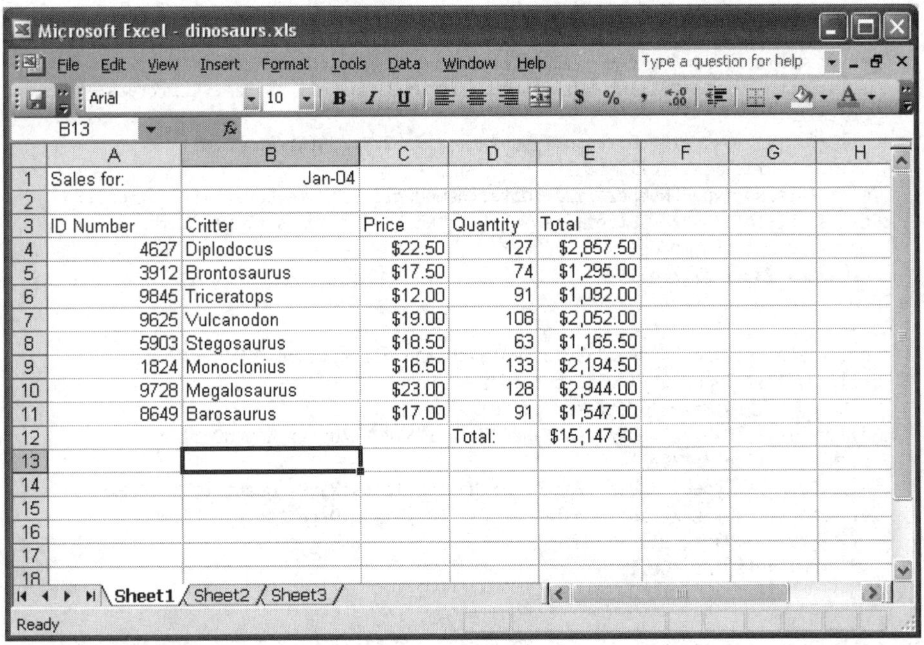

Figure 7-7. A spreadsheet with gaps and individual data components

The first row contains a date identifying when the data is from, the second row is blank, rows three to eleven contain the same data shown in Figure 7-6, and row twelve shows a total. Examining the Table element in the SpreadsheetML, listed in Example 7-6, shows how Excel treats these skipped rows and columns.

Example 7-6. More complex XML produced from the spreadsheet in Figure 7-7

```
<Table ss:ExpandedColumnCount="5" ss:ExpandedRowCount="12" x:FullColumns="1"
  x:FullRows="1">
  <Column ss:AutoFitWidth="0" ss:Width="73.5"/>
  <Column ss:AutoFitWidth="0" ss:Width="96.75"/>
  <Column ss:Index="5" ss:AutoFitWidth="0" ss:Width="56.25"/>
  <Row>
   <Cell><Data ss:Type="String">Sales for:</Data></Cell>
   <Cell ss:StyleID="s21"><Data ss:Type="DateTime">2004-01-01T00:00:00.000
     </Data><NamedCell
    ss:Name="Date"/></Cell>
  </Row>
  <Row ss:Index="3">
   <Cell><Data ss:Type="String">ID Number</Data></Cell>
   <Cell><Data ss:Type="String">Critter</Data></Cell>
   <Cell><Data ss:Type="String">Price</Data></Cell>
```

```
  <Cell><Data ss:Type="String">Quantity</Data></Cell>
  <Cell><Data ss:Type="String">Total</Data></Cell>
</Row>
<Row>
 <Cell><Data ss:Type="Number">4627</Data><NamedCell ss:Name="ID"/></Cell>
 <Cell><Data ss:Type="String">Diplodocus</Data><NamedCell ss:Name="Critters"/>
   </Cell>
 <Cell ss:StyleID="s22"><Data ss:Type="Number">22.5</Data><NamedCell
   ss:Name="Price"/></Cell>
 <Cell><Data ss:Type="Number">127</Data><NamedCell ss:Name="Quantity"/></Cell>
 <Cell ss:StyleID="s22" ss:Formula="=RC[-2]*RC[-1]"><Data ss:Type="Number">
   2857.5</Data><NamedCell
   ss:Name="Total"/></Cell>
</Row>
<Row>
 <Cell><Data ss:Type="Number">3912</Data><NamedCell ss:Name="ID"/></Cell>
 <Cell><Data ss:Type="String">Brontosaurus</Data>
   <NamedCell ss:Name="Critters"/></Cell>
 <Cell ss:StyleID="s22"><Data ss:Type="Number">17.5</Data><NamedCell
   ss:Name="Price"/></Cell>
 <Cell><Data ss:Type="Number">74</Data><NamedCell ss:Name="Quantity"/></Cell>
 <Cell ss:StyleID="s22" ss:Formula="=RC[-2]*RC[-1]"><Data ss:Type="Number">
   1295</Data><NamedCell
   ss:Name="Total"/></Cell>
</Row>
<Row>
 <Cell><Data ss:Type="Number">9845</Data><NamedCell ss:Name="ID"/></Cell>
 <Cell><Data ss:Type="String">Triceratops</Data>
   <NamedCell ss:Name="Critters"/></Cell>
 <Cell ss:StyleID="s22"><Data ss:Type="Number">12</Data><NamedCell
   ss:Name="Price"/></Cell>
 <Cell><Data ss:Type="Number">91</Data><NamedCell ss:Name="Quantity"/></Cell>
 <Cell ss:StyleID="s22" ss:Formula="=RC[-2]*RC[-1]"><Data ss:Type="Number">
   1092</Data><NamedCell
   ss:Name="Total"/></Cell>
</Row>
<Row>
 <Cell><Data ss:Type="Number">9625</Data><NamedCell ss:Name="ID"/></Cell>
 <Cell><Data ss:Type="String">Vulcanodon</Data>
   <NamedCell ss:Name="Critters"/></Cell>
 <Cell ss:StyleID="s22"><Data ss:Type="Number">19</Data><NamedCell
   ss:Name="Price"/></Cell>
 <Cell><Data ss:Type="Number">108</Data><NamedCell ss:Name="Quantity"/></Cell>
 <Cell ss:StyleID="s22" ss:Formula="=RC[-2]*RC[-1]"><Data ss:Type="Number">
   2052</Data><NamedCell
   ss:Name="Total"/></Cell>
</Row>
<Row>
 <Cell><Data ss:Type="Number">5903</Data><NamedCell ss:Name="ID"/></Cell>
 <Cell><Data ss:Type="String">Stegosaurus</Data>
   <NamedCell ss:Name="Critters"/></Cell>
 <Cell ss:StyleID="s22"><Data ss:Type="Number">18.5</Data><NamedCell
```

```
      ss:Name="Price"/></Cell>
    <Cell><Data ss:Type="Number">63</Data><NamedCell ss:Name="Quantity"/></Cell>
    <Cell ss:StyleID="s22" ss:Formula="=RC[-2]*RC[-1]"><Data ss:Type="Number">
      1165.5</Data><NamedCell
      ss:Name="Total"/></Cell>
  </Row>
  <Row>
    <Cell><Data ss:Type="Number">1824</Data><NamedCell ss:Name="ID"/></Cell>
    <Cell><Data ss:Type="String">Monoclonius</Data>
      <NamedCell ss:Name="Critters"/></Cell>
    <Cell ss:StyleID="s22"><Data ss:Type="Number">16.5</Data><NamedCell
      ss:Name="Price"/></Cell>
    <Cell><Data ss:Type="Number">133</Data><NamedCell ss:Name="Quantity"/></Cell>
    <Cell ss:StyleID="s22" ss:Formula="=RC[-2]*RC[-1]"><Data ss:Type="Number">
      2194.5</Data><NamedCell
      ss:Name="Total"/></Cell>
  </Row>
  <Row>
    <Cell><Data ss:Type="Number">9728</Data><NamedCell ss:Name="ID"/></Cell>
    <Cell><Data ss:Type="String">Megalosaurus</Data>
      <NamedCell ss:Name="Critters"/></Cell>
    <Cell ss:StyleID="s22"><Data ss:Type="Number">23</Data><NamedCell
      ss:Name="Price"/></Cell>
    <Cell><Data ss:Type="Number">128</Data><NamedCell ss:Name="Quantity"/></Cell>
    <Cell ss:StyleID="s22" ss:Formula="=RC[-2]*RC[-1]"><Data ss:Type="Number">
      2944</Data><NamedCell
      ss:Name="Total"/></Cell>
  </Row>
  <Row>
    <Cell><Data ss:Type="Number">8649</Data><NamedCell ss:Name="ID"/></Cell>
    <Cell><Data ss:Type="String">Barosaurus</Data><NamedCell ss:Name="Critters"/>
      </Cell>
    <Cell ss:StyleID="s22"><Data ss:Type="Number">17</Data><NamedCell
      ss:Name="Price"/></Cell>
    <Cell><Data ss:Type="Number">91</Data><NamedCell ss:Name="Quantity"/></Cell>
    <Cell ss:StyleID="s22" ss:Formula="=RC[-2]*RC[-1]"><Data ss:Type="Number">
      1547</Data><NamedCell
      ss:Name="Total"/></Cell>
  </Row>
  <Row>
    <Cell ss:Index="4"><Data ss:Type="String">Total:</Data></Cell>
    <Cell ss:StyleID="s22" ss:Formula="=SUM(R[-8]C:R[-1]C)">
      <Data ss:Type="Number">15147.5</Data><NamedCell
      ss:Name="GrandTotal"/></Cell>
  </Row>
</Table>
```

Excel doesn't report blank rows or cells. Instead, the first `Row` or `Cell` element after the blanks has an `ss:Index` attribute identifying its position. This means that stylesheets and other processors can't just count their way through the grid—they have to keep track of where the SpreadsheetML says things go.

Converting this spreadsheet to XML like that shown in Example 7-4 will be somewhat more difficult. There are two approaches that can be applied to this. The first approach, the stylesheet in Example 7-7, modifies the stylesheet shown in Example 7-4, and the changes are highlighted.

Example 7-7. A modified stylesheet for dealing with the new spreadsheet

```
<xsl:stylesheet version="1.0"
  xmlns:xsl="http://www.w3.org/1999/XSL/Transform"
  xmlns="http://simonstl.com/ns/dinosaurs/"
  xmlns:ss="urn:schemas-microsoft-com:office:spreadsheet"
 >
<xsl:output method="xml" omit-xml-declaration="yes" indent="yes" encoding="US-
    ASCII"/>
<xsl:template match="/">
  <xsl:apply-templates select="ss:Workbook"/>
</xsl:template>
<xsl:template match="ss:Workbook">
  <dinosaurs>
       <xsl:apply-templates select="ss:Worksheet[@ss:Name = 'Sheet1']"/>
  </dinosaurs>
</xsl:template>
<xsl:template match="ss:Worksheet">
   <date><xsl:value-of select="ss:Table/ss:Row/ss:Cell[@ss:StyleID = 's21']" />
       </date>
   <xsl:apply-templates select="ss:Table" />
</xsl:template>
<xsl:template match="ss:Table">
   <xsl:apply-templates select="ss:Row[position() &gt; 2]" />
<!--Note that because Excel skips the blank row, the third row is in position 2-->
</xsl:template>
<xsl:template match="ss:Row[ss:Cell[4]]">
<sale>
   <IDnum><xsl:apply-templates select="ss:Cell[1]" /></IDnum>
   <critter><xsl:apply-templates select="ss:Cell[2]" /></critter>
   <price><xsl:apply-templates select="ss:Cell[3]" /></price>
   <quantity><xsl:apply-templates select="ss:Cell[4]" /></quantity>
   <total><xsl:apply-templates select="ss:Cell[5]" /></total>
</sale>
</xsl:template>
<xsl:template match="ss:Row">
<total><xsl:apply-templates select="ss:Cell[2]" /></total>
</xsl:template>
</xsl:stylesheet>
```

Running this stylesheet against the SpreadsheetML produces XML much like that shown in Example 7-6, shown here in Example 7-8.

Example 7-8. XML produced by using XSLT on more complex SpreadsheetML

```
<dinosaurs xmlns="http://simonstl.com/ns/dinosaurs/" xmlns:ss="urn:schemas-microsoft-com:
office:spreadsheet">
<date>2004-01-01T00:00:00.000</date>
```

Example 7-8. XML produced by using XSLT on more complex SpreadsheetML (continued)

```
<sale>
<IDnum>4627</IDnum>
<critter>Diplodocus</critter>
<price>22.5</price>
<quantity>127</quantity>
<total>2857.5</total>
</sale>
<sale>
<IDnum>3912</IDnum>
<critter>Brontosaurus</critter>
<price>17.5</price>
<quantity>74</quantity>
<total>1295</total>
</sale>
<sale>
<IDnum>9845</IDnum>
<critter>Triceratops</critter>
<price>12</price>
<quantity>91</quantity>
<total>1092</total>
</sale>
<sale>
<IDnum>9625</IDnum>
<critter>Vulcanodon</critter>
<price>19</price>
<quantity>108</quantity>
<total>2052</total>
</sale>
<sale>
<IDnum>5903</IDnum>
<critter>Stegosaurus</critter>
<price>18.5</price>
<quantity>63</quantity>
<total>1165.5</total>
</sale>
<sale>
<IDnum>1824</IDnum>
<critter>Monoclonius</critter>
<price>16.5</price>
<quantity>133</quantity>
<total>2194.5</total>
</sale>
<sale>
<IDnum>9728</IDnum>
<critter>Megalosaurus</critter>
<price>23</price>
<quantity>128</quantity>
<total>2944</total>
</sale>
<sale>
<IDnum>8649</IDnum>
<critter>Barosaurus</critter>
```

```
<price>17</price>
<quantity>91</quantity>
<total>1547</total>
</sale>
<total>15147.5</total>
</dinosaurs>
```

A smarter approach uses the NamedCell element's ss:Name attribute, producing a similar result without relying on changeable details like row and cell positions. The stylesheet in Example 7-9 uses XSLT predicates to test for these attributes, yielding a stylesheet whose functionality is easier to discern. Places where this stylesheet references named ranges and cells are highlighted in bold.

Example 7-9. A SpreadsheetML transform that relies on named range information

```
<xsl:stylesheet version="1.0"
  xmlns:xsl="http://www.w3.org/1999/XSL/Transform"
  xmlns="http://simonstl.com/ns/dinosaurs/"
  xmlns:ss="urn:schemas-microsoft-com:office:spreadsheet"
 >
<xsl:output method="xml" omit-xml-declaration="yes" indent="yes" encoding="US-
    ASCII"/>
<xsl:template match="ss:Workbook">
  <dinosaurs>
      <xsl:apply-templates select="ss:Worksheet[@ss:Name = 'Sheet1']"/>
  </dinosaurs>
</xsl:template>
<xsl:template match="ss:Worksheet">
  <date><xsl:value-of select="ss:Table/ss:Row/ss:Cell[ss:NamedCell/@ss:Name =
      'Date']" /></date>
  <xsl:apply-templates select="ss:Table" />
<total><xsl:value-of select="ss:Table/ss:Row/ss:Cell[ss:NamedCell/@ss:Name =
'GrandTotal']" /></total>
</xsl:template>
<xsl:template match="ss:Table">
  <xsl:apply-templates select="ss:Row[position( ) &gt; 2]" />
</xsl:template>
<!--Only create sale elements for Rows which start with an ID-->
<xsl:template match="ss:Row[ss:Cell[1]/ss:NamedCell/@ss:Name='ID']">
<sale>
  <IDnum><xsl:apply-templates select="ss:Cell[ss:NamedCell/@ss:Name='ID']" />
  </IDnum>
  <critter><xsl:apply-templates select="ss:Cell[ss:NamedCell/@ss:Name='Critters']" /></
critter>
  <price><xsl:apply-templates select="ss:Cell[ss:NamedCell/@ss:Name='Price']" />
      </price>
  <quantity><xsl:apply-templates select="ss:Cell[ss:NamedCell/@ss:Name='Quantity']" /></
quantity>
  <total><xsl:apply-templates select="ss:Cell[ss:NamedCell/@ss:Name='Total']" />
      </total>
</sale>
```

```
</xsl:template>
<xsl:template match="ss:Row" />
</xsl:stylesheet>
```

This stylesheet will produce exactly the same output as the stylesheet in Example 7-7, which will look like the result in Example 7-8.

Creating XML Spreadsheets

There are two basic routes to creating a SpreadsheetML document. The first route is perhaps best described as "start from scratch," where you assemble a spreadsheet using the XML vocabulary. The other route uses Excel to build a template for the spreadsheets you create, accepting a certain amount of overhead for the convenience of using a familiar GUI (rather than a collection of XML parts) to create a spreadsheet. In general, especially where styles are involved, I strongly recommend using Excel to generate an initial SpreadsheetML file you can use as a model.

Whichever approach you choose, you don't need to provide as much information in your SpreadsheetML as Excel provides when you save information out. Most of the metadata can be discarded, and Excel can also reconstruct named ranges if necessary from the NamedCell elements inside of cells. Some data, like the ss: ExpandedColumnCount and ss:ExpandedRowCount attributes on the Table element, may actually be better left out, as it takes extra effort to generate and may produce errors when the spreadsheet is loaded if it's wrong. For the most part, you'll want to focus on creating the basic row and cell structures, along with styles.

You can use whatever tool you like to generate SpreadsheetML. XSLT, Java, C#, PHP, Perl, Python, Visual Basic, and many more will all work perfectly well. For complex spreadsheets with a lot of cross-references, I recommend working in whatever environment you're most comfortable in, as getting large numbers of cross-references right is a challenge, especially if they link among themselves. For simpler spreadsheets, though, XSLT's ready ability to take existing XML and add extra instructions to it makes it a very convenient tool for generating SpreadsheetML.

To demonstrate, the stylesheet in Example 7-10 will take the XML shown earlier in Example 7-8 and convert it back into SpreadsheetML. Critical pieces of logic are highlighted in bold.

Example 7-10. A stylesheet for generating SpreadsheetML

```
<xsl:stylesheet version="1.0"
  xmlns:xsl="http://www.w3.org/1999/XSL/Transform"
  xmlns:d="http://simonstl.com/ns/dinosaurs/"
  xmlns:ss="urn:schemas-microsoft-com:office:spreadsheet"
  xmlns="urn:schemas-microsoft-com:office:spreadsheet"
  xmlns="urn:schemas-microsoft-com:office:spreadsheet"
```

Example 7-10. A stylesheet for generating SpreadsheetML (continued)

```
  xmlns:o="urn:schemas-microsoft-com:office:office"
  xmlns:x="urn:schemas-microsoft-com:office:excel"
  xmlns:html="http://www.w3.org/TR/REC-html40"
 >
<xsl:output method="xml" omit-xml-declaration="no" indent="yes" encoding="US-
   ASCII"/>
<xsl:template match="d:dinosaurs">
<xsl:processing-instruction name="mso-application">progid=
   "Excel.Sheet"</xsl:processing-instruction>
<Workbook>
<!--Namespace declarations moved from Workbook to xsl:stylesheet-->
 <Styles>
  <Style ss:ID="Default" ss:Name="Normal">
   <Alignment ss:Vertical="Bottom"/>
   <Borders/>
   <Font/>
   <Interior/>
   <NumberFormat/>
   <Protection/>
  </Style>
  <Style ss:ID="s21">
   <NumberFormat ss:Format="mmm\-yy"/>
  </Style>
  <Style ss:ID="s22">
   <NumberFormat ss:Format="&quot;$&quot;#,##0.00"/>
  </Style>
 </Styles>
 <Worksheet ss:Name="Sheet1">
  <Table ss:ExpandedColumnCount="5" ss:ExpandedRowCount="{count(d:sale)+4}"
      x:FullColumns="1"
      x:FullRows="1">
   <Column ss:AutoFitWidth="0" ss:Width="73.5"/>
   <Column ss:AutoFitWidth="0" ss:Width="96.75"/>
   <Column ss:Index="5" ss:AutoFitWidth="0" ss:Width="56.25"/>
   <Row>
    <Cell><Data ss:Type="String">Sales for:</Data></Cell>
    <Cell ss:StyleID="s21"><Data ss:Type="DateTime"><xsl:value-of
       select="d:date"/></Data></Cell>
   </Row>
   <Row ss:Index="3">
    <Cell><Data ss:Type="String">ID Number</Data></Cell>
    <Cell><Data ss:Type="String">Critter</Data></Cell>
    <Cell><Data ss:Type="String">Price</Data></Cell>
    <Cell><Data ss:Type="String">Quantity</Data></Cell>
    <Cell><Data ss:Type="String">Total</Data></Cell>
   </Row>
<xsl:apply-templates select="d:sale" />
   <Row>
    <Cell ss:Index="4"><Data ss:Type="String">Total:</Data></Cell>
    <Cell ss:StyleID="s22" ss:Formula="=SUM(R[-{count(d:sale)}]C:R[-1]C)">
       <Data ss:Type="Number"></Data></Cell>
   </Row>
```

Example 7-10. A stylesheet for generating SpreadsheetML (continued)

```
  </Table>
  <WorksheetOptions xmlns="urn:schemas-microsoft-com:office:excel">
   <Print>
    <ValidPrinterInfo/>
    <HorizontalResolution>600</HorizontalResolution>
    <VerticalResolution>600</VerticalResolution>
   </Print>
   <Selected/>
   <Panes>
    <Pane>
     <Number>3</Number>
     <ActiveRow>12</ActiveRow>
     <ActiveCol>1</ActiveCol>
    </Pane>
   </Panes>
   <ProtectObjects>False</ProtectObjects>
   <ProtectScenarios>False</ProtectScenarios>
  </WorksheetOptions>
 </Worksheet>
 <Worksheet ss:Name="Sheet2">
  <WorksheetOptions xmlns="urn:schemas-microsoft-com:office:excel">
   <ProtectObjects>False</ProtectObjects>
   <ProtectScenarios>False</ProtectScenarios>
  </WorksheetOptions>
 </Worksheet>
 <Worksheet ss:Name="Sheet3">
  <WorksheetOptions xmlns="urn:schemas-microsoft-com:office:excel">
   <ProtectObjects>False</ProtectObjects>
   <ProtectScenarios>False</ProtectScenarios>
  </WorksheetOptions>
 </Worksheet>
</Workbook>
</xsl:template>
<xsl:template match="d:sale">
   <Row>
    <Cell><Data ss:Type="Number"><xsl:value-of
       select="d:IDnum" /></Data><NamedCell ss:Name="ID"/></Cell>
    <Cell><Data ss:Type="String"><xsl:value-of select="d:critter" /></Data><NamedCell ss:
Name="Critters"/></Cell>
    <Cell ss:StyleID="s22"><Data ss:Type="Number"><xsl:value-of
       select="d:price" /></Data><NamedCell
      ss:Name="Price"/></Cell>
    <Cell><Data ss:Type="Number"><xsl:value-of select="d:quantity" /></Data>
       <NamedCell ss:Name="Quantity"/></Cell>
    <Cell ss:StyleID="s22" ss:Formula="=RC[-2]*RC[-1]"><Data ss:Type="Number">
       <xsl:value-of select="d:total" /></Data></Cell>
   </Row>
</xsl:template>
<xsl:template match="d:date" />
<xsl:template match="d:total" />
</xsl:stylesheet>
```

There are a few pieces of this worth special attention. First, note that the Spread-sheetML is wrapped in XSLT; the SpreadsheetML becomes part of the stylesheet. There's one extra namespace declaration:

```
xmlns:d="http://simonstl.com/ns/dinosaurs/"
```

XSLT requires that references to parts of XML documents that have namespace URIs also have namespace prefixes. As a result, all references in the stylesheet to elements in the original document will look like d:sale instead of just sale.

There's also one piece of the SpreadsheetML we need to recreate explicitly, and not just by including it in the document: the processing instruction noted earlier that tells Windows this is an Excel spreadsheet. For that, we have to use:

```
<xsl:processing-instruction name="mso-application">progid=
  "Excel.Sheet"</xsl:processing-instruction>
```

Because the named ranges will vary depending on the number of sale elements in the original, this stylesheet won't generate the Names element and its contents. Excel will recreate the named ranges from the NamedCell elements in any case.

This stylesheet creates a Table element complete with (accurate) ss:ExpandedColumnCount and ss:ExpandedRowCount attributes.

```
<Table ss:ExpandedColumnCount="5" ss:ExpandedRowCount="{count(d:sale)+4}"
    x:FullColumns="1"  x:FullRows="1">
```

If calculating the number of rows or columns in your spreadsheet is going to be diffi-cult, it will be better to leave off this information, as it produces an error if wrong but little benefit if right.

The first row of the spreadsheet contains the date:

```
<Row>
  <Cell><Data ss:Type="String">Sales for:</Data></Cell>
  <Cell ss:StyleID="s21"><Data ss:Type="DateTime"><xsl:value-of select="d:date"/></
Data></Cell>
  </Row>
```

The xsl:value-of element pulls the information from the date element of the XML document and puts its value into the Data element. As we'll see at the end of the spreadsheet, regular processing of the date element (and the total element, which is handled similarly) will have to be suppressed.

The heart of this stylesheet is again the part that generates the Row and Cell ele-ments, like:

```
<xsl:template match="d:sale">
  <Row>
    <Cell><Data ss:Type="Number"><xsl:value-of select="d:IDnum" /></Data><NamedCell
ss:Name="ID"/></Cell>
```

The xsl:template element will collect every sale element in the original and produce a Row element which itself contains Cell elements matching its contents. Each Row contains the contents of one sale element. To keep XSLT from applying its default templates to the date and total elements, which would drop their values into the SpreadsheetML as (unexpected) text, the last code snippet explicitly specifies no processing for them with empty xsl:template elements.

```
<xsl:template match="d:date" />
<xsl:template match="d:total" />
```

The SpreadsheetML created by this stylesheet from the XML data in Example 7-8 looks like Example 7-11.

Example 7-11. A SpreadsheetML document created with XSLT

```
<?xml version="1.0"?>
<?mso-application progid="Excel.Sheet"?>
<Workbook xmlns="urn:schemas-microsoft-com:office:spreadsheet"
 xmlns:o="urn:schemas-microsoft-com:office:office"
 xmlns:x="urn:schemas-microsoft-com:office:excel"
 xmlns:ss="urn:schemas-microsoft-com:office:spreadsheet"
 xmlns:html="http://www.w3.org/TR/REC-html40"
 xmlns:d="http://simonstl.com/ns/dinosaurs/">
<Styles>
 <Style ss:ID="Default" ss:Name="Normal">
  <Alignment ss:Vertical="Bottom"/>
  <Borders/>
  <Font/>
  <Interior/>
  <NumberFormat/>
  <Protection/>
 </Style>
 <Style ss:ID="s21">
  <NumberFormat ss:Format="mmm\-yy"/>
 </Style>
 <Style ss:ID="s22">
  <NumberFormat ss:Format="&quot;$&quot;#,##0.00"/>
 </Style>
</Styles>
<Worksheet ss:Name="Sheet1">
 <Table ss:ExpandedColumnCount="5" ss:ExpandedRowCount="12" x:FullColumns="1"
  x:FullRows="1">
  <Column ss:AutoFitWidth="0" ss:Width="73.5"/>
  <Column ss:AutoFitWidth="0" ss:Width="96.75"/>
  <Column ss:Index="5" ss:AutoFitWidth="0" ss:Width="56.25"/>
  <Row>
   <Cell><Data ss:Type="String">Sales for:</Data></Cell>
   <Cell ss:StyleID="s21"><Data ss:Type="DateTime">2004-01-01T00:00:00.000</Data></Cell>
  </Row>
  <Row ss:Index="3">
   <Cell><Data ss:Type="String">ID Number</Data></Cell>
   <Cell><Data ss:Type="String">Critter</Data></Cell>
   <Cell><Data ss:Type="String">Price</Data></Cell>
   <Cell><Data ss:Type="String">Quantity</Data></Cell>
   <Cell><Data ss:Type="String">Total</Data></Cell>
```

Example 7-11. A SpreadsheetML document created with XSLT (continued)

```
 </Row>
 <Row>
  <Cell><Data ss:Type="Number">4627</Data><NamedCell ss:Name="ID"/></Cell>
  <Cell><Data ss:Type="String">Diplodocus</Data><NamedCell ss:Name="Critters"/>
    </Cell>
  <Cell ss:StyleID="s22"><Data ss:Type="Number">22.5</Data><NamedCell
    ss:Name="Price"/></Cell>
  <Cell><Data ss:Type="Number">127</Data><NamedCell ss:Name="Quantity"/></Cell>
  <Cell ss:StyleID="s22" ss:Formula="=RC[-2]*RC[-1]"><Data ss:Type="Number">
    2857.5</Data></Cell>
 </Row>
 <Row>
  <Cell><Data ss:Type="Number">3912</Data><NamedCell ss:Name="ID"/></Cell>
  <Cell><Data ss:Type="String">Brontosaurus</Data>
    <NamedCell ss:Name="Critters"/></Cell>
  <Cell ss:StyleID="s22"><Data ss:Type="Number">17.5</Data><NamedCell
    ss:Name="Price"/></Cell>
  <Cell><Data ss:Type="Number">74</Data><NamedCell ss:Name="Quantity"/></Cell>
  <Cell ss:StyleID="s22" ss:Formula="=RC[-2]*RC[-1]"><Data ss:Type="Number">
    1295</Data></Cell>
 </Row>
 <Row>
  <Cell><Data ss:Type="Number">9845</Data><NamedCell ss:Name="ID"/></Cell>
  <Cell><Data ss:Type="String">Triceratops</Data>
    <NamedCell ss:Name="Critters"/></Cell>
  <Cell ss:StyleID="s22"><Data ss:Type="Number">12</Data>
    <NamedCell
    ss:Name="Price"/></Cell>
  <Cell><Data ss:Type="Number">91</Data><NamedCell ss:Name="Quantity"/></Cell>
  <Cell ss:StyleID="s22" ss:Formula="=RC[-2]*RC[-1]"><Data ss:Type="Number">
    1092</Data></Cell>
 </Row>
 <Row>
  <Cell><Data ss:Type="Number">9625</Data><NamedCell ss:Name="ID"/></Cell>
  <Cell><Data ss:Type="String">Vulcanodon</Data>
    <NamedCell ss:Name="Critters"/></Cell>
  <Cell ss:StyleID="s22"><Data ss:Type="Number">19</Data><NamedCell
    ss:Name="Price"/></Cell>
  <Cell><Data ss:Type="Number">108</Data><NamedCell ss:Name="Quantity"/></Cell>
  <Cell ss:StyleID="s22" ss:Formula="=RC[-2]*RC[-1]"><Data ss:Type="Number">
    2052</Data></Cell>
 </Row>
 <Row>
  <Cell><Data ss:Type="Number">5903</Data><NamedCell ss:Name="ID"/></Cell>
  <Cell><Data ss:Type="String">Stegosaurus</Data>
    <NamedCell ss:Name="Critters"/></Cell>
  <Cell ss:StyleID="s22"><Data ss:Type="Number">18.5</Data><NamedCell
    ss:Name="Price"/></Cell>
  <Cell><Data ss:Type="Number">63</Data><NamedCell ss:Name="Quantity"/></Cell>
  <Cell ss:StyleID="s22" ss:Formula="=RC[-2]*RC[-1]"><Data ss:Type="Number">
    1165.5</Data></Cell>
 </Row>
```

Example 7-11. A SpreadsheetML document created with XSLT (continued)

```xml
<Row>
 <Cell><Data ss:Type="Number">1824</Data><NamedCell ss:Name="ID"/></Cell>
 <Cell><Data ss:Type="String">Monoclonius</Data>
    <NamedCell ss:Name="Critters"/></Cell>
 <Cell ss:StyleID="s22"><Data ss:Type="Number">16.5</Data><NamedCell
    ss:Name="Price"/></Cell>
 <Cell><Data ss:Type="Number">133</Data><NamedCell ss:Name="Quantity"/></Cell>
 <Cell ss:StyleID="s22" ss:Formula="=RC[-2]*RC[-1]"><Data ss:Type="Number">
    2194.5</Data></Cell>
</Row>
<Row>
 <Cell><Data ss:Type="Number">9728</Data><NamedCell ss:Name="ID"/></Cell>
 <Cell><Data ss:Type="String">Megalosaurus</Data>
    <NamedCell ss:Name="Critters"/></Cell>
 <Cell ss:StyleID="s22"><Data ss:Type="Number">23</Data><NamedCell
    ss:Name="Price"/></Cell>
 <Cell><Data ss:Type="Number">128</Data><NamedCell ss:Name="Quantity"/></Cell>
 <Cell ss:StyleID="s22" ss:Formula="=RC[-2]*RC[-1]"><Data ss:Type="Number">
    2944</Data></Cell>
</Row>
<Row>
 <Cell><Data ss:Type="Number">8649</Data><NamedCell ss:Name="ID"/></Cell>
 <Cell><Data ss:Type="String">Barosaurus</Data>
    <NamedCell ss:Name="Critters"/></Cell>
 <Cell ss:StyleID="s22"><Data ss:Type="Number">17</Data><NamedCell
    ss:Name="Price"/></Cell>
 <Cell><Data ss:Type="Number">91</Data><NamedCell ss:Name="Quantity"/></Cell>
 <Cell ss:StyleID="s22" ss:Formula="=RC[-2]*RC[-1]"><Data ss:Type="Number">
    1547</Data></Cell>
</Row>
<Row>
 <Cell ss:Index="4"><Data ss:Type="String">Total:</Data></Cell>
 <Cell ss:StyleID="s22" ss:Formula="=SUM(R[-8]C:R[-1]C)">
    <Data ss:Type="Number">15147.5</Data></Cell>
</Row>
</Table>
<WorksheetOptions xmlns="urn:schemas-microsoft-com:office:excel">
 <Print>
  <ValidPrinterInfo/>
  <HorizontalResolution>600</HorizontalResolution>
  <VerticalResolution>600</VerticalResolution>
 </Print>
 <Selected/>
 <Panes>
  <Pane>
   <Number>3</Number>
   <ActiveRow>12</ActiveRow>
   <ActiveCol>1</ActiveCol>
  </Pane>
 </Panes>
 <ProtectObjects>False</ProtectObjects>
 <ProtectScenarios>False</ProtectScenarios>
```

Example 7-11. A SpreadsheetML document created with XSLT (continued)

```
    </WorksheetOptions>
  </Worksheet>
  <Worksheet ss:Name="Sheet2">
   <WorksheetOptions xmlns="urn:schemas-microsoft-com:office:excel">
    <ProtectObjects>False</ProtectObjects>
    <ProtectScenarios>False</ProtectScenarios>
   </WorksheetOptions>
  </Worksheet>
  <Worksheet ss:Name="Sheet3">
   <WorksheetOptions xmlns="urn:schemas-microsoft-com:office:excel">
    <ProtectObjects>False</ProtectObjects>
    <ProtectScenarios>False</ProtectScenarios>
   </WorksheetOptions>
  </Worksheet>
</Workbook>
```

If you open the SpreadsheetML this stylesheet produces (which looks much like that in Example 7-2, minus some named ranges, metadata, and formatting) in Excel, we get the result shown in Figure 7-8.

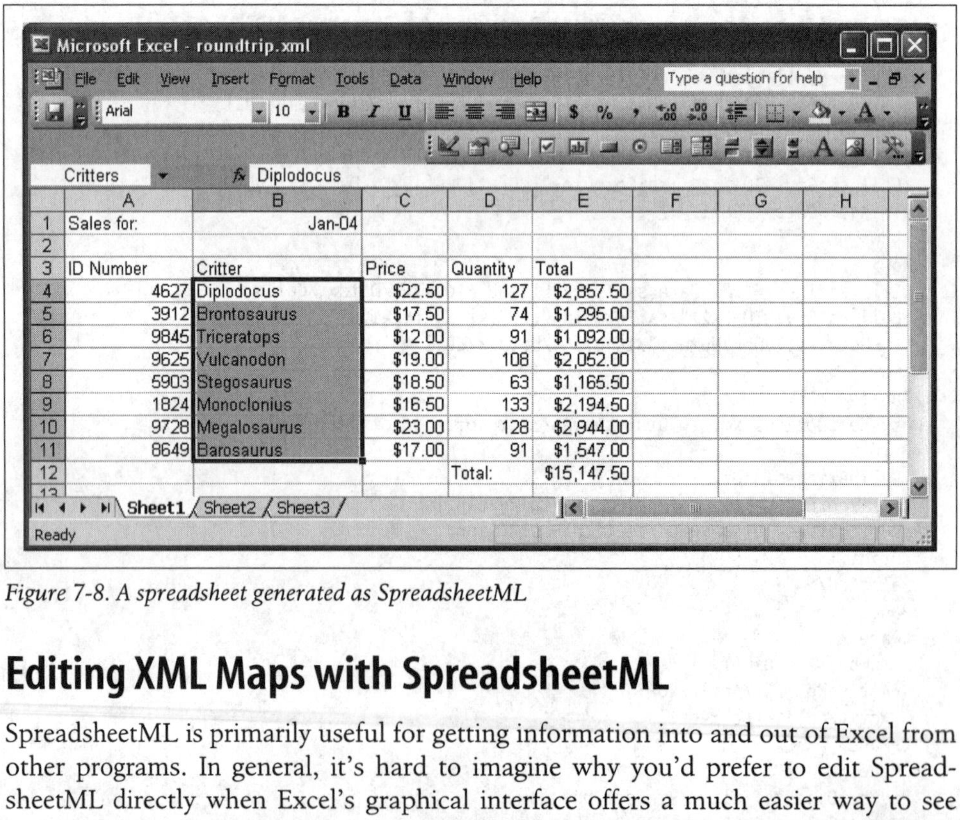

Figure 7-8. A spreadsheet generated as SpreadsheetML

Editing XML Maps with SpreadsheetML

SpreadsheetML is primarily useful for getting information into and out of Excel from other programs. In general, it's hard to imagine why you'd prefer to edit SpreadsheetML directly when Excel's graphical interface offers a much easier way to see and edit your information. There is, however, one case where Excel doesn't provide a graphical interface, and the SpreadsheetML provides a useful way to edit information that isn't otherwise accessible. Figure 7-9 shows a spreadsheet from Chapter 6 that uses an XML Map.

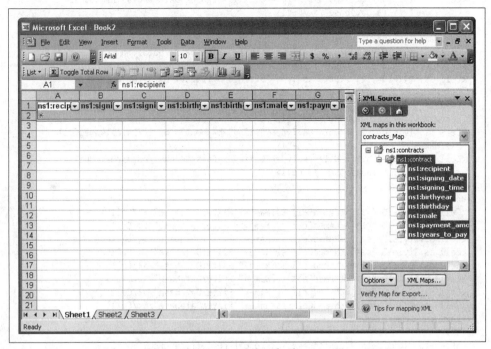

Figure 7-9. A spreadsheet using an XML Map, previously shown in Figure 6-25

Example 7-12 shows a portion of the SpreadsheetML that is produced when you save the spreadsheet itself as SpreadsheetML.

Example 7-12. Part of the SpreadsheetML for a spreadsheet containing an XML Map

```
<Worksheet ss:Name="Sheet1">
 <Names>
  <NamedRange ss:Name="_FilterDatabase" ss:RefersTo="=Sheet1!R1C1:R2C8"
   ss:Hidden="1"/>
 </Names>
 <Table ss:ExpandedColumnCount="8" ss:ExpandedRowCount="2" x:FullColumns="1"
  x:FullRows="1">
  <Column ss:AutoFitWidth="0" ss:Width="79.5"/>
  <Column ss:AutoFitWidth="0" ss:Width="75"/>
  <Column ss:AutoFitWidth="0" ss:Width="78"/>
  <Column ss:AutoFitWidth="0" ss:Width="58.5"/>
  <Column ss:AutoFitWidth="0" ss:Width="55.5"/>
  <Column ss:AutoFitWidth="0" ss:Width="38.25"/>
  <Column ss:AutoFitWidth="0" ss:Width="99.75"/>
  <Column ss:AutoFitWidth="0" ss:Width="78.75"/>
  <Row>
```

Example 7-12. Part of the SpreadsheetML for a spreadsheet containing an XML Map (continued)

```
    <Cell ss:StyleID="s21"><Data ss:Type="String">recipient</Data><NamedCell
      ss:Name="_FilterDatabase"/></Cell>
    <Cell ss:StyleID="s21"><Data ss:Type="String">signing_date</Data><NamedCell
      ss:Name="_FilterDatabase"/></Cell>
    <Cell ss:StyleID="s21"><Data ss:Type="String">signing_time</Data><NamedCell
      ss:Name="_FilterDatabase"/></Cell>
    <Cell ss:StyleID="s21"><Data ss:Type="String">birthyear</Data><NamedCell
      ss:Name="_FilterDatabase"/></Cell>
    <Cell ss:StyleID="s21"><Data ss:Type="String">birthday</Data><NamedCell
      ss:Name="_FilterDatabase"/></Cell>
    <Cell ss:StyleID="s21"><Data ss:Type="String">male</Data><NamedCell
      ss:Name="_FilterDatabase"/></Cell>
    <Cell ss:StyleID="s21"><Data ss:Type="String">payment_amount</Data><NamedCell
      ss:Name="_FilterDatabase"/></Cell>
    <Cell ss:StyleID="s21"><Data ss:Type="String">years_to_pay</Data><NamedCell
      ss:Name="_FilterDatabase"/></Cell>
   </Row>
   <Row>
    <Cell ss:StyleID="s22"><NamedCell ss:Name="_FilterDatabase"/></Cell>
    <Cell ss:StyleID="s23"><NamedCell ss:Name="_FilterDatabase"/></Cell>
    <Cell ss:StyleID="s24"><NamedCell ss:Name="_FilterDatabase"/></Cell>
    <Cell ss:StyleID="s25"><NamedCell ss:Name="_FilterDatabase"/></Cell>
    <Cell ss:StyleID="s26"><NamedCell ss:Name="_FilterDatabase"/></Cell>
    <Cell ss:StyleID="s27"><NamedCell ss:Name="_FilterDatabase"/></Cell>
    <Cell ss:StyleID="s27"><NamedCell ss:Name="_FilterDatabase"/></Cell>
    <Cell ss:StyleID="s27"><NamedCell ss:Name="_FilterDatabase"/></Cell>
   </Row>
  </Table>
  <WorksheetOptions xmlns="urn:schemas-microsoft-com:office:excel">
   <Selected/>
   <Panes>
    <Pane>
     <Number>3</Number>
     <ActiveRow>1</ActiveRow>
     <ActiveCol>1</ActiveCol>
    </Pane>
   </Panes>
   <ProtectObjects>False</ProtectObjects>
   <ProtectScenarios>False</ProtectScenarios>
  </WorksheetOptions>
 </Worksheet>
...
<x2:MapInfo x2:HideInactiveListBorder="false"
 x2:SelectionNamespaces="xmlns:ns1='http://simonstl.com/ns/example/contract'">
  <x2:Schema x2:ID="Schema1" x2:Namespace="http://simonstl.com/ns/example/contract"><xs:
schema xmlns:xs="http://www.w3.org/2001/XMLSchema" elementFormDefault="qualified"
targetNamespace="http://simonstl.com/ns/example/contract" xmlns:contract="http://simonstl.
com/ns/example/contract">
    <xs:element name="contracts">
        <xs:complexType>
            <xs:sequence>
                <xs:element maxOccurs="unbounded" ref="contract:contract"/>
```

```
                </xs:sequence>
            </xs:complexType>
        </xs:element>
        <xs:element name="contract">
            <xs:complexType>
                <xs:sequence>
                    <xs:element ref="contract:recipient"/>
                    <xs:element ref="contract:signing_date"/>
                    <xs:element ref="contract:signing_time"/>
                    <xs:element ref="contract:birthyear"/>
                    <xs:element ref="contract:birthday"/>
                    <xs:element ref="contract:male"/>
                    <xs:element ref="contract:payment_amount"/>
                    <xs:element ref="contract:years_to_pay"/>
                </xs:sequence>
            </xs:complexType>
        </xs:element>
        <xs:element name="recipient" type="xs:string"/>
        <xs:element name="signing_date" type="xs:date"/>
        <xs:element name="signing_time" type="xs:time"/>
        <xs:element name="birthyear" type="xs:gYear"/>
        <xs:element name="birthday" type="xs:gMonthDay"/>
        <xs:element name="male" type="xs:boolean"/>
        <xs:element name="payment_amount" type="xs:decimal"/>
        <xs:element name="years_to_pay" type="xs:integer"/>
</xs:schema>
    </x2:Schema>
    <x2:Map x2:ID="contracts_Map" x2:SchemaID="Schema1" x2:RootElement="contracts">
     <x2:Entry x2:Type="table" x2:ID="2" x2:ShowTotals="false">
      <x2:Range>Sheet1!R2C1</x2:Range>
      <x2:HeaderRange>R1C1</x2:HeaderRange>
      <x:FilterOn>True</x:FilterOn>
      <x2:XPath>/ns1:contracts/ns1:contract</x2:XPath>
      <x2:Field x2:ID="recipient">
       <x2:Range>RC</x2:Range>
       <x2:XPath>ns1:recipient</x2:XPath>
       <x2:XSDType>string</x2:XSDType>
       <ss:Cell>
       </ss:Cell>
       <x2:Aggregate>None</x2:Aggregate>
      </x2:Field>
      <x2:Field x2:ID="signing_date">
       <x2:Range>RC[1]</x2:Range>
       <x2:XPath>ns1:signing_date</x2:XPath>
       <x2:XSDType>date</x2:XSDType>
       <ss:Cell>
       </ss:Cell>
       <x2:Aggregate>None</x2:Aggregate>
      </x2:Field>
      <x2:Field x2:ID="signing_time">
       <x2:Range>RC[2]</x2:Range>
       <x2:XPath>ns1:signing_time</x2:XPath>
```

```
        <x2:XSDType>time</x2:XSDType>
        <ss:Cell>
        </ss:Cell>
        <x2:Aggregate>None</x2:Aggregate>
      </x2:Field>
      <x2:Field x2:ID="birthyear">
      <x2:Range>RC[3]</x2:Range>
      <x2:XPath>ns1:birthyear</x2:XPath>
      <x2:XSDType>gYear</x2:XSDType>
      <ss:Cell>
      </ss:Cell>
      <x2:Aggregate>None</x2:Aggregate>
      </x2:Field>
      <x2:Field x2:ID="birthday">
      <x2:Range>RC[4]</x2:Range>
      <x2:XPath>ns1:birthday</x2:XPath>
      <x2:XSDType>gMonthDay</x2:XSDType>
      <ss:Cell>
      </ss:Cell>
      <x2:Aggregate>None</x2:Aggregate>
      </x2:Field>
      <x2:Field x2:ID="male">
      <x2:Range>RC[5]</x2:Range>
      <x2:XPath>ns1:male</x2:XPath>
      <x2:XSDType>boolean</x2:XSDType>
      <ss:Cell>
      </ss:Cell>
      <x2:Aggregate>None</x2:Aggregate>
      </x2:Field>
      <x2:Field x2:ID="payment_amount">
      <x2:Range>RC[6]</x2:Range>
      <x2:XPath>ns1:payment_amount</x2:XPath>
      <x2:XSDType>decimal</x2:XSDType>
      <ss:Cell>
      </ss:Cell>
      <x2:Aggregate>None</x2:Aggregate>
      </x2:Field>
      <x2:Field x2:ID="years_to_pay">
      <x2:Range>RC[7]</x2:Range>
      <x2:XPath>ns1:years_to_pay</x2:XPath>
      <x2:XSDType>integer</x2:XSDType>
      <ss:Cell>
      </ss:Cell>
      <x2:Aggregate>None</x2:Aggregate>
      </x2:Field>
    </x2:Entry>
   </x2:Map>
  </x2:MapInfo>
</Workbook>
```

There are several types of information relating to the XML map here. The Worksheet element's Table contains the rows and cells that hold the actual data, with headers and style information, as well as a range named _FilterData. That really just reflects choices that can be made (and unmade) through the GUI.

The information in the x2:MapInfo element, which comes after all the Worksheet elements, however, is information that is created when you import an XML document or XSD schema. The only way to modify this information through Excel is to delete it. If, however, you just want to tweak something in the schema—perhaps Excel guessed that a given field in an XML document was a number rather than text or vice-versa—you can save the spreadsheet as SpreadsheetML, make the changes to the x2:MapInfo element's contents, and re-open it in Excel.

 Remember that SpreadsheetML doesn't represent everything in an Excel document. If the spreadsheet whose map you want to alter already contains VBA, Charts, or other features that SpreadsheetML doesn't capture, be certain to have them backed up and be prepared for some cutting from the original spreadsheet and pasting into the new.

Editing the schema in the x2:Schema element works fine, so long as you produce a valid schema that conforms to Excel's limited understanding of XSD. You'll need to manually ensure that the x2:Field elements still correspond to the contents of that schema; if you change a type in the schema, be sure to change it in the x2:XSDType element of the corresponding x2:Field element. You can also make changes to the x2:XPath element, if you need to change the location in the document from which Excel retrieves the field's contents, typically if you add or remove a container element from the XML document structure.

This kind of editing is definitely at your own risk, and likely best restricted to relatively small changes, but it does provide a useful set of tools that aren't (yet) in Excel itself.

CHAPTER 8

Importing and Exporting XML with Microsoft Access

Relational databases and XML aren't always the best of friends. XML documents store information in hierarchies, while relational databases store information in linked tables. XML document structures are typically much more open than relational databases, which focus on regularity for better performance. Because of these differences, it doesn't make sense to rebuild Microsoft Access as an XML application. Instead, Access uses XML as a means of communicating with the outside world, capable of representing the information it stores as XML and also able to accept new or changed information through XML messages. Add in a little XSLT, and you have a whole new interface for connecting Access to different applications.

 The XML features in Access are available in every copy of Office 2003; there's no Standard/Professional/Enterprise distinction for you to worry about.

Access XML Expectations

Unlike most of the other Office applications, Access doesn't really have a custom vocabulary, though it adds a few Office-specific pieces to things like the XML Schemas it generates. The vocabulary that Access speaks "natively" is largely determined by the structures of your database, particularly the names of tables and the fields they contain. If you've named your tables and your fields well, you may be pleasantly surprised to find that Access produces some very readable XML. If not, you can't blame Microsoft, but fortunately they provide XSLT facilities for improving your results in such cases.

While Microsoft doesn't provide an Access-specific vocabulary, Access definitely has expectations about the structures of incoming and outgoing XML. The basic structures are very simple, though cases like multi-table export can require more interpretation. The easiest way to learn about the expectations Access has for incoming data is to start with sample information inside the database, and then export it. Close analysis of the exported material should tell you what Access will want for an import.

Generally speaking, XML structures offer a range of structural possibilities that don't map easily to relational database tables. XML doesn't typically worry about things like primary keys and foreign keys, nor are its structures defined as relations between tables. Access does very well at working with a subset of XML structures that is (or can be made to be) relational-database friendly, but there are some natural limitations, as well as fields of work where other pieces of the Office suite are more appropriate tools.

 For a wealth of information about XML and databases, including information about mapping between XML and relational databases, see *http://rpbourret.com/xml/index.htm*.

Exporting XML from Access Using the GUI

Exporting XML from Access is much like exporting any other format from Access, though with a few extra pieces. There are a number of possible variations in the export process, depending on whether you need to export a single table, a linked group of tables, or a query.

Exporting a Single Table

For our initial example, we'll start with a database containing a table that defines a list of books. The design view for that table is shown in Figure 8-1. It includes six fields of three different types.

For the initial tests, there's just a little bit of information in this table. Exporting mature tables with thousands of records can produce large XML files very quickly—definitely useful in real life but difficult for initial analysis. Figure 8-2 shows a partial view of the content in the test table.

Exporting this table to XML involves a few steps, most of which will be familiar to developers who have exported information from Access databases before. The process starts by selecting the books table in the database, then selecting Export… from the File menu. The dialog box shown in Figure 8-3 will appear, and you'll need to select "XML (*.xml)" from the "Save as type" drop-down box.

When you perform the export, Access may actually create more files than just the XML file, but they'll all appear in the same directory with the XML. Once you click the Export button, a small dialog box with basic options, shown in Figure 8-4, will appear.

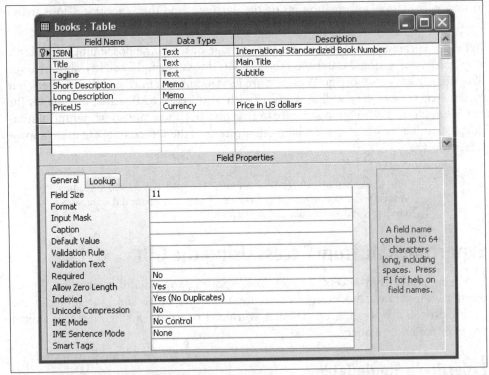

Figure 8-1. A simple table for export

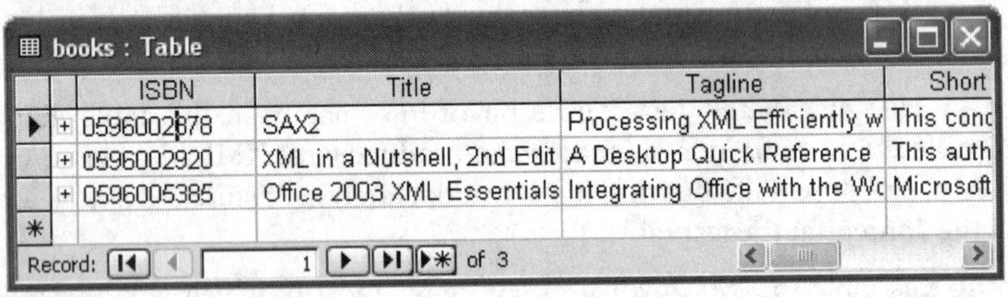

Figure 8-2. Test data in the books table

For now, we'll accept the defaults and just hit OK. The result will be two files, *books.xml* and *books.xsd*. The *books.xml* file will contain the information from the table, while *books.xsd* will contain an XML Schema description of that content, annotated with a bit of information specific to Access and its Jet database engine.

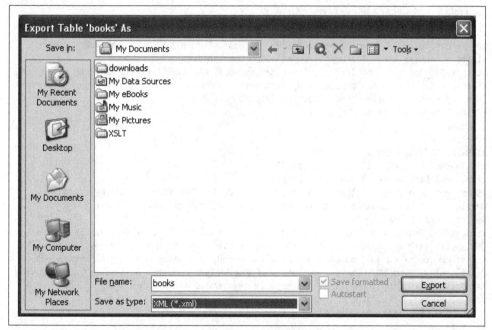

Figure 8-3. Selecting the destination for the export

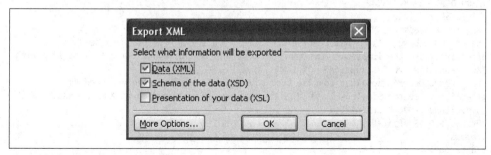

Figure 8-4. Basic export options

The *books.xml* file, shown in Example 8-1, reflects the structure and content of the original table closely.

Example 8-1. A simple table export

```
<?xml version="1.0" encoding="UTF-8"?>
<dataroot xmlns:od="urn:schemas-microsoft-com:officedata" xmlns:xsi="http://www.w3.org/
2001/XMLSchema-instance"  xsi:noNamespaceSchemaLocation="books.xsd" generated="2003-03-
26T13:49:17">
<books>
<ISBN>0596005385</ISBN>
<Title>Office 2003 XML Essentials</Title>
<Tagline>Integrating Office with the World</Tagline>
```

Example 8-1. A simple table export (continued)

```
<Short_x0020_Description>Microsoft has added enormous XML functionality to Word, Excel,
and Access, as well as a new application, Microsoft InfoPath.  This book gets readers
started in using those features.</Short_x0020_Description>
<Long_x0020_Description>Microsoft has added enormous XML functionality to Word, Excel, and
Access, as well as a new application, Microsoft InfoPath.  This book gets readers started
in using those features.</Long_x0020_Description>
<PriceUS>34.95</PriceUS>
</books>
<books>
<ISBN>0596002920</ISBN>
<Title>XML in a Nutshell, 2nd Edition</Title>
<Tagline>A Desktop Quick Reference</Tagline>
<Short_x0020_Description>This authoritative new edition of XML in a Nutshell provides
developers with a complete guide to the rapidly evolving XML space.</Short_x0020_
Description>
<Long_x0020_Description>This authoritative new edition of XML in a Nutshell provides
developers with a complete guide to the rapidly evolving XML space.  Serious users of XML
will find topics on just about everything they need, including fundamental syntax rules,
details of DTD and XML Schema creation, XSLT transformations, and APIs used for processing
XML documents.  Simply put, this is the only references of its kind among XML books.</
Long_x0020_Description>
<PriceUS>39.95</PriceUS>
</books>
<books>
<ISBN>0596002378</ISBN>
<Title>SAX2</Title>
<Tagline>Processing XML Efficiently with Java</Tagline>
<Short_x0020_Description>This concise book gives you the information you need to
effectively use the Simple API for XML, the dominant API for efficient XML processing with
Java.</Short_x0020_Description>
<Long_x0020_Description>This concise book gives you the information you need to
effectively use the Simple API for XML, the dominant API for efficient XML processing with
Java.</Long_x0020_Description>
<PriceUS>29.95</PriceUS>
</books>
</dataroot>
```

The root element of this document, dataroot, is the only piece of this document specific to Access:

```
<dataroot xmlns:od="urn:schemas-microsoft-com:officedata" xmlns:xsi="http://www.w3.
org/2001/XMLSchema-instance"  xsi:noNamespaceSchemaLocation="books.xsd"
generated="2003-03-26T13:49:17">
```

It makes a namespace declaration for the od prefix, which is not actually used in this document, and it also includes a pointer to the XML Schema describing this document's structure. Because the element names used here are not in any namespace, the document uses the xsi:noNamespaceSchemaLocation attribute to identify the schema that should be used for all of the elements in this document that have no namespace. It also includes one small bit of metadata in the generated attribute, identifying the time and date when this XML document was created.

The dataroot element contains three child books elements, each indicating a row in the books table. Their contents map fairly simply to the names and values of the table columns:

```
<books>
<ISBN>0596002920</ISBN>
<Title>XML in a Nutshell, 2nd Edition</Title>
<Tagline>A Desktop Quick Reference</Tagline>
<Short_x0020_Description>This authoritative new edition of XML in a Nutshell provides
developers with a complete guide to the rapidly evolving XML space.</Short_x0020_
Description>
<Long_x0020_Description>This authoritative new edition of XML in a Nutshell provides
developers with a complete guide to the rapidly evolving XML space.  Serious users of
XML will find topics on just about everything they need, including fundamental syntax
rules, details of DTD and XML Schema creation, XSLT transformations, and APIs used
for processing XML documents.  Simply put, this is the only references of its kind
among XML books.</Long_x0020_Description>
<PriceUS>39.95</PriceUS>
</books>
```

The only significant variation here involves the column names which included spaces. Instead of Short Description, we now have Short_x0020_Description, following a convention Microsoft has developed for representing spaces in XML element names. (XML forbids spaces in element names, as they make it difficult to separate the element name from the attributes, so Access uses _x0020_, the Unicode hex number for the space.)

The XML itself is pretty simple, and provides relatively little information about many of the things Access considers important, like datatype, length, and all the details you can set in the Design view for tables. That information is kept in the XML Schema, shown in Example 8-2.

Example 8-2. The schema Access created to describe its XML output

```
<?xml version="1.0" encoding="UTF-8"?>
<xsd:schema xmlns:xsd="http://www.w3.org/2001/XMLSchema" xmlns:od="urn:schemas-microsoft-
com:officedata">
<xsd:element name="dataroot">
<xsd:complexType>
<xsd:sequence>
<xsd:element ref="books" minOccurs="0" maxOccurs="unbounded"/>
</xsd:sequence>
<xsd:attribute name="generated" type="xsd:dateTime"/>
</xsd:complexType>
</xsd:element>
<xsd:element name="books">
<xsd:annotation>
<xsd:appinfo>
```

```
<od:index index-name="PrimaryKey" index-key="ISBN " primary="yes" unique="yes"
clustered="no"/>
</xsd:appinfo>
</xsd:annotation>
<xsd:complexType>
<xsd:sequence>
<xsd:element name="ISBN" minOccurs="0" od:jetType="text" od:sqlSType="nvarchar">
<xsd:simpleType>
<xsd:restriction base="xsd:string">
<xsd:maxLength value="11"/>
</xsd:restriction>
</xsd:simpleType>
</xsd:element>
<xsd:element name="Title" minOccurs="0" od:jetType="text" od:sqlSType="nvarchar">
<xsd:simpleType>
<xsd:restriction base="xsd:string">
<xsd:maxLength value="50"/>
</xsd:restriction>
</xsd:simpleType>
</xsd:element>
<xsd:element name="Tagline" minOccurs="0" od:jetType="text" od:sqlSType="nvarchar">
<xsd:simpleType>
<xsd:restriction base="xsd:string">
<xsd:maxLength value="100"/>
</xsd:restriction>
</xsd:simpleType>
</xsd:element>
<xsd:element name="Short_x0020_Description" minOccurs="0" od:jetType="memo" od:
sqlSType="ntext">
<xsd:simpleType>
<xsd:restriction base="xsd:string">
<xsd:maxLength value="536870910"/>
</xsd:restriction>
</xsd:simpleType>
</xsd:element>
<xsd:element name="Long_x0020_Description" minOccurs="0" od:jetType="memo" od:
sqlSType="ntext">
<xsd:simpleType>
<xsd:restriction base="xsd:string">
<xsd:maxLength value="536870910"/>
</xsd:restriction>
</xsd:simpleType>
</xsd:element>
<xsd:element name="PriceUS" minOccurs="0" od:jetType="currency" od:sqlSType="money"
type="xsd:double"/>
</xsd:sequence>
</xsd:complexType>
</xsd:element>
</xsd:schema>
```

The xsd:schema element includes the namespace for XSD itself as well as a namespace declaration for the additional Access-specific information that is used in the schema:

```
<xsd:schema xmlns:xsd="http://www.w3.org/2001/XMLSchema" xmlns:od="urn:schemas-
microsoft-com:officedata">
```

The next item is the declaration for the dataroot element. While Access always uses a dataroot element for its exports, the contents of that dataroot element vary from export to export. In this particular case, the dataroot element may contain zero or more books elements, as well as a dateTime attribute called generated:

```
<xsd:element name="dataroot">
<xsd:complexType>
<xsd:sequence>
<xsd:element ref="books" minOccurs="0" maxOccurs="unbounded"/>
</xsd:sequence>
<xsd:attribute name="generated" type="xsd:dateTime"/>
</xsd:complexType>
</xsd:element>
```

The remainder of the schema is the declaration for the books element, which itself contains the declarations for all of its child elements. (This style of schema is frequently referred to as "Russian doll," after the nesting wooden dolls, and works well for simple structures like those created here.) The declaration begins with an annotation used by Access to identify the primary key of the table:

```
<xsd:element name="books">
<xsd:annotation>
<xsd:appinfo>
<od:index index-name="PrimaryKey" index-key="ISBN " primary="yes" unique="yes"
clustered="no"/>
</xsd:appinfo>
</xsd:annotation>
```

Schemas permit any kind of markup in the xsd:appinfo element, and Microsoft has used that freedom along with an index element in its own od namespace to provide information Access can use to reconstruct the primary key.

The next element is an xsd:complexType, which contains an xsd:sequence containing the declarations for all of the child elements that appear in a books element. All of the child elements are declared using xsd:element elements that contain xsd:simpleType elements detailing the restrictions on the content of that particular component. For instance, the declaration for the ISBN element looks like:

```
<xsd:element name="ISBN" minOccurs="0" od:jetType="text" od:sqlSType="nvarchar">
<xsd:simpleType>
<xsd:restriction base="xsd:string">
<xsd:maxLength value="11"/>
</xsd:restriction>
</xsd:simpleType>
</xsd:element>
```

Most of this is basic XML Schema, saying that this is an element named ISBN, which may or may not appear, and whose contents are a string whose maximum length is eleven characters. The xsd:element itself contains two extra attributes, both of them Microsoft-specific. The first, od:jetType, identifies the type of this field in Access, while the second, od:sqlSType, identifies its type for Microsoft SQL Server.

Most of the other elements declared here follow a similar pattern with different xsd:maxLength values; those for the memo-typed values are especially large. One notably different declaration is that for the PriceUS element, which is done using attributes exclusively:

```
<xsd:element name="PriceUS" minOccurs="0" od:jetType="currency" od:sqlSType="money" type="xsd:double"/>
```

In this case, the type of xsd:double is enough to define the contents of the element—no further restrictions are needed, so no xsd:simpleType, xsd:restriction, or facet-specific elements are needed. W3C XML Schema has no notion of a currency type, so the data will be stored without a dollar sign. If you need to indicate explicitly that these are U.S. dollars, you may want to add a separate column to the table indicating the units used by the currency.

Exporting Linked Tables

Exporting individual tables is useful, but there are times when you may want to export multiple tables and preserve the relationships between them. Access allows you to export a set of tables, though it works most easily when only two tables are involved.

For our first example, we'll add a table that contains information about (very fictional) promotions for the various books. Figure 8-5 shows what this table looks like.

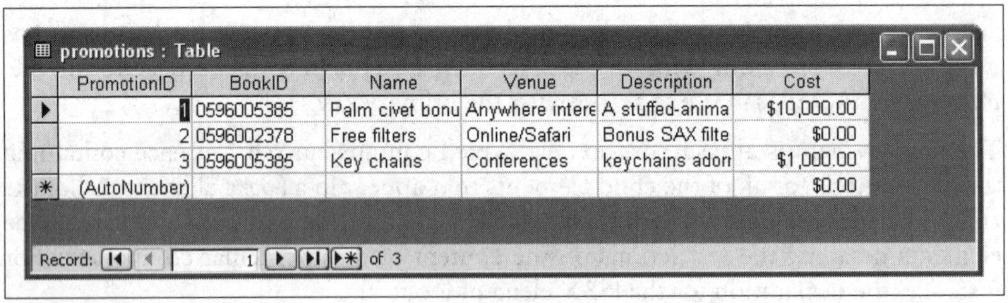

	PromotionID	BookID	Name	Venue	Description	Cost
▶	1	0596005385	Palm civet bonu	Anywhere intere	A stuffed-anima	$10,000.00
	2	0596002378	Free filters	Online/Safari	Bonus SAX filte	$0.00
	3	0596005385	Key chains	Conferences	keychains ador	$1,000.00
*	(AutoNumber)					$0.00

Figure 8-5. The promotions table

The promotions table links to the books table though its BookID field, as shown in Figure 8-6.

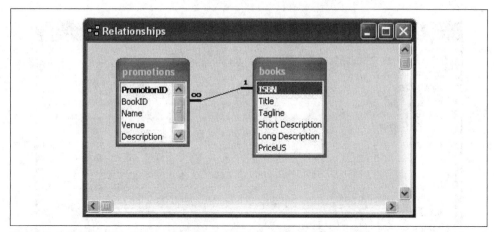

Figure 8-6. Relationships between the books and promotions tables

Exporting this pair of tables takes a few more steps, as Access lets you choose how the export works. The choice of which table is the base table makes a big difference in the results of the export, so the examples below will export it both ways. First, we'll start by exporting the books table again, but this time, we'll select More Options from the dialog box shown in Figure 8-7.

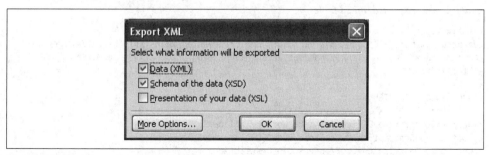

Figure 8-7. Basic export options

Clicking More Options brings up a larger dialog with many more choices, as shown in Figure 8-8.

In this case, all the information we need is on the first (Data) tab. Checking the "promotions" box and hitting the OK button tells Access to export both the books table and the linked records of the promotions table, in this case, all of them. Example 8-3 shows an abbreviated version of the export, with the new content from the promotions table in bold.

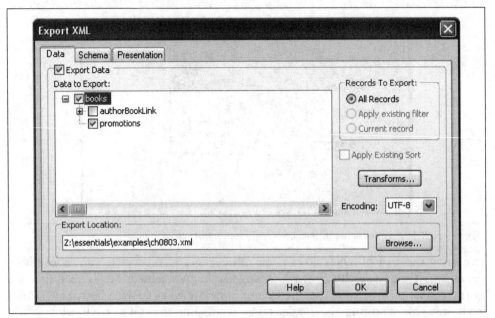

Figure 8-8. The full version of the Export XML dialog box

Example 8-3. Exported linked tables

```
<?xml version="1.0" encoding="UTF-8"?>
<dataroot xmlns:od="urn:schemas-microsoft-com:officedata" xmlns:xsi="http://www.w3.org/
2001/XMLSchema-instance"  xsi:noNamespaceSchemaLocation="ch0804.xsd" generated="2003-03-
31T16:37:01">
<books>
<ISBN>0596005385</ISBN>
<Title>Office 2003 XML Essentials</Title>
<Tagline>Integrating Office with the World</Tagline>
<Short_x0020_Description>...</Short_x0020_Description>
<Long_x0020_Description>...</Long_x0020_Description>
<PriceUS>34.95</PriceUS>
<promotions>
<PromotionID>1</PromotionID>
<BookID>0596005385</BookID>
<Name>Palm civet bonus</Name>
<Venue>Anywhere interested</Venue>
<Description>A stuffed-animal palm civet, lovingly screen-printed to match the cover, with
every copy of the book.</Description>
<Cost>10000</Cost>
</promotions>
<promotions>
<PromotionID>3</PromotionID>
<BookID>0596005385</BookID>
<Name>Key chains</Name>
<Venue>Conferences</Venue>
<Description>keychains adorned with lovely palm civets and the title of the book.
</Description>
```

Example 8-3. Exported linked tables (continued)

```
<Cost>1000</Cost>
</promotions>
</books>
<books>
<ISBN>0596002920</ISBN>
<Title>XML in a Nutshell, 2nd Edition</Title>
<Tagline>A Desktop Quick Reference</Tagline>
<Short_x0020_Description>...</Short_x0020_Description>
<Long_x0020_Description>...</Long_x0020_Description>
<PriceUS>39.95</PriceUS>
</books>
<books>
<ISBN>0596002378</ISBN>
<Title>SAX2</Title>
<Tagline>Processing XML Efficiently with Java</Tagline>
<Short_x0020_Description>...</Short_x0020_Description>
<Long_x0020_Description>...</Long_x0020_Description>
<PriceUS>29.95</PriceUS>
<promotions>
<PromotionID>2</PromotionID>
<BookID>0596002378</BookID>
<Name>Free filters</Name>
<Venue>Online/Safari</Venue>
<Description>Bonus SAX filters, open source-licensed, for developers who visit the SAX2
book site.</Description>
<Cost>0</Cost>
</promotions>
</books>
</dataroot>
```

The general pattern here is much like the original export of the books table, except that zero or more promotions elements—whose BookID holds the same value as the containing books element's ISBN element—now appear inside of each books element. This works the same way that zero or more books elements appeared inside of the dataroot element. All of the table columns are listed inside of each promotions element, making it easy to reconstruct the information in the promotions table or to treat the information as a complete set of information about each book.

The schema has also changed only a little, as shown in Example 8-4.

Example 8-4. A schema for a set of related tables

```
<?xml version="1.0" encoding="UTF-8"?>
<xsd:schema xmlns:xsd="http://www.w3.org/2001/XMLSchema" xmlns:od="urn:schemas-microsoft-
com:officedata">
<xsd:element name="dataroot">
<xsd:complexType>
<xsd:sequence>
<xsd:element ref="books" minOccurs="0" maxOccurs="unbounded"/>
</xsd:sequence>
<xsd:attribute name="generated" type="xsd:dateTime"/>
```

Example 8-4. A schema for a set of related tables (continued)

```
</xsd:complexType>
</xsd:element>
<xsd:element name="books">
<xsd:annotation>
<xsd:appinfo>
<od:index index-name="PrimaryKey" index-key="ISBN " primary="yes" unique="yes"
clustered="no"/>
</xsd:appinfo>
</xsd:annotation>
<xsd:complexType>
<xsd:sequence>
<xsd:element name="ISBN" minOccurs="0" od:jetType="text" od:sqlSType="nvarchar">
<xsd:simpleType>
<xsd:restriction base="xsd:string">
<xsd:maxLength value="11"/>
</xsd:restriction>
</xsd:simpleType>
</xsd:element>
<xsd:element name="Title" minOccurs="0" od:jetType="text" od:sqlSType="nvarchar">
<xsd:simpleType>
<xsd:restriction base="xsd:string">
<xsd:maxLength value="50"/>
</xsd:restriction>
</xsd:simpleType>
</xsd:element>
<xsd:element name="Tagline" minOccurs="0" od:jetType="text" od:sqlSType="nvarchar">
<xsd:simpleType>
<xsd:restriction base="xsd:string">
<xsd:maxLength value="100"/>
</xsd:restriction>
</xsd:simpleType>
</xsd:element>
<xsd:element name="Short_x0020_Description" minOccurs="0" od:jetType="memo"
    od:sqlSType="ntext">
<xsd:simpleType>
<xsd:restriction base="xsd:string">
<xsd:maxLength value="536870910"/>
</xsd:restriction>
</xsd:simpleType>
</xsd:element>
<xsd:element name="Long_x0020_Description" minOccurs="0" od:jetType="memo"
    od:sqlSType="ntext">
<xsd:simpleType>
<xsd:restriction base="xsd:string">
<xsd:maxLength value="536870910"/>
</xsd:restriction>
</xsd:simpleType>
</xsd:element>
<xsd:element name="PriceUS" minOccurs="0" od:jetType="currency"
    od:sqlSType="money" type="xsd:double"/>
<xsd:element ref="promotions" minOccurs="0" maxOccurs="unbounded"/>
</xsd:sequence>
</xsd:complexType>
```

Example 8-4. A schema for a set of related tables (continued)

```
</xsd:element>
<xsd:element name="promotions">
<xsd:annotation>
<xsd:appinfo>
<od:index index-name="PrimaryKey" index-key="PromotionID " primary="yes"
    unique="yes" clustered="no"/>
<od:index index-name="BookID" index-key="BookID " primary="no" unique="no"
    clustered="no"/>
<od:index index-name="bookspromotions" index-key="BookID " primary="no"
    unique="no" clustered="no"/>
<od:index index-name="PromotionID" index-key="PromotionID " primary="no"
    unique="no" clustered="no"/>
</xsd:appinfo>
</xsd:annotation>
<xsd:complexType>
<xsd:sequence>
<xsd:element name="PromotionID" minOccurs="1" od:jetType="autonumber"
    od:sqlSType="int" od:autoUnique="yes" od:nonNullable="yes" type="xsd:int"/>
<xsd:element name="BookID" minOccurs="0" od:jetType="text" od:sqlSType="nvarchar">
<xsd:simpleType>
<xsd:restriction base="xsd:string">
<xsd:maxLength value="11"/>
</xsd:restriction>
</xsd:simpleType>
</xsd:element>
<xsd:element name="Name" minOccurs="0" od:jetType="text" od:sqlSType="nvarchar">
<xsd:simpleType>
<xsd:restriction base="xsd:string">
<xsd:maxLength value="50"/>
</xsd:restriction>
</xsd:simpleType>
</xsd:element>
<xsd:element name="Venue" minOccurs="0" od:jetType="text" od:sqlSType="nvarchar">
<xsd:simpleType>
<xsd:restriction base="xsd:string">
<xsd:maxLength value="50"/>
</xsd:restriction>
</xsd:simpleType>
</xsd:element>
<xsd:element name="Description" minOccurs="0" od:jetType="memo" od:sqlSType="ntext">
<xsd:simpleType>
<xsd:restriction base="xsd:string">
<xsd:maxLength value="536870910"/>
</xsd:restriction>
</xsd:simpleType>
</xsd:element>
<xsd:element name="Cost" minOccurs="0" od:jetType="currency" od:sqlSType="money"
type="xsd:double"/>
</xsd:sequence>
</xsd:complexType>
</xsd:element>
</xsd:schema>
```

The declaration of the books element is the same as it was, except that it now includes an xsd:element that references the promotions element:

```
<xsd:element ref="promotions" minOccurs="0" maxOccurs="unbounded"/>
```

Because there may be more than one promotions element related to each book, the maxOccurs attribute is set to unbounded. The use of a ref attribute to connect to the definition of the promotions element is a change from the prior approach, which made all of these definitions in place. (This is pretty much a style choice—the earlier "Russian doll" approach would have worked as well.)

After the closing of the xsd:element element defining the books field, the declaration of the promotions element appears:

```
<xsd:element name="promotions">
```

The first feature of the promotions element is an annotation that includes information about the indexes for the promotions table, including a "bookspromotions" index on BookID, which is the connection between the books table and the promotions table.

```
<xsd:annotation>
<xsd:appinfo>
<od:index index-name="PrimaryKey" index-key="PromotionID " primary="yes" unique="yes"
    clustered="no"/>
<od:index index-name="BookID" index-key="BookID " primary="no" unique="no"
    clustered="no"/>
<od:index index-name="bookspromotions" index-key="BookID " primary="no" unique="no"
    clustered="no"/>
<od:index index-name="PromotionID" index-key="PromotionID " primary="no" unique="no"
    clustered="no"/>
</xsd:appinfo>
</xsd:annotation>
```

The contents of the promotions element are defined, just like those of the books element, in an xsd:complexType containing a sequence of declarations:

```
<xsd:complexType>
<xsd:sequence>
<xsd:element name="PromotionID" minOccurs="1" od:jetType="autonumber" od:
sqlSType="int" od:autoUnique="yes" od:nonNullable="yes" type="xsd:int"/>
```

Apart from the indexing information, these are pretty ordinary XML schemas, and the structures they describe are typical of XML data. There is very little to their structure that requires interpretation beyond "this books element contains these promotions, so I'll bet those promotions go with that book." Access can't, however, make that work for many-to-one relationships. If, for instance, you used promotions as the primary table for export instead of books, you'd be exporting a many-to-one relationship rather than one-to-many. As Figure 8-9 shows, Access warns you of the difference with an intermediary entry named [Lookup Data], indicating that it will effectively be creating a lookup table to connect the information.

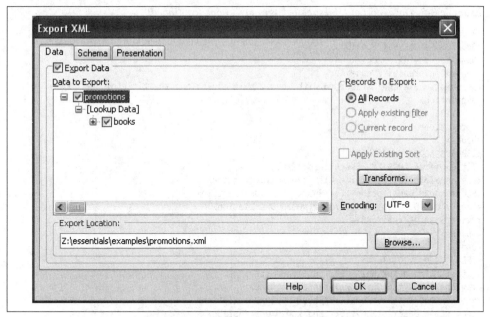

Figure 8-9. Exporting related tables with a many-to-one relationship

Example 8-5 shows the results of exporting the promotions table and the books table, but using the promotions table as the primary table.

Example 8-5. The export of tables related as many-to-one

```
<?xml version="1.0" encoding="UTF-8"?>
<dataroot xmlns:od="urn:schemas-microsoft-com:officedata" xmlns:xsi="http://www.w3.org/
2001/XMLSchema-instance"  xsi:noNamespaceSchemaLocation="promotions.xsd" generated="2003-
04-01T20:32:49">
<promotions>
<PromotionID>1</PromotionID>
<BookID>0596005385</BookID>
<Name>Palm civet bonus</Name>
<Venue>Anywhere interested</Venue>
<Description>A stuffed-animal palm civet, lovingly screen-printed to match the cover, with
every copy of the book.</Description>
<Cost>10000</Cost>
</promotions>
<promotions>
<PromotionID>2</PromotionID>
<BookID>0596002378</BookID>
<Name>Free filters</Name>
<Venue>Online/Safari</Venue>
<Description>Bonus SAX filters, open source-licensed, for developers who visit the SAX2
book site.</Description>
<Cost>0</Cost>
</promotions>
<promotions>
```

Example 8-5. The export of tables related as many-to-one (continued)

```
<PromotionID>3</PromotionID>
<BookID>0596005385</BookID>
<Name>Key chains</Name>
<Venue>Conferences</Venue>
<Description>keychains adorned with lovely palm civets and the title of the book.</
Description>
<Cost>1000</Cost>
</promotions>
<books>
<ISBN>0596005385</ISBN>
<Title>Office 2003 XML Essentials</Title>
<Tagline>Integrating Office with the World</Tagline>
<Short_x0020_Description>...</Short_x0020_Description>
<Long_x0020_Description...</Long_x0020_Description>
<PriceUS>34.95</PriceUS>
</books>
<books>
<ISBN>0596002920</ISBN>
<Title>XML in a Nutshell, 2nd Edition</Title>
<Tagline>A Desktop Quick Reference</Tagline>
<Short_x0020_Description>...</Short_x0020_Description>
<Long_x0020_Description>...</Long_x0020_Description>
<PriceUS>39.95</PriceUS>
</books>
<books>
<ISBN>0596002378</ISBN>
<Title>SAX2</Title>
<Tagline>Processing XML Efficiently with Java</Tagline>
<Short_x0020_Description>...</Short_x0020_Description>
<Long_x0020_Description>...</Long_x0020_Description>
<PriceUS>29.95</PriceUS>
</books>
</dataroot>
```

The connections between the tables are no longer represented in the XML structures themselves; you have to know that BookID and ISBN are connected to make the connections yourself. Once again, that information appears in the exported schema, as shown in the fragment in Example 8-6.

Example 8-6. The declarations for the promotions element and its index annotations

```
<xsd:element name="promotions">
<xsd:annotation>
<xsd:appinfo>
<od:index index-name="PrimaryKey" index-key="PromotionID " primary="yes" unique="yes"
clustered="no"/>
<od:index index-name="BookID" index-key="BookID " primary="no" unique="no"
    clustered="no"/>
<od:index index-name="bookspromotions" index-key="BookID " primary="no"
    unique="no" clustered="no"/>
<od:index index-name="PromotionID" index-key="PromotionID " primary="no"
    unique="no" clustered="no"/>
```

Example 8-6. The declarations for the promotions element and its index annotations (continued)

```
</xsd:appinfo>
</xsd:annotation>
<xsd:complexType>...
```

The last table export pattern we'll explore involves a many-to-many relationship between authors and books. As shown in Figure 8-10, this relationship is implemented with an intermediary table, which permits many authors to work on many books.

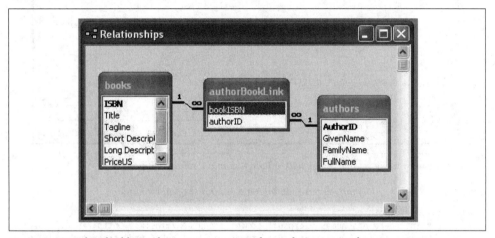

Figure 8-10. Related tables with a many-to-many relationship, expressed as two one-to-many relationships

Access will let you traverse this relationship in an XML export, as shown in Figure 8-11.

This time the export will use both of the styles shown above, whether you start by exporting the authors table with the books table, because the style of the export is determined by the nature of the join. One-to-many relationships are represented using containment, while many-to-one relationships are represented as separate pieces. In this case, the many-to-many relationship includes both of those choices.

Once again, the [Lookup Data] provides a warning that reassembling some of these relationships is going to require extra lookup work on the part of the consuming application. (Access does this extra work automatically, as we'll see in "Importing XML into Access Using the GUI," later in this chapter.) The results of this export are structurally a combination of our earlier exports, as shown in Example 8-7.

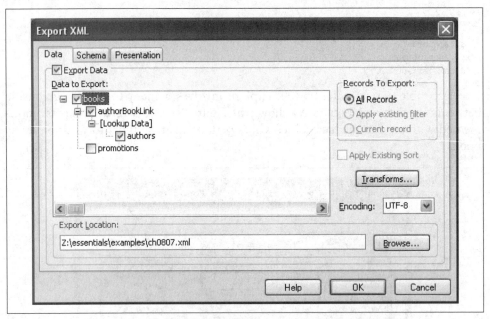

Figure 8-11. Exporting related tables with a many-to-many relationship

Example 8-7. A many-to-many export combining containment and lookup

```xml
<?xml version="1.0" encoding="UTF-8"?>
<dataroot xmlns:od="urn:schemas-microsoft-com:officedata" xmlns:xsi="http://www.w3.org/
2001/XMLSchema-instance"  xsi:noNamespaceSchemaLocation="ch0806.xsd" generated="2003-04-
01T21:01:50">
<books>
<ISBN>0596005385</ISBN>
<Title>Office 2003 XML Essentials</Title>
<Tagline>Integrating Office with the World</Tagline>
<Short_x0020_Description>...</Short_x0020_Description>
<Long_x0020_Description>...</Long_x0020_Description>
<PriceUS>34.95</PriceUS>
<authorBookLink>
<bookISBN>0596005385</bookISBN>
<authorID>1</authorID>
</authorBookLink>
</books>
<books>
<ISBN>0596002920</ISBN>
<Title>XML in a Nutshell, 2nd Edition</Title>
<Tagline>A Desktop Quick Reference</Tagline>
<Short_x0020_Description>...</Short_x0020_Description>
<Long_x0020_Description>...</Long_x0020_Description>
<PriceUS>39.95</PriceUS>
<authorBookLink>
<bookISBN>0596002920</bookISBN>
<authorID>3</authorID>
</authorBookLink>
```

```
<authorBookLink>
<bookISBN>0596002920</bookISBN>
<authorID>4</authorID>
</authorBookLink>
</books>
<books>
<ISBN>0596002378</ISBN>
<Title>SAX2</Title>
<Tagline>Processing XML Efficiently with Java</Tagline>
<Short_x0020_Description>...</Short_x0020_Description>
<Long_x0020_Description>...</Long_x0020_Description>
<PriceUS>29.95</PriceUS>
<authorBookLink>
<bookISBN>0596002378</bookISBN>
<authorID>2</authorID>
</authorBookLink>
</books>
<authors>
<AuthorID>1</AuthorID>
<GivenName>Simon</GivenName>
<FamilyName>St.Laurent</FamilyName>
<FullName>Simon St.Laurent</FullName>
</authors>
<authors>
<AuthorID>2</AuthorID>
<GivenName>David</GivenName>
<FamilyName>Brownell</FamilyName>
<FullName>David Brownell</FullName>
</authors>
<authors>
<AuthorID>3</AuthorID>
<GivenName>Elliotte</GivenName>
<FamilyName>Harold</FamilyName>
<FullName>Elliotte Rusty Harold</FullName>
</authors>
<authors>
<AuthorID>4</AuthorID>
<GivenName>Scott</GivenName>
<FamilyName>Means</FamilyName>
<FullName>W. Scott Means</FullName>
</authors>
</dataroot>
```

Each of the books elements now contains one or more authorBookLink elements that hold an authorID element. The value of that authorID element maps to an AuthorID element inside of an authors element. It takes a little traversing and sorting to reach an author's name from a book, but the connections are all still intact.

Exporting a Query

All this traversing isn't much fun for developers used to working with XML's container approach. Fortunately, relational databases have long offered another choice for interacting with their information: queries that provide specific views of information. Queries don't by themselves provide nested views, but they certainly make it easier to present some kinds of information, notably that with many-to-many relationships. The mechanics of exporting queries are much like those of exporting single tables, and the results are similar.

 Access supports SQL queries, obviously, as that's at the heart of its functionality. Access does not, however, support other standards for querying, like XQuery.

To demonstrate, we'll export a SQL query named booksByAuthor, which uses the books, authorBookLink, and authors tables to create a list of books sorted by author. The SQL for the query expresses the relationships that an XML processor working with the linked table export would otherwise have to deal with:

```
SELECT authors.GivenName, authors.FamilyName, books.ISBN, books.Title
FROM books INNER JOIN (authors INNER JOIN authorBookLink ON authors.AuthorID =
    authorBookLink.authorID) ON books.ISBN = authorBookLink.bookISBN
ORDER BY authors.FamilyName;
```

The interface for exporting a query is exactly the same as that for a table, except that there is no option for exporting linked information. When you export a query, all the information you want to export must be in that query. Exporting the query produces the result shown in Example 8-8.

Example 8-8. An exported query

```
<?xml version="1.0" encoding="UTF-8"?>
<dataroot xmlns:od="urn:schemas-microsoft-com:officedata" xmlns:xsi="http://www.w3.org/
2001/XMLSchema-instance"  xsi:noNamespaceSchemaLocation="booksByAuthor.xsd"
generated="2003-04-02T14:47:59">
<booksByAuthor>
<GivenName>David</GivenName>
<FamilyName>Brownell</FamilyName>
<ISBN>0596002378</ISBN>
<Title>SAX2</Title>
</booksByAuthor>
<booksByAuthor>
<GivenName>Elliotte</GivenName>
<FamilyName>Harold</FamilyName>
<ISBN>0596002920</ISBN>
<Title>XML in a Nutshell, 2nd Edition</Title>
</booksByAuthor>
<booksByAuthor>
<GivenName>Scott</GivenName>
<FamilyName>Means</FamilyName>
```

Example 8-8. An exported query (continued)

```
<ISBN>0596002920</ISBN>
<Title>XML in a Nutshell, 2nd Edition</Title>
</booksByAuthor>
<booksByAuthor>
<GivenName>Simon</GivenName>
<FamilyName>St.Laurent</FamilyName>
<ISBN>0596005385</ISBN>
<Title>Office 2003 XML Essentials</Title>
</booksByAuthor>
</dataroot>
```

Just as in a tabular representation of the query, information repeats, notably the ISBN and title of *XML in a Nutshell*, which has two authors. The schema exported for queries follows the same pattern as exports of a single table.

Presentation and Transformation

While the XML export features described above are certainly useful, the export formats shown are really only the beginning of what you can do. These formats represent the limits of what Access itself understands, but Access also provides hooks for other approaches, including a presentation form for web browsers and much broader capabilities for XSLT integration.

 Access' support for XSLT transformations on export works only when you export data using the GUI interface.

We'll transform the result of the query export shown above in Example 8-8 using an XSLT stylesheet. The stylesheet itself, shown in Example 8-9, is extremely simple, merely creating paragraphs and adding labels. The most exciting thing that happens is that the authors' GivenName and FamilyName end up on the same line, separated by a space.

Example 8-9. A simple stylesheet for producing HTML from the booksByAuthor query

```
<xsl:stylesheet version="1.0"
  xmlns:xsl="http://www.w3.org/1999/XSL/Transform"
>
<xsl:output method="xml" omit-xml-declaration="yes"
    encoding="US-ASCII"/>
<xsl:template match="dataroot" >
<html>

  <head>
    <title>Exported Query</title>
  </head>
```

Example 8-9. A simple stylesheet for producing HTML from the booksByAuthor query (continued)

```
  <body>
    <xsl:for-each select="booksByAuthor">

    <p>
      <xsl:text>Author: </xsl:text>
      <xsl:value-of select="GivenName"/>
      <xsl:text> </xsl:text>
      <xsl:value-of select="FamilyName"/>
    </p>

    <p>ISBN: <xsl:value-of select="ISBN"/></p>

    <p>Title: <xsl:value-of select="Title"/></p>
    <hr />
    </xsl:for-each>

  </body>
</html>

</xsl:template>

</xsl:stylesheet>
```

To apply this transformation to the data, follow the same process for exporting it normally, until you reach the Export XML dialog box shown previously in Figure 8-11. Here, you click the Transforms… button, revealing the dialog box shown in Figure 8-12.

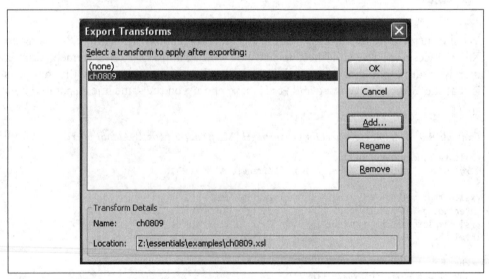

Figure 8-12. The Transforms dialog box

Click the Add... button, and you can browse your filesystem to add an XSLT stylesheet to your options. Once you've done that, you can select a transformation and click OK.

This time, when you perform the export, Access applies the XSLT stylesheet to the outgoing data, producing the result shown in Example 8-10.

Example 8-10. Results of an XSLT-enhanced export

```
<html>
<head><title>Exported Query</title></head>
<body>
<p>Author: David Brownell</p>
<p>ISBN: 0596002378</p>
<p>Title: SAX2</p>
<hr/>
<p>Author: Elliotte Harold</p>
<p>ISBN: 0596002920</p>
<p>Title: XML in a Nutshell, 2nd Edition</p>
<hr/>
<p>Author: Scott Means</p>
<p>ISBN: 0596002920</p>
<p>Title: XML in a Nutshell, 2nd Edition</p>
<hr/><p>Author: Simon St.Laurent</p>
<p>ISBN: 0596005385</p>
<p>Title: Office 2003 XML Essentials</p>
<hr/>
</body>
</html>
```

In a web browser, this looks like Figure 8-13.

 Unfortunately, Access will produce a blank file if the stylesheet includes `<xsl:output method="html" />`, so the HTML produced by this method will only work in more recent browsers.

These foundations will let you bypass the Access reports and HTML generation capabilities if you want to create custom reports, web views, or share information with systems that don't find the XML that Access generates directly amenable.

Importing XML into Access Using the GUI

Access provides fewer options for importing XML, but what it provides is simple and reasonably solid. Access lets you import data that looks roughly like the data it exports, and only as tables or additions to tables. This can be a great way to load new data into a database or add newly updated information, but it does make it difficult to transfer complex interrelated structures between databases. A single docu-

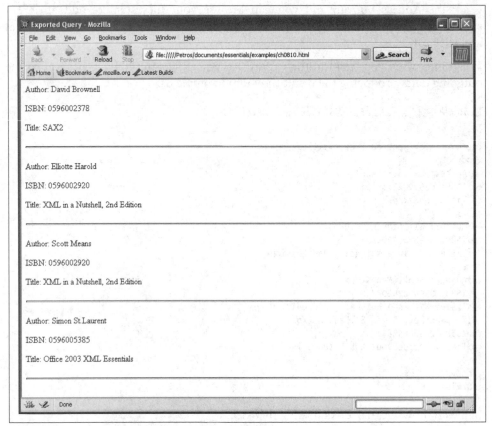

Figure 8-13. Transformed query results in a web browser

ment may contain XML that refers to multiple tables, of course, and XSLT transformations on import can help as well.

To get started, we'll import the code shown in Example 8-11 into the Access database previously used for exporting.

Example 8-11. New data for import

```
<?xml version="1.0" encoding="UTF-8"?>
<dataroot xmlns:od="urn:schemas-microsoft-com:officedata" xmlns:xsi="http://www.w3.org/
2001/XMLSchema-instance"  xsi:noNamespaceSchemaLocation="ch0802.xsd">
<books>
<ISBN>0596002637</ISBN>
<Title>Practical RDF</Title>
<Tagline>Solving Problems with the Resource Description Framework</Tagline>
<Short_x0020_Description>The Resource Description Framework (RDF) is a structure for
describing and interchanging metadata on the Web.</Short_x0020_Description>
```

Example 8-11. New data for import (continued)

```
<Long_x0020_Description>The Resource Description Framework (RDF) is a structure for
describing and interchanging metadata on the Web - anything from library catalogs and
worldwide directories to bioinformatics, Mozilla internal data structures, and knowledge
bases for artificial intelligence projects.</Long_x0020_Description>
<PriceUS>39.95</PriceUS>
</books>
<books>
<ISBN>0596003838</ISBN>
<Title>Content Syndication with RSS</Title>
<Tagline>Sharing Headlines and Information Using XML</Tagline>
<Short_x0020_Description>RSS is sprouting all over the Web, connecting weblogs and
providing news feeds.</Short_x0020_Description>
<Long_x0020_Description>RSS is sprouting all over the Web, connecting weblogs and
providing news feeds.  Originally developed by Netscape in 1999, RSS (which can stand for
RDF Site Summary, Rich Site Summary, or Really Simple Syndication) is an XML-based format
that allows Web developers to create a data feed that supplies headlines, links, and
article summaries from a web site</Long_x0020_Description>
<PriceUS>29.95</PriceUS>
</books>
<books>
<ISBN>0596002912</ISBN>
<Title>XPath and XPointer</Title>
<Tagline>Locating Content in XML Documents</Tagline>
<Short_x0020_Description>Referring to specific information inside an XML document can be
like looking for a needle in a haystack: how do you differentiate the information you need
from everything else?</Short_x0020_Description>
<Long_x0020_Description>Referring to specific information inside an XML document can be
like looking for a needle in a haystack: how do you differentiate the information you need
from everything else?  XPath and XPointer are two closely related tools that play a key
role in XML processing by allowing developers to find these needles and manipulate
embedded information.</Long_x0020_Description>
<PriceUS>24.95</PriceUS>
</books>
</dataroot>
```

To get started, select "Get External Data" from the File menu, and select "Import...." The dialog box shown in Figure 8-14 will appear.

You may have to select XML from the "Files of type" drop-down menu at the bottom, as the dialog initially defaults to Access formats. Select the file *ch0811.xml*, and click Import. The Import XML dialog box shown in Figure 8-15 will appear.

You can click on the plus sign to the left of "books" if you want to inspect the structure. If you just click OK right now, Access will create a new table, books1 (or whatever number avoids a conflict), to import the XML into Access without conflicting with the prior XML table. That may be perfectly fine, as it gives you a chance to compare the new data with the old before merging the two. Access provides two more options, however: one that lets you just create a new table based on the structure of the XML file, and another that lets you append the data in the XML file to an existing table. In this case, we know the new books are different from the old books, so

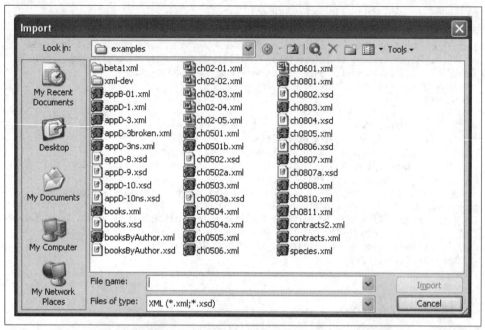

Figure 8-14. Initial import dialog box

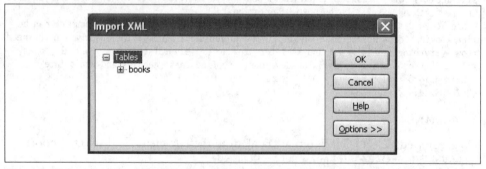

Figure 8-15. Import dialog box showing structure of XML documents

click on Options and select "Append Data to Existing Table(s)," as shown in Figure 8-16.

If you click OK now, the extra books will be added to the existing books table, as shown in Figure 8-17.

Access refuses to import XML data that causes a conflict with existing key relationships. For example, if you import that same document again the same way, you'll be rewarded with the ImportErrors table shown in Figure 8-18.

Using the Transform… button shown in Figure 8-16, you can also perform conversions that make it easier to import data that doesn't arrive in a form that meets

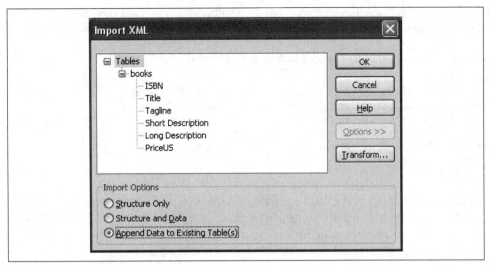

Figure 8-16. Import dialog box showing more complex structure of XML documents, as well as append options

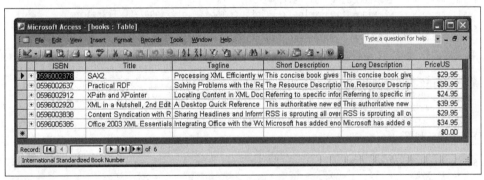

Figure 8-17. The results of importing a document and appending its data

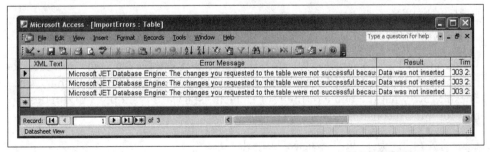

Figure 8-18. The results of importing a document and appending its data when the data is already there

Access' expectations. For example, suppose information about a new book arrived in the form shown in Example 8-12.

Example 8-12. An attribute-based XML document for import

```
<update>
<books ISBN="0596003277" Title="Learning XSLT" Tagline="A Hands-On
Introduction to XSLT and XPath" Short_x0020_Description="A gentle
introduction to the complex intricacies of XSLT" Long_x0020
_Description="A gentle introduction to the complex intricacies of
XSLT and XPath, walking through the spec from simple work to
complex." PriceUS="34.95" />
</update>
```

In Example 8-12, all of the data is stored in attributes, and Access won't even look at attributes during an import. To get this information into Access, you'll need to use a transformation, like the generic one shown in Example 8-13, which converts all attributes into child elements.

Example 8-13. A stylesheet for transforming attributes into elements

```
<?xml version="1.0" encoding="UTF-8"?>
<xsl:stylesheet version="1.0" xmlns:xsl="http://www.w3.org/1999/XSL/Transform">
<!--Derived from recipe 6.1 of Sal Mangano's XSLT Cookbook-->

<xsl:output method="xml" version="1.0" encoding="UTF-8" indent="yes"/>

<xsl:template match="@*">
  <xsl:element name="{local-name(.)}" namespace="{namespace-uri(..)}">
    <xsl:value-of select="."/>
  </xsl:element>
</xsl:template>

<xsl:template match="node( )">
  <xsl:copy>
    <xsl:apply-templates select="@* | node( )"/>
  </xsl:copy>
</xsl:template>

</xsl:stylesheet>
```

When applied to Example 8-12, the stylesheet in Example 8-13 will produce the result shown in Example 8-14, which Access can import easily. (Note that Access doesn't care what the name of the root element is; update is simply a useful description for human consumption.)

Example 8-14. An elementized version of Example 8-12

```
<?xml version="1.0" encoding="UTF-8"?>
<update>
<books>
<ISBN>0596003277</ISBN>
```

Example 8-14. An elementized version of Example 8-12 (continued)

```
<Title>Learning XSLT</Title>
<Tagline>A Hands-On Introduction to XSLT and XPath</Tagline>
<Short_x0020_Description>A gentle introduction to the complex intricacies of XSLT</Short_
x0020_Description>
<Long_x0020_Description>A gentle introduction to the complex intricacies of XSLT and
XPath, walking through the spec from simple work to complex.</Long_x0020_Description>
<PriceUS>34.95</PriceUS>
</books>
</update>
```

If you tell Access to import *ch0812.xml*, the file shown in Example 8-12, you won't have much to choose from in the Import XML dialog box, as shown in Figure 8-19.

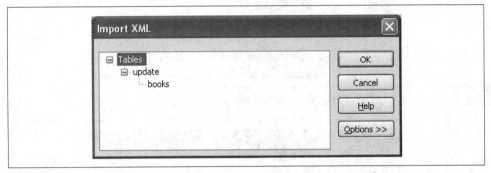

Figure 8-19. Access' initial reaction to the document that stores data in attributes

If you click on Options and then on Transform…, you'll be able to add the stylesheet, much as you did for the export transformation. Add the stylesheet to the list of transformations and select ch0813, as shown in Figure 8-20.

When you click OK, Access applies the transformation to the document, modifying the display of components you see, producing the result in Figure 8-21.

In this case, the table already exists, so be sure to select "Append Data to Existing Table(s)." When you click OK, the data from Example 8-12 will be added to the table books, as shown in Figure 8-22.

While transformations work well for some kinds of import problems, they suffer from one major limitation: they have to be applied manually. The techniques for importing XML with Visual Basic for Applications, explored in the next section, do not support the use of stylesheets for transformation on import.

Automating XML Import and Export

While the GUI is certainly the most flexible way to learn about Access' XML support, it can be tricky to explain if you're using XML to distribute information to users or collect information from them. Rather than tell users to go through a multi-step

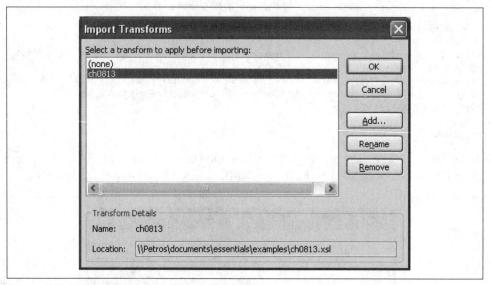

Figure 8-20. Selecting a stylesheet for transformation

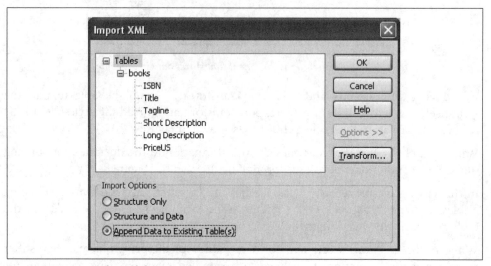

Figure 8-21. A transformed document ready for import

process, you can use the Visual Basic for Applications `Application.ImportXML` and `Application.ExportXML` methods to create buttons or other interfaces that let users get information in and out more easily.

Of the two methods, `Application.ImportXML` is by far the simpler. It only takes two argument: a data source—most likely a file reference or a URL—and an options constant. The choices for the options are `acAppendData`, `acStructureAndData` (the default),

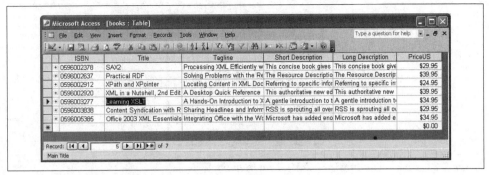

Figure 8-22. The result of importing a transformed document

and acStructureOnly. These correspond to the behaviors described in the section "Importing XML into Access Using the GUI."

For an example of how this might work, the XML in Example 8-15 is available at *http://simonstl.com/ora/updateBook.xml*.

Example 8-15. An online XML update file

```
<update>
<books>
<ISBN>0596003722</ISBN>
<Title>XSLT Cookbook</Title>
<Tagline>Solutions and Examples for XML and XSLT Developers</Tagline>
<Short_x0020_Description>A comprehensive collection of recipes for applying XSLT in a
variety of situations.</Short_x0020_Description>
<Long_x0020_Description>A comprehensive collection of recipes for applying XSLT in a
variety of situations, including structural changes, and conversion to XHTML, SVG, and
programming code.</Long_x0020_Description>
<PriceUS>34.95</PriceUS>
</books>
</update>
```

To import this, create a form with a button on it, and add this code to the button:

```
Private Sub Command0_Click( )
    Application.ImportXML "http://simonstl.com/ora/updateBook.xml", _
        acAppendData
End Sub
```

When you click on the button, which might look like Figure 8-23, your database will retrieve the XML from *http://simonstl.com/ora/updateBook.xml* and add its contents to the database.

If your books table looked like Figure 8-22, it will now look like Figure 8-24.

Figure 8-23. A button for importing XML data from the Web

	ISBN	Title	Tagline	Short Description	Long Description	PriceUS
+	0596002378	SAX2	Processing XML Efficiently w	This concise book gives	This concise book give	$29.95
+	0596002637	Practical RDF	Solving Problems with the Re	The Resource Descriptio	The Resource Descrip	$39.95
+	0596002912	XPath and XPointer	Locating Content in XML Doc	Referring to specific infor	Referring to specific in	$24.95
+	0596002920	XML in a Nutshell, 2nd Edit	A Desktop Quick Reference	This authoritative new ed	This authoritative new	$39.95
+	0596003277	Learning XSLT	A Hands-On Introduction to X	A gentle introduction to t	A gentle introduction t	$34.95
▶	0596003722	XSLT Cookbook	Solutions and Examples for X	A comprehensive collect	A comprehensive colle	$34.95
+	0596003838	Content Syndication with R	Sharing Headlines and Inform	RSS is sprouting all over	RSS is sprouting all ov	$29.95
+	0596005385	Office 2003 XML Essentials	Integrating Office with the Wc	Microsoft has added eno	Microsoft has added e	$34.95
*						$0.00

Record: [◀][◀] 6 [▶][▶][▶*] of 8

Figure 8-24. The result of the automated importation of an XML document

 As noted earlier, you can't apply a transformation when importing XML through Visual Basic for Applications, so the imported XML file must meet Access' structural expectations to start with. If you're providing XML specifically for the purpose of distributing it to Access databases, this shouldn't be a problem, but it may require some code, a temporary download, or some kind of proxy if your Access database has to import data that Access can't interpret automatically.

The `Application.ExportXML` method provides somewhat more control and functionality than its `ImportXML` companion, though it also lacks direct transformation capabilities. It takes eight arguments, listed here:

ObjectType
Most typically `acExportTable`, `acExportQuery`, or `acExportReport`, though you can also experiment with `acExportForm`, `acExportFunction`, `acReport`, `acServerView`, or `acStoredProcedure`.

DataSource
A string containing the name of the Access object—typically the table or query—you want to export.

DataTarget

The path to the XML document you want to export. Leave this blank if you're just exporting a schema.

SchemaTarget

The path to the XML Schema document you want to export. If you're just exporting data and not a schema, leave this blank.

PresentationTarget

The path to the XSLT that Access generates for creating an Internet Explorer interface to access data. Note that this is *not* a place for specifying an XSLT transformation.

ImageTarget

A path to a directory that will be used for exporting images if you're exporting a report.

Encoding

The encoding to use for the exported text files. This may be either acUTF16 (for UTF-16), or acUTF8 (for UTF-8). UTF-8 is the default.

OtherFlags

This field holds an integer that is the sum of several flags. Starting from a value of zero, add acEmbedSchema if you to embed a schema inside of the XML file instead of in a separate file. Add acExcludePrimaryKeyAndIndexes if you don't want the schema to contain index information. Add acLiveReportSource if this is to be connected to a Microsoft SQL Server database. Add acPersistReportML if you want to look at the ReportML Access uses internally. Add acRunFromServer if you want to create Active Server Pages (ASP) rather than HTML output for the PresentationTarget.

You can also specify additional objects to export as extra arguments after these, perhaps if you wanted to export multiple tables simultaneously. Most typically, you'll use just three arguments, as shown in this method:

```
Private Sub Command1_Click( )
    Application.ExportXML acExportTable, "books", _
        "C:\xml\booksExport.xml"
End Sub
```

When this code is used for the button shown in Figure 8-25, if you've done all the imports along the way, the results at *C:\xml\booksExport.xml* will look like Example 8-16.

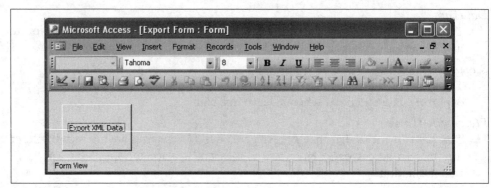

Figure 8-25. A button for exporting XML to your hard drive

Example 8-16. The results of exporting all of the data in the books table using the button

```
<?xml version="1.0" encoding="UTF-8"?>
<dataroot xmlns:od="urn:schemas-microsoft-com:officedata" generated="2004-02-06T15:42:40">
<books>
<ISBN>0596005385</ISBN>
<Title>Office 2003 XML Essentials</Title>
<Tagline>Integrating Office with the World</Tagline>
<Short_x0020_Description>Microsoft has added enormous XML functionality to Word, Excel,
and Access, as well as a new application, Microsoft InfoPath.  This book gets readers
started in using those features.</Short_x0020_Description>
<Long_x0020_Description>Microsoft has added enormous XML functionality to Word, Excel, and
Access, as well as a new application, Microsoft InfoPath.  This book gets readers started
in using those features.</Long_x0020_Description>
<PriceUS>34.95</PriceUS>
</books>
<books>
<ISBN>0596002920</ISBN>
<Title>XML in a Nutshell, 2nd Edition</Title>
<Tagline>A Desktop Quick Reference</Tagline>
<Short_x0020_Description>This authoritative new edition of XML in a Nutshell provides
developers with a complete guide to the rapidly evolving XML space.</Short_x0020_
Description>
<Long_x0020_Description>This authoritative new edition of XML in a Nutshell provides
developers with a complete guide to the rapidly evolving XML space.  Serious users of XML
will find topics on just about everything they need, including fundamental syntax rules,
details of DTD and XML Schema creation, XSLT transformations, and APIs used for processing
XML documents.  Simply put, this is the only references of its kind among XML books.</
Long_x0020_Description>
<PriceUS>39.95</PriceUS>
</books>
<books>
<ISBN>0596002378</ISBN>
<Title>SAX2</Title>
<Tagline>Processing XML Efficiently with Java</Tagline>
<Short_x0020_Description>This concise book gives you the information you need to
effectively use the Simple API for XML, the dominant API for efficient XML processing with
Java.</Short_x0020_Description>
```

Example 8-16. The results of exporting all of the data in the books table using the button (continued)

```
<Long_x0020_Description>This concise book gives you the information you need to
effectively use the Simple API for XML, the dominant API for efficient XML processing with
Java.</Long_x0020_Description>
<PriceUS>29.95</PriceUS>
</books>
<books>
<ISBN>0596002637</ISBN>
<Title>Practical RDF</Title>
<Tagline>Solving Problems with the Resource Description Framework</Tagline>
<Short_x0020_Description>The Resource Description Framework (RDF) is a structure for
describing and interchanging metadata on the Web.</Short_x0020_Description>
<Long_x0020_Description>The Resource Description Framework (RDF) is a structure for
describing and interchanging metadata on the Web - anything from library catalogs and
worldwide directories to bioinformatics, Mozilla internal data structures, and knowledge
bases for artificial intelligence projects.</Long_x0020_Description>
<PriceUS>39.95</PriceUS>
</books>
<books>
<ISBN>0596003838</ISBN>
<Title>Content Syndication with RSS</Title>
<Tagline>Sharing Headlines and Information Using XML</Tagline>
<Short_x0020_Description>RSS is sprouting all over the Web, connecting weblogs and
providing news feeds.</Short_x0020_Description>
<Long_x0020_Description>RSS is sprouting all over the Web, connecting weblogs and
providing news feeds.  Originally developed by Netscape in 1999, RSS (which can stand for
RDF Site Summary, Rich Site Summary, or Really Simple Syndication) is an XML-based format
that allows Web developers to create a data feed that supplies headlines, links, and
article summaries from a web site</Long_x0020_Description>
<PriceUS>29.95</PriceUS>
</books>
<books>
<ISBN>0596002912</ISBN>
<Title>XPath and XPointer</Title>
<Tagline>Locating Content in XML Documents</Tagline>
<Short_x0020_Description>Referring to specific information inside an XML document can be
like looking for a needle in a haystack: how do you differentiate the information you need
from everything else?</Short_x0020_Description>
<Long_x0020_Description>Referring to specific information inside an XML document can be
like looking for a needle in a haystack: how do you differentiate the information you need
from everything else?  XPath and XPointer are two closely related tools that play a key
role in XML processing by allowing developers to find these needles and manipulate
embedded information.</Long_x0020_Description>
<PriceUS>24.95</PriceUS>
</books>
<books>
<ISBN>0596003277</ISBN>
<Title>Learning XSLT</Title>
<Tagline>A Hands-On Introduction to XSLT and XPath</Tagline>
<Short_x0020_Description>A gentle introduction to the complex intricacies of XSLT</Short_
x0020_Description>
<Long_x0020_Description>A gentle introduction to the complex intricacies of XSLT and
XPath, walking through the spec from simple work to complex.</Long_x0020_Description>
```

Example 8-16. The results of exporting all of the data in the books table using the button (continued)

```
<PriceUS>34.95</PriceUS>
</books>
<books>
<ISBN>0596003722</ISBN>
<Title>XSLT Cookbook</Title>
<Tagline>Solutions and Examples for XML and XSLT Developers</Tagline>
<Short_x0020_Description>A comprehensive collection of recipes for applying XSLT in a
variety of situations.</Short_x0020_Description>
<Long_x0020_Description>A comprehensive collection of recipes for applying XSLT in a
variety of situations, including structural changes, and conversion to XHTML, SVG, and
programming code.</Long_x0020_Description>
<PriceUS>34.95</PriceUS>
</books>
</dataroot>
```

The facilities Access provides for getting XML into and out of databases, while not especially flexible, should be enough for you to transfer data among databases easily.

CHAPTER 9

Using Web Services in Excel, Access, and Word

The web services facilities in Microsoft Office are largely separate from the XML features covered elsewhere in this book, although Microsoft has often sold XML and web services as the same thing. Web services, after all, use XML as a key part of their program-to-program communication. On the other hand, most of the ways that Microsoft Office supports XML are very distinct from web services. The web services support in most parts of Office is completely separate from the rest of the XML support, relying on Visual Basic for Applications (VBA) and the Microsoft Office Web Services Toolkit, which generates code programmers can use to access Web Services.

 It's worth noting that the web services field is in significant flux. SOAP has moved from Version 1.1 to 1.2, a new version of WSDL is under development, and UDDI may eventually be replaced with other technologies. For now, be certain to test the services you use, and keep an eye out for new versions of the Office Web Services Toolkit.

What Are Web Services?

In a general sense, web services are programs you can access over the Web. In their broadest definition, tools like Google, Amazon, Mapquest, and other web-based applications are certainly web services. More typically, web services, as opposed to the regular Web, are about program-to-program communication. Web sites can make information available to other programs, and many are using XML to spare the other programs the difficulties of processing HTML. Over the last three years, web services has developed into a specialty of its own, built on a protocol called SOAP.

SOAP—formerly the Simple Object Access Protocol, but now an acronym without an official expansion—uses an XML vocabulary and a set of rules for sending XML over HTTP. (HTTP, the HyperText Transfer Protocol, is the protocol at the heart of the Web, most commonly used to transfer HTML from servers to clients.) SOAP is most frequently used as a framework for sending remote procedure calls (RPC) between programs, and that's how the examples in this chapter will use it. The Microsoft Office Web Services Toolkit creates code that makes Word or Excel a client application, capable of calling SOAP-based services on other computers.

There are two other layers to the web services supported by Office. Web Services Description Language (WSDL) provides a machine-readable description of a web service, identifying things like the methods it supports and the parameters and return values for those methods. Given a WSDL file, an application (or a programmer) can determine how to interact with a web service. The Microsoft Office Web Services Toolkit uses WSDL files to create its code. If the WSDL file is written correctly, the resulting code will be able to interact with the SOAP-based web service smoothly.

The WSDL file will tell the Toolkit what code to create, but there's still one problem: the Toolkit needs to know where to find the WSDL file. UDDI (Universal Description, Discovery, and Integration) is designed to help with this problem by providing a common framework for describing and organizing web services in public or private directories. UDDI servers store information describing services and their providers, helping developers to find services they trust and can use.

There are other ways to provide and use web services. XML-RPC, described at *http://xmlrpc.com/*, preceded SOAP and provides support for function calls over HTTP. Microsoft Office doesn't provide direct support for XML-RPC.

You can also use HTTP calls to send XML between clients and servers without using SOAP, in what is often called Representational State Transfer, or REST. For more on REST, see *http://internet.conveyor.com/RESTwiki/moin.cgi/FrontPage*. It's probably easiest to think of REST much as you think of the Web; it uses basic HTTP functionality to exchange information between programs and servers much the same way that browsers use HTTP to exchange information between browsers and servers. You can use some REST-based services in Office by combining HTTP calls with the built-in XML functionality described in earlier chapters, or through VBA.

The Microsoft Office Web Services Toolkit

Unlike the rest of the XML functionality in Word, Excel, and Access, if you want to use SOAP-based web services, you'll need to download a separate package, the Microsoft Office Web Services Toolkit. (InfoPath has web services support built into it.) As the URL for this package has changed a few times, it's easiest to go to *http://www.microsoft.com/downloads/search.aspx* and search for "Office Web Services Toolkit." Separate versions are available for Office XP and Office 2003. Once you've installed it, you'll be able to have Office generate VBA code for accessing and using web services. Microsoft's support for SOAP comes with the toolkit, and has also become part of Windows with Windows XP.

 It is possible to create VBA code that accesses SOAP services without using the Toolkit, but doing so requires much greater knowledge of both VBA and SOAP than this chapter assumes. If you're feeling intrepid, see Chapter 8 of Matthew MacDonald's *Office 2003 XML for Power Users* (APress).

Unlike the other XML features described in this book, using the Microsoft Office Web Services Toolkit works the same way across applications, except for InfoPath. Once you've learned how to interact with a web service in Excel, you can use the same code to work with it in Word or Access. The only thing that needs to change is the integration between your VBA code and the object model for the particular application and document you're working with. It's probably easiest to start your development in Excel, as the Excel grid makes it easy to set up test environments where inputs occupy particular cells and outputs are placed into particular cells by the VBA code.

Accessing a Simple Web Service from Excel

Once you've installed the toolkit, you can start connecting your spreadsheet to web services. To get to the Web Service References Tool (its name inside of all of the applications), you'll need to go to Tools → Macro → Visual Basic Editor. On the Tools menu of the Visual Basic Editor, you'll find Web Services References. Selecting that will bring up the dialog box shown in Figure 9-1.

You can use the search features in the top left of this dialog to find services through Microsoft's UDDI service, or you can choose instead to enter a URL for the WSDL file at the lower left. The toolkit defaults to UDDI, and UDDI hosted by Microsoft at that, as you'll see if you click the More button. If you'd like to try looking for a service through UDDI, enter a keyword or business name in the appropriate location, and then click the Search button at the bottom. If you enter "currency" under keyword, click the More button, and click Search, you'll have a brief wait while the toolkit queries Microsoft and then you'll see something like Figure 9-2.

The Currencyws service offers two methods: GetLicRate and GetRate. (As the documentation for them is identical, it's difficult to say what the difference is.) Clicking the Test button will let you visit a page where you can test the services, if the provider of the service offers testing. If you were to check the box next to "Currencyws" and click Add, the toolkit would generate code to let you access the service.

Instead, because UDDI hasn't really taken off, and most consumers of web services are using their own or other people's private services, we'll experiment with the other option, the Web Service URL. This lets you work with any service whose providers offer a WSDL file describing it, whether or not it's been registered with UDDI.

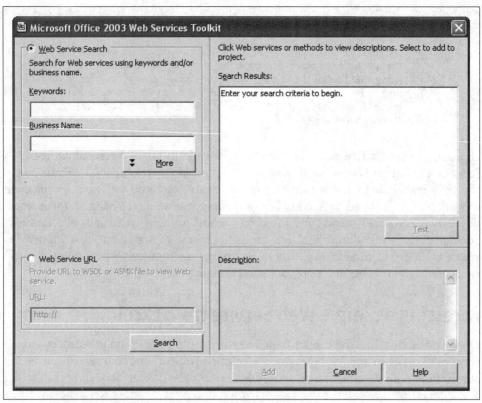

Figure 9-1. The Microsoft Office Web Services Toolkit in action

You can find a listing of public services at *http://xmethods.net/*, though you should definitely test to make sure that the services still work before you integrate them with your documents. Many services also require license keys and sometimes license payments, but for this example we'll use one that is available for free. It returns the IP address for a given domain name. We'll start by telling Excel which service we'd like to use, in this case, *http://www.cosme.nu/services/dns.php?wsdl*. Enter that value in the URL: box at the bottom left and click Search. A search result for the DNS service will appear in the top right, as shown in Figure 9-3. Check the box to its left.

Clicking the Add button will make Excel generate VBA code for invoking the service, as shown in Figure 9-4.

Next, close the Visual Basic Editor and set up a very simple spreadsheet like the one shown in Figure 9-5.

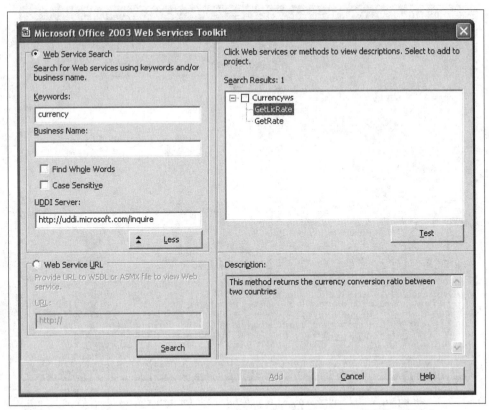

Figure 9-2. Searching for services using the UDDI support of the Microsoft Office Web Services Toolkit

To demonstrate how to call a service, add a button for calling the service. Display the Control Toolbar by right-clicking on a toolbar and choosing Control Toolbox from the pop-up menu. Click the button icon, and then click on the spreadsheet wherever you'd like the button to go. Right-click the button, and choose Properties from the pop-up menu. Under Name, enter `GetData`; under Caption, enter `Get IP Address`. (These names can be anything you like.) Close the Properties dialog box, and your spreadsheet should look something like Figure 9-6.

To add the final piece, right-click on the button and choose View Code. In the window that appears, enter the subroutine shown in Example 9-1.

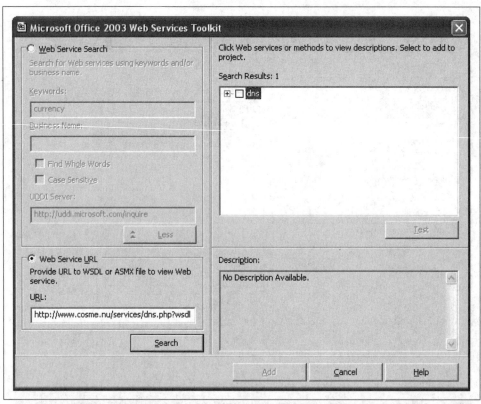

Figure 9-3. Telling the Web Services Toolkit to generate code for a specific web service

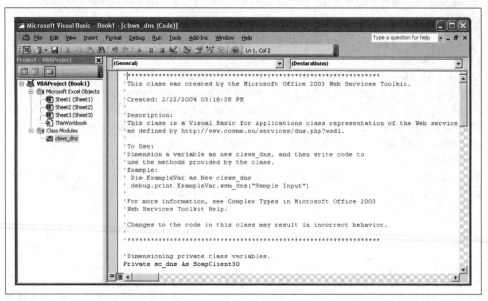

Figure 9-4. VBA code for accessing the DNS service generated by the Web Services Toolkit

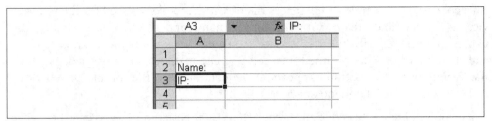

Figure 9-5. A spreadsheet for adding web services

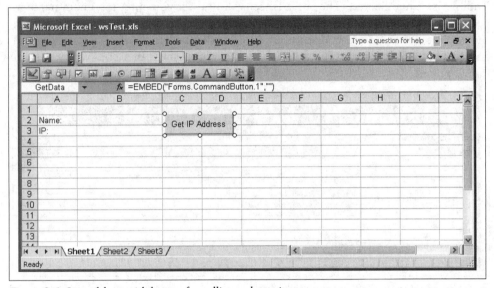

Figure 9-6. Spreadsheet with button for calling web services

Example 9-1. Code for calling simple web service

```
Private Sub GetData_Click()
    Dim info As New clsws_dns
    Dim name As String
    Dim IP As String

    name = Range("B2").Text

    IP = info.wsm_dns(name)

    Set IPRange = Range("B3")

    IPRange.Value = IP

End Sub
```

This code is pretty simple. It references the object the toolkit created for the web service, clsws_dns, and creates variables for the name and IP address. It collects the name from cell B2, calls the web service at wsm_dns with the name as an argument, and then puts the value returned into cell B3. The method name, wsm_dns, is set by the Web Services Toolkit and appears in the comments at the top of the generated code, as you can see if you look back to Figure 9-4.

Once you've entered this code and closed the Visual Basic Editor, you can then leave design mode by making sure the triangle and ruler icon at the left of the Control Toolbar isn't highlighted. The spreadsheet will now let you enter a domain name in cell B2. Clicking on the "Get IP Address" button will invoke the web service, using the generated wsm_dns method, and put the IP address corresponding to that domain name in cell B3. Figures 9-7 and 9-8 show this spreadsheet in action with different domain names.

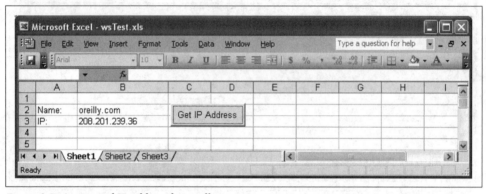

Figure 9-7. A retrieved IP address for oreilly.com

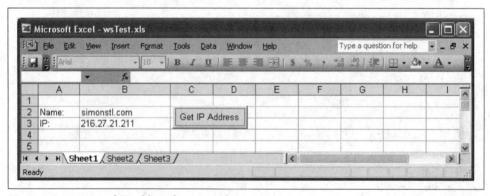

Figure 9-8. A retrieved IP address for simonstl.com

IP address resolution is one of the simpler services out there, but there are many cases where services this simple can be very useful in a spreadsheet, including currency convertors, price retrieval, postal code processing, and much more.

Accessing More Complex Web Services

While one return value for a method or function is a fairly normal approach in programming languages, SOAP is capable of returning values that are more complex. To demonstrate, the next example will test a service that returns information about a given US Zip Code, including the city, state, area code, and time zone.

Information about the service, including an HTML testing form that lets you see what results the service will produce, is available at *http://webservicex.net/uszip.asmx?op=GetInfoByZIP*. Its WSDL file is at *http://webservicex.net/uszip.asmx?WSDL*. If you test it with the Zip Code 13053, it will report back:

```
<?xml version="1.0" encoding="utf-8" ?>
<NewDataSet>
 <Table>
  <CITY>Dryden</CITY>
  <STATE>NY</STATE>
  <ZIP>13053</ZIP>
  <AREA_CODE>607</AREA_CODE>
  <TIME_ZONE>E</TIME_ZONE>
 </Table>
</NewDataSet>
```

The test reports back without a SOAP envelope. As the Web Services Toolkit will handle all the processing of the SOAP envelope and just hands your code the message inside, that won't be a problem for you. The Table here (and the <any /> in the schema in the WSDL file where these would appear) will lead the Web Services Toolkit to generate code that returns an IXMLDOMNodeList, as shown in Figure 9-9.

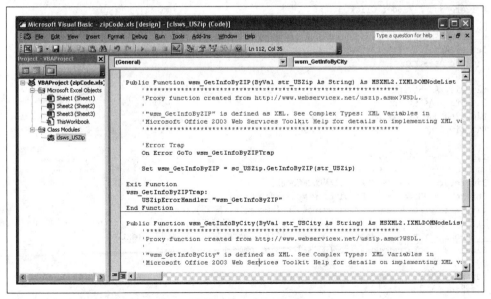

Figure 9-9. Generated code returning XML rather than a value

To work with this more complex data, the spreadsheet will have one source cell (for the Zip Code) and four result cells, as well as a button that will execute the web service call, as shown in Figure 9-10.

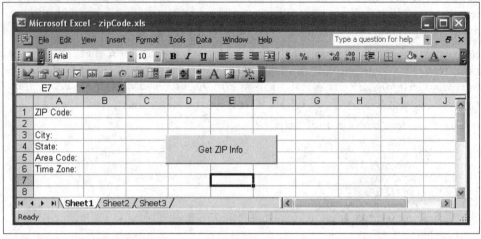

Figure 9-10. Spreadsheet base for running the web service

The code behind the "Get ZIP Info" button—which is named ZipCoder—is an extension of Example 9-1. It adds a few variables, and uses some XPath to extract the values of the XML elements returned by the SOAP call, as shown in Example 9-2.

Example 9-2. Calling a more complex web service

```
Private Sub ZipCoder_Click( )

Dim zipResolver As clsws_USZip
Set zipResolver = New clsws_USZip
Dim zip As String

Dim city As String
Dim state As String
Dim areaCode As String
Dim timeZone As String

zip = Range("B1").Text

Dim returnedNodes As MSXML2.IXMLDOMNodeList
Set returnedNodes = zipResolver.wsm_GetInfoByZIP(zip)
city = returnedNodes.Item(0).selectSingleNode("//CITY").Text
state = returnedNodes.Item(0).selectSingleNode("//STATE").Text
areaCode = returnedNodes.Item(0).selectSingleNode("//AREA_CODE").Text
timeZone = returnedNodes.Item(0).selectSingleNode("//TIME_ZONE").Text

Set cityRange = Range("B3")
cityRange.Value = city
```

Example 9-2. Calling a more complex web service (continued)

```
Set stateRange = Range("B4")
stateRange.Value = state

Set areaCodeRange = Range("B5")
areaCodeRange.Value = areaCode

Set timeZoneRange = Range("B6")
timeZoneRange.Value = timeZone

End Sub
```

The main difference is in the way that information is returned from the web services call. Instead of the data coming back as a string, it comes back as a list of XML nodes, more precisely an MSXML2.IXMLDOMNodeList. To extract the individual values from the XML, the selectSingleNode method takes an XPath and returns the first node matching the XPath, here returning the CITY element, the text of which is then put into the city variable:

```
Dim returnedNodes As MSXML2.IXMLDOMNodeList

Set returnedNodes = zipResolver.wsm_GetInfoByZIP(zip)

city = returnedNodes.Item(0).selectSingleNode("//CITY").Text
```

Once the information is extracted, it's put into cells. If you enter a Zip Code into cell B1 and then click "Get ZIP Info," it puts the corresponding information into cells B3-B6, as shown in Figure 9-11.

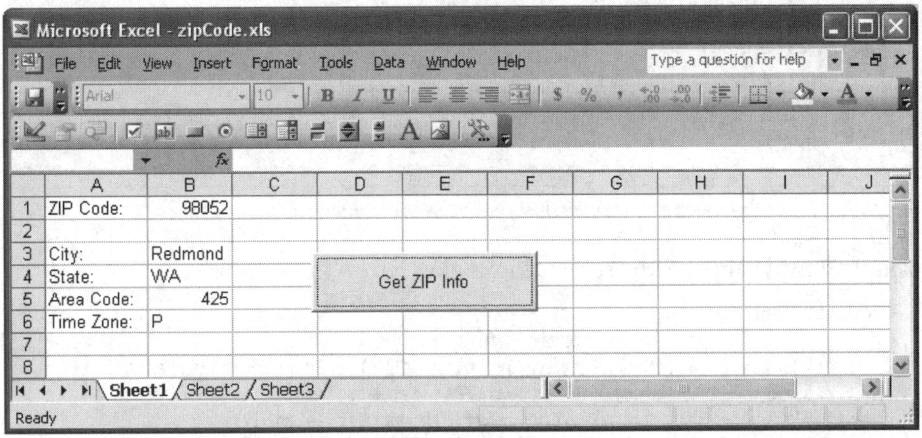

Figure 9-11. Information about a Zip Code retrieved through a web service

You may encounter a problem with some services in which they return XML as a string, and the Toolkit returns that string rather than a searchable node list. To demonstrate, we'll connect to a different service that returns complex information, but reports it in the WSDL as a string. It's a stock quote application, which you can explore at *http://www.webservicex.net/stockquote.asmx*. The test page looks like Figure 9-12; note that the placeholder shown in the SOAP response's GetQuoteResult element near the bottom is a string.

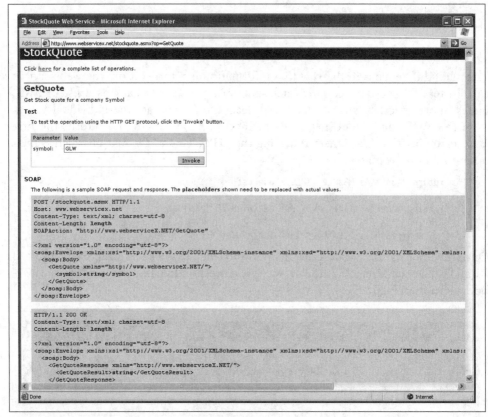

Figure 9-12. Test page for a web service that returns XML content as text

A sample return value for the service looks like:

```
<?xml version="1.0" encoding="utf-8"?>
<string xmlns="http://www.webserviceX.NET/">
&lt;StockQuotes&gt;&lt;Stock&gt;&lt;Symbol&gt;GLW&lt;/Symbol&gt;&lt;Last&gt;12.
90&lt;/Last&gt;&lt;Date&gt;2/20/2004&lt;/Date&gt;&lt;Time&gt;4:01pm&lt;/
Time&gt;&lt;Change&gt;-0.11&lt;/Change&gt;&lt;Open&gt;13.01&lt;/
Open&gt;&lt;High&gt;13.01&lt;/High&gt;&lt;Low&gt;12.66&lt;/
Low&gt;&lt;Volume&gt;15572300&lt;/Volume&gt;&lt;MktCap&gt;17.325B&lt;/
MktCap&gt;&lt;PreviousClose&gt;13.01&lt;/PreviousClose&gt;&lt;PercentageChange&gt;-0.
85%&lt;/PercentageChange&gt;&lt;AnnRange&gt;4.54 - 13.89&lt;/
AnnRange&gt;&lt;Earns&gt;-0.18&lt;/Earns&gt;&lt;P-E&gt;N/A&lt;/P-
E&gt;&lt;Name&gt;CORNING INC&lt;/Name&gt;&lt;/Stock&gt;&lt;/StockQuotes&gt;</string>
```

There's XML in there, but for some reason the service's creator chose to present it as text. It *should* look like:

```xml
<?xml version="1.0" encoding="utf-8"?>
<string xmlns="http://www.webserviceX.NET/">
  <StockQuotes>
   <Stock>
    <Symbol>GLW</Symbol>
    <Last>12.90</Last>
    <Date>2/20/2004</Date>
    <Time>4:01pm</Time>
    <Change>-0.11</Change>
    <Open>13.01</Open>
    <High>13.01</High>
    <Low>12.66</Low>
    <Volume>15572300</Volume>
    <MktCap>17.325B</MktCap>
    <PreviousClose>13.01</PreviousClose>
    <PercentageChange>-0.85%</PercentageChange>
    <AnnRange>4.54 - 13.89</AnnRange>
    <Earns>-0.18</Earns>
    <P-E>N/A</P-E>
    <Name>CORNING INC</Name>
   </Stock>
  </StockQuotes>
 </string>
```

When the toolkit returns the string value, it will at least convert the < to < and > to >, making it easy to parse with a different part of the MSXML toolkit. Once again, build a spreadsheet to hold the information, with a button to call the service, as shown in Figure 9-13.

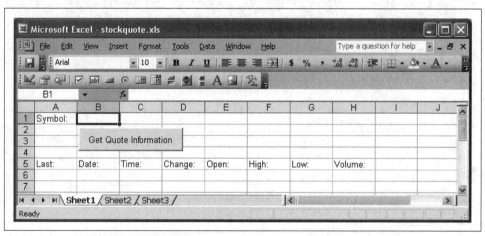

Figure 9-13. A spreadsheet for the stock quote service

Behind the button, the code shown in Example 9-3 will handle the conversion from text to XML and extract the contents of the XML to fields in the Excel spreadsheet.

Example 9-3. Processing XML returned by a web service as text

```
Private Sub GetQuote_Click()
Dim symbol As String
Dim stockObject As New clsws_StockQuote
Dim xmlDoc As MSXML2.DOMDocument
symbol = Range("B1").Text

Set xmlDoc = New MSXML2.DOMDocument

xmlDoc.LoadXml (stockObject.wsm_GetQuote(symbol))
Range("A6").Value = xmlDoc.selectSingleNode("//Last").Text
Range("B6").Value = xmlDoc.selectSingleNode("//Date").Text
Range("C6").Value = xmlDoc.selectSingleNode("//Time").Text
Range("D6").Value = xmlDoc.selectSingleNode("//Change").Text
Range("E6").Value = xmlDoc.selectSingleNode("//Open").Text
Range("F6").Value = xmlDoc.selectSingleNode("//High").Text
Range("G6").Value = xmlDoc.selectSingleNode("//Low").Text
Range("H6").Value = xmlDoc.selectSingleNode("//Volume").Text

End Sub
```

The highlighted portions show where `MSXML2.DOMDocument`, in particular its `LoadXML` method, is used in place of `MSXML2.IXMLDOMNodeList`. This accepts the string from the Toolkit, and parses it into XML, which can then be processed normally. The results look like Figure 9-14.

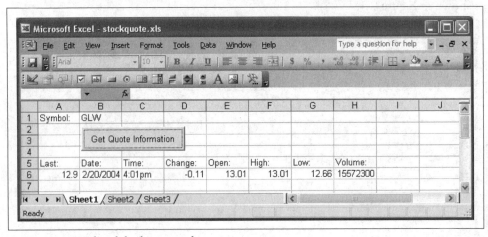

Figure 9-14. Results of checking a stock quote

If you ever have trouble with the values the toolkit hands you, take a close look at the generated code to see what type of data it is passing back to your application.

Depending on how the service was initially structured, you may have to do some extra work.

There is no intrinsic limit on the amount of information a web service can return, and you may in fact want to present more complex information than these examples have shown. If the service returns a lot of data, XPath combined with the `selectSingleNode` and `selectNodes` methods will become a critical tool for picking out just the information you want.

Accessing REST Web Services with VBA

While the Microsoft Office Web Services Toolkit doesn't provide direct support for REST-based services, REST is simple enough in practice that it doesn't really need a toolkit. All it requires is support for HTTP, which VBA offers through the `MSXML2.XMLHTTP` object. Using this object, you can create HTTP requests and process the responses. Since a lot of the SOAP web services described previously offer simple HTTP versions, it's easy to create a comparison, so this example will use the `GetInfoByZIP` service shown earlier. If you visit *http://webservicex.net/uszip. asmx?op=GetInfoByZIP*, you'll see the test form in Figure 9-15.

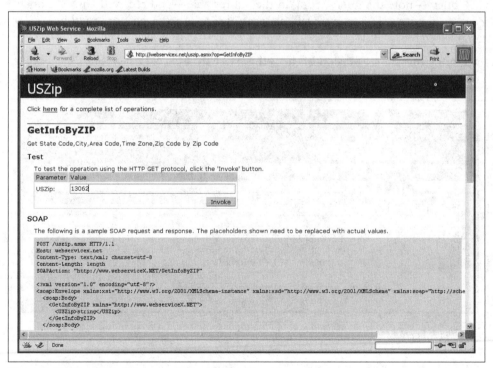

Figure 9-15. Test form that supports the web service

If you enter "13062" and click the Invoke button, you'll see something like Figure 9-16.

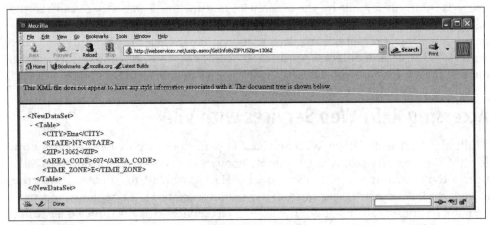

Figure 9-16. A test invocation of the web service using GET

What has happened here is that the form sent the zip code information as part of a GET query—note the query string in the address bar—and received an XML document in return. For many web services, there's no need for anything more complicated.

Integrating this simple version of the web service into Excel is easy. Start by creating a new spreadsheet that looks like Figure 9-17, itself an echo of Figure 9-10.

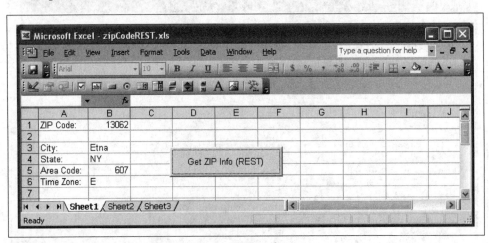

Figure 9-17. Spreadsheet base for running the REST web service

There's no need to use the Microsoft Office Web Services Toolkit for this example; the VBA code for the button in Example 9-4 alone is all you need.

Example 9-4. EREST-based code for retrieving Zip Code information

```
Private Sub ZipCoderREST_Click()

Dim zip As String
Dim query As String

zip = Range("B1").Text

'assemble query string
query = "http://webservicex.net/uszip.asmx/GetInfoByZIP?USZip=" + zip

'define XML and HTTP components
Dim zipResult As New MSXML2.DOMDocument
Dim zipService As New MSXML2.XMLHTTP

'create HTTP request to query URL - make sure to have
'that last "False" there for synchronous operation
zipService.Open "GET", query, False

'send HTTP request
zipService.send

'parse result
zipResult.LoadXml (zipService.responseText)

'extract result contents into appropriate cells
Range("B3").Value = zipResult.selectSingleNode("//CITY").Text
Range("B4").Value = zipResult.selectSingleNode("//STATE").Text
Range("B5").Value = zipResult.selectSingleNode("//AREA_CODE").Text
Range("B6").Value = zipResult.selectSingleNode("//TIME_ZONE").Text

End Sub
```

Instead of calling a generated object, this code constructs an HTTP request. If you enter "13062" into cell B1 and click the Get ZIP Info (REST) button, you'll see the result shown in Figure 9-18.

The REST HTTP version is both simpler and more portable, and demands less code on the server side as well. Why wouldn't you use REST rather than SOAP throughout your work? If you control both ends of the transaction, this is a very appealing option, as it lets you use whatever web tools you like, not just tools specifically oriented toward SOAP web services. However, there are many services that are available only through SOAP, and a growing number of programmers who know how to work with SOAP. It's best to have both approaches in your toolbox.

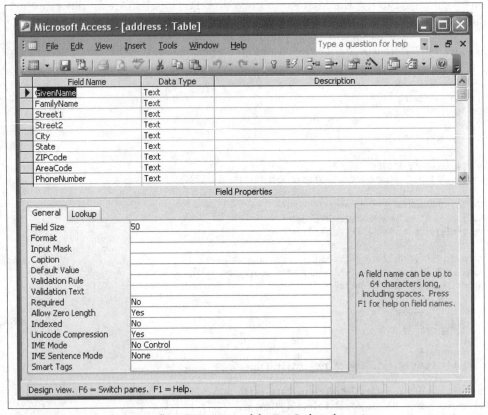

Figure 9-18. Result of running the REST version of the Zip Code web service

Using Web Services in Access

While web services aren't likely to factor into the tables at the heart of an Access database, they can be very useful in forms and reports. To demonstrate, the following example will use the Zip Code web service shown earlier as a way of filling in an address form without the user having to type in the city or state.

To get started, create a database, and then fire up the Microsoft Office Web Services Toolkit. The steps for generating code to work with a web service in Access are precisely the same as they were in Excel, so you can open the Visual Basic Editor and follow the same steps to create a web service wrapper associated with the WSDL file *http://webservicex.net/uszip.asmx?WSDL*. Once you have created that wrapper, make a table containing basic address information, like the address table shown in Figure 9-19.

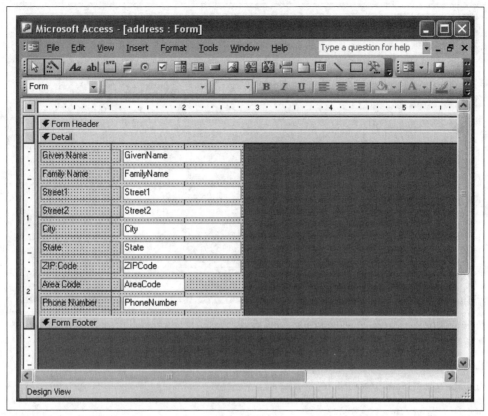

Figure 9-19. The address table that forms the base of the example

A basic form, created using the Form Wizard's "columnar" option, provides users (and the web service) with access to the information in the table. The design of the form is shown in Figure 9-20.

For my own convenience, I've set the Auto Tab property of the City, State, and Area-Code fields to "No," leaving them accessible if I need to change them but keeping them out of the way because that information should fill automatically once a Zip Code is entered into the ZIPCode field. (To set this property, right click on the field and select Properties. You can find Auto Tab under either the Other tab or the All tab.) The crucial modification this form needs, however, is adding the code shown in Example 9-5.

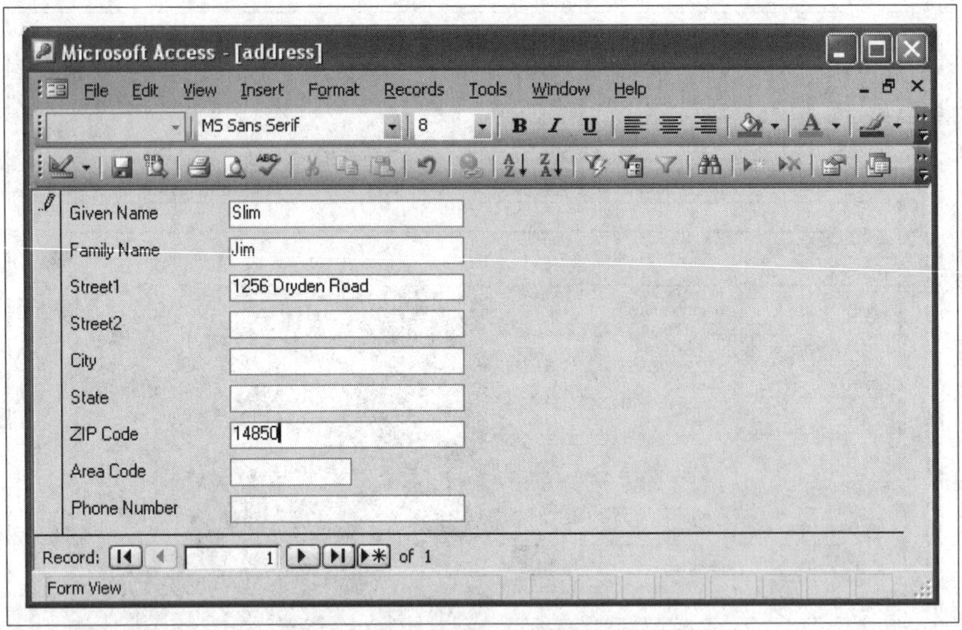

Figure 9-20. The form that will host the web service, shown just before the After Update event is triggered

Example 9-5. AfterUpdate code for updating fields when a Zip Code is entered

```
Private Sub ZIPCode_AfterUpdate()

Dim zipResolver As clsws_USZip
Set zipResolver = New clsws_USZip

Dim returnedNodes As MSXML2.IXMLDOMNodeList

'Send the web service the text value of the ZIPCode field
Set returnedNodes = zipResolver.wsm_GetInfoByZIP(Me.ZIPCode.Text)

'Put the results in the City, State, and AreaCode fields
Me.City = returnedNodes.Item(0).selectSingleNode("//CITY").Text
Me.State = returnedNodes.Item(0).selectSingleNode("//STATE").Text
Me.AreaCode = returnedNodes.Item(0).selectSingleNode("//AREA_CODE").Text

End Sub
```

To add the code, right-click on the ZIPCode field and select Properties.... In the Event tab, click in the field to the right of After Update, and then click on the ellipsis button to the right of that. Select Code Builder from the dialog box, and enter the code shown in Example 9-5. Close the Visual Basic Editor, and switch the form from Design View to Form View. As you enter values and reach the Zip Code value, the form should look like Figure 9-21.

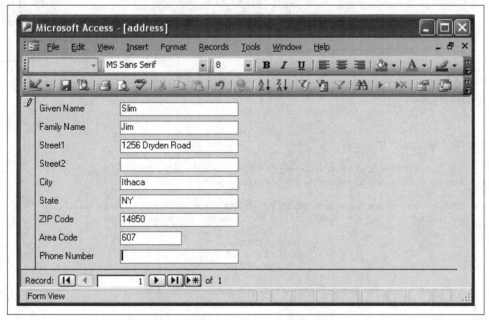

Figure 9-21. The data just after the Zip Code's After Update event is triggered

Once you tab to the next field, the VBA code will call the web service and enter the values it retrieves into the City, State, and Area Code fields, as shown in Figure 9-22.

Every time the user makes a change to the Zip Code and leaves the field, the City, State, and Area Code fields will update accordingly. The user can still make changes to those fields after the update, and those changes will remain provided that there are no further changes to the Zip Code.

You can also use the REST version of this service in Access by substituting the code shown in Example 9-6 for the code in Example 9-5. If you use this, there's no need to use the Web Services Toolkit at all.

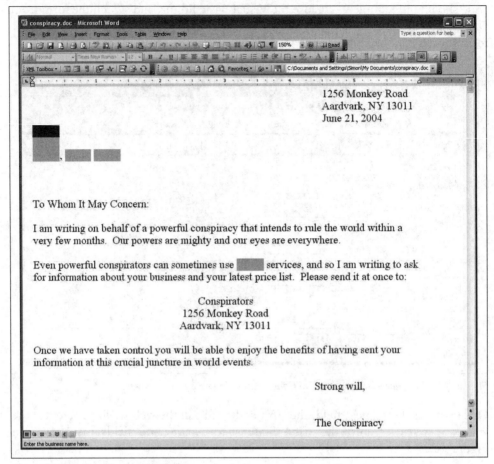

Figure 9-22. A form letter with fields

Example 9-6. REST version of Access web services call

```
Private Sub ZIPCode_AfterUpdate()

Dim query As String

'assemble query string
query = "http://webservicex.net/uszip.asmx/GetInfoByZIP?USZip=" + _
    Me.ZIPCode.Text

'define XML and HTTP components
Dim zipResult As New MSXML2.DOMDocument
Dim zipService As New MSXML2.XMLHTTP

'create HTTP request to query URL - make sure to have
'that last "False" there for synchronous operation
zipService.Open "GET", query, False

'send HTTP request
```

Example 9-6. REST version of Access web services call (continued)

```
zipService.send

'parse result
zipResult.LoadXml (zipService.responseText)

Me.City = zipResult.selectSingleNode("//CITY").Text
Me.State = zipResult.selectSingleNode("//STATE").Text
Me.AreaCode = zipResult.selectSingleNode("//AREA_CODE").Text

End Sub
```

The REST code produces exactly the same behavior shown in Figures Figure 9-21 and Figure 9-22. The core logic of this example is the same as it was in Example 9-4, just as Example 9-5 echoes Example 9-2. The only difference between using web services in Excel and using them in Access is the objects provided by the application context. This book can't begin to teach you everything about the object models in these applications, but once you learn those, the web services integration is simple.

Using Web Services in Word

Word uses the same facilities as Excel and Access, though it's a bit tougher to see how web services fit with Word. Unlike spreadsheets or databases, word processors rarely have discrete fields for entering particular data, and users don't typically expect calculations to happen (except perhaps for spell-checking) as they work on a document. Still, if you're reading this section you may have a critical use case in mind, so it's worth exploring how to integrate web services with Word.

One new feature of Word, the Research Pane, makes heavy use of web services. Unfortunately, it does so by requiring people who want to provide information to the Research Pane to create web services that meet the pane's expectations. Creating web services is far beyond the scope of this book, but a tutorial on creating services for the Research Pane with Visual Studio.NET is available at *http://www.devx.com/codemag/Article/18214?trk=DXRSS_XML*.

To demonstrate, the example uses a form letter, combining some regular text with text form fields entered from Word's Forms Toolbar. (The Insert → Fields menu option only lets you enter fields with calculated values, so the Forms Toolbar is definitely the way to go.) The form letter looks like Figure 9-23; hopefully your own form letter will be slightly more normal.

Making this into a SOAP web service–consuming document requires using the Microsoft Office Web Services Toolkit. Just as in Excel and Access, go to Tools → Macros → Visual Basic Editor (or Alt-F11). Once in the Visual Basic Editor, go to Tools → Web Services References…. As shown in Figure 9-24, enter the web service URL *http://webservicex.net/uszip.asmx?WSDL*, and click Add.

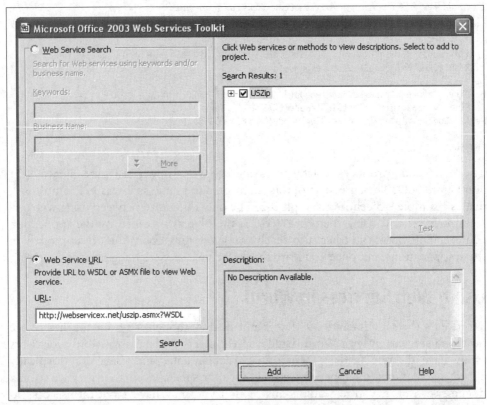

Figure 9-23. Adding the USZip service to the Word document

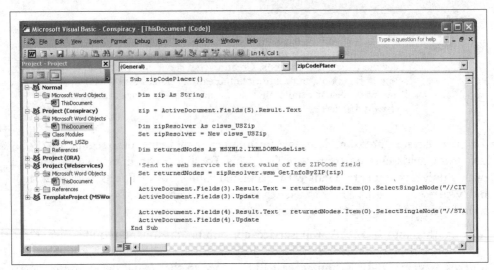

Figure 9-24. Entering code for field activity

Unlike Access or Excel, you'll need to add the code in the Visual Basic Editor directly, in the Project for this document—Project (Conspiracy) in this case—in "Microsoft Word Objects," "This Document," as shown in Figure 9-25.

The actual code is that in Example 9-7, which again resembles Examples 9-5 and 9-2.

Example 9-7. Code for putting information retrieved from a web service into Word forms

```
Sub zipCodePlacer( )

  Dim zip As String

  zip = ActiveDocument.Fields(5).Result.Text

  Dim zipResolver As clsws_USZip
  Set zipResolver = New clsws_USZip

  Dim returnedNodes As MSXML2.IXMLDOMNodeList

  'Send the web service the text value of the ZIPCode field
  Set returnedNodes = zipResolver.wsm_GetInfoByZIP(zip)

  ActiveDocument.Fields(3).Result.Text = _
      returnedNodes.Item(0).SelectSingleNode("//CITY").Text
  ActiveDocument.Fields(3).Update

  ActiveDocument.Fields(4).Result.Text = _
      returnedNodes.Item(0).SelectSingleNode("//STATE").Text
  ActiveDocument.Fields(4).Update
End Sub
```

This time the integration is with Word's form fields, accessible by number through the ActiveDocument.Fields( ) collection. The zip argument comes from field number 5 (Word counts fields from 1, not zero), and the results go into fields 3 and 4. This code still needs to be connected to the field for the Zip Code. To do that, right-click on the field and select Properties. From the Run Macro on Exit drop-down box, select zipCodePlacer, as shown in Figure 9-25.

(If you want, you can also uncheck "Fill-in enabled" on the properties for the city and state fields to take them out of the tab order for the document.) Once you've done this, there's one last step: protecting the document. Go to Tools → Protect Document (or select Protect Document in the Task Pane). You'll see the Protect Document pane, as shown in Figure 9-26.

Check the checkbox under "Editing restrictions," select "Filling in forms," and then click "Yes, Start Enforcing Protection." Click OK in the confirmation dialog box (you don't need to enter a password), and the document will be ready to use. Filling in the first few fields does nothing unusual; it's not until you enter the Zip Code field that anything will happen. Figure 9-27 shows a document just before tabbing out of the Zip Code field, and Figure 9-28 shows the document afterwards, when the web service call has filled in the city and state fields.

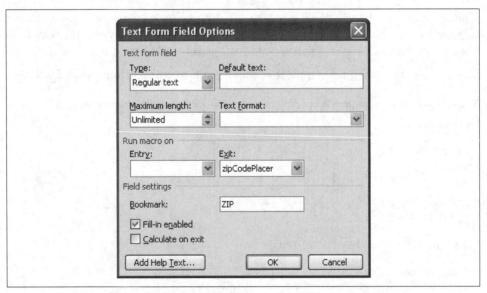

Figure 9-25. Connecting the field to the code

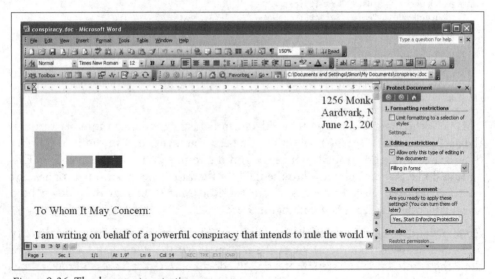

Figure 9-26. The document protection pane

This should spare the conspirator a small amount of typing, provided of course that their computer is on a network and the web service is operating. You can also do the same thing with the REST version of the service. The only change is in the code, shown in Example 9-8.

Figure 9-29 shows the result of entering a Zip Code in the document using the REST-based code. As usual, it's very much like its SOAP-based alternative.

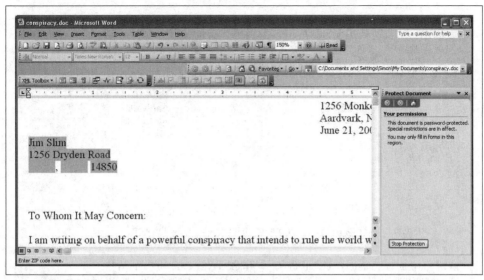

Figure 9-27. The document before the Zip Code web service is called

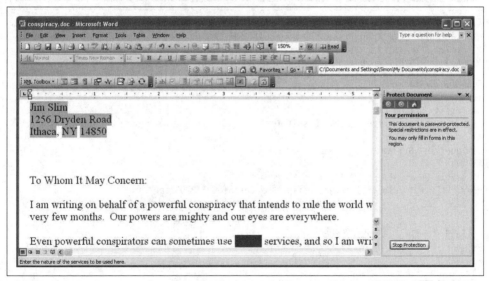

Figure 9-28. The document after the SOAP-based Zip Code web service is called, with city and state information filled in

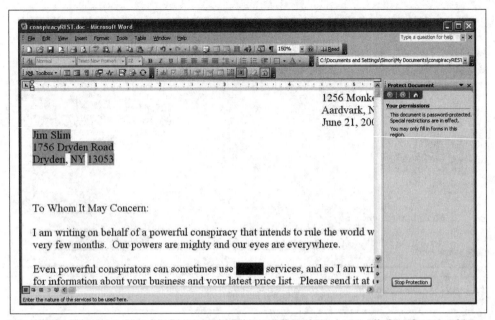

Figure 9-29. The document after the REST-based Zip Code web service is called, with city and state information filled in

Example 9-8. REST version of code for updating Word forms with retrieved information

```
Sub zipCodePlacer( )

Dim zip As String
zip = ActiveDocument.Fields(5).Result.Text

Dim query As String

'assemble query string
query = "http://webservicex.net/uszip.asmx/GetInfoByZIP?USZip=" + _
    zip

'define XML and HTTP components
Dim zipResult As New MSXML2.DOMDocument
Dim zipService As New MSXML2.XMLHTTP

'create HTTP request to query URL - make sure to have
'that last "False" there for synchronous operation
zipService.Open "GET", query, False

'send HTTP request
zipService.send

'parse result
zipResult.LoadXml (zipService.responseText)

ActiveDocument.Fields(3).Result.Text = _
    zipResult.SelectSingleNode("//CITY").Text
```

Example 9-8. REST version of code for updating Word forms with retrieved information (continued)

```
ActiveDocument.Fields(3).Update

ActiveDocument.Fields(4).Result.Text = _
    zipResult.SelectSingleNode("//STATE").Text
ActiveDocument.Fields(4).Update

End Sub
```

This just scratches the surface of what you can do with web services of various kinds in Office, but hopefully it's a start on which you can build your own projects.

CHAPTER 10

Developing InfoPath Solutions

InfoPath is a brand new product in the Microsoft Office System. Unlike Word, Excel, and Access, InfoPath was built from the ground up to create and edit XML. It carries much of the same promise as the rest of Office's new XML functionality: to bring XML to the masses. Or perhaps more precisely, it promises to *get* XML *from* the masses. By enabling everyday Office users to fill out XML-based business forms for everything from status reports to press releases to invoices to memos, InfoPath has the potential to open the floodgates to the creation of XML data in the enterprise.

What Is InfoPath?

InfoPath encompasses both a development environment for building business forms and a run-time forms application meant to be deployed on the end user's desktop. InfoPath "solutions," as they're called, are developed to enable end users to create and edit particular kinds of XML documents without having to know anything about XML. A different solution is developed for each kind of information that needs to be gathered, where "each kind of information" corresponds to an XML document type, or schema. Figure 10-1 shows one of the sample forms that come bundled with Info-Path. An average business user can fill out this form to create a valid instance of an XML schema—for meeting agendas in this case. Notable features of this form include the use of InfoPath's built-in date picker control and the use of repeating sections (one for each agenda item).

InfoPath solutions are heavily standards-based. Apart from an XML-based manifest file, called a form definition file, you can build a solution entirely using XSLT, XSD, and HTML. Form controls, text, and layout are described using HTML and CSS, supplemented with InfoPath-specific annotations. XSLT is used to transform the XML document being edited into the HTML-based form view. And information from an associated XSD schema serves to enforce validation on-the-fly, as the user fills out the form. By accessing the InfoPath object model, you can use ECMAScript and the DOM to further customize the behavior of the editor as necessary. Most

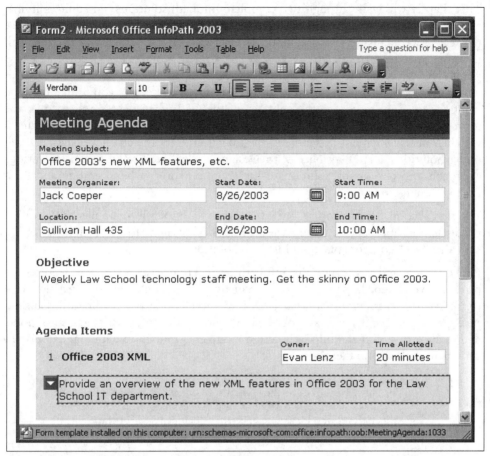

Figure 10-1. One of InfoPath's sample forms being filled out

importantly, when a user fills out a form, the data created by InfoPath is pure XML, valid according to your schema. Unlike Word, there is no InfoPath equivalent to the *.doc* proprietary format, or even to WordprocessingML, Word's proprietary XML vocabulary (see Chapter 2).

The InfoPath application supports two top-level tasks: filling out forms and designing forms. The task of filling out forms is the responsibility of end users, but the task of designing forms is up to you, the developer.* InfoPath running in design mode is an indispensable tool for building InfoPath solutions, but it ultimately is not the only way to develop solutions. Since solutions themselves are thoroughly XML-based, you can develop them "by hand," by using InfoPath in design mode, or by using your XML toolkit of choice. In many cases, a combination of these approaches is appropriate.

---

* When I refer to a "user" or "end user" in this chapter, I'm referring to someone who fills out forms in Info-Path, not someone who designs them.

This chapter will walk through two complete InfoPath solutions, one quite minimal and the other more feature-rich, that were developed "by hand," in order to expose the technical details of how a solution is put together. Only then will the InfoPath form designer be introduced in all its WYSIWYG convenience and power. At that point, you'll have a greater understanding of what InfoPath in design mode does under the hood, and you'll be able to use it to greater effect. If you're like me, you want the freedom to escape the confines of the GUI when necessary—to treat the form designer as just another tool in your arsenal, rather than the sole crutch on which your development depends. In the final section of the chapter, called "Developing Solutions That Play Nice with Design Mode," we'll take a look at various approaches to developing solutions using a combination of hand editing and Info-Path in design mode.

The first section, "InfoPath in Context," compares InfoPath to similar XML editing products and approaches. If you would rather go straight to the technical details, skip ahead to "Components of an InfoPath Solution."

Please understand that since the InfoPath application is an extremely feature-rich product, we cannot hope to cover it exhaustively in a single chapter. Instead, we'll try to cover the *essentials* of what goes into the creation of an InfoPath solution. Along the way, we'll make key observations about the InfoPath processing model and include tips on using InfoPath design mode in conjunction with manual modifications to the solution files themselves.

 For further study, see the "Microsoft Office 2003 XML Reference Schemas" package, available at *http://www.microsoft.com/office/xml/*. It includes a developer reference that documents all of the elements and attributes in the InfoPath form definition file format.

InfoPath in Context

While WYSIWYG (What You See Is What You Get) and forms-based XML editing together compose a relatively new field, InfoPath is by no means the first kid on the block. Before delving into the details of InfoPath's particular approach, let's take a step back and examine some of the common design problems that engineers of related products face, and how they are often solved. Then we'll be able to understand InfoPath's design in a wider context.

The Problem

Say you have an application that requires data to be gathered, stored, and presented. You also need to repurpose that data in different contexts, whether doing analysis on it or presenting it via different media. So you decide to use XML. Next you design an XML schema for your documents. So far, so good. Now you face a more difficult problem. How do you get your users to enter information in the format that you need? In other words, how do you get them to create XML? Well, you *could* try to teach them XML. While the thought of everyone in the world speaking our favorite language is a touching one, it's also unrealistic. Your job isn't quite done yet. You need to provide a user-friendly way for people to create XML without having to know or care that it's XML they're creating.

Alternative Approaches

XML editing applications such as InfoPath represent just one way to solve this problem. Two other approaches to gathering XML include building a custom application and using a generic server-side framework.

Building a custom application

Once you've decided on a particular XML schema, you could write a custom application designed to gather information in that schema. Whether you build this as a desktop application written in VB (Visual Basic) or as a web application using HTML forms, it will be hard-wired to your particular schema. The problem with this approach is that it tends to get reinvented every time a new kind of information needs to be gathered. After going through this experience two or three times, you'll long for a more generic framework that lets you just plug in an XML schema and make a few tweaks each time you need to gather a new kind of information.

Generic server-side frameworks

Chances are, someone has implemented a generic form-to-data management solution for your favorite server-side web application platform, whether J2EE, .NET, Perl, Python, or PHP. An example of an XML-oriented framework that is Java-based is called JXForms. Based on Apache Cocoon, it supports the automated mapping between HTML forms and XML documents according to the schema that you specify. It's also based on XForms, a W3C recommendation which we'll talk about shortly in "InfoPath versus XForms." For more information on the JXForms framework, see *http://cocoon.apache.org/2.1/userdocs/flow/jxforms.html*.

Server-side frameworks such as JXForms can save you a lot of development time building repetitive custom applications, but they also have some severe limitations:

- User interactivity is restricted to that provided by vanilla HTML forms, which does not allow for more sophisticated features such as structural editing (e.g., repeating and optional elements) and rich-text editing.
- The client-side implementation (using HTML forms) is tightly coupled to the server-side process that translates the submitted values to XML, i.e., the client-server contract includes not only the XML schema but an additional mapping between HTTP parameters and values in the generated document.

Rich-Client XML Editors

A number of products designed to address the limitations of HTML forms have been cropping up in various shapes and sizes in the last few years. In comparing the various rich-client XML editors, I've found it helpful to see where they land across different dichotomies. These aren't always true dichotomies, as some products clearly fall on both sides. InfoPath, for example, could be characterized as both data-oriented and document-oriented (to a limited extent). Rather than trying to navigate the shifting landscape of XML editors here, I'll limit my focus to InfoPath and how its approaches compare to other products in general.

Browser-based versus desktop deployment

There is a growing number of browser-based XML editors on the market, built to run on a variety of different platforms. Deployment formats include ActiveX controls (Windows only), Java applets, and Mozilla-only JavaScript modules. Browser-based editors, in many ways, provide the best of both worlds when it comes to XML editing and web functionality. As a browser plug-in, the editor is automatically installed or updated when a user loads a page in which it's embedded. This makes it possible to deploy XML editing applications over the Web at large. And in a corporate environment, it means that the IT department won't have to worry about yet another installation or upgrade on users' machines.

InfoPath is *not* a browser-based application, and at the time of this writing Microsoft has not revealed any plans to release it as such. As a member of the Office family, it must be installed on the desktop of each user who intends to use it to fill out forms. There are, however, some significant advantages of this approach. Most notable is the ability for users to save filled-out forms on their own machines, in addition to being able to submit them, for example, to a web service. Before a user has finalized his work, he can save it to his machine for later editing, or email it to a co-worker for further review just like any other Office document. Security restrictions make this impossible for the browser-based editors. As a desktop application, InfoPath also provides sophisticated native functionality not available in any of the browser-based editors, such as the ability to export to an Excel spreadsheet, or merge multiple filled-out forms into the same view.

Document-oriented versus data-oriented

The distinction between document-oriented and data-oriented XML is a tenuous but useful one. Whether a given XML editor can rightly be called document-oriented depends at least partially on its support for mixed content, i.e., elements that can contain both elements and text content. Mixed content is used wherever words or phrases within a passage need to be semantically marked up, or formatted, inline. Mixed content, in many ways, is where XML shines in comparison to other data formats.

Unfortunately, while InfoPath provides very powerful structural editing constructs, it does not currently support the use of mixed content. The one exception—and this may just suffice for many use cases—is InfoPath's support for "rich text" editing. The vocabulary used for embedded rich text is XHTML, to varying levels of restriction ranging from plain (no formatting) to rich (font formatting, paragraphs, lists, hyperlinks, etc.). Despite lack of general support for mixed content, the embedded XHTML editor makes it conceivable to use InfoPath as a frontend to a web content management system.

Bundled versus standalone development tool

Vendors of some XML editors provide a development tool that helps speed the development of XML editing solutions, in whatever format they're represented. To varying extents, you will need to rely on the development tool at least to get started developing editing applications. Unless the vocabularies and formats used to define a solution are fully documented and/or standardized (i.e., they use XForms), you should count on spending some time with the development tool.

InfoPath is no exception to this rule. It does not support XForms, and neither does it come, at least at the time of this writing, with documentation for every aspect of solution development. Fortunately, in the case of InfoPath, that doesn't mean you have to buy an extra license. On the question of whether the development tool comes "bundled" or "standalone," InfoPath has a unique answer: not only is the form design tool bundled with the run-time form module, but they are one and the same application. This peculiar packaging may make perfect sense from a marketing perspective, but it's potentially confusing from a user's perspective. Fortunately again, InfoPath solutions can be configured such that a form's design can be "protected," so that an end user filling out the form won't accidentally drop into design mode, in which they find themselves editing the controls themselves rather than their values.

Declarative versus procedural configuration

Most editors allow a certain amount of their behavior to be configured declaratively. For example, an XML Schema is a declarative specification of constraints on the values and structure of instance documents. It can be used to validate a document as it's being edited. And XSLT can be used to describe how the document looks while it's being edited. InfoPath employs both XSD and XSLT within editing solutions.

Most editors can also be configured through a procedural scripting interface, such as a JavaScript API (Application Programming Interface). Ideally, scripting will be kept to a minimum—used only in cases where the declarative configuration mechanisms do not suffice. For those kinds of customizations, InfoPath provides a complete object model and lets you choose between JScript and VBScript for accessing it.

The release of the InfoPath SP1 Preview introduced .NET programmability support. Microsoft has also released the InfoPath 2003 Toolkit for Visual Studio .NET. Searching for "InfoPath" at *http://www.microsoft.com/downloads/search.asp* should yield both results.

In addition to using XSD and XSLT, InfoPath allows a remarkable amount of custom functionality to be configured declaratively. The form definition file that's included with every solution allows you to create custom menus and buttons, associating them with named actions from a set of built-in "editing components." You can also specify custom error conditions for business rules that can't be or aren't described in your XSD schema. This too is done declaratively, using XPath expressions, which by the way is much like the approach that Schematron (*http://xml.ascc.net/schematron/*) takes to validating XML. Finally, InfoPath allows you to declaratively specify a remote submission mechanism, such as:

- Submitting XML to a web service
- HTTP POST of `text/xml` content

For other submission mechanisms, such as HTTP POST with `application/x-www-form-urlencoded` content, you can specify the submission behavior using custom scripting. We'll see an example of this in the second example solution in this chapter.

"Mapping" versus "Merging"

All XML editing products oriented to end users have the same basic problem to solve. They must somehow translate back and forth between the underlying XML being edited and the friendly editing view that the user sees. They generally have both of the following:

- An XML- or HTML-based editing view vocabulary
- A way of translating between the editing view vocabulary and the XML document being edited.

In Word and InfoPath, we have examples of each of the two broad approaches to solving this problem. Word's approach could be characterized as "merging," because its editing view consists of WordprocessingML with embedded custom XML tags from the XML document being edited. It translates between the editing view and pure XML by way of two XSLT stylesheets:

1. An *onload* stylesheet for merging the custom XML tags into a WordprocessingML editing view
2. An *onsave* stylesheet for extracting the custom XML tags from the merged WordprocessingML editing view

For more information, see "Word's Processing Model for Editing XML," in Chapter 4.

On the other hand, InfoPath's approach could be characterized as "mapping" rather than "merging." InfoPath's editing view vocabulary consists of HTML and CSS, as rendered by the Internet Explorer engine. Unlike Word, the editing view itself does not directly contain custom XML tags. Rather, HTML nodes in the editing view are mapped, or *bound*, to XML nodes in the source document being edited. This is done by way of a single XSLT stylesheet, supplemented as necessary with annotations in the InfoPath namespace. Separate onload and onsave stylesheets are not necessary. The bindings established by the stylesheet specify a complete, round-trip mapping between the source document and the editing view.

InfoPath versus XForms

A discussion of InfoPath in context would be incomplete without reference to XForms, a W3C recommendation for the next generation of web forms. XForms is slated to replace traditional HTML forms altogether in XHTML 2.0. It is completely XML-based, from the vocabulary through which a form's controls are declared to the format of the data as it is submitted back to a web server. InfoPath and XForms have some major similarities:

- They both provide a way for end users to create and edit XML documents using a user-friendly forms-based interface.
- They both use XSD schemas as a declarative validation mechanism.
- They both are designed to serve as a frontend to web services.

Despite their similarities, XForms and InfoPath ultimately have different emphases. InfoPath represents a single implementation that runs only on the Microsoft Windows PC platform. Accordingly, it is optimized for usability on that platform. In contrast, XForms is a specification meant to have many different implementations, enabling the interoperability of web forms on a wide range of different clients. Rather than optimizing for a single user interface, XForms abstracts away from the particular device by separating form controls from how they are presented. While InfoPath provides some minimal accessibility features such as tab indexes and access keys, XForms is designed from the ground up for accessibility. Illustrative of this design goal is XForms' requirement that every form control have a label.

Despite InfoPath's heavy emphasis on web services integration, it is ultimately not meant to serve as the next-generation web client. Rather, it is designed to thrive in corporate intranet environments, replacing paper forms and supporting enterprise data and content management applications. As a member of the Microsoft Office System, it provides sophisticated offline functionality not addressed by web-based technologies such as XForms.

There has been some hubbub over the fact that InfoPath does not support XForms even though in many ways it seems like just the type of application the XForms specification is meant to address. There is a wide range of perspectives one can choose to take on this. Some may decry InfoPath as yet another Microsoft product that chooses to go its own way rather than following the standards. While there may be some validity to this claim, it starts to appear untenable when you consider the actual extent to which InfoPath solutions are based on existing W3C standards, such as XSLT, XSD, and HTML.

Still others may side-step the debate altogether, choosing instead to go out and implement an XForms profile that compiles to an InfoPath solution (hint hint), something not entirely inconceivable given the open format of InfoPath's form templates.

Ultimately, it's hard not to get excited when products like InfoPath come on the scene, whether they support XForms or not. In either case, the most important electronic asset, our data, remains open. Products like InfoPath and implementations of XForms help to make vendor lock-in a thing of the past.

The XForms specification can be viewed at *http://www.w3.org/TR/xforms*. To learn more about XForms, consider these books:

- Micah Dubinko, *XForms Essentials* (O'Reilly)
- T. V. Raman, *XForms: XML Powered Web Forms* (Addison Wesley)

Components of an InfoPath Solution

A *form*, in InfoPath terms, is an XML document that is associated with a particular form template and that conforms to the XML schema defined by that form template, though as we'll see in our first example solution, the use of a schema is not required. Such files are created every time a user fills out a new form using an existing form template.* A *form template*, or solution, consists of a set of XML, XSLT, XSD, and optional script files that work together to define everything about how the form looks and behaves, how it binds to the underlying XML document's elements and attributes, and how the data is validated. A form template occurs as one of the following:

- A set of files, including an XML-based *form definition file* (an *.xsf* file) that declares all of the other files in the set, relative to its own location
- A form template package (an *.xsn* file), which consists of all of the form template files, including the form definition file, compressed into a single cabinet archive (just like a *.cab* file, only with the *.xsn* extension)

---

* The word "form" crops up a lot when talking about InfoPath. Attempting to restrict usage to the precise sense defined here would be awkward and misleading. Instead, context will clarify whether I'm referring to the XML document being edited, the InfoPath solution as a whole, or the actual files that make up the solution.

To fill out a new form, a user simply opens an existing form template (.*xsn* or .*xsf* file). The form template might reside on the user's own computer, but more often it is retrieved from a central location such as a web server. This allows multiple people to use the same form template. InfoPath then launches the form in its initial empty state. To make changes to a form that has already been filled out, a user would open the existing XML file, make changes, and save those changes, either locally on his or her own computer for later editing, or remotely via a submission mechanism defined in the form template. Saved forms can even be emailed to other InfoPath users for subsequent editing.

When InfoPath opens an existing, filled-out form, it checks whether it has write access to the document. When opening a file marked as read-only, InfoPath prompts the user with a warning that starts with "This form cannot be filled out", and asks the user "Do you want to open a read-only version of this form?" This is all well and good for XML files on the file system, but for a web server that doesn't have WebDAV or Front Page Server Extensions enabled, it is a bewildering and meaningless message, especially when the server otherwise perfectly handles form submissions. Until this issue is addressed by a newer version of InfoPath, the practical impact is that users either need to learn to ignore this message, or you need to expose write access on the web server to filled-out forms, even if you intend for users to normally *submit*, rather than *save*, completed forms.

One of the best ways to learn how InfoPath solutions work is to examine and experiment with the sample forms that come bundled with the application. First select File → Design a Form... → Customize a Sample. Then choose one of the many sample forms that can be customized. To view the individual form template files for that solution, or for any other .*xsn* file in design mode, select File → Extract Form Files... All of the files will be output into the directory that you choose.

The InfoPath Processing Instructions

XML documents edited by InfoPath retain their association with the InfoPath application in general and with a specific solution in particular through the use of special processing instructions (PI) inserted into the prolog of the instance document. All XML files created by or edited using InfoPath automatically include these PIs. To manually associate an XML document with the InfoPath application, use the now familiar mso-application PI:

```
<?mso-application progid="InfoPath.Document"?>
<doc>...</doc>
```

This will associate the file with the InfoPath application. Windows Explorer will render the file using the InfoPath icon and will launch InfoPath when a user opens the file. But if you only include an mso-application PI, InfoPath will display an error message when trying to open the file. To avoid this, you'll also need to associate the document with a particular solution, by using the mso-infoPathSolution PI. Example 10-1 shows a complete XML document whose PIs associate it with both the InfoPath application and a particular InfoPath solution.

Example 10-1. An InfoPath "form," myAnnouncement.xml

```
<?mso-application progid="InfoPath.Document"?>
<?mso-infoPathSolution href="manifest.xsf" PIVersion="1.0.0.0"?>
<announcement>
  <headline>Building closes early</headline>
  <body>The building will be closing an hour early today, at 9pm.</body>
</announcement>
```

The href pseudo-attribute in Example 10-1 points to the location of a form definition file (*.xsf*) or form template package (*.xsn*). The PIVersion pseudo-attribute is required. The current version of the PI is 1.0.0.0; future versions may introduce new features or be interpreted differently.

There are also two optional pseudo-attributes not shown here. The solutionVersion pseudo-attribute can be used to identify the version of the solution that was last used to edit the file. This is useful in the context of managing solution upgrades. And the productVersion pseudo-attribute is used to identify the version of the InfoPath application that was used to edit this file. Both of these pseudo-attributes are automatically included in the solution PI when InfoPath saves a filled-out form.

Some of the example XML document instances in this chapter use a relative pathname to refer to the form template in the mso-infoPathSolution PI. This makes it possible to experiment with these files on your own computer just by putting them into the same directory. However, when deploying the form, you should publish it to a central location such as a web server where multiple users can access it. Subsequent instance documents created by InfoPath (when a user saves or submits a filled-out form) will then refer to this absolute URL or network path. See "Publishing a Form from Design Mode," later in this chapter.

A Simple Form Definition File

The form definition file, or "solution manifest," is the starting point for defining an InfoPath solution by hand. Example 10-2 shows a simple form definition file that includes only the bare minimum of what's required to define a form template. No optional features are utilized.

Example 10-2. A minimal form definition file, manifest.xsf

```
<xsf:xDocumentClass solutionFormatVersion="1.0.0.0"
xmlns:xsf=
"http://schemas.microsoft.com/office/infopath/2003/solutionDefinition">
  <xsf:views>
    <xsf:view name="Announcement Form">
      <xsf:mainpane transform="announcement.xsl"/>
    </xsf:view>
  </xsf:views>
  <xsf:package>
    <xsf:files>
      <xsf:file name="announcement.xsl"/>
    </xsf:files>
  </xsf:package>
</xsf:xDocumentClass>
```

From this minimal example, we see that the root element, xsf:xDocumentClass, has a required attribute, solutionFormatVersion, and two required element children, xsf:views and xsf:package (whose relative order is insignificant). The attribute indicates the version of the form definition file format we're using; in this case, it's 1.0.0.0. The xsf:views element must contain at least one xsf:view element. Each view in turn must have one xsf:mainpane element that refers to an XSLT stylesheet in its transform attribute. The stylesheet referred to here is what transforms the source XML document into the form's HTML-based editing view. The xsf:package element contains a reference to each of the files used in the solution. This example declares only one file, the required XSLT stylesheet.

Filenames referred to by xsf:file elements must all be pathnames that are relative to the location of the form definition file itself. This will ensure that they are resolved correctly whether InfoPath opens the solution via the form definition file (*.xsf) or via a form template package (*.xsn).

All internal references to subordinate files, such as included or imported stylesheet modules or schema files, must be relative and must also be declared in the form definition file using corresponding xsf:file elements.

InfoPath keeps a local cache of a solution's files so that when an end user re-opens a document associated with a particular solution, Info-Path will check the form template files for updates *only if the form definition file has been modified since InfoPath last opened it*. If you want changes to your solution's XSLT stylesheet to take effect, for example, then you'll also need to re-save, or touch, the form definition file, even if you didn't make any changes to it. This will cause InfoPath to check for updates on all of the solution's files the next time it opens that solution. Understanding this ahead of time will keep you from pulling your hair out when trying to tweak individual files in unpackaged form templates.

Defining a Form Using Only an XSLT Stylesheet

The minimal form definition file we saw in Example 10-2 declares only one additional file, the XSLT stylesheet. To a limited extent, the stylesheet on its own is sufficient to define a round-trip mapping between a source document and an editing view. Even a schema is not necessary. This is how it works: the XSLT stylesheet is interpreted in such a way that implicit bindings are automatically created between HTML nodes in the editing view and XML nodes in the source document. We will explore two types of implicit bindings in this chapter:

- Text bindings
- Structural bindings

Our current solution example will illustrate text bindings. Our second solution example, which we'll see later in "A More Complete Example," will additionally illustrate structural bindings.

Text bindings are established in the following manner: any instances of the xsl: value-of instruction in the stylesheet will automatically be rendered as editable text boxes in the resulting InfoPath form, provided that the following two conditions hold:

1. In the stylesheet, the xsl:value-of element must occur as the only child element of a valid HTML element, such as span.

2. When the stylesheet is applied, the XPath expression in the select attribute must evaluate to a node-set containing exactly one element node or one attribute node.

If one of these conditions does not apply, then the value will still be displayed as instructed by the stylesheet, but the field will not be editable. In the event that both conditions apply but you nevertheless don't want the field to be editable, you can disable this behavior by annotating the XSLT instruction as follows:

```
<span ...>
  <xsl:value-of select="expression" xd:disableEditing="yes"/>
</span>
```

The presence of xd:disableEditing="yes" will keep InfoPath from automatically establishing the text binding and making the field editable. The xd prefix (recalling InfoPath's pre-release code name, "XDocs") in the above and subsequent examples must map to the InfoPath namespace URI:

```
http://schemas.microsoft.com/office/infopath/2003
```

Example 10-3 shows an XSLT stylesheet that transforms an XML document into a simple HTML view, displaying the values of two elements in the source document and establishing implicit text bindings for them.

Example 10-3. An XSLT-defined editing view, announcement.xsl

```
<xsl:stylesheet version="1.0"
  xmlns:xsl="http://www.w3.org/1999/XSL/Transform">

  <xsl:template match="/announcement">
    <html>
      <head>
        <title>Announcement</title>
      </head>
      <body>
        <h1>
          <xsl:value-of select="headline"/>
        </h1>
        <p>
          <xsl:value-of select="body"/>
        </p>
      </body>
    </html>
  </xsl:template>

</xsl:stylesheet>
```

We now have three files:

- A form definition file, *manifest.xsf*, shown in Example 10-2
- The declared stylesheet, *announcement.xsl*, shown in Example 10-3
- An instance document, *myAnnouncement.xml*, shown in Example 10-1

Provided that these three files are in the same directory, double-clicking the *myAnnouncement.xml* file will cause InfoPath to launch in editing mode and display the document using the editing view defined by *announcement.xsl*. The resulting view is shown in Figure 10-2.

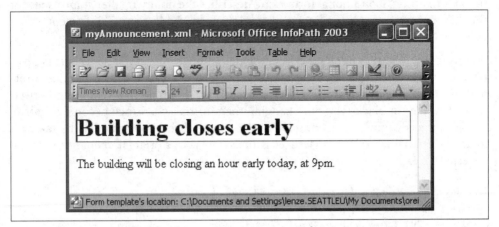

Figure 10-2. Opening a filled-out form, myAnnouncement.xml

Note that the headline field is highlighted with a box around it. This is what an editable text box looks like when instantiated as an HTML h1 element. The end user can make edits as necessary and then simply tab or click into the body field to make changes there as well. The HTML h1 and p element nodes are said to be *bound* to the XML headline and body nodes, respectively. Every time the user registers a change, that change is propagated to the underlying XML, and the XSLT stylesheet is immediately reapplied. The change is registered when the user takes the focus off the field that was changed (usually by tabbing to the next field).

The automatic bindings via the xsl:value-of instructions work in our example, because both of the two previously mentioned conditions are satisfied as follows:

- Each pertinent xsl:value-of instruction in the stylesheet occurs as the only element child of a valid HTML element (h1 and p, respectively).

- Each of the two XPath expressions evaluates to a node-set containing only one node (headline and body, respectively).

InfoPath's use of text bindings to create editable fields allows virtually any HTML element that can contain text to function as a text box. Thus, text boxes are created using text bindings, rather than using the HTML input element, as might otherwise have been expected.

This mechanism is certainly a convenient way to get started, but editing requirements tend to be more complex than what this feature supports. For all but the simplest document types, more will be needed.

Conditional formatting

Before moving on to further ways of binding HTML nodes in the view to XML nodes in the source, let's take a detour down the strange and wonderful road of conditional formatting. Conditional formatting describes the ability to alter some aspect of the editing view according to some condition in the XML source document. It's a commonly expected feature of forms-based XML editors.

A consequence of InfoPath's processing model, in which the XSLT stylesheet is reapplied every time the user registers a change, is that you can specify conditional formatting rules directly in XSLT. This is useful, for example, for rendering derived number values in black type but changing them to red when they become negative. Usefulness aside, you can get an idea of the potential this construct has by taking a look at Example 10-4. This stylesheet is the same as our original *announcements.xsl* stylesheet, except for the addition of a conditional statement.

Example 10-4. Conditional formatting expressed in XSLT

```
<xsl:stylesheet version="1.0"
  xmlns:xsl="http://www.w3.org/1999/XSL/Transform">

  <xsl:template match="/announcement">
```

Example 10-4. Conditional formatting expressed in XSLT (continued)

```
<html>
  <head>
    <title>Announcement</title>
  </head>
  <body>
    <xsl:choose>
      <xsl:when test="starts-with(headline,'SpEcIaL CoDe')">
        <div style="font-family: Arial;">
          <xsl:value-of select="headline"/>
        </div>
        <div style="font-family: Comic Sans MS;">
          <xsl:value-of select="headline"/>
        </div>
        <div style="font-family: Wingdings;">
          <xsl:value-of select="headline"/>
        </div>
        <p style="font-size: 50px;">
          CONGRATS! YOU UNLOCKED THE SPECIAL CODE!!
        </p>
      </xsl:when>
      <xsl:otherwise>
        <h1>
          <xsl:value-of select="headline"/>
        </h1>
      </xsl:otherwise>
    </xsl:choose>
    <p>
      <xsl:value-of select="body"/>
    </p>
  </body>
</html>
</xsl:template>

</xsl:stylesheet>
```

Our solution will continue to behave exactly as it did before, until some unsuspecting user enters a value in the headline field that starts exactly with the string SpEcIaL CoDe. At the moment the user takes the focus off the field (by tabbing to the next one), they'll get the surprise shown in Figure 10-3. The change is registered, the text content of the headline element is updated, the XSLT is reapplied, and, with great satisfaction, our condition succeeds.

Regardless of the presence of a conditional statement, this example also demonstrates another possibility: multiple HTML nodes in the view being bound to the same XML node in the source. In this view we have a total of four text boxes even though they are bound to a total of only two XML nodes. As you would expect, when the user registers a change to one of the three "SpEcIaL CoDe" fields, the other fields are updated accordingly—or they disappear altogether if the field's value no longer starts with our very special code.

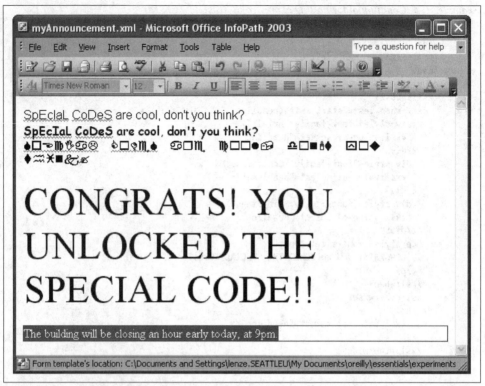

Figure 10-3. Fun with conditional formatting

Keep in mind that an HTML node in the view does not *have* to be bound to an XML node in the source for it to display its value, or some derivative thereof. As it happens, each of the HTML nodes in our example creates an implicit binding to the underlying XML node, resulting in the proliferation of text boxes. But if one of the xsl:value-of instructions had xd:disableEditing="yes", or if one of the two necessary conditions on it did not apply, then the binding would not occur and no text box would result. The value, however, would still display as instructed by the stylesheet. Another way to disable the automatic text binding is to wrap the select expression in the XPath string( ) function. In that case, the same result is displayed, but the binding is disabled, because the expression evaluates to a string rather than to a node-set.

One final thing to note about Figure 10-3 is the presence of the squiggly lines under each instance of "SpEcIaL CoDeS", even the Wingdings rendition. This is the Info-Path spelling checker in action. The spelling checker and AutoComplete features are turned on by default for HTML nodes that are implicitly bound to XML source nodes. To override this behavior, you need to declare and parameterize the corresponding xField control in the form definition file. See "The xField editing component" later in this chapter.

Explicitly Binding HTML Nodes to XML Nodes

We've now seen a mechanism by which HTML nodes in the view are implicitly bound to XML nodes in the source document being edited. You can also *explicitly* specify bindings in the HTML view by annotating the XSLT stylesheet with attributes in the InfoPath namespace. The most important of these attributes is xd: binding. (We'll see an example that uses the xd:binding attribute later in this chapter, under "Date picker control.") By attaching this attribute to an HTML element in the XSLT stylesheet, you are telling InfoPath to bind that element to a particular node in the XML source tree. The value of the xd:binding attribute is an XPath expression that is evaluated in the current XSLT context. It selects the element or attribute node to which this HTML element will be bound. This explicit binding takes precedence over any implicit binding that would otherwise occur.

The other primary annotation that InfoPath uses is the xd:xctname attribute, which identifies the type of control that a particular HTML element functions. While, under certain circumstances, the InfoPath editor will not work correctly if the xd: xctname attribute is not present (e.g., the date picker control requires its presence), it is primarily needed only by InfoPath design mode rather than editing mode. Except for the specific controls that require it, you can generally avoid this attribute when creating solutions by hand. That means you don't need to know the xd:xctname attribute's possible values, shown here:

```
PlainText
RichText
DropDown
ListBox
DTPicker
DTPicker_DTButton
CheckBox
OptionButton
Section
RepeatingSection
RepeatingTable
BulletedList
ListItem_Plain
NumberedList
PlainList
Button
InlineImage
ExpressionBox
inkpicture
```

Again, since you generally don't need to worry about the xd:xctname attribute, this list is not directly useful except to illustrate what kinds of controls InfoPath supports. The items in this list correspond to available controls in InfoPath design mode's Controls task pane (shown later in this chapter, in Figure 10-11).

Specifying an Initial XML Template

When a user opens an XML file that is already associated with an InfoPath solution via the InfoPath PIs, InfoPath launches the file with the form view defined by that solution. However, when a user directly opens a form definition file (*.xsf) or package (*.xsn) in order to fill out a new form, InfoPath needs an "empty" XML template, or skeleton, from which to begin. This initial XML template is specified in the form definition file, using the xsf:initialXmlDocument element child of the xsf:fileNew element. Example 10-5 shows our minimal form definition file with the additional specification of an initial XML template. Note that, as is the case with all of a solution's files, the initial XML template must also be declared in the list of files within the xsf:package element.

Example 10-5. Specifying the initial XML document

```
<xsf:xDocumentClass solutionFormatVersion="1.0.0.0"
xmlns:xsf="http://schemas.microsoft.com/office/infopath/2003/solutionDefinition">
  <xsf:views>
    <xsf:view name="Announcement Form">
      <xsf:mainpane transform="announcement.xsl"/>
    </xsf:view>
  </xsf:views>
  <xsf:package>
    <xsf:files>
      <xsf:file name="announcement.xsl"/>
      <xsf:file name="template.xml"/>
    </xsf:files>
  </xsf:package>
  <xsf:fileNew>
    <xsf:initialXmlDocument caption="Announcement" href="template.xml"/>
  </xsf:fileNew>
</xsf:xDocumentClass>
```

The initial XML template file normally consists mostly of empty elements and attributes but can also include default values, such as an initial value of 0 for a decimal-valued field. Example 10-6 shows an example initial XML template. Note that the mso-infoPathSolution PI must be included and must refer to the relative path of the form definition file.

Example 10-6. An example initial XML template, template.xml

```
<?mso-infoPathSolution href="manifest.xsf"
                       PIVersion="1.0.0.0"?>
<?mso-application progid="InfoPath.Document"?>
<announcement>
  <headline></headline>
  <body></body>
</announcement>
```

Adding a Schema

While using a schema is not required, it buys you a lot in terms of automatic data validation. Fields that should be dates, for example, will be flagged as invalid if anything other than a valid date is entered into it. Example 10-7 shows a schema that we could add to our example solution.

Example 10-7. A simple XSD schema, announcement.xsd

```
<xsd:schema xmlns:xsd="http://www.w3.org/2001/XMLSchema"
  elementFormDefault="unqualified">

  <xsd:element name="announcement">
    <xsd:complexType>
      <xsd:sequence>
        <xsd:element name="headline">
          <xsd:simpleType>
            <xsd:restriction base="xsd:string">
              <xsd:maxLength value="40"/>
            </xsd:restriction>
          </xsd:simpleType>
        </xsd:element>
        <xsd:element name="body" type="xsd:string"/>
      </xsd:sequence>
    </xsd:complexType>
  </xsd:element>

</xsd:schema>
```

This schema requires that the headline element's value not exceed 40 characters in length. To see what effect this will have on our solution, we first need to add it to the solution. Example 10-8 shows the final version of our minimal form definition file, with the schema declared using the xsf:documentSchema element.

Example 10-8. Declaring a schema in the form definition file

```
<xsf:xDocumentClass solutionFormatVersion="1.0.0.0"
xmlns:xsf="http://schemas.microsoft.com/office/infopath/2003/solutionDefinition">
  <xsf:views>
    <xsf:view name="Announcement Form">
      <xsf:mainpane transform="announcement.xsl"/>
    </xsf:view>
```

Example 10-8. Declaring a schema in the form definition file (continued)

```
    </xsf:views>
    <xsf:package>
      <xsf:files>
        <xsf:file name="announcement.xsl"/>
        <xsf:file name="template.xml"/>
        <xsf:file name="announcement.xsd"/>
      </xsf:files>
    </xsf:package>
    <xsf:fileNew>
      <xsf:initialXmlDocument caption="Announcement" href="template.xml"/>
    </xsf:fileNew>
    <xsf:documentSchemas>
      <xsf:documentSchema location="announcement.xsd"/>
    </xsf:documentSchemas>
  </xsf:xDocumentClass>
```

Finally, Figure 10-4 shows the resulting behavior of the InfoPath editor when the user types in a headline that exceeds 40 characters. Namely, it displays a friendly message alerting the user to the problem.

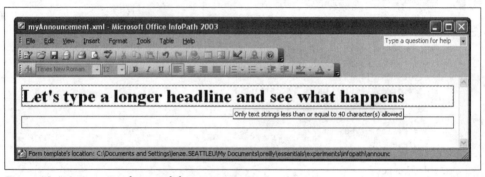

Figure 10-4. Automatic schema validation in action

A More Complete Example

So far we've looked at only the bare minimum of what goes into making an InfoPath solution. Now we'll jump in from the opposite extreme and show a complete, working example. In addition to illustrating more features of the form definition file, this example will further demonstrate how InfoPath interprets certain XSLT constructs to establish implicit bindings between HTML nodes in the form view and XML nodes in the source document. So far, we've seen how text bindings are established, using the xsl:value-of instruction. This example will additionally demonstrate the use of *structural bindings*, as we'll see in the section called "The XSLT Stylesheet."

While the example in this section illustrates a great deal of functionality, there are still a number of features not covered here. I recommend consulting the InfoPath online Help system to fill in the gaps. In particular, consult the "InfoPath XSF Reference" for comprehensive coverage of the form definition file format, including a reference for the XSF schema. From the InfoPath Help task pane, select Table of Contents → InfoPath Developer's Reference → InfoPath XSF Reference.

Figure 10-5 shows our example form from the user's perspective. It is a form for creating new "events," which might ultimately be displayed in the context of an event calendar. The "Title" field is surrounded by a blue border. This is InfoPath's built-in behavior for indicating the currently active field, which is independent of how the view stylesheet instructs the field to be rendered. The field is also underlined in red, because the schema requires the field to be non-empty (see "The XSD Schema" later in this section). Until the user fills out the field, the document will remain invalid. Likewise, the date and time fields remain underlined until the user enters valid data.

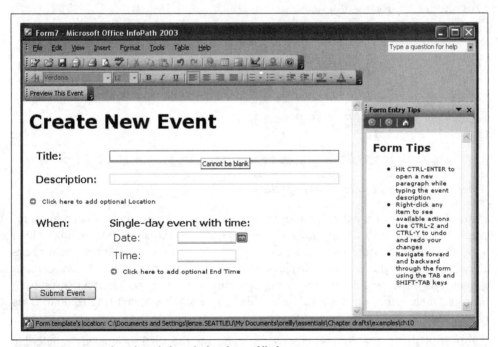

Figure 10-5. A sample InfoPath form before being filled out

The "Form Tips" task pane is a custom HTML-based task pane specific to our solution. Apart from giving the user some form entry tips, it actually serves some auxiliary roles in our solution, as we'll see in the section entitled "The HTML Task Pane."

Figure 10-6 shows the same form after being mostly filled out. The user has added the optional "Location" section and is currently selecting a date using InfoPath's built-in date picker control.

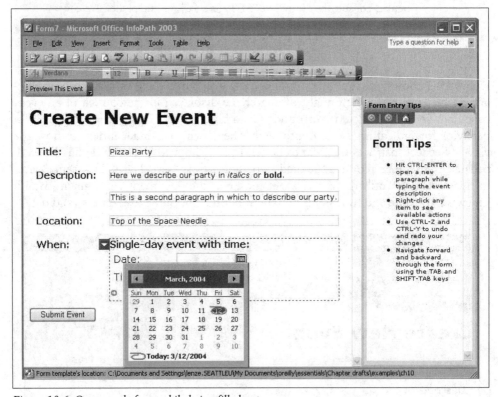

Figure 10-6. Our sample form while being filled out

Figure 10-7 shows that the "Description" field may contain more than one paragraph. This is called a "repeating section." The contextual editing menu, which appears either when the user clicks the blue down-arrow on the left or right-clicks anywhere inside the section, displays buttons for inserting and removing paragraphs. Also, the text within the paragraph can be formatted. The text formatting buttons, such as bold and italic, are enabled in InfoPath's formatting toolbar. This type of field is called a "rich text" field.

Figure 10-8 shows the contextual editing menu for the section labeled "Single-day event with time." The option to replace the element with another kind of scheduling for the event corresponds to a choice group in the XML schema.

Figure 10-9 shows the section and corresponding structural editing context menu after replacing the element.

Finally, whether the form is saved to the user's hard drive or submitted to a backend system, the resulting XML is shown in Example 10-9.

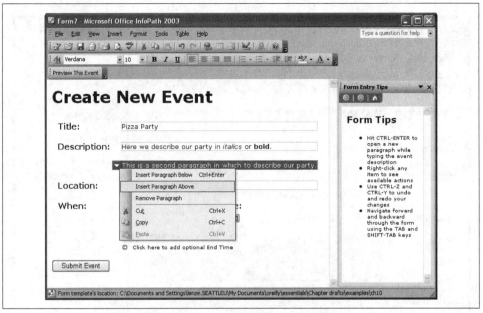

Figure 10-7. Structural context menu buttons for repeating elements

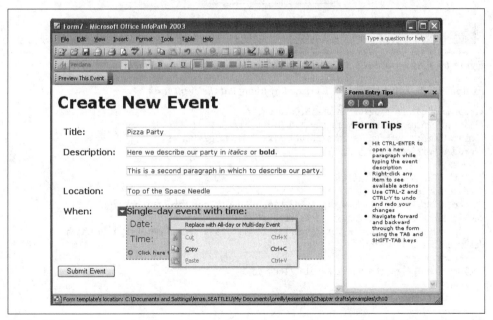

Figure 10-8. Structural editing context menu button for replacing an element in a choice group

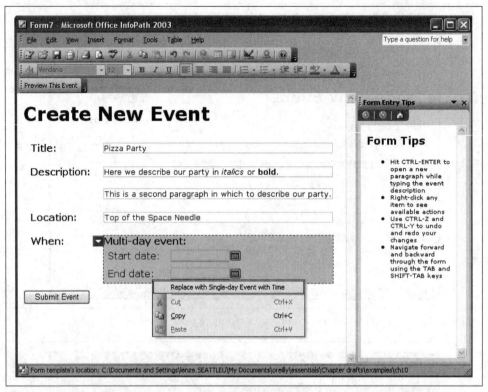

Figure 10-9. Structural editing context menu button after replacing element

Example 10-9. The instance XML created by filling out the event form

```
<?mso-application progid="InfoPath.Document"?>
<?mso-infoPathSolution PIVersion="1.0.0.0"
  href="http://myserver/events/solution.xsn" language="en-us"
  productVersion="11.0.5329" ?>
<event>
  <title>Pizza Party</title>
  <description>
    <p xmlns="http://www.w3.org/1999/xhtml">Here we describe our party in
<em>italics</em> or <strong>bold</strong>.</p>
    <p xmlns="http://www.w3.org/1999/xhtml">This is a second paragraph in which to
describe our party.</p>
  </description>
  <location>Top of the Space Needle</location>
  <when>
    <single-day date="2003-09-13" start-time="20:00:00" end-time="23:00:00"/>
  </when>
</event>
```

This XML document conforms to the schema included in our solution. Note that the
rich text vocabulary used is indeed XHTML, with em and strong elements for italic
and bold, respectively.

The XSD Schema

Example 10-10 shows the top-level schema document for our solution's XSD schema.

Example 10-10. The XSD schema for events, schema.xsd

```
<xs:schema xmlns:xs="http://www.w3.org/2001/XMLSchema"
  elementFormDefault="qualified" xmlns:xhtml="http://www.w3.org/1999/xhtml">

  <xs:import namespace="http://www.w3.org/1999/xhtml"
             schemaLocation="paragraphs.xsd"/>

  <xs:element name="event">
    <xs:complexType>
      <xs:sequence>
        <xs:element ref="title"/>
        <xs:element ref="description"/>
        <xs:element ref="location" minOccurs="0"/>
        <xs:element ref="when"/>
      </xs:sequence>
    </xs:complexType>
  </xs:element>

  <xs:element name="title">
    <xs:simpleType>
      <xs:restriction base="xs:string">
        <xs:minLength value="1"/>
      </xs:restriction>
    </xs:simpleType>
  </xs:element>

  <xs:element name="description">
    <xs:complexType>
      <xs:sequence>
        <xs:element maxOccurs="unbounded" ref="xhtml:p"/>
      </xs:sequence>
    </xs:complexType>
  </xs:element>

  <xs:element name="location" type="xs:string"/>

  <xs:element name="when">
    <xs:complexType>
      <xs:choice>
        <xs:element ref="single-day"/>
        <xs:element ref="multi-day"/>
      </xs:choice>
    </xs:complexType>
  </xs:element>

  <xs:element name="single-day">
    <xs:complexType>
      <xs:attribute name="date" use="required" type="xs:date"/>
```

Example 10-10. The XSD schema for events, schema.xsd (continued)

```
      <xs:attribute name="start-time" use="required" type="xs:time"/>
      <xs:attribute name="end-time" type="xs:time"/>
    </xs:complexType>
  </xs:element>

  <xs:element name="multi-day">
    <xs:complexType>
      <xs:attribute name="start-date" use="required" type="xs:date"/>
      <xs:attribute name="end-date" use="required" type="xs:date"/>
    </xs:complexType>
  </xs:element>

</xs:schema>
```

Primary things to note about this schema include:

- The title element must not be empty.
- The description element must contain one or more xhtml:p elements.
- The location element is optional.
- The content of when consists of a choice between a single-day element or a multi-day element.
- The date- and time-related fields must have xsd:date and xsd:time values, respectively.

Example 10-11 shows the imported schema document that declares the xhtml:p element. The (highlighted) content model of this element is precisely what InfoPath considers rich text content, i.e., mixed content with any number of elements in the XHTML namespace. If you want to use rich text editing in InfoPath, your schema must have a type definition that looks like this.

Example 10-11. The schema for XHTML paragraphs, paragraphs.xsd

```
<xs:schema targetNamespace="http://www.w3.org/1999/xhtml"
  elementFormDefault="qualified"
  xmlns:xs="http://www.w3.org/2001/XMLSchema">

  <xs:element name="p">
    <xs:complexType mixed="true">
      <xs:sequence>
        <xs:any namespace="http://www.w3.org/1999/xhtml"
                processContents="lax" minOccurs="0" maxOccurs="unbounded"/>
      </xs:sequence>
    </xs:complexType>
  </xs:element>

</xs:schema>
```

The constraints imposed by our schema are all enforced by InfoPath in editing mode. In particular, InfoPath notifies the user if the underlying document becomes invalid, whether by drawing a red underline or box around the invalid field, or showing a dialog box indicating that the user may not, for example, remove the one remaining xhtml:p element. As far as InfoPath in editing mode is concerned, validation is where the role of schemas ends. The schema is not directly used by the InfoPath XML editor to generate UI, but only to validate intermediate editing results. Another way of saying this is that the schema solely has restrictive, rather than generative, semantics.

However, InfoPath in design mode is another matter. In fact, should we decide to create a solution in design mode starting with this schema (which is exactly what we'll look at doing in "Creating a Simple Solution from an XSD Schema"), it turns out that we need to make one internal change to our schema in order for the full range of functionality in design mode to be available to us.

Making a concession for design mode

The schema as listed above works perfectly well for our hand-made solution in Info-Path editing mode. When starting with this schema in design mode, however, Info-Path fails to recognize the xhtml:p element as a "field" having data type "XHTML," ironically because of the fact that the complex type declaration (whether named or anonymous, as above) occurs inside a schema document whose target namespace is the XHTML namespace. To get around that, we can simply offload the type declaration to another imported schema document, using an arbitrary target namespace. Example 10-12 shows the updated *paragraphs.xsd* schema document. We'll use this revision from now on instead, in order to facilitate our design mode example later on.

Example 10-12. The revised schema document for XHTML paragraphs, paragraphs.xsd

```
<xs:schema targetNamespace="http://www.w3.org/1999/xhtml"
  elementFormDefault="qualified"
  xmlns:rich="http://oreilly.com/dummy-namespace-for-rich-text-decl"
  xmlns:xs="http://www.w3.org/2001/XMLSchema">

  <xs:import namespace="http://oreilly.com/dummy-namespace-for-rich-text-decl"
           schemaLocation="xhtmlType.xsd"/>

  <xs:element name="p" type="rich:xhtml"/>

</xs:schema>
```

Example 10-13 shows *xhtmlType.xsd*, which *paragraphs.xsd* imports.

Example 10-13. The XHTML type declaration schema document, xhtmlType.xsd

```
<xs:schema elementFormDefault="qualified"
  targetNamespace="http://oreilly.com/dummy-namespace-for-rich-text-decl"
  xmlns:xs="http://www.w3.org/2001/XMLSchema">

  <xs:complexType name="xhtml" mixed="true">
```

```
  <xs:sequence>
    <xs:any namespace="http://www.w3.org/1999/xhtml"
            processContents="lax" minOccurs="0" maxOccurs="unbounded"/>
  </xs:sequence>
 </xs:complexType>

</xs:schema>
```

This is not a concession you will normally have to make. (Of course, you'll never have to make it if you never use design mode.) It is unique to situations in which you want to use and edit specific elements in the XHTML namespace with greater control than what the black box of rich text editing gives you. We could have simply made the description element a rich text field, but in that case we would not have been able to enforce the rule that it contain only a sequence of xhtml:p elements.

The Initial XML Template

Example 10-14 shows the initial XML document template that InfoPath works from when a user tries to fill out a new form. The optional location element is absent by default, and the default choice for the content of the when element is single-day, without the optional end-time attribute. Also, the infoPathSolution PI refers to the relative path of the form definition file.

Example 10-14. The initial XML document, template.xml

```
<?mso-application progid="InfoPath.Document"?>
<?mso-infoPathSolution href="manifest.xsf" PIVersion="1.0.0.0"?>
<event>
  <title></title>
  <description>
    <p xmlns="http://www.w3.org/1999/xhtml"></p>
  </description>
  <when>
    <single-day date="" start-time=""/>
  </when>
</event>
```

The XSLT Stylesheet

Example 10-15 shows the complete XSLT stylesheet that defines our solution's default editing view. The stylesheet consists of pure XSLT sprinkled with some annotations in the xd namespace. The highlighted start and end tags in this example identify all of the HTML nodes in the result tree that have bindings to XML nodes in the source tree, whether implicitly or explicitly (using the xd:binding attribute).

Example 10-15. The default view stylesheet, default.xsl

```xsl
<xsl:stylesheet version="1.0"
  xmlns:xsl="http://www.w3.org/1999/XSL/Transform"
  xmlns:xd="http://schemas.microsoft.com/office/infopath/2003"
  xmlns:xdFmt=
      "http://schemas.microsoft.com/office/infopath/2003/xslt/formatting"
  xmlns:xhtml="http://www.w3.org/1999/xhtml">

  <xsl:template match="/event">
    <html>
      <head>
        <style type="text/css">
          body { font-family: Verdana; }

          .optionalPlaceHolder { padding-left: 20px;
                                 behavior: url(#default#xOptional);
                                 font-size: xx-small;
                                 font-weight: normal; }

          .field { border: 1pt solid #dcdcdc; font-size: x-small; }
        </style>
      </head>
      <body>
        <h1>Create New Event</h1>
        <table cellspacing="2" cellpadding="10">
          <colgroup span="1" width="100" valign="top"
                    style="font-weight: bold;"/>
          <colgroup span="1" width="450" valign="top"/>
          <tr>
            <td>Title:</td>
            <td>
              <div class="field">
                <xsl:value-of select="title"/>
              </div>
            </td>
          </tr>
          <tr>
            <td>Description:</td>
            <td>
              <xsl:apply-templates select="description/xhtml:p"/>
            </td>
          </tr>
          <xsl:choose>
            <xsl:when test="location">
              <xsl:for-each select="location">
                <tr>
                  <td>Location:</td>
                  <td>
                    <div class="field">
                      <xsl:value-of select="."/>
                    </div>
                  </td>
                </tr>
```

Example 10-15. The default view stylesheet, default.xsl (continued)

```
            </xsl:for-each>
          </xsl:when>
          <xsl:otherwise>
            <tr>
              <td colspan="2" class="optionalPlaceholder"
                  xd:xmlToEdit="locationElement" tabindex="0">
                <xsl:text>Click here to add optional Location</xsl:text>
              </td>
            </tr>
          </xsl:otherwise>
        </xsl:choose>
        <tr>
          <td>When:</td>
          <td>
            <xsl:apply-templates select="when/*"/>
          </td>
        </tr>
      </table>
      <input type="button" value="Submit Event" xd:CtrlId="btnCreate"/>
    </body>
  </html>
</xsl:template>

<xsl:template match="xhtml:p">
  <p class="field">
    <xsl:copy-of select="node( )"/>
  </p>
</xsl:template>

<xsl:template match="single-day">
  <div>
    <div style="font-weight: bold;">Single-day event with time:</div>
    <table>
      <colgroup span="1" width="100" style="padding: 5px;"/>
      <tr>
        <td>Date: </td>
        <td>
          <xsl:call-template name="make-date-picker">
            <xsl:with-param name="date-node" select="@date"/>
          </xsl:call-template>
        </td>
      </tr>
      <tr>
        <td>
          <xsl:if test="@end-time">Start </xsl:if>
          <xsl:text>Time: </xsl:text>
        </td>
        <td>
          <xsl:call-template name="make-time-field">
            <xsl:with-param name="time-node" select="@start-time"/>
          </xsl:call-template>
        </td>
```

Example 10-15. The default view stylesheet, default.xsl (continued)

```
          </tr>
          <xsl:choose>
            <xsl:when test="@end-time">
              <xsl:for-each select="@end-time">
                <tr>
                  <td>End time: </td>
                  <td>
                    <xsl:call-template name="make-time-field">
                      <xsl:with-param name="time-node" select="."/>
                    </xsl:call-template>
                  </td>
                </tr>
              </xsl:for-each>
            </xsl:when>
            <xsl:otherwise>
              <tr>
                <td colspan="2" class="optionalPlaceholder"
                    xd:xmlToEdit="end-time" tabindex="0">
                  <xsl:text>Click here to add optional End Time</xsl:text>
                </td>
              </tr>
            </xsl:otherwise>
          </xsl:choose>
        </table>
      </div>
  </xsl:template>

  <xsl:template match="multi-day">
    <div>
      <div style="font-weight: bold;">Multi-day event:</div>
      <table>
        <colgroup span="1" width="100" style="padding: 5px;"/>
        <tr>
          <td>Start date: </td>
          <td>
            <xsl:call-template name="make-date-picker">
              <xsl:with-param name="date-node" select="@start-date"/>
            </xsl:call-template>
          </td>
        </tr>
        <tr>
          <td>End date: </td>
          <td>
            <xsl:call-template name="make-date-picker">
              <xsl:with-param name="date-node" select="@end-date"/>
            </xsl:call-template>
          </td>
        </tr>
      </table>
    </div>
  </xsl:template>
```

Example 10-15. The default view stylesheet, default.xsl (continued)

```xsl
<xsl:template name="make-date-picker">
  <xsl:param name="date-node"/>
  <span xd:disableEditing="yes">
    <span class="field"
          xd:binding="$date-node"
          xd:xctname="DTPicker_DTText"
          contentEditable="true"
          style="BEHAVIOR: url(#default#CalPopup)
                          url(#default#urn::controls/Binder)
                          url(#default#Formatting);
                 width: 100;"
          xd:innerCtrl="_DTText"
          xd:boundProp="xd:num"
          xd:datafmt='"date","dateFormat:Short Date;"'>
      <xsl:attribute name="xd:num">
        <xsl:value-of select="$date-node"/>
      </xsl:attribute>
      <xsl:value-of select="xdFmt:formatString($date-node,
                                               'date',
                                               'dateFormat:Short Date;')"/>
    </span>
    <button style="height:18px; width:20px;
                   BEHAVIOR: url(#default#DTPicker);"
            tabindex="-1">
      <img src="res://infopath.exe/calendar.gif"/>
    </button>
  </span>
</xsl:template>

<xsl:template name="make-time-field">
  <xsl:param name="time-node"/>
  <span xd:disableEditing="yes">
    <span class="field"
          xd:binding="$time-node"
          contentEditable="true"
          xd:xctname="PlainText"
          xd:datafmt='"time","noSeconds:1;"'
          xd:boundProp="xd:num"
          style="BEHAVIOR: url(#default#urn::controls/Binder)
                          url(#default#Formatting);
                 width: 100;">
      <xsl:attribute name="xd:num">
        <xsl:value-of select="$time-node"/>
      </xsl:attribute>
      <xsl:value-of select="xdFmt:formatString($time-node,
                                               'time',
                                               'noSeconds:1;')"/>
    </span>
  </span>
</xsl:template>

</xsl:stylesheet>
```

Text bindings

The `title` field shows an example of a text binding:

```
<div class="field">
  <xsl:value-of select="title"/>
</div>
```

This is the same kind of binding that we saw in our first stylesheet, in Example 10-3. Our current example has one other implicit text binding, corresponding to the `location` field. As we've seen, text bindings cause the corresponding HTML element to be rendered as an editable field in the InfoPath editing view. To make these fields look more like actual text boxes, they are each associated with the CSS class, `field`, which is declared inside the HTML document head and which adds a thin border to the element:

```
.field { border: 1pt solid #dcdcdc; font-size: x-small; }
```

This serves no function other than to make the element look more like a form field to the user.

Rich text bindings

A rich text binding is essentially no different than a text binding, except that it maps an HTML element in the result tree to an XHTML-valued XML element in the source tree, i.e., an element that can contain XHTML elements. This stylesheet contains one rich text binding shown in the template rule for `xhtml:p` elements:

```
<xsl:template match="xhtml:p">
  <p class="field">
    <xsl:copy-of select="node( )"/>
  </p>
</xsl:template>
```

Like the rules for the implicit creation of regular text bindings, the following two conditions must be met for a rich text binding to be created when an `xsl:copy-of` instruction is present:

- The `xsl:copy-of` instruction must be the only child element of a valid HTML element (p in this case).

- The expression in the `select` attribute must evaluate to a node-set containing zero or more text nodes and elements in the XHTML namespace that share the same parent element in the source document (`xhtml:p` in this case).

This text binding causes the HTML p element in the editing view to be rendered as an editable field, just as with a regular text binding. However, for it to function as a rich text field, there is one further requirement:

- The form definition file must explicitly declare this field, with rich text editing enabled.

Until this final condition is met, the field will behave like any other text binding, with the formatting toolbar disabled. See "The xField editing component," later in this chapter, to learn how to declare a rich text binding using the xsf:xmlToEdit element.

Structural bindings

Unless explicitly disabled, structural bindings are implicitly created whenever an XSLT template rule, named template, or xsl:for-each instruction, if it has any literal result elements as immediate children, is invoked. The binding occurs between the "current node," in XSLT terms, and each HTML element in the result tree that is created by a literal result element that is the immediate child of the xsl:template or xsl:for-each element. For example, the template rule that matches xhtml:p elements creates a structural binding between the p element in the result tree and the xhtml:p element in the source tree:

```
<xsl:template match="xhtml:p">
  <p class="field">
    <xsl:copy-of select="node( )"/>
  </p>
</xsl:template>
```

This structural binding occurs because xhtml:p is the current node, and the HTML p literal result element is the immediate child of xsl:template. Thus, it turns out that the resulting HTML p element, unlike any other element created by our stylesheet, has not one, but *two* bindings: a (rich) text binding and a structural binding. Both bindings map between the same two nodes.

Our stylesheet creates a number of structural bindings, one for each literal result element that is an immediate child of xsl:template or xsl:for-each. All of their corresponding start and end tags are highlighted in Example 10-15. Scanning down the stylesheet, we see structural bindings for html, tr, p, div, tr, and div, each of which maps to the current node at that point in stylesheet processing. On the other hand, the last two templates in the stylesheet, which happen to be named templates (make-date-picker and make-time-field) as opposed to template rules, do not create structural bindings. This is because their respective span element children explicitly prevent those bindings from being created by invoking xd:disableEditing="yes".

All of this begs the question, "What is the point of a structural binding?" The answer is that, whereas text bindings (whether rich or not) enable text editing, structural bindings enable *structural editing*. Examples of structural editing actions were included in Figures 10-7, 10-8, and 10-9, under friendly names like "Insert Paragraph Below", and "Replace with All-day or Multi-day Event." However, structural editing actions are not automatically available just because there is a structural binding. The structural binding is merely a prerequisite for structural editing. To enable structural editing, the form definition file must explicitly declare buttons, associate them with editing actions, and map them to XML nodes in the source document.

These mappings, if they are to have any effect on the form, rely on the presence of corresponding structural bindings. To see how this is done, see "Editing components" later in this chapter.

Date picker control

The precise rules for how to create a date picker control are not documented by Info-Path. The best approach, at this point, is to learn and follow by example. The make-date-picker template, shown again below, explicitly establishes a binding with an XML source node through the use of the xd:binding attribute. It is evaluated in the current XSLT context; in this case, the bound node is whatever value is passed to the template through the date-node parameter. This allows us to reuse the template for each date picker control we need to create in our form.

```
<xsl:template name="make-date-picker">
  <xsl:param name="date-node"/>
  <span xd:disableEditing="yes">
    <span class="field"
          xd:binding="$date-node"
          xd:xctname="DTPicker_DTText"
          contentEditable="true"
          style="BEHAVIOR: url(#default#CalPopup)
                          url(#default#urn::controls/Binder)
                          url(#default#Formatting);
                 width: 100;"
          xd:innerCtrl="_DTText"
          xd:boundProp="xd:num"
          xd:datafmt='"date","dateFormat:Short Date;"'>
      <xsl:attribute name="xd:num">
        <xsl:value-of select="$date-node"/>
      </xsl:attribute>
      <xsl:value-of select="xdFmt:formatString($date-node,
                                             'date',
                                             'dateFormat:Short Date;')"/>
    </span>
    <button style="height:18px; width:20px;
                   BEHAVIOR: url(#default#DTPicker);"
            tabindex="-1">
      <img src="res://infopath.exe/calendar.gif"/>
    </button>
  </span>
</xsl:template>
```

The span element child of xsl:template (which prevents a structural binding via xd:disableEditing="yes") contains two child elements: span and button. These must occur as adjacent sibling elements for the correct behavior to result. The span element has a number of attributes in the xd namespace, most (if not all) of which must be present for the date picker control to work correctly. The xd:num attribute (which initializes the date picker control, determining what calendar date will be highlighted) is created using the xsl:attribute instruction only because that is how the InfoPath form designer outputs the attribute. It will also work just fine if you use a literal result attribute and an attribute value template instead (as in xd:num="{$date-node}").

The contentEditable attribute, which is an extension to HTML that's supported by Internet Explorer, is also required. The CSS BEHAVIOR property is part of IE's behavioral extensions to CSS. The URL-based values are specific to InfoPath. The xd:datafmt attribute defines a translation from what the user types in to the underlying value to be stored. Specifically, it allows the user to enter a wide range of date formats, such as 9/22/03 or September 22, 2003, while storing the value using the ISO 8601 format, i.e., 2003-09-23. Conversely, the xdFmt:formatString() extension function is used to translate from the XML source value in the standard format to the localized format indicated by the second two arguments passed to the function. When the user tabs out of the field, its value, regardless of how the user entered the data, will be displayed in the localized format, e.g., 9/22/03. Finally, the button element creates the calendar icon button that, when clicked, displays the calendar date picker shown back in Figure 10-6. When the user selects a date, that date value populates the node to which the preceding span element is bound.

Time field formatting

To create a time-valued field, as well as a number of other types of InfoPath form controls, you should again take the approach of learning and doing by example. This is where InfoPath's sample forms are indispensable. For many kinds of controls, the sample forms represent the only documentation that's currently available, if you want to create such controls by hand. The declaration of the time field in our example is similar to that of the date picker. A named template, make-time-field, can be reused for each time field we want to create in the form.

The Form Definition File

Example 10-16 shows the entire form definition file for our example solution.

Example 10-16. The form definition file, manifest.xsf

```
<xsf:xDocumentClass solutionFormatVersion="1.0.0.0"
  xmlns:xsf=
    "http://schemas.microsoft.com/office/infopath/2003/solutionDefinition"
  xmlns:xhtml="http://www.w3.org/1999/xhtml"
  publishUrl="http://myserver/events/solution.xsn">

  <xsf:package>
    <xsf:files>
      <xsf:file name="template.xml"/>
      <xsf:file name="schema.xsd"/>
      <xsf:file name="paragraphs.xsd"/>
      <xsf:file name="xhtmlType.xsd"/>
      <xsf:file name="script.js"/>
      <xsf:file name="helper.html"/>
```

Example 10-16. The form definition file, manifest.xsf (continued)

```
      <xsf:file name="default.xsl"/>
      <xsf:file name="view2.xsl"/>
    </xsf:files>
  </xsf:package>

  <xsf:fileNew>
    <xsf:initialXmlDocument caption="Event" href="template.xml"/>
  </xsf:fileNew>

  <xsf:documentSchemas>
    <xsf:documentSchema location="schema.xsd"/>
  </xsf:documentSchemas>

  <xsf:scripts language="jscript">
    <xsf:script src="script.js"/>
  </xsf:scripts>

  <xsf:taskpane caption="Form Entry Tips" href="helper.html"/>

  <xsf:views default="Event Form">
    <xsf:view name="Event Form">
      <xsf:mainpane transform="default.xsl"/>
      <xsf:toolbar caption="Views" name="switcher">
        <xsf:button name="SwitchToPreview" caption="Preview This Event"/>
      </xsf:toolbar>
      <xsf:menuArea name="msoStructuralEditingContextMenu">
        <xsf:button action="xCollection::insertAfter"
                    xmlToEdit="pRepeating"
                    caption="Insert Paragraph Below"
                    showIf="immediate"/>
        <xsf:button action="xCollection::insertBefore"
                    xmlToEdit="pRepeating"
                    caption="Insert Paragraph Above"
                    showIf="immediate"/>
        <xsf:button action="xCollection::remove"
                    xmlToEdit="pRepeating"
                    caption="Remove Paragraph"
                    showIf="immediate"/>
        <xsf:button action="xReplace::replace"
                    xmlToEdit="single-to-multi"
                    caption="Replace with All-day or Multi-day Event"
                    showIf="immediate"/>
        <xsf:button action="xReplace::replace"
                    xmlToEdit="multi-to-single"
                    caption="Replace with Single-day Event with Time"
                    showIf="immediate"/>
        <xsf:button action="xOptional::remove"
                    xmlToEdit="end-time"
                    caption="Remove End Time"
                    showIf="immediate"/>
        <xsf:button action="xOptional::remove"
                    xmlToEdit="locationElement"
```

Example 10-16. The form definition file, manifest.xsf (continued)

```
                    caption="Remove Location"
                    showIf="immediate"/>
    </xsf:menuArea>
    <xsf:editing>

      <xsf:xmlToEdit name="pRepeating" item="xhtml:p" container="/event">
        <xsf:editWith component="xCollection">
          <xsf:fragmentToInsert>
            <xsf:chooseFragment parent="description">
             <p xmlns="http://www.w3.org/1999/xhtml"/>
            </xsf:chooseFragment>
          </xsf:fragmentToInsert>
        </xsf:editWith>
      </xsf:xmlToEdit>

      <xsf:xmlToEdit name="pRich" item="xhtml:p">
        <xsf:editWith component="xField" type="formatted"/>
      </xsf:xmlToEdit>

      <xsf:xmlToEdit name="single-to-multi"
                     item="single-day"
                     container="event">
        <xsf:editWith component="xReplace">
          <xsf:fragmentToInsert>
            <xsf:chooseFragment parent="when">
             <multi-day start-date="" end-date=""/>
            </xsf:chooseFragment>
          </xsf:fragmentToInsert>
        </xsf:editWith>
      </xsf:xmlToEdit>

      <xsf:xmlToEdit name="multi-to-single"
                     item="multi-day"
                     container="event">
        <xsf:editWith component="xReplace">
          <xsf:fragmentToInsert>
            <xsf:chooseFragment parent="when">
             <single-day date="" start-time=""/>
            </xsf:chooseFragment>
          </xsf:fragmentToInsert>
        </xsf:editWith>
      </xsf:xmlToEdit>

      <xsf:xmlToEdit name="end-time"
                     item="@end-time"
                     container="event">
        <xsf:editWith component="xOptional">
          <xsf:fragmentToInsert>
            <xsf:chooseFragment parent="when/single-day">
             <xsf:attributeData attribute="end-time" value=""/>
            </xsf:chooseFragment>
          </xsf:fragmentToInsert>
```

Example 10-16. The form definition file, manifest.xsf (continued)

```
          </xsf:editWith>
        </xsf:xmlToEdit>

        <xsf:xmlToEdit name="locationElement"
                       item="location"
                       container="event">
          <xsf:editWith component="xOptional">
            <xsf:fragmentToInsert>
              <xsf:chooseFragment followingSiblings="when">
                <location/>
              </xsf:chooseFragment>
            </xsf:fragmentToInsert>
          </xsf:editWith>
        </xsf:xmlToEdit>

      </xsf:editing>
      <xsf:unboundControls>
        <xsf:button name="btnCreate"/>
      </xsf:unboundControls>
    </xsf:view>
    <xsf:view name="Preview Event">
      <xsf:toolbar caption="Views" name="switcher">
        <xsf:button name="SwitchToForm" caption="Go Back To Form"/>
      </xsf:toolbar>
      <xsf:mainpane transform="view2.xsl"/>
    </xsf:view>
  </xsf:views>

  <xsf:customValidation>
    <xsf:errorCondition match="single-day/@end-time"
      expression="translate(.,':','') &lt;= translate(../@start-time,':','')">
      <xsf:errorMessage type="modeless"
                        shortMessage="End time must come after start time.">
        The event's end time must be later than the event's start time.
      </xsf:errorMessage>
    </xsf:errorCondition>
    <xsf:errorCondition match="multi-day/@end-date"
      expression="translate(.,'-','') &lt;= translate(../@start-date,'-','')">
      <xsf:errorMessage type="modeless"
                        shortMessage="End date must come after start date.">
        The event's end date must be later than the event's start date.
      </xsf:errorMessage>
    </xsf:errorCondition>
  </xsf:customValidation>

  <xsf:submit caption="Submit Event" showStatusDialog="no">
    <xsf:useScriptHandler/>
  </xsf:submit>

</xsf:xDocumentClass>
```

This form definition file illustrates a number of advanced features:

- Support for multiple views—in this case, the default view (*default.xsl*), which was shown in Example 10-15, and a secondary view (*view2.xsl*, not shown in this chapter)
- The use of an HTML task pane (*helper.html*), shown later in Example 10-17
- The declaration of a script file that uses JScript (*script.js*), shown later in Example 10-18
- The declaration of custom buttons associated with structural editing actions
- The use of custom validation rules over and above the XSD schema (using the xsf:customValidation element)
- The declaration of a form submission mechanism whose behavior is defined by a custom script (using the xsf:useScriptHandler element)

All of these features and their corresponding XSF declarations are well documented in InfoPath's online Help system or secondary Microsoft documentation. For purposes of this tutorial, we'll take a closer look specifically at how structural editing actions are enabled.

Creating toolbars, menus, and buttons

To enable any structural editing action or a custom action, a button must first be created. The form definition file allows you to create custom toolbars that contain menus or buttons. Menus (described using the xsf:menu element), in turn, can contain buttons or more menus. The form definition file in Example 10-16 includes one custom toolbar declaration for each view. The declaration for the default view's custom toolbar is shown again below:

```
<xsf:toolbar caption="Views" name="switcher">
  <xsf:button name="SwitchToPreview" caption="Preview This Event"/>
</xsf:toolbar>
```

The button declared here is used to switch to the form's secondary view by invoking the OnClick handler for the named button, i.e., SwitchToPreview. The secondary view likewise has its own toolbar and button for switching back to the default view. See Example 10-18 for the script that contains the instructions that implement these actions.

In addition to custom toolbars, InfoPath contains nine built-in named menu areas:

```
msoFileMenu
msoEditMenu
msoInsertMenu
msoViewMenu
msoFormatMenu
msoToolsMenu
```

```
msoTableMenu
msoHelpMenu
msoStructuralEditingContextMenu
```

It should be obvious which menus in the UI each of these corresponds to. The last one, msoStructuralEditingContextMenu, is the only menu area used by our example solution, as declared in Example 10-16. This menu contains each of the buttons declared using the xsf:button declarations, shown again below:

```
<xsf:menuArea name="msoStructuralEditingContextMenu">
   <xsf:button action="xCollection::insertAfter"
        xmlToEdit="pRepeating"
        caption="Insert Paragraph Below"
        showIf="immediate"/>
   <xsf:button action="xCollection::insertBefore"
        xmlToEdit="pRepeating"
        caption="Insert Paragraph Above"
        showIf="immediate"/>
   <xsf:button action="xCollection::remove"
        xmlToEdit="pRepeating"
        caption="Remove Paragraph"
        showIf="immediate"/>
   <xsf:button action="xReplace::replace"
        xmlToEdit="single-to-multi"
        caption="Replace with All-day or Multi-day Event"
        showIf="immediate"/>
   <xsf:button action="xReplace::replace"
        xmlToEdit="multi-to-single"
        caption="Replace with Single-day Event with Time"
        showIf="immediate"/>
   <xsf:button action="xOptional::remove"
        xmlToEdit="end-time"
        caption="Remove End Time"
        showIf="immediate"/>
   <xsf:button action="xOptional::remove"
        xmlToEdit="locationElement"
        caption="Remove Location"
        showIf="immediate"/>
</xsf:menuArea>
```

The structural editing context menu is what the user sees when he or she right-clicks a section that has structural editing actions enabled on it, or left-clicks the blue down-arrow icon that automatically appears at the top left corner of a section when the mouse hovers over it. The showIf attribute on each button declaration causes the button to be displayed in the menu only when the user's selection is in certain contexts. The showIf attribute has three possible values:

```
immediate
enabled
always
```

The value immediate (which is used in all the instances above) is the most restrictive of the three. If showIf="immediate", then the button will only be included in the menu when its associated editing action is immediately applicable to the user's current HTML selection. What is precisely meant by "immediately applicable" depends on the particular editing action. A value of enabled means that the button will be displayed only when it is enabled (not otherwise grayed out). A button is enabled not only when the editing action is immediately applicable to the user's selection, but also when the user's selection is some descendant of that immediately applicable context. Finally, a value of always means that the button will be displayed in the context menu at all times, regardless of the user's current selection and regardless of whether the button is enabled or disabled (grayed out).

Rather than associating itself by name with custom OnClick event handling script (as with the buttons for switching between views), each of the xsf:button elements above declaratively associates itself with an action of a built-in *editing component* (see the next section, "Editing components"), by way of the action attribute. The value of this attribute is the name of the editing component, followed by a scope operator (::), followed by one of the actions available for that editing component. The button must also associate itself with an actual node in the source document, that node's view in the HTML document, and a configured instance of the editing component. This is all done in a single swoop by referring, in the xmlToEdit attribute, to an xsf:xmlToEdit element declared under the xsf:editing element inside the view's configuration. Finally, the caption attribute's value is what the user actually sees when using these buttons.

Editing components

An editing component is a collection of actions for editing certain kinds of XML nodes. Each component is configurable in its own way. There are six kinds of editing components. Table 10-1 shows the name, purpose, and associated actions of each.

Table 10-1. The six editing components and their associated actions

Name	Purpose	Actions
xCollection	For a repeating list, or table, of elements	insert, insertBefore, insertAfter, remove, removeAll
xOptional	For optional elements or attributes	insert, remove
xReplace	For choice groups of alternative elements	replace
xTextList	For plain, bulleted, or numbered lists (also corresponds to a repeating sequence of elements)	split, merge, remove
xField	For text bindings, i.e. text boxes and rich text boxes	(none)
xImage	For embedded images	(none)

Before continuing, let me warn you that the next several paragraphs are rather dense. They are an attempt to succinctly cover a complex topic, i.e., how editing control associations (declared using `xsf:xmlToEdit` elements) are established. If you get tripped up on a single point, don't stop reading. Try to forge on through the examples in the following sections. Things may become clear in retrospect. Most likely, they will only truly become clear after doing some experimentation of your own. In any case, this should get you started on the right track.

Each `xsf:xmlToEdit` element within the `xsf:editing` element in a view's configuration represents an XML editing control. It defines an association between nodes in the source document and a particular editing component, along with parameterization of the editing component's behavior.

The `item` and `container` attributes on each `xsf:xmlToEdit` element together define *where* the control is in the HTML editing view, by way of the structural and/or text bindings to XML source nodes that have already been established. The basic syntax is like this:

```
<xsf:xmlToEdit name="someID" item="pattern" container="pattern"...>
```

The required `name` attribute of the `xsf:xmlToEdit` element is a unique identifier and is what `xsf:button` elements refer to in their `xmlToEdit` attributes. The `item` attribute is always required, regardless of which editing component is being associated. The `container` attribute is only required for certain editing components and optional for others. For example, it is optional for xField, but it is required for xCollection, xOptional, and xReplace. (The editing component in question is determined by the value of the `component` attribute of the `xsf:editWith` child element.)

Whereas the `item` and `container` attributes determine *where* the control is in the HTML editing view, the `xsf:editWith` child element defines *what* the editing control is and does: which editing component it uses (through the `component` attribute), and how that editing component is configured (through any additional attributes and child elements of the `xsf:editWith` element). The basic syntax is like this:

```
<xsf:editWith component="xSomeComponent"...>
  <!-- other child elements, depending on which component is being used -->
</xsf:editWith>
```

The `xsf:xmlToEdit` element's `container` and `item` attributes' values must lie in the subset of XPath syntax that corresponds to the syntax for XSLT patterns. In fact, they are interpreted in essentially the same way as XSLT patterns. The precise definition of a pattern's behavior, as found in the XSLT recommendation, is that:

> A node matches a pattern if the node is a member of the result of evaluating the pattern as an expression with respect to some possible context; the possible contexts are those whose context node is the node being matched or one of its ancestors. — *http://www.w3.org/TR/xslt#patterns*

A helpful way to think about how editing control associations occur is to consider the procedural task that InfoPath performs while the user is editing. At any given point while a user is editing, InfoPath must determine whether or not to activate an XML editing control based on the user's current HTML node selection. Its criteria for doing so depend on the item and container attribute values of the various xsf:xmlToEdit declarations in the form definition file.

Here goes. Starting with the current HTML node selection, InfoPath traverses the ancestor nodes (in reverse document order) until it finds an HTML node that is bound to an XML node that matches the item pattern of an xsf:xmlToEdit element in the current view's configuration. If the container attribute is also present on a candidate xsf:xmlToEdit element, then InfoPath continues to traverse the ancestors until it finds an HTML node that is bound to an XML node that satisfies the container pattern. Provided that InfoPath finds an item node (and a container node, when specified) that is bound to the current HTML selection or one of its ancestors, then the current selection will behave as declared within the corresponding xsf:xmlToEdit element. Namely, the actions of the associated editing component will be available, and the actions will behave as customized by the xsf:editWith element's additional attributes and elements.

Moreover, both the container and item HTML nodes are control-selectable, i.e., a dashed border appears around them when the mouse hovers over them, and they can be selected by the user. An exception to this behavior is when the container node binds to an element that is not normally selectable within the body of an HTML document. This is the case with many of our example's declarations, in which the container XML node, the root event element, maps to the editing view's root html element. Though the container HTML node (html) is not selectable in this case, its binding to a node in the XML source document is still a necessary (and sufficient) condition for the editing control association to take place. If it were not for the structural binding between event and html, most of our solution's editing controls would be disabled.

An optional viewContext attribute on the xsf:xmlToEdit element can be added if there exists more than one HTML binding to the same XML node. (We saw a facetious example of this back in Example 10-4.) In that event, the viewContext attribute can be used to disambiguate two controls (i.e., xsf:xmlToEdit elements) that have the same context (item and container attributes), by referring to the value of an HTML element's xd:CtrlId attribute value. Then an editing control with a particular viewContext will apply only to an HTML selection that not only falls within the context specified by the item and container attributes but also is, or is a descendant of, an HTML element whose xd:CtrlId attribute value equals the value of the viewContext attribute.

That's how these things behave in the abstract. If you didn't comprehend it all, don't worry. Taking a look at some concrete uses of the individual editing components in our example may help.

The xCollection editing component

The xCollection component is used to edit a repeating list of elements. In our example, the xhtml:p element is associated with the xCollection editing component in order to enable actions such as xCollection::insertAbove and xCollection::insertBelow. This declaration is shown again below:

```
<xsf:xmlToEdit name="pRepeating" item="xhtml:p" container="/event">
  <xsf:editWith component="xCollection">
    <xsf:fragmentToInsert>
      <xsf:chooseFragment parent="description">
        <p xmlns="http://www.w3.org/1999/xhtml"/>
      </xsf:chooseFragment>
    </xsf:fragmentToInsert>
  </xsf:editWith>
</xsf:xmlToEdit>
```

When a user clicks inside the HTML p element in the editing view, the above-declared XML editing control is activated, because the p element falls within the context defined by the item and container attributes. Specifically:

- p is bound to the xhtml:p element in the source document, which of course matches this declaration's item pattern ("xhtml:p")
- p has an ancestor HTML element that's bound to an XML node that satisfies the container pattern ("/event"), namely the final ancestor element, the html root element of the editing view.

The xsf:editWith element, besides specifying which editing component to use (xCollection), in turn uses the xsf:fragmentToInsert element and its child, xsf:chooseFragment, to specify *what* XML fragment to insert when a user invokes the xCollection::insert, xCollection::insertAbove, or xCollection::insertBelow actions. When the user pushes the Insert Paragraph Below button, for example, a new XML fragment will be inserted, namely an empty p element in the XHTML namespace. *Where* the fragment will be inserted is determined by the parent attribute of the xsf:chooseFragment element. Its value is an XPath expression that is evaluated in the context of the container node, i.e., using the container XML node as the context node. If the parent attribute is absent, then the fragment is directly inserted as a child of the container node. In other words, the parent attribute's value, when absent, defaults to ".". In our example, the parent attribute is present, and the XPath expression description is evaluated using the root element, event, as the context node, yielding the source document's description element. Therefore, the fragment to insert will be inserted as a child of the description element.

The xOptional editing component

The xOptional editing component corresponds to an optional element or attribute in the source document. Our example contains an optional location element and an optional end-time attribute. The declarations for each are very similar, both in the form definition file and in the XSLT stylesheet. In both cases, the stylesheet uses an `xsl:choose` statement to test for the presence of the optional node. If present, the stylesheet processes the node using `xsl:for-each`, thereby establishing a structural binding. But when the optional node is absent, it has no way of creating a binding to the node, as there is no way to bind to an XML node that does not yet exist in the source document. The solution around this is to create a placeholder link that refers to the XML fragment to insert via the `xd:xmlToEdit` attribute:

```
<td colspan="2" class="optionalPlaceholder"
    xd:xmlToEdit="locationElement" tabindex="0">
  <xsl:text>Click here to add optional Location</xsl:text>
</td>
```

The `optionalPlaceholder` CSS class is declared in the HTML document head. The linking behavior of the placeholder element (a `td` in this case) is effected by using the CSS behavior, `url(#default#xOptional)`, an InfoPath-specific property included in our `optionalPlaceholder` class. The `xd:xmlToEdit` attribute refers to the `locationElement` editing control in the form definition file:

```
<xsf:xmlToEdit name="locationElement"
               item="location"
               container="event">
    <xsf:editWith component="xOptional">
      <xsf:fragmentToInsert>
        <xsf:chooseFragment followingSiblings="when">
          <location/>
        </xsf:chooseFragment>
      </xsf:fragmentToInsert>
    </xsf:editWith>
</xsf:xmlToEdit>
```

The above blurb shows that the fragment to insert when a user invokes the `xOptional::insert` action is simply an empty `location` element. The `followingSiblings` attribute on the `xsf:chooseFragment` element is necessary, because our schema dictates that the `location` element, if present, must come before the `when` element. Otherwise, the default insertion behavior would yield an invalid document. The default insertion behavior is to append the fragment as the last child of the parent node (the `event` element in this case, because the parent attribute is absent). The `followingSiblings` attribute can be used to override this default append behavior. Its value is an XPath expression evaluated in the context of the parent node (the `event` element, in this case). The effective behavior is that the fragment will be inserted before all the nodes in the node-set returned by the `followingSiblings` expression. In this case, that means the `location` element will be inserted immediately before the `when` element.

The end-time control declaration shows how attributes are inserted, using the `xsf:attributeData` element:

```
<xsf:xmlToEdit name="end-time"
               item="@end-time"
```

```
                container="event">
    <xsf:editWith component="xOptional">
      <xsf:fragmentToInsert>
        <xsf:chooseFragment parent="when/single-day">
          <xsf:attributeData attribute="end-time" value=""/>
        </xsf:chooseFragment>
      </xsf:fragmentToInsert>
    </xsf:editWith>
  </xsf:xmlToEdit>
```

The xReplace Editing Component

The xReplace editing component is usually used in conjunction with a choice group
in the schema between two or more alternative XML elements. In our example, the
XSLT stylesheet initially establishes a structural binding by applying templates to the
child of the when element, regardless of which element (single-day or multi-day) is
present:

```
<tr>
  <td>When:</td>
  <td>
    <xsl:apply-templates select="when/*"/>
  </td>
</tr>
```

The matching template rule is applied, thereby establishing a structural binding
between the single-day or multi-day element and the div element contained within
the matching xsl:template element, which will be one of these:

```
<xsl:template match="single-day">
  <div>
    ...
  </div>
</xsl:template>

<xsl:template match="multi-day">
  <div>
    ...
  </div>
</xsl:template>
```

The form definition file in turn declares two separate editing controls, one for each
possible element:

```
<xsf:xmlToEdit name="single-to-multi"
               item="single-day"
               container="event">
    <xsf:editWith component="xReplace">
      <xsf:fragmentToInsert>
        <xsf:chooseFragment parent="when">
          <multi-day start-date="" end-date=""/>
        </xsf:chooseFragment>
      </xsf:fragmentToInsert>
    </xsf:editWith>
  </xsf:xmlToEdit>
```

```
<xsf:xmlToEdit name="multi-to-single"
               item="multi-day"
               container="event">
  <xsf:editWith component="xReplace">
    <xsf:fragmentToInsert>
      <xsf:chooseFragment parent="when">
        <single-day date="" start-time=""/>
      </xsf:chooseFragment>
    </xsf:fragmentToInsert>
  </xsf:editWith>
</xsf:xmlToEdit>
```

As can be seen above, the xReplace component is configured in a similar way to the xOptional and xCollection components. It too uses the xsf:chooseFragment element to determine exactly what to replace the element with. In this case, the single-day element is replaced with a multi-day element that includes its two (required) empty attributes, and the multi-day element is replaced with a single-day element whose optional end-time attribute is absent.

The xField editing component

xField is the editing component that lets you customize the behavior of leaf node editing, or what we have been calling "text bindings". Our form definition file associates the xhtml:p element with the xField component so that it can customize its behavior—specifically by declaring type="formatted" on the xsf:editWith element, effectively making the text binding behave as a rich text binding:

```
<xsf:xmlToEdit name="pRich" item="xhtml:p">
  <xsf:editWith component="xField" type="formatted"/>
</xsf:xmlToEdit>
```

The other legal values for the type attribute (when the component is xField) are plain, plainMultiline, formattedMultiline, and rich.

 This example illustrates the fact that the same node in the source document can be associated with multiple editing components, since the form definition file also associates xhtml:p with the xCollection editing component. Another common use case for associating an element with multiple editing components is when an optional node can be removed (using xOptional::remove) or replaced (using xReplace:: replace). In that case, two separate xsf:xmlToEdit declarations are necessary, one for xOptional and one for xReplace.

The xField component also supports the use of the proofing and autoComplete attributes on xsf:editWith. The value of these attributes (yes or no) determines whether the given field will enable the proofing features (such as spell checking), and form field auto-completion, respectively.

The xTextList editing component

Although our example doesn't use the xTextList editing component, it turns out that it probably should. As useful as xCollection is in other contexts, it doesn't make editing paragraphs as easy as you might expect from a Microsoft product. In Word, for example, to create a new paragraph or split an existing paragraph in two, you simply hit Enter. And to merge paragraphs, you just hit the Backspace or Delete keys, depending on where the current insertion point is. Thankfully, in InfoPath, you can use the xTextList editing component to expose this split-and-merge behavior that the user expects. This is much better than forcing the user to switch back and forth between the keyboard and mouse, typing sentences and then clicking "Insert Paragraph Below," or copying and pasting from one paragraph into the other because xCollection doesn't automatically split or merge paragraphs.

So let's see what would be involved in updating our solution to use xTextList for paragraphs, rather than xCollection. The XSLT stylesheet and all files other than the form definition file can remain unchanged. All we need to do in *manifest.xsf* is delete all of the xCollection-oriented buttons, as well as the editing controls named pRepeating and pRich. In their place, we add the following simple declaration:

```
<xsf:xmlToEdit name="pList" item="xhtml:p">
  <xsf:editWith component="xTextList" type="formatted"/>
</xsf:xmlToEdit>
```

This single declaration does everything that we tried to achieve using the xCollection component, only better. No more buttons are necessary, because the split, merge, and remove actions are by default made available through the Enter, Backspace, and Delete keys. And a separate xField declaration is no longer necessary, because xTextList also supports the type attribute (with values of plain or formatted).

The HTML Task Pane

Our form definition file in Example 10-16 declared a custom HTML task pane:

```
<xsf:taskpane caption="Form Entry Tips" href="helper.html"/>
```

Example 10-17 shows the contents of *helper.html*, our custom task pane document.

Example 10-17. The HTML task pane, helper.html

```
<html>
  <head>
    <style type="text/css">
      body { font-family: Verdana; font-size: xx-small; }
    </style>
  </head>
  <body>
    <form name="finalForm" action="http://myserver/process-events/" method="post">
      <input type="hidden" name="xml"/>
    </form>
```

Example 10-17. The HTML task pane, helper.html (continued)

```
    <h3>Form Tips</h3>
    <ul>
        <li>Hit CTRL-ENTER to open a new paragraph while typing the event
description</li>
        <li>Right-click any item to see available actions</li>
        <li>Use CTRL-Z and CTRL-Y to undo and redo your changes</li>
        <li>Navigate forward and backward through the form using the TAB and SHIFT-
TAB keys</li>
    </ul>
  </body>
</html>
```

This task pane displays some common InfoPath editing shortcuts for the user, such as hitting Ctrl-Enter to trigger the xCollection::insertAfter action, which in this case functions to create a new paragraph. However, there is also a hidden HTML form embedded in the document. This demonstrates just one possibility of how XML created by InfoPath could be submitted to a web application other than through the built-in declarative submission mechanisms. The form doesn't do anything by itself, but a script can be written to access it and submit it, as we'll see in the next section, "The Script File." InfoPath's built-in HTTP submission mechanism only supports HTTP POST of text/xml content, but this form and the accompanying script used to populate and submit it generates an HTTP POST request with content of type application/x-www-form-urlencoded, with the value of the xml parameter being the XML document that was created. The advantage is that it can be integrated with an existing web application designed to work with HTML forms.

 Submission of XML as content of type application/x-www-form-urlencoded, while useful as an example, is not generally advisable, because it only supports ASCII characters. For an application that requires international characters or any other character outside the ASCII range, you should use a different submission mechanism.

The Script File

Our form definition file in Example 10-16 declared a script file:

```
<xsf:scripts language="jscript">
  <xsf:script src="script.js"/>
</xsf:scripts>
```

Example 10-18 shows the contents of *script.js*, our custom script file.

Example 10-18. The script file, script.js

```
function SwitchToPreview::OnClick( )
{
    XDocument.View.SwitchView("Preview Event");
}
```

Example 10-18. The script file, script.js (continued)

```
function SwitchToForm::OnClick( )
{
    XDocument.View.SwitchView("Event Form");
}

function XDocument::OnSubmitRequest(eventObj)
{
    var xdoc = eventObj.XDocument;
    try
    {
        var finalForm = xdoc.View.Window.TaskPanes(0).HTMLDocument.finalForm;

        finalForm.xml.value = xdoc.DOM.xml;
        doSubmitHTMLForm(xdoc);
    }
    catch (ex)
    {
        eventObj.ReturnStatus = false;
        throw ex;
    }

    eventObj.ReturnStatus = true;
}

function btnCreate::OnClick(eventObj)
{
    eventObj.XDocument.Submit( );
}

function doSubmitHTMLForm(xdoc)
{
    var taskpaneDoc = xdoc.View.Window.TaskPanes(0).HTMLDocument;
    var finalForm = taskpaneDoc.finalForm;
    var resultWindow = taskpaneDoc.open(
                    "http://myserver/pleaseWait",
                    "result","scrollbars=yes,menubar=yes," +
                    "resizable=yes,location=yes,toolbar=yes,status=yes");
    finalForm.target = "result";
    finalForm.submit( );
    resultWindow.focus( );
}
```

The functions defined in this short script file perform two primary tasks:

- Switching between views
- Submitting the created XML to a web server

The view-switching behavior is achieved by implementing the OnClick event handler for each of the two buttons that were declared in the form definition file, in

Example 10-16. The "Preview Event" view (defined by the *view2.xsl* stylesheet, not listed in this chapter) declared one of these buttons, named SwitchToForm:

```
<xsf:view name="Preview Event">
  <xsf:toolbar caption="Views" name="switcher">
    <xsf:button name="SwitchToForm" caption="Go Back To Form"/>
  </xsf:toolbar>
  <xsf:mainpane transform="view2.xsl"/>
</xsf:view>
```

To switch back to the default "Event Form" view (defined by *default.xsl*), the following single line of code is all that's needed:

```
XDocument.View.SwitchView("Event Form");
```

When the user clicks the Go Back To Form button, the editing view switches back to the default form view that was displayed when the form was first opened.

There is one other OnClick event handler implemented in this script file:

```
function btnCreate::OnClick(eventObj)
{
    eventObj.XDocument.Submit();
}
```

Unlike the view-switching buttons, this button (named btnCreate) was not declared in the form definition file but instead was declared directly in *default.xsl* (Example 10-15), identified by the value of its xd:CtrlId attribute:

```
<input type="button" value="Submit Event" xd:CtrlId="btnCreate"/>
```

To be successfully referenced, this button must also be declared within the xsf: unboundControls section of the form definition file, within the xsf:view element:

```
<xsf:unboundControls>
      <xsf:button name="btnCreate"/>
    </xsf:unboundControls>
```

Clicking on this button causes the solution's submission mechanism to be invoked. The form definition file specifies that the submit action should, in turn, be handled by a custom script (as opposed to one of the other options, such as xsf: useHttpHandler or xsf:webServiceAdapter):

```
<xsf:submit caption="Submit Event" showStatusDialog="no">
    <xsf:useScriptHandler/>
  </xsf:submit>
```

The XDocument::OnSubmitRequest event is fired when the user attempts to submit the form. Finally, our corresponding event handler populates the xml field in our HTML task pane's hidden form with the serialized XML document created by the user, and submits it to a web server. At this point, we are using Internet Explorer's HTML document object model API, accessible via the HTMLDocument property of the InfoPath TaskPane object:

```
var taskpaneDoc = xdoc.View.Window.TaskPanes(0).HTMLDocument;
```

Though our HTML task pane did not show an example of it, it is also possible to do the converse, i.e., access the InfoPath object model from script embedded in an HTML task pane document.

 The complete InfoPath object model is well documented in InfoPath's online Help system, under Table of Contents → InfoPath Developer's Reference → InfoPath Object Model Reference.

The Cabinet Manifest

When it comes time to deploy your solution, you have several deployment options:

- Individually publish all of the form template files, including *manifest.xsf*, to a shared location or web server
- Use InfoPath design mode's "Publish Form…" feature to create and publish a *.xsn* file (see "Publishing a Form from Design Mode" later in this chapter).
- Use the *makecab.exe* utility to create a *.xsn* file at the command-line prompt

Example 10-19 shows a DDF ("diamond directive file") that can be fed to the *makecab.exe* utility (included with Windows 2000 and XP) to package up all the form template files into a single CAB file, named *event.xsn*.

Example 10-19. A cabinet file manifest for solution deployment, cab-manifest.ddf

```
.Option Explicit
.Set CabinetNameTemplate=event.xsn
.Set Cabinet=on
.Set Compress=on

manifest.xsf
default.xsl
view2.xsl
template.xml
helper.html
schema.xsd
paragraphs.xsd
script.js
```

This file is not part of the InfoPath form template. Rather, it just provides a way to package the form template files into a single *.xsn* file, without having to open the solution in design mode with all of the potential issues that can create. (See "Developing Solutions that Play Nice with Design Mode," later in this chapter.) It can be executed using this command:

```
makecab.exe /F cab-manifest.ddf
```

You should ensure that when you do publish your form template, regardless of the deployment method chosen, you publish it to the same location as listed in the publishUrl attribute of the form definition file's root element, xsf:xDocumentClass.

Otherwise, InfoPath will refuse to open the form, complaining that it has moved from its original location. For more information on this topic, see "Publishing a Form from Design Mode," later in this chapter.

Using InfoPath Design Mode

By now you've probably noticed that this chapter is heavily biased toward the creation of solutions by hand. One of the reasons for this is that you can only use the full power of XSLT when creating a solution if you do it by hand, rather than through InfoPath design mode. Provided that you understand how InfoPath establishes implicit bindings from your stylesheet, you should be able to avoid potential pitfalls by writing your stylesheet in such a way that only the bindings you intend to create get created. You can do it, whether it means avoiding certain arrangements of XSLT instructions or invoking xd:disableEditing="yes" in the right places.

> The design mode of InfoPath is well documented in InfoPath's online Help system. The focus of this chapter has been to expose the technical details of InfoPath solutions, particularly where existing documentation is lacking, such as how InfoPath interprets view stylesheets to establish node bindings. For that reason, this section provides only a cursory overview of InfoPath design mode and happily refers you to the online Help system for a more in-depth investigation.

That said, there are a number of reasons InfoPath in design mode may be useful to you:

- As a tool for learning how valid solutions can be created
- As a form design tool for developers or IT workers who aren't as XML-savvy
- As an expedient way to create forms, given an existing XML schema, instance document, or web service
- As an expedient way to configure other aspects of a solution besides the default view, e.g., secondary views, submission behavior, web services integration, etc. (see "Developing Solutions that Play Nice with Design Mode" later in this chapter).
- As a solution packaging and deployment tool that supports automatic update notifications
- As an IDE for InfoPath scripting, with the help of Microsoft Script Editor

InfoPath design mode provides a WYSIWYG environment for creating forms meant to be run by InfoPath in editing mode. It has sophisticated support for the creation of

HTML layout tables and lets you drag and drop different kinds of form controls onto the form view canvas. You can begin creating a form in one of three ways:

1. From scratch.
2. From a "data source," which can be an XSD schema, an XML instance document, a WSDL-defined web service, or a Microsoft Access or SQL Server database.
3. By customizing one of the sample forms that come bundled with InfoPath.

Creating a Simple Solution from an XSD Schema

If we had decided to create our event form example from within design mode, rather than by hand, we would only need an example instance document, or better yet, a schema, to get started. Since we already have the schema (Example 10-10), let's take a quick look at what this would involve. Figure 10-10 shows a newly created form in design mode, not unlike the one we created by hand.

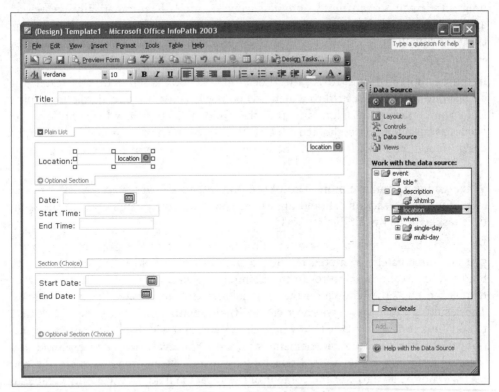

Figure 10-10. Designing a form starting from an XSD schema "data source"

To create a new form starting with an XML schema, select File → Design a Form... → New from Data Source. From within the Data Source Setup Wizard, choose "XML Schema or XML data file," click Next, and finally click Browse to find the XML schema file.

InfoPath design mode utilizes as much information as possible from the schema to aid you in creating your form. In fact, just by dragging and dropping from the Data Source task pane, shown on the right side of the window in Figure 10-10, we can create a functional form in just a few seconds.

The Data Source task pane provides an Explorer-like view of the underlying XML schema for the form you are designing. Some icons signify *groups*, and others *fields*, in InfoPath's terminology. A field is an attribute or an element that can contain only text, or rich text in the case of XHTML content. A group is an element that can contain element children, i.e., other groups or fields. In XSD terms, fields (except for rich text fields) have simple content and groups have complex content. When you drag an element or attribute onto the canvas, InfoPath automatically creates an appropriate section (for a group) or form control (for a field). When more than one choice is equally appropriate, it immediately prompts you to choose which control or section type you want.

In our example in Figure 10-10, the "Location" text box is selected. As a result, the corresponding location field to which it is bound is automatically highlighted in the Data Source task pane. Note also that the optional section in which the text box occurs is also bound to the location field. As you navigate through the form in design mode, you will see where the binding for each control is in the data source tree.

When you want to have more control (no pun intended) over exactly what kinds of form controls or sections should appear in your form, you can switch to the Controls task pane, shown in Figure 10-11.

When you drag a control or section onto the canvas from the Controls task pane, you are immediately prompted to choose what group or field in the data source to bind that control or section to. In the example shown in Figure 10-11, the location field is chosen as the binding for the optional section being dragged onto the canvas. The resulting XSLT view stylesheet created by InfoPath will include the "Click here to add" link for the location field when it is absent, and will display the optional section itself when the location element is present. However, this is an example of a structural binding, rather than a text binding, which means that, as such, the end user will not be able to edit the content of the location field, but will only be able to add or remove it. To provide editing support, we additionally need to create a text binding. We can do this either by dragging a Text Box control onto the canvas, inside the optional section, and then selecting the location field when prompted for a binding, or we can start from the Data Source task pane instead and simply drag

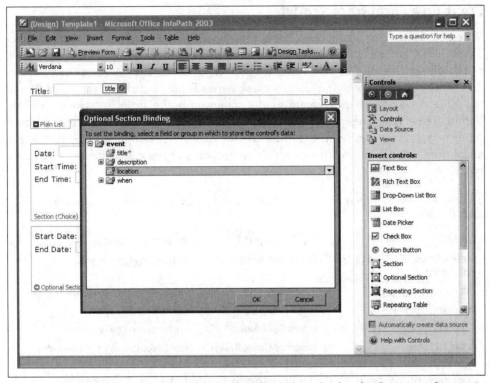

Figure 10-11. The Controls task pane and the prompt to select a binding for the "optional section" being dragged onto the canvas

the `location` field into the optional section we created for it. A corresponding Text Box control will automatically be created. Either way, we end up with the `location` field having two bindings, a text binding and a structural binding, just as was the case with the event form example we created by hand.

Another thing to note about Figure 10-10 is that the entire form appears exactly as InfoPath in design mode created it, as a result merely of dragging-and-dropping fields, groups, sections, or controls onto the canvas. No additional edits were made. Thus, it not only makes reasonable choices about what controls or section types to use, but it also automatically tries to make the field names friendlier, so "location" becomes "Location," "start-time" becomes "Start Time," etc.

We can relate some of these controls back to some terminology introduced earlier in the chapter under "The XSLT Stylesheet," for the event form solution created by hand. Specifically, the Text Box and Rich Text Box controls result in the creation of *text bindings*, and the various kinds of sections (optional, repeating, choice, etc.) result in the creation of *structural bindings* and corresponding editing control declarations (`xsf:xmlToEdit` elements) in the form definition file. Other kinds of bindings, such as those employed by the checkbox and radio button controls, can best be explored by perusing the sample forms that come bundled with the InfoPath application.

Creating a Form from Scratch

When creating a new blank form rather than starting from a schema or instance document, InfoPath automatically creates a schema for you as form controls are added to the design. To disable this default behavior, uncheck the "Automatically create data source" checkbox in the Controls task pane. Table 10-2 shows the controls and the XSD declarations they create in the schema for the fields to which they are bound. These mappings reveal not only how this handy feature works, but, perhaps more importantly, it gives you some clues about how to design your own schemas and forms. Specifically, it shows which controls make sense to bind to which data types.

Table 10-2. Controls for text and rich text bindings, and the automatically created data source fields they bind to

Control(s)	Data Source Type	XSD Element Declaration
Text Box, List Box, Drop-Down List Box, Option Button	Element field (string)	`xsd:string`-typed element
Rich Text Box	Element field (XHTML)	Complex-typed element with XHTML content.
Date Picker	Element field (date)	`xsd:date`-typed element
Check Box	Element field (boolean)	`xsd:boolean`-typed element
Picture, Ink Picture	Element field (base64binary)	`xsd:base64binary`-typed element

All of the controls that bind to automatically created element fields can also bind to attribute fields, with one exception. The Rich Text Box control binds to an element field that can contain XHTML elements. Since attributes cannot contain elements, Rich Text Box controls cannot bind to attribute fields. The Button, Hyperlink, and Expression Box controls can never have bindings. The Expression Box control is essentially a way for you to create an `xsl:value-of` instruction from within design mode. You specify the XPath expression whose value you want displayed. If necessary, editing will be explicitly disabled in the resulting stylesheet, through use of the `xd:disableEditing` annotation, because Expression Box controls are meant primarily to display derived information, such as a sum of numbers. They are not used to establish editing bindings.

The Layout and Views Task Panes

The Layout task pane provides a set of table-based layout templates to choose from and a set of table operations for manipulating them. The Views task pane allows you to manage multiple views in your form template, each of which corresponds to an instance of the `xsf:view` element in the form definition file.

Publishing a Form from Design Mode

Once you have finished designing your form, you have the option of publishing it through the InfoPath interface. Click on "Publish Form..." in the Design Tasks task pane, and a wizard will guide you through the process. You have a choice between three publication targets: shared folder, SharePoint form library, or web server. Publication to a web server requires that WebDAV be enabled on the server. All of the form's files will be packaged into an *.xsn* file and saved at the location that you specify.

Once you've selected your publishing target and location, you'll be prompted to provide a user-accessible location (URL or network path) for your solution. This dialog is shown in Figure 10-12. The value of this field is used to populate the `publishUrl` attribute of the `xsf:xDocumentClass` element, i.e., the root element of the form definition file. It identifies the central location from which all users will initially retrieve the form and receive form updates. InfoPath uses the value of the `publishUrl` attribute in two ways:

- InfoPath assigns this value to the `href` pseudo-attribute of the `mso-infoPathSolution` PI when InfoPath saves a filled-out form

- InfoPath checks this value to verify that the form template has not moved from its original published location.

You will want to modify this field only if the user-accessible URL or path is different from the URL or path where you originally put the file. Changing the value will be necessary, for example, if you need to publish the file to a web server using a network drive but require your users to download the file via an HTTP URL.

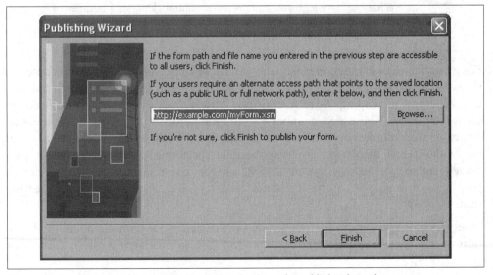

Figure 10-12. Final step of the publishing wizard, where the publishUrl attribute is set

Developing Solutions That Play Nice with Design Mode

There are a number of alternative approaches to developing InfoPath solutions. How much work should you do by hand?* And how much work should you do in design mode? Table 10-3 lists possible alternative solution development strategies.

Table 10-3. Alternative solution development strategies

Development strategy	Level of risk
1. Never use design mode.	Safe
2. Always use design mode.	Safe
3. Build a solution in design mode, but customize and maintain it by hand, never going back to design mode.	Safe
4. Build a solution in design mode, customize a portion of it by hand, and maintain it both ways.	Daring
5. Build a solution entirely by hand and later open it in design mode.	Crazy?

Options 1, 2, and 3 are safe because they never burden InfoPath design mode with having to read in a form template that it didn't itself create. Options 4 and 5 share the risk that InfoPath will have trouble opening your solution, because your dirty little fingers have been touching it. And if InfoPath opens your solution without complaining, you run the risk that parts of your solution will get overwritten. The primary problem is that, while the InfoPath XML editor will accept virtually any XSLT stylesheet you throw at it, the InfoPath form designer is much more finicky.

 From within design mode, changing a view that you have created by hand is always a risky proposition. While this section describes a mechanism by which you can preserve manual changes, a number of things could still go wrong. *Always* back up your form template files before opening them in design mode.

For example, the form designer requires the xd:binding and xd:xctname attributes to be explicitly present on all controls in the view stylesheet. Otherwise, it will not correctly identify all bindings or form controls, even though the editor has no problem identifying them. There are a number of other limitations that design mode imposes. For example, it chokes on common XSLT constructs such as xsl:call-template, but not without first displaying an error message specifying exactly what is not supported. Again, this is a limitation of design mode, not the InfoPath XML editor. If you build or modify a solution by hand, you can feel free to use any XSLT instruction you wish.

Does this effectively mean that, once you skirt design mode with a manual modification, there's no going back? Well, it would, if it wasn't for another InfoPath feature

---

* When I say "by hand," I really mean any way other than using InfoPath in design mode. One of the key advantages of the underlying XML syntax of solutions is not only that you can modify things manually, but you can also use XML tools to generate, modify, or otherwise process solutions.

called the *preserve code block*. This is a mechanism by which you can mark portions of an XSLT view stylesheet as untouchable regions, for your eyes only. Note that you won't be able to use the form designer to edit or customize the controls declared therein, and that's the whole point. This is done by wrapping your manual customizations in a template rule annotated with `mode="xd:preserve"`. The template rules in the `xd:preserve` mode and the `xsl:apply-templates` instructions that invoke them will remain untouched. Note that all template rules and named templates that you invoke from within a preserved code block will also need to be preserved, using `mode="xd:preserve"`. Otherwise, design mode will discard them, resulting in an invalid stylesheet, in the case of missing named templates. For named templates, you will also have to add an arbitrary `match` attribute, so that it will still be legal XSLT after you add a `mode` attribute. To ensure that your named-template-cum-template-rule doesn't match any nodes, you can use a pattern that is guaranteed to match nothing, such as `@*/*`.

Example 10-20 shows our first example stylesheet (Example 10-3) with the entire view protected by the `xd:preserve` mode.

Example 10-20. Using the xd:preserve mode to preserve manual stylesheet changes

```
<xsl:stylesheet version="1.0"
  xmlns:xsl="http://www.w3.org/1999/XSL/Transform">

  <xsl:template match="/announcement">
    <html>
      <head>
        <title>Announcement</title>
      </head>
      <body>
        <xsl:apply-templates select="." mode="xd:preserve"/>
      </body>
    </html>
  </xsl:template>

  <xsl:template match="announcement" mode="xd:preserve">
    <h1>
      <xsl:value-of select="headline"/>
    </h1>
    <p>
      <xsl:value-of select="body"/>
    </p>
  </xsl:template>
</xsl:stylesheet>
```

Figure 10-13 shows the result of opening the corresponding form template in design mode. We only see a red box that says "Preserve Code Block." This alerts us that custom stylesheet code is being skipped over. We can commence to drag and drop other controls onto the form canvas, add text before or after the block, or create layout tables around the block, moving it around as necessary.

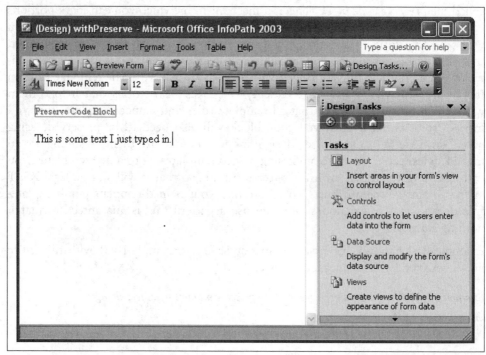

Figure 10-13. Preserve code block

Example 10-21 shows the XSLT stylesheet as output by the form designer after making a small change (adding some text to the bottom of the form). We see that it's much more verbose, including all of its CSS and namespace declaration boilerplate. However, our template rule in the xd:preserve mode is indeed preserved unaltered, and our solution will continue to work as expected in InfoPath's editing mode.

Example 10-21. Stylesheet output by InfoPath design mode, with code blocks preserved

```
<?xml version="1.0" encoding="UTF-8"?>
<xsl:stylesheet version="1.0" xmlns:xhtml="http://www.w3.org/1999/xhtml"
xmlns:xsl="http://www.w3.org/1999/XSL/Transform" xmlns:msxsl="urn:schemas-
microsoft-com:xslt" xmlns:xd="http://schemas.microsoft.com/office/infopath/2003"
xmlns:x="urn:schemas-microsoft-com:office:excel"
xmlns:xdExtension="http://schemas.microsoft.com/office/infopath/2003/xslt/extension
"
xmlns:xdXDocument="http://schemas.microsoft.com/office/infopath/2003/xslt/xDocument
" xmlns:xdSolution="http://schemas.microsoft.com/office/infopath/2003/xslt/solution"
xmlns:xdFormatting="http://schemas.microsoft.com/office/infopath/2003/xslt/formatti
ng" xmlns:xdImage="http://schemas.microsoft.com/office/infopath/2003/xslt/xImage">
    <xsl:output method="html" indent="no"/>
    <xsl:template match="announcement">
        <html>
            <head>
                <style tableEditor="TableStyleRulesID">TABLE.xdLayout TD {
```

```
    BORDER-RIGHT: medium none; BORDER-TOP: medium none; BORDER-LEFT: medium none;
BORDER-BOTTOM: medium none
}
TABLE {
    BEHAVIOR: url (#default#urn::tables/NDTable)
}
TABLE.msoUcTable TD {
    BORDER-RIGHT: 1pt solid; BORDER-TOP: 1pt solid; BORDER-LEFT: 1pt solid; BORDER-
BOTTOM: 1pt solid
}
</style>
                <title>Announcement</title>
                <meta http-equiv="Content-Type" content="text/html"></meta>
                <style controlStyle="controlStyle">BODY{margin-
left:21px;color:windowtext;background-color:window;layout-grid:none;}
    .xdListItem {display:inline-block;width:100%;vertical-align:text-top;}
    .xdListBox,.xdComboBox{margin:1px;}           .xdInlinePicture{margin:1px;
BEHAVIOR: url(#default#urn::xdPicture) }        .xdLinkedPicture{margin:1px;
BEHAVIOR: url(#default#urn::xdPicture) } url(#default#urn::controls/Binder) }
    .xdSection{border:1pt solid #FFFFFF;margin:6px 0px 6px 0px;padding:1px 1px 1px
5px;}        .xdRepeatingSection{border:1pt solid #FFFFFF;margin:6px 0px 6px
0px;padding:1px 1px 1px 5px;}        .xdBehavior_Formatting {BEHAVIOR:
url(#default#urn::controls/Binder) url(#default#Formatting);}
.xdBehavior_FormattingNoBUI{BEHAVIOR: url(#default#CalPopup)
url(#default#urn::controls/Binder) url(#default#Formatting);}
    .xdExpressionBox{margin: 1px;padding:1px;word-wrap: break-word;text-overflow:
ellipsis;overflow-
x:hidden;}.xdBehavior_GhostedText,.xdBehavior_GhostedTextNoBUI{BEHAVIOR:
url(#default#urn::controls/Binder) url(#default#TextField)
url(#default#GhostedText);}      .xdBehavior_GTFormatting{BEHAVIOR:
url(#default#urn::controls/Binder) url(#default#Formatting)
url(#default#GhostedText);}      .xdBehavior_GTFormattingNoBUI{BEHAVIOR:
url(#default#CalPopup) url(#default#urn::controls/Binder) url(#default#Formatting)
url(#default#GhostedText);}      .xdBehavior_Boolean{BEHAVIOR:
url(#default#urn::controls/Binder) url(#default#BooleanHelper);}
    .xdBehavior_Select{BEHAVIOR: url(#default#urn::controls/Binder)
url(#default#SelectHelper);}      .xdRepeatingTable{BORDER-TOP-STYLE: none; BORDER-
RIGHT-STYLE: none; BORDER-LEFT-STYLE: none; BORDER-BOTTOM-STYLE: none; BORDER-
COLLAPSE: collapse; WORD-WRAP: break-word;}.xdTextBox{display:inline-block;white-
space:nowrap;text-overflow:ellipsis;;padding:1px;margin:1px;border: 1pt solid
#dcdcdc;color:windowtext;background-color:window;overflow:hidden;text-align:left;}
        .xdRichTextBox{display:inline-block;;padding:1px;margin:1px;border: 1pt
solid #dcdcdc;color:windowtext;background-color:window;overflow-x:hidden;word-
wrap:break-word;text-overflow:ellipsis;text-align:left;font-weight:normal;font-
style:normal;text-decoration:none;vertical-align:baseline;}
    .xdDTPicker{;display:inline;margin:1px;margin-bottom: 2px;border: 1pt solid
#dcdcdc;color:windowtext;background-color:window;overflow:hidden;}
    .xdDTText{height:100%;width:100%;margin-
right:22px;overflow:hidden;padding:0px;white-space:nowrap;}
    .xdDTButton{margin-left:-21px;height:18px;width:20px;behavior:
url(#default#DTPicker);}        .xdRepeatingTable TD {VERTICAL-ALIGN:
top;}</style>
```

```
            </head>
            <body>
                <div>
                    <xsl:apply-templates select="." mode="xd:preserve"/>
                </div>
                <div> </div>
                <div>This is some text I just typed in.</div>
            </body>
        </html>
    </xsl:template>
    <xsl:template match="announcement" mode="xd:preserve">
        <h1>
            <xsl:value-of select="headline"></xsl:value-of>
        </h1>
        <p>
            <xsl:value-of select="body"></xsl:value-of>
        </p>
    </xsl:template>
</xsl:stylesheet>
```

One thing to note about the use of mode="xd:preserve" for a solution's default view is that InfoPath will *not* overwrite your stylesheet (and hence won't add any of the boilerplate shown above), as long as you do both of the following:

- Annotate all template rules in the stylesheet with mode="xd:preserve" (except for a root template rule that initially applies templates) until InfoPath opens it without complaining

- Do not make any changes to the default view from within design mode

You may be asking yourself, "then why should I bother opening the solution in design mode at all if I'm not going to make any changes to the default view?" The answer is that there are plenty of other things about a solution that you may want to configure or change from within design mode besides the default view, e.g., submission behavior, secondary views, scripting, custom validation, custom error messages, secondary data sources, and solution packaging and publication. In fact, I recommend avoiding option 5 in Table 10-3, unless you employ this precise strategy. Unless you particularly want to learn how InfoPath design mode generates XSLT stylesheets and you have some patience for experimentation, you should avoid making changes within design mode to XSLT views that you created outside of design mode.

Among the use cases for employing both design mode and hand-editing is the need to develop multiple views for a single solution. For example, you may already have an XSLT stylesheet that displays your document type in a particular way, e.g., on a web site, but you still haven't developed a form for gathering instances of that document type. You can use InfoPath design mode to rapidly develop the form as your default view, and you can then manually edit the form definition file (*manifest.xsf*) to

---

add your existing stylesheet as an alternate view for your users to see, like a preview of how the document will look when published. Unlike a default view stylesheet, a secondary view stylesheet doesn't need to be annotated with `mode="xd:preserve"` unless you specifically open that view from within design mode. If you never switch to that view in design mode, you won't have to worry about the form designer choking on it, and it will survive in your solution unaltered.

InfoPath's "preserve code block" feature is thus useful for both options 4 and 5 in Table 10-3. With option 4, you can isolate only the part of the stylesheet that you need to customize outside of design mode. With option 5, the safest approach, again, is to wrap your entire stylesheet (all but the root template rule) in a "preserve code block." Just to be sure that it's clear what it means to "wrap the entire stylesheet in a preserve code block." Example 10-22 shows an example of this technique.

Example 10-22. Wrapping an entire stylesheet in a single preserve code block

```
<xsl:stylesheet version="1.0"
  xmlns:xsl="http://www.w3.org/1999/XSL/Transform"
  xmlns:xd="http://schemas.microsoft.com/office/infopath/2003">

  <xsl:template match="/">
    <xsl:apply-templates select="/event" mode="xd:preserve"/>
  </xsl:template>

  <xsl:template match="/event" mode="xd:preserve">
    <html>
      <!-- ... -->
      <xsl:apply-templates select="location" mode="xd:preserve"/>
      <!-- (All xsl:apply-templates instructions use mode="xd:preserve")-->
    </html>
  </xsl:template>

  <xsl:template match="location" mode="xd:preserve">
    <!-- ... -->
  </xsl:template>

  <!-- ... -->
  <!-- (All template rules use mode="xd:preserve") -->

</xsl:stylesheet>
```

The XML You Need for Office

A knowledge of XML is essential if you want to build applications around the Office XML capabilities rather than just using other people's templates. If you're already acquainted with XML, you don't need to read this appendix. If you're not, you should read on.

The general overview of XML given in this appendix should be sufficient to enable you to work with XML documents. For a much more solid grounding in the many details of XML, you should consider these books:

- Erik T. Ray, *Learning XML* (O'Reilly)
- Elliotte Rusty Harold and W. Scott Means, *XML in a Nutshell* (O'Reilly)
- Elizabeth Castro, *XML for the World Wide Web: Visual QuickStart Guide* (Peach-pit Press)

You may also be interested in the "Annotated XML Specification," written by Tim Bray and published online at *http://xml.com/*, which an provides illuminating explanation of the XML 1.0 specification. You may also look to "What is XML?" by Norm Walsh, also published on *XML.com*.

What Is XML?

XML, the Extensible Markup Language, is an Internet-friendly format for data and documents invented by the World Wide Web Consortium (W3C). The "Markup" denotes a way of expressing the structure of a document within the document itself. XML has its roots in a markup language called SGML (Standard Generalized Markup Language), which is used in publishing. HTML was an application of SGML to web publishing. XML was created to do for machine-readable documents on the Web what HTML did for human-readable documents—that is, provide a commonly agreed-upon syntax so that processing the underlying format becomes common place and documents are made accessible to all users.

Unlike HTML, though, XML comes with very little predefined. HTML developers are accustomed both to the notion of using angle brackets (< >) for denoting elements, and also to the set of element names themselves (such as head, body, etc.). XML shares only the former feature (i.e., the notion of using angle brackets for denoting elements). Unlike HTML, XML has no predefined elements, but is merely a set of rules that lets you write other languages like HTML.

Because XML defines so little, it is easy for everyone to agree to use the XML syntax, and then to build applications on top of it. It's like agreeing to use a particular alphabet and set of punctuation symbols, but not saying which language to use. This offers immense flexibility, much like the flexibility you're used to having in creating your own Word templates, Excel spreadsheets, or Access databases.

Anatomy of an XML Document

The best way to explain how an XML document is composed is to present one. Example A-1 shows an XML document you might use to describe two authors.

Example A-1. A very simple XML document

```
<?xml version="1.0" encoding="us-ascii"?>
<authors>
    <person id="lear">
        <name>Edward Lear</name>
        <nationality>British</nationality>
    </person>
    <person id="asimov">
        <name>Isaac Asimov</name>
        <nationality>American</nationality>
    </person>
    <person id="mysteryperson"/>
</authors>
```

The first line of the document is known as the XML declaration. This tells a processing application which version of XML you are using—the version indicator is mandatory—and which character encoding you have used for the document. In this example, the document is encoded in ASCII. (The significance of character encoding is covered later in this appendix.)

If the XML declaration is omitted, a processor will make certain assumptions about your document. In particular, it will expect it to be encoded in UTF-8, an encoding of the Unicode character set. However, it is best to use the XML declaration wherever possible, both to avoid confusion over the character encoding and to indicate to processors which version of XML you're using. (1.0 is most common, but 1.1, which makes relatively minor though potentially incompatible changes, has recently appeared.) Encoding handling should be automatic with Office, but you may need to watch for documents you import from other sources.

Elements and Attributes

The second line of Example A-1 begins an element, which has been named authors. The contents of that element include everything between the right angle bracket (>) in <authors> and the left angle bracket (<) in </authors>. The actual syntactic constructs <authors> and </authors> are often referred to as the element start tag and end tag, respectively. Do not confuse tags with elements! Tags mark the boundaries of elements. Note that elements, like the authors element here, may include other elements, as well as text. An XML document must contain exactly one root element, which contains all other content within the document. The name of the root element defines the type of the XML document.

Elements that contain both text and other elements simultaneously are classified as mixed content. Word supports the use of mixed content, while the other applications in the Office suite generally do not.

The sample "authors" document uses elements named person to describe the authors themselves. Each person element has an attribute named id. Unlike elements, attributes can only contain textual content. Their values must be surrounded by quotes. Either single quotes (') or double quotes (") may be used, as long as you use the same kind of closing quote as the opening one.

Within XML documents, attributes are frequently used for metadata (i.e., "data about data"), describing properties of the element's contents. This is the case in our example, where id contains a unique identifier for the person being described.

As far as XML is concerned, it does not matter in what order attributes are presented in the element start tag. For example, these two elements contain exactly the same information as far as an XML 1.0 conformant processing application is concerned:

```
<animal name="dog" legs="4"></animal>
<animal legs="4" name="dog"></animal>
```

On the other hand, the information presented to an application by an XML processor on reading the following two lines will be different for each animal element because the ordering of elements is significant:

```
<animal><name>dog</name><legs>4</legs></animal>
<animal><legs>4</legs><name>dog</name></animal>
```

XML treats a set of attributes like a bunch of stuff in a bag—there is no implicit ordering—while elements are treated like items on a list, where ordering matters.

New XML developers frequently ask when it is best to use attributes to represent information and when it is best to use elements. As you can see from the "authors" example, if order is important to you, then elements are a good choice. In general, there is no hard-and-fast best practice for choosing whether to use attributes or elements, though elements can contain other elements and attributes, while attributes can contain only text.

The final author described in our document has no information available. All we know about this person is his or her ID, `mysteryperson`. The document uses the XML shortcut syntax for an empty element. The following is a reasonable alternative:

```
<person id="mysteryperson"></person>
```

Name Syntax

XML 1.0 has certain rules about element and attribute names. In particular:

- Names are case-sensitive, e.g., `<person/>` is not the same as `<Person/>`.
- Names beginning with `xml` (in any permutation of uppercase or lowercase) are reserved for use by XML 1.0 and its companion specifications.
- A name must start with a letter or an underscore, not a digit, and may continue with any letter, digit, underscore, or period. (Actually, a name may also contain a colon, but the colon is used to delimit a namespace prefix and is not available for arbitrary use as of the Second Edition of XML 1.0.)

A precise description of names can be found in Section 2.3 of the XML 1.0 specification, at *http://www.w3.org/TR/REC-xml#sec-common-syn*.

XML Namespaces

XML 1.0 lets developers create their own elements and attributes, but leaves open the potential for overlapping names. `title` in one context may mean something entirely different than `title` in a different context. The Namespaces in XML specification (which can be found at *http://www.w3.org/TR/REC-xml-names/*) provides a mechanism developers can use to identify particular vocabularies using Uniform Resource Identifiers (URIs).

URIs are a combination of the familiar Uniform Resource Locators (URLs) and Uniform Resource Names (URNs). From the perspective of XML namespaces, URIs are convenient because they combine an easily used syntax with a notion of ownership. While it's possible for me to create namespace URIs that begin with `http://microsoft.com`, general practice holds that it would be better for me to create URIs that begin with `http://simonstl.com`, a domain I own, and leave `http://microsoft.com` to Microsoft. In general, organizations and individuals who create XML vocabularies should choose a namespace URI in a space they control. This makes it possible (though it isn't required) to put information there documenting the vocabulary, or other resources for processing the vocabulary.

The rules for XML names don't permit developers to create elements with names like `http://simonstl.com/ns/mine:Title`, and it's not clear that working with names like that would be much fun anyway. To get around these problems, the Namespaces in XML specification defines a mechanism for associating URIs with element and attribute names through prefixes. Instead of typing out the whole URI, developers can work with a much shorter prefix, or even set a default URI that applies to names without prefixes.

To create a prefix, you use a namespace declaration, which looks like an attribute. For example, to create a prefix of xhtml associated with the URI http://www.w3.org/1999/xhtml, you would use an xmlns:xhtml attribute as shown below:

```
<container xmlns:xhtml="http://www.w3.org/1999/xhtml" >
....
</container>
```

To apply a prefix, you put it in front of the element or attribute name, with a colon separating the prefix from the name. To put an XHTML p element inside of that container, you could write:

```
<container xmlns:xhtml="http://www.w3.org/1999/xhtml" >
<xhtml:p>This is an XHTML paragraph!</xhtml:p>
</container>
```

When a program encountered the xhtml:p, it would know that p was the local name of the element, xhtml was the prefix, and http://www.w3.org/1999/xhtml was the URI for that element. The namespace declaration applies to all elements inside the element where it appears, as well as the element containing the declaration. For example, the xhtml prefix works for all three of these paragraphs:

```
<container xmlns:xhtml="http://www.w3.org/1999/xhtml" >
<xhtml:p>This is XHTML paragraph 1!</xhtml:p>
<xhtml:p>This is XHTML paragraph 2!</xhtml:p>
<xhtml:p>This is XHTML paragraph 3!</xhtml:p>
</container>
```

In most XML processing, the prefix doesn't matter—the local name and the URI are what count, and the prefix is just a mechanism for associating them. (This is especially important in XSLT processing and XML Schemas.) In some documents, especially documents that use only structures from one namespace or where one vocabulary is dominant, developers choose to use the default namespace rather than prefixes. When the default namespace is used (assigned with an xmlns attribute), elements without a prefix are associated with a given URI. In XHTML, an XML derivative of HTML, this is the most typical path, since HTML developers aren't used to putting prefixes on all of their element names. A typical XHTML document might look like this:

```
<html xmlns="http://www.w3.org/1999/xhtml">
  <head>
    <title>My Document</title>
  </head>
  <body>
    <p>Could use some content here</p>
  </body>
</html>
```

In this case, the URI http://www.w3.org/1999/xhtml applies to every element in the document, including html, head, title, body, and p. The default namespace has one quirk, though: it doesn't apply to attributes. Attributes can be given a namespace by explicitly using a prefix in their name, but unprefixed attributes have no namespace URI. This often doesn't matter, but it can be important when writing XSLT stylesheets and creating XML Schemas.

Typically, the namespaces used by a document are declared on the root element of the document, which lets them apply to all the content inside that document. They can, of course, also be declared throughout the document, though this makes it more difficult to read. Declarations can override each other as well, and the declaration closest to a given use of a prefix in the hierarchy will be used. This lets developers mix and match XML vocabularies even when they use the same prefix.

Namespaces are very simple on the surface but are a well-known field of combat in XML arcana. For more information on namespaces, see Tim Bray's "XML Namespaces by Example," published at *http://www.xml.com/pub/a/1999/01/namespaces.html*; *XML In a Nutshell*; or *Learning XML*.

Well-Formedness

An XML document that conforms to the rules of XML syntax is known as *well-formed*. At its most basic level, well-formedness means that elements should be properly matched, and all opened elements should be closed. A formal definition of well-formedness can be found in Section 2.1 of the XML 1.0 specification, at *http://www.w3.org/TR/REC-xml#sec-well-formed*. Table A-1 shows some XML documents that are not well-formed.

Table A-1. Examples of poorly formed XML documents

Document	Reason why it's not well-formed

`<foo>`
  `<bar>`
  `</foo>`
`</bar>`
	The elements are not properly nested because foo is closed while inside its child element bar.

`<foo>`
  `<bar>`
`</foo>`
	The bar element was not closed before its parent, foo, was closed.

`<foo baz>` `</foo>`	The baz attribute has no value. While this is permissible in HTML (e.g., `<table border>`), it is forbidden in XML.
`<foo baz=23>` `</foo>`	The baz attribute value, 23, has no surrounding quotes. Unlike HTML, all attribute values must be quoted in XML.

Comments and Processing Instructions

As in HTML, it is possible to include comments within XML documents. XML comments are intended to be read only by people. With HTML, developers have occasionally employed comments to add application-specific functionality. For example, the server-side include functionality of most web servers uses instructions embedded in HTML comments. In XML, comments should not be used for any purpose other than those for which they were intended, as they are usually stripped from the document during parsing.

The start of a comment is indicated with `<!--`, and the end of the comment with `-->`. Any sequence of characters, aside from the string `--`, may appear within a comment. Comments can appear at the start or end of a document as well as inside elements. They cannot appear inside attributes or inside of a tag. A comment might look like:

```
<!--Hello, this is a comment -->
```

Comments tend to be used more in XML documents intended for human consumption than those intended for machine consumption. If you want to pass information to an XML application without affecting the structure of the document, you can use processing instructions, or PIs. Processing instructions use `<?` as a starting delimiter and `?>` as a closing delimiter, must contain a target conforming to the rules for XML names, and may contain additional data. A typical PI might look like:

```
<?xml-style type="text/css" href="mystyle.css" ?>
```

In this case, `xml-style` is the target and `type="text/css" href="mystyle.css"` is the data. For more information on PIs, see Section 2.6 of the XML 1.0 specification, at *http://www.w3.org/TR/REC-xml#sec-pi*.

Entity References

You may occasionally need to use the mechanism for escaping characters. Because some characters have special significance in XML, there needs to be a way to represent them. For example, in some cases the `<` symbol might really be intended to mean "less than" rather than to signal the start of an element name. Clearly, just inserting the character without any escaping mechanism would result in a poorly formed document because a processing application would assume you were starting another element. Another instance of this problem is needing to include both double quotes and single quotes simultaneously in an attribute's value. Here's an example that illustrates both these difficulties:

```
<badDoc>
  <para>
    I'd really like to use the < character
  </para>
  <note title="On the proper 'use' of the " character"/>
</badDoc>
```

XML avoids this problem by the use of the predefined entity reference. The word "entity" in the context of XML simply means a unit of content. The term "entity reference" means just that, a symbolic way of referring to a certain unit of content. XML predefines entities for the following symbols: left angle bracket (<), right angle bracket (>), apostrophe ('), double quote ("), and ampersand (&).

An entity reference is introduced with an ampersand (&), which is followed by a name (using the word "name" in its formal sense, as defined by the XML 1.0 specification), and terminated with a semicolon (;). Table A-2 shows how the five predefined entities can be used within an XML document.

Table A-2. Predefined entity references in XML 1.0

Literal character	Entity reference
<	&lt;
>	&gt;
'	&apos;
"	&quot;
&	&amp;

Here's our problematic document revised to use entity references:

```
<badDoc>
  <para>
    I'd really like to use the &lt; character
  </para>
  <note title="On the proper &apos;use&apos;  of the &quot;character"/>
</badDoc>
```

Being able to use the predefined entities is often all you need; in general, entities are provided as a convenience for human-created XML. XML 1.0 allows you to define your own entities and use entity references as "shortcuts" in your document. Section 4 of the XML 1.0 specification, available at *http://www.w3.org/TR/REC-xml#sec-physical-struct*, describes the use of entities.

Character References

You may find character references in Office 2003 XML documents. Character references allow you to denote a character by its numeric position in Unicode character set (this position is known as its code point). Table A-3 contains a few examples that illustrate the syntax.

Table A-3. Example character references

Actual character	Character reference
1	&#48;
A	&#65;
~	&#xD1;
®	&#xAE;

Note that the code point can be expressed in decimal or, with the use of x as a prefix, in hexadecimal.

Character Encodings

The subject of character encodings is frequently a mysterious one for developers. Most code tends to be written for one computing platform and, normally, to run within one organization. Although the Internet is changing things quickly, most of us have never had cause to think too deeply about internationalization.

XML, designed to be an Internet-friendly syntax for information exchange, has internationalization at its very core. One of the basic requirements for XML processors is that they support the Unicode standard character encoding. Unicode attempts to include the requirements of all the world's languages within one character set. Consequently, it is very large!

Unicode encoding schemes

Unicode 3.0 has more than 57,700 code points, each of which corresponds to a character. (You can obtain charts of all these characters online by visiting *http://www. unicode.org/charts/*.) If one were to express a Unicode string by using the position of each character in the character set as its encoding (in the same way as ASCII does), expressing the whole range of characters would require four octets for each character. (An octet is a string of eight binary digits, or bits. A byte is commonly, but not always, considered the same thing as an octet.) Clearly, if a document is written in 100 percent American English, it will be four times larger than required—all the characters in ASCII fitting into a 7-bit representation. This places a strain both on storage space and on memory requirements for processing applications.

Fortunately, two encoding schemes for Unicode alleviate this problem: UTF-8 and UTF-16. As you might guess from their names, applications can process documents in these encodings in 8- or 16-bit segments. When code points are required in a document that cannot be represented by one chunk, a bit-pattern is used that indicates that the following chunk is required to calculate the desired code point. In UTF-8 this is denoted by having the most significant bit of the first octet set to 1.

This scheme means that UTF-8 is a highly efficient encoding for representing languages using Latin alphabets, such as English. All of the ASCII character set is represented natively in UTF-8—an ASCII-only document and its equivalent in UTF-8 are byte-for-byte identical. UTF-16 is more efficient for representing languages that use Unicode characters represented by larger numeric values, notably Chinese, Japanese, and Korean.

This knowledge will also help you debug encoding errors. One frequent error arises because of the fact that ASCII is a proper subset of UTF-8—programmers get used to this fact and produce UTF-8 documents, but use them as if they were ASCII. Things start to go awry when the XML parser processes a document containing, for example, characters such as Á (replace with accented A). Because this character cannot be represented using only one octet in UTF-8, this produces a two-octet sequence in the output document; in a non-Unicode viewer or text editor, it looks like a couple of characters of garbage.

Other character encodings

Unicode, in the context of computing history, is a relatively new invention. Native operating system support for Unicode is by no means widespread. For instance, although Windows NT offers Unicode support, Windows 95 and 98 do not have it.

XML 1.0 allows a document to be encoded in any character set registered with the Internet Assigned Numbers Authority (IANA). European documents are commonly encoded in one of the ISO Latin character sets, such as ISO-8859-1. Japanese documents commonly use Shift-JIS, and Chinese documents use GB2312 and Big 5.

A full list of registered character sets may be found at *http://www.iana.org/assignments/character-sets*.

XML processors are not required by the XML 1.0 specification to support any more than UTF-8 and UTF-16, but most commonly support other encodings, such as US-ASCII and ISO-8859-1. Although many XML transactions are currently conducted in ASCII (or the ASCII subset of UTF-8), there is nothing to stop XML documents from containing, say, Korean text. You will, however, probably have to dig into the encoding support of your computing platform to find out if it is possible for you to use alternate encodings.

Validity

In addition to well-formedness, XML 1.0 offers another level of verification called *validity*. To explain why validity is important, let's take a simple example. Imagine you invented a simple XML format for your friends' telephone numbers:

```
<phonebook>
  <person>
    <name>Albert Smith</name>
```

```
      <number>123-456-7890</number>
   </person>
   <person>
      <name>Bertrand Jones</name>
      <number>456-123-9876</number>
   </person>
</phonebook>
```

Based on your format, you also construct a program to display and search your phone numbers. This program turns out to be so useful, you share it with your friends. However, your friends aren't so hot on detail as you are, and try to feed your program this phone book file:

```
<phonebook>
   <person>
      <name>Melanie Green</name>
      <phone>123-456-7893</phone>
   </person>
</phonebook>
```

Note that, although this file is perfectly well-formed, it doesn't fit the format you prescribed for the phone book, because there's a phone element where there should have been a number element. You will likely need to change your program to cope with this situation. If your friends had used number as you did to denote the phone number, there wouldn't have been a problem. However, as it is, this second file probably won't be usable by programs set up to work with the first file; from the program's perspective, it isn't valid.

For validity to be a useful general concept, we need a machine-readable way of saying what a valid document is; that is, which elements and attributes must be present and in what order. XML 1.0 achieves this by introducing document type definitions (DTDs). Office doesn't use DTDs, preferring to use W3C XML Schemas, as described in Appendix C.

Document Type Definitions (DTDs)

The purpose of a DTD is to express which elements and attributes are allowed in a certain document type and to constrain the order in which elements must appear within that document type. A DTD is generally composed of one file or a group of connected files, containing declarations defining element types, attribute lists, and entities. DTDs are explored in Appendix D.

Connecting DTDs to documents

Even if you don't work with DTDs, you should be aware of how DTDs are linked to XML documents. This is done with a document type declaration, <!DOCTYPE ...>, inserted at the beginning of the XML document, after the XML declaration in our fictitious example:

```
<?xml version="1.0" encoding="us-ascii"?>
<!DOCTYPE authors SYSTEM "http://example.com/authors.dtd">
```

```
<authors>
    <person id="lear">
        <name>Edward Lear</name>
        <nationality>British</nationality>
    </person>
    <person id="asimov">
        <name>Isaac Asimov</name>
        <nationality>American</nationality>
    </person>
    <person id="mysteryperson"/>
</authors>
```

This example assumes the DTD file has been placed on a web server at *example.com*. Note that the document type declaration specifies the root element of the document, not the DTD itself. You could use the same DTD to define person, name, or nationality as the root element of a valid document. Certain DTDs, such as the DocBook DTD for technical documentation (see *http://www.docbook.org*), use this feature to good effect, allowing you to use the same DTD while working with multiple document types.

A validating XML processor is obligated to check the input document against its DTD. If it does not validate, the document is rejected. To return to the phone book example, if your application validated its input files against a phone book DTD, you would have been spared the problems of debugging your program and correcting your friend's XML because your application would have rejected the document as being invalid. Office 2003 doesn't perform validation against DTDs; instead, it validates against XML Schemas.

The XSLT You Need for Office

XSLT plays a huge role in Office 2003. This book contains numerous examples of XSLT stylesheets for use in Word, Excel, InfoPath, and Access. Since proficiency in XSLT is a prerequisite for understanding much that's in this book, your best bet (if you don't already know XSLT) is to pick up one of the excellent books on XSLT that are already available. Here are some good books to choose from for learning XSLT:

- Michael Fitzgerald, *Learning XSLT* (O'Reilly)
- Jeni Tennison, *Beginning XSLT* (Wrox)
- Michael Kay, *XSLT Programmer's Reference* (Wrox)
- Doug Tidwell, *XSLT* (O'Reilly)
- G. Ken Holman, *Definitive XSLT and XPath* (Prentice Hall)
- John E. Simpson, *XPath and XPointer* (O'Reilly)
- Sal Mangano, *XSLT Cookbook*, (O'Reilly)

If you are already comfortable with XSLT, then great—you might not need to read this appendix at all. For those of you who are new to XSLT, this appendix provides a brief introduction and tutorial, illustrating just a few aspects of this powerful language. Truthfully, when developing XML solutions for Office, the more XSLT you know, the better. While this appendix may provide a good start, it only scratches the surface.

After a brief overview of what XSL-FO, XSLT, and XPath are, we'll look at three example stylesheets. The first two illustrate the most common use case for XSLT: transforming XML documents into HTML. The last example converts between one XML format and another XML format.

The examples in this appendix do not pertain specifically to Office. For Office-specific examples of XSLT stylesheets, see the main content of the book (specifically Chapters 3, 4, 5, 7, 8, and 10). The highest concentration of XSLT examples is in Chapter 3.

Sorting Out the Acronyms

When learning XSLT, there are three primary specifications to be aware of: XSL (sometimes referred to as XSL-FO), XSLT, and XPath. Originally, these three languages were just parts of a single language, XSL, or "Extensible Stylesheet Language". But before being released as W3C recommendations, they were re-factored into three separate specifications. They essentially have a subset relationship, as depicted in Figure B-1. XPath is used by XSLT, which is in turn used by XSL.

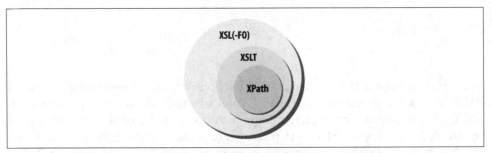

Figure B-1. The subset relationship between XSL, XSLT, and XPath

This appendix is concerned only with the inner two circles in Figure B-1, XSLT and XPath. We'll see how XSLT and XPath relate to each other—and what they actually look like—in the tutorial later on. First, let's briefly look at the role each language plays.

What Is XSL?

As we've seen, XSL stands for "Extensible Stylesheet Language." It is a language for expressing stylesheets for XML. It consists of two primary parts:

- An XML formatting vocabulary
- An XML transformation language

This appendix is concerned only with XSLT, which is the transformation component of XSL. The other component—the formatting vocabulary—is commonly called XSL Formatting Objects, or XSL-FO. It theoretically can function apart from XSLT as a standalone formatting vocabulary, but it is usually used as a part of XSL (i.e., with XSLT). The most common use case for XSL-FO is transforming XML documents into documents suitable for printing, particularly in PDF format.

The XSL 1.0 recommendation is located at *http://www.w3.org/TR/xsl*.

What Is XSLT?

XSLT stands for "Extensible Stylesheet Language Transformations." It is a language for transforming XML documents into other XML documents or other formats, such as HTML and plain text. An XSLT *stylesheet* is a program that declaratively defines the transformation from a *source tree* (input) to a *result tree* (output). Since XSLT stylesheets themselves are represented in XML format, that means there are three essential XML documents, or "trees," involved in any XSLT transformation. Figure B-2 shows a diagram depicting the relationships of these three trees.

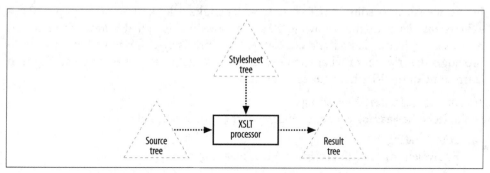

Figure B-2. The three trees involved in every XSLT transformation

The input to the XSLT processor (depicted by the rectangle in Figure B-2) consists of the source XML document (the source tree) and the XSLT program itself (the stylesheet tree). The output of the transformation is a new XML document (the result tree).

The XSLT 1.0 recommendation is located at *http://www.w3.org/TR/xslt*.

> The XSLT and XPath supported by Office 2003 are strictly limited to version 1.0. As of the time of this writing, XSLT 2.0 and XPath 2.0 are still works in progress.

> When Microsoft was first getting started with XML, it released a preliminary version of XSL (before it was re-factored as XSLT) as a part of Internet Explorer 5. Microsoft has deprecated that version of "XSL," and you should avoid it. Any time you see the namespace URI http://www.w3.org/TR/WD-xsl, the developer was using this older version, and you'll have difficulties integrating that code with newer projects. Always check XSLT code and documentation to make sure it uses the correct XSLT namespace URI: *http://www.w3.org/1999/XSL/Transform*. For more information, see the "Unofficial MSXML XSLT FAQ" at *http://www.netcrucible.com/xslt/msxml-faq.htm*.

What Is XPath?

XPath is short for "XML Path Language." It is an expression language for addressing parts of an XML document. XPath is an essential part of XSLT and is used to select "nodes" in the XML source tree for further processing.

The XPath "data model" is fundamental to XSLT. Mathematically speaking, it defines the entire domain and range of XSLT "functions"—in other words, the input to and output from XSLT stylesheets. It defines what a "tree" is, the seven kinds of nodes that can occur in a tree (root, element, attribute, comment, processing instruction, namespace, and text nodes), and how they relate to XML.

Before we get into some XSLT examples, let's take a look at some example XPath *expressions*. Each of the following XPath expressions is called a *location path* and returns an object called a *node-set*. Rather than precisely defining its behavior, we'll provide a description of what each expression selects. In that way, you can begin to learn some of the XPath language by example.

/child::article/child::heading
: Selects the heading element children of the root article element.

/article/heading
: Equivalent to /child::article/child::heading.

/article/para[position( )=1]
: Selects the first para element child of the root article element.

/article/para[1]
: Equivalent to /article/para[position( )=1].

/article/para[position( )=last( )]
: Selects the last para element child of the root article element.

/article/para[last( )]
: Equivalent to /article/para[position( )=last( )].

self::node( )
: Selects the context node.

.
: Equivalent to self::node( ).

./order
: Selects the order element children of the context node.

order
: Equivalent to ./order.

order/attribute::price
: Selects the price attribute of each order element child of the context node.

order/@price
: Equivalent to order/attribute::price.

order[@price > 30]/shipTo
: Selects the shipTo element children of each order element child of the context node whose price attribute's value is greater than 30.

These examples only illustrate a few of XPath's operators and functions. Aside from location paths, XPath also supports the operators that you'd expect to find in a programming language, such as arithmetic (+, -, *, div, and mod) and logic (and, or). You can use XPath to do math and to manipulate strings, as well as to select nodes. For a more thorough investigation (as well as an explanation of how exactly such expressions are evaluated), see one of the books cited at the beginning of this appendix. We'll come across a few more XPath expressions in this appendix (in the context of XSLT).

XPath expressions appear as the values of various attributes in XSLT. For example, the select attribute of a number of XSLT instructions (including the xsl:value-of, xsl:for-each, and xsl:apply-templates elements) contains an XPath expression.

The XPath 1.0 recommendation is located at *http://www.w3.org/TR/xpath*.

A Simple Template Approach

All three of the approaches in this appendix include a source document, stylesheet, and result document.

 To execute the example stylesheets in this appendix, you will need an XSLT processor. See the sidebar in Chapter 3 called "Command-Line Tools" for more information on obtaining and using a command-line XSLT processor.

Example B-1 shows the source document for our first example transformation.

Example B-1. An XML source document containing people's names

```
<people>
  <person>
    <givenName>Joe</givenName>
    <familyName>Johnson</familyName>
  </person>
  <person>
    <givenName>Jane</givenName>
    <familyName>Johnson</familyName>
  </person>
  <person>
    <givenName>Jim</givenName>
    <familyName>Johannson</familyName>
  </person>
  <person>
    <givenName>Jody</givenName>
    <familyName>Johannson</familyName>
  </person>
</people>
```

The stylesheet in Example B-2 looks much like the result document that it creates. Specifically, the content of the `<xsl:template match="/">` element is essentially an HTML template of the result, along with some placeholders for dynamic content. The dynamic parts of the stylesheet below are highlighted.

Example B-2. A very simple stylesheet for combining people's names with HTML

```
<xsl:stylesheet version="1.0"
  xmlns:xsl="http://www.w3.org/1999/XSL/Transform">

  <xsl:output method="html" indent="yes"/>

  <xsl:template match="/">
    <html>
      <head>
        <title>Name list</title>
      </head>
      <table>
        <tr>
          <th>Given Name</th>
          <th>Family Name</th>
        </tr>
        <xsl:for-each select="/people/person">
          <tr>
            <td>
              <xsl:value-of select="givenName"/>
            </td>
            <td>
              <xsl:value-of select="familyName"/>
            </td>
          </tr>
        </xsl:for-each>
      </table>
    </html>
  </xsl:template>

</xsl:stylesheet>
```

Let's look at each element in this stylesheet, drilling down into the hierarchy as we go.

First, the root element, xsl:stylesheet, contains one required attribute, the version attribute, which has a value of 1.0. The root element also declares the XSLT namespace, mapped to the xsl prefix. It doesn't matter what prefix you use, of course, but the xsl prefix is the most widely accepted convention:

```
<xsl:stylesheet version="1.0"
  xmlns:xsl="http://www.w3.org/1999/XSL/Transform">
  ...
</xsl:stylesheet>
```

The xsl:output instruction gives the XSLT processor hints on how to serialize the result tree. In this case, method="html" instructs the processor to output the result tree using HTML serialization rules (not necessarily well-formed XML), and indent="yes" instructs it to insert some indentation into the result (to facilitate readability):

```
<xsl:output method="html" indent="yes"/>
```

In this stylesheet, the root element contains an xsl:template element. In XSLT, any xsl:template element that has a match attribute is called a *template rule*. The value of the match attribute determines what parts of the source document will trigger this template rule. This stylesheet's one and only template rule matches the *root node* of the source document, as indicated by the value of the simple slash (/):

```
<xsl:template match="/">
  ...
</xsl:template>
```

Many stylesheets contain a template rule that matches the root node in this way. It is often called the "root template rule" and is sometimes considered analogous to the main function in a C or Java program, because it is effectively where processing begins. The analogy breaks down however because it is possible to write a stylesheet that doesn't explicitly include a root template rule. But for now, it's okay to think of it as the starting point for all processing.

 The "root node" is not the same thing as the "root element." In XPath/XSLT, every document contains a root node, which is the top-level, "invisible" container of everything in the document, including the root, or document, element.

Inside the root template rule, we see some regular HTML markup:

```
<html>
  <head>
    <title>Name list</title>
  </head>
  <table>
    <tr>
      <th>Given Name</th>
      <th>Family Name</th>
    </tr>
    ...
  </table>
</html>
```

These elements (as a whole, including their end tags) are called *literal result elements*, because they effectively create literal html, head, title, etc. elements in the result of the transformation (the result tree). In fact, any element not in the XSLT namespace that occurs inside (as a child or descendant of) the xsl:template element is interpreted as a literal result element.

Next, we see an element in the XSLT namespace, xsl:for-each. This element is an example of an XSLT *instruction*. An instruction is any element inside (as a child or descendant of) the xsl:template element that *is* in the XSLT namespace.

```
<xsl:for-each select="/people/person">
  ...
</xsl:for-each>
```

The xsl:for-each instruction iterates over certain nodes from the source document (Example B-1), repeating the content inside the element once for each selected node. In this case, the XPath expression /people/person returns a node-set consisting of the person element children of the people element in the source document. For each of those elements, a new table row (tr element) is created in the result, using a tr literal result element:

```
<tr>
  ...
</tr>
```

Then, inside each table row, there are two placeholders for dynamic content. The xsl:value-of instruction inserts the *string-value* of the selected node into the result document. In this case, the first table column (a td element) will contain the value of the givenName element child of the *current node* in XSLT processing (the person element being processed), and the second table column contains the value of the familyName element:

```
<td>
  <xsl:value-of select="givenName"/>
</td>
<td>
  <xsl:value-of select="familyName"/>
</td>
```

The HTML result of this transformation is shown in Example B-3.

Example B-3. The result of running the stylesheet in Example B-2 against the XML document in Example B-1

```
<html>
  <head>
    <META http-equiv="Content-Type" content="text/html; charset=UTF-16">
    <title>Name list</title>
  </head>
  <table>
    <tr>
      <th>Given Name</th>
      <th>Family Name</th>
    </tr>
    <tr>
      <td>Joe</td>
      <td>Johnson</td>
    </tr>
    <tr>
```

```
      <td>Jane</td>
      <td>Johnson</td>
    </tr>
    <tr>
      <td>Jim</td>
      <td>Johannson</td>
    </tr>
    <tr>
      <td>Jody</td>
      <td>Johannson</td>
    </tr>
  </table>
</html>
```

The number and order of table rows in the result (besides the first row, which is the table heading) corresponds to the number and order of person elements in the source document. And, as you can see, the table column values correspond to the values of the givenName and familyName elements in the source document.

> The META HTML element in Example B-3 is automatically added to the result of the transformation, according to XSLT's serialization rules for HTML. The XSLT processor does not always have control over (or responsibility for) serialization, but when it does, it must output a META element that indicates the document's character encoding. See *http://www.w3.org/TR/xslt#section-HTML-Output-Method* for the precise rules.

A Rule-Based Stylesheet

All XSLT processing is rule-based, it's just that some stylesheets take advantage of this fact more than others. Our first stylesheet (Example B-2) only used one template rule (where match="/"). Now we'll look at a stylesheet that uses multiple template rules.

Example B-4 shows the source document for this example transformation. It is a simple article that contains a heading and multiple paragraphs. Inside the paragraphs, there is some "mixed content," i.e., elements that contain both text and elements (e.g., the emphasis element).

Example B-4. A simple XML document containing marked-up text

```
<article>
  <heading>This is a short article</heading>
  <para>This is the <emphasis>first</emphasis> paragraph.</para>
  <para>This is the <strong>second</strong> paragraph.</para>
</article>
```

Example B-5 shows a simple XSLT stylesheet that is designed to process documents that look like the XML document in Example B-4.

Example B-5. An XSLT stylesheet with multiple template rules

```
<xsl:stylesheet version="1.0"
  xmlns:xsl="http://www.w3.org/1999/XSL/Transform">

  <xsl:output method="xml" indent="yes"/>

  <xsl:template match="/">
    <html>
      <head>
        <title>
          <xsl:value-of select="/article/heading"/>
        </title>
      </head>
      <body>
        <h1>
          <xsl:value-of select="/article/heading"/>
        </h1>
        <xsl:apply-templates select="/article/para"/>
      </body>
    </html>
  </xsl:template>

  <xsl:template match="para">
    <p>
      <xsl:apply-templates/>
    </p>
  </xsl:template>

  <xsl:template match="emphasis">
    <i>
      <xsl:apply-templates/>
    </i>
  </xsl:template>

  <xsl:template match="strong">
    <b>
      <xsl:apply-templates/>
    </b>
  </xsl:template>

</xsl:stylesheet>
```

This stylesheet contains an xsl:output element too:

```
<xsl:output method="xml" indent="yes"/>
```

In this case the result document will be serialized in XML format, so that the result will be well-formed XML (all elements will have end tags, etc.).

The root template rule is very similar to the stylesheet we saw in Example B-2, except that here the values of the title and h1 elements are dynamic:

```
<xsl:template match="/">
  <html>
    <head>
      <title>
        <xsl:value-of select="/article/heading"/>
      </title>
    </head>
    <body>
      <h1>
        <xsl:value-of select="/article/heading"/>
      </h1>
```

The xsl:value-of instructions see to it that both the title and h1 elements in the result will have the same value as the heading element in the source document (Example B-4).

This snippet demonstrates how you can re-use the same text in the source document in multiple places in the result. The string This is a short article will appear both as the resulting HTML document's title and as its top-level heading.

> In fact, you can use as little or as much of the source tree as you want when creating a result tree. XSLT leaves it up to you. You could copy the source tree verbatim into the result tree (called an "identity transformation"), or you could create an entirely unrelated result tree, ignoring what's in the source tree. The most useful stylesheets are usually those that do something in between these two extremes.

So far, there is not much difference between this example and the first stylesheet we looked at (Example B-2). The root template rule contains a basic template of the result document, along with some placeholders for dynamic content (xsl:value-of instructions). What distinguishes this stylesheet from the first one is the use of the next XSLT instruction that we see, the xsl:apply-templates instruction:

```
<xsl:apply-templates select="/article/para"/>
```

The purpose of this instruction is to tell the XSLT processor to find a matching template rule for each of the nodes returned by the XPath expression in the instruction's select attribute. In this case, the XPath expression /article/para returns a node-set consisting of two elements. Looking back at the source document (Example B-4), we see that the article root element contains two para elements. For each of these element nodes, the XSLT processor tries to find a matching template rule.

The xsl:apply-templates instruction is similar to the xsl:for-each instruction, in that both instructions iterate over a set of nodes that is selected using the instruction's select attribute. The difference between them is what happens to each node. The content of the xsl:for-each element statically dictates what content to insert into the result tree; the same thing happens for each node in the node-set. On the other hand, the xsl:apply-templates instruction *dynamically* decides what to do with each node in the node-set. It acts like a big, invisible if/else statement, determining which template rule to apply based on which node is currently being processed. Unlike the xsl:for-each instruction, it has the potential of doing something different for every node that it processes.

In this case, it first looks for a template rule for the first para element. After it has found a matching template rule and has finished applying it, it then looks for a template rule for the second para element. If there were more than two para elements in the source document, then it would continue to do this until it has finished finding and applying a template rule for each of the nodes in the node-set.

Where does the XSLT processor find these template rules? Well, the first place it looks is inside your stylesheet. We've already seen that a template rule is any xsl:template element that has a match attribute, which means that our stylesheet contains four template rules. (Their order doesn't matter.) In this case, since we're processing para elements, the second template rule in the stylesheet matches, as determined by the value of its match attribute:

```
<xsl:template match="para">
```

The value of the match attribute is called a *pattern*. In this case the pattern para successfully matches the para elements that are being processed via xsl:apply-templates.

Inside this template rule, there is a p literal result element. Effectively, there will be one p element in the result tree for each para element in the source tree:

```
<p>
  <xsl:apply-templates/>
</p>
```

The xsl:apply-templates instruction inside the p element has no select attribute. When the select attribute is absent, the instruction is equivalent to <xsl:apply-templates select="child::node( )"/>. This means "Process all child nodes, regardless of their type." In this case, the current node being processed is a para element. The para elements in our source document contain both elements and text, so the node-set to process will consist of both elements and text nodes. Since our stylesheet does not explicitly define a template rule for *text nodes*, then one of XSLT's *built-in template rules* is applied. The built-in rule for text nodes is to copy the node to the result tree. Thus, the p elements in the result tree will effectively contain the same text as their corresponding para elements in the source tree.

Our stylesheet contains two other template rules, one for emphasis elements and one for strong elements:

```
<xsl:template match="emphasis">
  <i>
    <xsl:apply-templates/>
```

```
    </i>
  </xsl:template>

  <xsl:template match="strong">
    <b>
      <xsl:apply-templates/>
    </b>
  </xsl:template>
```

The effect of these rules is that emphasis elements in the source document get transformed into i elements in the result document, and strong elements in the source document get transformed into b elements in the result document.

Finally, we see the result of applying the stylesheet (Example B-5) to our simple XML source document (Example B-4). Example B-6 shows the XML serialization of the result tree of this transformation.

Example B-6. The resulting XML document
```
<?xml version="1.0" encoding="utf-8"?>
<html>
  <head>
    <title>This is a short article</title>
  </head>
  <body>
    <h1>This is a short article</h1>
    <p>This is the <i>first</i> paragraph.</p>
    <p>This is the <b>second</b> paragraph.</p>
  </body>
</html>
```

As you can see, the title and h1 elements have the same value (from the source document's heading element). Also, the para elements have been converted to p elements, the emphasis element has been converted to an i element, and the strong element has been converted to a b element.

A More Advanced Example

Our final example triplet of source document, stylesheet, and result document involves converting an XML format into another XML format, rather than HTML. Example B-7 shows a simple XML document containing order information.

Example B-7. An XML document containing orders
```
<orders>
  <order>
    <item>Widget</item>
    <price>50</price>
    <quantity>3</quantity>
  </order>
  <order>
```

Example B-7. An XML document containing orders (continued)

```
    <item>Thingamajig</item>
    <price>25</price>
    <quantity>2</quantity>
  </order>
  <order>
    <item>Whatchamacallit</item>
    <price>35</price>
    <quantity>1</quantity>
  </order>
</orders>
```

Example B-8 shows an XSLT stylesheet for converting this document into a summary format.

Example B-8. An XSLT stylesheet for processing orders

```
<xsl:stylesheet version="1.0"
  xmlns:xsl="http://www.w3.org/1999/XSL/Transform">

  <xsl:output indent="yes"/>

  <xsl:template match="/">
    <orderSummary>
      <expensiveItems>
        <xsl:apply-templates select="/orders/order[price >= 30]"/>
      </expensiveItems>
      <cheapItems>
        <xsl:apply-templates select="/orders/order[price &lt; 30]"/>
      </cheapItems>
    </orderSummary>
  </xsl:template>

  <xsl:template match="order">
    <xsl:element name="{item}">
      <xsl:attribute name="totalPrice">
        <xsl:value-of select="price * quantity"/>
      </xsl:attribute>
    </xsl:element>
  </xsl:template>

</xsl:stylesheet>
```

This stylesheet introduces some more features of XPath and XSLT. Let's step through the stylesheet just as we did with the first two examples.

This time, the xsl:output method does not include a method attribute. Since it defaults to xml (as long as the result document's root element name is not html), the result will be serialized as a well-formed XML document. The indent attribute asks the processor, once again, to add line breaks and indentation to make the resulting document easy to read:

```
    <xsl:output indent="yes"/>
```

Inside the root template rule, we see some literal result elements. The orderSummary element will end up as the root, or document, element of the result document. And it will contain two child elements, expensiveItems and cheapItems:

```
<xsl:template match="/">
  <orderSummary>
    <expensiveItems>
      ...
    </expensiveItems>
    <cheapItems>
      ...
    </cheapItems>
  </orderSummary>
</xsl:template>
```

Inside the expensiveItems element, we see the xsl:apply-templates instruction:

```
<xsl:apply-templates select="/orders/order[price >= 30]"/>
```

The XPath expression /orders/order[price >= 30] selects all order element children of the root order element where the price child element's value is greater than or equal to 30. This test occurs inside square brackets and is called a *predicate*. (XPath predicates are similar to WHERE clauses in SQL.) Predicates are useful for filtering out all but the nodes you want from a given node-set. In this case, we only want to process certain orders—where the price is greater than 30.

Inside the cheapItems element, we see a similar instruction:

```
<xsl:apply-templates select="/orders/order[price &lt; 30]"/>
```

The XPath expression /orders/order[price < 30] also contains a predicate. But in this case, the expression selects all the order elements that the first xsl:apply-templates instruction filtered out, namely the order elements where the price value is less than 30.

> Certain markup characters in XML have special meaning and must be escaped when they occur inside element or attribute values. The XPath less-than operator (<), for example, must be escaped (as <) when it occurs inside an attribute value (as in XSLT).

As we learned in the last section, the xsl:apply-templates instruction tells the XSLT processor to find matching template rules for each of the nodes in the node-set selected by the select attribute. Our stylesheet in Example B-8 includes only one other template rule:

```
<xsl:template match="order">
```

This template rule happens to match all of the nodes selected by each of the two xsl:apply-templates instructions. In other words, all of the order elements being processed match the pattern order (in the match attribute).

Inside the template rule, we see a new XSLT instruction, xsl:element:

```
<xsl:element name="{item}">
    ...
</xsl:element>
```

The purpose of the xsl:element instruction is to create an element in the result document. In that respect, it is similar to a literal result element. However, unlike literal result elements, xsl:element instructions allow you to make the element name dynamic. In this case, the name of the element will be the value of the item child element of the current node (the item child of the order element being processed). The curly braces ({ }) are called an *attribute value template* and are replaced with the value returned by the XPath expression between them (item in this case). Without the curly braces, the XSLT processor would just create an item element (using the string item as the name of the new element, rather than evaluating item as an XPath expression).

Inside the xsl:element instruction, we see an xsl:attribute instruction:

```
<xsl:attribute name="totalPrice">
    ...
</xsl:attribute>
```

As you may have already guessed, the xsl:attribute element creates an attribute in the result. In this case, the name of the attribute will be totalPrice. The value of the totalPrice attribute is determined by the content of the xsl:attribute element. Looking inside the xsl:attribute element, we see an xsl:value-of instruction:

```
<xsl:value-of select="price * quantity"/>
```

Unlike previous examples, the XPath expression shown here is an arithmetic expression, consisting of a location path multiplied by a location path. Actually, what happens is this: the location paths (price and quantity) are first evaluated and converted to numbers. Then those numbers are multiplied by each other. Thus, the value of the totalPrice attribute in the result will be the product of the values of the price and quantity child elements of the order element currently being processed.

Finally, Example B-9 shows the result of applying the XSLT stylesheet (Example B-8) against the source document (Example B-7).

Example B-9. The result of applying the stylesheet in Example B-8 against the XML document in Example B-7

```
<?xml version="1.0"?>
<orderSummary>
  <expensiveItems>
    <Widget totalPrice="150"/>
    <Whatchamacallit totalPrice="35"/>
  </expensiveItems>
  <cheapItems>
    <Thingamajig totalPrice="50"/>
  </cheapItems>
</orderSummary>
```

As you can see, there is an element to correspond to each of the original order elements from Example B-7. The name of each element varies according to the value of the original item child element (Widget, Whatchamacallit, or Thingamajig). They are divided up into "expensive" and "cheap" items depending on their original price values. For example, since the "Thingamajig" item's price was only 25 (which is less than 30), it ended up inside the cheapItems element. Finally, the totalPrice attribute in each case consists of the original price value multiplied times the original quantity value.

Conclusion

XSLT can be a difficult language to learn, and, for that reason, it's often been derided as an overly complex language. In truth, XSLT is a small language with few primitives, few operators, and few functions. While there's no shame in consulting the reference manual, it is easily a candidate for a language that you can learn comprehensively. So take heart! With the right guidance and a little patience, it can be done.

Probably XSLT's most difficult construct to learn is also its most powerful: template rules. It is quite possible to work with XSLT while avoiding this construct (thereby missing out on much of XSLT's power), and this is often how people learn XSLT. The problem with this avoidance is that it tends to catch up with you sooner or later. If you can just master this one aspect of XSLT (how template rules work), then you will have overcome the most difficult hurdle. After that, everything should fall into place, and you will have a powerful new tool in your XML processing arsenal.

The XSD You Need for Office

The purpose of this appendix is to introduce you to XML Schema Definitions (XSD). Microsoft uses XSD, or subsets of XSD, throughout the Office suite. While XSD is a subject worthy of a book or several of its own, and many people prefer to work with it only through tools, there is a core set of XSD features that will let you describe and define XML vocabularies as well as understand how Office interprets XML information.

What Is XSD?

XML Schema Description (XSD), sometimes referred to as W3C XML Schema (WXS), is an XML vocabulary that lets you describe other XML vocabularies so that programs can test whether a given document meets rules laid down in the schema. XSD is defined by a set of three W3C Recommendations:

XML Schema Part 0: Primer
> A tutorial for XML Schema, explaining Parts 1 and 2 in simpler terms with more examples and integration. Available at *http://www.w3.org/TR/xmlschema-0/*.

XML Schema Part 1: Structures
> An XML vocabulary for describing the structures of XML vocabularies, based on a mixture of markup and object-oriented design. Available at *http://www.w3.org/TR/xmlschema-1/*.

XML Schema Part 2: Datatypes
> A set of extensible types for describing the contents of XML elements and attributes, including things like integers, decimals, and dates. Available at *http://www.w3.org/TR/xmlschema-2/*.

The mechanisms for defining structures and datatypes allow schema designers to create type systems that may be extended or restricted. This brief appendix will focus on the parts of XSD you need to define document structures, and leaves advanced features like extension, restriction, substitution groups, and keys for more detailed exploration in other books.

 For more information on XSD generally, see Eric van der Vlist's *XML Schema* (O'Reilly) or Priscilla Walmsley's *Definitive XML Schema* (Prentice-Hall). The Primer noted above may also be a good place to start.

Creating a Simple Schema

As a simple example to get you started building schemas, examine the structure of Example C-1. You may have seen the document before (it was Example A-1 in Appendix A), but this time do an inventory of the parts it contains.

Example C-1. A simple XML document for definition in a schema

```
<?xml version="1.0" encoding="us-ascii"?>
<authors>
    <person id="lear">
        <name>Edward Lear</name>
        <nationality>British</nationality>
    </person>
    <person id="asimov">
        <name>Isaac Asimov</name>
        <nationality>American</nationality>
    </person>
    <person id="mysteryperson"/>
</authors>
```

This document contains an authors element, which itself contains multiple person elements. Each person element has an id attribute and may contain a name and a nationality element. For now, we'll treat all of the textual content of the elements and attributes as text. One way to define this document in a schema is with a schema whose structure mirrors the document shown in Example C-2, called a "Russian doll" schema after the wooden *matruschkas*. The names of the elements being defined are in bold to make it easier to read.

Example C-2. A "russian doll" schema that describes Example C-1.

```
<xs:schema xmlns:xs="http://www.w3.org/2001/XMLSchema" >
  <xs:element name="authors">
    <xs:complexType>
      <xs:sequence>
        <xs:element name="person" maxOccurs="unbounded">
          <xs:complexType>
            <xs:sequence minOccurs="0" >
              <xs:element name="name" type="xs:string" />
              <xs:element name="nationality" type="xs:string"  />
            </xs:sequence>
```

Example C-2. A "russian doll" schema that describes Example C-1. (continued)

```
                <xs:attribute name="id" type="xs:string" use="required"/>
            </xs:complexType>
        </xs:element>
    </xs:sequence>
  </xs:complexType>
 </xs:element>
</xs:schema>
```

This schema starts by defining the authors element, which will be the root element for the document, and its contents. Because the authors element contains more than simple text, it is defined as an xs:complexType. That type contains a sequence of person elements. The parts of the declaration that pertain only to the authors element are shown here:

```
<xs:element name="authors">
    <xs:complexType>
        <xs:sequence>
            <xs:element name="person" maxOccurs="unbounded">
                ...
            </xs:element>
        </xs:sequence>
    </xs:complexType>
</xs:element>
```

The definition of the person element itself contains an xs:complexType containing an xs:sequence, this time specifying that name and nationality elements (each of which only contain a string) may appear in that sequence. The xs:complexType for the person element also contains a definition for the id attribute.

```
<xs:element name="person" maxOccurs="unbounded">
    <xs:complexType>
        <xs:sequence minOccurs="0" >
            <xs:element name="name" type="xs:string" />
            <xs:element name="nationality" type="xs:string" />
        </xs:sequence>
        <xs:attribute name="id" type="xs:string" use="required"/>
    </xs:complexType>
</xs:element>
```

Because the name and nationality elements and the id attribute just contain strings, they are "simple" relative to the complex types used for the elements that contain them, so a declaration like:

```
<xs:element name="name" type="xs:string" />
```

is sufficient to say "the name element will appear here and contain a string."

There are a few other pieces to examine in Example C-2, notably the maxOccurs and minOccurs attributes on xs:element, and the use attribute on xs:attribute.

You can write the same schema in a more modular way, shown in Example C-3. Again, the names of elements are bolded.

Example C-3. A different style of schema that describes Example C-1

```xml
<?xml version="1.0" encoding="UTF-8"?>
<xs:schema xmlns:xs="http://www.w3.org/2001/XMLSchema" >

  <xs:element name="authors">
    <xs:complexType>
      <xs:sequence>
        <xs:element maxOccurs="unbounded" ref="person"/>
      </xs:sequence>
    </xs:complexType>
  </xs:element>

  <xs:element name="person">
    <xs:complexType>
      <xs:sequence minOccurs="0">
        <xs:element ref="name"/>
        <xs:element ref="nationality"/>
      </xs:sequence>
      <xs:attribute ref="id" use="required"/>
    </xs:complexType>
  </xs:element>

  <xs:element name="name" type="xs:string"/>

  <xs:element name="nationality" type="xs:string"/>

  <xs:attribute name="id" type="xs:string"/>

</xs:schema>
```

Instead of nesting all the declarations into one xs:element, this version separates all the declarations into separate pieces. Only one new piece is needed to do this, the ref attribute on xs:element and xs:attribute. Writing schemas this way is frequently simpler, as it allows you to reuse the same elements in multiple places and because it separates information about how often an element or attribute may appear (maxOccurs, minOccurs, and use, which go with the ref) from the information about an element or attribute's content (the type attribute, xs:complexType child element, and so on).

When the xs:element and xs:attribute declarations are moved out to be immediate children of the xs:schema element, they become global elements and attributes, accessible for use in any declaration. Elements also become possible root elements for the document, so Office applications may ask which element to use as the root if given schemas written in this style. (It's generally easier to keep xs:attribute declarations inside of the elements that use them, or in attribute groups, described later, rather than as globals.)

If you load either of these schemas into an Excel XML map (as described in Chapter 6) and load Example C-1 into the map, you'll get the result shown in Figure C-1.

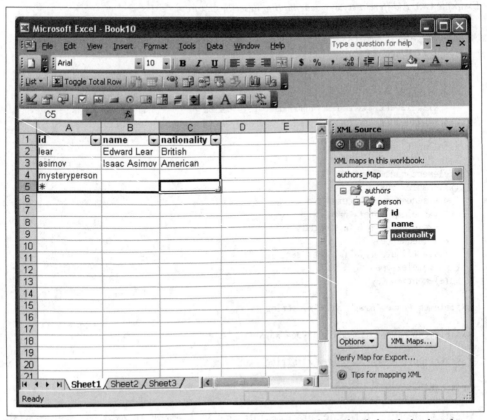

Figure C-1. An XML map using the schema in Examples C-2 and C-3, loaded with the data from Example C-1

While the two schemas are different, the model they describe to Excel (or Word, or any other schema-processing software) is exactly the same. For some record/field based vocabularies, the simple structures presented in Examples C-2 and C-3 are more than enough to get work accomplished.

Schema Parts

The simple schemas in Examples C-2 and C-3 use a lot of pieces of XSD, and you can use them as models for future schemas, but there are a lot more options available, even in the most readily usable subset of XSD.

Namespaces

The only namespace declaration to appear in either example was the namespace declaration for XSD itself:

```
xmlns:xs="http://www.w3.org/2001/XMLSchema"
```

In this case, the schema was defining a vocabulary that was not in a namespace, so there was no need to define an additional namespace. If, as is typical, your schemas define vocabularies that are in a namespace, you'll need to define the namespace on the root xs:schema element. Example C-4 shows a slightly modified version of Example C-3, defining the vocabulary as belonging to the http://simonstl.com/ns/authors/ namespace. Changes to the schema appear in bold.

Example C-4. Example C-3 rewritten to support a namespace

```
<?xml version="1.0" encoding="UTF-8"?>
<xs:schema xmlns:xs="http://www.w3.org/2001/XMLSchema"
           targetNamespace="http://simonstl.com/ns/authors/"
           xmlns="http://simonstl.com/ns/authors/"
           elementFormDefault="qualified"
           attributeFormDefault="unqualified" >

  <xs:element name="authors">
    <xs:complexType>
      <xs:sequence>
        <xs:element maxOccurs="unbounded" ref="person"/>
      </xs:sequence>
    </xs:complexType>
  </xs:element>

  <xs:element name="person">
    <xs:complexType>
      <xs:sequence minOccurs="0">
        <xs:element ref="name"/>
        <xs:element ref="nationality"/>
      </xs:sequence>
      <xs:attribute ref="id" use="required"/>
    </xs:complexType>
  </xs:element>

  <xs:element name="name" type="xs:string"/>

  <xs:element name="nationality" type="xs:string"/>

  <xs:attribute name="id" type="xs:string"/>

</xs:schema>
```

All of the changes in this case are at the top. The targetNamespace attribute tells the XSD processor what namespace is being defined here, and the xmlns attribute that follows declares the default namespace to use that same namespace URI. (If you leave off the xmlns attribute, the connections between the ref attributes and their corresponding xs:element and xs:attribute declarations will break.) The elementFormDefault and attributeFormDefault attributes declare whether local elements and attributes will be namespace-qualified by default. To match typical XML 1.0 practice, elements are qualified and attributes are not.

Namespace handling in XSD can get extremely complicated if you start using unqualified elements, qualified attributes, or mixing all of them by using the form attribute on individual declarations. The easiest approaches are definitely either to work without namespaces at all or to use qualified elements and unqualified attributes.

It's also worth noting that you don't have to define attributes used in documents for namespace declarations. XSD doesn't consider them attributes and doesn't validate them.

Named and Anonymous Type Definitions

All of the types defined in Examples C-2, C-3, and C-4 were anonymous. Only the xs:elements and xs:attributes had names, not the xs:complexType elements. Some of the declarations referenced a named type, xs:string (a predefined datatype), but these schemas didn't create any named types of their own. If you want to create named types for the complex type content of Example C-4, you could further modularize it as shown in Example C-5.

Example C-5. Example C-4 rewritten to break out complex types

```
<?xml version="1.0" encoding="UTF-8"?>
<xs:schema xmlns:xs="http://www.w3.org/2001/XMLSchema"
           targetNamespace="http://simonstl.com/ns/authors/"
           xmlns="http://simonstl.com/ns/authors/"
           elementFormDefault="qualified"
           attributeFormDefault="unqualified" >

  <xs:element name="authors" type="authorsContent" />

  <xs:complexType name="authorsContent">
    <xs:sequence>
      <xs:element maxOccurs="unbounded" ref="person"/>
    </xs:sequence>
  </xs:complexType>

  <xs:element name="person" type="personContent" />

  <xs:complexType name="personContent">
    <xs:sequence minOccurs="0">
      <xs:element ref="name"/>
      <xs:element ref="nationality"/>
    </xs:sequence>
    <xs:attribute ref="id" use="required"/>
  </xs:complexType>

  <xs:element name="name" type="xs:string"/>

  <xs:element name="nationality" type="xs:string"/>
```

Example C-5. Example C-4 rewritten to break out complex types (continued)

```
  <xs:attribute name="id" type="xs:string"/>

</xs:schema>
```

Instead of this definition of the authors element:

```
    <xs:element name="authors">
      <xs:complexType>
        <xs:sequence>
          <xs:element maxOccurs="unbounded" ref="person"/>
        </xs:sequence>
      </xs:complexType>
    </xs:element>
```

the schema now uses:

```
    <xs:element name="authors" type="authorsContent" />

    <xs:complexType name="authorsContent">
      <xs:sequence>
        <xs:element maxOccurs="unbounded" ref="person"/>
      </xs:sequence>
    </xs:complexType>
```

The actual xs:element now looks more like its simpler cousins that simply refer-enced a datatype, while the xs:complexType is a separate component. This approach means that the xs:complexType can be referenced by multiple elements that have the same content model, and it also means that advanced schema developers can derive additional types from the authorsContent type to create variations. (If you don't have an explicit reason to create named types, it is frequently easier to avoid them alto-gether.)

Datatypes

The examples have been using datatypes, a special kind of named type, since Example C-2. This xs:element refers to the xs:string datatype:

```
    <xs:element name="nationality" type="xs:string"/>
```

The xs:string datatype is probably the most commonly used type, and it may be okay during the early development of your schemas to define all content as being of type xs:string and then go through later and define more specific types. XSD includes over forty types that you can use without further work, described briefly below.

xs:anyURI
: Contains any URL or URI as its value.

xs:base64binary
: Contains Base 64 encoded binary content, as defined in RFC 2045.

xs:boolean

Contains a true/false value, expressed as true, false, 0, or 1.

xs:byte

Contains an integer value between -128 and 127.

xs:date

Contains a date in the ISO 8601 [-]*CCYY-MM-DD*[Z|(+|-)*hh:mm*] format. The optional negative at the start indicates if the year is before 0 AD, *CC* is the century, *YY* the year, *MM* the month, and *DD* the day. The [Z|(+|-)*hh:mm*] is an optional time zone, where Z indicates Universal Time (UTC). For example, August 5, 2004 as experienced in London might be written 2004-08-05Z, while December 7, 1941 BC on the east coast of the United States would be written -1941-12-07-05:00.

xs:dateTime

Much like xs:date above, except that it adds time information, making the complete format [-]*CCYY-MM-DDThh:mm:ss*[Z|(+|-)*hh:mm*], where the T is a capital letter T used as a divider, and *hh:mm:ss* is hours, minutes, and seconds. Hours are expressed in 24-hour time. For example, August 5, 2004 at 9:51 P.M. as experienced in London might be written 2004-08-05T21:51:00Z, while December 7, 1941 BC at 11:37:42 A.M. on the east coast of the United States would be written -1941-12-07T11:37:42-05:00.

xs:decimal

Contains a number with one decimal point and an arbitrary number of digits. A leading negative sign is permitted, as are any number of insignificant leading or following zeros. There is no restriction on the number of digits used, but scientific notation (12.04E+2, for instance) is prohibited. Legal decimals include 0, 4.624, -4.6424, 0010.1111220, and 11221523432399322146838572919572399102.556.

xs:double

A 64-bit floating point number, expressed using a decimal format with optional scientific notation, as well as the values 0 (positive zero), -0 (negative zero), INF (positive infinity), -INF (negative infinity), and NaN (not a number). Doubles are expressed internally as powers of two rather than powers of ten, so some rounding errors may appear in calculations made with doubles.

xs:duration

A length of time, expressed using the format P*n*Y*n*M*n*DT*n*H*n*M*n*S. The leading P is mandatory and the T marks the boundary between date and time measurement, but the other letters are required only if used. For example, P1Y is a duration of one year, P2M is a duration of two months, P1DT2H is one day and two hours, and PT20M03S is twenty minutes and three seconds. You should probably avoid combining years or months with days and smaller units, as comparisons can become very complicated.

xs:ENTITIES

Maps to the ENTITIES type in DTDs, used for unparsed entities. This is included for completeness, but your odds of seeing or using it are slim.

xs:ENTITY

Like xs:ENTITIES, maps to the ENTITY type in DTDs, used for unparsed entities. This is included for completeness, but your odds of seeing or using it are slim.

xs:float

Exactly like xs:double, except only a 32-bit floating point space.

xs:gDay, xs:gMonth, xs:gMonthDay, xs:gYear, xs:gYearMonth

These types represent durations of calendar time with an optional time zone. The first three refer to repeating times (every 15th of the month, every June, every June 15th, respectively), while xs:gYear and xs:gYearMonth refer to specific years and months within a year (the year 2110, June 2110).

xs:hexBinary

Like xs:base64binary, this holds encoded binary content, except that data is encoded by representing every byte in text as its hexadecimal value.

xs:ID

Maps to the DTD type ID, which is used for attribute values that must be unique within a document. Unlike its use in DTDs, it can be applied to both attribute and element content. Its value must start with a letter or underscore, and be composed of letters and numbers, underscores, periods, and hyphens.

xs:IDREF

Maps to the DTD IDREF, which is used for attribute values that must match an ID value elsewhere in the document. Unlike its use in DTDs, it can be applied to both attribute and element content. Like ID, its value must start with a letter, underscore, or colon, and be composed of letters and numbers, underscores, periods, and hyphens.

xs:IDREFS

Maps to the DTD IDREFS, and is just like xs:IDREF, except that multiple identifiers pointing to IDs may appear, separated by spaces.

xs:int

Represents 32-bit integers, in the range from -2147483648 to 2147483647. Any number of leading zeros is permitted, but no decimal points, scientific notation, INF, or NaN. Legal values include 20, -9743, 0, and 2147483645.

xs:integer

Like decimal, this represents all positive and negative integers with any number of digits allowed. No decimal point may appear. -0 and +0 are permitted, but they are considered equal. Legal values include -200, 420, and 2147483649.

`xs:language`

A language code like those used by the `xml:lang` attribute, based on RFC 1766. Values might include en-`US` for English as spoken in the United States, `fr-CA` for Canadian French, or `fr` for French.

`xs:long`

A 64-bit integer, in the range -9223372036854775808 to 9223372036854775807. No decimal points, scientific notation, `INF`, or `NaN` are permitted.

`xs:Name`

An XML Schema version of the XML 1.0 Name production, which must start with a letter, underscore, or colon, and be composed of letters, numbers, periods, underscores, hyphens, and colons.

`xs:NCName`

Like `xs:Name`, except that colons are prohibited.

`xs:negativeInteger`

Exactly like `xs:integer`, except that no positive integers or zero are allowed.

`xs:NMTOKEN`

An XML Schema version of the XML 1.0 NMTOKEN production, which allows values containing letters, numbers, periods, colons, underscores, and hyphens.

`xs:NMTOKENS`

Just like `xs:NMTOKEN`, except that multiple tokens may appear separated by whitespace.

`xs:nonNegativeInteger`

Exactly like `xs:integer`, except that negative values are prohibited. Zero is allowed.

`xs:nonPositiveInteger`

Exactly like `xs:integer`, except that positive values are prohibited. Zero is allowed.

`xs:normalizedString`

A string of characters that will be reported as if all whitespace characters are spaces—no tabs, linefeeds, or carriage returns will be reported to the program.

`xs:NOTATION`

An XML Schema version of the rarely-used XML 1.0 NOTATION type for attributes.

`xs:positiveInteger`

Exactly like `xs:integer`, except that negative values are prohibited. Zero is not allowed.

xs:QName
> A namespace-qualified name. The prefix used in the value must be in scope, declared in this element or in an ancestor element, and the application will be told of the namespace URI and the local portion of the name.

xs:short
> A 16-bit integer, in the range -32768 to 32768. Decimal points are forbidden.

xs:string
> Any legal XML text you like.

xs:time
> Time information represented in a 24-hour format as *hh*:*mm*:*ss*[Z|(+|-)*hh*:*mm*], where *hh*:*mm*:*ss* is hours, minutes, and seconds and the rest is an optional time-zone. For example, 9:51 A.M. as experienced in London might be written 09:51:00Z, while 11:37:42 P.M. on the east coast of the United States would be written 23:37:42-05:00.

xs:token
> Just like xs:string, except that all whitespace is collapsed down to single spaces and leading and trailing whitespace is removed.

xs:unsignedByte, xs:unsignedInt, xs:unsignedLong, xs:unsignedShort
> Positive 8-bit, 32-bit, 64-bit, and 16-bit integers, respectively. Zero is permitted in all of these, but negative numbers, decimal points, INF, and NaN are not.

XML Schema Part 2 provides a set of facilities for creating additional constraints on these datatypes using a facet-based system, but those facilities definitely deserve a book of their own. For most applications, one of these basic types will be acceptable.

Varied Document Structures

While some XML documents, particularly those spreadsheet or database contents, only need to define containers and possibly a sequence, richer documents often contain a much wider variety of possibilities. Sections may be optional or appear repeatedly, but may also be replaced with a variety of different choices. Choices may themselves include or be included by sequences. XML Schema offers support for many different kinds of document structure.

Examples C-2 through C-5 all used the xs:sequence element and the minOccurs and maxOccurs attributes shown below.

```
<xs:element name="person">
  <xs:complexType>
    <xs:sequence minOccurs="0">
      <xs:element ref="name" />
      <xs:element ref="nationality" />
    </xs:sequence>
    <xs:attribute ref="id" use="required"/>
  </xs:complexType>
</xs:element>
```

The xs:sequence element is called a *compositor*, imposing order on its child xs:element particles. There are two other compositors available: xs:choice and xs:all. The xs:choice element permits one of a list of particles to appear, while xs:all requires that all particles must appear but doesn't put constraints on the order in which they appear. In addition to setting rules for their particles, compositors also act as a group, and you can specify minOccurs or maxOccurs for the group as a whole. (The default value for both the minOccurs and maxOccurs is one.)

If you wanted to define a person element that included both name and nationality but weren't concerned about the order in which they appeared, you could use:

```
<xs:element name="person">
  <xs:complexType>
    <xs:all>
      <xs:element ref="name"/>
      <xs:element ref="nationality"/>
    </xs:all>
    <xs:attribute ref="id" use="required"/>
  </xs:complexType>
</xs:element>
```

(Note that the xs:attribute isn't part of the group. Attributes are part of the type, but the compositors only apply to element content.)

If, on the other hand, you wanted to define a person element that could contain a choice of a name or an alias, you might use:

```
<xs:element name="person">
  <xs:complexType>
    <xs:choice minOccurs="0" >
      <xs:element ref="name" />
      <xs:element ref="alias" />
    </xs:choice>
    <xs:attribute ref="id" use="required"/>
  </xs:complexType>
</xs:element>
```

The particles inside of an xs:sequence or xs:choice may be xs:element, xs:sequence, xs:choice, xs:any, or xs:group elements. (xs:all may only contain xs:element.) For example, a choice might be between an element and sequence of choices:

```
<xs:element name="pachinko">
  <xs:complexType>
    <xs:choice>
      <xs:element name="simple" type="xs:string" />
      <xs:sequence>
        <xs:choice>
          <xs:element name="choice1" type="xs:string" />
          <xs:element name="choice2" type="xs:string"
        </xs:choice>
        <xs:choice>
          <xs:element name="choiceA" type="xs:string" />
          <xs:element name="choiceB" type="xs:string"
        </xs:choice>
```

```
    </xs:sequence>
   </xs:choice>
  </xs:complexType>
 </xs:element>
```

In this case, the pachinko element may contain an element named simple, or it may contain the sequence. The sequence requires either a choice1 or a choice2 element (but not both), followed by either a choiceA or a choiceB element (again, not both.)

XML Schema prohibits certain combinations of compositors, requiring that schema structures always provide a deterministic path to a particular combination of elements; the processor should never have to keep two possible choices in mind while it works out which particle a particular element matches. Most simple schemas will never encounter these problems, but more complex ones can fall afoul of them. For more detail, see Chapter 7 of Eric van der Vlist's *XML Schema*.

When Anything Is Allowed

If you aren't concerned about what goes into a particular element or particle, you can use the xs:any element for its content and xs:anyAttribute to specify its attributes. You can limit the contents to particular namespaces using the namespace attribute and tell the schema validator to skip the contents using the processContents attribute. For example, if you wanted to create an extension element that permitted any content and had any namespaces, you might declare it like:

```
<xs:element name="extension">
  <xs:complexType>
    <xs:sequence minoccurs="0" maxOccurs="unbounded">
      <xs:any namespace="##any" processContents="skip" />
    </xs:sequence>
    <xs:anyAttribute namespace="##any" processContents="skip" />
  </xs:complexType>
</xs:element>
```

The namespace attribute can hold a namespace URI (or URIs, separated by whitespace), as well as one of four wildcards:

##local

Only elements (or attributes, for xs:anyAttribute) in no namespace at all may appear.

##targetNamespace

Only elements (or attributes, for xs:anyAttribute) in the schema's target namespace may appear.

##any

Elements (or attributes, for xs:anyAttribute) in any namespace at all may appear.

##other

Only elements (or attributes, for xs:anyAttribute) that are not in the schema's target namespace may appear.

The xs:any element must appear within an xs:sequence or xs:choice, while the xs:anyAttribute may appear in xs:attributeGroup as well as xs:complexType and related elements.

Model Groups

If you have lots of declarations you'll be using frequently but don't need to be able to extend or restrict them, you can use the xs:group element, first to define a group of declarations and then to reference them.

For example, the declaration for the person element in Example C-3 looked like:

```
<xs:element name="person">
  <xs:complexType>
    <xs:sequence minOccurs="0">
      <xs:element ref="name"/>
      <xs:element ref="nationality"/>
    </xs:sequence>
    <xs:attribute ref="id" use="required"/>
  </xs:complexType>
</xs:element>
```

If you planned to reuse this combination of name and nationality but not the id attribute, you could create a model group holding the sequence and reference it inside the xs:complexType. The new version would look like:

```
<xs:element name="person">
  <xs:complexType>
    <xs:group ref="name-nationality" />
    <xs:attribute ref="id" use="required"/>
  </xs:complexType>
</xs:element>

<xs:group name="name-nationality">
  <xs:sequence minOccurs="0">
    <xs:element ref="name"/>
    <xs:element ref="nationality"/>
  </xs:sequence>
</xs:group>
```

You can do the same thing to attributes if you have a group of attributes to be applied repeatedly. To create a set of attributes referring to URLs and giving MIME types of the desired content, you might create an xs:attributeGroup like this one:

```
<xs:attributeGroup name="retrievalInformation" >
  <xs:attribute name="href" type="xs:anyURI" />
  <xs:attribute name="mime-type" type="xs:string"/>
</xs:attribute>

<xs:element name="link">
  <xs:complexType>
    <xs:attributeGroup ref="retrievalInformation" />
  </xs:complexType>
</xs:element>
```

The link element could now have attributes named href and mime-type.

The xs:group element may contain any compositor (xs:sequence, xs:choice, or xs:all) and its contents, while xs:attributeGroup is limited to containing xs:attribute, xs:attributeGroup, or xs:anyAttribute. If you need to put both elements and attributes in a group, use xs:complexType instead.

Empty Content, Mixed Content, and Default Values

XML Schema can support a few more types of content than have been shown so far, as well as supply content to documents in some cases. The simplest case that hasn't been shown yet is the creation of an element (like br in HTML) that must always be empty. The easiest way to do this is to use an xs:complexType element that doesn't reference any elements, like this:

```
<xs:element name="br">
    <xs:complexType>
    </xs:complexType>
</xs:element>
```

If you want to add attributes, they can be placed in the xs:complexType element without changing the emptiness of the br element.

Another common case is mixed content, where text and elements appear on the same level of a document. A classic case is a paragraph that contains bold, italic, and underlined text. In simple HTML, this might look like:

```
<p>This is <b>bold</b>, this is <i>italic</i>, and this is
<u>underline</u>.</p>
```

To make this work, you need to create a definition of the p element that contains an xs:complexType element whose mixed attribute is set to true:

```
<xs:element name="p">
    <xs:complexType mixed="true">
        <xs:choice minOccurs="0" maxOccurs="unbounded">
            <xs:element name="b" type="xs:string" />
            <xs:element name="i" type="xs:string" />
            <xs:element name="u" type="xs:string" />
        </xs:choice>
    </xs:complexType>
</xs:element>
```

The choice will permit as many b, i, and u elements as necessary, while mixed="true" will permit text to be mingled with any of them.

If instead of these fancy features you just want to create a definition that provides a default value to an element or attribute if one is not provided, you can use the default attribute on simple element or attribute declarations. To create an element called name whose value defaults to Winky if the element is present but empty, you would write:

```
<xs:element name="name" default="Winky" />
```

To create an attribute named `flavor` whose value defaults to `vanilla`, you would write:

```
<xs:attribute name="flavor" default="vanilla" />
```

Unlike the element, the default value will only be applied if the attribute is absent. You can also fix a value to an attribute or element. If you insisted that the `flavor` must always be `vanilla`, you could instead use:

```
<xs:attribute name="flavor" fixed="vanilla" />
```

The `flavor` attribute's value will default to `vanilla` if the attribute isn't present in the document, and an error will be reported if a document contains a `flavor` attribute with any other value.

Annotations

The last feature of XML Schema worth noting here is its support for annotations. Every single element in XML Schema permits an `xs:annotation` element as its first child (except `xs:annotation` itself, that is). The `xs:annotation` element may contain any number of `xs:documentation` and `xs:appinfo` elements, and the content models for both of those are wide open.

The `xs:appinfo` element is intended for machine-readable content, while the `xs:documentation` element is intended for human-readable content. Both accept a source attribute that points to a URI, and `xs:documentation` also accepts an `xml:lang` attribute that specifies the human language in which the documentation appears. At present, Office ignores both of these, but `xs:documentation` in particular is an opportunity for you to provide additional information in your schemas. For example, to document the `flavor` attribute's peculiar status, a careful schema writer might modify its definition:

```
<xs:attribute name="flavor" fixed="vanilla">
  <xs:annotation>
    <xs:documentation xml:lang="en-US">
      While many people like multiple flavors of ice cream,
      the manager of this project insists that everyone must
      have vanilla, and accepts no questions on the matter.
    </xs:documentation>
  </xs:annotation>
</xs:attribute>
```

You can also use HTML, DocBook, or the XML vocabulary of your choice within `xs:documentation`, and then use other programs or stylesheets to create more formal documentation using this information.

Other Features

XML Schema defines a wide variety of other features, including extension and restriction of both structural types and datatypes, combining types, inclusion and export of external schemas, substitution groups, keys for establishing uniqueness among parts of a document, a mechanism for suggesting which schema applies to a document, and attributes that let parts of a document identify which types within the schema apply to them. Office doesn't support many of these features, and many of them have complex interactions with data models. If you need more information on these features, please consult a book dedicated to XML Schema.

Working with XML Schema

While XML Schema is at the heart of many XML-based projects, it has a few usability issues. You've no doubt noticed that it's verbose, a common problem for anything using XML. Its structures, even using the relatively simple subset of features shown here, can rapidly become complicated, and hunting through these structures to figure out in which choice or sequence a particular component is used is really not much fun. When you've created a schema yourself, it's generally tolerable, but interpreting large schemas created by other people is a challenge, especially when you're reading the structure through XML tags.

Most people who work with XML Schema seem to do so from behind the relative safety of tools, notably the commercial XML Spy (*http://www.xmlspy.com/*). There are many schema editors, some free, some not, all with their own pluses and minuses. Graphic diagrams can be a relief after pointy brackets. Some developers still like to work in text, but not directly in XML Schema, and they may be able to use the tools described in Appendix D for much of their schema creation work.

For some cases, it may be enough to infer schemas from existing documents. Excel 2003 has this capability built into, but getting to those schemas is a bit difficult, as described in Chapter 7. Both the Trang program described in Appendix D and Microsoft's XSDInference toolkit, at *http://msdn.microsoft.com/library/default. asp?url=/library/en-us/dnxmlnet/html/xsdinference.asp*, can give you an instant schema if you need to work with the schema separately.

The enormous feature set provided by the XML Schema recommendations gives developers a huge project to work on, and interoperability between schema tools remains tricky. The applications within Microsoft Office generally work directly with their own preferred subsets of XML Schema, and those subsets seem generally reliable, but you should definitely expect to test your schemas in Office and make sure they behave as you (and your users) expect.

Using DTDs and RELAX NG Schemas with Office

While Microsoft has chosen to use XSD as the schema language throughout its product line, there are at least two other strong schema languages in regular use today. Both Document Type Definitions (DTDs) and RELAX NG (pronounced "relaxing" but no longer an acronym) are much simpler than XSD, and both offer features that go beyond those in XSD, though in different ways. Developers who need or prefer to integrate DTDs or RELAX NG with Microsoft Office can do so by converting these schemas into XSD with Trang, a very simple but powerful translation tool.

If you need a more detailed explanation of DTDs, any introductory XML book should provide a lot of information. For a more thorough explanation of RELAX NG, see Eric van der Vlist's *RELAX NG* (O'Reilly).

XML.com also has a number of excellent articles on RELAX NG and RELAX NG compact syntax that go beyond the coverage in this appendix. To test RELAX NG schemas and perform conversions of either DTDs or RELAX NG schemas into XSD, you'll want to download James Clark's Trang package from *http://www. thaiopensource.com/relaxng/trang.html*. Trang requires that you have a Java runtime installed, but includes all the Java classes it needs in two Java JAR packages.

 If you're working with existing vocabularies that use DTDs, you'll definitely need to know how to work with DTDs. Otherwise, if you're creating new vocabularies, you may want to work with RELAX NG instead.

What Are DTDs?

Document Type Definitions express the allowed elements and attributes in a certain document type and constrain the order in which elements must appear within that document type. A DTD is often composed of a single file, which contains declarations defining the element types and attribute lists. (In theory, a DTD may span more than one file; however, the mechanism for including one file inside another—parameter entities—is outside the scope of this appendix.)

Element Type Declarations

An element is the actual instance of the structure as found in an XML document, whereas the element type defines the element, giving it a name and a structure. The form of an element type declaration is:

```
<!ELEMENT element-name contentspec>
```

The allowable content defined by *contentspec* is defined in terms of a simple grammar, which allows the expression of sequence, alternatives, and iteration within elements. For a formal definition of the element type declaration, see Section 3.2 of the XML 1.0 specification at *http://w3.org/TR/REC-xml#NT-elementdecl*. Table D-1 introduces the most common constructs.

Table D-1. Element type content specifications

Content specification	Meaning
`<!ELEMENT e (#PCDATA)>`	The e element may contain character data—that is, text (and possibly entity and character references).
`<!ELEMENT e EMPTY>`	The e element has no content—that is, it can only appear as `<e/>` or `<e></e>`.
`<!ELEMENT e ANY>`	The e element may contain character data or any other element defined in the DTD.
`<!ELEMENT e (a+)>`	The e element must contain at least one a element and may contain multiple a elements. (The plus means "one or more.")
`<!ELEMENT e (a,b*,c+)>`	The e element must contain the following sequence: one a element, followed by zero or more b elements, followed by one or more c elements. The asterisk means "zero or more."
`<!ELEMENT e (#PCDATA|b)*>`	The e element may contain b elements or character data, and they can all be mixed together.
`<!ELEMENT e (a|b|c)* >`	The e element may contain zero or more a, b, or c elements, in any order.

For a document to be valid, the DTD must provide an element type declaration for every element used in the document and the contents of all of those elements must conform to the content models specified in the element type declaration. Element type declarations leave off one important aspect of elements, however: attributes.

Attribute List Declarations

Inside a DTD, permissible attributes are specified on a per-element basis. An attribute list declaration takes this form:

```
<!ATTLIST element-name attribute-definitions >
```

In the attribute definitions, you have to identify the attribute's name and type, whether the attribute is optional or required, and, if necessary, the attribute's default value. Unlike elements, you can specify default values for attributes, which are inserted by an application when it parses the XML document, even if they're not explicitly written in the document. Attributes can store all kinds of content, but the main types used are CDATA (character data, including entity and character references), ID (identifiers whose value must be unique within the document), and IDREF and IDREFS (which point to ID values). Attribute definitions may also specify a list of acceptable values rather than a generic type. Attribute types are only a subset of the XSD types described in Appendix C—all of them are textual. Table D-2 shows some common attribute definitions.

Table D-2. Attribute definitions

Attribute definition	Meaning
`subject CDATA #REQUIRED`	The `subject` attribute must always be present and it should contain only character data. It has no default value.
`rating CDATA #IMPLIED`	The `rating` attribute is allowed, but not mandatory. It has no default value.
`play (scissors|paper|stone) "stone"`	The `play` attribute may take only the values `scissors`, `paper`, or `stone`. If it is not specified, it is assumed to take the default value `stone`.
`color CDATA #FIXED "purple"`	The `color` attribute must take the value `purple`. If it is not specified on the element, the processing application provides `purple` as a default value.

Here's a complete attribute declaration for a fictitious `animals` element, which must have a name, either two or four legs, and, optionally, a note field:

```
<!ATTLIST animal
    name CDATA #REQUIRED
    legs (two|four) "four"
    notes CDATA #IMPLIED >
```

While attributes can be very useful for annotations, Microsoft Office tends to use element content for information that's presented directly. You can certainly use attributes, but you may find it easier to stick with elements unless you have a particular reason to choose attributes.

Putting it Together

To demonstrate a complete DTD, we'll explore a document and its DTD. The document is shown in Example D-1, while the DTD is shown in Example D-2.

Example D-1. A valid XML document

```
<?xml version="1.0" encoding="us-ascii"?>
<!DOCTYPE authors SYSTEM "http://example.com/authors.dtd">
<authors>
```

```
    <person abbrev="edd">
        <name>Edd Dumbill</name>
        <nationality>British</nationality>
    </person>
    <person abbrev="simonstl">
        <name>Simon St.Laurent</name>
        <nationality>American</nationality>
    </person>
    <person abbrev="vdv">
        <name>Eric van der Vlist</name>
        <nationality>French</nationality>
    </person>
</authors>
```

The DOCTYPE declaration at the top of Example D-1 assumes that the DTD file shown in Example D-2 has been placed on a web server at *example.com*. Note that the document type declaration specifies the root element of the document, not the DTD itself. (You could use the same DTD for documents that used person, name, or nationality as the root element of a valid document.)

Example D-2. The DTD for Example D-1

```
<!ELEMENT authors (person)* >

<!ELEMENT person (name,nationality)>
<!ATTLIST person
   abbrev CDATA #REQUIRED>

<!ELEMENT name (#PCDATA)>
<!ELEMENT nationality (#PCDATA)>
```

The DTD defines the structures you find in the document. There is an authors element type that may contain zero or more person elements. In this document, we have three person elements. There is a person element type that must contain a name element followed by a nationality element. Each of the person elements in the document has those parts in that order. The person elements are required to have an attribute named abbrev, and all of them do. Finally, the name element type and the nationality element type can only hold textual content. All of the name and nationality elements here do that.

A validating XML 1.0 processor is required to check the input document against its DTD. If it does not validate, errors are reported to the application, which typically rejects the document. Non-validating processors will accept the document even if it doesn't conform to structures defined by the DTD, and just use the DTD for things like default values for attributes. Microsoft Office and most Microsoft tools use non-validating XML 1.0 parsers. (Schema validation is a separate process, defined long after XML 1.0 was finished.)

Other DTD Features

DTDs include a number of other features that aren't covered here. Parameter entities and conditional sections make it possible for developers to create more flexible DTDs, turning features on and off or reusing them. Documents can contain internal subsets in the DOCTYPE declaration, adding their own information to the document type declaration. Entity declarations make it possible for developers to create named references to content, making it simpler to include external files or characters not easily accessed from the keyboard. Notation declarations and unparsed entities make it possible to create metadata and include non-XML content, though these are rarely used. DTD do not support namespaces or XML Schema datatypes directly at all.

While Microsoft Office applications can process these features when opening a file (except for notations and unparsed entities, which it ignores), all of the DOCTYPE information is removed when the document is saved back out. Because XSD provides no support at all for entities, you can't preserve the entity information from an XML DTD in a schema and use that with Office.

What Is RELAX NG?

The W3C XML Schema process began with high ambitions to be a more powerful alternative to DTDs, but many people found XSD to be more trouble than it was worth. XSD is difficult for many people to create, difficult to process, has areas (notably block and final) that are fairly contentious, and not everyone wants to define their documents in terms of object inheritance anyway. While XSD has done well in some fields of XML work, and Microsoft has implemented it throughout its product line, there was a plain need for an alternative.

RELAX NG, which has developed largely from work done by XML pioneers Murata Makoto and James Clark, has mathematical foundations rather than the ad hoc object structures used by XSD. Fortunately, you don't need to know the math to use the schemas, but these foundations make it a lot simpler to both use and process RELAX NG. RELAX NG comes in both an XML syntax and a compact syntax, but we'll focus on the compact syntax here because it's generally quite approachable.

RELAX NG is being developed at the Organization for the Advancement of Structured Information Standards (OASIS), a different specification development organization from the W3C, and standardized through the International Organization for Standardization (ISO) as part of the Document Schema Definition Languages (DSDL) effort. For more on OASIS development of RELAX NG, see *http://www. oasis-open.org/committees/relax-ng/*. For more on the DSDL work, see *http://dsdl.org*.

A Basic RELAX NG Schema

For our first RELAX NG schema, we'll start with Example D-3, which is the same document shown in Example D-1 except without the DOCTYPE declaration.

Example D-3. A sample XML document

```
<?xml version="1.0" encoding="us-ascii"?>
<authors>
    <person abbrev="edd">
        <name>Edd Dumbill</name>
        <nationality>British</nationality>
    </person>
    <person abbrev="simonstl">
        <name>Simon St.Laurent</name>
        <nationality>American</nationality>
    </person>
    <person abbrev="vdv">
        <name>Eric van der Vlist</name>
        <nationality>French</nationality>
    </person>
</authors>
```

Described in RELAX NG Compact syntax, the schema for this document can resemble the schemas shown in Examples D-4 and D-5. Example D-4 uses a nested syntax.

Example D-4. A nested RELAX NG schema

```
element authors {
  element person {
    attribute abbrev {text},
    element name {text},
    element nationality {text}
  }*
}
```

The curly braces work much like those in C structs, defining the contents of named components. This schema defines an authors element, which contains zero or more person elements. (The zero or more comes from the asterisk after the closing brace for person.) The person elements have mandatory abbrev attributes and name and nationality elements, all of which store their contents as text. If you prefer a more declarative approach, RELAX NG also supports that option. Example D-5 uses a more DTD-like declaration approach.

Example D-5. A declarative RELAX NG schema

```
start=authors

authors = element authors { person* }
person = element person { abbrev, name, nationality }
abbrev = attribute abbrev {text}
name = element name {text}
nationality = element nationality {text}
```

This approach reads differently, but describes the same structure. Instead of just starting with the authors element, it explicitly lists possible root elements in the start declaration. Each declaration describes the contents of one element or attribute. The difference between attribute and element declarations is much smaller in RELAX NG than in XSD or in DTDs, and the abbrev attribute is attached to the person element just like the name and nationality elements. Elements and attributes that contain text just list text as their content.

To validate documents against these schemas, you can use James Clark's Jing tool, which is included with Trang, the tool we'll be using later in this appendix to convert RELAX NG types into XSD. Go to the directory where you've unzipped Trang, and you can run the validator by typing the following:

```
java -jar jing.jar -c appD-4.rnc appD-3.xml
```

If there aren't any errors in the document, Jing does its work and doesn't report anything. Otherwise, it reports errors like:

```
C:\trang>java -jar jing.jar -c appD-4.rnc appD-3broken.xml
C:\trang\appD-3broken.xml:5: error: attribute "country" not allowed at this point;
ignored
C:\trang\appD-3broken.xml:9: error: unknown element "address"
```

This can be a useful diagnostic, but in work with Office you'll probably convert your RELAX NG to XSD.

Advanced Features: Namespaces and Datatypes

RELAX NG goes well beyond the capabilities of DTDs and into the features that XSD provides. RELAX NG provides simple support for namespaces, so adding a namespace to the schema shown in Example D-5 requires adding only one line, as shown in Example D-6.

Example D-6. A declarative RELAX NG schema with namespaces

```
default namespace = "http://example.com/authors/"
start=authors

authors = element authors { person* }
person = element person { abbrev, name, nationality }
abbrev = attribute abbrev {text}
name = element name {text}
nationality = element nationality {text}
```

Now all of the elements without prefixes—authors, person, name, and nationality—are in the http://example.com/authors/ namespace. Applying this to the non-namespaced Example D-3 produces an error:

```
C:\trang>java -jar jing.jar -c appD-6.rnc appD-3.xml
C:\trang\appD-3.xml:2: error: unknown element "authors"
```

Adding a default namespace declaration to the root element clears things up:

```
<authors xmlns="http://example.com/authors/">...
```

Jing no longer reports any errors. You can also define namespaces for prefixed elements and attributes, using slightly different syntax:

```
namespace auth = "http://www.example.com/authors/"
start=auth:authors
auth:authors=element auth:authors {auth:person * }
...
```

These namespace declarations are most commonly made at the top of the schema, and they apply to all the declarations that follow them.

RELAX NG doesn't provide its own set of datatypes, preferring to let developers choose their own set. For the most part—and conveniently compatible with Office's expectations—RELAX NG developers use the datatypes defined by XML Schema. This requires an extra declaration, and then you can use XSD types. For example, to define the text contents of the name and nationality elements as xsd:string and the abbrev attribute's contents as xsd:token, we'll change the RELAX NG schema to use datatypes, as in Example D-7.

Example D-7. A declarative RELAX NG schema using datatypes

```
default namespace = "http://example.com/authors/"
datatypes xsd = "http://www.w3.org/2001/XMLSchema-datatypes"

start=authors

authors = element authors { person* }
person = element person { abbrev, name, nationality }
abbrev = attribute abbrev {xsd:token}
name = element name {xsd:string}
nationality = element nationality {xsd:string}
```

You can use any of the of the XML Schema datatypes and constrain their facets, if needed.

> For a more thorough introduction to RELAX NG Compact syntax, see Michael Fitzgerald's tutorial at *http://www.xml.com/pub/a/2002/06/19/rng-compact.html*. The specification for RELAX NG compact syntax is available at *http://www.oasis-open.org/committees/relax-ng/compact-20020607.html*.

How Do I Convert DTDs and RELAX NG to XSD?

Whether you're working with legacy schemas or simply prefer to work in these simpler frameworks, you need to convert these forms to XSD for work in Office. As noted earlier, Trang, available from *http://www.thaiopensource.com/relaxng/trang.html*, offers an extremely easy path from DTDs or RELAX NG to XSD. At its core, Trang is a simple command-line utility that takes XML sample documents, DTDs, RELAX NG, RELAX NG Compact syntax, or XSD and converts them into DTDs, RELAX NG, RELAX NG Compact syntax, or XSD. For working with Office, you'll mostly be converting DTDs and RELAX NG to XSD, though perhaps you'll want to convert XSD to other forms to use with other systems.

 RELAX NG is more expressive than XSD in a number of ways. If you really take advantage of RELAX NG, the limitations of XSD will be fairly apparent, and Trang can't convert all of RELAX NG's capabilities to XSD. If you stick with the subset shown in this appendix, however, you should not encounter such losses.

The basic syntax for using Trang looks like:

```
java -jar trang.jar sourceFile destinationFile
```

By default, the kind of transformation Trang performs depends on the file extensions of the source and destination files, shown in Table D-3.

Table D-3. File extensions used by Trang

File extension	Meaning
.xsd	W3C XML Schema (XSD) file (output only)
.dtd	XML 1.0 Document Type Definition (DTD)
.rng	RELAX NG file, XML syntax
.rnc	RELAX NG file, compact syntax
.xml	XML instance file (source only)

Converting the DTD shown in Example D-2 to XSD is as easy as typing:

```
java -jar trang.jar appD-2.dtd appD-8.xsd
```

at the command prompt. The resulting XSD file is shown in Example D-8.

Example D-8. The result of converting the DTD in Example D-2 to XSD

```
<?xml version="1.0" encoding="UTF-8"?>
<xs:schema xmlns:xs="http://www.w3.org/2001/XMLSchema"
elementFormDefault="qualified">
  <xs:element name="authors">
    <xs:complexType>
      <xs:sequence>
        <xs:element minOccurs="0" maxOccurs="unbounded" ref="person"/>
      </xs:sequence>
    </xs:complexType>
  </xs:element>
  <xs:element name="person">
```

```
    <xs:complexType>
      <xs:sequence>
        <xs:element ref="name"/>
        <xs:element ref="nationality"/>
      </xs:sequence>
      <xs:attribute name="abbrev" use="required"/>
    </xs:complexType>
  </xs:element>
  <xs:element name="name" type="xs:string"/>
  <xs:element name="nationality" type="xs:string"/>
</xs:schema>
```

Next, we'll convert the RELAX NG schema shown in Example D-7 to the XSD shown in Example D-9:

```
    java -jar trang.jar appD-7.rnc appD-9.xsd
```

The RELAX NG schema in Example D-7 included some features that weren't in the DTD, notably namespaces and datatypes, reflected in the resulting XSD, which now includes a targetNamespace attribute and an xs:token for the abbrev attribute. Trang also prefixes child element names with authors—not necessary, but it does make some aspects of the schema clearer if there are multiple namespaces used.

Example D-9. The result of converting the RELAX NG in Example D-7 to XSD

```
<?xml version="1.0" encoding="UTF-8"?>
<xs:schema xmlns:xs="http://www.w3.org/2001/XMLSchema"
elementFormDefault="qualified" targetNamespace="http://example.com/authors/"
xmlns:authors="http://example.com/authors/">
  <xs:element name="authors">
    <xs:complexType>
      <xs:sequence>
        <xs:element minOccurs="0" maxOccurs="unbounded" ref="authors:person"/>
      </xs:sequence>
    </xs:complexType>
  </xs:element>
  <xs:element name="person">
    <xs:complexType>
      <xs:sequence>
        <xs:element ref="authors:name"/>
        <xs:element ref="authors:nationality"/>
      </xs:sequence>
      <xs:attributeGroup ref="authors:abbrev"/>
    </xs:complexType>
  </xs:element>
  <xs:attributeGroup name="abbrev">
    <xs:attribute name="abbrev" use="required" type="xs:token"/>
  </xs:attributeGroup>
  <xs:element name="name" type="xs:string"/>
  <xs:element name="nationality" type="xs:string"/>
</xs:schema>
```

If you need to create an XSD from a sample document, you can also do that. Running Trang on our sample document to create an XSD from Example D-3 produces the result shown in Example D-10.

Example D-10. The result of converting the XML document in Example D-3 to XSD

```xml
<?xml version="1.0" encoding="UTF-8"?>
<xs:schema xmlns:xs="http://www.w3.org/2001/XMLSchema"
elementFormDefault="qualified">
  <xs:element name="authors">
    <xs:complexType>
      <xs:sequence>
        <xs:element maxOccurs="unbounded" ref="person"/>
      </xs:sequence>
    </xs:complexType>
  </xs:element>
  <xs:element name="person">
    <xs:complexType>
      <xs:sequence>
        <xs:element ref="name"/>
        <xs:element ref="nationality"/>
      </xs:sequence>
      <xs:attribute name="abbrev" use="required" type="xs:NCName"/>
    </xs:complexType>
  </xs:element>
  <xs:element name="name" type="xs:string"/>
  <xs:element name="nationality" type="xs:NCName"/>
</xs:schema>
```

Example D-10 handles the attribute declaration for abbrev differently from the other transformations, and has less information generally than the ones generated from the DTD and the RELAX NG schema. For quick and dirty work, this kind of transformation may be very useful, though the results are only as good as the sample documents you provide.

> For a more sophisticated approach to generating schemas from sample documents, see *http://examplotron.org*. Examplotron lets you annotate the sample documents to provide additional information used in generating schemas. Examplotron produces RELAX NG, which Trang can then convert to XSD.

Once you've created the XSD files, you can use them in conjunction with Office just like any other XSD.

Index

We'd like to hear your suggestions for improving our indexes. Send email to *index@oreilly.com*.

B

Base64-encoded data
  line endings and, 103
  objects, attributes relating to, 28
  in WordprocessingML, 112
Beginning XSLT (Tennison), 505
block-level context, 48
block-level elements, 149–151, 184
boilerplate text, in templates, 224
bold property, 45
bookmarks, 72, 75
Bornstein, Niel (.NET & XML), xii
Bray, Tim
  "Annotated XML Specification", 493
  "XML Namespaces by Example", 498
breaks, 42, 45
browser-based XML editors, 430
built-in template rules, 111, 516
bundled XML editors, 431
Burke, Sean M. (RTF Pocket Guide), 23
business forms (see forms)
buttons, InfoPath, 466–468

C

Castro, Elizabeth
  XML for the World Wide Web, xi
  XML for the World Wide Web: Visual
    QuickStart Guide, 493
Cell element, 333, 337
cell-level elements, custom, 153
cells
  in spreadsheets, 333, 337
  in tables, 40, 58, 61
Cerami, Ethan (Web Services Essentials), xii
character encodings, 501
character references, in XML, 500
character styles, 32, 47, 86
  conflicts between, 91–94
  linked, removing from Word
    documents, 122
Clark, James
  Jing tool, 546
  Trang package, 540
comments
  extracting from Word
    documents, 115–116
  in WordprocessingML, 72, 75
  in XML, 499
compact syntax, RELAX NG, 544
compatibility options, 37
compositors, XSD, 534, 535

conditional formatting, XSLT
    stylesheet, 440–442
contact information for this book, xiii
content, mixed
  in WordprocessingML, 20
  in XML, 495
  in XML as Excel source data, 280
  XML editor support for, 430
  in XSD, 537
content, separating from presentation, 11, 12
ControlCaptionFromID member,
    ISmartDocument interface, 240
ControlCount member, ISmartDocument
    interface, 239
ControlID member, ISmartDocument
    interface, 239
ControlNameFromID member,
    ISmartDocument interface, 240
controls, Smart Document
  defining, 239–244
  document actions for, 250–263
  populating, 244–249
  types and associated methods, 264
ControlTypeFromID member,
    ISmartDocument interface, 242
create-onload-stylesheet.xsl
    stylesheet, 193–198
CRLF (carriage return linefeed pair), as line
    ending in WordprocessingML, 103
curly braces ({}), 520
Cygwin, XML processor, 103

D

"Data only"view, Word, 142, 147
data view
  editing restrictions and, 204
  limitations of, 205
  options for, 133
  (see also onload XSLT stylesheet)
databases
  creating XML documents from, 11
  generating data-driven Word tables
    using, 104–110
  generating documents and spreadsheets
    from, 10
  Smart Documents accessing, 206
  XML and, 360
  (see also Access)
data-oriented XML editor, 430
dataroot element, 364, 367

datatypes
    RELAX NG, 547
    XSD, 529–533
    XSD to Excel mappings, 294
date picker control, InfoPath, 461
DDF file, 479
default values, XSD, 537
Definitive XML Schema (Walmsley), xii, 523
Definitive XSLT and XPath (Holman), 505
derived styles, 89
diamond directive file, 479
direct formatting, 91
    font settings, 43
    paragraph settings, 49, 90
    removing from Word documents, 121
.dll files
    permissions for, with managed code, 273
    Smart Documents distributed as, 208
.doc files (see documents, Word)
Docbook, converting WordprocessingML
    to, 128
DOCTYPE declaration, 503, 544
document actions, 224, 227–228, 234,
    249–263
Document Actions task pane, 224, 227–228
document protection, Word, 74, 163–167,
    188–191, 192, 204
document type declaration, 503
Document Type Definition (see DTD)
document-oriented XML editor, 430
DocumentProperties element, 330
documents, Word
    annotating, 13, 72, 75
    as basis for onload XSLT stylesheet, 180
    attaching schema to, 181
    changing font sizes in, 123–125
    cleaning up for publishing, 118–120
    converting
        special-purpose translations, 128
        to Docbook, 128
        to HTML, 125
        to OpenOffice.org, 128
        to PDF, 128
    copying, 117
    direct formatting, removing, 121
    embedded XML data in, 130
    extracting information from
        comments, 115–116
        metadata, 113
        text content, 110–113
    generating from databases, 10, 104–110
    linked character styles, removing, 122

metadata
    embedding as XML, 130
    extracting, 113
    removing, 118–120
    modifying, 116–125
    saving as WordprocessingML, 16
    (see also Word; WordprocessingML)
documents, XML (see XML)
double quotes ("), 495, 500
Drake, Fred L. (Python & XML), xii
dt namespace prefix, 28
DTD (Document Type Definition), 503,
    540–544
    converting to XSD, 540, 547–550
    creating Smart Document schemas
        from, 212
    resources for, xii
.dtd files (see DTD)
Dubinko, Micah (XForms Essentials), 434
dummy styles, 97–99

E

editing components, InfoPath, 468–475
editing permissions, ranges of, 72, 74
editing restrictions, 163–166, 188–191, 204
Eisenberg, David (SVG Essentials), 10
ELEMENT type declaration, 541
element type declarations, DTD, 541
elements, XML, 495, 496
    (see also specific elements)
embedded images, 112
    generating with XSLT, 110
    line endings and, 103
Enterprise Edition, Office 2003, 1
entity references, 499
EpicEditor, Smart Documents and, 207, 213
escaping characters in XML, 499
Excel
    creating XML Maps in, 295–298
    disadvantages in previous versions of, 276
    editing XML with, 12, 306–316
    editions of, supporting XML, 276
    grid structure of, 278
    HTML data, opening in, 281
    loading and saving XML from
        VBA, 316–323
    "Open as a read-only workbook"
        option, 289
    "Open as an XML List" option, 282–289
    opening XML spreadsheets, 325
    saving XML spreadsheets, 326
    separating content from presentation, 12

Excel (*continued*)
    Smart Documents for, 207, 208
    Web Services, accessing, 15, 399–411
    XML as source data for
        opening using XML Maps, 293–306
        opening XML documents
            directly, 280–293
        requirements, 278–280
    XML features in, 6, 276, 277
    XML Schema and, 280, 294–295
    XML Source task pane, 290, 296, 298
    XSD datatypes mapped to, 294
    (see also SpreadsheetML; spreadsheets)
ExcelWorkbook element, 331
expansion pack, for Smart Documents, 208,
        270, 273, 275
explicit binding, XSLT stylesheet, 443
Extensible Markup Language (see XML)
Extensible Stylesheet Language
        Transformations (xee XSLT)

F

Ferrara, Alex (Programming .NET Web
        Services), xii
field instruction text, 112
fields, in Word, 41, 49
file element, 265
Fitzgerald, Michael (Learning XSLT), xi, 505
fonts
    default, 31
    properties, conflicts between, 91–94
    properties for, 46
    run properties for, 43
    size, 46, 87, 123–125
    TrueType, WordprocessingML not
        embedding, 16
footers, 40, 112
form definition file, InfoPath, 434, 436,
        462–475
form template, InfoPath, 434
form template package, InfoPath, 434
formatting restrictions, 166, 191, 204
formatting (see styles)
forms, InfoPath, 434
formulas, in spreadsheets, 333
FrameMaker, Smart Documents and, 207,
        213
FrontPage, creating XSLT stylesheets with, 9

G

generic server-side frameworks, 429

Glenn, Walter
    Word 2000 in a Nutshell, 222
    Word Pocket Guide, 17, 222
grammar checker, 36, 72, 74
graphics (see embedded images; SVG)
> entity reference, 500
guidgen.exe utility, 265

H

Harold, Elliotte Rusty (XML in a
        Nutshell), xi, 493
headers, 40, 112
help files, for Smart Documents, 268
hierarchical document structures,
        representing in Wordprocessing
        ML, 23
Holman, G. Ken (Definitive XSLT and
        XPath), 505
HTML
    binding to XML, 438–444, 459–461, 484
    converting WordprocessingML to, 125
    converting XML to, with XSLT, 509–517
    lists, compared to WordprocessingML
        lists, 62
    opening in Excel, 281
html namespace prefix, 330
HTML Task Pane, InfoPath, 475
HTTP (HyperText Transfer Protocol), 397
hyperlinks, in Word, 41, 49
HyperText Transfer Protocol (HTTP), 397

I

IANA (Internet Assigned Numbers
        Authority), 502
identity transformation, 116
"Ignore mixed content" option, Word, 161,
        168, 171, 186
ImageClick method, ISmartDocument
        interface, 249
images (see embedded images)
indentation of paragraph, 52
InfoPath, 8, 14, 426–428
    alternatives to Design Mode, 486–491
    binding XML to HTML, 438–444,
        459–461, 484
    buttons, 466–468
    compared to XForms, 433
    date picker control, 461
    declarative configuration in, 432
    deploying solution for, 479

Microsoft FrontPage (see FrontPage)
Microsoft InfoPath (see InfoPath)
Microsoft Office 2003 (see Office 2003)
Microsoft Outlook (see Outlook)
Microsoft PowerPoint (see PowerPoint)
Microsoft Visio (see Visio)
Microsoft Word (see Word)
Microsoft Word Visual Basic Reference, 229
mixed content
    in WordprocessingML, 20
    in XML, 495
    in XML as Excel source data, 280
    XML editor support for, 430
    in XSD, 537
model groups, XSD, 536
mso-application PI, 17
    for Excel, 329
    for InfoPath, 435
    generating, 104, 108
    removing to open document in Internet
        Explorer, 21
mso-infoPathSolution PI, 436, 444
mso-solutionextension PI, 201, 264
msxsl.exe, XSLT processor, 103

N

name syntax, XML, 496
named cells, 338, 346
named ranges, 346, 350
named types, in XSD, 528
NamedCell element, 338
Names element, 338
namespaces
    attributes, namespace-qualified, 24
    default, in WordprocessingML, 18
    for XSD, 526–528
    for XSLT, 507
    list of, in WordprocessingML, 27
    prefixes for, 18, 496
    RELAX NG, 546
    resources for, 498
    SpreadsheetML, 329, 350
    XML, 496–498
    XML schema one-to-one correspondance
        with, 203
nested markup, 23
.NET & XML (Bornstein), xii
Newcomer, Eric (Understanding Web
        Services: SOAP, WSDL, and
        UDDI), xii
node-set, resulting from XPath
        expression, 508

O

o namespace prefix, 28
o:CustomDocumentProperties element, 172
o:DocumentProperties element, 29, 112, 113
Office 2003, ix, 10
    Enterprise Edition, 1
    XML's role in, 2, 4–10
Office 2003 XML for Power Users
        (MacDonald), 399
OfficeDocumentSettings element, 331
OnCheckboxChange method,
        ISmartDocument
        interface, 255–259
OnListOrComboSelectChange method,
        ISmartDocument interface, 251
onload XSLT stylesheet, 137, 139
    automatically applied, requirement
        for, 203
    creating, 179–200
    determining whether schema is
        attached, 156
    editing attributes and, 161
    method of selecting, 141–144
    multiple, for one schema, 144
    preserving PIs in document with, 173
    utility for generating, 193–200
onOffProperty type, 38
OnPaneUpdateComplete method,
        ISmartDocument interface, 263
OnRadioGroupSelectChange method,
        ISmartDocument
        interface, 259–263
onsave XSLT stylesheet, 138, 147
    editing attributes and, 161
    preserving PIs when saving
        documents, 174
    save options for, choosing, 178
    used for creating onload XSLT
        stylesheet, 193–200
OnTextboxContentChange method,
        ISmartDocument interface, 250
"Open as a read-only workbook" option,
        Excel, 289
"Open as an XML List" option,
        Excel, 282–289
OpenOffice.org, converting
        WordprocessingML to, 128
operators, in XPath, 508
o:processingInstructions element, 172
Options dialog, Word, 35
outline levels, 79–83
Outlook, XML not supported with, 9

W

About the Authors

Evan Lenz is an XML developer whose primary area of expertise is XSLT. He recently joined Infopop Corporation as an interface engineer. He has served on the W3C XSL Working Group, spoken at various XML conferences, and written XML-related articles and book chapters. Evan holds a Bachelor of Music degree from Wheaton College (IL), with majors in Piano Performance and Philosophy. He lives in Seattle, Washington, with his wife Lisa, son Samuel, and daughter Morgan. See what latest geekery he's up to at *http://www.xmlportfolio.com*.

Mary McRae is Senior Vice President and Principal XML Technologist for DMSi (*http://www.dmsi-world.com*), a consultancy specializing in structured markup solutions for document-focused organizations. She helps her clients avoid the pitfalls that she first encountered as an early adopter of SGML through training and support in project management, needs analysis, requirements definition, product selection, schema development, application customization, and middleware development. Since the first beta release of Office 11, Mary has immersed herself in the nuances of Microsoft Office Word 2003 and its application in a structured authoring environment. She has led the development of DMSi SyntoniX—Smart Document solutions for industry-standard and customer-specific schemas, and is a frequent speaker at industry conferences, seminars, and user group gatherings. She continues to write about Microsoft Office and XML at *http://www.office-xml.com*.

Simon St.Laurent is an editor with O'Reilly Media, Inc. Prior to that, he'd been a web developer, network administrator, computer book author, and XML trouble-maker living in Ithaca, NY. His books include *XML: A Primer, XML Elements of Style, Building XML Applications, Cookies*, and *Sharing Bandwidth*. He is also an occasional contributor to *XML.com*.

Colophon

Our look is the result of reader comments, our own experimentation, and feedback from distribution channels. Distinctive covers complement our distinctive approach to technical topics, breathing personality and life into potentially dry subjects.

The animal on the cover of *Office 2003 XML* is a Malay palm civet (*Viverra tanga-lunga*). These mammals are native to the Malay peninsula, including parts of Thailand, Singapore, Myanmar, and Malaysia. Like other palm civets, the Malay is around 17–28 inches long with a tail length of 16–26 inches. It weighs from 3 to 10 pounds, and their its color ranges from gray to brown. The markings on its face resemble those of a raccoon. The civet has four anal glands that it uses to expel an extremely strong-smelling secretion that is used to discourage attackers. This musk was once used by perfume makers in their products. However, animal rights groups objected to the cruel harvesting process and most manufacturers now use synthetic alternatives to approximate the scent.

Civets are nocturnal and prefer wooded areas where they can sleep in trees during the day. At night, they hunt for small vertebrates, insects, fruits, and seeds, which they wash down with palm juice. This juice is called "toddy" by the natives, so civets are often referred to as "toddy cats." They are also extremely fond of coffee, and usually ingest the ripest and reddest coffee beans available. They eat only the outer covering of the bean; the rest of it passes through their digestive process unscathed. These excreted beans are then used to roast the world's most expensive and rarest coffee, Kopi Luwak.

Philip Dangler was the production editor and proofreader, and Jane Ellin was the copyeditor for *Office 2003 XML*. Emily Quill and Darren Kelly provided quality control. Angela Howard wrote the index.

Emma Colby designed the cover of this book, based on a series design by Edie Freedman. The cover image is a 19th-century engraving from *Royal Natural History*. Emma Colby produced the cover layout with QuarkXPress 4.1 using Adobe's ITC Garamond font.

David Futato designed the interior layout. This book was converted by Joe Wizda to FrameMaker 5.5.6 with a format conversion tool created by Erik Ray, Jason McIntosh, Neil Walls, and Mike Sierra that uses Perl and XML technologies. The text font is Linotype Birka; the heading font is Adobe Myriad Condensed; and the code font is LucasFont's TheSans Mono Condensed. The illustrations that appear in the book were produced by Robert Romano and Jessamyn Read using Macromedia FreeHand 9 and Adobe Photoshop 6. The tip and warning icons were drawn by Christopher Bing. This colophon was written by Philip Dangler.

Whenever possible, our books use a durable and flexible lay-flat binding. If the page count exceeds this binding's limit, perfect binding is used.

Related Titles Available from O'Reilly

XML

Content Syndication with RSS
Java and XML
Java and XSLT
Learning XML, *2nd Edition*
Learning XSLT
Perl & XML
Practical RDF
Programming Jabber
Programming Web Services with SOAP
Python & XML
SAX2
SVG Essentials
Web Services Essentials
XForms Essentials
XML CD Bookshelf, *Version 1.0*
XML in a Nutshell, *2nd Edition*
XML Pocket Reference, *2nd Edition*
XML Schema
Xpath and Xpointer
XSL-FO
XSLT
XSLT Cookbook

O'REILLY®

Our books are available at most retail and online bookstores.
To order direct: 1-800-998-9938 • *order@oreilly.com* • *www.oreilly.com*
Online editions of most O'Reilly titles are available by subscription at *safari.oreilly.com*

Keep in touch with O'Reilly

1. Download examples from our books

To find example files for a book, go to:

www.oreilly.com/catalog

select the book, and follow the "Examples" link.

2. Register your O'Reilly books

Register your book at *register.oreilly.com*

Why register your books?
Once you've registered your O'Reilly books you can:

- Win O'Reilly books, T-shirts or discount coupons in our monthly drawing.
- Get special offers available only to registered O'Reilly customers.
- Get catalogs announcing new books (US and UK only).
- Get email notification of new editions of the O'Reilly books you own.

3. Join our email lists

Sign up to get topic-specific email announcements of new books and conferences, special offers, and O'Reilly Network technology newsletters at:

elists.oreilly.com

It's easy to customize your free elists subscription so you'll get exactly the O'Reilly news you want.

4. Get the latest news, tips, and tools

www.oreilly.com

- "Top 100 Sites on the Web"—PC Magazine
- CIO Magazine's Web Business 50 Awards

Our web site contains a library of comprehensive product information (including book excerpts and tables of contents), downloadable software, background articles, interviews with technology leaders, links to relevant sites, book cover art, and more.

5. Work for O'Reilly

Check out our web site for current employment opportunities:

jobs.oreilly.com

6. Contact us

O'Reilly & Associates
1005 Gravenstein Hwy North
Sebastopol, CA 95472 USA

TEL: 707-827-7000 or 800-998-9938
       (6am to 5pm PST)

FAX: 707-829-0104

order@oreilly.com
For answers to problems regarding your order or our products. To place a book order online, visit:

www.oreilly.com/order_new

catalog@oreilly.com
To request a copy of our latest catalog.

booktech@oreilly.com
For book content technical questions or corrections.

corporate@oreilly.com
For educational, library, government, and corporate sales.

proposals@oreilly.com
To submit new book proposals to our editors and product managers.

international@oreilly.com
For information about our international distributors or translation queries. For a list of our distributors outside of North America check out:

international.oreilly.com/distributors.html

adoption@oreilly.com
For information about academic use of O'Reilly books, visit:

academic.oreilly.com